Praise for
Longing for Daddy

"The father issue affects the very core of a woman's life. Monique Robinson has done a fine job of addressing this very special relationship between a woman and her father by giving those who have struggled in this area practical principles for healing unreconciled wounds and reminding us that God is the only perfect Father."

—MICHELLE MCKINNEY HAMMOND, author of *In Search of the Proverbs 31 Man*

"In *Longing for Daddy*, Monique Robinson compassionately and insightfully helps women recover from the devastations of failed fathering. Through self-examination, inspiration, and prayer, readers learn to break free of their negative behaviors and embrace real healing. A must-read for those serious about journeying toward spiritual maturity."

—RONN ELMORE, PSY.D., author of *An Outrageous Commitment: The 48 Vows of an Indestructible Marriage*

"For those women who know the pain of having been wounded or rejected by their father, Monique Robinson has unlocked the secret door that leads us to understanding, healing, forgiveness, and in some cases restoration. I thank God that she was inspired to write such an amazing book."

—TERRI MCFADDIN, author of *Only a Woman* and *Sapphires and Other Precious Jewels*

"Every little girl yearns to be 'daddy's girl.' No relationship is more pivotal to a woman's emotional development and identity than her relationship with her father, and many women have relationship issues because of absent fathers. In a deeply personal account, Pastor Monique Robinson examines the heartaches she faced growing up 'longing for daddy.' Her journey to healing, wholeness, and happiness is a must-read for every woman who always wanted to sit on her father's lap and hear, 'Never forget that your daddy loves you, no matter what.' *Longing for Daddy* is a breakthrough book that is a watershed of revelation, inspiration, and hope."

—PAMELA PERRY, newspaper columnist, magazine journalist, and president of American Christian Writers/Detroit

Longing for Daddy

HEALING FROM THE PAIN OF AN ABSENT
OR EMOTIONALLY DISTANT FATHER

MONIQUE ROBINSON

WATERBROOK
PRESS

LONGING FOR DADDY
PUBLISHED BY WATERBROOK PRESS
12265 Oracle Boulevard, Suite 200
Colorado Springs, Colorado 80921

Details in some anecdotes and stories have been changed to protect the identities of the persons involved.

Trade Paperback ISBN 978-1-57856-687-7
eBook ISBN 978-0-307-45753-0

Published in the United States by WaterBrook Multnomah, an imprint of the Crown Publishing Group, a division of Penguin Random House LLC, New York.

WATERBROOK and its deer colophon are registered trademarks of Penguin Random House LLC.

Library of Congress Cataloging-in-Publication Data
Robinson, Monique.
    Longing for daddy : healing from the pain of an absent or emotionally distant father / Monique Robinson.   1st ed
        p. cm.
Includes bibliographical references (p. 187).
    ISBN 1-57856-687-8
    1. Christian women—Pastoral counseling of. 2. Fathers and daughters—Religious aspects—Christianity. 3. Paternal deprivation—Religious aspects—Christianity. I. Title.
    BV4445.R63 2004
    248.8'43—dc22

                                                            2003018610

Printed in the United States of America
2015

10 9

For
my heavenly Father,
my earthly father, Willie Moore,
my surrogate father, Emanuel Shedrick,
and
my spiritual father, Bishop Kenneth C. Ulmer

CONTENTS

FOREWORD

"If my father...should desert me, you [Lord] will take care of me" (CEV).

"My God, my God, why hast thou forsaken me?" (KJV).

"I will never leave you nor forsake you."

Three dimensions of hidden hurt and hope! The first declaration follows a plea not to be forsaken. The second is bellowed out of a context of pain, despair, and destiny. The third is an eternal promise of a faithful Savior, who exhorts contentment and comfort in His perpetual presence.

I am constantly amazed at the painful realities of biblical revelation. I think one of the ways we know that Scripture is written by God Himself is that He left in the hard parts. Scripture never attempts to paint a utopian portrait of life. It shows life with warts and all, valleys and hills, victories and defeats. On the one hand, the Word of God speaks of the permanent bonds of matrimony, yet it helps us wrestle with the realities of divorce. It even presents the divine gift of salvation through faith and yet also unveils the calamity and condemning consequences of rejecting the Way, the Truth, and the Life. Likewise, as tender, blessed, and holy as the relationships between parent and child, father and son, mother and daughter are, the Word of God examines the possibility that these relationships run the risk of ruin.

David grew up in the loving family of a faithful father, Jesse. He knew what it was like to be surrounded by the loving affirmation of a godly father. He and his brothers were exposed to the environment of a home committed to the God of Israel. These truths make David's proclamation all the more significant. When he says in Psalm 27:10, "If my father and mother should desert me...," he is hyperbolically speaking of the unthinkable. In other words he is saying, "I know it would be unthinkable and unlikely, but EVEN IF my father and mother would forsake me, the

Lord would be there to take care of me." His words create an image of a child being gathered up into the arms of a loving parent.

David's words make a significant point. In the natural, he did not know what it was like to grow up abandoned by his father. He did not live in a home with an absentee father. He had no problem with the void of a father figure. Yet he could imagine what to him would be the impossible: "Even if my father—the one who has been here, the one who I know loves me, the one who has been there for me—even if THAT father forsook me, abandoned and deserted me, I know the Lord would be there for me." The statement is really more about his faith in God than it is a fear about his father. He declared faith in the faithfulness of a heavenly Father even in the face of the possibility of a faithless earthly father. For David this powerful declaration was a hypothetical possibility but an unlikely probability. Yet during the challenges, trials, attacks, and grief of his later life, at times he certainly *felt* all alone and abandoned, not only by family, but by God Himself (Psalm 22).

At times David felt so forsaken, abandoned, and alone that he could no longer see God's face. At times he felt God was hiding from him (Psalms 10:1; 13:1; 69:17). When David wrote these words, both his father and mother were probably dead. It may be in the sense of his parents being dead that he felt abandoned or alone. However he makes this pronouncement as if to say, "God will gather me in His arms, pick me up, and carry me even if my parents do leave me. I will still make it. I will not be left alone." What words of encouragement for those who've been abandoned by their earthly fathers!

The lack of true fathers is not a contemporary phenomenon. It is interesting to note the number of biblical characters who made the pages of eternal history with little or no mention of a father. That fact is particularly noteworthy in light of the patriarchal society in which most of the Bible was written. Although the psalmist heralds the blessing of children by declaring that children are a gift from God and pronounces the man with many of them as blessed (Psalm 127:3-5, NASB), we are struck by the lack of direct fatherly influence on several prominent biblical characters. We know nothing significant about Paul's father, although Scripture implies that he was probably a Roman Jew. Acts 16:1 tells us that Timothy's father was a Greek, but we clearly learn that Timothy was influenced greatly in the things of the Lord by his mother and grandmother (2 Timothy 1:5) rather than by his father, who would normally have played that role (Deuteronomy 6:1-7). Jabez, the man who made history for his prayer that God heard, is not spoken of in relationship to a father. In fact, the Bible says that his mother named him *Jabez,* which means "sorrow or pain." That mere fact is a revelation since, in the custom of the day, most often the father named the boy child. The text gives us no information about the identity of his father. It might not be too much of a stretch to suggest that maybe the pain of his mother's delivery was related to the absence of the father!

Paul adds another dimension. He suggests there is a shortage of spiritual fathers (1 Corinthians 4:15). We don't have enough fathers providing spiritual protection, serving spiritual food, or offering spiritual guidance. He speaks of those God-given relationships where sons and daughters are knit in the womb of the spirit and come forth to the glory and service of God the Father. He calls attention to parent-child relationships that are produced by the life-giving seed of the gospel. Paul then encourages his spiritual children to imitate him. It is challenge enough to live in the role of father; it is quite another thing to then ask those children to be like you. It assumes that your example is portable and reproducible. It requires accountability, responsibility, integrity, and godliness and that you walk in the Spirit. It does not imply perfection, but it demands a sensitivity that recognizes that godly relationships are part of the stewardship of life. It makes you wonder what kind of tracks you are leaving for your children to walk in.

The Bible implies that a man's life cannot be truly evaluated or assessed until the third generation. "A good man leaves an inheritance to his children's children" (Proverbs 13:22). One of the great joys of my life has been to see my three children accept Christ and now live a life of service to the Lord. So often I wish my own father had been here to see how the Lord is using his grandchildren. He would be so proud of them. I often feel the responsibility, the challenge, and the encouragement of carrying on the godly legacy left by him and my mother (who at eighty-six still clings to life). I count it a sovereign blessing of God to have been raised in a home where I saw my father and mother serve the Lord, work in the church, and cover their children with prayer. Although several of the kids in our neighborhood were in single-parent homes, I find it hard to relate from a firsthand perspective to a father abandoning his children. My dad was always there.

However, while I grew up in a home where my dad was present—providing, protecting, and presiding—I lived with years of guilt and hidden shame over the fact that I was not present in the home that raised my two daughters. The loving, solid relationship that we have today is only by the grace of God. My perpetually plaguing question was whether my daughters felt abandoned and forsaken. It was a feeling of distress, discouragement, and despair that could be healed only by the cleansing power of the living Lord. We often joke, often weep, and always rejoice that our relationship is a *miracle!*

Father's Day 2003 was a red-letter day I'll treasure for the rest of my life. As I sat at the dinner table surrounded by my wife, three children, and a dear friend and his wife, my oldest daughter passed me a Father's Day card addressed to "Grandfather." I thought she had made a mistake and had passed me the card from her younger sister, who blessed us last year with our first grandchild. However, when I opened the card, it said "SURPRISE!" *She was having a baby!* I thought it was a hoax. I thought it was a joke. But as I looked at her and saw the gleam in her eyes and the glow on her countenance, tears welled up in my eyes. My firstborn was carrying my second grandchild. It was all the more special because she herself had been born on Father's Day many (I guess I can't really say how many) years ago. I was surprised at the euphoria I felt. I just hugged her, and before I knew it, both she and I were mixing tears. God had allowed me to live to see my third generation.

In addition to my experiences as a son and as a father whose mistakes have been miraculously redeemed, I have another vantage point on the issue of father abandonment. I have been blessed of God to have several boys and girls come into my life, and I am the closest thing to a father they have ever known. Upon my arrival at the church that I have now pastored for more than twenty years, I was struck by the weekly presence of a little boy who always ran to me to get a hug. Week after week he would wait patiently for the lingering crowd to disperse and then run to me, grab me around my legs, and hug me tightly. One Sunday his mother was obviously in a hurry to go home, and after calling for her son repeatedly, she approached me quite apologetically and said she was sorry if her son was bothering me. She said, "Pastor, this boy just won't leave until he gets a hug from you." And then with a small tear trickling down her cheek and yet with a twinkle in her eye, she announced, "Pastor, you are the only man who ever hugged my boy!"

One of the challenges we have in ministering to children in a large, growing congregation is teaching children to know and love God as Father. We have taught several to pray the model prayer that begins "Our Father…," only to have some say with inquiring tones, "What's a father?" I dare not bore you or bring you down with the distressing statistics about the number of fatherless homes in America. I don't have to. You know of one. You may be in one. You may have grown up in one. You certainly know someone who did.

As we turn to the Word of God for insight, we see again the relevance of the verses I quoted earlier. The Bible lifts up a word that relates to this topic: *forsake*. David uses it. Jesus uses it. God Himself uses it.

Saying, "When my father…forsake[s] me," David speaks of a possibility.

Asking, "My God, My God, why hast thou forsaken me?" Jesus speaks of our pain.

Declaring, "I will never leave you nor forsake you," God the Father makes a promise.

David, the sweet psalmist of Israel, almost seems schizophrenic in Psalm 27 as he extols the faithfulness of God and his faithful confidence in Him. He declares that his heart's one desire is to live in the presence and glory of his God. He boldly declares that God will protect him in the day of trouble and vindicate him when he is under attack by the enemy. In chiasmic style David alternates between talking *about* God (verses 1-6) and talking *to* God (verses 7-12) and again talking *about* God (verses 13-14). However, an interesting revelation comes forth in the stanza in which he talks to God. He implores God not to hide His face and not to turn away from him. He then petitions the Lord in verse 9, "Do not leave me nor forsake me." It almost sounds like he either stutters or intentionally hyperbolizes his request: "Don't leave me; don't forsake me!" It seems repetitious since most of us would consider *leaving* and *forsaking* to be synonymous. However, I would suggest a slightly different spin that distinguishes the two words.

"To leave" is more psychological, whereas "to forsake" carries a more physical, even geographical, connotation. When David says to the Lord, "Do not leave me," he means, "Do not reject me," which adds emphasis to the preceding plea: "Do not hide Your face from me" (verse 9). When he says, "Do not...forsake me," the emphasis is on departure from a location and leaving someone behind and alone. It indicates the idea of releasing or letting go of that which desires to be held. To forsake includes but goes beyond emotional and psychological to include relocation.

The word used here in Psalm 27 first appears in the injunction that covers the marriage commitment modeled in the relationship between Adam and Eve. God says for this reason shall a man "leave" and cleave. The word *leave* is the same word, *àzab*, for "forsake" in Psalm 27:10 (compare with Genesis 2:24). The New King James word *leave* in Psalm 27:9 is *natash* in Hebrew, a different word with a slightly different meaning. But when juxtaposed to *àzab*, the two become a revelation of the dual dynamic a child feels when abandoned by a father. Psychological and emotional: leaving. Physical and geographic: forsaking. Another way to look at it is this painful equation: leaving + forsaking = abandonment. Abandonment is psychological and physical, as much emotional as it is geographical.

With this in mind, we see that Jesus' words while hanging on the cross were the epitome of his humanity. It is as the God-man that the humanity of the Christ cries out: "My God, my God, why hast thou forsaken me?" The holiness of the Father had turned from the hellishness of man placed on the righteousness of His Son. Dr. K. S. Wuest speaks of this scene this way:

> He was abandoned and deserted by God the Father, and for the reason that God "appointed Him to be sin for us who knew no sin; that we might become the righteousness of God in Him" (II Cor. 5:21). A fellowship had been broken that had always existed, a fellowship that had continued all during our Lord's earthly life. But now the Father's smiling face was turned away. Understand the "how" of it, we cannot. Feel the awfulness of it, we may not. Believe the fact of it, we must. Our Lord said His God had abandoned Him, deserted Him.[1]

Whom do you turn to when God forsakes you? You are never more alone than when you feel God has forsaken you. There is no more dramatic example of the human eyes and manly heart of the Master than these words. Here, as in no other scenario, He is touched with our infirmities (Hebrews 4:15). He is a son forsaken by a father. He wonders where God is. How did God allow him to get in such a mess? Ever felt that way? Ever wondered where God was? Ever felt abandoned by God? It is in the face of such perplexing queries from us, as well as the declaration of David and the dereliction felt by Jesus, that God says, "I will never leave you nor forsake you."

The promise is never to leave nor forsake. Herein lies the basis of the literary journey you have embarked upon.

These two actions, to leave and to forsake, take on an added dimension when we examine their use in the letter to the Hebrews (13:5). Therein lies the prevailing promise that covers and hovers over this work. The word *leave* is not from the usual Greek word that means "to leave" but from a word that means "to uphold" or "sustain." In the Greek there are two negatives before the word *leave,* presenting a very strong negation. The promise is, "I will not, I will not cease to uphold or sustain thee."[2]

Again Dr. Wuest helps us gain a deeper understanding of this promise. The word *forsake* is a composite of three words, "to leave," "down," and "in." The first has the idea of forsaking one. The second suggests rejection, defeat, helplessness. The third refers to some place or circumstance in which a person may find himself helpless, forsaken. The meaning of the word is that of forsaking someone in a state of defeat or helplessness in the midst of hostile circumstances. The word means, in its totality, "to abandon, to desert, to leave in straits, to leave helpless, to leave destitute, to leave in the lurch, to let one down." There are three negatives before this word, making the promise one of triple assurance. It is, "I will not, I will not, I will not forsake thee." Not only do we have the assurance of God's all-sufficient sustaining power to hold us true to Him and in perfect peace as we go through testing times, but we have His promise that He will never abandon us, never desert us, never leave us in dire straits but will come to our help. He will never leave us destitute but will supply all our need. He will never leave us in the lurch but will see to it that we are rescued from the difficulties in which we sometimes find ourselves. *He will never let us down.*[3]

Monique Robinson ventures into a personal examination of the very pain that David sought to avoid: the pain of an absent or emotionally distant father. With a vivid yet flowing style, she invites us to wrestle with this very real emotional and psychological dilemma that all of us can directly or vicariously relate to. She is tough but transparent. She writes with vision and vulnerability. She pictures her pain with persistence and passion. All the while she leads us on a journey to deliverance and liberty. Minister Robinson is my beloved daughter in whom I am well pleased. As her spiritual father, I am so very proud of the gift that she is to the body of Christ and the gifts God has placed in her. I have been blessed to watch her grow in her walk and service to the Lord. In this work God will use her as an instrument of blessing for you. You will weep. You will rejoice. You will remember. You will thank God for His power, His presence, and His promise. He still says to you—even if you have been or have felt forsaken by an earthly father—"I will never leave you nor forsake you."

I can never fill the void or role of an earthly father, but I declare to my daughter Monique, "I am forever proud of you. I will never leave you nor forsake you."

—KENNETH C. ULMER, PH.D.

ACKNOWLEDGMENTS

To my Lord and Savior Jesus Christ, who gave me wisdom and guidance in writing this book. May it give You glory and honor.

To my husband, Andre—thank you for your love and continued support. At my weariest points, your prayers and encouragement strengthened me.

Mom, thank you for your love, strength, care, and support every day of my life, at every milestone in my life. You are my greatest cheerleader, and I love you. Thank you for allowing me to tell our story.

To my sister and best friend, Dee Dee Everett—thank you for being my support, my sounding board, and a shoulder to lean on.

To my niece Candice Cooper—thank you for your teenage love and support. Continue walking with the Lord, and may you know Him as Father.

To my mother-in-law, Sandra Robinson—thank you for serving as a prayer warrior throughout this process. You're a gift to our family.

To my editor, Adrienne Ingrum—your expertise, biblical knowledge, and polish helped bring forth a great book. Your love for the Lord, sweet spirit, and encouragement brought ease to the editing process. You were an answer to prayer.

Paulette Bowman, thank you for standing by me and encouraging me every step of the way. You read every word and offered sound, candid advice. You are my sister, my mentor, my friend.

Terri McFaddin and Michelle McKinney Hammond, thank you for believing in me and this project and for assisting me in getting published. I praise God for the two of you.

LaVerne Tolbert, thank you for showing me how to write a winning proposal and encouraging me to write.

Donielle Cole, your hands are a wonder! Thank you for helping me input the corrections.

Stephanie Diani, thank you for an awesome photo shoot. Your eyes are a gift to the world, capturing its beauty.

Jordan Allen, you always check up on me, encourage me, and support me. You, too, serve as a godly father figure in my life, and I praise God for you.

Karen Husband, God used this book to develop a new, lifelong relationship. Thank you for your candor. You are family, my sister, my friend.

Michele Barnwell, Donielle Cole, Ailia Coley, Andrea Cook, Sheryl Durden, Ronn and Aladrian Elmore, Verbenia Gant, John Grier, Kimberly Jones, Valerie Long, Shelby McNeil, Aron Roberts, Selena Spann, Geney Warner, Beverly Winton, Kirk and Miranda Williams, and Sharon Woods—thank you for your diligent prayers and support.

To every woman who wrote her story—thank you. May God use your testimonies to touch many women around the world.

And to Laura Barker and the staff at WaterBrook Press—thank you for making my first writing experience a joyful one. The love of God and a spirit of excellence truly flow through your organization.

Chapter 1

Message from a Fatherless Daughter

When my father and my mother forsake me,
then the LORD will take care of me.

PSALM 27:10

An epidemic of absentee fathers is plaguing our society, and it's no respecter of persons. It has hit homes from east to west, north to south, affecting the wealthiest and the poorest, male and female, as well as all races and ethnicities. Society has allowed it, and the church hasn't been able to stop it. Children, teens, adults, even the elderly are all crying on the inside because of it.

Fear, a need to overcompensate, low self-confidence, no self-worth, crippled identity, bitterness, and anger are all manifestations of this growing scourge. The absence of a father affects how we relate to God and others and how we view and treat ourselves. Many fatherless children grow into pleasers who fail to set boundaries for fear of abandonment and rejection. Others become perfectionists; they keep everything in order externally to shield their internal, emotional chaos. Many women overcompensate for their lack of self-esteem and become overachievers to prove to others (and themselves) that they *are* somebody. All find it difficult to put God in control because either they have no reins on their life, or they hold on to them too tightly.

Alarming statistics reveal that teen pregnancy is on the rise. *Marriage Partnership* notes the rate of divorce has soared to around 50 percent and over 60 percent for remarriage.[4] And 83 percent of marriages that take place within two years of a divorce also end up in a divorce.[5] The incarceration of men in general, and black men in particular, cripples homes and breaks down the family structure. Older single women are resorting to artificial insemination for selfish reasons and choosing to parent alone or with another woman. How do we combat absentee fatherhood in the face of these realities? Only by turning our hearts to our heavenly Father. Despite the statistics, you can live a victorious, healthy life if you'll seek God in prayer and recognize Him as your true Father.

This book is designed to enlighten you regarding the role of God in the life of the fatherless and to heal wounds and scars from your relationships—or lack thereof—with your earthly father. If you have experienced physical, emotional, or spiritual absence or abuse from a father or father figure, this book is written for you.

However, it is *not* designed to bash men or degrade fathers. By offering insight and godly perspective, I pray it will bring healing to father-daughter relationships.

My desire is that you learn about God as Father on an intellectual and spiritual level by studying the Bible and on a practical level by doing the Word of God (James 1:22). Throughout this book I will underscore father figures in Scripture and will point out forefathers in Scripture who serve as our spiritual role models. Studying their character prayerfully will develop your character. You'll learn from their mistakes and catalog their godly actions. You can glean from their words of wisdom and follow in their footsteps.

This book is *not* about mothers. If anyone knows the beauty, strength, wisdom, wit, tenacity, stamina, commitment, unconditional love, and continued support of a mother, I do. Mine was a teenage mother who raised two daughters alone, and I celebrate her. But the design, purpose, and function of mothers and fathers are different. The love, nurture, and care of a mother cannot be weighed against the love, nurture, and care of a father. Try with all your might not to compare your mother to your father.

This book is your opportunity to step back, change the lens on the camera, and take a panoramic snapshot of your earthly father once you recognize God is your real Father. Get on your tiptoes, stretch, and reach for *the* Father. Discover His love and affection. He can and wants to be present in your life.

Our Father in heaven has everything we need. He can fill every void that He designed our fathers to fill. David, in Psalm 68:5, reminds us that God is a father to the fatherless.

Feed on the promises of God, for He cannot lie, and His Word will not return void. Cling to His promise in Psalm 27:10, cited at the opening of this chapter, for our heavenly Father will take care of you.

God wants to tuck you in bed at night, be the shoulder you cry on, wipe away your tears, hold and care for you, walk hand in hand with you. Invite Him to be there for you as a Father. God won't impose; God only comes when invited. Jesus asked the man at the pool of Bethesda, "Do you want to be healed?" (John 5:6, CEV). Do you?

THE ROAD TO HEALING

I write this book out of the sincere passion of personal experience. My own childhood years were bittersweet. My mother graduated from high school in Mississippi at age sixteen. Her parents told her and her four older siblings to go to Los Angeles to pursue a "better" life. They believed prosperity was in California. At the time of my birth, my mother was already a twenty-year-old single parent of a two-and-a-half-year-old. My older sister, Deatrice "Dee Dee" Everett, and I have different fathers. Her father played a vital role throughout her life. My father dated my mother two years, saw me once as a newborn, and never returned.

As a child I was unable to articulate my feelings, but, in retrospect, I acknowledge how lonely and disconnected I felt when my sister's father regularly picked her up from our home, took her to his, and left me behind. I never wanted her to go with him, and the few times I accompanied her I felt out of place. I wanted us *both* to be at home with Mama. He was always cordial, but he never embraced me as a daughter. I certainly do not fault him.

I needed and longed for a father. I was ashamed and embarrassed when I discovered my last name wasn't my father's last name. That further contributed to my identity crisis and removed all connection to my father. My birth certificate reads Monique Marcella *Moore* (my biological father's name), but I was called Monique Marcella *Everett*, Dee Dee's last name, for thirty-six years until I married. My mother wanted us to have the same last name, so I grew up an Everett. But I never truly fit in with the Everett family.

I believed God loved everyone except me. When I accepted Jesus Christ as my Lord and Savior at age eleven, I was *so* happy Jesus loved me! I wholeheartedly believed it and embraced it. Love was the highlight and focus of salvation for me more than eternal life. However, no one explained and modeled the importance of an intimate *relationship* with the Lord. Therefore, God and His love became a distant memory.

I told myself I was dumb and would never finish college. I dropped out of Southern University before I entered, because I knew when I received my acceptance letter that I couldn't meet the challenge. After an eight-year journey of dropping in and out of colleges and finally obtaining my bachelor of science degree, I still feared someone would "uncover" the truth—that I knew absolutely nothing! My life was aimless, but I masked it with confidence.

I passed many years in an aimless circle before I painfully acknowledged the root of my problems. When I was finally ready to move from denial, hurt, and pain to the arms of the Father, I freed God's hands to heal my wounded heart, to repair what was shattered when my father walked out.

In 1992, when I was twenty-seven, God led me to Dallas, where He isolated me from family and friends and forced me to face my inner self. I was an ugly sight. For the first time, I realized the negative impact my biological father had on my life. The thought of him (whoever he was) instantly brought me to tears. I continually wondered in despair, *How could he leave me?*

My healing process began with a confession to God similar to the introduction at an Alcoholics Anonymous meeting. I said, "Lord, my name is Monique Marcella Everett, and I am fatherless." God and the angels in heaven resonated in my mind, "Hello, Monique."

The Lord showed me the impact being fatherless had had on my *entire* life—my attitudes, my actions, my beliefs, my decisions, my identity. When my father walked out of my life, confusion stepped in. I never believed in myself. I was fearful of life and fearful of death. In relationships, I longed for love and would do anything to prevent a man from leaving me. I lost my virginity to keep my first boyfriend from breaking up with me and subsequently equated sex with love. Men thought I was cool because whatever they wanted—time, sex, money, a meal—I provided. I viewed the inevitable end of these relationships as abandonment.

While I was in Dallas, the Lord led me to Psalm 27:10—"When my father and my mother forsake me, then the LORD will take care of me"—and I embraced this promise for five painful years as the Lord healed me. My life was transformed, my mind reshaped. I gained joy and peace as I learned to lean on my Daddy—God. I viewed Him as my Father and treated myself as His beautiful daughter. I envisioned myself at His throne, on Jesus' lap; prayer became intimate Father-daughter talks; His Word was a bedtime story; and walking with the Lord included my hand in His big hand.

I began to equate discipline with love, not abandonment. I realized I could come to my Father for anything. I understood the noes of God meant protection, for my Father would not withhold any good thing from me. I felt at liberty to express my anger toward Him and knew He wouldn't "get me back" by punishing and leaving me. During those five years I fell in love with God. By September 1997, God had become my Father.

A Traumatic Experience

Perhaps you, too, endured a painful childhood, longing for your daddy's love, but you've never fully dealt with the trauma of your experience. You may even believe *trauma* is too strong a word, not wanting to recognize the impact of fatherlessness on your life. *Trauma* is defined as any distressing experience. Lack of a father's love and presence disturbs the inner self and certainly qualifies to be described as a trauma.

- It was traumatic if you entered this world without a father.
- It was traumatic if you lived in a household with a physically or sexually abusive father.
- It was traumatic if your father walked out on your family.
- It was traumatic if your father and mother divorced, leaving you torn between the two. When you were asked by a judge, "With whom do you want to live?" your soul wanted to cry out, "Both of them!"
- If your father and mother engaged in premarital sex and bore children out of wedlock, all of you experienced the traumatic consequences of sin.
- If you packed and toted a suitcase every other week to visit Daddy, that was traumatic. Fourteen days' absence is dangerous! The Enemy has too much room to infiltrate children's impressionable hearts and minds with negativity, lies, and manipulation. Yet, not visiting at all is more traumatic.

If you have lived with any of these situations as normal, recognize that they're not. The disconnection of father and daughter is distressing. Our earthly father was designed to be a representation of our heavenly Father, and if he is absent, we are deprived of exposure to an accurate image of God.

God made man and woman in His image (see Genesis 1). But both are needed to reflect His image! *Together* a husband and wife bring stability to their offspring.

Separation from your father is a calamity, but the good news is that such a tragedy is a platform for the Lord to introduce Himself to you and evidence Himself as both a loving God and a loving Father.

Throughout this book, I will be encouraging you to do the work necessary to understand and know God as Father. At the close of each chapter, I've included a self-evaluation section labeled "Growth Chart." Answering these questions will help you face the wounds created by separation from your earthly father and will lead you to accept the healing touch of your heavenly Father. I've also included a "Growth Spurt" section that leads you directly into relationship with the Father through the Word and prayer. Often we expect God to do miracles and give us extraordinary blessings while we do the ordinary. That won't work here, my sister. Move out of your comfort zone or lazy zone, and do the work of praying, fasting, studying, meditating, and listening to God's voice.

In 1992, when I began my five-year journey to completely know God as Father, the road was not easy. Those years were tough, bumpy, rough, and lonely, but they were definitely rewarding. I was liberated, and God will liberate you, too.

≡ GROWTH CHART

1. Check all that apply:
   ___ I'm angry most of the time and don't know why.
   ___ I struggle to connect with God.
   ___ I inadvertently sabotage relationships.
   ___ Love is a foreign language.
   ___ I smother those closest to me.
   ___ I have little or no self-confidence.
   ___ I rarely take risks or step out in faith.

_____ I have minimal self-worth.

_____ There's an undercurrent of anxiety in most tasks I perform.

_____ I never feel like I fit in or belong.

2. List specific challenges you faced as a result of your father's absence.

3. What specific baggage needs unloading on your journey toward healing and restoration?

⊒ GROWTH SPURT

Scripture Memorization

"A father of the fatherless, a defender of widows, is God in His holy habitation." Psalm 68:5

Prayer

Lord, I desire to know You as my Father. I don't understand all the details of my earthly father's absence, but I ask You to fill every void. I'm ready to begin this new journey of trusting You with my life.

Chapter 2

The Father's Day

I will be a Father to you,
and you shall be My sons and daughters,
says the LORD Almighty.

2 CORINTHIANS 6:18

Today is the Father's day. Not a day Hallmark set aside, but our *heavenly* Father's day. His day comes not just once a year; every day is a day of surrender to the Father's everlasting, unending, and unconditional love, an opportunity to hear what He says about you—His beautiful daughter—in His Word, the Bible.

In my quest to know God as Father I wanted to know what He said about fathers and mothers, the fatherless and the motherless. My accounting background prompted me to seek out who was mentioned and how many times. The word *father* occurs 979 times in Scripture, in 852 verses. The word *mother* occurs 350 times—only a third as often as *father*. The word *fatherless* is mentioned 41 times and in 39 instances is coupled with the widow who has lost her husband to death. *Widow* is mentioned 50 times, more than *fatherless*.

The words *motherless* and *widower* (a man who loses his wife to death) are never used in Scripture.

These calculations show God's plan, position, and purpose for the male and the impact of his presence in our lives. The Bible places special emphasis on the father. Children can rightly be called orphans if their father is absent for any reason. Even the presence of a loving mother cannot replace a father.

THE ROAD TO THE FATHER

When my husband and I honeymooned in Cancún, we took an all-day tour of the Mayan ruins at Chichén Itzá. Our tour guide was vibrant and passionate about his culture and its history. He instructed us American tourists to "undress" from our Western culture in order to understand and appreciate Mayan culture. I would not undress from my biblical culture to accept the worship of their gods and ancestors, but I liked his concept of undressing.

We can become so accustomed to our environment and our cultural background we forget that our way of thinking and our way of life are not the only ways. Closed thinking precludes us from having an open heart and mind, so let's "undress" mentally to grasp the concept of God as our Father.

Undress from the physical realm—what we see, touch, and feel—to get clothed in the spiritual realm. God is Spirit, and the beginning of knowing God as Father is to worship Him in spirit and in truth. We connect with God through Jesus Christ. Through Him alone do we have access to the Father (Ephesians 2:18).

If you haven't done so, take a moment to pray and ask Jesus Christ to connect you to the Father, to be Lord of your life, to rule every aspect of your life.

Lord Jesus, I need my life to change, and that change only comes through You. I want God to be my Father, and that relationship only comes through You. I am a sinner, and I need You to cleanse me. I believe that You died for my sins and were raised from the dead so I can have an abundant and eternal life. Thank You for new life. Thank You for saving me. Be Lord of my life. In Your name I pray. Amen.

If you just prayed that prayer, you now have access to the Father. God's Spirit, the Holy Spirit, now gives you guidance and direction, serving as your Helper and your Teacher. (See Appendix A.)

Jesus Christ bridged the gap between humans and God, giving us a permanent Father-daughter relationship. We can now experience an intimate relationship with the Father by doing what God tells us to do.

One day when I was struggling with my father wounds, I announced, "Okay, God, since You allowed my father to leave me at birth, *You* have to be my Father!" God responded with an announcement of His own: "You will obey Me, be responsible for your actions, stop whining about your past, and look forward to your future with Me. You must come to Me for *everything*—no exceptions. Enough with the temper tantrums and lying down, kicking and screaming. I've taught you and equipped you to do the right thing. We're in this together. You'll always be My child, but I want you to know who you are—royalty, a godly woman, a lady. Practice until you get it right. No excuses. When you fall, I'll be right there to pick you up. And in the process you will grow to resemble Me."

If you have accepted Jesus Christ, an intimate relationship with the Father awaits you. If you've never been taught about intimacy with God or have backslid, don't shut Him out. In Revelation 3:20 Jesus said, "I stand at the door and knock. If anyone hears My voice and opens the door, I will come in to him and dine with him, and he with Me."

He longs to be active in your life. He is knocking and wants you to let Him in to build an intimate relationship with you.

You can break out of that emotional rut when you let the Father in. Trust Him to navigate your path of healing and deliverance.

STAGES OF LIFE

James Vander Zanden, in *Human Development,* charts psychoanalyst Erik Erikson's stages of development.[6] Erikson described the physical, emotional, and psychological stages of life accompanied by positive developments in a healthy environment versus the results of neglect:

Stages of Development	Positive	Negative	Favorable Outcome
Infant (0-2)	Trust	Mistrust	Trust is developed in self, parents, and in the world
Toddler (2-4)	Autonomy	Shame and Doubt	A sense of self-control is developed without a loss of self-esteem
Early School Age (5-7)	Initiative	Guilt	Learns to acquire direction and purpose in activities
Middle School Age (8-12)	Industry	Inferiority	Acquires a sense of mastery and competence
Adolescent (13-18)	Identity	Alienation	Develops a coherent sense of self

Erikson was not speaking from a biblical perspective or about fathers in particular, but I believe his analysis captures what a fatherless child experiences during the foundational, formative stages of life.

If you'll examine the stage of development you were in when your father departed, you'll be able to pinpoint some of the challenges you faced. My father departed when I was days old; therefore I experienced all the negative components listed in the third column of the diagram. His leaving created a domino effect from birth that was realized in my early adult years.

But though the challenges created by our fathers' absence are very real, it's important to remember that what you *believe* affects how you *think*, affects how you *feel*, affects how you *behave*. Your belief in God, your Father, can change the behavior that results from having an absent father.

Paul, in his letter to the Romans, succinctly said:

1. Change your belief system (Romans 10:9).
2. Change your thinking (Romans 12:2).
3. You'll have the energy and ability to prove the good, acceptable, and perfect will of God (Romans 12:2).
4. These changes will affect your behavior (Romans 12:9–13:4).

Following his advice will lead you to a new Father, a new foundation, and a new outlook on life.

HONOR YOUR FATHER

Sometimes I wish I could skip over the challenging and seemingly impossible commands in Scripture: "Love your enemies" (Matthew 5:44), "Do not fret because of…the man who brings wicked schemes to pass" (Psalm 37:7), "Be angry, and do not sin" (Ephesians 4:26), and "Let no corrupt word proceed out of your mouth" (Ephesians 4:29).

On my road to healing I came across a verse I'd read before but which now had new meaning:

> "Honor your father and mother," which is the first commandment with promise: "that it may be well with you and you may live long on the earth." (Ephesians 6:2-3)

There was *no way* the first part of that verse applied to me! Was the Father asking me to honor a man I've never met? A man whose face I've never seen? A man who never gave me a chance to know him? A man who abandoned me? Surely not! So I closed the Bible and tried to ignore the words. But God kept bringing them back to me. I couldn't run away from the truth of His Word. Neither can you. This may be the most challenging scripture you'll face.

We are commanded to honor our father and mother, without any stipulations. It does not read, "*If your father was supportive financially, emotionally, and spiritually,* honor your father," or "*If your father was a provider,* honor your father," or "*If your father was not abusive,* honor your father," or "*If your father kept his promises,* honor your father." That would contradict the character of our loving, forgiving, and merciful Father.

According to *Webster's,* the word *honor* has several closely related meanings, which include:

- to revere
- to esteem
- to show respect
- to show a courteous regard for
- integrity in one's actions[7]

The greatest sense of the word *honor* is to place one upon a pedestal; the lowest sense is to give people the respect due them, which *always* prohibits disrespect. This is the command given to us regarding our fathers. It is not easy, but God asks us to do it and gives us His strength.

Let's look at Ephesians 6:2 in context. Paul wrote this letter to the church in Ephesus while he was imprisoned in Rome. Chapters 1–3 lay the foundation of Christ—what He did for us, His purpose for us, and our position in Him. Chapters 4–6 reveal our overall responsibilities in relationships, which include Christ, our brothers and sisters in Christ, our spouse, parents, children, and bosses. Paul ended the letter by putting everything in perspective and exhorting us to gear up for the continuous spiritual fight of our lives.

Chapter 5, which just precedes our troublesome command to honor our fathers no matter what, talks about being filled with the Spirit. God gives you the Holy Spirit the moment you confess with your mouth that Jesus is Lord and believe that God raised Him from the dead (Romans 10:9). However, being *filled* with the Holy Spirit is different. It does not automatically happen. You must want to be filled, and you must ask God. Being filled is like having a tank full of gas in your car, running the gas out, and going back to the station for a refill. Where you travel, the road conditions, and the state of your vehicle determine the frequency of refills.

Despite the circumstances, you *can* adhere to the Father's command to honor your father if you are filled with the Holy Spirit. However, only the Spirit of God can help you honor a man who may not be honorable or a man whom you've never seen. It can only be accomplished by total submission.

God may lead you to honor your father by initiating peace in your relationship. He may lead you to honor him by accepting his apology. He may lead you to apologize! He may lead you to honor your father by simply closing your mouth and not allowing your tongue to offend.

The first challenge I had to overcome in honoring my father was renewing my mind toward him. Shame prevented me from telling others, but the Lord knew my internal battle. I tore him down in my *mind*.

The Father showed me how these thoughts affected me. I wasn't tearing my father down; I was tearing my spirit down!

Paul told the Ephesians to let no corrupt word proceed out of their mouths (4:29). I had to make sure no corrupt words were in my head. God showed me that entertaining and dwelling on evil thoughts dishonored my father. I had to speak and think good, not evil, of him. Since I didn't know him, the good was generic, but it was *much* better than the bad. I had to rid my thoughts of negativity and speculation and focus solely on the truth: My father is created in the image of God, and *everything* God creates is good. As odd as it may seem, I honor my father by thanking him for leaving me. Because he left, I know God as Father. The way I know Him now, having pursued the Father with such desperation and determination, would not be my experience had he stayed in my life. I might not otherwise have had the privilege of glorifying God in this way.

I honor my earthly father with my mind, tongue, and thanks. Likewise, I honor the Father with my mind, mouth, thanksgiving, and praise.

Honoring is the final destination in your healing process, but you will get there. It took me five challenging and frustrating years. Nevertheless, when I arrived, the Father gave me lightness, a refreshing freedom, and peace I wouldn't trade for the world.

LONGEVITY

In Exodus 20, the fifth commandment is, "Honor your father and your mother, that your days may be long upon the land which the LORD your God is giving you" (verse 12). This instruction was reiterated throughout Scripture: by Moses in Deuteronomy, by Jesus five times in the Gospels, and by Paul in Ephesians 6:

> "Honor your father and your mother," which is the first commandment with promise: "that it may be well with you and you may live long on the earth." (Ephesians 6:2-3)

Honoring our father is tied to long life. Dishonor and vile actions toward your father will only hurt *you*, feeding deep-seated anger, bitterness, and a hardened heart that will cause your premature death. The *actions* that created the father-daughter wounds don't lead to death. Your father will answer to God for his actions. The father-daughter *wounds* don't lead to death. The Father can heal them. How you *respond* to your father who wounded you can lead to death. Dishonor can shorten your life.

The scripture in Ephesians 6 about honoring your father is sandwiched between being filled with the Spirit and spiritual warfare. Both of these are necessary to our success in honoring our fathers. Be filled and fight!

We do not wrestle against flesh and blood or, specifically (Ephesians 6:12). Meditate on this scripture, and ask the Lo and soften your heart as you travel down this bumpy section of the road to healing. Honoring your father is not an option; therefore, do not ignore, dismiss, or gloss over this command.

May your days be long on the earth.

≡GROWTH CHART

1. Journal your journey through this book.
2. What is your view of your earthly father?
3. What is your view of your heavenly Father?
4. On a forgiveness scale from 1 to 10 (1=Completely unforgiven, 10=Completely forgiven) how close are you to forgiving your father? | 1   2   3   4   5   6   7   8   9   10 |
5. How do you honestly feel about Ephesians 6:2-3? Are you obeying these verses?

≡GROWTH SPURT

Scripture Memorization
"When my father and my mother forsake me, then the LORD will take care of me." Psalm 27:10

Prayer
Father, from this day forward, it is Your day and a new season in my life. I want to know You as my Father. Remove anything or anyone who would hinder me from knowing You as my Daddy.

Chapter 3

Why Fathers Leave

And He said, "...Have you eaten from the tree
of which I commanded you that you should not eat?"

GENESIS 3:11

I agonized for years over the departure of my father, asking God over and over, "Why did he leave me?" I wondered what he thought when he saw me for the first and last time. As a six-pound-three-ounce baby girl, did I frighten him when he looked into my eyes? Or *did* he look into my eyes? Did he plan his escape when I still was in my mother's womb, or did he panic after my birth? Those questions may go unanswered for eternity, but the Father's answer gave me peace. His answer took me back to the beginning of time to search for the primary reason fathers leave.

THE FALL OF MAN

When God told Adam not to eat from the tree of the knowledge of good and evil, He meant it. But Adam chose to disobey God and turned order into chaos.

Failure to adhere to the command of God led to spiritual, emotional, and physical devastation and passed world dominion to Satan.

Every second of the day we face the devastating consequences of the Fall. When you watch television or read the paper, you take in a litany of tragedy. Yet we don't understand the catastrophic dimensions of the Fall.

We expect life to be neat, not chaotic. We expect our family structure and each member to be ideal. We expect God to say yes to everything we ask. We expect perfect marriages, children, churches, parents, and jobs.

A panoramic view of the width and depth of the Fall changes these expectations. It becomes no surprise that my father chose to abandon his responsibilities to me. Every family shows up somewhere on the wide spectrum of the dysfunction scale. Some families are more dysfunctional than others, but we *all* experience spiritual, emotional, and physical consequences of the Fall.

As a result of the Fall, your father was, like all of us, born innately depraved. He desperately needed an intimate relationship with God to deter him from his collision course with you. If he had no relationship with God, or a superficial one, he was totally vulnerable. This does not excuse his actions, but it lays the foundation for you to understand and forgive.

Scripture clearly points to the one ultimately responsible for our fallen world. The Lord God said to the serpent, "Because *you* have done this…" (Genesis 3:14, emphasis added). The serpent represents Satan. He is the ruler over the systems of this world, and, unfortunately, we live in his domain.

Your earthly father is *not* the enemy! The man you despise, disrespect, avoid, and speak ill of is not the one to fight. Take your focus off your father (in the physical realm), and see evil forces (in the spiritual realm) as the problem, and fight the battle there.

This statement is not a license for fathers to sin freely, nor does it excuse past, present, and future ungodly behavior—including how *we* respond to such ungodliness. Your father is responsible and will be held accountable for his actions. However, the first step you must take on the path of healing is recognizing the innumerable ways Satan operates.

The demon *Fear* is assigned to one father, telling him the only answer to his problems is to flee and never return. Another demon taints the mind of a father and tells him to resolve his problems by suicide. The demon *Depression* is assigned to another father, encouraging him that the answer to the stresses of life is in a bottle of alcohol. The demon *Violence* is assigned to another, conditioning him to strike his wife and children. The demon *Abuse* is assigned to one father, telling him his sexual desires can be fulfilled through his daughter.

With the path of destruction laid out through her father, the demon *Deception* tells a daughter all men are dogs. Another demon, *Homosexuality*, tells her sister that her physical, emotional, and sexual needs can only be fulfilled by a woman.

These are merely a few examples of how we're attacked spiritually. When you recognize our fallen nature and the world system undermining the family, you begin to see how our lives have been complicated by the Fall.

Satan is called the father of lies (John 8:44, NIV). He's the author of them and seeks to plant them in our minds. We must combat him and his lies, not our earthly fathers.

So how are we equipped to do combat? The Word of God must influence our emotions and thoughts. Remember Ephesians 6:12: "We do not wrestle against flesh and blood, but against principalities, against powers, against the rulers of the darkness of this age, against spiritual hosts of wickedness in the heavenly places." You are engaged in a spiritual war, not a father-daughter battle.

THE LEGACY OF THE FALL

Throughout Scripture, we can observe the many reasons fathers become disconnected from their children. "There is nothing new under the sun" (Ecclesiastes 1:9). We can also, through these powerful examples, gain insight into how God can use our pain, redeeming the legacy of sin and using it to bring glory to Himself.

Death

Death was not God's original design for man. I used to think of death as a natural occurrence and believed it did not produce the same emotional and psychological challenges as a father who walks out. But it, too, traumatizes children. It's still a direct result of the Fall.

The Old Testament heroine Esther experienced the death of both parents as a child. We don't know if her father and mother died together or if her father died first and then her mother (based on word order in Scripture); either way, their deaths restructured her life.

Her loving cousin, Mordecai, raised her as his own daughter, responding to the need for a father figure in her life. She came to him as a teenager. We don't know the challenges they faced while she grieved the death of her parents, but we do know that the Father had His hand on her life all along.

The death of a father did not halt the favor and hand of God but positioned her to be elevated as queen of the Persian king Ahasuerus. God used her to save the lives of the Jews, and, likewise, He wants to use you to draw men and women to Him.

Jealousy

Sarai plotted and schemed and decided to take matters into her own hands when she could not give Abram a son. She gave her servant, Hagar, to him as his wife, and she conceived and gave birth to Ishmael, whose name means *God hears* (Genesis 16:1-16).

Ishmael was fourteen years of age when Isaac was born and seventeen years old when Sarai (now called Sarah) in her jealousy pushed him and his mother out of their abode and away from his father (now called Abraham). How devastating to be torn from his father at the threshold of manhood, and how much worse to endure the pain of having his own father usher him away.

While Hagar was in the wilderness, she lifted her voice and cried to God, but God heard the voice of the lad (Genesis 21:16-17). That verse alone shows the love God has for fatherless, abandoned children. And God blessed Ishmael despite his father's sin, even though Isaac, not Ishmael, was the one promised by God.

Maybe you were born as a result of an adulterous or unfavorable relationship and were sent away or went unrecognized to prevent the "disruption" of your father's family. Your father may have done everything he could to usher you out of his life to please another woman. Whatever the circumstances of your past, you can rest in the certainty that the Father sees you, hears your cry, will take care of you, and has a great blessing in store for you.

Family Members

One of the greatest heartbreaks is when family members—fathers, mothers, siblings, aunts, uncles—turn their backs and seek to destroy you. In Genesis 37:17-35 Joseph experienced this nightmare when his brothers launched a plot to kill him.

As the firstborn of Israel's second wife, Rachel, who was the love of Israel's life, Joseph was beloved by his father. But Israel's older sons, by his first wife, Leah, and his concubines, greatly despised Joseph. The brothers threw Joseph into a pit with the intent to kill him but later sold him into slavery to Midianite traders. Jealousy divided a family. Hatred separated a loving father from his child. God, the protective Father, responded to Joseph's pain and isolation.

Sometimes family members hinder a father-child relationship with manipulation and distance. Your father's departure may very well be the result of your mother's heel in his back, pushing him out the door. She may have been emotionally wounded, discovered abusive behaviors, or selfishly didn't want him to love anyone else—including you—if he didn't love her. She may have adopted an "I'll fix him" attitude and denied him visits, calls, and letters. She intended to hurt him but inadvertently damaged you.

Children are often used as bait or punishment for fathers who refuse to be in relationship with the mother. Such behavior is ungodly and unacceptable. Regardless of the relationship between parents, children need their fathers.

If you are a mother who deliberately denies your child visits with, or from, his or her father for selfish reasons, I implore you to pray and ask God to reveal to you the long-term effects such actions will have on your child. Bitterness and unforgiveness will hurt you and the child the most. Allow God to heal you of that relationship, and do what's best for your child.

Family members usually have good intentions in "protecting" a child from a man they deem unworthy of a relationship with the child, but they hurt the child in the long run. Again, children need their fathers—no matter how rotten the family thinks he is.

If you know a father who has to struggle to see his child, let him know that it only reaffirms his love. Encourage him not to give up. The truth will be revealed, and he and the child will one day appreciate it.

Distance

Another hindrance to a father-child relationship is distance. When a father moves hundreds or thousands of miles away from his children or a mother moves the children far away, it creates a gulf and rift in the relationship that can lead to noncommunication and permanent separation.

Again, look at Hagar and Ishmael. Abraham gave Hagar bread, water, and her son and sent her away (Genesis 21:14). The wilderness represents a barren and desolate place. There Ishmael made his home (Genesis 21:20-21).

If a father is not in the home, parents can work together to find ways for the children to see him often. Summers or holidays are not enough for healthy development of the father-child relationship. If you are not living with the father of your child, consider ways you can close the distance between them, such as living in the same community until the children are grown.

Another aspect of the distance problem is the fact that our prisons are overpopulated with fathers. Robbery, murder, drugs, sex offenses, domestic violence, and child abuse are reasons many fathers are separated from their children. Children of incarcerated fathers experience a heightened level of shame and embarrassment. Not only did Daddy leave, but everybody knows why. Despite the offense or what people say, a child longs to see, touch, and embrace his or her father, no matter where he is. Extreme frustration and rebellion often result when visitation is refused.

Was your father incarcerated during a portion or all of your formative years? Forgive him for his parental *and* legal offense. Reacquaint yourself with him if you can, and develop a relationship. If your child's father is incarcerated, do not refuse visitation simply because the father is imprisoned. Refuse only if he is a threat to you or your child.

Despite his location, a child needs a connection and bond with his father. If shame is the barrier, pray and work through it. If anger is the barrier, go in anger but don't sin. If visitation is impossible, write a letter or send a card to make the connection. The enemy is not behind bars.

Misplaced Priorities

Some fathers don't physically leave, but they do leave their daughters vulnerable to abuse and neglect. One of the most traumatic stories in Scripture is found in Judges 19:22-30, when a father perpetuates the abuse of his virgin daughter. He invited sin into their home and left his daughter vulnerable to the perverted men of the world. She was saved only by the grace of God, but her visiting counterpart suffered abuse and death.

This father valued his position, man's perception, and a new acquaintance more than he treasured his family. He protected and elevated a stranger over his daughter.

Daughters are subject to the ills and perversions of the world when fathers do not protect them. The wrong boss, friend, colleague, minister, or family member can be an enemy seeking to devour, and the father's role is to shelter his daughter rather than being distracted by worldly esteem or pressures.

Without extreme vigilance, care, and protection by fathers, daughters can be abused or even killed on their front porch.

Adoption

In some instances fathers and/or mothers must give up their children for adoption for the good of the children. A great example of adoption is found in Exodus 1 and 2.

Following Joseph's death, a new king of Egypt (Pharaoh) arose and felt threatened by the increasing number of Hebrews. He created a hostile and ruthless environment, subjecting them to hard bondage. When that was unsuccessful in controlling their increase, he instructed the midwives to kill the Hebrew women's newborn sons.

Fear, paranoia, and fatigue likely gripped Moses' mother as she frantically hid her newborn for three months to shield him from death. When all her options were exhausted, she carefully prepared a place to lay him by the river's bank. Moses was later found and adopted by Pharaoh's daughter.

Many daughters were adopted for known and unknown reasons. You may have been filtered through the foster-care system before you were adopted, but the Father prepared a place for you. The Father has a purpose for your life, and your adoption, like Moses', was intended by God to save your life and to help others.

Sexual Immorality

David peered over the top of his castle and lusted for Bathsheba, the wife of Uriah. His lack of self-control caused him to commit sexual sin and then murder Uriah. His sin resulted in the death of David and Bathsheba's son.

But each one is tempted when he is drawn away by his own desires and enticed. Then, when desire has conceived, it gives birth to sin; and sin, when it is full-grown, brings forth death. (James 1:14-15)

Like David, fathers who engage in sexual immorality often put themselves and the people closest to them in jeopardy.

Adultery, lust, sexual immorality, and pornography kill the heart, mind, spirit, physical body, marriage, emotions, love, and children. Selfishness and the lack of self-control leave long-term effects from generation to generation, "visiting the iniquity of the fathers upon the children and the children's children to the third and the fourth generation" (Exodus 34:7).

Teen and even preteen pregnancy has become frighteningly prevalent. Sex is glamorized on television, videos, billboards, movies, magazines, and books. Teenagers have less supervision because of working mothers. And so many parents have set an example that suggests sexual immorality is no big deal.

Many teenagers today believe they are invincible and are careless with their lives. It's hard for them to think past high school or college, and others don't expect to live long because they're inundated with violence almost daily. It's a recipe for teenage pregnancy and absent fathers, because most teenage boys who impregnate teenage girls will not raise their children.

Lamentations 5:7 captures this concept best: "Our fathers sinned and are no more, but we bear their iniquities."

Everyone is affected, and it is no secret that *we* suffer the consequences of our father's sin. *We* experience the associated pain, heartache, ripping apart of the family, and even death. *We* die emotionally when our dads father babies out of wedlock. *We* see unborn children die via abortion. *We* see our physical bodies growing while our emotional growth is stunted.

Generational Curses

Many fathers leave because they watched their father leave and their father's father left their father. And Uncle John left Aunt Mae and their kids. Uncle Pete left Aunt Elma and their kids. In their nuclear and extended family, men never endured through the rough times. The Enemy came into the family structure, wreaked havoc, and manipulated the father into believing that the only solution was to leave.

Generational curses are passed down from father to child to grandchild and so on until someone decides, "Enough is enough!" and engages in spiritual battle to break the curse. Consider the story of Josiah in 2 Kings 22. His father, Amon, and grandfather Manasseh led Israel away from God, engaging in idol worship and other evil practices. Despite their legacy, when the high priest discovered the Book of the Law—God's instructions for the people of Israel—Josiah broke the generational chain of sin and led his people in humble repentance.

Strongholds can be broken if you are willing to tarry in prayer and educate your children and your children's children about the stronghold laced throughout your family tree.

Divorce

Divorce disrupts and devastates the family structure, ripping apart the union God created between man and woman. No wonder God spoke so bluntly in Malachi 2:16, saying, "For the LORD God of Israel says that He hates divorce, for it covers one's garment with violence." The Father views divorce as a violent act, leaving scarred men, women, and children behind.

God allowed divorce because of the hardness of man's heart (Matthew 19:8), and statistics prove that today our hearts are harder than ever.

Entrapment

Some of our mothers were spiritually immature when they birthed us. They lacked wisdom and guidance and were not sure how to handle their emotions. Perhaps they had their own issues of fatherlessness. They may have made the mistake of manipulating, deceiving, or sexually entrapping a man—privately planning their pregnancy without his knowledge or consent.

Various scenarios lie beneath entrapment: a deep longing for love, acceptance, and commitment from a man; loneliness; fear of abandonment and the desperate hope that a child will make him stay; a deep longing to be loved and seeking that love solely through a child; and, as a single woman, the fear of getting older and never having a baby.

Despite their ungodly behavior and its long-term consequences, many women who entrap men develop into beautiful, wise, caring, and loving mothers—celebrated by their daughters and sons.

The pregnancies that result from such unions may anger fathers. Some opt to remove themselves from the mother and "her" child, refusing physical, emotional, and financial support—never to be heard from again. Others disappear physically but are forced to support the child financially. Such fathers are immobilized by a flood of negative emotion, which creates a wide gulf between them and the children.

If the above describes your mother's past, don't be dismayed. Your story is not an isolated event, for acts of sexual deception can be traced back to biblical times. In Genesis 19:30-38 we read about the deception of two daughters who plotted and sexually entrapped their own father.

Then Lot went up out of Zoar and dwelt in the mountains, and his two daughters were with him; for he was afraid to dwell in Zoar. And he and his two daughters dwelt in a cave. Now the firstborn said to the younger, "Our father is old, and there is no man on the earth to come in to us as is the custom of all the earth. Come, let us make our father drink wine, and we will lie with him, that we may preserve the lineage of our father." So they made their father drink wine that night. And the firstborn went in and lay with her father, and he did not know when she lay down or when she arose.

It happened on the next day that the firstborn said to the younger, "Indeed I lay with my father last night; let us make him drink wine tonight also, and you go in and lie with him, that we may preserve the lineage of our father." Then they made their father drink wine that night also. And the younger arose and lay with him, and he did not know when she lay down or when she arose.

Thus both the daughters of Lot were with child by their father. The firstborn bore a son and called his name Moab; he is the father of the Moabites to this day. And the younger, she also bore a son and called his name Ben-Ammi; he is the father of the people of Ammon to this day.

Hopelessness, fear, and lack of trust in God gripped these two widowed, motherless sisters. Understand that your mother lacked spiritual sustenance and substance and probably had deep-seated wounds and fears. Your father was wounded by her actions and his weak flesh. *Both* parents are responsible for your lack of an earthly dad—not just your father. Both must take ownership and confess their sin. Prayerfully each must learn that only the Father can satisfy those insatiable needs, settle fears, and soothe all hurts.

Sometimes the truth hurts, but the Father wants to heal you completely. He wants the whole truth revealed to help you reshape your view of your earthly father. If you've formulated a negative view of your father, God wants to steer you away from the blame game and usher you into acceptance and forgiveness. It helps to put ourselves in our parents' shoes to understand and forgive them. My mother's story was not sexual entrapment, but I had to realize that she was sixteen years old when she moved to Los Angeles with her sisters and brother with no parental direction and spiritual guidance in a new land. I probably would have made the same mistakes she did.

Make every effort not to criticize your parents. Take your negative energy and redirect it to the throne of God. Cry out to the Father. Intercede on behalf of both parents. Honor them by praying for them.

I Will Never Leave You

Your Father in heaven promises to never leave you nor forsake you (Joshua 1:5). God knew before time began that your father would abandon his responsibilities, so He made plans before you were born to cradle you in His loving arms and take care of you. With the Father, everyone can have joy, because His grace and mercy always prevail.

Agree that you will not spend your life in anger asking why. Instead, ask the Father how He can be glorified through your life.

Jesus speaks the same words to you as He said to Lazarus's sisters: "This sickness is not unto death, but for the glory of God, that the Son of God may be glorified through it" (John 11:4). The emotional, psychological, mental, and spiritual "sickness" you're experiencing about your father's absence will not kill you, if you allow God to be glorified through your life's experiences.

◢Growth Chart

1. In what area(s) of your life was your father absent? Check all that apply:
   ___ Physical
   ___ Financial
   ___ Emotional
   ___ Spiritual
   ___ Mental
2. How did your father leave you?
3. Why did your father leave you?
4. How did your father's absence affect you? Check all that apply:

   ___ Low self-image   ___ Fear of success

   ___ Low self-worth   ___ Anger

   ___ Panic attacks   ___ Bitterness

   ___ Fear of abandonment   ___ Loneliness

   ___ "I don't belong"   ___ Depression

   ___ Longing for love   ___ Instability

   ___ "I'm a pleaser"   ___ Unaccomplished tasks

5. Identify at least five ways God has revealed Himself as a father in your life.

6. Look at your maternal and paternal family trees. How many fathers abandoned their children?

⬛ GROWTH SPURT

Scripture Memorization

"For all have sinned and fall short of the glory of God." Romans 3:23

Prayer

Father, help me to know without a shadow of a doubt that You will never leave me nor forsake me.

Chapter 4

Why Daughters Leave

If you have anything against anyone, forgive him,
that your Father in heaven
may also forgive you your trespasses.

MARK 11:25

One of our greatest struggles as individuals is to understand our humanity. We know about the fall of man, but we have difficulty grasping what that concept means for us.

We expect perfection in an imperfect world. We place high, unrealistic demands on ourselves and then beat ourselves when we fail. And when our earthly fathers fall from our impossibly high pedestals, our lives are shattered. Remember Ephesians 6:12 in the previous chapter. Your father is not your enemy. He is flesh and blood—fallible—and he *will* make mistakes.

⎯⎯⎯

A DAUGHTER'S STORY: ALMA

When I was young, my father was always there, and he *never* missed a beat. He was my best friend, and I would always say, "I want my husband to be just like my dad." But at the tender age of thirteen, disappointment burst through the front door of my life when I discovered that my father led another life, with another woman.

I felt unwanted, that he had left me when he had other kids, that I wasn't good enough. He was never there emotionally. He was always upset and seemed to take his anger out on me. He betrayed me. From that day forward he stepped down from his position of father and became a stranger.

I've been on the road to healing from a broken heart for literally seven years. I know I've made much headway because prayer and personal experiences have taught me that no man or woman is perfect and that I must do three things to experience complete healing: forgive my father, allow God to help me stop judging my father, and rebuild our relationship and friendship.

In retrospect, my actions and responses to this crisis made things a lot worse. My immaturity produced a rebellious spirit, and I despised my dad. I began telling people I didn't have a father (even though he came home every night), and I ran from my pain rather than calling on God for help. The rocky road I traveled—filled with pain and suffering—would have been much smoother had I initially trusted God.

My father and I are still working on our relationship. He has openly acknowledged that his actions caused a separation between us and has vowed that he will do *whatever* it takes to restore my confidence in him. But I am not quite ready to believe him.

I have decided I don't want God to bring back the relationship I once had with my father. I want God to make me a better daughter and my dad a better father.

A FATHER-FIGURE KING

One of my favorite father figures in Scripture is King David. Initially described as a ruddy, bright-eyed, good-looking youth, he blossomed into a man after God's own heart who would do all of God's will (Acts 13:22).

Listen to God's description of David in Psalm 89:20-29:

I have found My servant David;
With My holy oil I have anointed him,
With whom My hand shall be established;
Also My arm shall strengthen him.
The enemy shall not outwit him,
Nor the son of wickedness afflict him.
I will beat down his foes before his face,
And plague those who hate him.

But My faithfulness and My mercy shall be with him,
And in My name his horn shall be exalted.
Also I will set his hand over the sea,
And his right hand over the rivers.
He shall cry to Me, "You are my Father,
My God, and the rock of my salvation."
Also I will make him My firstborn,
The highest of the kings of the earth.
My mercy I will keep for him forever,
And My covenant shall stand firm with him.
His seed also I will make to endure forever,
And his throne as the days of heaven.

This passage reveals God's heart for an imperfect child. David was an anointed king, filled with the Holy Spirit. However, as mentioned in the previous chapter, David erred. He killed Uriah and brought pain and suffering on Bathsheba and himself. Their newborn son died.

Some of our fathers are great men like David who made a mistake and are sorry for their sin. They want God to create a clean heart in them and renew their spirit (Psalm 51:10). They long for those affected by their sin to forgive them and let them off the hook of anger, bitterness, and athers can identify with David—longing to be forgiven for addictions to work, church, sex, alcohol, drugs, or gambling; for committing adultery, stealing, lying, or swindling. Their sin may be ever before them with a constant reminder from family or friends. But they must remember the key verse is 2 Samuel 11:27: "But the thing that David had done displeased the LORD."

Oh, how this verse captures the heart of the Father! He did not hate or despise David but hated and despised the offense. When David acknowledged his sin, he wrote Psalm 51, and God forgave him. Psalm 89, with God's loving appraisal of His servant, was written *after* David's offense. Likewise, fathers must know that the Father loves and forgives them. He's not holding any confessed sin over their head.

Wives and mothers can identify with Bathsheba—grieving over the consequences of her husband's sin, fighting and clawing to put the pieces of her life back together, and heartbroken at the death of her child. Life seems out of control, unfair, and God seems cruel and distant, but she discovers that He is her only lifeline.

Daughters experience an emotional, psychological, and spiritual death when a father's actions shatter his image. Maybe you're one of many daughters whose father didn't leave, but you left him because of one or many mistakes. Your buried feelings produced a superficial relationship, a "keep it short and sweet, 'Hi, Dad…let me speak to Mom,' syndrome." If he asks too many questions, you retort and retreat to your most effective weapon—avoidance.

A TIME TO FORGIVE

We wrongly place a hierarchy on sin: Adultery, homosexuality, and drug addiction are at the peak, and lying, gossiping, and procrastination are at the base. But in truth all sin is on level ground. *All* have sinned and fallen short of the glory of God (Romans 3:23). Do not allow the Enemy to divert your focus by measuring sin, somehow believing that your errors are more heinous than your own sin.

In the midst of your father's offense, he may be a man after God's own heart. Perhaps you have been blessed with a good dad, and it's time you acknowledge it. Yes, he hurt and disappointed you and possibly disrupted your family, but the Father has seen your justifiable disappointment, and He's nudging at your spirit for reconciliation and restoration.

Maybe you're thinking, *You don't know how many times he's made the same mistake!* Remember when Peter asked Jesus in Matthew 18:21, "Lord, how often shall my brother sin against me, and I forgive him? Up to seven times?" Jesus responded in verse 22, saying, "I do not say to you, up to seven times, but up to seventy times seven." God places no limits on forgiving your brother (or father).

The Father desires that you forgive your father. Kathy Rodriguez mentions in *Healing the Father Wound* that forgiveness is remembering and releasing. It doesn't, however, change the consequences. We must release our fathers from their debt to us, but we may have to maintain safe boundaries set around our relationship to prevent future offenses.[8]

Unforgiveness subtly permeates every aspect of your life, especially relationships. Face your father and/or your heavenly Father about your pain. It won't go away by itself.

Because of a mistake her father made, a friend of mine has a distorted view of men. She's constantly complaining about them and is annoyed by them. She mistrusts most men. They better *not* make a mistake, for every mistake is magnified. She meets them with a furrowed or raised brow or a pinched lip. Despite her desire for marriage, she truly believes there are no good men. My heart hurts for her.

If that's your story, look to our infallible Father to usher you into the arena of forgiveness. Ask Him to use His balm to heal your damaged emotions. Ask Him to give you a new perspective about your father and about men. Ask Him to quench any complaining or critical spirit. Jesus said, "Ask, and it will be given to you; seek, and you will find; knock, and it will be opened to you" (Luke 11:9). The Father wants to return the daughter who left her father. He eagerly awaits your cue. He specializes in reconciliation.

A TIME TO FORGET

The Word of God, the Bible, can help you forget your troubled past. Being completely submerged in God's Word transforms, renews, and reveals His perfect will for your life.

Paul, in his letter to the church in Philippi, mentioned the importance of putting the past behind us and getting our minds—our thought life—under control:

> One thing I do, forgetting those things which are behind and
> reaching forward to those things which are ahead, I press toward
> the goal for the prize of the upward call of God in Christ Jesus.
> Therefore let us, as many as are mature, have this mind.
> (Philippians 3:13-15)

Your positive future requires forgetting your negative past. The word *forgetting* in this passage literally means to lose out of your mind, to liberate your mind, or to neglect.

The Word of God is a purifier, able to extract the painful memories associated with your father and replace them with a strong hunger and desire to strain, stretch, and reach on tiptoe for His intangible prize. Have you ever asked the Lord to remove the painful memories of your past?

Do not underestimate the power of your Father. He can "do exceedingly abundantly above all that we ask or think" (Ephesians 3:20), and erasing a memory is easy stuff for God.

≡GROWTH CHART

1. List a major mistake in your past that you wish you could reverse.
2. How many people were affected by that mistake? How many of those people have forgiven you?
3. What was your father's offense? What died in your relationship that you need the Father to bring back to life?
4. Turn to Appendix B. Where are you on the Grief Cycle? Where are you stuck?
5. What behavioral changes do you need to make to move to acceptance and forgiveness?

≡GROWTH SPURT

Scripture Memorization

"You ought rather to forgive and comfort him, lest perhaps such a one be swallowed up with too much sorrow. Therefore I urge you to reaffirm your love to him." 2 Corinthians 2:7-8

Prayer

Father, I cannot forgive my father without Your help. Where he has hurt me, I look to You for healing. Where he fell because of his humanity, I look to You for empathy, new insight, and understanding. Show me where my anger was accompanied by sin so that I may ask forgiveness from You. And in the same manner that You forgive me, help me to forgive my father. Push and encourage me to move forward to experience the new relationship You have in store for us. Restore our relationship, I pray.

Chapter 5

Daddy's Love

We love Him because He first loved us.

1 John 4:19

God intended that a father's love and care would mirror His own tender affection for His people. But when our relationships with our earthly fathers result in brokenness and wounds, that reflection of His love becomes warped or even shattered. The only one who can repair our understanding of true love is the Father.

A Daughter's Story: Beatrice

I'm the third oldest in our family of nine girls and three boys, and I know all too well what it's like to grow up without knowing a father's love. My father was in the home and provided for us financially, but he was never there emotionally for any of his children or our mother.

My father and I never spent any quality time together, and I grew up feeling very insignificant. I tried desperately to be good at everything in hopes that he would notice me, but he never did. He *never* said an encouraging word, he *never* told me I was pretty, and he *never* told me he loved me.

Each of my sisters and brothers suffered, all because we longed for love from an unloving father. We have low self-esteem, division, failed marriages, and failed relationships.

For so long I was angry with *both* of my parents. I was livid with my father for not loving me and furious with my mother for tolerating his behavior. He was cruel and unloving to her, unfaithful in their marriage, and he played around, literally until the day she died—refusing to come home and care for her and their children.

Prior to his death, I tried to convey my feelings, but he refused to hear or accept it, saying, "You don't know what you're talking about!"

But in spite of everything, I forgave him. At least I thought I did.

Over the years I realized I had suppressed my pain. I couldn't face the hurt that haunted me, and I didn't want to hear others tell me I should be over it by now.

I'm sixty-five years old now, and, many tears later, I'm finally going through the healing process. God never allowed my spirit to rest until I carried my burdens to Him in prayer. Through my growing relationship with Him, He's healing every wound.

He unfolded my father's background, and I was surprised to know that my father didn't know a father's love either. He was raised by his mother, and she used him to solicit men for her. How humiliating that must have been for him as a child. Likewise, my mother was raised by her grandmother apart from a mother and a father.

Neither of them knew the love of a father—or how to show that love to me. But I thank God that He is a Father to me now—showing me daily I am loved.

━━━━━

EXPERIENCE HIS LOVE

If you don't capture how much He loves and adores you, you will never know God as your Father. I struggled with how to communicate His love to you—frequently battling on my knees—asking the Father to help me. "Lord, how can I compare Your love? A warm, gentle breeze is not gentle enough. Snuggling by a fire on a cold winter night is not warm enough. A colorful, fragrant bouquet of flowers is not beautiful enough. A much-needed hug from a loved one is not close enough. And a father's caressing and stroking his wife's stomach that carries their first child is not joyous and exciting enough."

No words can describe the Father's love. You must *experience* God's love. You need not understand it to receive it, but you must *surrender* to His love to fully know it.

I'll never forget the day I was sitting in my apartment in Dallas and I got the tingles. There wasn't a man in my life. I wasn't remotely close to dating. No one was even calling me. I was dwelling on the Lord, and I got the tingles. It happened periodically over and over again.

As I matured in Christ, my love for Him grew daily, but that day I knew I had fallen in love with the Lord. I felt His outpouring of love like never before.

The Father loves you. His precious thoughts of you outnumber the sand (Psalm 139:17-18)! He loves you so much that He pays attention to the minuscule details of your life. He knows the number of strands of hair on your head. He loves you despite you. In spite of your past, in spite of your mistakes, in spite of your disobedience, in spite of your future mistakes, He loves you.

The Father's love is the *only* love that cleanses, purges, and makes us whole. The blood of Jesus Christ, His Son, cleanses us from all sin (1 John 1:7).

Two years ago I had the joy of sharing my home with a professional chef for three months. I gleaned as much as I possibly could about food preparation and cooking. One day she taught me about clarifying butter—the process of making butter pure.

Cut the butter into small pieces and place them in a small, deep saucepan. Turn on the heat to melt the butter very slowly. Your flame should be low, because if it's too high, it will melt too fast and burn. Heat slowly for about twenty minutes until it crackles or bubbles. Turn off the heat and let it sit for a few minutes. While it sits, all the impurities in the butter will rise to the top, leaving the pure butter below. Scrape off the residue or impurities and strain the pure butter to complete the process. The pure butter remaining is a clear liquid that won't burn and will keep indefinitely.

The Father wants to use us in many of His recipes to draw men and women to Christ, but He needs us to be pure. He turns on the heat to purify us, to get the junk out of our lives. He's not going to burn us, so the heat is on low, and the process is slow.

When He sees that our lives are bubbling, He turns off the heat and lets us sit still for a while. He hasn't forgotten about us. He's just making sure all the impurities and residue rise to the surface. Then He scrapes us and strains us to ensure that nothing impure remains. We may think He's cruel, unfair, and unloving for allowing us to suffer, but it's a true demonstration of His love.

Once we're pure, we keep indefinitely; we will spend eternity with Him. Our lives here on earth—our thinking, our vision, our direction—are clear. We can't be burned by the Enemy.

Loving Your Father

God's love is not only purifying, His love is unchanging, unending, and unconditional. God's love is defined in the Greek language as *agapao*—a love that does not need a chemistry, an affinity, or a feeling. It's a committed, loyal, and sacrificial love. It is faithful, everlasting, and absolute.

This love suffers long and is kind; does not envy; does not parade itself, is not puffed up; does not behave rudely, does not seek its own, is not provoked, thinks no evil; does not rejoice in iniquity, but rejoices in the truth; bears all things, believes all things, hopes all things, endures all things. This love *never* fails (1 Corinthians 13:4-8).

And this love that we receive from the Father is the love we need to give Him. Loving God was not our idea. We didn't wake up one day and say, "Oh, I think I'll love God today." We love God because He first loved us (1 John 4:19). Now that you have a Father-daughter relationship with God, love Him with all your heart, with your entire mind, and with all your soul. Love Him with your whole being—your emotions, intellect, and spirit.

The first time the word *love* is mentioned in Scripture is Genesis 22:2 where God told Abraham to take his only son, Isaac, whom he loved, to the mountain and offer him as a burnt sacrifice. The next day Abraham obeyed the Lord, took his questioning son to the altar, and laid him on top of the wood to slay him.

That's the kind of love God desires from you—a willingness to give Him what you love most. It's a committed, unconditional love that says, "Whatever you ask, Lord, no matter how challenging, I will obey."

God didn't require Abraham to kill Isaac. He was testing Abraham's faith, love, and commitment to Him. If God has not tested your love for Him, He will.

LOVING YOURSELF

Healing our father wounds involves not only learning to love God but also ourselves. Sometimes we're our own worst enemy—verbally abusing ourselves with our self-talk. We say things like, "I can't do anything right," "I'm stupid," "I look horrible," "I'm fat," or "I don't know anything." If someone else said those words to us, we'd be ready to fight! If you engage in this destructive thought and speech pattern, catch yourself and re-inforce the biblical truths of who you are in Christ.

The Lord commands you to love yourself, and your refusal to do so is a private and public denouncement of Christ. When you accepted Jesus Christ as your personal Lord and Savior, you died, and your life is now hidden in Him (Colossians 3:3). You are joined to Christ—He is in you, and you are in Him. So the things you say about or do to yourself, you say and do unto Christ.

Jesus said, "You shall love your neighbor *as yourself*" (emphasis added). He quoted Leviticus 19:18, where the word *love* also means "to esteem." Loving yourself precedes loving your neighbor; hating yourself precludes loving your neighbor; you must have *self*-esteem before you can esteem your neighbor.

The word *shall* in Scripture signifies the promises of God and the commands of God. This verse represents a command. Disobeying it can lead to a destructive chain of events: Disobedience produces sin; sin breaks your fellowship with the Father; broken fellowship produces separation; separation leads to destruction.

As you seek to obey the command to love yourself, it's essential to remember that you cannot love yourself without an intimate relationship with the Father. If you love and absolutely adore yourself apart from Him, you're self-righteous, vain, prideful, narcissistic, arrogant, and conceited. This self-love is not of God. It's self-absorbed, self-serving, and self-centered. It is sin.

When you surrender to the Father's love, your life will change. You'll have a healthy sense of love for God and yourself, and others will notice. My life changed, and I marvel as He reveals more of His love each day.

≡GROWTH CHART

1. What was your definition of love as a child? as an adult?
2. How was love demonstrated in your home? Was it one-sided or from both parents?
3. Who or what stands in the way of your completely knowing and receiving the Father's love?

4. Do you really believe the Father loves you?
5. Do you love God? yourself?

≡Growth Spurt

Scripture Memorization
"You shall love the LORD your God with all your heart, with all your soul, and with all your mind." Matthew 22:37

Prayer
Father, tug my spirit throughout the course of each day to remind me of Your love. Renew my mind about You as my Father, and don't allow the pain my earthly father caused to overshadow or distort the true essence of Your love. May I know, experience, and surrender to Your unconditional love.

A Shoulder to Cry On

Weeping may endure for a night, but joy comes in the morning.
PSALM 30:5

The wounds inflicted by an absent or emotionally distant father can sometimes be subtle, but there's no escaping the fact that our lives have been profoundly affected on multiple levels. Still, many of us are tempted to "stuff" our pain, pretending we're just fine and attempting to ignore the signs of our inner turmoil. The day comes, however, when our grief won't stay hidden any longer.

A DAUGHTER'S STORY: CONSUELA

I was driving home alone one night thinking about my dad—how his life had gone, how he died. Several other things were on my mind at the same time. I was exhausted; it was very late in the evening, and all I wanted to do was get home. But just that quick, I was swallowed up by sadness. I missed him. I was mad at him—for dying, for saying cool things to me that I needed to hear and then dying, for being emotionally unavailable while he was healthy. I hit every chord I could think of, and that particular night every chord "hit back."

It had never struck me this hard before. Still driving, I eventually began crying so hard that I had to widen my eyes just to see. The tears were blurring my vision. Even with all of this, I still felt that more was coming and that any attempt to circumvent these feelings would not end well for me.

So I drove around some corners and parked in the most deserted place I could find. I checked my locked doors, reclined my seat, curled up, and just wailed.

I had not cried this hard at my father's funeral (a few years before). In fact, I had never cried this hard in my life, and I hesitated to let it happen at this point. I wasn't sure I could return from wherever "letting it all out" takes a person. I didn't want to be out of control, and I had succeeded to that point of my life in avoiding that experience. Never mind how lame it was to procrastinate grief; it was about survival and, of course, control. I prayed for the Lord's company (insurance that I would return). Then I just totally let go. I unloaded an emotional trunkful, and, ultimately, it felt great.

For a couple of years following, I experienced "unscheduled" crying, although that scene has never repeated itself.

Even today—ten years after my father's passing—I still grieve. He's not here anymore, and sometimes I'm reminded. Whether it comes out as tears, anger, or pain, or whether it's something funny, quaint, or totally "invented" (What would Daddy be doing today?), on those days I just indulge in a good memory, a good cry, a huge ice cream cone, a pretty walk, or something else good. Whatever happens, I let the feeling come, and I let the feeling pass. It always passes eventually.

THE BEREAVED DAUGHTER

The first time I cried actual tears for my father was in Dallas, where God isolated me to deal with my daddy issues. I was flabbergasted that tears were falling over a man I had never met. But the more I thought about our nonencounter and nonrelationship, the faster the tears fell. I was grieving his overall absence in my life.

The fifth dirge of Lamentations indicates that one becomes an orphan solely through the loss of a father, even if the mother is still present: "We have become orphans and waifs, our mothers are like widows" (Lamentations 5:3). The *New American Standard Bible* reads, "We have become orphans *without a father*" (emphasis added).

The word *orphan* means "to be lonely" and refers to a bereaved person. And bereaved people need to grieve both their tangible and intangible losses.

GRIEVING THE LOSS

Grief is a cycle of several stages that leads to acceptance and forgiveness. The stages include shock, denial, outward anger, inward anger, depression, and acceptance and forgiveness. (See Appendix B.)

In the past I associated grief primarily with physical death. But death is not the only loss we grieve. We need to grieve lost relationships, jobs, homes, dreams. The absence of a father is worth grieving. The Father revealed to me that I needed to grieve the tangible and intangible losses surrounding my absent father.

The tangible losses were his presence, along with his financial and material support. Associated tangible losses were my virginity and an aborted child when I was twenty years old because he wasn't there to teach me about men.

The intangible losses were my identity, trust, hope, self-worth, self-confidence, a sense of belonging, love, protection, words of wisdom, encouragement, praise, a piggyback ride, a push on a swing, a reprimand, and support.

These "losses" are not excuses to point the finger at my father, to place blame, or to relieve myself of my responsibilities. My ungodly actions were my personal sins—sins I had to confess to the Father to receive forgiveness.

Catalog in detail the many losses you *felt*. Grieving is all about feelings. Then keep those losses in mind as we look at the stages of grief.

Shock

Shock is always your entryway into the grief cycle. Fatherless children experience shock at the hand of physical, sexual, or verbal abuse. When Mommy and Daddy announce they are getting a divorce, when it's revealed that Daddy has another woman or even another family, or when a father dies, the first feeling is shock. (See Appendix B.)

A temporary state of numbness, mental paralysis, or immobilization usually accompanies shock. Then from shock, one normally moves to some degree of denial.

Denial

Many women live in their own little cosmos called fantasyland. They refuse to face reality, insisting, "This is not happening to me" and continuing on as if nothing has happened. A daughter might tell her friend, "He's going to call," knowing he made that promise five years ago and has never called.

"I don't need a father! All I need is my mama!" also are words of denial. *Everyone* needs a father.

Denial makes excuses for an absent father. "He just doesn't know how to express himself." It makes you pretentious before family and friends. "Dad didn't pick me up again. I'm sure something important came up." Denial covers up our fathers' ill behaviors out of shame and embarrassment. Sometimes we tell a lie for so long about our fathers that we believe it! "Since we moved, my daddy doesn't know how to find me." Such behavior is unacceptable.

Getting stuck in denial and living your life under this canopy precludes you from facing reality. Lying to yourself and others will keep you stuck in grief and prolong your healing. Don't allow denial to be a refuge from fear, heartache, and pain.

Reality says, "My father was an alcoholic, and we were all codependent." Or, "It's been three years, he has a new family, and he's not coming back." "I needed a father, and he betrayed me." From there you can move forward to face the anger.

Outward Anger

When your father is absent, you tend to be mad at the world. Anger can be directed, of course, at your father; at your mother, who possibly encouraged your father to leave or prevented you or him from visiting; at family members who verbally degraded your father; and at God for allowing him to leave.

It is not a sin to be mad at God. He can handle your anger. Remember *He* said, "Be angry, and do not sin" (Ephesians 4:26). He did *not* say, "Be angry...except with Me." We all have been mad at God. Talk about it to the Father.

Sandra's parents divorced when she was ten years old. At her father's hand she experienced sexual abuse, alcohol and drug abuse, and later, as a young adult, public shame. As he was dying of AIDS, he repeatedly apologized to her, leaving out the specifics and hoping his general apologies would do an overall sweep of the messes he had made in her life.

In a counseling session she acknowledged that he had made horrible choices and mistakes, but she genuinely forgave him. She periodically mourned and grieved her father's death at transitional points in her life.

Sandra, with tears in her eyes, said, "God let me down. I was a child! Why didn't *He* protect me?"

I was proud of Sandra. So many believers suppress their anger toward the Father, fearing that it is a sin, that believers are not supposed to be mad at God. Many think, *I can't say I'm mad at God! He's God!* Your actions will, however, reflect your anger: not going to church, not praying, not reading His Word, not trusting Him.

Instead of mouthing agreement with others that He's a good God when you're thinking, *He's good to everyone else but me,* be real with God. God can handle your disappointment with Him.

He longs to talk to you about your pain toward Him. It's no secret to Him. He's omniscient and ubiquitous.

One of the greatest challenges you will have mentally and spiritually is understanding that every aspect of your life was orchestrated by God—that He had, and still has, full control over what He will allow in your life.

God did not turn His back on you or take His eyes off you for one millisecond. God knew what you could handle, for He will not put *anything* on you that you cannot handle.

What happened to Sandra was the result of man's decision to live apart from God, but naturally she blames God. Yes, He allowed it, but no, He did not cause it. Man caused it.

Your anger will begin to dissipate when you understand God's purpose for your life and that your life is not for you but for God and His kingdom. The abuse, the abandonment, the torture not only made you stronger; they furthered the kingdom of God.

The Father can use your testimony to bring a lost soul to Christ. He wants to use your experience, your testimony to reveal that His Word is true. Bring your anger to God, and He will let you see that you are more than a conqueror (Romans 8:37).

Be mindful of misdirected anger. When anger with your absent father is suppressed or repressed, it usually manifests itself in your closest relationships. Annoyance with your husband (who just may remind you of your father), frustrations with your children, struggles with your boss or colleagues, or rigidity with friends and family—all these are symptoms of misdirected anger, especially when you can't pinpoint the root of the problem. If you find yourself saying, "I don't know why, but we just can't get along," you may want to pull out the microscope and examine where the true anger lies.

Don't be alarmed if you visit and revisit and revisit this stage of grieving. Remember each time that you're just passing through.

Inward Anger

Inward anger is self-blame for your irresponsible actions, for what you could have intercepted or prevented, or for actions against you by another. Often this is misdirected anger because the events were out of your control.

You may partially blame yourself for your father's departure or in some ways blame yourself for abuse you endured. You may blame yourself because you had anger and bitterness in your heart for your father and he died before your issues were resolved.

The most classic example of misdirected anger is when sexually abused women blame themselves because they obeyed their abuser and kept silent. They were emotionally and psychologically torn and confused about the abuse and their love for Daddy. Now, as adults, they say, "If I had only told someone," or "If I had just done *this or that*, it would not have happened."

Remember, children do not think like adults. It is physiologically impossible because a child's cognition is not fully developed.

Others are angry with themselves because they experienced a sensation that was pleasurable in a context that was unpleasant. With this you must understand the human body, its design, and the fall of man. God designed certain parts of the body to experience sexual pleasure. God's order is for sexuality to be expressed within the context of marriage. Anything outside the context of marriage is distorted, confusing, and debilitating. In instances of abuse, pleasure is mixed with pain and shame.

It's okay to be angry with yourself because you sinned or made some unwise choices in life. Remember, be angry but do not sin against yourself. Self-degradation, sexual immorality, self-mutilation, and badgering are all sin.

Do not defile your temple! It will surely hamper your grieving and delay your healing.

Depression

Depression is a normal response to loss. Everyone experiences some form of depression at one time or another, for we all have highs and lows. However, while traveling through the grief cycle, it can set in at any time and usually comes when everything seems to settle. Insomnia, overeating or a loss of appetite, and feelings of helplessness, hopelessness, or anger are symptoms of depression. The question you must ask to see if you're in a danger zone is, "Am I in control of this depression, or is it controlling me?"

A common form of depression among the fatherless is *dysthymic disorder*. According to the American Psychiatric Association, dysthymia—a depressed mood for most of the day, for more days than not, for at least *two years*—is a subtle disorder that's hard to detect.

This form of depression is silent, vicious, and overtakes and consumes your identity. The presence of a poor appetite or overeating, insomnia or hypersomnia, low energy or fatigue, low self-esteem, poor concentration or difficulty making decisions, and feelings of hopelessness become a way of life. It becomes your friend, the norm, and is seen by you and others as your personality. New friends and acquaintances meet the clinically depressed person and not the true you.

If these symptoms or other symptoms of major depression describe you, seek professional help immediately. Emotional ailments need treatment just as physical ailments do. It's time to rediscover and reacquaint yourself with the personality God gave you before you were wounded.

Acceptance and Forgiveness

Acceptance and forgiveness are the goals of the grieving process. When you arrive there, you have found a peaceful place. You have unloaded heavy weights and baggage, your back straightens up, your countenance is brighter, your head is held higher. You can see and think clearly, for the light of the Lord has removed dreariness and can now shine through you. You are liberty and freedom personified, and you, like Paul, can say, "The things which happened to me have actually turned out for the furtherance of the gospel" (Philippians 1:12).

Joseph—whose brothers stripped him of everything, including a loving relationship with his father, and sold him into slavery—grieved over the betrayal, jealousy, and losses. Scripture records Joseph crying eight times before he says to his brothers, "But as for you, you meant evil against me; but God meant it for good, in order to bring it about as it is this day, to save many people alive" (Genesis 50:20).

When you realize your father's absence was not about you, healing is complete. Accepting your plight and forgiving your father, yourself, and others puts you in the right position to be used by God. It's a serving position and a platform where the Father will use your life as a testimony for His goodness.

CRY ON HIS SHOULDER

Weeping was not intended to be for life. Grief is only for a season, and the Father wants to be the shoulder you cry on to usher in that new, refreshing season of joy.

Climb on His lap, wrap your arms around Him as He wraps His loving arms around you, and release the hurt that has plagued you for so long.

Read Revelation 4 to get a visual image of the throne of God. Then, with that image in mind, allow your heart and mind to enter into His presence. Walk around those four living creatures and bowing elders, and take a seat on His lap. That's right, you have access! Be held and caressed by Him as you lay your head on His shoulder and release tears that He wipes away.

You don't need to suppress your pain any longer, because your heavenly Father understands your shock, denial, anger, and depression. He's waiting for you to surrender the pain and frustrations to Him.

Minister Pat Ashley said, "God is grieved when we're wounded, but He is more grieved when we refuse to be healed." Grab Him, hold on to Him, embrace Him, and trust Him. He faithfully healed me, and He wants to do the same for you.

≣GROWTH CHART

1. God allows us to be angry without sinning. Following that guideline, stop right now and tell the Father about your anger toward your earthly father.
2. Write a letter to your father in your journal to express your feelings about his absence.
3. List tangible and intangible losses associated with your earthly father.
4. Where are you in the grieving cycle? (See Appendix B.)

≣GROWTH SPURT

Scripture Memorization

"For I know the thoughts that I think toward you, says the LORD, thoughts of peace and not of evil, to give you a future and a hope." Jeremiah 29:11

Prayer

Father, I cry out to You with a broken and wounded heart. You allowed my father's behaviors, and I need Your healing touch. Hold me as I grieve. I need Your shoulder to cry on. Let every tear that falls move me closer to healing, forgiveness, and knowing You as my Father.

Chapter 7

A Father-Daughter Talk

Call to Me, and I will answer you,
and show you great and mighty things,
which you do not know.

JEREMIAH 33:3

*L*ong before I met Christ, I was introduced to the Holy Ghost. He was the One who made the women at Big Grandmother's church in Mississippi jump around, cry, scream, and fall out on the floor. The church people said you had to have the Holy Ghost to get to heaven, but in fear I thought, *I don't want the Holy Ghost!* So I knew I would miss heaven.

Happily, when I was in the sixth grade, a classmate and now my very close friend, Cheryl Brown, introduced me to Christ. This cute, bright-eyed eleven-year-old was on fire for the Lord, spreading the gospel through the Four Spiritual Laws of Campus Crusade for Christ. I remember every law:

Law One: God loves you and offers a wonderful plan for your life.

Law Two: Man is sinful and separated from God. Therefore, he cannot know and experience God's love and plan for his life.

Law Three: Jesus Christ is God's only provision for man's sin. Through Him you can know and experience God's love and plan for your life.

Law Four: We must individually receive Jesus Christ as Savior and Lord; then we can know and experience God's love and plan for our lives.[9]

One day during recess I was God's project for her, and she led me to

Christ. I was *so* happy I was saved and, moreover, that Jesus loved me. Immediately I developed a deep hunger for His Word and excitedly talked to my friend Jesus all the time.

Whom Do You Talk To?

The Person and function of the Holy Spirit (or Holy Ghost) became clear to me when I was a young adult and learned about the triune God. I understood that I received Him at recess with Cheryl by my side. But I had not yet been introduced to the Father. He seemed to stay in the shadows, a mere backdrop of the Son and the Spirit.

I made it a priority to know the role, function, and nature of Jesus and the Holy Spirit. On the other hand, the Father was absent, just like my father. When I prayed, I talked to Jesus. When He spoke, it was the Holy Spirit. My God was not triune; He was dyadic. My relationship was with Jesus and the Spirit, and the Father's name was only mentioned if I recited the prayer in Matthew 6:9-13. He simply had no place in my life.

I later discovered, in my fatherless quandary, a series of interesting verses:

But you, when you pray...pray to your Father. (Matthew 6:6)

Now it came to pass...that one of His disciples said to Him, "Lord teach us to pray, as John also taught his disciples." So He said to them, "When you pray, say: Our Father in heaven." (Luke 11:1-2)

Jesus directed us to pray to the Father, not to Himself, nor to the Holy Spirit who had not yet come. We are never instructed in Scripture to pray to Jesus Christ—only in His name (Colossians 3:17). Of course that does not mean we should not talk to Him, call on Him, thank Him, or praise Him. He *is* God and more than worthy of our worship and praise. He is King of kings and Lord of lords, the Alpha and Omega, the

Beginning and the End. To that end, do not let a day go by without giving Him the reverence due to Him.

Nevertheless, He was sent *by* the Father to give us access *to* the Father, and now that we have access, we must talk to Him.

> For through Him we both have access by one Spirit to the Father.
> (Ephesians 2:18)

When I moved beyond the mundane recital of the model prayer in Matthew 6:9-13, I began to earnestly pray to the Father as Jesus instructed. It was uncomfortable, a struggle. I didn't know Him, and my initial thought was, *Who are you?*

I had to discover through His Word who He was and His role in my life. It was surprisingly simple. He wanted me to know Him as Father, and He wanted to manifest His love to me, His daughter.

The more I talked to Him, the more He revealed Himself to me, and the more He revealed Himself to me, the more I desired to pour out my heart to Him. Only then was I able to refute the subtle lies that were planted in my head by the Enemy: "God doesn't love you." "If He loved you, your father would be with you." "He cares for everyone else but you." "A loving God wouldn't allow you to be neglected."

We parallel our earthly father with our heavenly Father. In other words, our expectations of the Father are similar to those of our earthly father. The Father went unacknowledged in my life because my father was not acknowledged. He, like my earthly father, was reduced solely to a name on a piece of paper without connection. He only existed "somewhere out there." If your father was verbally or physically violent, you most likely view the Father as a God who sits on His throne waiting for you to mess up so He can "get you" and punish you. If your father was abusive, you probably view the Father as cruel, unloving, and uncaring.

To break free from this distorted view of God, you must learn and embrace what the Father says about Himself in the Word. Read what He says and then talk to Him about it. Talking to Him will recondition your mind, and you'll discover that you cannot compare or parallel Him to man or any created thing. He's immeasurable. He will tip every scale and go off every chart.

Talk to Him about your thoughts of Him (and don't worry—He can handle your *true* thoughts). I promise you, the more you talk, the more you'll discover that His Word is truth. He is Majesty, high above the heavens, and cannot be reduced to the small box called "my life experiences."

TALKING TO THE FATHER

Jesus Christ gave you access to the Father, so it's time to go talk to Him and get to know Him!

A Father-daughter talk is prayer—talking and listening to the Father. It is a dialogue between humanity and divinity—a platform where humanity enters the spirit realm to connect with a holy God. It's an arena where your deepest, most intimate thoughts, desires, and concerns can be shared with assured confidentiality.

You need neither catchy phrases nor eloquent words. You don't have to hum or shout at God. Just talk and listen, listen and talk. There's only one prerequisite: Come as you are. And if you must "put on," still come.

Getting to know the Father is like getting to know the next-door neighbors. They've been there all along; you've just never conversed with them. You've been introduced, but there's no relationship. You may know *about* them, but you don't *know* them intimately. To know your neighbors you must initiate conversation and invite them into your personal space.

To know your heavenly Father you must do the same. He's been there all along; you've just never conversed with Him. You were introduced when you accepted Jesus Christ, but the relationship is superficial, lacking intimacy. You're always cordial, speaking to Him on a Sunday morning, but He wants so much more.

The Father loves you, and He is waiting for you, His daughter, to have many Father-daughter talks. He wants to talk, and He wants to listen. He wants you to talk, and He wants you to listen. He has so much to share with you, but your days are preoccupied. You have career, school, children, husband or boyfriend, mother, and friends. There's the dance, doctor's appointment, softball practice, and movie night. He watches as you exhaust yourself each day and fill up your planner for the next. He's grieved because there's no room for Him.

He watches as you struggle; yet, you won't turn and ask Him for help. You are completely silent.

He has the answers. He knows the path you should take, but you choose not to seek His direction. But you have high expectations of Him. You expect Him to take care of you, protect you, and love you. You expect Him to show you the way without asking.

The Father, throughout history, has never imposed Himself on His children or His creation. He gave us a will. Read the Word of God closely, and you'll discover many provisional statements are conditional. Our silence and unrighteousness will cancel many, many blessings.

LISTENING TO THE FATHER

The Father speaks through His Holy Spirit, the most influential—and most ignored—voice in the world. Throughout history He has spoken, seeking the attention of His creation.

Scripture is laced with phrases like "listen to Me," "hear the voice of the Lord," "thus says the Lord," "incline your ear to the Lord," "listen carefully to the word of the Lord." He's fervently urging His children to listen.

The Father speaks to me in varied ways. Sometimes He speaks to me in clear sentences through His Word or through others. But most of the time He speaks to my spirit with a thought, a word, an idea, or an unsettled spirit when He does *not* want me to move and I'm ready to zoom forward or when He *wants* me to move and I want to park on the scripture that says, "Be still" (Psalm 46:10).

Two of the five sensory receptors are used to listen to the Father: our eyes and our ears. We must open our eyes to hear His voice. What an oxymoron! We listen with our eyes when He shows us a person's actions, a house in which He wants us to reside, a godly man who will be a husband and a father figure for our children, or His truths in His Word. If we don't read His Word (with our eyes), we won't know what He's saying.

We also listen with our ears. Our great, majestic, omniscient, omnipresent Father does not speak in a loud, thunderous, immense voice. In His sovereignty He could, but most of the time the Holy Spirit speaks in a still, small voice—directly to your spirit, in the midst of your chaos and bewilderment.

> Then He said, "Go out, and stand on the mountain before the LORD." And behold, the LORD passed by, and a great and strong wind tore into the mountains and broke the rocks in pieces before the LORD, but the LORD was not in the wind; and after the wind an earthquake, but the LORD was not in the earthquake; and after the earthquake a fire, but the LORD was not in the fire; and after the fire a still small voice. (1 Kings 19:11-12)

Elijah looked for God in the spectacular—a strong wind, an earthquake, a fire. But God spoke in a whispering voice.

If you're weary, worn out, and frightened—ready to give up on life— the Father will pass by and speak to you in a soft, delicate voice. He doesn't sound like the blowing wind, shaking earth, and raging fire you're already experiencing. He will speak calmly and peacefully.

Another common phrase in Scripture regarding God speaking is "and the word of the Lord came a second time." This means the person *heard* God but chose *not* to obey. The book of Jonah is a prime example.

God spoke, and Jonah heard Him clearly when He told him to get up and go to Nineveh and cry out against its people on His behalf because of their wickedness. After hearing God's voice, Jonah arose and fled to

Tarshish. That is *not* what God told him to do! He deliberately went the opposite way to run from God.

Jonah found a ship going to Tarshish, paid the fare, and thought he had successfully escaped the presence of the Lord. But the Lord sent a great wind to rock his world, discharged him from the ship, and sent a great fish to swallow him. It took three murky days and nights for Jonah to lay aside his stubbornness and talk to God. Only then did God release him, and the *same* word of the Lord came to Jonah the second time.

Hearing the Father's voice and choosing to disobey will always cost you something. Jonah had to pay to go in the opposite direction, and we, too, pay when we choose the route of disobedience. Disobedience delays the Father's plan for us, and if we stubbornly choose disobedience long enough, we will not fulfill the plan He has for our lives.

Choosing to ignore the voice of the Father has consequences. Your world will be shaken. No matter how hard you try, you cannot run from God. He will allow turbulence in your life to get you to talk to Him.

Once you surrender, you'll discover His Word and marching orders have not changed. He does not alter His Word or plan for our lives because of our disobedience, but He will *use* our disobedience to bless and save others. Initially the tempest made the men on the ship headed for Tarshish cry out to other gods, but as the sea continued to grow more violent, they met the Lord, feared Him exceedingly, offered sacrifices, and took vows (Jonah 1:5,14-16).

THE PRACTICE OF LISTENING

God wants your ear. Jesus said, "My sheep hear My voice, and I know them, and they follow Me" (John 10:27). Listening to God is an art. It requires focus, attentiveness, concentration, laying down defenses, and disposing of presuppositions. He wants to speak *to* you. He needs you to listen so He can speak *through* you to someone else.

Practice listening. Get on your knees a few times a week to pray, and don't say a word. Just listen carefully and don't ask for anything. Enter His presence with both ears open. Keep silent, listen, and when you get off your knees, follow Him and obey. Don't get frustrated. Keep practicing and you'll hear Him.

The Father wants to talk to you about your life. Talking to the Father results in greater intimacy and a fuller manifestation of the glory of the Lord in your life. If you talk to Him, He will show you that right now life controls *you*, and He will help you walk in truth.

Fatherless children tend to keep a tight rein on their lives. They want control, since their lives and emotions in the past were out of their control. Their actions say, "I don't need to pray; I have life under control." Until life is navigated by the Father, it is *still* out of control.

Satan's plan is to find new, tantalizing things to absorb your time and deter any conversations with God. He knows the power of talking to the Father and will do anything to distract you. Recognize the voice of your heavenly Father but know Satan's voice as well. It will *always* contradict Scripture.

Meet your loving Father at His throne. Even if you *feel* you're in control, share your plans, strategies, and even your to-do list with God. Ask Him in prayer to give you His view on them. Then listen to that still, small voice, always confirming it with Scripture. More and more you'll find yourself letting go of your own way and loving God's rule over your life.

Silence of the Lamb

Silence—the ability to hear what's *not* being said—is an artful form of communication to be mastered.

Five months into our marriage Andre and I had our biggest fight. It lasted two days. On day three, he awoke, got dressed, and said he was going to his best friend's house to avoid the tension. I rushed to get dressed and told him, "*You* stay in the house; I'll leave!" So I jumped in the car, turned on my cell phone, and headed to the beach.

The Father always met me there, and I was starving for a word from

Him. I needed to talk to Him about the character flaws Andre had pointed out the day before. His feedback had pierced my heart. (I had been warned that marriage magnified your flaws, but no one told me about the sting.)

I began talking to the Father, begging Him to speak. *Nothing.*

I ran down the hill to the beach in hopes of hearing His voice in the waves. *Nothing.*

I walked along the pedestrian path, but there was no word from the Lord. I heard a bird chirping in a palm tree, and *I* decided to come up with a word: "He covers me under the shadow of His wings." No, *that* wasn't the word.

I frantically continued walking north two miles, wrestling with the Father's silence, begging Him to speak. *Nothing.*

I turned to walk back. In tears, I began to question if I could truly hear from God, but instantly I knew *that* thought was a lie from the Enemy, because I've learned that what contradicts Scripture is not a word from God. Scripture says, "I will hear what God the LORD will speak, for He will speak peace to His people and to His saints" (Psalm 85:8).

As I approached my car, I resolved that the Father had nothing to say. A lady sat on the bench, facing the water, rocking her infant daughter to sleep. The stroller was parked by the bench, and the baby was lying on her shoulder, facing me with her bright eyes wide open.

As I neared, the mother turned to me and silently asked, "Is she asleep?" I read her lips, smiled, and shook my head no. She smiled, turned, faced the water, and continued rocking.

Minutes before I approached, that baby was probably in the stroller, crying and fussing. Without a word her mommy had picked her up, placed her head on her shoulder, and rocked her until she calmed down and, her mother hoped, went to sleep.

And without a word, the Father—with His maternal nature—showed me I was that crying, fussy baby. He didn't need to speak to me. He was comforting me until I calmed down.

I was moved to tears. I could imagine Him rocking me and turning

His head to Jesus to ask, "Is she asleep?" and Jesus, with a smile, shaking His head no.

When the Father is silent, be still and know that He is God (Psalm 46:10). He will never leave you nor forsake you (Joshua 1:5). He is the Father of mercies and God of all comfort (2 Corinthians 1:3). He will cover you as a hen gathers her chicks under her wings (Matthew 23:37).

Maybe you've talked to the Father, yet silence echoes in your ear. Keep praying, keep listening, keep believing, and keep rocking in His arms. Your answer is on the way.

Pillow Talk

Praying on our knees and praying prostrate are postures that keep us humble, reverent, and focused before God. Yet there are times when we need to create an intimate, nonformal environment to talk with the Father, to help us view Him as Daddy—talking over a cup of tea, conversing during breakfast or dinner, listening to Him while sitting on the patio, or talking while lying on our pillows.

I love to cuddle up with the Father on my bed, resting on my two fluffy pillows. I call this our pillow talk. It's usually on a cold winter night when I'm freezing or when I'm not feeling well or when, after praying on my knees, I want to continue our conversation. When I fall asleep, I know I've fallen asleep in His arms. Or we will have pillow talk when I wake up and it's not quite time to get up. It's a great place to talk to Him before I begin my day.

It's one of the places where I have the most intimate communion with the Father. It's quiet, the phone is off, and I can place all my attention on the throne.

I keep a prayer pad on my side of the bed to remind me to pray on my knees. When I don't want to get on my knees, I ask the Father, "May we have pillow talk?" He always says no when it's an issue of laziness or if I really need to intercede on someone's behalf. Then I fall on my knees.

Choose a place where you can be yourself. Remove all distractions—television, beeper, phones—and talk to the Father. It will heighten your prayer life.

Sacrificial Prayer

During my healing process I was angry with my complete-stranger father for leaving me and outraged at the Father for allowing him to leave. I was so mad I thought I would lose control. I had never experienced such anger toward God. I remember my prayers to the Father during that season of my life. I would get on my knees once a day before bedtime, close my eyes, clasp my hands, and say, "Father, I'm not talking to you. Amen." (*Amen* means "it is so," and was *that* so!) This lasted four days, after which I longed for Daddy, and there was an outpouring of words *and* tears.

I realize now that my prayers those four days were not irreverent or wrong. They were obedient, sacrificial prayers. As believers we are commanded to pray. I was angry, but I did not sin. I had to talk to the Father, and that was *all* I had to say. God doesn't ask us to apologize for our anger.

Jesus commands us to pray (Luke 18:1), and that I did. When you don't feel like praying or when you're mad at God, pray anyway. Don't neglect your Father-daughter talks. Pour out your heart to the Father. It's therapeutic and will bring wellness to your soul.

⩽GROWTH CHART

1. Examine your schedule. What can be removed to make room for the Father?
2. Make an appointment to sit down and talk with the Father daily. The hour may fluctuate each day. Make adjustments each week where necessary. Commit to your meeting time.
3. Journal your prayers and catalog the Father's answers. Likewise, begin a prayer list for others.

4. Are you angry with God regarding your father? Write a letter to Him in your journal to express your feelings.

5. List negative messages you say about yourself. Now refute them with the Word of God.

≡GROWTH SPURT

Scripture Memorization

"The LORD is near to all who call upon Him, to all who call upon Him in truth." Psalm 145:18

Prayer

Father, forgive me for not talking to You as often as I should. Show me the encumbrances in my life that hinder intimacy with You. May I approach Your throne with honor and excitement—never perceiving my time with You as burdensome or mundane. I look forward to our daily heartfelt and rich conversations.

Chapter 8

Daddy's at Work

His work is honorable and glorious,
and His righteousness endures forever.

PSALM 111:3

One morning during the first winter in my new townhouse, I awoke to the cold air that had seeped in overnight through every nook and cranny in the house. I wrapped myself in a blanket, hurried downstairs to turn up the central heat, and climbed back into bed until the warmth thoroughly overtook the cold.

The heat and cold were in a tug of war. The heat would blow and take over the house, but as soon as the heater cut off, the cold air would rush in and swallow all the heat.

When the heater ignited again, I took advantage of it and rushed to the shower. Combined, the heater and the hot water were heavenly. When I turned off the shower, the heater cut off, and once again the room was cold. I stormed out of the bathroom, rushed downstairs, and furiously turned up the heat.

One year later, on a cold winter morning, I faced the *exact* same scenario in the cold bathroom. This time I noticed three switches on the wall: one for the light, one for the light and fan, and, yes, one for the *heater*. An overhead heater, separate from the central unit, had been installed in each bathroom upstairs.

The Father had done His work in providing me a well-heated home. I needed to do mine by simply flipping a switch.

Our heavenly Father is *always* at work in our lives behind the scenes, preparing the way, molding and shaping us to be more like Christ. God meets every need imaginable, as well as ones unimaginable—for He knows what we need before we do. He's eons ahead.

The only areas where God is not at work in our lives are those we've closed off to Him or where we won't do our part—as when I didn't flip the switch. His healing work in our mind, emotions, and relationships can begin only when we surrender them.

DESTRUCTION OF THE WALL

Nehemiah served as an advisor and cupbearer to the king in Persia. His primary responsibility was to prevent the king from being poisoned. He laid his life on the line for another person several times a day.

While on duty, he received a visit from his brother and some other men from Judah. They informed him of the children of Israel's distressful state, saying, "The survivors who are left from the captivity in the province are there in great distress and reproach. The wall of Jerusalem is also broken down, and its gates are burned with fire" (Nehemiah 1:3). The city called "the habitation of peace" was now a habitation of pandemonium—vulnerable, agonizing, and in great pain.

The survivors who escaped from bondage under the hand of the Chaldeans faced hopeless and helpless circumstances that left them susceptible to attack. Their physical and emotional position grieved Nehemiah so much that it ushered him into the practice of fasting and intercessory prayer on their behalf—and then into a leadership role in the rebuilding of the city walls.

The greatest testimony we can glean from Nehemiah is his continuous and consistent posture of prayer. Ten prayers are laced throughout the book of Nehemiah, denoting his total dependence on the Father. He offered prayers of repentance, continuous prayers on behalf of the people, and prayers for mercy in the sight of man. He prayed without ceasing, and his prayers gave him boldness in the face of the king and the enemy.

Like the destruction wrought in the battle over Jerusalem, your father's emotional or physical departure symbolically broke down walls of trust and security, and your gate of protection was burned. You were left vulnerable—scrambling to build new walls.

You entered adulthood acquiring a new trade as an architect to rebuild your life, but your efforts were unsuccessful, frustrating, and futile. Replacing tenderness with toughness, trust with skepticism, and freedom with shame has worn you out.

You built a wall with the inferior material of defense mechanisms, trying to shield yourself from people who have the potential to hurt, harm, or let you down.[10] You may be living life in a shell, afraid to break out because you don't trust people. Skepticism keeps you on the periphery of relationships, not allowing anyone to get too close.

Toughness, indecisiveness, and irresponsibility are common walls that keep people away. They successfully shield inner pain. Pretentious living draws people near temporarily, then turns them away.

Life cannot be lived to its fullest in the shadow of fear or under the umbrella of self-protection. Fear and self-protection will cause you to live in a vacuum. The Father is your protector and the restorer of life, and He wants to send believers to walk with you in your healing.

Model Nehemiah and pray! Pray earnestly. Pray without ceasing (1 Thessalonians 5:17). Pain, sorrow, or frustration may dominate your life right now, but if you cry out to God, He will hear you, and His work on your life will begin. Simply cry, "Help!"

> In my distress I called upon the LORD,
> And cried out to my God;
> He heard my voice from His temple,
> And my cry came before Him, even to His ears. (Psalm 18:6)

The Father specializes in brokenness and will send someone to partner with you to help rebuild your life. You are not alone. Everyone has a part: God, the body of Christ, and you.

A MIND TO WORK

I had a part to play that winter morning by flipping the switch and turning on the heat, but I didn't allow my mind to work! I fussed and complained and wanted God to turn on the central heating. I prayed earnestly to nudge Him into action, but I learned that He will not allow us to sit idle while we beckon for Him to do all the work. We are workers together with Him (2 Corinthians 6:1).

Nehemiah and the people succeeded in rebuilding the wall because they had a *mind* to work (Nehemiah 4:6). In the midst of mockery, negativity, and criticism, the people united in a collaborative effort, and *together* they rebuilt what was torn down.

Chapter 3 of Nehemiah details the names of men, sons, and priests who united to rebuild the wall. Daughters also had a part and purpose in rebuilding the wall. Shallum, the leader of half of the district of Jerusalem, worked *with* his daughters to make repairs (3:12). This mention of women on the wall denotes our position: working alongside our Father.

Imagine working with your father in a communal effort to reestablish a broken people. Well, you can! The Father works *with* you to restore your life. Then He wants to use you to help restore others.

We delay our healing and helping others when our minds dwell on the past. Pondering on the who, where, what, and why of the past will immobilize you. Laziness and procrastination will slow you down. You have work to do!

Start with obedience. The restoration process begins with obeying the Word of God. Anything that keeps you from living by the Word of God must be discarded. Anyone who diverts your attention from God must be guarded. Habitual, continual sin must stop. Free yourself from complacency and complaining. All of these delay the restoration process.

Work on your healing. Call for counseling or join a support group. Turn off the television, open the Word of God, and allow the truth of His Word to soothe your pain. Research what the Word of God says about your situation. Purchase books and workbooks that assist in your healing. Fall on your knees and talk to your Father who hears, empathizes, and longs to help.

Confess your sins to the Lord. Repent from sin and dead works. Deny your flesh and go on a fast. Journal daily your thoughts, desires, challenges, fears, milestones, and answered prayers. Find a prayer partner who will intercede on your behalf. Set your mind on things above.

WORKING ON THE WALL

Even with all the people working together, the wall of Jerusalem could not be rebuilt overnight, and neither can your life. It took fifty-two days of backbreaking, muscle-straining work. They fought, stood, watched, rebuked, prayed, and received constant encouragement to remind them of God's presence and faithfulness.

Everything seemed bleak. The enemy was all around, lying in wait, trying to instill fear; the cries and complaints of wives, sons, and daughters echoed in the ears of Nehemiah; a famine was in the land; financial hardships became the norm; the nobles and rulers practiced usury; and hopelessness filled the air. But God fought for them (Nehemiah 4:20).

Restoring our lives to health and recovering from our father wounds takes time. It's not an overnight process. My healing process took five years, and I've learned that the Father's work never ends. Expect opposition, frustration, confusion, challenges, and fatigue while your life is being rebuilt, but don't give up on the Father. He is working alongside you.

Once your life is rebuilt, the Enemy does not pack up and leave.

Notice that on the fifty-third day the enemies of Israel were *not* laid to rest. They were disheartened because they perceived that God had done the work (6:16), so their threats intensified.

Press through the attacks of the Enemy. Look beyond your natural vision to see God's supernatural hand on your life. And when you get tired, pray *exactly* as Nehemiah did: "O God, strengthen my hands" (6:9).

The rebuilding process is intensive and extensive but rewarding. Anger, bitterness, negative thoughts, and ungodly behaviors are discarded and replaced with tenderness, kindness, humility, meekness, and forgiveness (Colossians 3:12-13). New dreams are birthed. Vision is broadened. Blessings abound. Peace is released. A biblical perspective and positive attitude are given. "Old things have passed away; behold, all things have become new" (2 Corinthians 5:17).

What's in Your Hands?

Harriet Tubman escaped north by the Underground Railroad in 1849 and later frequented the South to lead over three hundred slaves to freedom. Opposition surrounded her as she risked her life for personal freedom and the freedom of others, but Harriet was well equipped for the battle—a Bible in one hand and a gun in the other.

Nehemiah and the people of Israel were surrounded by opposition as they risked their lives to rebuild the wall of Jerusalem, but they were well equipped for the battle—one hand worked at construction and the other held a weapon.

Sanballat and Tobiah were Satan's chief emissaries, wreaking havoc every step of Nehemiah's way. They were on assignment and expressed disdain at the mention of someone seeking the well-being of the children of Israel (Nehemiah 2:10).

The Enemy is not excited about your restored life, and he will do anything to distract and discourage you. His strategy is to laugh (2:19), mock (4:1), and criticize (4:3) your efforts. If that doesn't work, the Enemy will grow in number (4:7) and create confusion (4:8) with the overall goal to destroy you (4:11). He will do *anything* in his power to abort the work that the Father has begun.

I wonder how many slaves in 1849 chose to remain in bondage for fear of freedom. I wonder how many men and women in Nehemiah's day chose not to work on the wall but opted to chime in with the enemy, complaining and discrediting God. I wonder if you will choose to clutch the pain of the past rather than freedom with the Father. Fight for healing and deliverance. Don't ally with the Enemy. Construction is needed on the walls and gates of your life, but opposition is all around. Are you well equipped for the battle? What is in your hands?

Send Me, Lord!

God says, "No more hiding." He's at work tearing down the inferior walls you have built. He tears them down layer by layer until He unveils His beautiful daughter hiding behind. Then He will rebuild your self-worth, self-confidence, self-image, and character. Afterward He will use you as a spiritual architect to rebuild the lives of others.

When your life is rebuilt, my prayer is that you, like Nehemiah, will go before the King of kings and Lord of lords and say, "Send me, Lord, to rebuild the lives of my people" (see 2:5). That's what this Christian walk is all about—rebuilding the people and building the kingdom.

◢Growth Chart

1. What signs were posted toward man and God as a result of your father's absence?
   ___ Men at Work
   ___ Keep Out
   ___ Open Trench
   ___ Construction Zone

_____ Detour

_____ Road Closed

_____ Loading Zone

_____ No Entry

2. List the areas of your life where the Father is working.

3. What specific areas have a "Keep Out!" sign posted toward God?

4. Are you willing to work with the Father to restore emotional and spiritual health to your life? What will that look like?

◢GROWTH SPURT

Scripture Memorization

"His work is honorable and glorious, and His righteousness endures forever." Psalm 111:3

Prayer

Father, chip away the dead things in my life like a bad attitude, unforgiveness, selfishness, and a hardened heart, and never stop working to build my character and self-esteem. Create in me a clean heart, and make me a holy and righteous woman of God.

Chapter 9

Daddy's Gifts

*If you then, being evil,
know how to give good gifts to your children,
how much more will your Father who is in heaven
give good things to those who ask Him!*

MATTHEW 7:11

My mother was tall, thin, sassy, and looked too cute in her hot pants and bouffant hairdo when my sister and I were growing up. The few men she dated absolutely adored her but had a superficial relationship with Dee Dee and me. Their interest was in the beautiful woman Patsy, not her kids.

When I was sixteen and Dee Dee was away at college, Manuel entered my mother's life. I met him before my mother did. A close friend invited me to spend the night with her at her father's house, and when Mom dropped me off, Manuel saw her and fell in love.

My friend and I couldn't enjoy ourselves outside because he kept interrupting us. "You two come inside so Monique can call her mother," he nagged. I thought, *Why does he want me to call my mother? I'm spending the night.*

Mom and Manuel did date, and over the course of time he proved to be different from the other men she dated. He was not only interested in my mother, but he also cared for me. Shortly after, he began to call me his daughter, and I called him Dad.

He was concerned about my school, grades, dating, job, finances, clothes, and car. He taught me how to fix a flat tire, change spark plugs, and drive a stick shift. He talked about the Lord, taught me about "no-good men," and encouraged me to "keep my skirt down."

Once when I was sick and cooped up in the house all week, he and Mom put me in the car and drove me around the neighborhood, just so I could get some fresh air and sunlight. I remember slouching in the backseat, looking out the window and wishing I could enjoy the day as much as they did.

That seemingly small gesture showed his great love, care, and concern for me, and seventeen years later the thought *still* warms my heart. It's the small things a father does that have the greatest impact on our lives—not money and material things. It's time spent—even if riding silently in a car.

For twenty-one years his love has been consistent. He has supported every milestone in my life—graduations, moving across the country, accepting the call to ministry, quitting a job with no other job in sight. He gave me money when I was broke, and he taught me about the importance of saving and purchasing a home. He gave me away on my wedding day. The list goes on.

I didn't realize it for many years, but God—through His love, grace, and mercy—gave me a father in the man called Emanuel. We call him Manuel for short, but his name, Emanuel, means *God is with us*.

When I put more emphasis on my biological father than my spiritual Father, God was with me and gave me a surrogate father who has never abandoned me physically, emotionally, or spiritually.

Many godly father figures can be found in Scripture. Moses was given Jethro; Samuel, Eli; Esther, Mordecai; Elisha, Elijah; Joshua, Moses; Timothy, Paul; and the disciples, Jesus.

The Father wants to strategically place a father figure in your life. Look around—a Mordecai or Elijah may already be there. He may be a stepfather like Joseph was to Jesus or a grandfather like Jacob was to

Manasseh and Ephraim. Or maybe, like Emanuel, he's not biologically related to you, but he can certainly serve the purpose of an earthly father.

God said He would take care of us when our fathers forsake us, and He has fulfilled His promise via stepfathers, grandfathers, uncles, and nonbiological fathers. Please don't overlook, dismiss, or discount them. Celebrate them!

Regardless of your age, if you don't have an earthly father figure, pray for one. It's a need, and the God who supplies all our needs will meet it.

WEEKEND DADS

It's time to celebrate the most overlooked and underrated father—the weekend dad. He faithfully commits to pick up his children and care for them, even in weekend segments.

His past mistakes may be apparent, or perhaps the situation is not due to his mistakes at all. Either way, he loves you, his daughter. Your role is to focus on your love for each other and build the best relationship you can under the circumstances.

When I married Andre, two daughters accompanied him—Sheena, age nine, and Andrea, age three. They came home biweekly, Friday through Sunday, and I would think, *I wish they could spend every day with their dad. I wish Sheena and Andrea lived in the same household with each other. I wish they could meet their dad at the front door each day when he arrives home. I wish we lived in a perfect world!* Then I shifted my focus from the negative, the past that will not change, to center on the positive and the blessings.

These girls were blessed and highly favored, fearfully and wonderfully made, here on purpose, and their lives were orchestrated by God. God knew them before they entered their mother's womb (Jeremiah 1:5). Both are loved and adored by *all* their parents. Sheena is doubly blessed with a loving mother and father *and* a loving stepmother and stepfather—calling all four Mom and Dad. What a blessing to have a stepfather fill the gap when

Andre can't be present and a stepmother to fill the gap when her mom is not present.

Christ is the fabric of our marriage and central in our lives, so our girls have a biblical model of a godly marriage and home. Four months after we married I led Sheena to Christ, and we're currently teaching Andrea about baby Jesus, hoping she will make the decision to accept Him as her Lord and Savior.

Both are learning to pray. One morning Andre was praying on his knees by our bed, and I was sitting on the other side reading when Andrea ran into our room. She looked at her dad, then walked over to me and whispered, "What is my dad doing?" I whispered, "Praying." She looked at him silently, absorbing the scene. What a teachable moment on the *weekend!* God meets us where we are and moves mightily, despite how we got there.

More daughters today under age eighteen have weekend dads than ever before. These daughters must press through the frustration of toting a bag on weekends; anger at their father's remarriage or visitation issues; longing for both parents to be in the same home; shame from comparing their friends' two-parent homes to their one-parent home. If you have a weekend dad, look for the many blessings that encircle you. Praise your father for his love, commitment, and adoration for you. Praise your father for fighting to have visitations with you. And praise God that no matter where we are, He will never leave us nor forsake us.

As fathers, mothers, and stepparents, we must make our sons and daughters feel like both houses are home. Visiting Daddy should not be a weekend getaway to Disneyland with the father always looking for something to do. It should be viewed as going to their other home.

Children need clothes, shoes, toothbrushes, toys, books, friends, chores, and responsibilities at their father's home. If you can, discard the suitcase so they don't feel like a visitor. This is the responsibility of the father, but, mothers, feel free to assist for your child's sake.

Our goal in the first year of marriage was to make our house a home for our girls. It was a slow process, building up their wardrobe, books, games, and toys and remodeling their bedroom, but now weekends are a smoother transition. No more packing to come and go.

STEPFATHERS

Loving stepfathers are a godsend. They serve both as husbands to our mothers and as fathers to their sons and daughters.

Mary, an unwed, virgin teenager, was impregnated by the Holy Spirit, and Jesus was born. Jesus did not have a biological father but was given Joseph—a loving stepfather who covered and protected Him before and after birth. Joseph served as His earthly father, but Jesus solely depended on His Father in heaven.

We can learn from Jesus how to develop intimacy with the Father. He always slipped away from the multitude and His disciples to pray to the Father; He asked and received instructions from the Father; and He never moved without seeking direction from the Father. Following His encounters, lives were changed, the disciples were named, water was walked on, unclean spirits were rebuked, people were healed, the dead were resurrected, and the list goes on.

Jesus is our model of how to live a victorious life on earth with an absent biological father. Cherish your relationship with your stepfather. He's one of Daddy's gifts. But also spend quality time with your heavenly Father and depend on Him for guidance.

SPIRITUAL FATHERS

Another gift from God is the man who fathers the congregation of God's people—your pastor. God sent him to teach you His truths and to model godliness as a man, husband, and father. He is the father of God's house, supporting major pivots and milestones in your life—baptism, marriage, death of a loved one, baby dedications, counseling, and prayer. He is your spiritual father figure, and you are his spiritual child.

I know we can all take turns bragging about our pastors, so I pray you can chime in as I celebrate mine. The Father expressed His love for me by ordering my steps to Faithful Central Missionary Baptist Church (now Faithful Central Bible Church), where He chose Bishop Kenneth C. Ulmer to fill the spiritual void that my biological father could not.

As He did with the prophet Jeremiah (Jeremiah 1:9), God put His words in Bishop Ulmer's mouth and anointed him as a phenomenal expositor of the Word of God. And like Paul, he encourages over thirteen thousand members to imitate him just as he also imitates Christ (1 Corinthians 11:1). He loves, fears, and reverences God without compromise and teaches me daily to follow his lead.

A few years ago Bishop Ulmer was the guest speaker at a neighboring church, and he taught them how to pray for their pastor based on Paul's exhortation for prayer in Ephesians 6:18-19:

- Pray for his priorities (keeping God first).
- Pray for his pride (keeping it in check, for pride steals God's glory).
- Pray for his protection (include temptations).
- Pray for power (spending time with God).

I've used the same model to pray for him, and I encourage you to adopt it when you intercede *daily* on your pastor's behalf. One of the greatest expressions of love for your pastor is the gift of prayer. Pray for him without ceasing!

FATHERLESS MEN

Many fatherless men have a heart for fatherless children and adults. Their ministry is to father them, offering a relationship they never had.

Genealogies are prevalent in Old Testament writings. Throughout Scripture we see the thread connecting men to their fathers, grandfathers, and great-grandfathers. Unfortunately, many believers skip over the genealogies, missing a wealth of knowledge and understanding.

In 1 Kings, a common thread is found among most of the men mentioned—reference to their biological father. Here are a few examples: Prior to chapter 17, it's recorded that Jesse is the father of King David, David is the father of Solomon, and Solomon is the father of Rehoboam. Adonijah is the son of Haggith; Joab the son of Zeruiah; and Jeroboam the son of Nebat, whose mother's name was Zeruah.

Following chapter 17 we find Elisha the son of Shaphat; Micaiah the son of Imlah; Zedekiah the son of Chenaanah, and so on. (Don't let the pronunciation of names make you miss the point.)

As we arrive at chapter 17, we meet Elijah the prophet, who is introduced with only a nebulous account of his lineage. We know he's a Tishbite, from the city of Tishbe in Gilead. His biological father is not mentioned, and whether he grew up with him is uncertain.

Nonetheless, look at the vision the Father had for this man's life on earth and in the future. He ministered to the fatherless (17:21), served as a spiritual father (19:19-21), was taken up by the Father (2 Kings 2:11), and his spirit and power were deposited in John the Baptist to turn the hearts of the fathers to the children and the hearts of the children to their fathers (Malachi 4:5-6; Luke 1:17). What a great and powerful account of his life.

Scripture reveals how the Father wants to use the fatherless to impact the world. He will raise godly men to serve as fathers to meet our needs.

Don't minimize and underrate the "Elijahs" in your life.

CHILD SUPPORT

Children need financial *and* emotional support from their fathers on a *daily* basis. "Child support" is a misnomer—limited to finances dictated by our government and legal systems.

Unfortunately, many children are not supported by their fathers, but our heavenly Father is the *greatest* supporter of His children. He covers all the bases and supplies all our needs according to His riches in glory through Christ Jesus.

We can help by offering a canopy of prayer over our children. Ask the Father to step in where their earthly fathers can't or refuse to step in. And we must praise God for the fathers who *do* support their children.

If your earthly father failed to provide the support you needed as a child, turn that disappointment over to the Father, and let Him answer your heart's cry.

⩙GROWTH CHART

1. Identify all the surrogate fathers the Father has placed in your life.
2. In what areas of your life have they been a gift to you?
3. Who is your spiritual father? How much time do you spend each day in prayer for him? Stop right now to pray for his priorities, pride, protection, and power.
4. Write a personal psalm to thank God for your surrogate father (no shorter than Psalm 117 and no longer than Psalm 119).
5. What was positive about your weekends with your dad?
6. What did you learn, and how did you grow?

⩙GROWTH SPURT

Scripture Memorization

"Every good gift and every perfect gift is from above, and comes down from the Father of lights, with whom there is no variation or shadow of turning." James 1:17

Prayer

Father, I thank and praise You for the gift of my surrogate father. You sent him especially to meet a physical, emotional, spiritual, or financial need in me, and I rejoice in You. May I never minimize our relationship or dishonor him in any way. I celebrate his love today.

Chapter 10

Clean Up Your Room

Wash me thoroughly from my iniquity,
and cleanse me from my sin.

PSALM 51:2

In an effort to fill the gaping hole left by their father's absence, many daughters reach for food, alcohol, sex, drugs, work—anything that might satisfy their hunger. Of course, the only thing that can answer that aching need is an intimate relationship with the Father. But if our lives are too cluttered with useless substitutes, we need to clean up and make room for God to do His healing work.

───

A DAUGHTER'S STORY: LEI

"Mommieeeeee, Daddy is home!"

My mother timed my daddy's arrival from work to the minute on my screams of delight. Even now, I chuckle as I recall how incredibly happy and carefree I was in the presence of my daddy. I can still hear him saying proudly—declaring, in fact—"You are my big, beautiful princess." Hearing him say this as often as he did established my position as his firstborn daughter and affirmed the value placed on me, and only me. Daddy provided for me. And he took great pride in meeting the needs and desires of my mom, sister, baby brother, and me. After all, he was Daddy, and "that's what daddies are supposed to do," he would say. And I believed him. I believed in him, because my daddy never lied. Consequently, the memories of these wonderfully satisfying and jolly times of my past make my experiences with reconciling present hurt, resentment, and bitterness all the more perverse and potent.

Seeing a child blow out ten, eleven, twelve birthday candles may be a celebration to most, but it was heartbreaking for Daddy. School friends, extracurricular activities, sports, and time alone took me away from him. Special moments watching afternoon sports events and evening boxing with my daddy were replaced by sleepovers with the girls. And Daddy did not like it. The freer I *felt,* the more trapped I became. My teenage years were filled with daily retaliations with my daddy in an effort to assert my independence.

The playful banter metamorphosed into hurtful exchanges. Open conversations on ordinarily random topics were cryptic and short, often leaving us frustrated, confused, and angry. The greatest indication of the change in his manner toward me was report-card day. I walked home quickly—proud of the five A+'s and one B+. In the place of hugs and a special allowance, he yelled his disgust at how much of a disappointment I was and how I would not amount to anything, then quickly dismissed me to bed without dinner. I challenged myself to meet his expectations, to make him change his mind about what he had said and how he felt. I tap-danced, walked on eggshells, and jumped at my daddy's every command. The results were damaging.

What had happened to my daddy, whom I now referred to as "Dad"? I spent my days, weeks, months, and summers attempting to meet his unrealistic and unattainable hopes and dreams.

Dad had his ideas about me, and he wouldn't budge. Any infraction was handled with screaming and yelling, coupled with slaps across the face, and graduated to beatings that left me breathless. His frustrations with my growing up were translated in black-and-blue bruises, welts,

Clean Up Your Room   89

and my sobbing for relief. My dad laid down the law, and all of us in the house feared him. I looked for things to get involved in to avoid going home. It became increasingly more difficult to manage a civil relationship with my dad, so I was determined to move out and escape the hurt.

I left home at age sixteen after another fight and beating session. Leaving home didn't rescue me from the hurt but rather forced me to deal with me. And admittedly, I did not like me. I had spent so much time trying to please everyone, I didn't know myself. Although I was geographically distant from the path of my dad's destruction, I was in no way clear of the ruins. I needed to numb myself from the memories, so years of abuse with alcohol followed.

By the time I graduated from high school, I had become a functional alcoholic. But I steered forward to meet the requirements for attending an acclaimed university. The highlight of my freshman year was the introduction to sex. Sex usually kept some utilities from being turned off or garnered me dinner and gifts. Then on one occasion of lust and passion, my established drinking buddy and I stupidly decided to get married. I was nineteen.

I fought with my husband, behaved like a kid, in public took care of business, and privately died in my basement studio apartment with my new husband watching. We separated a year later, and when he asked me what I wanted for graduation, I very coyly asked for a divorce.

More than eight years later, the day after my twenty-ninth birthday party, I began to take inventory of myself—my life being spared miraculously after one incredible drunken binge. I had to ask, who could have...what could have...driven me this far?

A power greater than my desires needed to take control. The impact of acknowledging Jesus Christ as my personal Lord and Savior and His accepting me was overwhelming and humbling.

The most challenging things I had to confront were my self-abuse with sex and alcohol and seeing my father. Staying sober was not easy when alcohol had been my leaning post and my comforter for more than ten years. Releasing my physical sexual urges had been ruinous. I had to cut off contact with men who wanted me, and I was not excited about my choice not to be touched and caressed physically. But as a new believer, I had to give up the old for the new.

Currently I live a much more stable and free life, completely celibate and without alcohol abuse.

About five years ago, I decided to contact my father by mail. I was armed with a new attitude, grown up, mature with Christian love—and I deeply wanted to confront my father. I took pains to communicate my intentions and shared my feelings for him in a letter. I was slowly encouraged by our regular correspondence for seven months, and I was joyfully surprised when he called my home one Saturday morning.

But suddenly the letters stopped coming, and so did his communication with me. I wrote one final time in which I conveyed my desire to know once and for all if he wanted to have a renewed relationship with me. He didn't respond.

It disappoints me that my father isn't ready to make the kind of commitment it takes to relearn a relationship with an estranged daughter. But I am still waiting for him to change his mind. He is missing out on a beautiful relationship.

THE TASKS ASSIGNED BY THE FATHER

Most families have a rule that if the children haven't completed their chores, the parents will withhold their privileges. Likewise, God withholds blessings when our lives are not clean. As the Father's daughter, you must live a holy life. Your room represents your life, and you are responsible for keeping it clean. When you receive your mansion in heaven, it will be spotless and won't need cleaning, but your temporary home on earth—your life—constantly needs work.

When your father abandoned you, hurt, frustration, and resentment slowly settled in your life, like dust. Those emotions formed layers of bitterness, depression, and unforgiveness that now manifest themselves in ungodly habits like being judgmental and overly critical, backbiting, cursing, abusing alcohol, and overeating.

We are responsible for certain daily, weekly, and seasonal chores to prevent the accumulation of dust and clutter in our lives. David wrote in Psalm 19:12, "Cleanse me from secret faults." Cleaning up your room means getting rid of those secrets you think you're hiding from God. (Remember, He's omniscient.)

We must clean up our bad habits and attitudes, confess our sins, work to rid our lives of unforgiveness, and incorporate health into our lifestyles. Your outward appearance is almost as important as the inward.

DAILY CLEANSING

The Bible says, "If we confess our sins, He is faithful and just to forgive us our sins and to cleanse us from all unrighteousness" (1 John 1:9). Confession is simply the earnest acknowledgment of sin and should be done throughout the day, every day.

The Bible also says, "Confess your sins to one another, and pray for one another so that you may be healed" (James 5:16, NASB). Confession is not only the avenue to God for cleansing but also for healing. The practice of clearing out your sins daily will help usher in healing from your father-inflicted wounds.

You may be thinking, *My father sinned against* me, *not the other way around!* Well, ask yourself, *Have I sinned in my conversation, attitude, and treatment toward my father? Am I working toward forgiveness, or have I resolved that I will hold on to this hurt, anger, and bitterness?* And don't forget to ask the same questions about those who were contributors to your father's flight (for example, your mother, grandmother, aunt, uncle, another woman).

I know what it's like to be overwhelmed with excruciating pain from a father's absence. Forgiveness seems unimaginable and healing unreachable. God showed me the first step was to stop sinning against Him with my mouth and mind.

Forgiveness did not happen overnight for me, and it won't for you. The goal was confession and working *toward* forgiveness. It's a process. Since I never met my father, my confessions were made to the Father along with writing a letter to my father that I could never mail. These steps ushered in complete healing. I'm still in awe at how the Father changed my heart. It *still* surpasses my understanding.

My colleague and good friend Pastor Camille Wooden introduced me to a verse one day that I will never forget:

I have purposed that my mouth shall not transgress. (Psalm 17:3)

Two other translations phrase it this way:

I have resolved that my mouth will not sin. (NIV)

I have made up my mind never to tell a lie. (CEV)

Purpose in your mind that you won't be a gossiper, backbiter, curser, or liar. Don't entertain the sins associated with the tongue. It's unladylike, unattractive, and undesirable. The Enemy loves it when we tear people apart with our tongue, forgetting that our battle is not against flesh and blood. Resolve to stop sinning with your tongue.

It's a personal tragedy when we hold unforgiveness in our heart. Not only do we hurt others, we hurt ourselves and delay healing. The Father can help. He can liberate your heart, mind, emotions, and spirit.

Clean this area of your life daily to remove the inevitable barrier of unforgiveness that will prevent you from moving forward.

WEEKLY CLEANING

A chore that few daughters undertake is the spiritual discipline of fasting. Living in a chaotic world that promotes and publicly displays sin from every angle, we are vulnerable and prone to get out of tune spiritually. Fasting cleans the mental, spiritual, and physical impurities that block our relationship with the Father. It restores our focus and draws us closer to Him.

Feelings should never dictate whether you should fast. Most times you won't "feel" like it. Sometimes your flesh will dread a fast before it begins, but out of obedience and sacrifice you'll succumb to God's call. Other times when you're weighted down with heavy burdens, you will welcome it with open arms.

> "Now, therefore," says the LORD, "turn to Me with all your heart,
> with fasting, with weeping, and with mourning." (Joel 2:12)

The goal of fasting is a heart turned toward God. Look at God's Word concerning the purpose and results of fasting:

> Is this not the fast that I have chosen:
> To loose the bonds of wickedness,
> To undo the heavy burdens,
> To let the oppressed go free,
> And that you break every yoke?
> Is it not to share your bread with the hungry,
> And that you bring to your house the poor who are cast out;
> When you see the naked, that you cover him,

And not hide yourself from your own flesh?
Then your light shall break forth like the morning,
Your healing shall spring forth speedily,
And your righteousness shall go before you;
The glory of the LORD shall be your rear guard.
Then you shall call, and the LORD will answer;
You shall cry, and He will say, "Here I am."
(Isaiah 58:6-9)

Fasting should be a weekly discipline in the life of the believer. Stormie Omartian, in *Greater Health God's Way*, highlights prayer and fasting as one of the seven steps to inner and outer beauty, noting that fasting is not a torture but the key to a better quality of life. She teaches four types of short fasts that will liberate your life. (See Appendix C.)

She also makes it clear that how you break a fast is just as important as the fast itself. Last month my husband and I fasted for our family Monday through Friday, from six in the morning to six in the evening. Although we know it's best to break a fast with live, healthy fruits or vegetables, we instead opted to end our fast with burritos from a favorite Mexican restaurant. We couldn't wait until six o'clock to throw self-control out the window and dive in. Our stomachs stuffed from the heavy meal, we were both sick an hour later. The sickness lasted twenty-four hours! We were miserable and prayed that God would forgive us for our lack of self-control.

Denying the flesh is a challenge, but prayer and fasting say to the Father, "I'm serious about sin, holiness, and restoration." If you can't fast due to medical restrictions, choose instead to sacrifice television, media, or the telephone. Fast and pray about your life: your husband, children, family, friends, relationship with the Father, and earthly father. You'll be amazed at how your life will change when you commit to this cleaning each week.

SPRING CLEANING

To hone and strengthen our relationship with the Father, we must integrate quarterly and annual sabbaticals into our schedule.

Quarterly retreats can include a day away at the park; walking or sitting on the beach; a drive along the coast in the silence of your own car—alone, just you and God; or going to a day spa to pamper yourself. Don't limit retreats to having someone always preach and teach in your ear. We need to get alone, be silent, and learn to hear the Father's voice.

Author and minister Terri McFaddin took the female pastoral staff at our church on a day retreat to Oxnard (an hour away from Los Angeles), and we shared a two-story suite that slept six. In eight hours we had the time of our lives doing absolutely nothing! We ate lunch together, walked on the beach, prayed, and then went our separate ways. Terri swam; Camille cuddled up with a book by the fire in our room, although it was a warm, sunny day; Beverly crawled in the bed and slept; and I went to the gym. Later we gathered, talked, packed our bags, and returned home. That one-day getaway was a vacation. It was refreshing and revitalizing and gave me the burst of energy I needed to continue in ministry without burnout.

The total cost for the day was less than forty dollars per person. We spend more than that on shoes! Getaways don't have to be costly.

Annual getaways may include retreats and conferences. Make sure these retreats incorporate rest—even if you have to miss a class or two. I've seen women's retreats where every hour of the day is jam-packed with classes, workshops, and preaching. By the time you leave, you need a retreat from the retreat!

In 2001 the women's ministry at my church hosted our first women's retreat at Alhatti Private Christian Resort. Having a passion for women's health, I purposefully included five hours of relaxation: Women had the opportunity to get a massage; play tennis, basketball, or miniature golf; go hiking; read at the lake; or go to their cabins and relax.

My volunteers and I were amazed when we noticed an unusual silence hovering over the campus. We discovered later that 85 percent of the women had gone to their cabins, curled up in their beds, hugged their pillows, and gone to sleep.

Women juggle work, home, children, school, husband, ministry—and we are unaware of how deprived of rest our bodies are. The Father wants to get your attention, and He is calling you to slow down and leave some tasks undone. You are *not* a superwoman.

Schedule in your planner rest each day, a miniretreat every quarter, and a full retreat each year. You will be amazed how your life will change for the better.

CLEANING YOUR CLOSET

You have entered a new season with the Father, so let's make sure your wardrobe is up-to-date. You'll need to discard last season's clothing if it represents the world. Scan your closet and drawers, and note what is displeasing to God—things such as old letters, memoirs, clothing, jewelry, and phone numbers that represent your former life before your commitment to Christ.

Our clothes make profound statements about who we are and how we view ourselves. I'll never grow accustomed to women attending church wearing very tight pants or extremely short skirts, backless tops, or with their stomachs or cleavage showing.

If that describes your wardrobe, I want to give you the benefit of the doubt and assume you were not taught how to dress appropriately as a woman of God, especially in the house of God. It's easy to adopt the media's and society's false belief that the less clothing you wear and the more skin you show, the more attractive you are. Not so. Attractiveness and beauty lie within and are shown all the more when covered with tasteful clothing.

Here are some guidelines for your wardrobe that apply any time but particularly when you're dressing for church. Remember, you're entering the house of the Lord.

Do not wear the following:
- See-through clothing
- Tight clothing
- Backless tops
- Blouses or shirts that reveal your stomach or cleavage
- Spaghetti-strap tops
- Skirts higher than the top of your knee. (Skirts should never be midthigh.)
- Clothing that reveals or outlines your undergarments. (Bra specialists at Victoria's Secret state that 85 percent of women wear the wrong size or type of bra.)
- Any open split above the knee

Do the following:
- Wear a full-coverage, semipadded bra.
- Carry a scarf for your legs for skirts above the knee.
- Cross your legs at the ankle and not at the knee. (It's ladylike and also has health benefits.)
- Sit up straight.
- Ask yourself these simple questions before you leave the house:
  "What statement am I making today with my clothing?"
  "How will people view me?"
  "Am I wearing this to be attractive or to attract the attention of a man?"
  "When I sit, are my thighs revealed?"
  "Will my clothing hinder my worship?"
  "When I raise my arms to worship, does my midriff show?"
  "Does my clothing represent Christ?"

In God's house, your audience is the Lord, not your neighbor or yourself. If anything you wear contradicts the Word of God, defames the name of Christ, hinders worship, or brings attention to you, wear something else. It will never be in style in the house of the Lord.

The Father calls us to live and dress virtuously, not so He can rain on our fashion parade, but because He wants to protect us. He knows that men deal with lust and are easily distracted when a woman is dressed inappropriately. If your goal is to distract and gain attention from a man, a greater issue is at hand: your identity and unresolved issues with both fathers—earthly and heavenly.

Out of honor for Him, it's time to literally clean your closet. Sentimental keepsakes from a sinful lifestyle are not a virtue of Daddy's girls.

POLISHING YOUR ATTITUDE

Despite our earthly father's plight and flight, we are responsible for our actions as adult women. Our past is not a valid excuse for ungodly behavior. Nor are these justification for a bad attitude:

"I'm not a morning person."

"That's just me. I've always been like that."

"He gets on my nerves."

"I'm moody. It runs in my family."

"I'm PMS*ing*." (The P in PMS includes Pre-, Present-, and Post-Menstrual Syndrome. Translation: a bad attitude all the time.)

If you and various family members are moody, ask the Father to break that generational curse. Grumpiness and temperamental behaviors are not of God.

Stop speaking negatively, and instead be controlled by the Holy Spirit. Seven of the fruit of the Spirit—joy, peace, patience, kindness, goodness, faithfulness, and gentleness—are sandwiched between *love* and *self-control* (Galatians 5:22-23, NASB).

If you are born again, you have love and self-control. The Holy Spirit does not need to germinate. He was fully developed when He indwelled you and sealed you at your invitation to have Jesus Christ in your life. Our responsibility is to ask Him to fill us and control us daily.

If you are constantly irritable, it's time for a self-examination. Most likely the problem is you. There may be a physical imbalance or illness, suppressed anger or bitterness, unforgiveness, or unconfessed sin. Let your prayer be that of Psalm 139:23-24:

> Search me, O God, and know my heart;
> Try me, and know my anxieties;
> And see if there is any wicked way in me,
> And lead me in the way everlasting.

Meditate on 2 Corinthians 13:5:

> Examine yourselves as to whether you are in the faith. Test yourselves. Do you not know yourselves, that Jesus Christ is in you?— unless indeed you are disqualified.

PHYSICAL CHECKUP

Many fatherless women inflict physical abuse against their bodies because they have a low sense of self-worth. How we treat our bodies cannot be detached from our identity.

Emotional imbalance evolves into physical imbalance, abuse, neglect, poor eating habits, and sometimes eating disorders. I have yet to find a depressed person who wants to go home and make a salad. Fatty, unhealthy foods or no food at all wins every time. The Father is calling us to clean up our temple (1 Corinthians 6)—an often overlooked component to spiritual maturity.

Our daily intake is directly connected to our physiological, psychological, emotional, and spiritual well-being. Our diet affects how we think, feel, and act. If one component is out of balance, the others follow suit.

When we deprive our bodies of proper nutrients, we experience a plethora of ailments. We are then extremely susceptible to disease. Constantly feeding our bodies chemicals—tap water, processed foods, fast foods, canned goods, cigarettes, and alcohol—activates disease. When we pass down poor eating habits to the next generation, we may inadvertently pass down diseases like hypertension, diabetes, or certain cancers.

One sunny Saturday in August 1997 I was rushed to the emergency room with a racing heart rate of 133 beats per minute (normal is 70-90), uncontrollably trembling hands, an enlarged liver pushing out my stomach, fluid in my lungs, an enlarged heart, and severe dehydration.

Several doctors and nurses surrounded me, put an IV in my arm and a thick tube through my nose, traveling down my throat to pump my stomach. Semilucid, I watched as panic showed on their faces. In shifts they asked me questions about my health, my recent intake, and the events leading up to the emergency room visit. I could barely think, but the one thought I did have was, *What is happening to me?*

Over the course of three years in seminary, I drank coffee to wake up and coffee to stay up. Daily I ate at fast-food restaurants at all hours of the day and night. Approximately three times a week at two o'clock in the morning, when Southern Methodist University's library closed, I'd drive through McDonald's around the corner from my house to get my last bite. Or if I wanted to treat myself, I would drive to Hal's Chicken and purchase two pieces of fried chicken with fries, white bread, and pickles. Fruits, vegetables, water, baked and grilled meats were foreign concepts to me, along with rest and exercise.

When my hands began to shake, I attributed it to the coffee. When I gradually became more and more fatigued, I attributed that to the extensive and intense homework and the early morning classes. My weight gain was due to my overconsumption of Blue Bell Ice Cream, and I was irritable all the time because everybody was crazy and got on my nerves. My hair was thinning because of the stressors of school, work, and practicum and not having enough money for hair care. The excuses ran on.

Not knowing my father's medical history should have made me extremely cautious about my intake, because I could be susceptible to any disease. But I wasn't cautious. The thought didn't cross my mind. However, I *did* know my heavenly Father's history, and He teaches that our bodies are not our own but the temple of the Holy Spirit (1 Corinthians 6:19). Should we dare defile it in any manner? Absolutely not! But I limited my application of that verse to sexual sin.

I lay numb in Baylor Hospital in Dallas, Texas, for a week after the doctors ran tests from AIDS to Z, trying to discover why my body was shutting down. At age thirty-two my diagnosis was acute hyperthyroid disease and congestive heart failure, and my prognosis was bleak. My life was out of control, and God had to put me on my back to get my attention, because I was treating His temple like the city dump.

I left the hospital weary and weak, with eleven different medications to restore my body to health. When I went to my two-week checkup, my endocrinologist said, "I'm so glad to see you! We didn't think you would make it in the hospital!" Those words startled me, and for the first time God showed me the destructive path I had traveled. I was blind—bound spiritually and physically. It was only God's grace, mercy, and forgiveness that saved me.

I hope you will learn from my experience. My mother always said, "Every lesson doesn't have to be a bought lesson. Some lessons can be taught." You are Daddy's girl. Your temple is beautiful, and it is important that you take good care of it. Busyness is not an excuse. Laziness is not an excuse. And taking out the pains of the past on your vessel is certainly not an excuse. You will only cause yourself harm.

If sedating yourself with a glass of wine every night helps you sleep, seek help. If you can't stop smoking, seek help. If you are not exercising regularly, start. If you are poisoning your body with fast foods, canned goods, and bleached products—stop! They lead to heart disease, cancers, diabetes, high blood pressure, and strokes.

We are stewards of our bodies, and one day we will have to give an account to the Father for how we handled (or mishandled) them. The Father wants you healthy. It grieves Him to see you suffer from self-inflicted wounds. The Father is showing you what areas to clean up, and He is willing to help.

A Deep Cleansing

After twenty-two years of chemically treating my hair, I allowed my natural hair to grow. I discovered beautiful, thick, jet-black hair that grows all over my scalp. I stress "all over" because permanents had prevented growth in the back and side edges of my hairline. For twenty-two years beauticians had attributed it to my nerves, the weakest areas of my hair, and dryness. What folly!

After I stripped away the unnatural, I saw my natural beauty. I had struggled with acne from ages twelve to thirty-six. My wedding coordinator and beauty consultant gave me a gift of facial products to deep clean my skin daily. In less than two months the acne and blotchy skin vanished. Now I don't have to hide behind makeup.

These are two illustrations to point you to the Father, who wants to deep clean your life and remove anything that causes breakage. Colabor with Him to remove anything that strips you of your outer and inner beauty. Deep clean your life using principles in this chapter—introspection, isolation, confession, and repentance. You will experience health and growth, just as the Father desires.

≡Growth Chart

1. Are you willing to open the door of your life and let Christ in to help you clean up?

2. What bad habits need to be swept from under your personal rug, faced, and discarded?

3. What secrets are hiding in your closet? in your family's closet?

4. On a scale from 1 to 10 (1=Never, 10=Always), how disciplined are you with the following:

___ Confession

___ Fasting

___ Retreats

___ Rest

___ A good attitude

___ Eating healthy

___ Exercise

≡GROWTH SPURT

Scripture Memorization

"Create in me a clean heart, O God, and renew a steadfast spirit within me." Psalm 51:10

Prayer

Father, I want to be like You—holy, pure, and righteous. Clean up my life, and remove everything that displeases You. I surrender all.

Chapter 11

Spankings

For whom the LORD loves He corrects.

PROVERBS 3:12

R andi scurried frantically into the garage, jumped in her car, and raced to the grocery store to exchange the brand of Caesar salad dressing she'd purchased earlier that day. She darted into the store, grabbed the right product from the shelf, and ran to the express line—only to discover three people ahead of her. *Come on, hurry up,* she thought as her heart pulsated and her hands trembled.

Finally reaching the front of the line, she exchanged products, charged out of the store, and jumped into her car. Her car seemed to creep home, for every light was red, and every car around her poked along. She was sweating and nervous but thanked God she had made it home five minutes before her husband. If Byron's dinner wasn't on the table *and* he witnessed her error in salad dressing, she'd die—literally.

Byron was later incarcerated for attempted murder. Randi spent three weeks in the hospital fighting for her life, a bullet lodged in her upper chest.

A slap in the face, a push down the stairs, blows to her body—even looking down the barrel of a gun—were the norm in her home and commonplace in her life. She had watched her mother, with trepidation and fear, experience the same physical and verbal abuse. She had vowed as a teen never to be like her mother. Now, seated at the desk of a biblical counselor, on the road to recovery, she realized that constant exposure to her father's abusive characteristics subconsciously gave her an attraction to such men.

Fear continuously shouted, "No!" when she and her older siblings *begged* their mother to leave their father. Randi's anger escalated toward her father *and* mother because they *both* put her in danger. Relief came to her family after her father died in a car accident when she was sixteen.

Grieving over her many losses and fighting to keep her sanity, Randi found herself at the feet of the Father, determined to know and receive His love. The greatest challenge she faced was refuting ideas that God was out to get her and punish her for every mistake. She pressed forward to negate the distorted thought that her heavenly Father's nature was equivalent to her earthly father's abusive nature.

OUR FATHER'S NATURE

We struggle to understand the disciplining hand of the Father when our earthly fathers were absent or when there was any type of abuse. Most children with absent fathers were either disciplined inappropriately by their fathers or not disciplined at all. In adulthood that distorts our view of the disciplining hand of our heavenly Father.

Scripture teaches that fathers are responsible for raising, teaching, and disciplining their children (Ephesians 6:4). Failure to do so causes individual, familial, and social chaos. But once the fatherless belong to the Father, we are not exempt from His correction.

Jesus Christ is the only person in Scripture who specifically refers to the Father as our *heavenly* Father. The phrase *heavenly Father* appears in only six verses, but each verse and its context capture key characteristics of our Father.

Two verses in Matthew speak of His forgiving nature:

> For if you forgive men their trespasses, your heavenly Father will
> also forgive you. (6:14)

So My heavenly Father also will do to you if each of you, from his
heart, does not forgive his brother his trespasses. (18:35)

Both verses exhort man to adopt the forgiving heart of the Father and forgive one another. Not doing so precludes man from receiving His forgiveness. The Father only models our heart when it comes to forgiveness.

In Matthew 6:26 and 32 we see Christ highlighting the immense love
and value the Father places on His children:

Look at the birds of the air, for they neither sow nor reap nor
gather into barns; yet your heavenly Father feeds them. Are you
not of more value than they? (verse 26)

For your heavenly Father knows that you need all these things.
(verse 32)

These verses declare that God alone is our caregiver, desperately desiring
to submerge us in a deluge of blessings. Our end of the bargain is simple:
Seek the kingdom of God *first*, and everything we need will be added to
us—eliminating stress, fatigue, and worry.

Luke 11:13 underscores the Father as a giver of good gifts, specifically
the Holy Spirit:

If you then, being evil, know how to give good gifts to your
children, how much more will your heavenly Father give the
Holy Spirit to those who ask Him!

Fathers, mothers, friends, husbands, boyfriends, and bosses can never sur-
pass the Father in giving His children great gifts, and the greatest of all is
eternal and abundant life through His Son, Jesus Christ.

I want to conclude with Matthew 15:13, which so eloquently captures His disciplining nature:

But He answered and said, "Every plant which My heavenly Father has not planted will be uprooted."

A distinction must be noted between disciplining and purging. This passage speaks of discipline: excavating the things we've planted in our lives that are not of Him, that don't bear good fruit. Matthew refers to matters of the heart like adultery, murder, evil thoughts, fornication, false witness, and blasphemy. The Father has promised to uproot such evils. Expect to experience His disciplining hand if any of these characterize your life and you refuse to modify it.

Purging, on the other hand, *feels* the same as the disciplining hand of the Father, but it's not connected to sin. A skilled gardener—with love and care for the plant—carefully trims the leaves, pulls off dead leaves, brushes away fallen debris, and waters so that the plant will remain healthy and continue to grow properly. Periodically the gardener has to change the pot and add new soil to accommodate a growing plant that has outgrown its environment.

Likewise, Jesus, referring to Himself as the true vine and the Father as the vinedresser, said:

Every branch in Me that does not bear fruit He takes away; and every branch that bears fruit He prunes, that it may bear more fruit. (John 15:2)

Your heavenly Father is a skilled Gardener who loves you and wants to make sure you continue to grow. So He comes in and removes deadness and debris from your life and oh so delicately trims what appears to be growing just fine. As we outgrow our environment, He uproots us from certain jobs, certain friends, and certain ministries.

The trial you're facing right now is either a result of discipline for sin or part of the pruning process. Either way, both represent the loving hand of the Father.

HIS LOVE AND DISCIPLINE

The Father is not sitting on His throne, looking down from heaven and just waiting for His children to blow it so He can punish us. That's cruelty, not discipline, and it's definitely not the character of our heavenly Father.

Discipline is love, designed to keep you alive and on the path to which God called you. When you disobey the Word of God, the Father—with love—pulls out His spiritual shovel to uproot the sin. Many believers can attest that this disciplining process can be painful because we feel and see what He's extracting.

Discipline is designed to point you in the right direction. It's an indicator that you've gotten beside yourself, tuned out His voice to selfishly do your own thing, and—if the Father doesn't intervene—your life will soon derail.

It can be hard to tell a believer from a nonbeliever since some believers have skillfully adopted the ways of the world and a childish "I can do what I want to do" posture. When the Father steps in and exercises discipline, He's viewed as unloving, cruel, and a killjoy. But any loving parent disciplines his child, and the Father is our loving spiritual parent. He is serious about our reputation despite our past. As His daughters, we must abide by His rules, and if we choose not to, discipline is inevitable. When we refuse to adhere to the Father's Word and fulfill our responsibilities, we shame God's name.

Wearing the name of Jesus Christ puts you on public display, and every time you sin (whether publicly or privately), you put God's reputation on the line. You should be distinct from the world so you'll have a testimony to lead an unsaved person to Christ or a ministry to another believer in Christ.

Examine yourself. Are you exercising wisdom in your conversations, or does your speech parallel the world's? Are you walking upright before the Lord, or are you a believer incognito?

Who is wise and understanding among you? Let him show by good conduct that his works are done in the meekness of wisdom.... For where envy and self-seeking exist, confusion and every evil thing are there. But the wisdom that is from above is first pure, then peaceable, gentle, willing to yield, full of mercy and good fruits, without partiality and without hypocrisy. Now the fruit of righteousness is sown in peace by those who make peace. (James 3:13,16-18)

No believer is exempt from the Father's hand of discipline—especially the fatherless. He won't allow His daughters to take a woe-is-me stance and live as victims. He knows you were abandoned. He knows you were left behind. He knows you were abused. He allowed it so He can use you to transform the world for the kingdom of God. Don't allow your past to define and dictate your future. You are royalty, fearfully and wonderfully made, beautiful, holy, a new creation, and chosen for greatness. That's your future, and the Father is working to keep you focused and on track.

Grieving your losses means you're on track. Being angry and not sinning means you're on track. Pressing forward to forgive means you're on track. Accepting your plight and moving forward in the Father's plan definitely means you're on track.

All children, at one time or another, test their parents. They try to see just how far they can go to get their way before Daddy or Mommy pulls out the belt. If the parents never discipline the children, they will lack boundaries, self-discipline, control, and respect.

We test God to see how far we can go before He steps in. But like a good parent, He warns us, instructs us, and then delivers the rod of discipline. The rod of discipline is not an option, and it hurts us.

Spankings are the consequence of disobedience—designed to help us remember and never forget. It helps us remember rules set forth by a loving parent, and it helps us never forget the pain endured for breaking the rule.

Dee Dee and I had our share of spankings and punishments while growing up because my mother understood Proverbs 23:13-14 all too well:

Do not withhold correction from a child,
For if you beat him with a rod, he will not die.
You shall beat him with a rod,
And deliver his soul from hell.

Any time we disobeyed my mother, we were in for it! Dee Dee was a little bolder than I and would roll her eyes or smack her lips. No doubt she got spanked. If we were acting out in public, Mama wouldn't pull out her belt, but she'd pull out her index finger and thumb and pinch the life out of us. That was *worse* than the belt. The pain was so excruciating we couldn't even let out a scream. We laugh now, but then it was serious business.

For us who are adopted by the Father and no longer fatherless, sin is a decision. When we disobey the Word of God, consequences follow. There is no such thing as "getting away with it." Our Father in heaven is omniscient and omnipresent, and *nothing* occurs without His knowledge.

Your current suffering may be tied to sin. Sin is never an isolated event. It affects others, and it will cost you a spanking from the Lord every time.

But there is grace! Psalm 103:10 says, "He has not dealt with us according to our sins, nor punished us according to our iniquities."

His Promises and Discipline

The recent parenting philosophy that labels spankings as abuse contradicts Scripture and will destroy generations to come. Repeatedly the Word of God speaks of the rod of discipline and the dangers of withholding it from our children. It's so dangerous when we buy into the philosophy of the world rather than accepting the truths of the Father's Word.

King Solomon, the son of David and Bathsheba, would have been remiss to allow society to dictate what he taught his children. His busy schedule didn't overshadow his paternal responsibilities; he didn't abdicate his role as a father just because he was the king of Israel. He understood the importance of speaking wisdom to his children and cataloging his words for the generations to come.

The book of Proverbs gives directives specifically to his son about life, repeating the intimate phrase "my son" over twenty times. However, the word *son* in this book is not restricted to the male gender. It includes sons, daughters, grandchildren, generations, and nations.

Solomon's theme in chapter 3 is obedience and wisdom as he sets the stage for one of the pinnacles of the chapter:

> My son, do not despise the chastening of the LORD,
> Nor detest His correction;
> For whom the LORD loves He corrects,
> Just as a father the son in whom he delights. (Proverbs 3:11)

Verse 1 speaks of the matters of the mind and heart. He exhorts us not to forget the law of the Lord. If we remember to walk under the guidelines of the Word, long life and peace will be added to us.

How awesome are the promises of God! The Lord equates obedience to His Word with…

- longevity on earth (verse 2)
- favor and high esteem in the sight of God *and* man (verse 4)
- a safe walk and safety from stumbling (verse 23)
- sweet rest without trepidation (verse 24)
- being guarded against entrapment by the Enemy (verse 26)

We disqualify ourselves from these promises when we disobey the Word of the Lord. Our loving Father disciplines us to get our attention so we won't miss out on these treasures of life. That's why Solomon warns us not to despise or detest His chastening.

Don't overlook the promise sandwiched in verse 3:25, the sudden terror and trouble that will come from the wicked. Obeying God's Word signals the Enemy, and he moves into action to terrorize and taunt you. God's only instruction to you is "do not be afraid."

LITTLE THINGS MEAN A LOT

If you lack peace in your life, something is out of order, and the Father is trying to get your attention. Solomon equated peace with obedience, so examine your life and find where you're outside the will of God. And don't look for something real deep. You may be entertaining the sin of worrying, gossiping, lying, laziness, or procrastination.

The Father is also serious about what we deem as "little" things, those commands we ignore or put off until later, commands God has told us over and over to act on now—paying our bills on time, arriving to work and church on time, exercising, calling the doctor for a physical, apologizing to your spouse, reading the Word, and praying.

When He tells us to move, He expects an *immediate* response. As His daughters, we usually say, "As soon as I do this, Lord, then I'll do what You told me to do." If we don't put God first, our priorities are out of order.

In a biweekly discipleship group, the Holy Spirit led us to discuss procrastination. Procrastination is a sin, and every time we procrastinate, it costs.

Dawn was absolutely livid with the police officer who pulled her over and gave her a ticket for driving with expired tags. "He ruined my day!" she cried. "I told him they were at the house!"

Dawn had received her car registration in the mail and had not put the sticker on her rear license plate. You're thinking, *Maybe she delayed because she would've had to walk down the street on a cold, windy, rainy day and peel off the sticker while trying to hold on to her umbrella.* On the contrary! It was a sunny day, and her car was parked in her attached garage. She didn't even have to step outside! Procrastination—which is disobedience—cost Dawn a sixty-dollar spanking.

Sheila received a letter in the mail from her storage company, informing her to call them no later than May 27 to settle her account. Busy with the Memorial Day holiday and other things, she planned to call them early in the morning of May 28. At noon, not early morning, she placed her call, only to discover that at eleven o'clock that morning all of the items in her storage unit had been sold at an auction. Frantic, scrambling, and praying, she arrived at the storage company pleading and begging to reclaim her belongings.

She prayed as she watched her items, sold for four hundred dollars, loaded onto a truck. Sheila made one last plea to the buyer, and he agreed to sell her *his* newly purchased property for a thousand dollars. Procrastination cost Sheila a thousand-dollar spanking.

We daughters cannot afford to ignore our Father's command. Doing so grieves His Spirit and causes *us* harm. He teaches us how to be responsible even over the "little things." Be faithful over a few things, and God will trust you with great things (Luke 16:10).

Procrastination is similar to laziness. Both involve delay and misuse of time. Both kill dreams. Both make you miss opportunities. Both cry "tomorrow" and "later," then when you look up, years have passed with tasks, ideas, and goals unaccomplished.

The book of Proverbs names the cost of procrastination: poverty (6:9-11; 24:33-34), hard labor (12:24), futile work (12:27), a poor soul (13:4), and lack of wisdom (26:16). These are harsh consequences for dragging our feet.

Self-discipline in the Word of God is the key to a decent and ordered life. Lack of discipline creates disorder. My pastor reminds the congregation often that, "We are educated far beyond our obedience." We know our responsibilities, but we neglect them.

SETTING BOUNDARIES

Boundaries are parameters we set to keep ourselves and others from hurting us. Boundaries must be concrete and solid, not loose and abstract. It takes a strong person—one who knows her full identity in Christ—to constantly uphold the standard that our heavenly Father has set.

The simplest yet most challenging boundary is the Word of God. No one should be able to plow through your biblical barricade.

A lack of boundaries in your home, job, classroom, around your friends, and especially with your boyfriend will cause you to fall every time. I mentioned earlier that when I lacked self-worth, I was a yes-woman. Today I experience freedom, peace, and confidence knowing who my Father is, knowing that I'm a daughter of the King. No one can cross the boundaries He set for my life—not my husband, children, mother, surrogate father, sister, pastor, or friends.

If the request is outside the will of God, "Sorry, no." If it's during my personal pamper and relaxation time, "Sorry, no." If it's during the time my husband and I have scheduled for one another or family time, "Definitely not."

We are called to live a holy and righteous life. Holy means to be pure, consecrated, and set apart. "As He who called you is holy, you also be holy in all your conduct" (1 Peter 1:15). Righteousness, simply put, is right living.

Go against the grain of the world. Be a leader and not a follower. Stand on God's Word and do not waiver. You will not regret it. You may get talked about, mistreated, ostracized, and stigmatized, but you will excel, and God will honor your faithfulness. Take a stand for righteousness—live right!

≡ GROWTH CHART

1. How were you disciplined as a child? By whom? Was it appropriate?
2. What is your view of discipline? Is it in line with the Word of God?
3. What is your view of the disciplining hand of the Father? Does

it parallel the disciplining hand of your earthly father or the lack thereof?

4. Where does the Father's disciplining hand show up most in your life? What's preventing you from learning your lesson?

5. Is your life a godly representation of God's family name? If not, what sins need to be confessed?

6. What boundaries have you set?

7. Who can come in and completely deactivate the Word from your life, leaving you totally defenseless and susceptible to sin?

8. In what area of your life do you compromise the Word of God the most?

9. How many "spankings" do you receive in a day, week, or month because of disobedience or procrastination?

≡GROWTH SPURT

Scripture Memorization

"For whom the LORD loves He corrects, just as a father the son in whom he delights." Proverbs 3:12

Prayer

Father, thank You that Your hand of discipline is a manifestation of Your love for me. I want to be mindful of those things that are not pleasing in Your sight. Keep me on the path of righteousness for Your name's sake.

Chapter 12

A Man Like Dad

The righteous man walks in his integrity.

PROVERBS 20:7

*G*rowing up without a father or a father figure generates a dire need for love, attention, affirmation, and affection from a man. The indelible mark of a healthy father's love was not placed in our hearts and minds in our tender formative years, leaving us with an insatiable longing to be loved. Subconsciously we search for this love through male, even female relationships—depending on the level of bitterness toward men.

A DAUGHTER'S STORY: ELAINE

Were my father to repay all the loans I made to him under the "Let me borrow twenty dollars until I get paid" promise, I would have a nice chunk of change in my pocket.

My mother was the breadwinner, and my father was the house-husband. He cooked, he went looking for us if we were a little late making the walk from school, and he kept the house clean. That's what dads did in my world.

Until close examination, the concept of having issues that were symptomatic with absent fathers was hard for me to process because my father has been around as long as I can remember. Even during a period of separation when I was around seven or eight years old, he still had regular visits with us. But even though my father was there physically, he fell short in the areas of emotional and financial support.

Growing up as the oldest of three children, I watched my mother be the provider in my house, and that was what I perceived to be a normal marital relationship. I learned early that if I needed anything, Mommy was the one to ask. The concept of a God whom I can call on at anytime, who will always supply my needs, was a mental struggle. It never occurred to me in my own dating relationships that there was even the remote possibility of another model.

I went on with my version of normality for years. My life was pretty good (so I thought). I didn't need anyone, and just like my mother, I, too, could be a superwoman.

The relationship my siblings had with my father was quite different than mine, and I longed for something I couldn't articulate—the need for a daddy. I developed a need to be needed to fill that emptiness. I got involved in a series of relationships that ultimately left me feeling used and abandoned. Those feelings were familiar, but I wondered where they came from. Many of my friends attributed their abandonment issues to the absence of their fathers, but that wasn't my story. Or was it?

Life went on, and that question stayed in the back of my mind. Something was missing in my relationship with my father. He was right there, but he seemed so far away from me. He hung out with my brother, watched television and played games with my sister, but never spent time with me.

I attempted to camouflage my desire for an emotional connection with my father. We weren't connecting because *I* was too busy. I didn't need him anyway because I always had a boy or a man in my life, including my grandfather.

I was the apple of my grandfather's eye, his baby girl. My grandfather was the best grandfather a girl could have. He was my protector, provider, friend, comforter, encourager, advisor, and so much more. But at some point when my grandfather was doing all the things a father should, I wondered why my own father wasn't doing them. My grandfather was everything I needed from my father, but as great as he was, he wasn't my father.

I always ended up dating older men. When I found the love of my life (or so I thought), he was twelve years my senior and unemployed—just like Daddy. He was neither looking for a job nor in between gigs. He was simply unemployed.

When I picked him up for our first date (yeah, I picked him up), I thought this could be the beginning of a beautiful relationship because, after all, it was strangely familiar. We fell in love and were married ten months later. Five months later we were separated, and I haven't seen him since the day he left. I was devastated and subsequently ended up in counseling.

My motive for attending counseling was to find out how to bring him home, but God had another plan. In the midst of my grief I discovered some hard truths about myself. I had very little self-esteem; I expected very little out of life and often got it. My worth was in what I could do to make others happy—only to discover it was never enough. I was dramatic, tragic, the perpetual victim.

I was hurt by my father, and I needed the Father to heal my heart. I thank God for my grandfather and the role he played in my life, because I can see in retrospect that God used him to supply my paternal needs. I'm learning that my healing is a process of deliverance, growth, and liberation—not an event. Therefore I must be still and know that He is God.

For me the process continues.

LOOKING FOR LOVE

A father's love defines a daughter's femininity, shapes her character, affirms her identity, and validates her womanhood. When *paternal* nurture and care are neglected, daughters are stifled emotionally and subconsciously begin a quest for this love. So we get on our mark as teenagers and young adults, get set, and take off into the world of relationships and find ourselves emotionally handicapped, extremely vulnerable, and *more* susceptible to compromising God's Word.

Failing to receive nurture from our fathers and instruction about men causes many women to enter relationships blindly and sometimes desperately. We choose the first man who pays us any attention. Insecurities, promiscuity, or fear tend to saturate and dominate these relationships.

Fatherless women face fear of abandonment in their relationships with men. This fear moves them to reject truth and rationalize unhealthy behavior. Unhealed, we are prone to latch on to men with loose spiritual boundaries. We accept and believe almost anything they say, just to keep the relationship intact. Mistreatment and abuse are common.

The good news is that this fear can be eradicated when we are led by the Spirit. Cry out profusely and unashamedly to your Daddy! "For you did not receive the spirit of bondage again to fear, but you received the Spirit of adoption by whom we cry out, 'Abba, Father'" (Romans 8:15).

RECLAIMING PURITY

Society bombards us with sex. Most ads, magazines, commercials, and television shows are inundated with sexual overtones and innuendos. Movie ratings are watered down, explicit sex is exposed, and premarital sex is celebrated and glorified. Even believers are desensitized by the deluge of sex.

I spent my entire young adult life searching for love, validation, and commitment from men. The energy I displayed was neediness—a magnet for unfaithful, untrustworthy, insecure men. Neediness turns solid, healthy men away.

Neediness couldn't coexist with self-respect and integrity in my life, so in desperation, I threw the latter two out the window. Tying my soul to most men I dated resulted in numerous heartbreaks and disappointments. I stooped even lower at age twenty-one and dated a married man, and at age twenty-four decided to live with my boyfriend. I had no self-worth and was clearly on a path of destruction. I was a mess—a perfect candidate for the healing power of God.

When the Father took hold of me, He had to peel away layers of deadness to get to the core of my heart. He spent years purging me—cleaning me up physically, mentally, emotionally; breaking soul ties; renewing my mind; and making me holy, pure, and virtuous.

Initially I thought deliverance was unattainable. Rededication launched me into a repeated cycle of following God, stumbling, falling, wallowing in guilt, and repentance. I repeated the cycle so often that I began to question the love and power of God. Did He really forgive me? *Surely* He was disgusted with me each time I fell. Could He truly pacify my strong desire for male love and attention? Why wouldn't He just zap the desire and heal me instantly?

The Father and I were in a tug of war with my life. Our wills battled, and I didn't understand why He wouldn't just give up on me. I fought for almost three years until I was weary and then made the greatest decision of my life—following Christ.

My struggle was prolonged because I wasn't committed to the Lord. He did forgive me. He wasn't disgusted with me. He could pacify my desires. But I didn't adopt the spiritual disciplines necessary to live victoriously. I knew intellectually that I should pray, study the Word, and surround myself with godly relationships, but in practical terms I was wishy-washy and lazy with God. My actions proved that God was secondary to my own agenda.

My mind was messed up. I felt sorry for myself and continued to feed my faulty beliefs about God's lack of love for me and power in my life. In turn, my irrational thinking became a springboard for doubt, frustration, and ungodly actions.

I was warring against an unseen Enemy who wanted my mind. Psychologist Gary Oliver said, "The mind is the battleground for the heart. The enemy knows that if we choose to focus our attention or set our mind on something we shouldn't, it won't be long before we'll act on those thoughts."[11] The Enemy is targeting our minds. In this war we must pray that the peace of God will guard our hearts and minds through Christ Jesus (Philippians 4:7).

Stop believing the lies of the Enemy and cease rehearsing them in your head. Record the truth of God's Word over every lie spoken and believed. Find scriptures that contradict untruths, and read them aloud so you can *hear* the truth.

Write them on notes, and stick them on your bathroom mirror and in your car. Write them on index cards, and put them on your refrigerator and by your bed. Write them on your heart through memorization. The Bible tells us to meditate on things that are true, noble, just, pure, lovely, and of good report (Philippians 4:8). This is how to renew your mind.

"Walk in the Spirit, and you shall not fulfill the lusts of the flesh" (Galatians 5:16). That's a command and a promise. Walking refers to your lifestyle. You cannot commit sexual sin if you are living your life controlled by the Spirit.

Go against the tide of society that contradicts God's Word, and remain sexually pure at all cost.

> Present your bodies a living sacrifice, holy, acceptable to God,
> which is your reasonable service. And do not be conformed to this
> world, but be transformed by the renewing of your mind, that you
> may prove what is that good and acceptable and perfect will of
> God. (Romans 12:1-2)

We owe it to our husbands and husbands-to-be to remain pure. No greater gift can be given than the precious gift of chastity. Andre never pressured me for sex, lewd acts, or inappropriate behavior. He was committed to purity, and we're reaping the benefits of obedience in our marriage.

Follow Christ. Doing so will untangle you from the web of sexual sin. Spiritual laziness and following your own agenda will stifle your growth. A commitment to Christ ushers in liberty, serenity, and health to your emotions and relationships. Only Christ sustains us. He will make a way of escape for every temptation (1 Corinthians 10:13).

MAKING A LIST AND CHECKING IT TWICE

Many women have been taught to make a detailed prayer list describing the man they desire to marry. My advice: Get rid of the list! Lists are limited. Praying specifically is good, but your Father will do exceedingly, abundantly above all that you ask or think.

The Father is not seeking lists from His daughters. He's looking for a contrite, sincere, and yielded heart. Simply pray His will. He will see your heart and answer from the heart. He will meet needs you're unaware of and will meet new needs ushered in at the threshold of marriage.

When I married, I was unaware of many of my own physical, emotional, and spiritual needs. God met them through my husband. Andre was everything I needed and so much more.

He loves the Lord and is commitment personified. Whatever he puts his hand to, he finishes, whether he likes it or not.

I knew I needed a praying husband, but I didn't know I needed to *see* my husband praying daily or *hear* the silence downstairs and know that prayer is going forth. It sends a surge of peace, confidence, and security through my soul. With that I can trust that he hears from God.

He studies the Word of God daily. If I don't physically see him, there's evidence that he's been studying—a Bible moved, new study materials around, a filled writing pad.

I needed him to have godly male friends who hold each other accountable, but I didn't know I needed to overhear them praying, confronting, and exhorting one another with such masculine energy, authority, and tender strength.

I knew I had the gift of giving, but I didn't know I needed a husband with the same giving heart. If he were a miser with God and others, we would have constant conflict.

In our two years of marriage and nine-month engagement period, I have never heard any filthy language proceed out of his mouth. He won't mimic someone cursing or retell a story that includes curse words. I needed a man for whom I had a great level of respect.

His emotions are consistent. He's rarely moody or cranky—even when I am! God used him to show me I needed to get it together! A bad attitude for no reason is unacceptable.

I didn't know I needed to see a man love his daughters. He models before them what I missed. Initially I felt jealous, but I knew it was a fleeting reminder of my absent father. God continues to show me how He loves His daughters through their relationship.

I've always likened Andre to young David—the one least expected to be God's chosen one. He's always behind the scenes serving and tending the sheep; a man of valor and (spiritual) war; gifted; anointed; handsome; and the Lord is with him. Is he perfect? No. Is he a man like Dad? Absolutely. He is a man after God's own heart, the Father's love personified, and I'm honored that the Father gave him to me.

Don't miss a blessing because the man God sends might not match your list. Discard the list and change the prayer. Pray for wisdom and discernment in all your relationships with men. Pray that you will look to the Father to meet every need that man is incapable of meeting. And pray that God will develop your character and mold you into a godly wife—a chosen vessel prepared by God to meet the needs of your spouse.

THE FORMULA

Sometimes I cringe when I hear a testimony of the spiritual exercises done by a Christian woman before she met her husband. It's usually a great testimony, but other single women tend to think, *If I do those things, I'll get a husband too!* Not so. There is no formula. God moves differently with every person. It's simply His will and timing.

I know the gamut of emotions and frustration of waiting on the Lord for a mate. I began praying for a husband in June 1992 at age twenty-seven and married in February 2002 at age thirty-six. God answered my prayer four months shy of ten years. The Father was certainly *not* working by my timetable.

Imagine the array of emotions I experienced in those years—hope, hopelessness, contentment, frustration, shame, depression. I became weary of waiting, sick of female friends, sick of no date, sick of baby and bridal showers. I boycotted weddings. Then I found peace that surpasses all understanding and hope again. It was a roller coaster with highs and lows.

I now know that my prayer shifted God into gear to shape me into a wife. It included chipping away my father wounds and additional baggage I had picked up along life's way. His grace didn't allow me to pray for a wonderful, godly man and then enter a relationship with him needy and insecure myself. So He continued with His spiritual chisel. And through a difficult process, He taught me to see myself as His daughter and to depend solely on Him.

The more chipping the Lord did, the more mature I became. I started out praying for a *saved* man, then a man *walking* with the Lord, and finally a man who absolutely, wholeheartedly, unashamedly *loves* the Lord. The Father showed me that if a man loves Him, everything else will fall into place—especially his love and commitment to me.

In year four of praying for a husband, God chose an unusual way to teach me about marriage. As the director of counseling at Friendship West Baptist Church in Dallas, one of my responsibilities was facilitating approximately three premarital counseling classes per year. I was single, yet I taught and counseled these couples for two years!

I didn't understand God's assignment or His method, but I taught faithfully from His Word and the experiences of others. Many days I'd fall on my knees in despair in my office before going out to teach, for I desired what those couples had: companionship and the excitement of planning a life together with a spouse.

Sometimes I felt ashamed or believed that God was insensitive. I shied away from discussions directed toward my nondating, no-man-in-sight, desiring-to-be-married status. I would quickly redirect the conversation back to the lesson.

I didn't have a model of marriage while growing up, so the Father chose that I study His Word and teach it over and over again until it was embedded in my heart and mind. I would have *never* chosen that route, but each class brought new discoveries about mankind, relationships, self, and God's purpose and design for marriage. I honestly believe my marriage is healthy because of what God taught me for two years in the classroom.

The desire in your heart to marry should not be accompanied by shame. Your loving Father, who originated the beautiful institution of marriage, placed it there. We are relational beings, created to be in relationship with both God and man. *He* said it's not good for man to be alone (Genesis 2:18). Pray that every detail of your desire to marry lines up with His will.

Our Father answered my prayer. He can do the same for you. There is no partiality with God (Romans 2:11), and He is no respecter of persons. Become a healed, uncompromising woman of God. Godly men are attracted to those qualities; ungodly, unbelieving men are not. God's instruction to us about romance with unbelievers is emphatic: "Do not be unequally yoked together with unbelievers" (2 Corinthians 6:14). "Do not be deceived: 'Evil company corrupts good habits'" (1 Corinthians 15:33).

Since you're Daddy's girl, the men you date and marry must possess the characteristics of your holy, loving, caring, committed Father. You cannot afford to compromise by allowing the strong desire to be loved to overshadow ungodly qualities. That's a price you *don't* want to pay.

If you're already married to a man who is *not* conformed to your Father, don't worry. Pray the Scriptures over his mind (Romans 12:1-2; 2 Corinthians 10:3-5; Philippians 2:5; Colossians 3:2; 2 Timothy 1:7) and his heart (Matthew 22:37; John 7:38; Acts 15:8-9; Romans 10:9; Ephesians 5:25-28; Colossians 3:14-15,19), then watch God transform your husband into a man like Dad. Make your relationship with the Father attractive and inviting to your husband by becoming a healed, uncompromising woman of God.

EXAMINE YOURSELF

Until you are healed, be extremely wise and vigilant when a man desires a romantic relationship. Understand your limitations and weaknesses, and learn from your past mistakes. Be aware of your areas of vulnerability, and know which words and actions feed your emotions and weaken your defenses. Ask yourself what happens emotionally and physiologically when a man holds your hand, touches your shoulder, hugs you, or gives you a kiss. These scenarios seem simplistic, even elementary, but are very important when you are extremely vulnerable to the flesh and its need for touch, attention, and affection.

Catalog how you respond to positive and negative emotions—loneliness, hopelessness, fatigue, excitement—and the actions that follow. Many times women inadvertently let their defenses down when they're excited about the opportunities in a relationship.

Review previous destructive patterns. What were your pitfalls, and how could they have been avoided? Now extend that research to your entire family. One of the greatest tools used in counseling is called the genogram, wherein three to four generations are charted on a piece of paper. This visual allows a person to see both positive and negative traits that are passed down from generation to generation.

Learn about authentic love. We must understand love as a demonstration of integrity, respect, commitment, and obedience to God's Word. Love *never* contradicts your Father's Word.

Love suffers long and is kind; love does not envy; love does not parade itself, is not puffed up; does not behave rudely, does not seek its own, is not provoked, thinks no evil; does not rejoice in iniquity, but rejoices in the truth; bears all things, believes all things, hopes all things, endures all things.

Love never fails. (1 Corinthians 13:4-8)

Stern boundaries must be set around your male relationships. When Andre and I dated, he was not allowed upstairs. The only rooms upstairs were bedrooms and bathrooms—none of which concerned him, since there was a bathroom downstairs. Our curfew in the house was ten o'clock. I know that sounds primitive and corny, but that was the extreme measure I needed to stay pure.

I'll never forget the night we decided to rent a movie at my house that would end far beyond our curfew. Since we were under surveillance by Aron and Shanell and George and Paulette (two accountability couples), I told Andre to move his car from the street and put it in the garage to hide his presence. He did, and we hung out late with our movie and ordered pizza.

When the movie ended, Andre helped me clean the living room and kitchen, then grabbed his keys to go home. When he opened the back door leading to the garage, we discovered that the garage door had been up the entire time. Andre swore he had closed the garage when he pulled his car in.

God spoke clearly to us that night. We can outsmart others, but we cannot outsmart or hide from God. He is serious about every commitment and will expose disobedience and sin. The curfew was established that we might glorify God with our bodies and avoid every *appearance* of evil (1 Thessalonians 5:22). Disobeying it was sin. A man's car in a single pastor's garage until midnight looks evil no matter how innocent the actions are inside. That was a direct warning from God to me not to have loose boundaries. I was vulnerable and could not afford to fall or have a tarnished reputation.

Neither can you. Loose boundaries cause falls. Playing with your purity or testing how close you can get to the edge will cause you to fall, and a bit of "innocent pleasure" is not worth the cost. God's grace and mercy kept and shielded us that night—not a movie, pizza, or our own strength. Prepare a strategic plan to remain holy. If you're lax in any area, you will fall.

ONE DAY AT A TIME

Purity is a day-by-day decision. Each day when you awake, ask to be filled with the Holy Spirit, who gives you power to remain holy and sexually pure. To be filled simply means to be controlled by the Spirit. Paul said in Ephesians 5:18, "Do not be drunk with wine, in which is dissipation; but be filled with the Spirit." He's directing us not to live our lives out of control like a drunkard but in control, navigated by the Spirit. It's an invitation for His wisdom, guidance, conviction, and power throughout the course of the day.

Make a declaration each morning that you will flee fornication (1 Corinthians 6:18). Declare that you will not entertain or flirt with sin but run from it. The Holy Spirit will give you running power! Again, feed your spirit daily through prayer, worship, and reading the Word of God. These spiritual disciplines change our lives.

Place all your energy and focus on the Father. Your responsibility is an unconditional commitment to Him before *and* after marriage. If you seek first the kingdom of God and all His righteousness, everything else will be added to you (Matthew 6:33). Trust Him. Be nurtured by His faithfulness. If you delight yourself in the Lord, He will place His desire in your heart. If you commit your way to Him and trust also in Him, He will bring it to pass (Psalm 37:3-5).

God will not let you down. Obey His Word, and favorable results will accompany your obedience. The web of frustration and disappointment that's spun from negative behaviors will dissipate. Blessings will be released, not delayed. "And the peace of God, which surpasses all understanding, will guard your hearts and minds through Christ Jesus" (Philippians 4:7).

≡Growth Chart

1. What needs are you looking for a man to fulfill that can only be met by the Father?
2. On a scale from 1 to 10, measure your fear of abandonment. Has fear thrust you into overdrive to please your spouse, fiancé, or boyfriend in hopes that he won't abandon you?

    | 1   2   3   4   5   6   7   8   9   10 |

3. What's your plan to stay sexually pure? Develop a detailed strategic plan.
4. Find scriptures that command holiness and purity. Write them on index cards. Recite and memorize them.
5. What pitfalls from past relationships do you need to avoid?
6. Define love. Parallel your definition with 1 Corinthians 13:4-8. Compare and contrast.

≡Growth Spurt

Scripture Memorization

"He who walks in his uprightness fears the LORD, but he who is perverse in his ways despises Him." Proverbs 14:2

Prayer

Father, make me secure in my identity as Your daughter that I may attract a man like You—loving, committed, holy, and righteous. May I never settle for less.

Chapter 13

Daddy's Girl

How precious...are Your thoughts to me, O God!

PSALM 139:17

When our fathers abandoned us, it changed the way we viewed ourselves. We were no longer daughters but orphans. No longer treasured jewels but castoff rubbish. We became lost, confused, and alone, drifting without clear purpose and convinced we were of little worth.

But the Father reaches out to embrace us and give us a new identity—Daddy's girl—and once we accept His offer, things can never be the same.

A Daughter's Story: Francis

"I am going to see my daddy! I am going to see my daddy!" I must have shouted that for about three hours, but the wait seemed like three years! Between shouts I thought to myself, *I'm going to have my very own daddy!*

My mother pressed my hair early that day, combing it in my favorite style. She also let me wear my favorite powder-blue dress with a white-ruffle trim around the sleeves and collar. Everyone in the house had heard my shouts and told me how cute I looked. I hunted for a present to give my daddy; all I could find was a large pine cone in the front yard.

Seven years earlier, in 1964, I had attended my mother's high school graduation. I had the best seat in the house—in her stomach. My father couldn't join us because he was incarcerated and would remain there for seven years.

When I was three years old, my mother met another man and soon became pregnant with my sister. I was jealous of my sister and her relationship with her daddy, feelings that did not heal until we were adults.

Her daddy never did anything wrong to me, nor did he treat me like an outsider; he was just not *my* daddy. I didn't feel I could cuddle up to him the same way my sister did.

My mother didn't talk much about my father, but she often allowed me to visit his relatives. Those visits continued to spark my curiosity about my father, and although I had several uncles who were crazy about me, they never took the place of my very own daddy. I don't remember the one visit to my father in prison when I was less than a year old, but I do vividly remember being so excited to see my father for what felt like the very first time.

Finally the car pulled up. I ran outside as fast as I could and jumped right into his arms. I gave him the pine cone, and my daddy picked me up and kissed and hugged me for what seemed like an eternity! Tears of excitement ran down his face, and we instantly felt love and acceptance. I didn't realize until that hug how much I had missed having my very own daddy. I felt so special, so wanted. At seven years old I was overwhelmed by so many emotions at one time.

Nothing excited me more than to see my father regularly. I continued to live with my mother, sister, and her father, but he and my mother were beginning to have problems. Eventually my mother asked him to move out, and soon thereafter, my mother and my daddy began to date. I couldn't have been happier. We went everywhere together. We had family outings almost every weekend. Now I had *my* daddy, and my sister could feel what I had felt for the past four years.

After about a year, my mother and father announced they were getting married! I really had it all now. I was the flower girl in their wedding, and we were a real family.

Several months later their relationship changed drastically. I often heard my mother crying. They argued more and more. But I was still happy that we were together as a family.

The summer before my ninth birthday, we moved to a four-bedroom house in Carson, California. It was the nicest house I had ever seen. It was surrounded by other large houses in a nice neighborhood and near a new school. I had my very own bedroom. I thought, *Everything is going to be all right.*

My mother didn't seem happy. She enrolled in junior college and attended evening classes, which kept her away from home more than usual.

My father no longer doted on me but frequently yelled and screamed—using profanity I had never heard. I found it more and more difficult to be around him. He was this mean man who took care of us financially, not the daddy I thought I had.

My mother was gone most evenings. I started a new school where I didn't know anyone. My father was absent emotionally, and my mother was physically absent most of the time.

One evening my mother asked me to clean up my room, and on inspection she discovered I had put my clean clothes behind my bean-bag chair instead of taking the time to fold them. She was furious! She took out her belt and began to whip me as if I had stolen something from her.

When she left for school, I was still crying, and my father called me into their room to console me. But the way he touched me seemed unusual. This was not a regular touch, and it scared me.

My father asked me if I had ever had sexual intercourse. I was nine years old. Then my "daddy" stripped me of my purity, innocence, identity, and self-worth. As scared as I was, I did not scream; I did not try to stop him. I was afraid of this man. I did not feel I could ever trust another man again. The man I looked to for protection, provision, and acceptance had misused my body and misused his authority in my life.

My father sexually molested me for five years, until I was fourteen. Even my parents' separation didn't stop the molestation. Following a series of rebellious acts, my mother threatened to make me live with my father. That threat gave me the boldness I needed to tell my mother about the abuse.

She was completely devastated and blamed herself. In some ways, so did I. She filed for divorce and was awarded full custody of me. I didn't see or hear from my father again until I was an adult.

I often wondered why God allowed this to happen to me. My feeling was, if God loved me, He would have stopped my father.

For years I felt dirty and ashamed of who I was. Naturally, I allowed myself to be mistreated in my relationships with men. Wasn't that normal and what I deserved? If they were too nice, I created some drama, because life just didn't seem normal without it.

At age thirty I discovered two themes in my life: self-inflicted turmoil and a pattern of unfinished business—broken relationships and an inability to keep a job for longer than a year.

Finally I grew weary and knew I had to make critical decisions about my future, the way I wanted to live the rest of my life. I needed to decide whether I would allow my damaged emotions to affect my two children's lives, whether I'd take responsibility for my actions, and whether I'd continue to blame my father *and* mother for the bad choices I had made in life. Sure, some of my actions (and reactions) were a result of being molested, but as an adult the choices were always mine.

Deep inside I knew that what my father had done to me and his absence didn't define God's destiny for me. I believed in my soul that I was more worthy than the path I was on and that I deserved much more from life. Things had to change. My first change was to trust

God, knowing I only needed a small amount of faith. I cried out to God to heal me.

God led me to read a book that had been given to me several years earlier—*Woman, Thou Art Loosed* by T. D. Jakes. After reading it, I spent days and weeks alone, in one little room with my BIG God, and He began to deliver me. He delivered me from shame, self-doubt, low self-esteem, bitterness, and the resentment of being dealt what I felt was an unfair hand in life.

Over the years I have watched God use my life to help others with their struggles while He showed me that devastating things happen to us (sometimes through no fault of our own), but we have a choice to remain at the place of devastation or to move into what God has for us. We can choose to be pitiful or to walk in His power! We can choose to obey or to disobey His Word.

God does not waste anything. All that we go through is to His glory. My life in its entirety was designed to help someone else along the way, and the greatest gift I can give is the gift of transparency. I will never hide where I have been and what I have gone through. If I do, I hide God's glory.

When I allowed God to become my *Daddy*, He blessed me beyond my wildest imagination. I am happily married with three children I adore and who adore me. I have a heart and ministry for teenage girls. And God has so much more He wants to do with my life.

God eventually restored my relationship with my mother and blessed me with a wonderful stepfather, but God will always be the only Daddy I need. My relationship with my biological father is still disconnected, but I have forgiven him, and I pray earnestly for his salvation.

I know I'm healed because I am extremely grateful for all that I have gone through—the good and the bad. Thank You, heavenly Father. Thank You, *my very own Daddy*.

A New Identity

A daughter who wears the title "Daddy's girl" knows there is nothing her father won't do for her. She is the apple of his eye and therefore is secure in her identity. She runs to her father for everything because she knows he has her best interest at heart. When she's in trouble, he is there, and he comes to her defense without question or doubt. Breaking his heart devastates her, so she's careful to abide by Daddy's rules.

His love is immeasurable, and he won't withhold any good thing from her. Most men shy away from her because they know they must measure up to his model, for she amplifies his name to all.

This may not be your testimony about your earthly father, but it would be your testimony about your heavenly Father if you embraced Him. A father's love for his daughter cannot compare or outweigh the love our heavenly Father has for us.

You are the apple of your Father's eye. David cried out to the Lord in Psalm 17:8 and said, "Keep me as the apple of Your eye; hide me under the shadow of Your wings." The Hebrew word *apple* is a feminine, relational word that literally means *daughter*. So David is saying, "The way you view, cherish, and have compassion for your daughters, look at me in that manner and protect me from the enemy." The Father never turns His attention from you but peers down continuously with you in His sight.

The Father has your best interest at heart, for "no good thing will He withhold from those who walk uprightly" (Psalm 84:11). Therefore whatever He does *not* give you is not good for you—contrary to what you believe. Our responsibility is to walk uprightly—or in Daddy terms, be a good girl. So "let us not grow weary while doing good, for in due season we shall reap if we do not lose heart" (Galatians 6:9).

I remember a time when this concept of new identity was brought home to me in a personal way.

"Mom," Sheena called.

"Mom!" Sheena exclaimed.

"MOM!!!" Sheena shouted.

"Oh! Yes, sweetie?" I finally answered after I realized she was calling me.

"Look at my bag of goodies I get to take home from the party!" Sheena said with pure excitement.

Sheena was ten years old when we attended the birthday party of my best friend's son. Approximately twenty children, ages two to twelve, were running, screaming, and playing in the backyard while the parents lounged in the shade, ate, and talked. In the company of four other mothers and against the background of screams, my daughter had been calling my "new" name.

Months before my wedding Sheena had asked if she could call me Mom. Immediately and comfortably she adopted the name change. She did not wait until after her dad and I were married. Since *stepmother* sometimes holds a negative connotation in our society and *stepdaughter,* for me, seems disconnected, we decided not to preface our names with *step.* God created a beautiful, new mother-daughter relationship (one that respects and does not displace or replace her biological mother), and we both cherish it.

It took several months to adjust to my new name. Now, in a crowd of children, I know her cry for Mom. My new identity represents a special connection and bond to my daughter.

Your name has changed from God's *creation* to God's *daughter.* Viewing God as Father and wearing your new name will be an adjustment. Don't be surprised if the concept doesn't capture your heart at first. You may liken your heavenly Father to your earthly father. But press through what you've seen and experienced with your earthly father to embrace the love Daddy has for His girl in the spiritual realm. There's a special bond awaiting you that no one can break.

In my second year at Dallas Theological Seminary, Reverend D. Z. Coffield taught me the importance of my identity from one verse—Romans 1:1: "Paul, a bondservant of Jesus Christ, called to be an apostle, separated to the gospel of God…" It gives a holistic overview of our identity in Christ.

A New Person

Paul's Jewish name was Saul, and Saul was a tyrant! He condoned the murder of Stephen (Acts 7:58; 8:1); persecuted believers—entering homes uninvited, dragging men and women to prison (Acts 8:3); and obtained a decree from the high priest to transport believers from Damascus to Jerusalem (Acts 9:1-2).

The road to Damascus was a road to destruction for believers until Christ intercepted Saul's path and made it his pathway to destiny (Acts 9:3-9). Four chapters later Saul's name was changed to Paul.

When our fathers abandoned us, we were symbolically issued a decree to travel the path of destruction. But the Lord intercepted our lives, changed our paths, and changed our names. Your name was *creation*—a general term encompassing all of mankind, separated from God. Your name was changed to *daughter*—a relational term signifying intimacy, connectedness, and inheritance. *Daughter* is the new creation Paul spoke about in 2 Corinthians 5:17: "Therefore, if anyone is in Christ, he is a new creation; old things have passed away; behold, all things have become new."

From Acts 13 on, Paul *never* referred to himself as Saul, nor did he continue the practices of Saul. Saul was dead.

In a similar way, as you adopt your new identity, you must let old ways of thinking and behaving die. Tearing yourself apart over past mistakes is useless. Walk in your new nature. Proudly wear the name of Christ.

Too often we pull out our spiritual shovel and dig up the dead—the old self that is familiar to us. Rigor mortis and the stench of death have set in, yet we pick up the old self, drape her over our shoulders, and carry her around.

She represents the old lifestyle—friends, music, addictions, outbursts of anger, bitterness, depression, and vengeance. Carrying dead weight makes you weary, depressed, frustrated, angry, and exhausted.

Shake off the dead and become familiar with your new life in Christ. He will mold you into an awesome woman of God. Your life will change, and your destiny will be fulfilled.

A New Position

Paul referred to himself as a "bondservant" of Jesus Christ. Bondservants came from all walks of life and were not permitted to resign and work for another employer. They served until they died.

Your position is in Christ. The Holy Spirit is in you (Ephesians 4:30); you are in Christ (Colossians 3:3); Christ is in the Father; and the Father is in Christ (John 14:11). You are now in a secure position to serve.

When you accepted Christ, you died, and your life became hidden in Him. You work for Him now (Mrs. or Ms. Bondservant), and there is no room for selfishness. Life is about serving the true and living God.

The Father wants to use you to serve your husband, your children, your parents, your friends, your brothers and sisters in Christ, and, yes, even your boss. Your lifestyle, attitude, conversation, and relationships should reflect the gospel of Jesus Christ. We must be the gospel personified, prompting men and women to ask us, "What must I do to be saved?" (Acts 16:30).

A New Calling

I accepted Jesus Christ at age eleven and rededicated my life at age twenty-five when I joined Faithful Central Bible (then Missionary Baptist) Church. I was a babe in Christ for those thirteen years. I returned to the Lord broken and bruised from not living a life yielded to Christ.

Had the Lord revealed to me *then* that I would be an ordained associate pastor—overseeing the training, discipleship, and mentoring of women—I would have run away from Him and the church. The Father couldn't unveil His calling on my life during that time because I was not able to comprehend it. Even now, as a mature believer, I'm sometimes overwhelmed by the calling. If I think about it too long, fear and insecurity try to settle in. God loves us too much to devastate us. He knows how much we can handle.

Many babes in Christ anxiously ask the Father to show them their calling. It's equivalent to taking a newborn baby to a restaurant and expecting him to eat a steak and lobster dinner. As we serve and grow, God begins to unfold, piece by piece, the calling He has on our lives.

When I was a babe in Christ, the Father took me from Los Angeles to Dallas and separated me from family and friends. There He began chipping away and healing the deep-seated pangs of my father's abandonment. He had to isolate, heal, and *then* commission me.

I became tired of the heavy load wearing me down and made a decision to surrender to the healing hand of God. He could not use me while I carried the baggage of low self-worth, no self-confidence, fear, panic attacks, and insecurities. Had I chosen to hold on to bitterness, resentment, and unforgiveness, you would not hold this book in your hand today. Drs. Frank Minirth and Paul Meier wrote a book entitled *Happiness Is a Choice.* The title speaks for itself. We must choose whether we will live in depression and despair or in happiness, joy, and wholeness.

I urge you to choose happiness, not despair. Release the baggage you carry each day. Walk securely in the calling God has on your life. If it's unclear, serve in ministry until He reveals it. You will not "hear" your calling if you're lazy, complacent, or remain despondent about the future.

You have a custom-made calling, and there's work to do for the kingdom of God. Declare that your "daddy" issues will not delay the revelation of your calling another day. Begin to live life through the clear glasses of a victor, not through the shaded glasses of a victim.

A New Purpose
Paul knew the purpose for his existence on earth: to glorify God. Your purpose is the same. Comprehending and accepting that your life is not about you will be one of your greatest challenges. Everything that happened in your life was orchestrated by God to bring glory to God.

It was ordained before the beginning of time for my father to take flight. Why did my father abandon me at birth? So that somebody would be saved. Why did I experience excruciating emotional pain? So you would hear my testimony and be healed. Why did I stumble upon knowing God as Father? So you may know God as Father. Why did I struggle for years with my identity? So you would know your identity as Daddy's girl.

If you were physically, sexually, or emotionally abused by your father or if your father left you by death or decision, God held you so you could bear it. He allowed it, but He did *not* cause it. He knew you would make a decision to accept Jesus Christ as Lord and Savior and use your life experiences to draw men and women to Him.

Don't anchor your life on the abandonment or abuse. There's so much more to your life than your past and pain. Your life has purpose. The Father wants to nurse you back to health to use you to further the kingdom. The goal is that you see the big picture—God's picture that is larger than our finite minds.

Make Daddy proud, and strive to be a daughter who serves Jesus Christ and glorifies the Father through the calling He has for your life.

SELF-TALK

One crucial aspect of practicing your new identity is changing the way you talk to yourself. Verbal abuse was the bedrock of my conversations with myself. As I mentioned earlier, I constantly recited such phrases as, "I can't do it," "That was stupid," "I will never finish college," "Don't try that," "You'll never make it," "I don't know anything," "Someone's going to uncover how dumb I really am."

I habitually popped in negative tapes and pushed Play on my mental tape player until the Father revealed to me that I was negating who Christ said I was. As royalty, my crown is lovingkindness and tender mercies (Psalm 103:4). The Father directed my speech to be in line with my headpiece. So I practiced speaking lovingly and tenderly until the truth of His Word penetrated my heart and mind.

Record over those negative messages with the Word of God:

- I am fearfully and wonderfully made. (Psalm 139:14)
- I am regarded with numerous precious thoughts. (Psalm 40:5; 139:17)
- I am loved. (John 3:16; 17:23)
- I am more than a conqueror. (Romans 8:37)
- I am bought at a price. (1 Corinthians 6:20)
- I am a new creation. (2 Corinthians 5:17)
- I am chosen. (John 15:16; 1 Peter 2:9)
- I am royalty. (1 Peter 2:9)
- I am holy. (1 Peter 2:9)
- I am His own special daughter. (1 Peter 2:9)
- I am a child of God. (1 Peter 2:10)
- I can do all things through Christ who gives me strength. (Philippians 4:13)

Memorize and personalize these verses. Place them on your mirror, in your car, on your desk at work, *in* the refrigerator when you're searching for comfort foods, under your pillow when you're burdened in the midnight hour. Allow them to overshadow the faults in your belief system and saturate your heart and mind.

Creating new messages reconditions the mind. Paul wrote in Romans 12:2, "And do not be conformed to this world, but be transformed by the renewing of your mind." Let your new message solely consist of the Word of God, and the transformation process will begin.

▤ GROWTH CHART

1. Read Psalm 139 in its entirety. List in your journal everything the Lord says about you.

2. Measure the following on a scale from 1 to 10:
    Self-worth (1=I'm not valued; 10=I'm invaluable)

    | 1 2 3 4 5 6 7 8 9 10 |

    Self-confidence (1=I won't try; 10=I'll try, even if I fail)

    | 1 2 3 4 5 6 7 8 9 10 |

    Self-belonging (1=I never fit in; 10=I fit in anywhere)

    | 1 2 3 4 5 6 7 8 9 10 |

    Self-image (1=I'm distorted; 10=I view myself as Christ views me)

    | 1 2 3 4 5 6 7 8 9 10 |

3. In what area above do you tend to overcompensate? Explain why.
4. How would you describe God's perception of you? Is this helpful?
5. Record your self-talk. Is it pleasing to the Father?
6. What does your self-talk sound like? If someone said to you what you say to yourself, how would you feel? Would you feel cherished—or ready to fight?
7. Let's do a self-check. How often do you encourage yourself? How often do you put yourself down? How often do you speak the Word of God over your life?

◢GROWTH SPURT

Scripture Memorization

"But you are a chosen generation, a royal priesthood, a holy nation, His own special people, that you may proclaim the praises of Him who called you out of darkness into His marvelous light." 1 Peter 2:9

Prayer

Father, I want to fully know my identity in Christ. Remind me daily that I am fearfully and wonderfully made and that all Your works are marvelous, and that includes me. May I never negate this truth.

Chapter 14

Walking Hand in Hand

For I, the LORD your God, will hold your right hand,
saying to you, "Fear not, I will help you."

ISAIAH 41:13

Although I never had the opportunity to hold my father's hand, I love to see fathers holding the hands of their toddler daughters who are just learning to walk—the little ones concentrating on tiptoes and holding on for dear life to a pinky. I also love to glimpse the adult woman who holds her elderly father's hand and takes him for a walk. Their experience parallels walking hand in hand with the Father.

We have a permanent place, an indelible mark in His hand, reason enough we should take hold of it. God said, "I have inscribed you on the palms of My hands" (Isaiah 49:16).

Walking with the Father means committing to Christ, living for Christ, knowing the lordship of Christ, and surrendering to Christ. It is to live according to the Word of God. It's *not* "a walk in the park."

Initially, I was like the toddler who held on tight to her father's pinky, but I found myself in a cycle of frustration: holding on, letting go, falling down, crying, getting helped up by the Father, and holding on again—only to let go again. I would pull away from the Father, try to walk independently, and fall on my face. Or I would let go of the Father and hold on to a man. Then he'd shake me loose, and once again I would fall on my face. The cycle continued for about two and a half years until I got sick and tired of falling, depending on myself and others, and being wounded. Finally I learned to walk with the Father.

LEARNING TO WALK

Let me show you five keys to walking hand in hand with your heavenly Father:

1. **Rid your life of habitual, continual sin**. Ask your Father if your relationships, living arrangements, attitude, and speech are pleasing to Him. Be prepared for an honest answer.

2. **Recognize areas of perfectionism**. Perfectionism is not the same as a spirit of excellence. Perfectionists carry with them an obsessive-compulsive behavior that makes them fixate on a task until it's completed and in "perfect" order. Nothing can steer you away from it—except surrendering to the Father.

3. **Relinquish control of your life.** The purpose is to align your lifestyle with the Word of God so it reflects the character of God. Many believers use the phrase "my Lord and Savior Jesus Christ" too loosely. He may be your Savior, but to call Him "Lord" means He governs and rules your life.

4. **Restructure and prioritize your schedule.** Daily quality time with the Father develops and makes straight your walk. Make an appointment with Him, and stick to it—even if you show up only to be still and listen. Remember, He speaks through His Word!

5. **Rehearse your walk.** Most likely you won't master this overnight, especially if Jesus Christ is your Savior and *not* Lord—governor of your life. Make every day a dress rehearsal. Clothe yourself with the Word of God, learn the lines, and obey it. When you mess up, confess your mistakes (1 John 1:9) and start renewed. The more you practice walking with the Lord, the less you'll stumble.

These five Rs are challenging but rewarding. If you choose to walk with the Father, prepare yourself, like Jesus, to be ostracized, stigmatized, and criticized, components of our salvation that we tend to overlook. The gift of salvation is accompanied by the gift of suffering.

> For to you it has been granted on behalf of Christ, not only to believe in Him, but also to suffer for His sake. (Philippians 1:29)

MOVING FORWARD WITH THE FATHER

Walking with the Father is not necessarily easy. He will sometimes lead you through paths strewn with challenges and circumstances designed to help you grow strong and develop muscles of faith. But He has promised to walk alongside you as long as you cling to His hand.

The greatest troubles come, however, when we introduce our own challenges to the walk, bringing along burdens He never asked us to carry.

Walking on Crutches

Absent fathers unknowingly hand their daughters a crutch of "victim" when they walk out of their lives. If you have walked on that crutch for too long, you probably cannot imagine walking without it. Decide today to relinquish the crutch associated with your father.

Hobble to the Father, take His hand, and let Him teach you a new walk and guide you in all facets of your life. Let go of that crutch, grab the hand of the Father, and practice walking securely as His daughter.

Walking with Distractions

One of the greatest ploys of the Enemy is to distract the believer. If you want to walk hand in hand with the Father, you'll have to discard those things or persons that distract, tempt, or turn you away from Him.

A modern-day encumbrance that subtly stifles the believer's walk is technology. Our world has soared to new and exciting heights in the area of technology and communication, but with that some believers have taken a nosedive in their walk with the Lord. We are mesmerized by digital, flat-screen televisions; DVDs; satellite dishes; surround-sound stereos; camcorders; digital cameras; PDAs; pagers; cellular phones; the Internet; e-mail; caller ID; call-waiting ID; and laptop computers. The list is lengthy and grows daily.

Please don't misunderstand. Technology is not sin. It's our lack of self-discipline and control that allows it to preoccupy us and shift our attention away from God. That makes us vulnerable to sin. It has become the spiritual demise for many believers.

When my husband and I were dating, he didn't own a cellular phone, pager, caller ID—nothing. He was from the "old school" and was happy with simply a home phone. When we married, I insisted that I trade in my premarriage cellular phone to purchase the family-share-plan cellular phones. We did, and Andre had a new toy.

He programmed phone numbers, set the time, created a new greeting and lock code, decided on the tune for the ringer, changed the settings, and called all of his family and friends to give them his new cell number. It was set on "loud ring" in the car and "vibrate" at the job. The phone never left his side.

When our first bill arrived, we were both stunned. It wasn't the dollar amount that took us aback but the hours of usage. In thirty days, Andre was on his cell phone eleven hundred minutes. He went from zero to eleven hundred minutes in thirty days. That's eleven hundred minutes of added distractions.

We are busy people—much busier than we need to be. If the truth were told, we could probably scrape off half the tasks on our plates. Examine your daily, weekly, and monthly tasks and routines. Minimize those activities that pull you away from God and family. Keep your life balanced and prioritized. This pleases God.

Maybe your father spent most of his time in front of the television—giving you minimal attention. You probably discovered that joining him on the sofa and watching television with him offered very little interaction and quality time. Relationships can't be built when your attention is directed away from one another.

I exhort you not to mimic the father who was inattentive. As heartbreaking as it was for you, the same inattentiveness breaks the heart of the Father.

WALKING IN DARKNESS

When I first moved into my new home, I had a little bedtime ritual. Before I would go upstairs to retire, I would walk to the entryway and turn on the light, go back and turn off the kitchen light, turn on the light for the stairwell, turn off the entryway light, and walk upstairs to my room.

Two months later I grew tired of the extra steps. Changing my routine, I turned off the kitchen light, stretched my arms in front of me, and felt my way to the stairs. When I found the round post at the bottom of the rail, I knew to step up onto the entryway, step up to the platform of the stairwell, feel for the light switch, and turn on the light to begin my climb upward.

A month later I decided not to feel for the light switch in the stairwell, walking upstairs without the light. When I reached the top of the stairs, I turned the light on to have a lighted path to my bedroom. I gradually became accustomed to walking in the dark. Today I can turn the lights off and walk to my room as if I were walking in the light. I have mastered walking in the dark in my home.

I sought darkness over the light because I wanted to avoid making additional steps. So often we believers choose the dark to avoid the extra effort it takes to walk in the Light. Succumbing to laziness tops the list for why we walk dangerously in the dark. Searching for shortcuts has become our unspoken motto in our walk with Christ.

We train ourselves to walk in the dark, jeopardizing our lives. A lighted path ensures safety. Walk independently of the Father, and the Enemy will happily hold your hand and guide you to the road of destruction.

We insult the Lord when we choose to walk in darkness and pray for the benefits that come only from walking in the Light. You cannot entertain adultery and simultaneously pray for your marriage to work. You cannot rob God with your tithes and offerings and simultaneously pray for a financial breakthrough. You cannot habitually and continually feed your temple junk food and simultaneously pray for physical health and strength. These are behavioral signs of an erratic walk with the Father.

Walking in the Light can become laborious and wearisome at times, but we cannot surrender to darkness. Going against the grain of the world takes stamina, endurance, and determination, leaving no room for laziness.

Twice I've missed a step in my home, in the *daylight,* and have slid down the steps! Recently Andre slipped and fell down the stairs, injuring his arm and ankle. It was two o'clock in the afternoon! We're vulnerable even in the light!

Don't opt to pull your hand away from the Father and walk in darkness. "For you were once darkness, but now you are light in the Lord. Walk as children of light…finding out what is acceptable to the Lord" (Ephesians 5:8,10).

WALKING IN YOUR HEALING

The process of emotional healing is unusual. One would think that God would peel away the protective layers of woundedness until He reaches the core. On the contrary, His light pierces the solid mass of woundedness until it reaches and reveals the core, leaving a sliced mass that can gently be peeled away, layer upon layer.

I was dumbfounded when God revealed that my low self-worth, low self-confidence, need for love from a male, perfectionism, and pleasing qualities were the layers covering the root of my absent father. After He shed light on the core, it took years to peel away the layers of hurt and pain. Today I still struggle with the layer of perfectionism. I've tried to dress it up and call it "a spirit of excellence," but members of my discipleship group confronted me and called it what it was. Another layer the Father wants to heal was exposed.

A great challenge awaits you. As God begins to peel away the layers and heal the wounds left by your absent father, you must immediately begin to walk in your healing. Practice living as a woman who is already healed while waiting to be completely healed. Obey His Word—even when you feel the throb and sting of the bruises, scars, cuts, and wounds of your father.

Practice Your Walk

I visit the gym a minimum of three times a week to stay fit and to alleviate stress. My routine includes thirty minutes of cardiovascular exercise and thirty minutes of strength training. Eventually I will move to the free weights, located in the back of the gym, but I shudder and say, "Never mind" when I hear the thunderous moans and groans as metal clanks against metal.

I have noticed a pattern among the men who work out in that area. The buff guys walk slowly with their arms bent, slightly angled away from their sides, in a seemingly continuous flexed position. Their muscles appear to preclude them from straightening their arms.

The average fellows with medium-sized muscles walk slowly with their arms bent, slightly angled away from their sides in a flexed position.

The skinny, nonmuscular ones also pass by with their arms bent, slightly angled away from their sides, flexing what isn't there.

Muscular strength is their vision, and even though they do not have it yet, they are walking in it. That says, "I know what I want. I know the process it takes to get there (which is sometimes painful), and I am committed to the process—even at the risk of embarrassment." Initially I shook my head and laughed, but now I commend them.

Remember the old cliché "Practice makes perfect"? We're never "perfectly" healed as long as sin abounds. You must begin to practice walking in your healing. Find a believer who is healed from father wounds, and begin to imitate her. Mimic her discipline, consistency, strength, and triumph over pain. Begin to act as if you are healed while you're on the road to being healed.

"Act as if" is a counseling technique used in the Adlerian theory of psychology. This incredible technique can show us our potential and the power of self-control. And when you are following the Word of God, don't confuse *act as if* with *faking it*. You are not faking it; you are walking in truth! Choosing *not* to let your feelings dictate your life denotes growth.

Practicing your new walk means trying on new behaviors while walking by faith and not by sight (2 Corinthians 5:7). If feelings of fear and discomfort overshadow and threaten to immobilize you, don't be alarmed. Change is uncomfortable. Therefore, press forward to walk in the truth of God's Word, and watch your loving Father shepherd you with His healing hand.

Walking in Obedience

Another element of walking in your healing is to live your life under the authority and full counsel of God. That means you must obey every command He has written, despite your current spiritual, emotional, and physical conditions. From the sunniest day to the typhoons of life, you must obey. No exceptions, no options, no compromise.

Unsurprisingly our innate nature wants to retaliate because our fathers harmed us or caused us severe pain. But the Father says:

Only let your conduct be worthy of the gospel of Christ. (Philippians 1:27)

Only (monos) means "alone, solitary, or one way." It does not suggest multiple options. There's no more to the concept and no less. You can't add to it and can't take away from it. It is *the* way to behave. The *New*

International Version translates the Greek word *monos* as *whatever happens.* So whatever happens or whatever has happened, let your conduct be worthy of the gospel of Jesus Christ.

The word *conduct (agoge)* refers to our course and manner of life, our attitude, behaviors, conversation, and posture. All should be worthy of Jesus and your Father, *Yahweh-Rapha*—the Lord who heals. The key to this challenging walk with the Father is found in Galatians 5:16: "Walk in the Spirit, and you shall not fulfill the lust of the flesh." Allow the Holy Spirit to govern your life, and you will never pull your hand away from the Father's hand.

⟩GROWTH CHART

1. What is your position in your walk with the Father?
   ___ Ahead of Him
   ___ Staggering behind, refusing to keep up
   ___ Running away
   ___ By His side, holding His hand
2. The Father wants to walk alongside you in every aspect of your life. In what area of your life are you walking alone?
3. Whom are you walking with that prevents you from walking with the Father?
4. Take a walk (just you and the Father) at the beach, lake, park, or in your neighborhood, and let it symbolize a new walk with Him. As you walk, share your heart with Him—your hurts, pains, fears, and concerns.

⟩GROWTH SPURT

Scripture Memorization

"Nevertheless I am continually with You; You hold me by my right hand."
Psalm 73:23

Prayer

Father, I want my feet planted in the footsteps of Christ. When I try to slip away from You, stop and nudge me to stay on course. Hold my hand and never let it go. I can't walk successfully in this life apart from You.

Chapter 15

Story Time

I will delight myself in Your statutes;
I will not forget Your word.

PSALM 119:16

Snuggling with the Father and His Word will draw you unimaginably close to Him. His voice will resound from every page. Filled with morals, life-changing stories, humor, romance, suspense, mysteries, good guys and bad guys, and tailor-made instruction, the Father's Book has a very happy ending for all who believe in its hero, Jesus. His Word is not an antiquated, make-believe fairy tale. It's an up-to-date guide to truth—applicable to every area of your life.

Whoever first coined the acrostic B-I-B-L-E as Basic Instructions Before Leaving Earth was right on target.

Relax, and read along with Him.

A FAMILIAR STORY

Let's commence with a story of Jerusalem and parallel it with the formative years of your life as a fatherless daughter. Tune in closely and hear the voice of the Lord and what He says about you from birth. After you read the following passage, read it again. Then close your eyes and meditate on what the Word of the Lord says about you, His daughter, when you were abandoned by your father:

"Your birth and your nativity are from the land of Canaan; your father was an Amorite and your mother a Hittite. As for your nativity, on the day you were born your navel cord was not cut, nor were you washed in water to cleanse you; you were not rubbed with salt nor wrapped in swaddling cloths. No eye pitied you, to do any of these things for you, to have compassion on you; but you were thrown out into the open field, when you yourself were loathed on the day you were born.

"And when I passed by you and saw you struggling in your own blood, I said to you in your blood, 'Live!' Yes, I said to you in your blood, 'Live!' I made you thrive like a plant in the field; and you grew, matured, and became very beautiful. Your breasts were formed, your hair grew, but you were naked and bare.

"When I passed by you again and looked upon you, indeed your time was the time of love; so I spread My wing over you and covered your nakedness. Yes, I swore an oath to you and entered into a covenant with you, and you became Mine," says the Lord GOD.

"Then I washed you in water; yes, I thoroughly washed off your blood, and I anointed you with oil. I clothed you in embroidered cloth and gave you sandals of badger skin; I clothed you with fine linen and covered you with silk. I adorned you with ornaments, put bracelets on your wrists, and a chain on your neck. And I put a jewel in your nose, earrings in your ears, and a beautiful crown on your head. Thus you were adorned with gold and silver, and your clothing was of fine linen, silk, and embroidered cloth. You ate pastry of fine flour, honey, and oil. You were exceedingly beautiful, and succeeded to royalty. Your fame went out among the nations because of your beauty, for it was perfect through My splendor which I had bestowed on you," says the Lord GOD. (Ezekiel 16:3-14)

This analogy of the Father's love takes me back to the day of my birth to remind me that He was there. When my father wasn't present to cut my umbilical cord—symbolizing intimacy and involvement with the mother and child—my heavenly Father was there. He washed me, cleaned me up, clothed me in the finest attire, fed me with His Word, spoke of my beauty, and entered into a covenant with me.

And when I, like Jerusalem, turned from Him during my teenage and young adult years, He said to me, "Cast away from you all the transgressions which you have committed, and get yourselves a new heart and a new spirit" (Ezekiel 18:31). So I repented, and He created in me a clean heart and renewed a steadfast spirit within me (Psalm 51:10) and lovingly repeated the process—washing, cleansing, clothing, feeding, adoring, and restoring me.

If you continue reading the story past Ezekiel 16:14, you'll discover Jerusalem's rebellion and later restoration. Read on, and ask the Holy Spirit to speak to you about your relationship and commitment to the Lord. The time is now to respond to the voice of the Lord, which echoes throughout His Word.

Jesus said, "My mother and My brothers are these who hear the word of God and do it" (Luke 8:21). He also said, "My sheep hear My voice, and I know them, and they follow Me" (John 10:27).

You cannot follow if you do not hear. You cannot hear if you do not read. You will not obey if you do not know the Word of God.

A STORY TO DESIRE

I found myself in the backseat of a Volvo on a clear winter night, arrested by laryngitis, a sore throat, and sneezing as I traveled southeast from Johannesburg to Swaziland. Alongside me were two of my teammates, Vanessa and Kim, with similar symptoms.

We were taken by surprise when we left Dallas in the summer of 1994 and twenty hours later arrived in South Africa in the *winter* of 1994. A minor detail our travel agent had forgotten to share with us, and we were *not* dressed for the occasion. Everyone on our team had packed improperly, and, consequently, every team member became sick during our mission trip.

Traveling at night, we three pitiful ones sat in the backseat sneezing, sniffling, and coughing. Vanessa and I had window seats, and I couldn't help but marvel at the clear, star-filled skies.

Traveling farther east, I was captivated by a mass of lights in the sky, and I strained to ask if what I was viewing was the Milky Way. Vanessa confirmed it. For the first time, I saw the Milky Way galaxy—a cluster of 100 billion stars that's approximately 150,000 light-years in diameter—and I was utterly amazed.

I couldn't stop gazing at this marvelous wonder. It consumed every thought. I lost sight of my surroundings and forgot that I was sick. It captivated me. I relished and followed it for miles until it was out of view.

Six years later the Lord brought His Word to life through that experience. The Lord's Word is captivating, a marvelous wonder. It should consume every thought. Studying it takes your focus off yourself—your problems, fears, and shortcomings—and puts it completely on the Lord. We must relish and follow His Word.

David wrote:

One thing I have desired of the LORD,
That will I seek:
That I may dwell in the house of the LORD
All the days of my life,
To behold the beauty of the LORD,
And to inquire in His temple. (Psalm 27:4)

David speaks of a heart issue and priorities in this verse. The *one* thing he speaks of is a unit in three parts—dwelling, beholding, and inquiring. He purposed in his heart and mind to follow his desire.

Dwelling is the prerequisite of beholding and inquiring. It means to sit down and to remain. Translation: Stop what you're doing, reprioritize your life, and take a seat in the presence of the Lord. David's desire was to camp out in the presence of God every day of his life. We must make the same lifetime commitment.

Rearrange your life. Sit down, take a load off, be still, and keep silent. Open the Word of God and listen as He speaks. The Father wants you stationary to become familiar with His character.

Second, David desired to behold the Lord's beauty. The word *behold* means to gaze at or to look at something steadily and intently with pleasure. He desired to affix his eyes solely on the Lord, allowing him to lose sight of the perils around him.

That was me in South Africa. Gazing at the Milky Way made me lose sight of my surroundings, my illness, my companions, where I was going, and where I had come from. The Milky Way, illuminating the night sky, was that pleasurable. I marveled at God's work.

His Word, too, is that pleasurable—giving joy, hope, and direction. You'll marvel at His work in your life and His love for you. Engaging in the spiritual realm will make you forget your troubles in the physical realm. Sit down, remain in His presence, and focus intently on Him.

The last component of this unit is inquiring. Inquiring involves more than a dialogue with the Father through prayer. It means to uncover and inspect. It means opening His Word to read and dissect it with pen and paper in hand, taking copious notes, asking questions, expecting answers.

We could compare the task of inquiring with the role of an appraiser. Before you purchase a home, the bank's first task is to confirm the value of the house. They send an appraiser with a keen eye to inspect every nook and cranny of the home.

The buyer superficially sees a beautiful home inside and out, but the appraiser looks underneath the surface. He checks the pipes, turns on all the water faucets, flushes the toilets, runs the dishwasher, fills the tubs, checks the ceilings and walls for leaks, looks for cracks in the walls and tile, and examines the insulation. He documents all his findings.

We should approach God's Word like an appraiser. The banks won't take the word of the buyer that the property is great, and don't you take the word of anyone else regarding the Word of God. Don't take my word, your pastor's word, or Mama's word. Inspect it for yourself! Find out for yourself that His Word is inerrant, life-changing, transforming, soothing, and refreshing.

Watch out. While you're inspecting, you're being inspected. The Father is also performing His own appraisal on your life to know its worth and value. He knows it's invaluable with great potential, but He's looking for the leak and cracks. He'll reveal every damaged area that needs fixing. Then He will upgrade every area of your life.

David made a shift in Psalm 27 from praise, proclamation, and declaration in verses 1-6 to prayer in verses 7-13. He was looking for answers in the midst of trouble, and God answered him in verse 8. He said, "Seek My face." With trouble all around, God told him to dwell, behold, and inquire.

Seek God's face. Dwell in the presence of the Lord, and behold His beauty all the days of your life.

Make-Believe

My first mentor, Dr. LaVerne Tolbert, taught me the importance of creating a mental picture of the throne of God. What's great about this technique is that your image is unique and private, and it's an escape to the lap of the Father. Sometimes I'm sitting on the Father's lap, and sometimes I'm on Jesus' lap. Sometimes I'm prostrate before the throne, and sometimes I'm sitting at His feet.

When I intercede in prayer for somebody, that person is right there with me, holding my hand while I talk to the Father on his or her behalf. When my discipleship sisters hold hands for opening or closing prayer, we are right there at the Father's feet, holding hands, talking to Him.

For thirteen years I've carried this picture of being at God's throne, and it has blessed me. It has created greater intimacy and focus on the Lord. I won't describe my image in too much detail, because I want you to create your own—unique and special to you. There are some clues in the Word, particularly in Revelation 4. Search the Scriptures, and ask the Holy Spirit to reveal it to you the next time He reads you His story. Creating such an image will keep you focused while studying the Word of God. It will help you minister to Him as He ministers to you.

Envision bowing down before His throne. Enter His gates with thanksgiving and His courts with praise. Enter with a clean heart.

Echo David's words in Psalm 51: "Wash me thoroughly from my iniquity, and cleanse me from my sin" (verse 2). Ask God to purge you, wash you, and make you hear joy and gladness (verses 7-8). He will remove the sin that prevents you from hearing Him. Ask Him to create in you a clean heart and renew a steadfast spirit within you (verse 10).

Now you can study—renewed, restored, and refreshed. No one can take your image away. Never mind what rigid scholars, theologians, or legalists may think of your make-believe throne. The Father's children can play make-believe too! The difference is that we know our finite minds cannot capture or fathom the true essence, ambiance, and splendor of the real throne room of God.

The Word has cleansing power and gives you pressing power, like Paul, to push through opposition, trials, naysayers, tribulations, sleepless nights, and mornings when you don't want to get out of bed. It gives resistance, endurance, stamina, and resilience when life knocks you off your feet or when you're face to face with your past. And it gives you a new heart and mind to forgive others—including your father.

≣GROWTH CHART

1. Make an appointment with the Father to meet Him in His Word. Literally put Him down in your day planner. Make adjustments each week where needed. Commit to your meeting time.
2. Based on how often you read the Word of God, what is your spiritual condition?

___ Malnourished

___ Starving

___ Hunger pangs

___ Feasting

___ Full, sharing the Word with others

3. Where has your spiritual condition landed you?

___ ICU (Intensive Care Unit)

___ CCU (Critical Care Unit)

___ Serious but stable

___ Bed rest

___ Ill

___ Symptoms of illness

___ Healthy

4. Read Revelation 4:2-11. Create your personal make-believe image of the throne of God.

5. Read Luke 8:21. Can Christ say that about you? Can you honestly replace *My mother and My brothers* with your name and the sentence remain accurate?

≡ GROWTH SPURT

Scripture Memorization

"Your word I have hidden in my heart, that I might not sin against You."
Psalm 119:11

Prayer

Father, help me shift my schedule around to make studying Your Word a priority. Show me those persons or things that have replaced You, and I will be obedient to remove such distractions from my life. Open my ears to hear Your voice as You bring Your Word to life.

Chapter 16

Daddy, Pick Me Up

He...took her by the hand and called, saying,
"Little girl, arise."
Then her spirit returned,
and she arose immediately.

LUKE 8:54-55

Scripture reveals that Jesus lifted many daughters physically, emotionally, and spiritually from their infirmities. He can do the same for you. Lay aside all doubts and reservations, and cry out to the Father with your hands lifted, and ask Him to pick you up. No one is too heavy for Him. Actually, the heavier the daughter—weighed down internally with sorrow—the more strength and power He provides.

As you read the stories in Scripture about the women Christ healed, you'll notice a common denominator: touch. He either touched them or their children, or He was touched by them! Peter's mother-in-law, sick with fever, was raised from her sickbed (Matthew 8:14-15; Mark 1:29-31; Luke 4:38-39); the woman with the issue of blood touched Christ and was healed (Matthew 9:20-22; Mark 5:25-34; Luke 8:43-48); a twelve-year-old girl was raised from her deathbed (Matthew 9:18-26; Mark 5:21-42; Luke 8:40-56); a widow's dead son was touched, and both were made alive again (Luke 7:11-15); the woman with the alabaster flask washed Jesus' feet with her tears, wiped them with her hair, kissed and anointed them, and was made whole (Luke 7:37-50); and the woman with a spirit of infirmity, bent over for eighteen years, was touched and made straight (Luke 13:11-13).

TOUCHED BY THE FATHER

Jairus humbly came to Christ, worshiped Him, and cried out about his dying twelve-year-old daughter. He invited Christ to his home that He might touch her and make her alive again.

> While He spoke these things to them, behold, a ruler came and worshiped Him, saying, "My daughter has just died, but come and lay Your hand on her and she will live." So Jesus arose and followed him, and so did His disciples....
>
> When Jesus came into the ruler's house, and saw the flute players and the noisy crowd wailing, He said to them, "Make room, for the girl is not dead, but sleeping." And they ridiculed Him. But when the crowd was put outside, He went in and took her by the hand, and the girl arose. And the report of this went out into all that land. (Matthew 9:18-19, 23-26)

A loving father interceded on behalf of his dying daughter. He stated the problem and the solution to Christ. You may not have a father who will intercede on your behalf, but *anyone* can offer intercessory prayer—including you. State the problem and the solution. Christ, our Intercessor, knows your heartache, and the solution is a touch from Him.

He's waiting on you to come to Him. All He needs is an invitation. A simple cry, "Help!" with shortness of breath, lack of energy, or a nonverbal plea from the depths of your soul, and Jesus will come immediately, without question. He didn't question Jairus or hesitate when he cried out to Him, and He won't question or hesitate with you.

When Jesus arrived at Jairus's house, the scene was dampened with tears and dreary with a noisy crowd of wailing professional mourners.

Flute players filled the air with the sounds of a funeral dirge, and wails rang out from the mother, family, and friends. Then Christ entered the room. Not only did He observe the environment; He changed it. He announced that life still flowed through the veins of the young girl. He brought hope to the family and indignation to the crowd, so He put the naysayers out.

Clearing the periphery of your life makes room for Him to move closer to you. Christ will take inventory, observing those around you. He will put out the discouragers, distracters, disbelievers, and disenchanted that line the borders of your life. Separation from them strengthens your spiritual vital signs. Allow Him to clear the room that you may live.

The crowd was put out, and Christ went in. Apparently Jairus's daughter was in an inner room, apart from the crowd, lying on her deathbed. I'm sure her mother, drenched with tears, sat by her side, holding her limp, lifeless hand. But when Christ entered the room, she, too, had to step aside. An abundance of love, care, and concern from a mother is not powerful enough to raise a daughter from the dead. Only Christ's love and touch gives life.

Jesus didn't enter the girl's room by calling her name aloud, asking her to come forth, as He did for Lazarus, who was dead and buried in a cave (John 11:43). Neither did He enter with questions like, "What happened?" "How long has she been in this state?" or "Who caused this to happen?"

He came in without a word, without blame, and without judgment. He went in silently, touched her gently, and spoke to her softly. She needed the release of power from His hand to hers to get up from her deathbed. Christ took her by the hand, and she arose.

You need the tender, powerful touch of Christ to pick you up from your emotional deathbed. He won't judge, punish, or drill you with questions. He's coming to touch you, speak to you, and lift you. Mark and Luke record Jesus' words: "Little girl, arise." That's His word for you.

He specializes in resurrecting wounded daughters who grew physically into womanhood but died emotionally in childhood. Once you're resurrected, you will feel again, care again, and smile again. That critical spirit toward yourself and others will dissipate. Attitudes and arguments will cease in your relationships. Confusion will be bound. The Enemy can't use your life and mind as his playground another day. Christ's touch and His spoken word will make you get up and walk in holiness, righteousness, and wholeness.

Your healing is coming. We don't know the distance Christ traveled or the time it took to reach Jairus's daughter, but He heard the cry, immediately moved in her direction, touched her, spoke to her, and raised her to life.

I cannot tell you how long it will take before you become completely alive. Some paths are longer than others. But Christ is on the way, and your healing is absolute.

Don't be discouraged. I walked the healing path for five years, and it was worth every minute and every step. Christ brought me life, freedom, peace, and joy. Hold on, my sister. He's coming, bearing imperishable gifts. Be willing to travel the road with the Father no matter how long it takes. Commence with this daily declaration, "Because He lives, I will live!"

Let me make one other observation from this story: Sandwiched between these verses about Jairus's daughter is a woman who was devastated and weary from twelve years of blood flow (Matthew 9:20-22). She was on the path that Jesus walked to reach the dying girl. In desperation, she touched only the hem of His garment and was healed.

Similarly, when you cry out to the Lord, your call leads other daughters into the path of healing. The Father uses the fatherless as tools for healing.

OPEN THE DOOR TO THE FATHER

Christ is standing at the door of your life knocking, waiting for you to cry out and let Him in. He enters only by invitation, refusing to invade or intrude.

You have a choice: Leave the door closed (which precludes victorious living), or invite Him in and place every concern, fear, frustration, and pain in His hands. I pray that you choose the latter. Your life must be an open door, giving God free rein in every area.

Last year I received a new client in dire need of an emotional, psychological, and spiritual lift from the Father. I could almost envision her looking up to the Father, crying with outstretched arms, waiting for Him to pick her up.

At her wit's end, Katrina found herself slumped over in the chair in front of my desk with years of tears flowing from the depths of her soul. She struggled to express the mixed emotions that continue to run through her veins over the death of her father: anguish, joy, grief, anger, relief. Katrina was ridden with guilt for years because of the relief she had felt at his death.

Twenty years earlier she had stepped over her dead father who she believed was—for the thousandth time—passed out drunk. It was commonplace to find him completely intoxicated, passed out at the first-floor landing. When he'd awaken, he would quietly take another drink.

But not this time. The substance he drank to drown his sorrows and take his life was household bleach. Apparently the alcohol no longer eased the pain. Therefore death, he believed, was his only escape.

Now years later, this thirty-nine-year-old lived "safely" in the home of her verbally abusive mother. Since her father's suicide, Katrina's mother had repeatedly and continuously sung this song to her: "You can't do nothin', you won't be nothin', and you won't have nothin'. You're just like your father!" And Katrina believed every word.

As she sat, reflecting on her life, she realized that every memory and frayed emotion since childhood included an alcoholic father and a verbally abusive mother.

Her father was a silent alcoholic, and the noisemaker was her mother, whose life encompassed anger, frustrations, and loneliness—breeding verbal abuse toward Katrina and her younger sibling. Their codependence was centered on their mother more so than their father, but he was definitely the trigger. His level of drunkenness set the mood and tone for her mother and subsequently the atmosphere for the house.

"I don't ever recall him sober," she wailed. "As a little girl I thought Daddy was funny and Mommy was mean, but now I know he was drunk, and Mom is *still* mad."

As I empathized with her over the pain of a lifelong absent father, I silently prayed, "Lord, what words do You want me to say to comfort Your daughter? How do I lift her emotionally and spiritually and help put her on the road to becoming a victorious woman of God?" Over the course of several months, God revealed His answer.

Jesus was knocking on her sequestered, shattered life, and He wanted to come in to heal her brokenness. She had so many chains, latches, deadbolts, and locks on the door of her life that I (in my humanity) wondered if Christ could get through.

After many months of counseling, support groups, discipleship groups, and prayer, the Father is unveiling His beautiful daughter who hid behind a mask for thirty-nine years.

Coming to her wit's end brought new life. She opened her life and now dines daily with the Lord to develop intimacy with Him. She's deprogramming the negative messages the Enemy (not her parents) planted, grieving the many losses associated with her father, discovering who she is as a woman of God, and, with determination, learning about her heavenly Father and His overabundance of love.

Many women have chains, latches, deadbolts, and locks on the issues surrounding their fathers. We look through the peephole at Christ, turn, and walk away in hope that He'll go away. We yell through the door, "Come back later! I'm not presentable!"

If you let Him in, He may ask you, as He did the man at the pool of Bethesda, "Do you want to be made well?" (John 5:6). Most of the time His healing includes the painful process of purging and pruning to remove any deadness that lingers in your life. He wants you whole, and any*body* or any*thing* that does not represent Him must go.

No matter the depths of your anguish, it's not too late. You may *feel* dead, but in Christ's eyes you are sleeping in your sorrows and dormant in your dilemma. He sees you, wants to touch you, and longs to lift your hopes, dreams, career, marriage, relationships, and spirit.

Lay aside all formalities and formulas, and cry out to the Father with all your heart, mind, and soul. You're not a lost cause. Stop right now, lift up your arms, and cry out to Him in the same posture as a small child who wants to be picked up by her daddy or mommy. Notice that the position of reaching to be picked up is the same as the posture for worship.

HE'S PASSING BY

The Lord wants to show you His glory. He wants your countenance to glow simply because you've been in His presence.

Jesus encountered two blind men in Matthew 20:30-34. They believed the word on the street that Jesus was Lord and the Healer. When Jesus passed by, they cried out profusely. The throng attempted to silence them, but they became more boisterous. No one would interfere with their encounter with Jesus.

Their faith, persistence, and belief moved the heart of Jesus, and He asked them an important question: "What do you want Me to do for you?"

Their answer was very specific. "Lord, that our eyes may be opened." And Jesus answered their prayer.

I pray that your eyes will be opened—seeing yourself as God sees you, your father as God sees him, your vision as God has given it. When Daddy picks us up, we have a clearer view of life.

◢GROWTH CHART

1. Are you living life as a victim or a victor? How does the Father want to use your life to bless others?

2. What steps have you taken to begin honoring your father? Explain.

3. Remember the forgiveness scale in chapter 2? On a forgiveness scale from 1 to 10 (1=Completely unforgiven, 10=Completely forgiven), how much closer are you now to forgiving your father? |—1——2——3——4——5——6——7——8——9——10—|

4. Based on your attitude, actions, and integrity, can you truly say you know and love the Lord? If not, once again I invite you to visit Romans 10:9 to confess with your mouth and believe in your heart that Jesus Christ is Lord.

5. Take a moment to intercede on behalf of your father. Then confess your sins and the sins of your father (Nehemiah 9:2).

◢GROWTH SPURT

Scripture Memorization

"Humble yourselves in the sight of the Lord, and He will lift you up." James 4:10

Prayer

Thank You, Father, for sending Your Son, Jesus Christ, to die for me that I might live abundantly on earth and eternally with You in heaven. If He hadn't bridged the gap between us, I would still be a fatherless daughter. Thank You that You are my Father. Thank You for picking me up.

Chapter 17

Raised by the Father

He who raised Christ from the dead
will also give life to your mortal bodies
through His Spirit who dwells in you.

ROMANS 8:11

As we conclude our journey together, I want to send you off with some powerful reminders that will help you on your path of healing.

Remember, God is your Deliverer from your father wounds. He will restore health to you and heal you and your wounds (Jeremiah 30:17). He will bring health and healing and reveal to you the abundance of peace and truth (Jeremiah 33:6). *Nothing* is too hard for God (Jeremiah 32:17). There is hope in your future (Jeremiah 31:17).

The first commandment reads, "I am the LORD your God, who brought you out of the land of Egypt, out of the house of bondage. You shall have no other gods before Me" (Exodus 20:2-3). God is the only map to freedom, the only Deliverer from bondage. Place Him first in your home, marriage, family, friendships, dating relationships, job, finances, and ministry. Placing Him first restores order and stability to your life.

Anything that precedes God is deemed "the other god." Your father can be your god. If your attention and energy are on his mistakes and the pain he caused you, outweighing prayer and worship to the Lord, he is your god. Depression can be your God if you choose to remain in that state. Bitterness can be your god if you refuse to work toward forgiveness. Beware. God is jealous (Exodus 20:5).

Choose life. Honor your father. Give him respect because God said so. Honor him merely out of obedience to His Word, and live a long, prosperous, fulfilling life in the Lord.

Pray for your father. If he's an unbeliever, pray that he will recognize his need for a Savior. If he's a believer, pray for a heart of obedience and a love for the Lord. Pray against pride. Pray for a compassionate and contrite heart. Pray that your father will heal from *his* father's wounds. If he's deceased, pray that his impact on those he encountered (whether positive or negative) will point them to Christ.

Jesus said, "Love your enemies, bless those who curse you, do good to those who hate you, and pray for those who spitefully use you and persecute you" (Matthew 5:44). It's a challenging verse, but it's not impossible. Nothing is impossible with God (Luke 1:37). Prayer changes lives. You may be the chosen vessel God wants to use to change your father's heart.

Keep in mind that your father is not the enemy. "For though we walk in the flesh, we do not war according to the flesh" (2 Corinthians 10:3). Memorize Ephesians 6:12:

> For we do not wrestle against flesh and blood, but against principalities, against powers, against the rulers of the darkness of this age, against spiritual hosts of wickedness in the heavenly places.

These verses will change how you view your life. Take your focus off your father. Take your focus off our spiritual enemies. Place your focus on the Lord. Lift your head and look up to Him. Strain to keep your eyes on your Daddy in heaven.

Use the tools He gave you to break every shackle from your past. Grieve your tangible and intangible losses, but don't let your anger affect and infect your relationship with others. Extract misdirected anger, and ask forgiveness from those you've wronged.

Cry unashamedly, for God created tears! They were designed to release internal joy, sorrow, turmoil, and pain. When the pain seems unbearable, remember, "We are hard-pressed on every side, yet not crushed; we are perplexed, but not in despair; persecuted, but not forsaken; struck down, but not destroyed" (2 Corinthians 4:8-9).

Pray without ceasing (1 Thessalonians 5:17). Ask Him to teach you His Word (Psalm 119:26), then meditate on it day and night that you may observe to do according to all that is written in it (Joshua 1:8). Hide the Word in your heart that you may not sin against Him (Psalm 119:11).

You have a Father. Your belief in Christ gave you access to Him (John 14:6). He's infallible, omniscient, omnipresent, all-powerful, wise, and wonderful. He will not withhold anything good from His daughters who walk uprightly (Psalm 84:11). He will never leave you nor forsake you (Joshua 1:5). He will *never* let you down.

Get to know the Father. He loves you, and He knows everything about you. Before He formed you in the womb, He knew you (Jeremiah 1:5). His thoughts of you are precious! The sum of them is great! If you should count them, they would be more in number than the sand (Psalm 139:17-18). They are thoughts of peace and not of evil, to give you a future and a hope. When you call upon Him and go and pray to Him, He will listen to you. You will seek Him and find Him when you search for Him with all your heart (Jeremiah 29:11-13). Strive for intimacy with the Father. Don't procrastinate. Laziness prolongs deliverance.

May we never neglect our relationship with our Father in the same manner our fathers neglected us. Spend quality time with Him. Keep your promises. Adore Him. Speak well of Him. Praise Him.

Consistently pray and study His Word. Spend time together, dialogue often, and ask questions. Be creative with your time together to avoid a mundane relationship. Ask Him to make your time together enjoyable. The Father has no problem initiating great new ideas. The more time you spend, the closer the relationship. Time develops trust. Trust develops intimacy.

He has already begun to soften your heart, plant seeds of forgiveness, restore your joy, penetrate your life with peace, give you wisdom and understanding, and give you a new perspective on life. He's holding, comforting, and caressing you as He sustains you. His power has restored your life.

You are not dead. You are alive in Christ Jesus—a beautiful woman of God. You are the daughter of the Most High God. You were adopted into the family of the King. Your status is royalty, and your title is Queen. The bonds over your life are broken. From this day forward, your past will not dictate your future. The Holy Spirit dwells in you, and where the Spirit of the Lord is, there is liberty (2 Corinthians 3:17)!

Today is like the first day of spring in your life. It's your new season. Winter is past. Flowers are blooming. The sun is shining. Time has moved forward, but no time has been lost. You're in the right place. You're in the right season.

Now clean the daddy dust that has settled from seasons past. Open the windows of your life, and let some fresh air in.

Arise, my sister! You have been raised by the Father. Long for your heavenly Daddy!

Assurance of Salvation

For by grace you have been saved through faith,
and that not of yourselves; it is the gift of God.

EPHESIANS 2:8

*I*f you have prayed the prayer of salvation, you have become God's precious daughter. The Enemy will try to discourage you and convince you that nothing has changed. When you feel a twinge of doubt or fear, cling to the hand of your Daddy and spend time in the Word so you can lay claim to His wonderful promises.

HOW DO I KNOW I AM SAVED?

You are saved because God said so! The Word of God is unadulterated truth—written by man, inspired by God. Carefully read what God said through the apostle Paul:

> If you confess with your mouth the Lord Jesus and believe in your heart [intellect, emotions, will] that God has raised Him from the dead, [then] you will be saved. (Romans 10:9)

When we confess, from the core of our being, and believe, we receive the absolute promise of eternal security with Jesus Christ. This concept can be difficult for task-oriented people like us to grasp. Yet God does not require any prerequisites, tasks, formulas, fees, or tedious processes. Salvation is free, not earned.

CAN I LOSE MY SALVATION?

> In Him…having believed, you were sealed with the Holy Spirit of promise. (Ephesians 1:13)

Salvation and perfection are not the same. We are *all* sinners and will continue to have imperfections, shortcomings, and iniquities as long as we are human.

You may fear that life is like musical chairs and that when the music stops, you may not be in the right chair or position with God to receive eternal life. This concept creates stress and confusion, which is contradictory to God's character and nature. First John 1:9 declares, "If we confess our sins, He is faithful and just to forgive us our sins and to cleanse us from all unrighteousness." You cannot lose your salvation. The Holy Spirit sealed us (Ephesians 1:13) like an envelope that can never be opened by anyone but the Father.

WHO AM I IN CHRIST?

> If anyone is in Christ, he is a new creation; old things have passed away; behold, all things have become new. (2 Corinthians 5:17)

Believers, whether spiritually young or old, must embrace their new identity in Christ. Often we are defeated and our growth in Christ is stunted because we hold on to past experiences, beliefs, hurts, pains, and behaviors. With Christ comes a new you—a new nature, a new will, a new perspective on life. That newness includes completeness (Colossians 2:9-10), the fruit of the Spirit (Galatians 5:22-23), the power of the Spirit (Acts

1:8), and a lifestyle that does not continually, habitually, and deliberately practice sin (1 John 3:9).

Paul is an admirable example for knowing who and whose you are despite past and present experiences. Look at how he identified himself in the salutation of the following epistles:

- "Paul, a bondservant of Jesus Christ, called to be an apostle" (Romans 1:1)
- "Paul, called to be an apostle of Jesus Christ" (1 Corinthians 1:1)
- "Paul, an apostle of Jesus Christ by the will of God" (2 Corinthians 1:1)
- "Paul, an apostle of Jesus Christ" (Ephesians 1:1; see also Colossians 1:1; 1 Timothy 1:1; and 2 Timothy 1:1)
- "Paul and Timothy, bondservants of Jesus Christ" (Philippians 1:1)
- "Paul, a servant of God and an apostle of Jesus Christ" (Titus 1:1)
- "Paul, a prisoner of Christ Jesus" (Philemon 1)

Paul did not identify himself in these salutations as a former persecutor of Christ and the church, a very strict Pharisee from the tribe of Benjamin, a Roman citizen from Tarsus in Cilicia. He dropped the name Saul along with any identifiers of his lifestyle *before* Christ.

Unfortunately, we often define our identity by *what* we do instead of *who* we are in Christ. We wrap ourselves so tightly in our careers, children, and relationships that when we're laid off or our children leave for college or a relationship ends, our identity is lost. Those who have been traumatized in the past tend to view life as victims and therefore live defeated lives.

A healthy or faulty view of self is characterized by our behavior. What we do is the manifestation of what we believe about life and ourselves. We must actively reshape, reinforce, and constantly adjust our belief system to make what we believe congruent with the truths of God's Word. Paul told the church in Rome not to conform to the beliefs and practices of this world but to be transformed and changed by renewing their minds (Romans 12:2). *Renewing* suggests a continuous process of purging the old and replacing it with the new, over and over and over again.

Paul did refer to his past on five occasions, with hope of winning men and women to Christ (Acts 21:33–22:29; 26:1-29) and to give glory to God (Galatians 1:10-24; 1 Timothy 1:12-17; 1 Corinthians 15:8-10). Past experiences and present challenges are merely building blocks for a testimony manifesting God's love, grace, and mercy. Consider your past, no matter how great or horrific, as an essential tool to leading a lost soul to Jesus Christ.

So who are you? You are chosen! You are royalty! You are holy! You are special! You are fearfully and wonderfully made! Remember that your true identity is not based on past experiences or how you *feel* about yourself. It is rooted in the infallible, factual Word of God. Do not allow your emotions to dictate your life. Whether or not you *feel* chosen, regal, holy, or special is irrelevant. God says you are; therefore, celebrate your newness in Christ!

STUDY THE WORD!

Study to shew thyself approved unto God…rightly dividing the
word of truth. (2 Timothy 2:15, KJV)

God's Word is powerful and pragmatic. Although some look for a spectacular way for God to speak—words written in the sky, a cloud by day and a fire by night, or hearing His voice like the thunder roaring on a stormy day—one evident way God speaks today is through His written Word.

What a sad commentary to hear that the Bible is the number-one best-selling book in America but among the least read, or that only 1 percent of most congregations attend midweek Bible study. When believers neglect and reject spiritual sustenance, starvation is near.

Imagine eating once a week, biweekly, bimonthly, or annually. The prognosis for such a diet is an inability to think, irritability, a plummeted energy level, physical weakness, a weakened immune system that is unable to fight off disease, and, finally, death.

Now let's look at this principle from a spiritual perspective. The outcome is the same—death on a spiritual level. When we retreat from His Word and His presence, we are vulnerable to attack. Our spiritual immune system is down; we can't think properly; we lack energy and vitality; every aspect of our lives becomes frazzled; and the Enemy hits us head-on to strike us down and count us out. However, the Word of God replenishes our lives and supplies us with the intangible armor of God needed for spiritual warfare.

Does your life need restoration, revitalization, and rejuvenation? Do you have symptoms of spiritual starvation? Open the Bible, invoke the presence of the Holy Spirit, and ask Him to pour into your life His words of wisdom and understanding that speak directly to your situation. Allow God to speak words of love into your heart and soul, for the Word of God is truly a love story. When we refuse to read the Bible, we reject His love. He's waiting for you. He stands at the door and knocks, waiting for believers to invite Him in for fellowship, communion, and intimacy. Feed on the Word of God to know His character, His promises, and ultimately His love.

MEMORIZE THE WORD!

Your word I have hidden in my heart,
That I might not sin against You. (Psalm 119:11)

Creating a mental file you can pull from in times of doubt and trouble is essential to the Christian faith. Therefore, the more we study, recite, and memorize the Word of God, the more it saturates our hearts and minds and the better equipped we are to fight in this spiritual war. Begin by memorizing the following verses:

Assurance

"I will not leave you nor forsake you" (Joshua 1:5).

"For I am persuaded that neither death nor life, nor angels nor principalities nor powers, nor things present nor things to come, nor height nor depth, nor any other created thing, shall be able to separate us from the love of God which is in Christ Jesus our Lord" (Romans 8:38-39).

"In Him you also trusted, after you heard the word of truth, the gospel of your salvation; in whom also, having believed, you were sealed with the Holy Spirit of promise" (Ephesians 1:13).

"For by grace you have been saved through faith, and that not of yourselves; it is the gift of God" (Ephesians 2:8).

Forgiveness

"In Him we have redemption through His blood, the forgiveness of sins, according to the riches of His grace" (Ephesians 1:7).

"If we confess our sins, He is faithful and just to forgive us our sins and to cleanse us from all unrighteousness" (1 John 1:9).

Identity

"I will praise You, for I am fearfully and wonderfully made; marvelous are Your works, and that my soul knows very well" (Psalm 139:14).

"Therefore, if anyone is in Christ, he is a new creation; old things have passed away; behold, all things have become new" (2 Corinthians 5:17).

"I have been crucified with Christ; it is no longer I who live, but Christ lives in me" (Galatians 2:20).

"But one thing I do, forgetting those things which are behind and reaching forward to those things which are ahead, I press toward the goal for the prize of the upward call of God in Christ Jesus" (Philippians 3:13-14).

"But you are a chosen generation, a royal priesthood, a holy nation, His own special people, that you may proclaim the praises of Him who called you out of darkness into His marvelous light" (1 Peter 2:9).

The Word of God

"Your word I have hidden in my heart, that I might not sin against You" (Psalm 119:11).

"Every word of God is pure" (Proverbs 30:5).

"Study to shew thyself approved unto God...rightly dividing the word of truth" (2 Timothy 2:15, KJV).

"For the word of God is living and powerful, and sharper than any two-edged sword" (Hebrews 4:12).

"All Scripture is given by inspiration of God, and is profitable for doctrine, for reproof, for correction, for instruction in righteousness, that the man of God may be complete, thoroughly equipped for every good work" (2 Timothy 3:16-17).

Grief Cycle

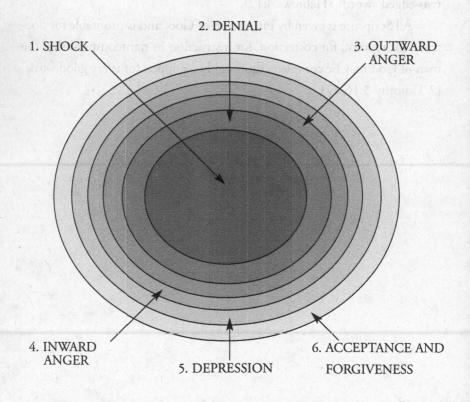

1. SHOCK

2. DENIAL

3. OUTWARD ANGER

4. INWARD ANGER

5. DEPRESSION

6. ACCEPTANCE AND FORGIVENESS

Types of Fasts

A Twenty-Four-Hour Fast
- Stop eating after dinner on Monday night at six.
- Eat nothing and drink only water all day Tuesday.
- After six o'clock on Tuesday night eat a fruit salad, or a vegetable salad, or a baked potato and a steamed vegetable. If you do have something more, like meat or cheese, go very, very lightly.

A Slightly Longer Fast
- Stop eating after lunch on Monday at noon.
- Eat nothing and drink only water for the remainder of Monday and all day Tuesday.
- For dinner on Tuesday evening at five or six o'clock, eat a fruit salad, or a vegetable salad, or a steamed vegetable and baked potato.

A Thirty-Six-Hour Fast
- Stop eating after dinner on Monday night at six.
- Eat nothing, and drink only water all day Tuesday and Tuesday night.
- On Wednesday morning break the fast with a raw or steamed apple and a papaya. Eat a lunch consisting of a raw vegetable salad and/or a steamed vegetable and a baked potato.

A Three-Day Fast

- Stop eating after dinner on Monday night at six.
- Eat nothing and drink only water all day Tuesday, Wednesday, and Thursday.
- Break the fast either Thursday evening or Friday morning with a raw apple or homemade applesauce plus an orange or a papaya. Nothing more.
- For lunch on Friday have something like a small, fresh raw vegetable salad or a baked potato with plain yogurt on top and a steamed vegetable (like broccoli or carrots).[12]

SUGGESTED READING LIST

Dr. Bill Bright, "Four Spiritual Laws," Campus Crusade for Christ, copyright © 1965, 2003 Campus Crusade for Christ. For more information, visit www.greatcom.org/laws/.

T. D. Jakes, *Woman, Thou Art Loosed* (Shippensburg, Pa.: Treasure House, 1993).

Frank Minirth and Paul Meier, *Happiness Is a Choice* (Grand Rapids, Mich.: Baker, 1994).

Paul D. Meier et al., *Introduction to Psychology and Counseling: Christian Perspectives and Applications,* 2d ed. (Grand Rapids: Baker, 1994).

Stormie Omartian, *Greater Health God's Way* (Eugene, Oreg.: Harvest House, 1996).

Kathy Rodriguez, *Healing the Father Wound* (Gresham, Oreg.: East Hill Church, 2001).

NOTES

1. K. S. Wuest, *Wuest's Word Studies from the Greek New Testament: For the English Reader* (Grand Rapids: Eerdmans, 1997), 88.

2. Wuest, *Wuest's Word Studies*, 25.

3. Wuest, *Wuest's Word Studies*, 87.

4. Karen L. Maudlin, "Succeeding at Second Marriages," *Marriage Partnership* 18, no. 3 (fall 2001): 52.

5. Thomas Whiteman, "Broken Promises...Broken Lives," *Christian Counseling Today* (fall 1994): 19.

6. James W. Vander Zanden, *Human Development*, 5th ed. (New York: McGraw-Hill, 1993), 40.

7. *Webster's American Family Dictionary*, s.v. "honor."

8. Kathy Rodriguez, *Healing the Father Wound* (Gresham, Oreg.: East Hill Church, 2001), 67.

9. The Four Spiritual Laws were written by Dr. Bill Bright, copyright © 1965, 2003 Campus Crusade for Christ. For more information visit http://www.greatcom.org/laws/.

10. For further information on defense mechanisms, see Paul D. Meier et al., *Introduction to Psychology and Counseling: Christian Perspectives and Applications*, 2d ed. (Grand Rapids: Baker, 1994), 230-8.

11. Carrie Oliver and Gary Oliver, "My Husband Isn't Honest," *Marriage Partnership* 20, no. 1 (spring 2003): 20.

12. Taken from: *Greater Health God's Way* by Stormie Omartian, pages 194-5. Copyright © 1999 by Harvest House Publishers, Eugene, OR 97402. Used by permission.

To learn more about WaterBrook Press and view
our catalog of products, log on to our Web site:
www.waterbrookpress.com

Praise for

American Gospel

"Thoughtful . . . The vitality of Americans' religious faith explains the persistence of a 'public religion' that continues to trouble unbelievers and secular thinkers."

—*The Washington Post*

"[A] sensibly balanced and engaging narrative account of religion's role in our nation's history." —*Los Angeles Times*

"Jon Meacham has given us an insightful and eloquent account of the spiritual foundation of the early days of the American republic. It is especially instructive reading at a time when the nation is at once engaged in and deeply divided on the question of religion and its place in public life."

—TOM BROKAW, author of *The Greatest Generation*

"Employing the cadence and elegance of language crafted by America's Founding Fathers, *Newsweek* managing editor Jon Meacham has written a thoughtful history of America in which religion imbued, but did not overpower, its construction. . . . A lively combination of history and literature. At a time when the mix of religion and politics is fraught with tension and toxicity, Meacham's book is a deft reminder of the carefully planted American roots that have given freedom and religion such fertile ground in this country." —*The Atlanta Journal-Constitution*

"A nimble examination of how American leaders . . . have wrestled with God personally and publicly . . . an enlightening look at how the founders discovered ways to tame but not extinguish the fires of faith." —*USA Today*

"In his *American Gospel* Jon Meacham provides a refreshingly clear, balanced, and wise historical portrait of religion and American politics at exactly the moment when such fairness and understanding are much needed. Anyone who doubts the relevance of history to our own time has only to read this exceptional book." —DAVID MCCULLOUGH, author of *1776*

"Lively, accessible, and persuasive . . . [a] wonderful new book." —*The New York Sun*

"Jon Meacham is one of our country's most brilliant thinkers about religion's impact on American society. In this scintillating and provocative book, Meacham reveals the often-hidden influence of religious belief on the Founding Fathers and on later generations of American citizens and leaders up to our own. Today, as we argue more strenuously than ever about the proper place of religion in our politics and the rest of American life, Meacham's important book should serve as the touchstone of the debate."

—MICHAEL BESCHLOSS, author of *The Conquerors: Roosevelt, Truman and the Destruction of Hitler's Germany, 1941–1945*

"Well-written . . . Meacham [has a] remarkable grasp of the intricacies and achievements of a nascent nation."

—*Publishers Weekly*

"An absorbing narrative full of vivid characters and fresh thinking, *American Gospel* tells how the Founding Fathers—and their successors—struggled with their own religious and political convictions to work out the basic structure for freedom of religion. For me this book was nonstop reading."

—ELAINE PAGELS, professor of religion, Princeton University, and author of *Beyond Belief: The Secret Gospel of Thomas*

"At a time when faith and freedom seem increasingly polarized, *American Gospel* recovers our vital center—the middle ground where, historically, religion and public life strike a delicate balance. Well researched, well written, inspiring, and persuasive, this is a welcome addition to the literature."

—JONATHAN D. SARNA, Joseph H. & Belle R. Braun
Professor of American Jewish History, Brandeis
University, author of *American Judaism: A History*

"Jon Meacham's reading is deep and wide, inspiring great confidence in the resulting text. His writing is graceful, forceful, and marked by sparkling clarity. Well beyond all this, however, his take on America's public religion is of critical importance in these divisive times; he offers both healing and hope."

—EDWIN S. GAUSTAD, emeritus professor of history,
University of California, Riverside, and author of *Faith of the
Founders: Religion and the New Nation, 1776–1826*

AMERICAN GOSPEL

THE·CHURCH·AND·MAGNA·CHARTA

THE·PRAYER·IN·THE·FIRST·CONGRESS·A·D·1774

RANDOM HOUSE TRADE PAPERBACKS
NEW YORK

AMERICAN
GOSPEL

GOD,
THE FOUNDING FATHERS,
AND
THE MAKING OF A NATION

JON MEACHAM

To Mary and Sam

Remember the days of old, consider the years of many

generations: ask thy father, and he will show thee;

thy elders, and they will tell thee.

—THE SONG OF MOSES, DEUTERONOMY 32:7

CONTENTS

AMERICAN GOSPEL

INTRODUCTION

AMERICAN GOSPEL: FAITH AND FREEDOM

The God who gave us life gave us liberty at the same time.
—THOMAS JEFFERSON, "A SUMMARY VIEW OF THE RIGHTS
OF BRITISH AMERICA," JULY 1774

*Religion and liberty must flourish or fall together in
America. We pray that both may be perpetual.*
—REVEREND WILLIAM SMITH, D.D., IN A SERMON
PREACHED AT CHRIST CHURCH, PHILADELPHIA, ON FRIDAY,
JUNE 23, 1775, THE DAY GEORGE WASHINGTON LEFT THE
CITY TO TAKE COMMAND OF THE CONTINENTAL ARMY

*A*s the sad news from the house on the hill reached town, the courthouse bell in Charlottesville tolled in tribute. Thomas Jefferson was dead, succumbing at ten minutes to one on the afternoon of Tuesday, July 4, 1826, the fiftieth anniversary of the Declaration of Independence. Secretive and ambitious, brave and curious, committed to liberty, the Enlightenment, and the American experiment, Jefferson was among the most eloquent and forceful of the Founders on the fraught subject of religion. Intellectually daring, Jefferson had little time for the intricacies of creeds, talk of miracles, and the familiar tenets of the faith that grew out of the life and, for believers, resurrection of Jesus. "I am of a sect by myself, as far as I know," Jefferson said.

As a student of history he also knew Europe had fought wars and led crusades over faith and that the first English colonies in North America had hardly been models of religious freedom. As a man of science he believed in the primacy of rational observation, dismissing much of the supernatural as superstition. Confident in the power of the mind to discern natural and moral truths, he once spent a few evenings in the White House going through the Gospels with a razor, excising passages he found implausible in order to arrange his own version of Jesus' teachings. On another occasion, he waved away talk of the Holy Trinity. "Ideas must be distinct before reason can act upon them, and no man ever had a distinct idea of the trinity," Jefferson said. "It is the mere Abracadabra of the mountebanks calling themselves priests of Jesus."

Nothing was simple about Jefferson, and nothing is simple about the debates over religion and public life nearly two centuries after him. Neither conventionally devout nor wholly unbelieving, Jefferson surveyed and staked out an American middle ground between the ferocity of evangelizing Christians on one side and the contempt for religion of secular *philosophes* on the other. The right would like Jefferson to be a soldier of faith, the left an American Voltaire. He was, depending on the moment, both and neither; he was, in other words, a lot like many of us.

In the opening years of the twenty-first century, some Americans believe the country has strayed too far from God; others fear that zealots (from the White House to the school board) are waging holy war on American liberty; and many, if not most, seem to think that we are a nation hopelessly divided by religion.

None of these dire views is quite right. The great good news about America—the American gospel, if you will—is that religion shapes the life of the nation without strangling it. Belief in God is central to the country's experience, yet for the broad center, faith is a matter of choice, not coercion, and the legacy of the Founding is that the sensible center holds. It does so because the Founders believed themselves at work in the service of both God and man, not just one or the other. Driven by a sense of providence and an acute appreciation of the fallibility of humankind, they created a nation in which religion should not be singled out for special help or particular harm. The balance between the promise of the Declaration of Independence, with its evocation of divine origins and destiny, and the practicalities of the Constitution, with its checks on extremism, remains perhaps the most brilliant American success.

This victory over excessive religious influence and excessive secularism is often lost in the clatter of contemporary cultural and political strife. Looking back to the Founding is neither an exercise in nostalgia nor an attempt to deify the dead, but a bracing lesson in how to make a diverse nation survive and thrive by cherishing freedom and protecting faith. And faith and freedom are inextricably linked: It is not for priests or pastors or presidents or kings to compel belief, for to do so trespasses on each individual's God-given liberty of mind and heart. If the Lord himself chose not to force obedience from those he created, then who are men to try?

There is a vast and growing literature about the Founding Fathers, much of it quite wonderful, and a stream of strong scholarship about the problem of church and state. Yet because faith is such an emotional subject for both believers and nonbelievers, discussion of the question of religion and public life can often be more divisive than illuminating. Secularists reflexively point to the Jeffersonian "wall of separation between church and state" as though the conversation should end there; many conservative Christians defend their forays into the political arena by citing the Founders, as though Washington, Adams, Jefferson, and Franklin were cheerful Christian soldiers.

The real saga of God, the Founding Fathers, and the making of the nation is a tale that opens with swashbuckling adventurers searching for gold in Virginia and sturdy but strict Puritans trying to create a Christian commonwealth in New England. The drama is America's drama, from George Washington to Ronald Reagan, from the Civil War to civil rights. The story of how the Founders believed in faith and freedom, and grappled with faith and freedom, has a particular resonance for our era. Given the world in which they lived—a time of divisive arguments about God and politics—the Founders repay close attention, for their time is like our time, and they found a way to honor religion's place in the life of the nation while giving people the freedom to believe as they wish, and not merely to tolerate someone else's faith, but to respect it.

America's early years were neither a golden age of religion nor a glowing hour of Enlightenment reason. Life was shaped by evangelical fervor and ambitious clergy, anxious politicians and determined secularists. Some Christians wanted to impose their beliefs on the rest of the country; other equally committed believers thought faith should steer clear of public life. In the fulcrum stood the brilliant but fallible political leadership of the new nation. The Founding Fathers struggled to assign religion its proper place in civil society—and they succeeded. Our best chance of summoning what Abraham Lincoln called "the better angels of our nature" may lie in recovering the sense and spirit of the Founding era and its leaders, for they emerged from a time of trial with an understanding of religion and politics that, while imperfect, averted the worst experiences of other nations. In that history lies our hope.

In one of the last letters of his life, written, his doctor said, with "all the striking characteristics of his vigorous and unfaded intellect," Jefferson spoke of America's hard-won freedom from monarchs who used church and state to reign over others, acting as though only kings could draw strength and standing from God. "All eyes are opened, or opening, to the rights of man," he wrote on Saturday, June 24, 1826. "The general spread of the light of science has already laid open to every view the palpable truth that the mass of mankind has not been born with saddles on their backs, nor a favored few booted and spurred, ready to ride them legitimately, by the grace of God."

For the Founding Fathers, God's grace was universal. In his first draft of the Declaration of Independence, Jefferson linked fundamental American ideals—that freedom is the gift of "Nature's God," that "all men are created equal," and that all "are endowed by their Creator with inherent and inalienable rights"—to a religious vision of the world with roots both in classical philosophy and in holy scripture. From antiquity, he drew on Aristotle and Cicero; from what was called Christendom, he owed much to John Locke (author of a book called *The Reasonableness of Christianity*), Algernon Sidney, Joseph Priestley, and Lord Bolingbroke, all Enlightenment thinkers. To Jefferson, the "Creator" invested the individual with rights no human power should ever take away.

What separated us from the Old World was the idea that books, education, and the liberty to think and worship as we wished would create virtuous citizens who cherished and defended reason, faith, and freedom. In our finest hours, we have been neither wholly religious nor wholly secular but have drawn on both traditions.

The Founders were politicians and philosophers, sages and warriors, churchmen and doubters. They knew history and literature, politics and philosophy, theology and business, statecraft and soldiering. They could be vain yet selfless, shortsighted yet shrewd and far-seeing, temperamental yet forbearing, bigoted yet magnanimous. They delved and dabbled in religion; while Jefferson edited the Gospels, Benjamin Franklin rephrased and rearranged the Book of Common Prayer. Franklin may have rendered the Lord's Prayer into the eighteenth-century vernacular, but his piety had its limits: on his first day in Philadelphia as a young man, Franklin recalled falling sound asleep in a Quaker meetinghouse. Many of the Founders were influenced by Deism, an Enlightenment vision of religion which held that there was a single creator God; some Deists, including Jefferson and Franklin, believed this God worked in the world through providence. For them, Jesus of Nazareth was a great moral teacher—even the greatest in all history—but he was not the Son of God; the Holy Trinity was seen as an invention of a corrupt church more interested in temporal power than in true religion. The mind of man, not the mysteries of the church, was the center of faith. When Thomas Paine wrote *The Age of Reason*, a tract attacking traditional Christianity, an American statesman, Elias Boudinot, sat down and whipped out a reply. Its title: *The Age of Revelation*. John Adams considered the ministry but chose law instead; for the rest of his life he was a Unitarian who privately confessed a weakness for the beauty of Episcopal liturgy. In an intensely anti-Catholic age, Franklin helped advance the career of John Carroll of Maryland, the priest who became the first American to be made a bishop in the Catholic Church.

As the light faded in the summer of 1826, Jefferson, now eighty-three, read Aeschylus, Sophocles, Euripides, and the Bible. During his final days, Jefferson said to his physician, "A few hours more, Doctor, and it will be all over."

On the night of July 3, Jefferson took his medicine for the last time, saying "Oh God!" with what one observer thought was "a tone of impatience." Pressed again later to take something, Jefferson declined: "No! nothing more." At one point his imagination drifted, and he gestured as though he were once again writing on his small desk. Moving in his mind between past and present, he gave his grandson instructions about his funeral arrangements. Struggling to be reassuring, a member of the family said that everyone hoped it would be a long time before those orders would have to be executed. With a smile, Jefferson replied, "Do you imagine I fear to die?"

He had long contemplated what he was to face on the other side of the grave, and he found the prospect bright. Once we left "our sorrows and suffering bodies," Jefferson had once told John Adams, then they would "ascend in essence to an ecstatic meeting with the friends we have loved and lost and whom we shall still love and never lose again."

He was thinking of his beloved wife and a child who had died before him, and he had written a short poem to his living daughter, saying that as he went "to his fathers . . . the last pang of life is in parting from you!" Yet "two seraphs await me, long shrouded in death," Jefferson said, and "I will bear them your love on my last parting breath."

He seems to have comforted himself, too, with a passage from the Gospel of Luke—a passage he had eliminated in his own Bible, for it spoke to the divinity of Jesus. Jefferson's family recalled hearing him repeat the song of Simeon, the old man who is told he will not die until he sees Christ. When Joseph and Mary bring the infant Jesus to the temple, Simeon takes the baby in his arms and recognizes the child as the Messiah. Content now to die, Simeon says, "Lord, now lettest thou thy servant depart in peace"—a prayer Jefferson is said to have murmured near the time of his death.

Finally, when the end came, as Jefferson was carried through the low stone wall of the Monticello cemetery in a wooden coffin, Reverend Frederick Hatch, whom Jefferson knew and liked, was called on to read the Episcopal burial office. The day was wet, and planks were placed over the grave to hold the casket. " ' "I am the resurrection and the life," saith the Lord,' " Hatch said, " ' "he that believeth in me, though he were dead, yet shall he live: and whosoever liveth and believeth in me, shall never die." ' " And so Jefferson, no conventional Christian, took his leave in the most Christian of ceremonies, in the manner dictated by the faith of his fathers.

VERY HUMAN HEROES

Jefferson had given his death and legacy much thought and left instructions to note only three achievements on his tombstone: the founding of the University of Virginia and his authorship of both the Declaration of Independence and of the Virginia statute for religious freedom, a bill he had written in 1777. These were the things for which "I wish most to be remembered," he said in a note that included a design for the grave, for they were the things for which he had lived.

The Virginia statute's opening words—*"Whereas Almighty God hath created the mind free"*—encapsulated Jefferson's twin obsessions: liberty and faith. The fight for the law came when Jefferson was abroad, in Paris, and it fell to his neighbor James Madison to carry it through. "Whilst we assert for ourselves a freedom to embrace, to profess and observe the religion which we believe to be of divine origin," wrote Madison, "we cannot deny an equal freedom to those whose minds have not yet yielded to the evidence which has convinced us." In these words written to press Jefferson's case, Madison captured a crucial paradox at the heart of the nation's life. Many, if not most, believed; yet none must. In Virginia, Jefferson's bill was "meant to comprehend, within the mantle of its protection, the Jew and the Gentile, the Christian and the Mahometan, the Hindoo, and infidel of every denomination." With his fellow Founding Fathers and America's early presidents, Jefferson knew that the nation was likely to grow ever more diverse.

All of the Founders were devoted to liberty, but most kept slaves. All were devoted to virtue, but many led complex private lives. All were devoted to the general idea of religion as a force for stability, but more than a few had unconventional personal faiths. George Washington would not kneel to pray and was not known to take communion, yet could only explain the American victory in the Revolution as an act of "the hand of Providence," going on about God's role in defeating the British empire at such length that he interrupted himself in a letter, saying there would be "time enough for me to turn preacher when my present appointment ceases. . . ." Jefferson's creed included elements of Deism, Anglicanism, and Unitarianism, and he argued for the moral life, yet he fathered at least one child with a woman he owned and controlled. John Jay, the first chief justice and a traditional Episcopalian, hated Catholicism. At a crowded party in France, Jay, one of the more orthodox believers among the Founders, found himself amid clever French philosophers who were, he recalled, speaking "freely and contemptuously of religion." Silent and perhaps sullen—he was a serious, sometimes overly grave man—Jay let the conversation roll on. "In the course of it," he recalled, "one of them asked me if I believed in Christ. I answered that I did, and that I thanked God that I did."

Samuel Adams, a fierce advocate of independence, was a Puritan who looked askance at other faiths, but knew that faith and political warfare were a deadly combination: "Neither religion nor liberty," he said, "can long subsist in the tumult of altercation and amidst the noise and violence of faction." Franklin was so supple in matters of religion that he drove a frustrated John Adams to write: "The Catholics thought him almost a Catholic. The Church of England claimed him as one of them. The Presbyterians thought him half a Presbyterian, and the Friends believed him a wet Quaker." Franklin was always a practical man. "He that spits against the wind, spits in his own face," he counseled a correspondent who was about to publish a tract against traditional Christianity. "I would advise you, therefore, not to attempt unchaining the tiger."

Many of the Founders both grew up and grew old in religious households. In the fall of 1775, Abigail Adams, daughter of a Harvard-educated clergyman—her mother had not thought much of the young man Abigail was marrying—wondered whether a dysentery epidemic in Boston was divine retribution for slavery. Martha Washington, the biographer Patricia Brady wrote, set aside an hour every morning for devotions, "praying and reading from the New Testament and the Anglican Book of Common Prayer." In addition to popular works by Anglican divines, Martha also read the *Works of Josephus*, the history of the tumultuous first century in Judea, including the Jewish rebellion against Roman occupation and the destruction of the Temple in Jerusalem. Benjamin Franklin's parents and siblings worried about his soul, prompting him to write them reassuring letters about the "uneasiness" his eclectic theology had caused them.

Religion has always been woven into American politics. John Quincy Adams liked to read the Bible in the mornings and would plunge naked into the Potomac for a swim before attending his weekly Sunday church service. Andrew Jackson summoned two Presbyterian ministers to be cross-examined at a Cabinet meeting concerning rumors about the loose sexual morals of his secretary of war's new wife, tales that included an alleged extramarital pregnancy. When Lincoln was running for the House of Representatives from Illinois, he was charged with being "a scoffer at religion," wrote the historian William J. Wolf, because he belonged to no church. During the campaign, Lincoln attended a sermon delivered by his opponent in the race, Reverend Peter Cartwright, a Methodist evangelist. At a dramatic moment in his performance, Cartwright said, "All who do not wish to go to hell will stand." Only Lincoln kept his seat. "May I inquire of you, Mr. Lincoln, where you are going?" the minister asked, glowering. "I am going to Congress" was the dry reply. When he was president, Lincoln also liked the story of a purported exchange about him and Jefferson Davis between two Quaker women on a train:

"I think Jefferson will succeed," the first said.

"Why does thee think so?"

"Because Jefferson is a praying man."

"And so is Abraham a praying man."

"Yes, but the Lord will think Abraham is joking."

"ALL MEN NEED THE GODS"

From the planting of the Virginia and Plymouth colonies forward, professions of faith in God—usually what George Washington called "that Almighty Being who rules over the universe"—have been at the center of the country's public life. This should not be surprising. Human beings are what scholars refer to as *homo religiosus*: we are by nature inclined to look outside ourselves and beyond time and space to a divine power (or, as in antiquity, powers) that creates, directs, and judges the world and our individual lives. "All men," said Homer, "need the gods."

The God who is spoken of and called on and prayed to in the public sphere is an essential character in the American drama. Washington improvised "so help me, God" at the conclusion of the first presidential oath and kissed the Bible on which he had sworn it. Lincoln saw the Civil War as an act of divine will that passed all understanding: it was, Lincoln thought, one of God's impenetrable mysteries. The only public statement Franklin D. Roosevelt made on D-Day 1944 was to read a prayer he had written drawing on the 1928 Episcopal Book of Common Prayer. Dwight Eisenhower opened Cabinet meetings with prayers. Ronald Reagan was not afraid to say that he saw the world as a struggle between light and dark, calling the Soviet empire "the focus of evil in the modern world" and, after launching strikes against Libya in retaliation for a terrorist bombing, declaring: "We have done what we had to do. If necessary, we shall do it again." Our finest hours—the Revolutionary War, abolition, the expansion of the rights of women, fights against terror and tyranny, the battle against Jim Crow—can

George Washington, at Federal Hall, New York City, April 30, 1789, improvised "so help me, God" at the conclusion of the first presidential oath and kissed the Bible. *(The Granger Collection, New York)*

partly be traced to religious ideas about liberty, justice, and charity. Yet theology and scripture have also been used to justify our worst hours—from enslaving black people to persecuting Native Americans to treating women as second-class citizens.

Now, nearly two and a half centuries after the Founding, the religious and political climate in America would seem a prime exhibit to support the Old Testament's lesson that there is no thing new under the sun. In 1822, Jefferson worried aloud about evangelical fervor: "The atmosphere of our country is unquestionably charged with a threatening cloud of fanaticism, lighter in some parts, denser in others, but too heavy in all." While a biblical case can be made for aggressive evangelization in public and private life, scripture also teaches that believers are to practice charity toward all.

Religion is one of the most pervasive but least understood forces in American life. The point of this book is to explore the role faith has played in the Republic and to illustrate how the Founding Fathers left us with a tradition in which we could talk and think about God and politics without descending into discord and division. It is not a full-scale history of religion in America or of the issue of the separation of church and state. It is, rather, a narrative essay that covers much ground quickly and briefly. From the blood-soaked holy wars of the Old World to ecclesiastical imprisonments and executions in their own midst, the Founders understood the dangers of mixing religious passions with the ambitions of politics. Their example can help us move forward in this, yet another age in which religion and politics provoke the most corrosive of debates.

Why do so many feel the country is so divided at the moment? For the left, one factor is that it has been a very long time since the high-water mark of post–World War II liberalism, Lyndon B. Johnson's Great Society. For the right, the same era has been a time both of great strides and grave setbacks. Conservative Christians are more influential today than in the past, but their power has come in reaction to what they view as threats to society, especially the Supreme Court decisions banning school prayer and permitting abortion. Both sides feel they are fighting for the survival of what is best about America: liberals for openness and expanding rights, conservatives for a God-fearing, morally coherent culture. When such conflicts are cast in stark, often religious terms, they become ferocious. If totalitarianism was the great problem of the twentieth century, then extremism is, so far, the great problem of the twenty-first.

It need not be this way. Extremism is a powerful alliance of fear and certitude; complexity and humility are its natural foes. Faith and life are essentially mysterious, for neither God nor nature is easily explained or understood. Crusades are for the weak, literalism for the insecure. Believers should heed Saint Paul, who conceded the limits of the human endeavor on this side of paradise. "O the depth of the riches and wisdom and knowledge of God! How unsearchable are his judgments and how unscrutable are his ways!" he wrote, and then alluded to Isaiah: " 'For who has known the mind of the Lord, or who has been his counselor?' " The secular can find a similarly instructive text in a remark of Hamlet's: "There are more things in heaven and earth, Horatio, than are dreamt of in your philosophy."

That, at least, was the view of many of the Founding Fathers. "I hate polemical politics and polemical divinity," said John Adams. "My religion is founded on the love of God and my neighbor; on the hope of pardon for my offenses; upon contrition; upon the duty as well as the necessity of [enduring] with patience the inevitable evils of life; in the duty of doing no wrong, but all the good I can, to the creation of which I am but an infinitesimal part."

There is always a risk that politically active believers may assume an off-putting air of moral superiority, just as politically active secularists may assume an off-putting air of intellectual superiority. Yet the religiously observant, however conservative, can find much in common with the fiercely secular, however liberal—and vice versa. Properly understood, both religion and America were forged through compromise and negotiation. They are works in progress, open to new interpretation, amendment, and correction. It would be wrong to give up hope that things can get better, our conversations more civil, our culture more tolerant, our politics less virulent. The acts of reading, of contemplation and discovery, of writing poems and finding cures and composing symphonies are, for the religious, acts of piety, and of thanksgiving. For the secular, such things may be about the wonders of nature, or of rationality, or of logic. So be it: the point is that we are all on the same odyssey, if for different reasons. In either case, the story is about moving forward, through the darkness, searching for light. Or at least it should be. Extremes make the journey more perilous.

The right's contention that we are a "Christian nation" that has fallen from pure origins and can achieve redemption by some kind of return to Christian values is based on wishful thinking, not convincing historical argument. Writing to the Hebrew Congregation in Newport, Rhode Island, in 1790, President Washington assured his Jewish countrymen that

America "gives . . . bigotry no sanction." In a treaty with the Muslim nation of Tripoli initiated by Washington, completed by John Adams, and ratified by the Senate in 1797, the Founders declared that "the government of the United States is not in any sense founded on the Christian Religion. . . ." Washington's expansive view of liberty also extended to those Christians who felt shut out of the mainstream. When American Catholics wrote him asking for "the equal rights of citizenship, as the price of our blood spilt under your eyes," Washington agreed, replying: "As mankind becomes more liberal, they will be apt to allow that all those who conduct themselves worthy members of the community are equally entitled to the protection of civil government."

Conservatives are not alone in attempting to appropriate the Founding for their own ends. Many Americans, especially secular ones, tend to stake everything on Jefferson's wall between church and state. The wall metaphor originated with the Anglican divine Richard Hooker, was used by the dissenter Roger Williams, the Scottish intellectual James Burgh, and by Jefferson, and gained its current weight when, in 1947, Supreme Court Justice Hugo Black quoted Jefferson's phrase.

The wall Jefferson referred to is designed to divide church from state, not religion from politics. Church and state are specific things: the former signifies institutions for believers to congregate and worship in the private sphere, the latter the collective milieu of civic and political and legal arrangements in which we live while in the public sphere. The church is private religion—be it evangelical or mainline Protestantism, conservative or liberal Catholicism, Orthodox, Reform, or Conservative Judaism, or any variant of Islam, Buddhism, Hinduism, and so on. The specific beliefs, practices, and positions of any faith are protected from government interference by the First Amendment, which mandates religious freedom. Yet the Founders consciously allowed a form of what Benjamin Franklin called "public religion" to take root and flower at the same time they were creating a republic that valued private religious liberty.

In 1749, laying out his thoughts on the proper education of

To Benjamin Franklin, history taught that "public religion" was ultimately good for society. The concept of public religion includes a spirit of charity to others, a generous moral disposition, and rituals acknowledging a dependence on divine providence. (© Bettmann/Corbis)

the young, Franklin placed the study of history at the heart of the undertaking, partly on the grounds that examples from the past would illuminate morality and religion: "Morality, by descanting and making continual observations on the causes of the rise or fall of any man's character, fortune, power, &c. mentioned in history [will demonstrate] the advantages of temperance, order, frugality, industry, perseverance, &c. &c. . . . *History* will also afford frequent opportunities of showing the necessity of a public religion, from its usefulness to the public; the advantages of a religious character among private persons; the mischiefs of superstition, &c, and the excellency of the Christian religion above all others ancient or modern."

Despite Franklin's generous words about Christianity, his idea of an American public religion was ecumenical, not sectarian. Writing to Yale president Ezra Stiles on Tuesday, March 9, 1790, fourteen years after the Declaration and just before his own death, the aged Franklin described his own faith—one he shared with many of the Founders—with clarity and wit:

I believe in one God, creator of the universe. That he governs it by his Providence. That he ought to be worshiped. That the most acceptable service we can render to him is doing good to his other children. That the soul of man is immortal, and will be treated with justice in another life respecting its conduct in this. These I take to be the fundamental principles of all sound religion, and I regard them as you do, in whatever sect I meet with them.

As to Jesus of Nazareth . . . I think the system of morals and his religion as he left them to us, the best the world ever saw, or is likely to see; but I apprehend it has

received various corrupting changes, and I have . . .
some doubts as to his divinity; though it is a question I
do not dogmatize upon, having never studied it, and
think it needless to busy myself with it now, when I expect soon an opportunity of knowing the truth with less
trouble.

AMERICA'S PUBLIC RELIGION

The nation's public religion, then, holds that there is a God, the
one Jefferson called the "Creator" and "Nature's God" in the
Declaration of Independence. The God of public religion made
all human beings in his image and endowed them, as Jefferson
wrote, with sacred rights to life, liberty, and the pursuit of happiness. What the God of public religion has given, no king, no
president, no government can abridge—hence the sanctity of
human rights in America. The God of public religion is interested in the affairs of the world. The God of public religion may
be seen as capable of rewarding or punishing individuals or the
nation either here and now or later, beyond time. And the God
of public religion is sometimes spoken of as a God bound to the
American nation, in Jefferson's words, "as Israel of old."

Properly understood, the God of public religion is not the
God of Abraham or God the Father of the Holy Trinity. The
Founding Fathers had ample opportunity to use Christian imagery and language in the Declaration of Independence and
Constitution, but did not. At the same time, they were not absolute secularists. They wanted God in American public life,
but, given the memory of religious warfare that could engulf and
destroy whole governments, they saw the wisdom of distin-

guishing between private and public religion. In churches and in homes, anyone could believe and practice what he wished. In the public business of the nation, however, it was important to the Founders to speak of God in a way that was unifying, not divisive. "Nature's God" was the path they chose, and it has served the nation admirably. Despite generations of subsequent efforts to amend the Constitution to include Jesus or to declare that America is a "Christian nation," no president across three centuries has made an even remotely serious attempt to do so.

Public religion is not a substitute for private religion, nor is it a Trojan horse filled with evangelicals threatening the walls of secular America. It is, rather, a habit of mind and of heart that enables Americans to be at once tolerant and reverent—two virtues of relevance to all, for the Founders' public religion is consummately democratic. When a president says "God bless America" or when we sing "America! America! God shed his grace on thee," each American is free to define God in whatever way he chooses. A Christian's mind may summon God the Father; a Jew's, Yahweh; a Muslim's, Allah; an atheist's, no one, or no thing. Such diversity is not a prescription for dissension. It is part of the reality of creation.

Scripture advises the faithful on how to conduct themselves in a world of sundry tongues and tribes. "Love thy neighbor as thyself" is rooted in Leviticus. "I exhort therefore, that, first of all, supplications, prayers, intercessions, and giving of thanks, be made for all men," Saint Paul wrote in I Timothy. "Beloved, let us love one another," says the First Epistle of John, "for love is of God; and every one that loveth is born of God, and knoweth God." The long-expected result of such counsel? For Isaiah, there is the image of a day in which the divisions of blood or creed disappear and the Almighty shall "swallow up death for ever, and the Lord God will wipe away tears from all faces." If and until such an hour strikes, the faithful must struggle and squint, as Saint Paul wrote, to "see through a glass, darkly."

For believers, God may guide history, but men remain its makers. The connection between public religion and private religion is therefore often close. As John T. Noonan, Jr., the scholar and judge, wrote, "nations do not worship, persons do," and a president's private faith inevitably informs his public life. The task of the citizen is to discern as clearly as possible the extent to which that president's private religious belief influences how he governs, and to speak out and to vote accordingly if the intermingling of personal conviction and public affairs is found to be unsettling.

As in so many things, the wise American president can learn much from Lincoln, who once told some visiting ministers that he did not worry whether God was on his side or not, "for I know that the Lord is *always* on the side of the *right*." It was, Lincoln said, "my constant anxiety and prayer that I and *this nation* should be on the Lord's side."

In crisis and in tranquillity, Americans have invoked the protection of the Founders' God, prayed for his guidance, and thanked him for safe passage through storm and struggle. At every significant point in the four centuries since English settlers laid the foundations for the nation we know—at *every* significant point—American leaders and the great majority of the American people have explicitly said or acted as though they understood history in terms of this public religion. As King George III's British troops moved toward New York City in the summer of 1776, Gershom Seixas, leader of the first Jewish synagogue in America, Shearith Israel, led his people into what they called their "exile." Armed with the Torah scrolls, the congregation linked the ancient story of its forbears with the young country's, referring to the Revolution as "the sacred cause of America." Once victory was won, the congregation prayed in thanksgiving: "We cried unto the Lord from our straits and from our troubles He brought us forth." The Lord delivered Israel; now he had delivered the United States.

Four decades ago, the sociologist Robert N. Bellah published a landmark essay, "Civil Religion in America," identifying "a set of beliefs, symbols, and rituals" in public life that illumined the country's understanding of itself as a nation set apart by God. "Europe is Egypt; America, the promised land," wrote Bellah. "God has led his people to establish a new sort of social order that shall be a light unto all the nations." The cultural sensibility Bellah spoke of was not, he said, "in any specific sense Christian" but American. The idea has deep roots. In antiquity Plato spoke of the notion that a civic faith could unite a people (in either allegiance to a common deity or to the nation itself as a kind of god); in the first decades of the sixteenth century, in *The Discourses,* Machiavelli noted that the Romans "turned to religion as the instrument necessary above all others for the maintenance of a civilized state"; in 1762, Rousseau coined the term "civil religion" in Book IV of *The Social Contract.*

I have chosen to talk about "public religion" because the phrase comes from Franklin, one of the greatest of the American Founders, and the idea was shared by men like Washington, who envisioned a republic in which "religion and morality" were "indispensable supports" for society, adding, "A volume

A man of generous religious spirit, Washington once said, "We have abundant reason to rejoice that in this Land the light of truth and reason has triumphed over the power of bigotry and superstition, and that every person may here worship God according to the dictates of his conscience." *(Courtesy of Barewalls.com)*

could not trace all their connections with public and private felicity." There are important distinctions between civil religion and public religion. Rousseau's civil religion is manufactured, not nurtured, and is about the power of the king, not the freedom of the people. Meanwhile, the religion described by Bellah emphasizes the idea of America as God's chosen, which can offer automatic justification for any course the country wishes to take, and risks elevating the nation itself as an object of worship. The Declaration envisions human liberties as gifts of nature's God to all men, wherever they may be—not exclusively to Americans. From the beginning we were to be a family in the neighborhood of nations.

To my mind, public religion is less about the veneration of the idea of country and more about the sacred origin of individual rights, the virtue of the populace—virtues that require constant cultivation—and the American sense of duty to defend freedom at home and, at times, abroad. On the eve of the Civil War, Lincoln spoke of America's "great struggle" to preserve liberty in a world given to tyranny and prayed that he would be able to lead what he called God's "almost chosen people"—a wonderful image, one capturing that our hearts are inclined toward the good, no matter how many rebukes and reminders it takes to make us see and do the right thing.

THE QUESTION OF MORALITY

In looking to the past, the Founders came to believe that religion, for all its faults, was an essential foundation for a people's moral conduct and for American ideas about justice, decency, duty, and responsibility. "And let us with caution indulge the supposition that morality can be maintained without religion," said George Washington. "Whatever may be conceded to the influence of refined education on minds of peculiar structure, reason and experience both forbid us to expect that national morality can prevail in exclusion of religious principle."

Though morality can be rooted in any number of secular sources, from appeals to reason or natural law without reference to a deity, many of the Founders thought religion and moral conduct were bound up together. "Without religion," John Adams wrote Jefferson, "this world would be something not fit to be mentioned in polite company, I mean Hell." To Benjamin Rush, the physician-patriot, Adams said: "Religion I hold to be essential to morals. I have never read of an irreligious character in Greek or Roman history, nor in any other history, nor have I known one in life, who was not a rascal. Name one if you can, living or dead." Rush was more ecumenical but struck the same notes in drafting a plan for educating the young: "Such is my veneration for every religion that reveals the attributes of the Deity, or a future state of rewards and punishment, that I had rather see the opinions of Confucius or Mohammed inculcated upon our youth than see them grow up wholly devoid of a system of religious principles." In a draft of Washington's farewell address, Alexander Hamilton echoed the thrust of Rush's argument. "Can we in prudence suppose that national morality can be maintained in exclusion of religious principles? Does it not require the aid of a generally received and divinely authoritative religion?"

There were times Franklin and Jefferson would have answered Hamilton in the negative. "A virtuous heretic shall be saved before a wicked Christian," said Franklin. Jefferson also cautioned against reflexively assuming a cause-and-effect connection between religious belief and moral conduct. "On the dogmas of religion, as distinguished from moral principles," he said, "all mankind, from the beginning of the world to this day, have been quarreling, fighting, burning and torturing one another, for abstractions unintelligible to themselves and to all others, and absolutely beyond the comprehension of the human mind."

And what about caring, law-abiding, generous unbelievers? Jefferson wondered. Part of the genius of the Founding was the creation of a culture in which men and women of goodwill—whatever the wellspring of that goodwill, be it a fear of God or a secular moral framework—could live together and prosper together. "If we did a good act merely from the love of god, and a belief that it is pleasing to him, whence arises the morality of the atheist?" Jefferson once asked. "It is idle to say, as some do, that no such being exists." Religion, then, could not claim to be the universal source of individual moral conduct. The virtue of atheists, Jefferson said, "must have had some other foundation than the love of god."

Still, on the whole, Jefferson tended to see the moral impulse as a gift of God's. "The Creator would, indeed, have been a bungling artist, had He intended man for a social animal, without planting in him social dispositions," Jefferson wrote in 1814; two years later, he told John Adams that "the moral sense is as much a part of our constitution as that of feeling, seeing, or hearing; as a wise Creator must have seen to be necessary in an animal destined to live in society."

Practical men—they were, after all, politicians—many of the Founders based their belief in the connection between religion and morality on the threat of future reward or punishment. People would be more likely to do right on earth if they believed they were to be held accountable before God. To Hamilton, "morality *must* fall without religion," and Adams believed that "every man, woman, and child" would be well advised "to take opium" if there were no afterlife. "For, I am certain," Adams said, "there is nothing in this world worth living for but hope, and every hope will fail us, if the last hope, that of a future state, is extinguished."

If religious freedom was, as Madison once said, "a lustre to our country," then religion itself—public or private—was not only about the threat of damnation, either. For many, faith in God fueled lives of goodness and charity and selflessness. "*Real* Christians will abstain from violating the rights of others," said John Jay, and the religious habit of mind played a role in fostering the American insistence on freedom. In 1751, to commemorate the Quaker William Penn's founding of Pennsylvania as a haven for religious dissenters, the colony had a bell made in his honor. The inscription was eloquent: "Proclaim liberty throughout all the land unto all the inhabitants thereof." The words were drawn from the Book of Leviticus, and, after cracking, the bell was to come down to history as the Liberty Bell—a symbol of freedom emblazoned with words of faith, created as a memorial to a man who believed in both. There could be no more fitting relic of the American public religion.

The distinctive feature of that religion lies in the meaning of the verse from Leviticus: that individual liberty for all—*all*, of any color or creed—is at the very center of the broad faith the Founders nurtured and passed on to us. Our minds and hearts, as Jefferson wrote, are free to believe everything or nothing at all—and it is our duty to protect and perpetuate this sacred culture of freedom. "The God who gave us life gave us liberty at the same time," said Jefferson, and "the hand of force may destroy but cannot disjoin them." The principles of God-given life and God-given human rights are the two wings on which the nation rose, and on which it still depends.

THE HAND OF THE DIVINITY

So is religion in America a necessary evil, or can it be a positive force for good? Taken all in all, I think history teaches that the benefits of faith in God have outweighed the costs. "The sacred rights of mankind are not to be rummaged for among old parchments or musty records," said Alexander Hamilton. "They are written, as with a sunbeam, in the whole volume of human nature, by the Hand of the Divinity itself. . . ." Guided by this religiously inspired idea of God-given rights, America has created the most inclusive, freest nation on earth. It was neither easy nor quick: the destruction of Native American cultures, the ravages of slavery, the horrors of the Civil War, and the bitterness of Jim Crow attest to that. And there is much work to be done. Yet while the tides of history are infinitely complex, other major Western powers have had a worse time of it than America, and our public religion, with its emphasis on the supremacy of the individual and its cultivation of moral virtue, is one reason why. France's revolution gave way to Napoleonic despotism. Russia's czarism helped bring about a revolution, the murder of the royal family, and the totalitarian Soviet state. Germany's absolutism partly provoked World War I, which opened the way for the rise of Adolf Hitler. Religion alone did not spare America, but the Founding Fathers' belief in the divine origin of human rights fundamentally shaped our national character, and by fits and starts Americans came to see that all people were made in the image of "Nature's God," and were thus naturally entitled to dignity and respect.

To argue against a role for faith in politics is essentially futile. The more useful enterprise is to ask, first, what *kind* of religion—either public or private—is at work in a given situation and, if it is predominately private, how much that religious thought or belief ought to shape one's opinion or vote.

The trickier part comes when private religious values involving emotional issues enter the public square—abortion rights, for example, or fetal–stem cell research. One could argue, and the faithful often do, that the Declaration's guarantee of the rights of life, liberty, and the pursuit of happiness (an element of public religion) extends to such questions. How much weight should politicians and judges give such theological views? In other words, how much religion is too little, just right, or too much in politics and legislating and policy making? The American experience suggests that religious convictions should be a factor but not the dominant one in many such difficult arenas of life and law.

Some conservative Christian believers think that that is exactly the problem: faith is not driving the bus, it is only one of many passengers. In word if not always in deed, however, the ideal of religious freedom lies near the heart of the American experience. "Let every man speak freely without fear, maintain the principles that he believes, worship according to his own faith, either one God, three Gods, no God, or twenty Gods; and let government protect him in doing so," said John Leland, a Baptist evangelist who worked with Jefferson and Madison to secure religious freedom in Virginia. The nation, the agnostic Robert Ingersoll said in 1876, was a place where religion had to make its own way; there would be no preferential treatment: "Our fathers founded the first secular government that was ever founded in this world. The first secular government; the first government that said every church has exactly the same rights and no more; every religion has the same rights, and no more. In other words, our fathers were the first men who had the sense, had the genius, to know that no church should be allowed to have a sword; that it should be allowed only to exert its moral influence." A tolerant, pluralistic democracy in which religious and secular forces continually contend against one another may not be ideal, but it has proven to be the most practical and enduring arrangement of human affairs—and we must guard that arrangement well.

THE TEST OF A LIFE

On the day Jefferson died, the sixth president of the United States, John Quincy Adams, attended Fourth of July ceremonies at the Capitol, then returned to the White House to receive callers before slipping off to work at three in the afternoon. He soon heard of Jefferson's death; Adams thought it "a strange and very striking coincidence that the author of the Declaration should have died on its 50th anniversary." A few days later came a letter written on the morning of July 4 from Quincy, Massachusetts, where Adams's father, the second president, in his ninety-first year, had taken a turn for the worse. In terrible midsummer heat, the president climbed into his carriage to go to his father. Stopping for breakfast at Waterloo, Maryland, Adams was told his father had died—on the Fourth, too, four hours after Jefferson. "The time, the manner, the coincidence with the decease of Jefferson, are visible and palpable marks of Divine favor," President Adams told his diary. For the Lord to call two soldiers of the Republic home in such a way, Adams thought, was biblical in scope, as though they had been taken up in an act of ascension. Adams believed it an occasion, as he put it, for "grateful and silent adoration before the Ruler of the Universe." As he buried his father, Adams hoped that one day he, too, might die "in peace with God and man" and be "sped to the regions of futurity with the blessings of my fellow-men."

John Adams and Thomas Jefferson had talked with each other about those regions of the afterlife, and Jefferson believed that one's works, not adherence to a particular faith, determined one's future fate. "I must ever believe that religion substantially good which produces an honest life," he wrote. But traditional Christians still thought Jefferson unsound. On a summer day in 1816 at Monticello, Jefferson opened a letter from an old friend, Margaret Bayard Smith, an author who was a fixture in Washington society from the time of her move to the capital as a new wife in the last months of the Adams presidency in 1800 until her death in the last year of John Tyler's presidency in 1844. Mrs. Smith was a fervent admirer of Jefferson's; parting from him after a visit to Monticello, she cried that it might be "the last time . . . in this world, at least, that I shall ever see you—But there is another world"—prompting Jefferson to calm her, saying, "God bless you, dear madam. God bless you." There was, she now wrote Jefferson, yet another round of rumors in circulation about his religion, and, as he replied, he took a middle course. "I never told my religion nor scrutinized that of another," Jefferson wrote. "I never attempted to make a convert, nor wish to change another's creed. I have ever judged of the religion of others by their lives. . . ." For Jefferson, liberty and religion, freedom and God, and goodness and faith were intertwined, each an indissoluble element in the American experiment. "For it is in our lives, and not from our words, that our religion must be read," Jefferson said. "By the same test the world must judge me." Whatever our doubts, whatever our faith, that is perhaps the supreme test for us all.

I. GOD AND MAMMON

FORTUNE, FEAR, AND THE FIRST COLONIES

For we must consider that we shall be as a City upon a Hill, the eyes of all people are upon us; so that if we shall deal falsely with our God in this work we have undertaken, and so cause Him to withdraw His present help from us, we shall be made a story and a by-word through the world.

—JOHN WINTHROP,
"A MODEL OF CHRISTIAN CHARITY," 1630

No man . . . can be so stupid to deny that all men naturally were born free, being the image and resemblance of God himself.

—JOHN MILTON, "THE TENURE OF KINGS AND MAGISTRATES," 1649

*A*merica as we like to think of it had nearly ended before it began. In the North Atlantic in the autumn of 1620, the passengers aboard the *Mayflower*—102 English Puritans seeking religious freedom, new lands, and better livelihoods—found themselves in the midst of a storm at sea. As the crew struggled to save the *Mayflower,* the Pilgrims, as William Bradford called them, thought they were going to die.

When the ship finally came within sight of Cape Cod after sixty-five days, wrote Bradford, "they were not a little joyful," and when at last they reached land, "they fell upon their knees and blessed the God of Heaven who had brought them over the vast and furious ocean, and delivered them from all the perils and miseries thereof."

Bradford and his company saw the hand of God in their journey, the God of Israel who had, in the Christian worldview, redeemed the sins of the world through the death and resurrection of Jesus Christ. In his account of the voyage and of the founding of Plymouth, Bradford suggested his own generation's epitaph: "May not and ought not the children of these fathers rightly say: 'Our fathers were Englishmen which came over this great ocean, and were ready to perish in this wilderness; but they cried unto the Lord, and he heard their voice.'"

God's kindness might be boundless, but the Pilgrims' kindness had its limits. En route, one of the hired sailors—a "proud and very profane young man, one of the seamen, of a lusty, able body"—was difficult, sneering at seasick passengers, cursing and swearing. Bullying and unsettling, the man frightened the Pilgrims so much that Bradford was not unhappy to see him dead. "But it pleased God . . . to smite this young man with a grievous disease, of which he died in a desperate manner, and so was himself the first that was thrown overboard." It is not exactly Christian to see the death of a man, however filthy-mouthed, as "a special work of God's providence," to use Bradford's words, but contradiction between profession and practice, between the dictates of faith and man's darker impulses, was to be an enduring theme in the history of the nation the Pilgrims were helping to found.

A decade later, John Winthrop would urge another company of Puritans to think of the New World as "a city upon a hill," a source of light to all the world. Shine it would, but it has also long been a place of shadows—of persecution, of slavery, of poverty. Still, with courage and with conviction, the settlers fought on. "So they committed themselves to the will of God," said Bradford of the *Mayflower*'s Pilgrims, "and resolved to proceed."

As it was in the beginning, so it has been since. Succeeding generations of Americans have moved through war and hardship, believing themselves committed to, and frequently alluding to, God, a supernatural force who created the world and remains interested in—and engaged with—history. The common story of America from the Pilgrims onward is a powerful one; it draws on some of the most vivid and important themes of Israel, investing the United States with a sense of earthly grandeur and divine purpose. "The civilization of New England has been like those fires lit in the hills that, after having spread heat around them, still tinge the furthest reaches of the horizon with their light," wrote Alexis de Tocqueville. There is a persistent idea in the popular American imagination that the nation was founded by what are sometimes called Planting Fathers seeking religious freedom—a vision of the past which gives religion pride of place as the country's earliest reason for being. In recent times conservative Christians have been particularly attracted to this version of our beginnings, and a 1755 observation of John Adams's suggests the same nar-

The first permanent American Jewish settlers came to New Amsterdam (later New York) fleeing persecution in Brazil in 1654. "As much as I love, esteem, and admire the Greeks," John Adams said, "I believe the Hebrews have done more to enlighten and civilize the world. Moses did more than all their legislators and philosophers." *(© Bettmann/Corbis)*

rative had already taken shape by the time of the Revolution. "Soon after the Reformation, a few people came over into this new world for conscience sake," Adams wrote. "Perhaps this apparently trivial incident may transfer the great seat of empire into America."

The reality is more complex, for many motives propelled the English across the Atlantic. The first years of the country's history were full of pious pilgrims, dashing gold hunters, ambitious London investors, anxious Jews in flight from persecution in Brazil, intense spiritual seekers guided by an "Inner Light," and stern Puritan politicians intent on building a City of God in the middle of a fallen world. It was an eclectic cast of characters, some in search of God, others on the prowl for mammon—and even those for whom freedom of religion was a driving force soon found themselves doing unto others what had been done unto them.

LAWS DIVINE, MORAL, AND MARTIAL

The first permanent English settlers arrived in search of gold, not God. The language of the First Charter of Virginia was lovely, the sentiments warm, the king's expectations clear. Issuing the document to the Virginia Company of London on Thursday, April 10, 1606, James I said he was happy to bless "so noble a work" in the hope that the mission to the New World would carry the "Christian religion to such people as yet live in darkness and miserable ignorance of the true knowledge and worship of God. . . ."

With the Lord out of the way, James quickly turned to mammon. The company was to take possession of "all the Lands, Woods, Soil, Grounds, Havens, Ports, Rivers, Mines, Minerals, Marshes, Waters, Fishings, Commodities . . ."—and on and on, for three paragraphs. Then came the order to "dig, mine, and search for all Manner of Mines of Gold, Silver, and Copper." To defend the enterprise, no "Robbery or Spoil" would ever go unpunished, and the company was authorized to "pursue with hostility the said offenders" in the event of plunder. The First Charter of Virginia is 3,805 words long; only 98 of those words, or about 3 percent, are about God. Faith, Captain John Smith wrote of the Virginia Company, was "their color, when all their aim was nothing but present profit."

Armed with the king's commission, three ships—the *Discovery,* the *Godspeed,* and the *Susan Constant*—with 144 men, led by Captain Christopher Newport, left London in December 1606. They reached the banks of the James River in May 1607, just thirteen months after the charter was issued. They knew about the ninety-eight words referring to God and built a makeshift chapel for morning and evening prayer, and two services on Sundays. Before long the colony's minister died, and Captain John Smith recalled that it took two or three years before "more preachers came," a sign, Smith thought, that God had "most mercifully hear[d] us." On the whole, however, evidence of God's care was scanty. Within weeks of the Jamestown landing Indians attacked, killing two and wounding ten. Smith went on an expedition, was captured and saved from execution only, he believed, by the intervention of the chief's daughter Pocahontas. When Smith returned to the settlement, he found only a third of the original company still alive. Things were at their bleakest.

Word of the colony's dismal beginnings soon reached London. Instead of taking delivery of "Gold, Silver, and Copper," the officers of the Virginia Company—and King James—were hearing of starvation and slaughter. Smith denounced those Englishmen whose disappointed hopes of discovering new riches drove them to return to London, where they told all who would listen that America was "a misery, a ruin, a death, [and] a hell." In June 1609, Sir Thomas Gates was sent from England to bring order to the chaos with instructions whose title left little doubt as to their content: "Laws Divine, Moral and Martial."

Gates set sail aboard the *Sea Venture;* one other ship accompanied it. On Monday, July 24, 1609, a hurricane struck. The *Sea Venture* fought the storm for three days. "Prayers might well be in the heart and lips but drowned in the outcries of the officers," wrote William Strachey, a *Sea Venture* passenger. "Nothing [was] heard that could give comfort, nothing seen that might encourage hope." Miraculously, the ship came upon a reef at Bermuda, and the 150 or so survivors built two boats out of the wreckage, christened them *Deliverance* and *Patience,* and set sail again, arriving at Jamestown on Monday, May 23, 1610. While the episode became celebrated in England when Strachey's account circulated in London (Shakespeare is said to have drawn on it as he wrote *The Tempest*), the hosannas in Virginia were more muted, for Gates immediately imposed martial law—a new code rife with ecclesiastical requirements and penalties for those who fell short of stringent religious rules.

The "Laws Divine, Moral and Martial" were severe, legislating religious observance "upon pain of death." Those who failed to come to services twice daily would first lose their food for the day. A second offense brought a whipping, and a third six months in the gallows. To break the Sabbath "by any gaming, public or private" or to miss church on Sunday was, on the third offense, a capital crime.

Sex was of particular interest. Sodomy, incest, rape, and adultery carried the death penalty, though fornication led only to serial whippings and the compulsory begging of forgiveness. To disobey the governor or his lieutenants (even to "murmur" against them) led to whippings and a required public confession on one's knees during Sabbath services. In short order the first enduring English settlement had become not an outpost of freedom or an inspired missionary base but a New World stage on which the Old World imposed its most suffocating and absolutist tactics. Writing of the *Sea Venture,* William Strachey spoke wonderingly of the mercies of the Almighty God who had delivered them—yet they were turning their Promised Land into a place that used force to control its subjects in realms both temporal and spiritual. It was hardly an auspicious beginning, hardly what Lincoln would later call "a new birth of freedom."

Pious Puritans like Bradford, or Elder William Brewster, or, after 1630, Winthrop, the governor of the Massachusetts Bay Colony, loom large in many American minds—larger, for instance, than the essentially forgotten Sir Thomas Gates of Jamestown. From the story of the *Mayflower* to the first Thanksgiving and beyond, the Pilgrim tale is much more appealing than Jamestown and the accounts of its seventeenth-century equivalent of venture capitalists swashbuckling their way through the Virginia wilderness, who turned to religious and civil martial law, and who, in 1619, the year before the *Mayflower* arrived in New England, took delivery of black slaves from a Dutch man-of-war.

The "African diaspora" and its religious and cultural implications for the faiths and customs of those brought here in bondage is a largely overlooked story in American history. Some slaves were Muslims, and they struggled to keep their faith; many others practiced native African religions despite aggressive, and successful, Christian evangelism within slave communities. The scholar Albert J. Raboteau calls the courageous preservation of native beliefs and rituals the "invisible institution" of the antebellum South; another scholar, Jon Butler, bluntly says white Americans carried out an "African spiritual holocaust." What is beyond argument, as John Adams would write, is that slavery was irreconcilable with "reason, justice & humanity"—a truth the nation would take a tragically long time to recognize.

Another tragedy—the criminal treatment of Native Americans—was born in and played out in both the South and the North, and it, too, had a religious cast. The Virginia Company was to consider the Christianization of the Native Americans as "the most pious and noble end of this plantation," and Massachusetts looked to "win and incite the Natives . . . to the only true God and Saviour of Mankind." But, as the

Pilgrims at the first Thanksgiving. The founding of Plymouth Colony by the *Mayflower* Pilgrims in 1620 marked the beginning of an early New England tradition of intolerance of those with dissenting religious views. *(The Granger Collection, New York)*

scholar Francis Paul Prucha put it, "The great distinguishing feature of English relations with the Indian groups was replacement of the Indians on the land by white settlers, not conversion and assimilation of the Indians into European colonial society." By 1622 in Virginia and by 1637 in New England, the dismal cycle of incursion, massacre, and war had begun, a bloody story that, like slavery, was to play a perennial role in the history of the country for more than two and a half centuries.

"THE WRATH OF THE DEVIL"

But most Americans do not want to think much about that Dutch ship and its human cargo, nor about the failure to treat the native population justly. We would rather imagine the voyage of the *Arbella,* the journey that brought Winthrop to our shores in 1630. Either just before leaving for the New World or en route—it is unclear which—Winthrop, a layman trained as a lawyer, wrote a sermon titled "A Model of Christian Charity":

> Now the only way to avoid this shipwreck and to provide for our posterity is to follow the counsel of Micah: to do justly, to love mercy, to walk humbly with our God. We must be knit together in this work as one man, we must entertain each other in brotherly affection . . . we must delight in each other, make others' condition our own, rejoice together, mourn together, labor, and suffer together . . . for we must consider that we shall be as a city upon a hill, the eyes of all people are upon us; so that if

we shall deal falsely with our God in this work we have undertaken, and so cause Him to withdraw His present help from us, we shall be made a story and a by-word through the world . . . we shall shame the faces of many of God's worthy servants, and cause their prayers to be turned into curses upon us. . . .

The allusion to the Sermon on the Mount—that we are "a city upon a hill"—is one of the most oft-cited images of the United States as a kind of Promised Land that the early New England settlers, playing the part of the ancient Israelites, reached after an exodus of peril and crisis. Winthrop's text is frequently used as a source of reassurance about our exceptional national destiny, yet we should not be so quick to think that an ancient phrase of his can help us smooth over the rougher passages of our history, or that telling ourselves we are a special people entitles the country or any element within it to impose its will on others under the cloak of divine sanction.

Looking back at Winthrop and Massachusetts Bay, the question is how to draw the good out of the New England Puritan experience while learning from the bad. By the standards of his own day, Winthrop was more moderate than most, but he was engaged in a very particular enterprise: the construction of a Christian commonwealth. Winthrop was no blithe optimist. He understood that the powers of darkness were often more formidable than the forces of light, and like prophets of old he thought that God's favor could be withdrawn at any time. His God, like Israel's, was an attentive actor. Man is a morally responsible agent, Winthrop believed, and will be called to account for what he does and leaves undone. To spurn Micah's injunction "to do justly" and "to love mercy" will invite divine judgment—probably on earth and beyond. Whatever one wishes to believe in religious terms, such a view can be dangerous in democratic societies. If a community (or a nation) is dominated by the idea that God specifically punishes sinners and the milieu in which they live, then it is all too easy for that community (or nation) to demand absolute adherence to certain moral codes on the grounds that the well-being of all is dependent on the personal conduct of the individual. The distance between a culture informed by religiously inspired values but governed by civil institutions that respect personal liberties to a kind of theological totalitarianism is a short one. A nation can feel called to a special role without descending into paranoia and moral dictatorship—a balancing act Americans have come to handle well, but which was not achieved in the New England of John Winthrop and William Bradford.

Early in the *Arbella* sermon Winthrop says: "There are two rules by which we are to walk one towards another: JUSTICE and MERCY." Winthrop was less interested, however, in being just and merciful to the extent of complete religious liberty. Having fled European conformity, the Puritans sought conformity of their own. The irony was not lost on the Old World. "Every party cries out for Liberty & toleration," said the Lord Bishop of Salisbury, "till they get to be uppermost, and then will allow none."

Anyone who did not believe as the Puritans did "shall have free liberty to keep away from us," said the Massachusetts minister Nathaniel Ward in 1647. In 1630, the historian Edmund S. Morgan wrote, the colony provided for the public support of ministers. In 1631, it limited the suffrage and the right to hold office to members of the church. In 1635 came an order for non-members of the church to attend church services, followed by a directive three years later that nonmembers should, as Morgan put it, "help pay for the preaching that might lead ultimately to their conversion." Ministers were not magistrates, but the influence of the clergy was no less real for its informality. "The ministers have great power with the people," said Winthrop, and the populace was "more easily governed" when the clergy and civil authorities cooperated closely.

ANNE HUTCHINSON'S EXILE

The case of Anne Hutchinson was a dark hour for Winthrop and Massachusetts Bay. A devoted Puritan, Mrs. Hutchinson came to the colony in 1634 with her husband, William, and eleven children. Conversant with the Bible, she became a popular religious figure, arguing in favor of the doctrine of salvation by faith, not works (or obedience to temporal laws). The Puritan leadership thought her an "Antinomian"—someone who rejected the power of the clergy or of religious authorities. By the autumn of 1637 she was on trial for heresy. In a showdown with Winthrop and others, Mrs. Hutchinson largely held her own, but eventually snapped, Winthrop recalled, and informed the court that God had told her He would "ruin us and our posterity and the whole state" to punish them for persecuting her.

For Winthrop, that was more than enough. She had to go; he ordered her expelled from Massachusetts Bay.

"I desire to know wherefore I am banished?" Hutchinson asked.

In 1637, Anne Hutchinson stood trial in Massachusetts Bay Colony for her dissenting religious views. She was forced into exile and was ultimately killed by Indians. *(The Granger Collection, New York)*

"Say no more," Winthrop said, cutting her off. "The court knows wherefore and is satisfied."

Winthrop remained fascinated by Hutchinson. Ten months after her sentencing, she suffered a terrible miscarriage—what Winthrop called "a monstrous birth." On first hearing of it, Winthrop wrote to Dr. John Clarke, a physician and preacher in

Rhode Island, asking for details. Clarke described seeing "innumerable distinct bodies in the form of a globe, not much unlike the swims of some fish . . . confusedly knit together by so many strings (which I conceive were the beginning of veins and nerves)."

Anxious to learn more even after reading this lugubrious account of the lost fetus, Winthrop spoke with Clarke, who added still further clinical details. Four years later, after her husband's death, Mrs. Hutchinson moved from Rhode Island to what is now the Bronx in New York. There, in September 1643, she and the family she had with her were massacred by Indians. Like William Bradford before him when the difficult seaman died on the *Mayflower*, Winthrop saw the hand of God in the murders. "These people had cast off ordinances and churches," Winthrop wrote in his journal, and had paid the price.

The idea that those still living were targets of divine retribution for sins committed on earth was a critical element in the Puritan worldview. In the last journal entry of the man's life, Winthrop recorded a story about a church member from Boston who had worked on a mill dam on the Sabbath. Toward the end of the man's task, "his conscience began to put him in the mind of the Lord's day and he was troubled," but he finished the job. The next evening, the man and his wife put their two children to bed, walked to a neighbor's, and returned to find their five-year-old daughter missing. Frightened, the parents began a hurried search, and the mother found the little girl had drowned in a well in the cellar of the house. Winthrop, who recounted the details, believed "a special hand of God" was responsible for the death, and the father agreed. The tragedy, Winthrop recalled the father telling a meeting of the congregation, was the work of "the righteous hand of God for his profaning His holy day against the checks of his own conscience."

CATHOLICS, QUAKERS, AND "DEVILS"

The middle of the seventeenth century brought hope and fear. In Maryland, founded by a powerful Catholic family, the legislature passed the Religious Toleration Act in 1649 to protect all "Trinitarian Christians"—not exactly the most liberal policy, but it did benefit Catholics in what was already a predominantly Protestant culture. The next year the term "Quaker" was coined in England. George Fox, one of the founders of the movement, was on trial when the judge in the case said they were "quakers" because, Fox recalled, they tended to "tremble at the word of God." Quakerism was based on the idea that each person has an "Inner Light" which enables the individual to forego churchly sacraments controlled by clergy and ecclesiastical authority, and experience God directly. This theology put the Quakers at odds with both Anglicans (who upheld the sacraments) and with the Puritans (who believed in conformity to church authorities). Facing persecution from every quarter, the Quakers found a welcome champion in William Penn, a rich Englishman who, with others, received a royal charter for what became Pennsylvania in 1681. The author of the eloquent 1670 "The Great Case of Liberty of Conscience," Penn said Pennsylvania was to be a "holy experiment" in religious and civil freedom, a land to the west and the south of New England in which Quakers and others could live in peace and goodwill. And it largely worked—at least in Pennsylvania.

To the north the news was worse. Connecticut's Code of 1650 was a brutal one. "If any man shall have or worship any God but the Lord God, he shall be put to death," it said. Reviewing the history of the New England colonies, Tocqueville remarked that "the legislator, forgetting completely the great principles of religious liberty he himself demanded in Europe, forces attendance at divine service by fear of fines, and he goes as far as to strike with severe penalties, and often death, Christians who wish to worship God according to a form other than his."

From the early seventeenth century to the revolutionary era, America's religious spirit was more sectarian than ecumenical, more closed than open, more likely to look inward rather than outward. Cotton Mather, a minister at Boston's Old North Church, wrote a history of the New World in 1702 titled *Magnalia Christi Americana* (*The Great Works of Christ in America*). Mather believed America was in the grip of evil; he played a critical role in the Salem witch trials. Though Jonathan Edwards's "Sinners in the Hands of an Angry God" is more widely known, Mather's less-quoted words in "The Wonders of the Invisible World: Observation as well Historical as Theological, upon the Nature, the Number, and the Operations of the DEVILS" capture the apocalyptic spirit of the age: ". . . If you do not by a speedy and thorough conversion to God escape the *wrath* of the Devil, you will yourselves go *down* where the Devil is to be . . . not for a *short time,* but *world without end;* not for a *short time,* but *Infinite Millions of ages.*" Conversion and conformity—these were the answers for such preachers. The alternative was hell without end.

"A WALL OF SEPARATION"

One early voice arguing to free faith from the power of government in Winthrop's world was Roger Williams, a minister who had followed Winthrop to Massachusetts Bay. Williams was mostly interested in saving the church from the state, not the state from the church. The world was the world; the kingdom of God was something else entirely. "Render to Caesar the things that are Caesar's," Jesus said, "and to God the things that are God's." Williams called for a "hedge or wall of separation between the Garden of the church and the wilderness of the world." Note that Williams was not planting a hedge or building a wall to protect the state, but rather religion, believing that the ambitions and vices of men could pervert the church, turning faith into a means of temporal power.

Far from securing Christianity's place in the world, Williams believed, Constantine's conversion early in the fourth century marked the beginning of the corruption of the faith as the church moved from being concerned with God to an obsession with the rise and fall of earthly empires. Williams's goal "was not freedom of thought for its own sake: he did not think that one way of seeking God was as good as another," wrote Edmund S. Morgan. "He wanted freedom because it was the only way to reach the true God." To Williams, "the gardens of Christ's churches turned into the wilderness of national religion, and the world (under Constantine's dominion) to the most un-Christian Christendom."

It was a hard case to refute. From 1534, the year Henry VIII broke with Rome, forward, chaos over religion and politics had been a central feature of life in England. Henry's daughter Mary, a Catholic, returned the realm to her faith, executing so many that she comes down to us as "Bloody Mary." Her sister and successor, Elizabeth, set a middle course, but after her came a century of civil strife and war, including the beheading of Charles I. The dizzying ecclesiastical swirl in England—from Catholicism to Anglicanism to Catholicism to a combination of the two under Elizabeth—led Williams to take a broad view. "I commend that man, whether Jew, or Turk, or Papist, or whoever, that steers no otherwise than his conscience dares," said Williams.

For such opinions Williams was exiled from the Massachusetts Bay Colony in 1635–36 and spent the rest of his embattled life working to found and secure Rhode Island. It was not easy. Winthrop watched the experiment with care. "At Providence also the devil was not idle," Winthrop wrote of Williams's colony, describing controversies like a wife-beating husband's anger at Williams when the minister tried to protect the wife.

And yet the views on religious freedom Williams articulated until his death in 1683 or 1684 (the exact date is unknown) gradually moved to the mainstream. What changed? Roughly put, it was a combination of the Reformation, the Enlightenment, and American political reality. Despite Anglican, Puritan, and Separatist experiments with re-creating absolutist churches or communities, the general trend after the European break with Rome created a culture of dissent within Christianity that grew down the centuries—and the occasional excesses of places like Jamestown and Massachusetts Bay fueled the colonists' desire for religious liberty.

The Enlightenment emphasis on the free play of the human mind was another factor. From John Milton's mid-seventeenth-century work to John Toland's *Christianity Not Mysterious* to the thought of Joseph Priestley and Lord Bolingbroke, people in Britain and the American colonies were coming to think of God and man in different ways in the late-seventeenth and eighteenth centuries. The result: these Reformation and Enlightenment sensibilities led many colonists to take their own theological and political stands in the New World. Rebelling against calls for conformity, those hungry for freedom of thought and religion struck out on their own, founding new places like Rhode Island and Pennsylvania. Even those like Jefferson and Madison and Adams who remained in Virginia and Massachusetts were coming to view religion and politics in a different light—a light in which individual conscience was beginning to take precedence over forced conformity of any kind, either Catholic, Anglican, or Puritan. As the seventeenth century gave way to the eighteenth, and more people believed and practiced faiths falling outside legislated religion (usually Anglicanism in the South and Congregationalism in the North), politics began to change, too, for America was becoming religiously diverse. Created by Christians dissenting from the first generations of English dissenters, the upheaval in the world of faith helped produce a democratic spirit, for people who chose their own spiritual path wondered why they could not choose their own political path as well.

LESSONS FOR THE FOUNDERS

Studying the stories of Massachusetts, Virginia, Pennsylvania, and Maryland, the young men about to construct a new nation detected a consistent theme: civil societies dominated by compulsory religious rigidity were unhappy and intolerant, while religious liberty seemed to produce more prosperous, stable, and popular cultures.

Pennsylvania, for instance, impressed young James Madison. "You are happy in dwelling in a land where . . . inestimable privileges are fully enjoyed and [the] public has long felt the good effects of their religious as well as civil liberty," he wrote a Philadelphia friend. "Foreigners have been encouraged to settle among you. Industry and virtue have been promoted by mutual emulation and mutual inspection, commerce and the arts have flourished and I can not help attributing those continual exertions of genius which appear among you to the inspiration of liberty. . . . Religious bondage shackles and debilitates the mind and unfits it for every noble enterprise [and] every expanded prospect."

Jefferson found Virginia and Massachusetts wanting. "They cast their eyes on these new countries as asylums of civil and religious freedom; but they found them free only for the reigning sect," Jefferson noted of early settlers. He knew of New England's history of applying the death penalty for religious offenses and regretted Virginia's persecution of Presbyterians, Quakers, and others.

The 1774 Massachusetts resolution calling for a Continental Congress noted the colonists' need "for the recovery and establishment of their just rights and liberties, civil and religious." When Jefferson, in writing his *Notes on the State of Virginia* in 1781 and 1782—the book was at first published in a private edition in 1785—came to Query XVII, his mind turned to the early days of Jamestown. The question—What of religion and Virginia?— led him to a cold-eyed report on his state's underwhelming record on liberty of conscience. "The first settlers in this country were emigrants from England, of the English church, just at a point of time when it was flushed with complete victory over the religious of all other persuasions"—an allusion to the Elizabethan conquest of Catholicism in England. "Possessed, as they became, of the powers of making, administering, and executing the laws," Jefferson said of the early settlers, "they showed equal intolerance in this country. . . ." In the decades after Jamestown, the Quakers were a particular target. In 1659, 1662, and 1693, Jefferson reported, Virginia made it a crime not to have children baptized in the Anglican Church. A century's worth of compulsion, though, did little good, Jefferson said, laying out the human costs of a 1705 act. If "a person brought up in the Christian religion" denied the existence of God, the Holy Trinity, disbelieved the divine authority of scripture or asserted there was more than one God or that Christianity was untrue, he was prohibited from office, including the military. A second offense meant the stripping of the rights of guardianship to a child and three years in prison without bail. Jefferson's disgust is palpable: "A father's right to the custody of his own children, being founded in law on his right of guardianship, this being taken away, they may of course be severed from him and put, by the authority of a court, into more orthodox hands." It was the most unnatural and perverse of laws, Jefferson said; it was nothing less than "religious slavery." Little wonder, then, he added, that "two-thirds of the people had become dissenters at the commencement of the present revolution."

JUDAISM SETTLES IN AMERICA

That the New World was to be home not only to Christians but to those of diverse faiths was clear from the start. In 1654, the

French ship *Ste. Catherine* brought a small number of Jewish refugees fleeing persecution in Catholic Brazil to New Amsterdam (later New York). They were, as the historian Jonathan D. Sarna has written, the first Jewish people to settle permanently and live their lives in North America. Doing so required enormous courage and resilience, for Peter Stuyvesant, the director-general of the New Netherlands, made it clear that they were not welcome. "The Jews . . . would nearly all like to remain here," he wrote home to Amsterdam, but he hoped, he said, that "the deceitful race—such hateful enemies and blasphemers of the name of Christ—be not allowed further to infect and trouble this new colony." Stuyvesant's superiors at the Dutch West India Company disagreed, directing him to allow the settlers to "travel," "trade," "live," and "remain" in the colony "provided the poor among them shall not become a burden to the company or to the community, but be supported by their own nation."

In 1730, Shearith Israel consecrated its synagogue on Mill Street in lower New York; there were also Jewish communities in Savannah, Charleston, Philadelphia, and Newport. The culture and character of religion in America worked to Judaism's benefit. "Whereas in so many other diaspora settings Judaism stood all alone in religious dissent, Jews in America shared this status with members of other minority faiths—for example, Huguenots, Quakers, and Baptists," wrote Sarna. To underscore this link with other faiths, synagogue leaders began referring to their flocks as the Jewish Society, echoing the Quakers' Society of Friends.

On the eve of the Revolution, answering a call from the Continental Congress for prayer, Shearith Israel asked the Lord to protect the colonies: "O Lord: the God of our Fathers Abraham, Isaac and Jacob, may it please thee, to put it in the heart of our sovereign lord, George the third, and in the hearts of his councillors, princes and servants, to turn away their fierce wrath from against North America." It was not to be.

As the revolutionary era opened, the freedom of any and all to pray as Shearith Israel did—in the manner and to the deity one pleased, or to no deity—was a crucial concern. America had been undertaken for many things, including the glory of God, but whose God? And what kind of God was so weak he needed the authorities of the colony of Virginia, or of Massachusetts, or of Connecticut, or any other to prop him up? "It is error alone which needs the support of government," Jefferson said. "Truth can stand by itself." Franklin agreed: "When a religion is good, I conceive that it will support itself; and, when it cannot support itself, and God does not take care to support [it], so that its professors are obliged to call for help of the civil power, it is a sign, I apprehend, of its being a bad one."

FAITH, REASON, AND JOHN LOCKE

In some private *Notes on Religion* jotted down in 1776, Jefferson wrote that "we have no right to prejudice another in his civil enjoyments because he is of another church. If any man err from the right way, it is his own misfortune, no injury to thee . . . on the contrary, according to the spirit of the gospel, charity, bounty, and liberality is due to him." Jefferson's arguments were partly drawn from the work of John Locke, an English Christian, philosopher, and politician who published *A Letter concerning Toleration* in 1689—a document that, along with other of Locke's works, helped fuel the rise of the American vision of religious liberty, a vision to be enshrined in the Bill of Rights a century later. In contrast to later figures such as Voltaire, Locke was no radical, no deep agnostic. He was not even a very vivid character. Yet his *An Essay concerning Human Understanding* and two *Treatises of Government* were essential pieces of Enlightenment political philosophy, arguing for the centrality of human reason, the natural rights of life, liberty, and property, and the idea that the authority of the state should be derived from "the consent of the governed."

Locke is significant, too, because he confronted the dilemma of the thinking believer: How does one reconcile faith and reason? Is all religion, given that it is based on ideas of a supernatural order, superstition, or can faith be an intellectually satisfying and respectable undertaking? Locke's answer was an emphatic, cogently argued yes. For him, reason—which he called "that faculty whereby man is supposed to be distinguished from beasts"—proved the existence of an all-powerful, all-knowing God. Following Aristotle, Locke wrote that man knows he himself exists, at least as much as he knows anything. Since being cannot logically come from nonbeing but from something or somewhere, Locke argued, then something greater than man created man.

In the Lockean scheme of things—as in the pagan philosophers', from Aristotle to Cicero—the majesty of creation and the marvels of man's own capacity for understanding lead to God. Revelation—the often miraculous accounts of God's interventions in history—is crucial, but for Locke revelation cannot trump reason: "Nothing that is contrary to, and inconsistent with, the clear and self-evident dictates of reason has a right to be urged or assented to as a matter of faith." Reason, in this sense, is the capacity of the mind to absorb history, testimony, and tradition, weigh them as probabilities, and reach a conclusion about whether one can comfortably choose to hold and defend a belief that someone else's reason might lead him to reject.

For Locke, toleration was both a religious and a political virtue. In 1689 he called religious liberty "the chief characteristic mark of the true Church," believing that the Pauline virtues of faith, hope, and love trumped the impulse to compel others to accept the Gospel. For too long the world had been rocked by "men's striving for power and empire over one another," Locke said, and the Christian's duty was to practice "charity, meekness, and good-will in general towards all mankind, even to those that are not Christians." By limiting religious strife as a source of controversy and unrest, civil society stood a better chance of being stable and harmonious. "I esteem it above all things necessary to distinguish exactly the business of civil government from that of religion and to settle the just bounds that lie between the one and the other." In his voice we can detect the notes that would, in America, swell to a chorus.

Musing amid the Revolution, Jefferson drew a distinction between Britain's America and the very new United States. "I doubt whether the people of this country would suffer an execution for heresy, or a three years imprisonment for not comprehending the mysteries of the Trinity," he said. "But is the spirit of the people an infallible, a permanent reliance?" No, Jefferson answered, it was not. History teaches us that "the spirit of the times may alter, will alter. Our rulers will become corrupt, our people careless." Best, then, to make the most of moments like the American Revolution, moments when precious things can be provisionally secured against ambition and avarice. "It can never be too often repeated, that the time for fixing every essential right on a legal basis is when our rulers are honest, and ourselves united." Such a time was at hand.

II. AND NONE SHALL BE AFRAID

THE REVOLUTION, THE CONSTITUTION, AND
THE CREATION OF THE PRESIDENCY

*The cause in which America is now in arms is the cause
of justice, of liberty, and of human nature.*
—REVEREND JOHN WITHERSPOON,
PRINCETON UNIVERSITY,
MAY 17, 1776

*Ye Sovereigns of the European world, continue your
religious oppression at your peril. So sure as you persist,
thousands of your present subjects, transplanted to the
fertile fields, the healthful villages and populous cities of
America, shall remind you of your impiety and error,
when it shall be too late for you to retrieve the loss.*
—"A FRIEND OF SOCIETY AND LIBERTY,"
THE PENNSYLVANIA GAZETTE, JULY 23, 1788

*T*heir first fight was over faith. As the Founding Fathers gathered for the inaugural session of the Continental Congress on Tuesday, September 6, 1774, at Carpenters' Hall in Philadelphia, an elegant Georgian brick building on Chestnut Street, Thomas Cushing, a lawyer from Boston, moved that the delegates begin with a prayer. Both John Jay of New York and John Rutledge, a rich lawyer-planter from South Carolina, objected. Their reasoning, John Adams wrote his wife, Abigail, was that "because we were so divided in religious sentiments"—the Congress included Episcopalians, Congregationalists, Presbyterians, and others—"we could not join in the same act of worship."

That Jay and Rutledge, both wealthy Episcopalians, did not want to pray was surprising, and betrayed a possible Anglican disdain for other Christian sects. Jay, a future warden of Trinity Church on Wall Street, and Rutledge, a leader in Christ Church Parish in Charleston, were observant but may have felt that a moment of public prayer would elevate each denomination to the same level, thus investing each sect with equal dignity and legitimacy. Their stated reason for going directly to the business of the day—that "we were so divided in religious sentiments"— would only grow truer as the country moved beyond a diversity of Christian denominations into a pluralistic mainstream that included people of all faiths, and avowedly of no faith. Whatever Jay's and Rutledge's motives, their objection, if successful, had the power to set a secular tone in ceremonial life at the very outset of the American political experience.

Things could have gone either way. Samuel Adams of Boston spoke up. "Mr. S. Adams arose and said he was no bigot, and could hear a prayer from a gentleman of piety and virtue who was at the same time a friend to his country," wrote John Adams to his wife. "He was a stranger in Philadelphia, but had heard that Mr. Duché (Dushay they pronounce it) deserved that character, and therefore he moved that Mr. Duché, an Episcopal clergyman, might be desired to read prayers to the Congress tomorrow morning." Then, in a declarative nine-word sentence, John Adams recorded the true birth of the culture of public religion: "The motion was seconded and passed in the affirmative." Samuel Adams, a onetime tax collector, had carried the day.

In "The Rights of the Colonists" in 1772, Sam Adams had written: "As neither reason requires nor religion permits the contrary, every man living in or out of a state of civil society has a right peaceably and quietly to worship God according to the dictates of his conscience." His motion for prayer, then, was not reflexive, and may have been motivated by his concern for the fate of his city. What John Adams called "the horrible rumor of the cannonade of Boston" had reached them, and everything the men gathered in Carpenters' Hall longed to defend was thought to be in jeopardy. (The rumors would prove unfounded.)

The next morning Reverend Duché appeared, dressed in clerical garb. As it happened, the psalm assigned to be read that day by Episcopalians was the Thirty-fifth. In the hall, the priest read: " 'Plead my cause, O Lord, with them that strive with me: fight against them that fight against me. Take hold of shield and buckler, and stand up for mine help.' "

John Adams was at once stunned and moved. "I never saw a greater effect upon an audience," he told Abigail. "It seemed as if Heaven had ordained that Psalm to be read on that morning." Then, without warning, Duché "struck out into an extemporary prayer," Adams wrote, "which filled the bosom of every man present."

Ten days later, Adams still tingled from the drama of the moment—the close quarters of the room, the mental vision in every delegate's head of the patriots facing fire to the north, and, with

Duché's words, the summoning of divine blessing for the cause of freedom. "It has had an excellent effect upon everybody here," Adams told Abigail. "I must beg you to read that Psalm."

"DIABOLICAL PERSECUTION"

As the delegates debated and deliberated in the Philadelphia autumn of 1774, a young man in Orange County, Virginia, devoured a friend's letters reporting the scene in and around Carpenters' Hall. James Madison, called "Jemmy," was only twenty-three years old but was already fascinated by politics, revolution, and religion. Preternaturally solemn, Madison thought the Virginia delegation notable for its "glowing patriots and men of learning and penetration," and was anxious for the Congress to "illuminate the minds of thinking people among us."

Madison had been a sickly child; as an adult he had, he said, "a constitutional liability to sudden attacks, somewhat resembling epilepsy, and suspending the intellectual functions." At a critical moment, though, his affliction changed the course of his life. Born to Virginia gentry in 1751, Madison was held back a year for health reasons, spending the time with a tutor who was an alumnus of Princeton—formerly the College of New Jersey, whose past presidents included Jonathan Edwards and Samuel Davies. The tutor thought Madison would like Princeton, and Madison did—immensely. The school was enjoying a kind of golden age under John Witherspoon, a Presbyterian clergyman who took a great interest in the Scottish Enlightenment, a movement that had produced Adam Smith, Francis Hutcheson, and David Hume. (Smith's *Wealth of Nations*, published in 1776, ultimately suffused American politics and government with its argument that the government which governs best governs least.)

An advocate of religious freedom, Witherspoon himself appears to have impressed Madison the most. Princeton, where Madison studied from 1769 to 1772, said it offered "free and equal liberty and advantage of education [to] any person of any religious denomination whatsoever." In 1774, the year Madison was following the Continental Congress so closely, the Anglican establishment was imprisoning dissenting preachers in Virginia. Madison argued against the oppression, but to no avail. The historian William Lee Miller reports a legend that "young Madison actually heard one of the Baptists continuing his preaching unsquelched from the jail." The incident consumed Madison, who denounced "that diabolical Hell conceived principle of persecution" which, Madison said, "vexes me the most of any thing whatever." Angry at his own failure to secure the release of the ministers, he said he had run out of "common patience" with the whole matter. "So I leave you to pity me and pray for Liberty of Conscience to revive among us," Madison wrote a classmate. Only two years later, in May 1776, Madison had a chance to do more than fulminate about religious freedom. He had a chance to help bring it into being.

As a delegate to the state convention drafting the Virginia Declaration of Rights, a forerunner of the Declaration of Independence to be shortly crafted in Philadelphia, Madison read George Mason's version of Article XVI:

That as religion, or the duty which we owe to our divine and omnipotent Creator, and the manner of discharging it, can be governed only by reason and conviction, not by force or violence; and therefore that *all men should enjoy the fullest toleration in the exercise of religion* [italics mine], according to the dictates of conscience, unpunished and unrestrained by the Magistrate, unless, under color of religion, any man disturb the peace, the happiness, or safety of society, or of individuals. And that it is the mutual duty of all to practice Christian forbearance, love and charity towards each other.

The idea of "toleration" bothered Madison. Liberty was the issue, not tolerance, for "tolerance" could mean the action of allowing something or granting permission. He seems to have asked Patrick Henry to make the case for a new phrase: "the free exercise of [religion]." After legislative to-ing and fro-ing, the convention at last accepted Madison's language. In the end, Article XVI read:

That religion, or the duty which we owe to our Creator, and the manner of discharging it, can be directed only by reason and conviction, not by force or violence; and therefore, *all men are equally entitled to the free exercise of religion* [italics mine], according to the dictates of conscience, and that it is the mutual duty of all to practice Christian forbearance, love, and charity, towards each other.

The vote on Virginia's declaration took place on Wednesday, June 12, 1776. Approval was unanimous. "Although it is not clear that the members of the Virginia convention knew that they were doing it," wrote William Lee Miller, "they had, by Madison's amendment, removed freedom of religion from the purview of what lawyers today call 'legislative grace'—with the implicit assumption that what is thus given can be withdrawn by the power that grants it—and made it instead what the Declaration of Independence . . . would call an inalienable right, equally possessed by all. That was new." It was indeed.

The months between the autumn of 1775 and the spring of 1776 were dark ones for Jefferson. He and his wife, Martha, lost a year-and-a-half-old daughter in September, and soon after the little girl's death he was away for several months on political business. For some reason the mails were erratic, and Jefferson heard so little of his wife and eldest child, a girl also named Martha, that he became agitated, worried that perhaps tragedy had struck again. "The suspense under which I am is too terrible to be endured," Jefferson wrote his brother-in-law, anxious to know how his wife and daughter were. "If anything has happened for God's sake let me know." They were fine, but after his return his wife's health grew more precarious (biographers speculate that there was a miscarriage). He tried to comfort himself with details of life at Monticello, stocking deer on his property, drinking good Madeira, and tending to his stables. Then, on Sunday, March 31, 1776, Jefferson's mother died. Word of her collapse from a stroke was quickly followed by his own five-week bout with a headache so severe that he could not travel.

Serious business awaited in Philadelphia, however—the issue of independence, what John Adams called not only "the greatest question" ever considered in America, but perhaps the greatest that would ever "be decided among men." In May, Jefferson left behind Monticello's sorrows and consolations to journey to the Continental Congress, where he arrived, Adams recalled, with "a reputation for literature, science, and a happy talent of composition." Jefferson was also intensely curious

Franklin, Jefferson, and Adams drafting the Declaration of Independence. Written and debated in Philadelphia in 1776, the final document spoke of a "Creator," "Nature's God," "the supreme judge of the world," and "divine providence"—the God of America's public religion. *(© Bettmann/Corbis)*

about what was happening in Williamsburg, where George Mason, James Madison, Patrick Henry, and others were simultaneously debating Virginia's Declaration of Rights and the state's new constitution—documents with far-reaching language on religious liberty. From Philadelphia, Jefferson sent down his own draft of a state constitution, one that included this provision: "All persons shall have full and free liberty of religious opinion; nor shall any be compelled to frequent or maintain any religious institution." He soon settled into rented rooms on the second floor of a three-story brick house at Seventh and Market streets. There was a bedroom where he slept and a larger parlor where he could work; he had brought along a small portable writing desk of his own design.

He would need it. On Friday, June 7, 1776, Richard Henry Lee of Virginia moved for a declaration of independence. John Adams offered the second. A committee of five was appointed to draft a statement on behalf of the Congress: Adams of Massachusetts, Franklin of Pennsylvania, Roger Sherman of Connecticut, Robert Livingston of New York, and Jefferson of Virginia. Jefferson was asked to put pen to paper, and he adjourned to his quarters at Seventh and Market for much of the rest of the month. The document, he said, was "intended to be an expression of the American mind," and he thought of the writing as an act of synthesis of the "sentiments of the day, whether expressed in conversation, in letters, printed essays, or in the elementary books of public right, as Aristotle, Cicero, Locke, Sidney, &c." God was essential in the declaration Jefferson put together in his rented parlor, but the God he wrote of was in no explicit way the God of Abraham, much less God the Father of the Holy Trinity.

The opening lines ultimately approved by Congress on Thursday, July 4 were:

> When in the course of human events it becomes necessary for one people to dissolve the political bands which have connected them with another, and to assume among the powers of the earth the separate and equal station to which *the Laws of Nature and of Nature's God* [italics mine] entitle them, a decent respect to the opinions of mankind requires that they should declare the causes which impel them to the separation.
>
> We hold these truths to be self-evident; that all men are created equal; that they are *endowed by their Creator* [italics mine] with certain unalienable rights . . .

Jefferson had mentioned God only twice—as "Nature's God" and "Creator"—but in the editing process his colleagues added two more allusions to the Almighty. One noted that the Congress was *"appealing to the supreme judge of the world for the rectitude of our intentions* [italics mine]," and the other asserted the Founders' *"firm reliance on the protection of divine providence* [italics mine]" as they pledged "to each other our lives, our fortunes, and our sacred honor." But "the supreme judge of the world" and "divine providence" were no more specific to the God of the Bible than "Creator" and "Nature's God."

In Philadelphia, Jefferson's draft went to the Congress on Friday, June 28. Jefferson hated the ensuing debate. The author of the document would one day come to believe that it was sacred scripture and that his writing desk was a holy object. "Politics, as well as religion, has its superstitions," Jefferson said of the desk. "These gaining strength with time may one day give imaginary value to this relic, for its associations with the birth of the Great Charter of our Independence."

In real time, Jefferson tried to show no emotion as the delegates parsed his words, but Franklin—another writer—detected the truth. "During the debate I was sitting by Dr. Franklin, and he observed that I was writhing a little under the acrimonious criticisms of some of its parts," Jefferson recalled.

The God of the Declaration does not choose nations or peoples to favor, or others to curse. Americans, Jefferson had written, simply wanted to "assume among the powers of the earth *the separate and equal station* [italics mine] to which the laws of Nature and of Nature's God entitle them. . . ." Jefferson was not claiming that America was particularly exalted; he was seeking, as he writes, a "separate and equal station" among the family of nations.

The founding religion—at least in the Declaration—was based more on a religion of reason than of revelation. But it was still religion. From Bolingbroke to Jefferson, even the most cerebral of Deists were making a leap of faith when they ascribed the discernible attributes of nature to a divine author. "The Liberty of a People is the gift of God and Nature," wrote Algernon Sidney in his *Discourses concerning Government,* a work much on Jefferson's mind as he wrote in Philadelphia. Sidney's book, published in 1698, was a reply to a treatise by Sir Robert Filmer titled *Patriarcha, or the Natural Power of Kings.* Sidney's view of individual rights became the American view, but from a strictly intellectual point of view there is no reason to ascribe "the Liberty of a People" to "God *and* [italics mine] Nature" unless one wishes to involve the divine in the equation. In other words, a secular case can be made that experience and inferences from nature (defined as what we find before us in observable reality or can reasonably discern intellectually) suggest it is best for a society to consider all men equal and work from there. It is a matter of choice—a matter of faith—to bring God into the picture at all. The Founding Fathers made that choice, linking the cause of liberty to the idea of God while avoiding sectarian religious imagery or associations.

The God of the Declaration is a divine force that created the universe, endows all men with human rights, and is an actor in the drama of the world he made. Jefferson's God may not favor one nation over another, but his God, Jefferson said, "watches over our country's freedom and welfare." It was this God who became the God of America's public religion. "We are not a world ungoverned by the laws and the power of a superior agent," Jefferson said. "Our efforts are in his hand, and directed by it; and he will give them their effect in his own time." His God merited attention and prayer, for mysteriously, by grace, God could, Jefferson said, "enlighten the minds" of the people and guide the nation's leaders. As far as possible, religious debate belonged outside politics. Jefferson, for one, relished theology, but saw such arguments as private intellectual affairs, not fit subjects for government. "I write with freedom," he said to one correspondent, "because, while I claim a right to believe in one God, I yield as freely to others that of believing in three. Both religions, I find, make honest men, and that is the only point society has any right to look to."

While a final version of the Declaration was being prepared, Franklin, Jefferson, and Adams met again to discuss a seal and motto for the new nation. Meanwhile, John Hancock of Massachusetts, the Congress's presiding officer, signed the Declaration of Independence with only Charles Thomson of Pennsylvania as a witness.

Later in the summer, when the delegates gathered to sign their names to the document, they were bedeviled by horseflies, which came buzzing through the hall's open windows from a nearby stable. According to the nineteenth-century biographer James Parton, Jefferson liked to recall that the uninvited guests moved the ceremony along at a brisker than normal pace. There were, Parton reported, "swarms of flies" laying siege to "the silk-stockinged legs of honorable members. Handkerchief in hand, they lashed the flies with such vigor as they could command . . . but the annoyance became at length so extreme as to render them impatient of delay, and they made haste to bring the momentous business to a conclusion."

The flies were the least of the Americans' worries. All summer the delegates worked with the sure and certain knowledge that if they lost the war to George III, they would face capital punishment. There was nervous joking about the risk they were taking. For the rest of his life, Jefferson loved the story of how Benjamin Harrison, an enormously fat Virginian, once told the wispy Elbridge Gerry of Massachusetts, "Gerry, when the hanging comes, I shall have the advantage; you'll kick in the air half an hour after it is all over with me!"

They might hang for treason, but they trusted they were in the right. In Williamsburg, where Madison was representing Orange County in the Virginia state convention, the delegates immediately voted to suppress the standard Anglican prayer for the king and the royal family, directing congregations to ask God to guide "the magistrates of the commonwealth." In Philadelphia, Adams recalled, "The bells rung all day and almost all night. Even the chimers chimed." In New York, some soldiers of the Continental Army took part in a kind of riot as ecstatic colonists tore down a statue of King George III. General Washington was not amused. "The general hopes and trusts," Washington told his troops, "that every officer and man will endeavor so to live and act as becomes a Christian soldier, defending the dearest rights and liberties of his country."

PROTECTING CHURCH FROM STATE

Washington's use of phrases like "Christian soldier" have long fed a sense that the nation was much more explicitly sectarian in its early years. By most measures it is true that the colonies were full of religious people, and most of these were Christian. Washington laced his military orders with references to the Almighty, but usually in the same vein as Jefferson's God in the Declaration of Independence. "Let every face brighten and every heart expand with grateful joy and praise to the supreme disposer of all events who has granted us this signal success," Washington wrote after the American victory at Saratoga. "The chaplains of the army are to prepare short discourses suited to the joyful occasion to deliver to their several corps. . . ." The chaplains, of course, were Christian ministers, and Washington appears to have thought religion a useful tool in leading his troops and, later, his nation. Washington believed that every man was "accountable to God alone for his religious opinions" and "ought to be protected in worshipping the Deity according to the dictates of his own conscience." Bishop William White, who knew Washington in Philadelphia and in New York, said, "I do not believe that any degree of recollection will bring to my mind any fact which would prove General Washington to have been a believer in the Christian revelation. . . ." Respectful of both the predominant faith and of the rights of conscience, Washington's use of the word "Christian" and his reliance on chaplains was a pragmatic acknowledgment of the cultural reality of his day. The people who looked to him for leadership were largely Christian, and so he spoke to them and supported them in the language and rituals of their faith. This, too, was to become an element of public religion: a delicate blending of allusions to a broadly defined God and to the spirit of religious liberty with the symbolism of Christianity. (Shortly after taking the presidential oath in 1789, for example, Washington attended services at St. Paul's Chapel in New York.)

Still, the language of the Declaration marked an important shift in early American history. Prior to Philadelphia and the Revolution, most public professions of faith were Christian, whether the words came from Anglicans in Jamestown or Puritans in New England. In declaring the colonies' independence from Great Britain, though, the Founders were also making another declaration: that Americans respected the idea of God, understood the universe to be governed by moral and religious forces, and prayed for divine protection against the enemies of this world, but were not interested in establishing yet another earthly government with official ties to a state church.

Even the preachers of the day saw the wisdom of keeping Williams's garden and wilderness separate. The reasoning was rooted in both conviction and in pragmatism: church and state would be more powerful apart than they would have been if joined together. Separation did not mean the affairs of the Commonwealth, to use Locke's term, and the concerns of the faithful were to be hermetically sealed off one from the other. That was impossible on practical grounds, for the nature of a republic was dependent on the nature of its people, and if the people held religious values, there was no escaping the projection of those values into the republic. "From the beginning, politics and religion were in accord," Tocqueville said, "and they have not ceased to be so since."

Accord, though, is crucially different from attachment. "The magistrate is to govern the *state,* and Christ is to govern the *church,*" said Reverend Samuel Stillman in a 1779 sermon to the Supreme Court of Massachusetts. "The former will find business enough in the complex affairs of government to employ all his time and abilities. The latter is infinitely sufficient to manage his own kingdom without foreign aid." The religious knew, too, that to ally themselves with the powers of the temporal world might result in momentary gain, but only momentary. In Tocqueville's analysis, religion in America nurtures the moral life, which in turn creates basically virtuous citizens who are able to maintain a republic that is itself basically virtuous. "I do not know if all Americans have faith in their religion—for who can read to the bottom of hearts?—but I am sure that they believe it necessary to the maintenance of republican institutions. This opinion does not belong only to one class of citizens or to one party, but to the entire nation; one finds it in all ranks." It was for the benefit of the church, Tocqueville thought, that it, as an institution, should steer clear of direct political engagement. Interviewing clergyman after clergyman, he found that "all attributed the peaceful dominion that religion exercises in their country principally to the complete separation of church and state." Earthly influence was tempting but impermanent. "[In] allying itself with a political power," Tocqueville said, "religion increases its power over some and loses the hope of reigning over all."

Such was a particular risk in a democratic republic like the United States. "If the Americans, who change their head of state every four years, who every two years make a choice of new legislators and replace provincial administrators each year; if the Americans, who have delivered the political world to the attempts of innovators, had not placed their religion somewhere outside of that, what could it hold onto in the ebb and flow of human opinions?" Tocqueville asked. "In the midst of the parties' struggle, where would the respect be that is due it? What would become of its immortality when everything around it was perishing?" He was not speaking theoretically, but from experience and history. "In Europe, Christianity has permitted itself to be intimately united with the powers of the earth," he said. "Today these powers are falling and it is almost buried under their debris."

"GOD HAS FAVORED OUR UNDERTAKINGS"

For the Founders, religious freedom was not equivalent to a public life free of religion. Franklin and Jefferson played with the idea of America as a New Israel. In *Common Sense,* Thomas Paine referred to George III as the "hardened, sullen tempered Pharaoh of England." Preachers took up the theme. On Thursday, December 11, 1783, in the Third Presbyterian Church in Philadelphia, Reverend George Duffield spoke of the "Ameri-

AMERICAN GOSPEL | 81

can Zion" in a sermon about the American victory in the Revolution. To Duffield, Washington was Joshua; the king of France, Cyrus, the ruler who helped free Israel from Babylon.

The clergy were reflecting a widespread public conviction. When on the afternoon of July 4, 1776—one of the most eventful of days—the Continental Congress asked Franklin, Jefferson, and Adams to propose a seal, Franklin's vision was biblical, as was Jefferson's. Franklin wanted an image along these lines: "Moses standing on the shore, and extending his Hand over the Sea, thereby causing the same to overwhelm Pharaoh who is sitting in an open Chariot, a Crown on his Head and a Sword in his Hand. Rays from the Pillar of Fire in the Clouds reaching to Moses, to express that he acts by Command of the Deity. Motto, Rebellion to Tyrants is Obedience to God." According to the historian Derek H. Davis, Jefferson's design included a depiction of "the Children of Israel in the wilderness, led by a cloud by day and a pillar of fire by night."

The final seal would not take shape for another six years, and the ultimate emblem was simpler—the now familiar eagle. But in the work of the early committee, Franklin, Jefferson, and Adams suggested *E Pluribus Unum*—"out of many, one"—as the first of the country's three mottoes, words underscoring the pluralistic nature of the American experiment. And God did not disappear entirely. The reverse side of the final seal (it is the image to the left on the back of the dollar bill) depicts the "Eye of Providence" above an unfinished pyramid with the words of the second motto: *Annuit Coeptis*—"God (or Providence) has favored our undertakings." There is also a third Latin motto: *Novus Ordo Seclorum*—"a new order of the ages."

The *Annuit Coeptis* phrase comes from Virgil, not from the

Bible or from Christian tradition. Charles Thomson, the secretary of the Congress, is credited with the design of the seal. A classicist, Thomson apparently thought better of the initial idea of using one particular religious tradition, that of the God of Abraham, as the nation's, when he successfully proposed the final design to an approving Congress in 1782. By including the Eye and quoting Virgil's *Georgics* in speaking of God (and by skipping the Exodus imagery altogether), the Founders honored "the many signal interpositions of providence in favor of the American cause," Thomson wrote, without making Franklin's public religion overtly biblical. The God alluded to and prayed to could be interpreted however one liked. It was one of many shrewd compromises, and it was in keeping with the precedent Jefferson had set by invoking "Nature's God" in the Declaration.

From appointing chaplains, opening legislative sessions with prayer, and declaring days of fasting and thanksgiving, the Founders' public piety has fueled a conservative view that the "wall" between church and state was erected only recently, in the more secular twentieth century. There is a distinction, however, between professing conviction (which traditions like legislative prayer do) and using an established church to coerce not only belief but conformity with political and cultural mores. In America a kind of "wall" between church and state—albeit a low one—has always been there, or at least has been since the last state (Massachusetts) disestablished its church in 1833. Given that a large majority do believe in a transcendent power, and given that the evocations of a transcendent power grew organically from the habits and hearts of the early Americans, it would be as unsound to ban the use of the word "God" from all arenas of public life as it would be to require every American to

The "Eye of Providence" was included in the final great seal of the United States. Franklin and Jefferson had initially proposed designs evoking the Israelites' deliverance from Egypt, but in the end Congress chose a less sectarian symbol. (© Stefano Bianchetti/Corbis)

attend church services every Sunday. There are infinite shades of gray and nuance about when religious expression in public places is appropriate, and we will be forever engaged in sorting out those things. God did not give us easy answers; we should not expect the world he created to provide them, either.

One answer that has much to recommend it is simple conversation between those who disagree. Such a point may seem obvious or naive, but it has roots in the Founding. Jefferson was always uncomfortable with one aspect of public religion: the declaration of days of national prayer. He and Adams once clashed on the floor of Congress over such a proclamation, but the episode says as much about Jefferson's deft political skill as it does about religion and politics. Benjamin Rush recalled the scene to Adams long afterward: "You rose and defended the motion [for a day of prayer], and in reply to Mr. Jefferson's objections to Christianity you said you were sorry to hear such sentiments from a gentleman whom you so highly respected and with whom you agreed upon so many subjects, and that it was the only instance you had ever known of a man of sound sense and real genius that was an enemy to Christianity. You suspected, you told me, that you had offended him, but that he soon convinced you to the contrary by crossing the room and taking a seat in the chair next to you." Sometimes foes, sometimes friends, Jefferson and Adams shared much, and conversation in such matters generally trumps combat.

The hunger on the part of many later generations of evangelical believers to see the nation's founding as a Christian event from which we have fallen is understandable; the myth of sin and redemption is as old as Genesis and is the motive power of the story of Jesus' death and resurrection. The preponderance of historical evidence, however, suggests that the nation was not "Christian" but rather a place of people whose experience with religious violence and the burdens of established churches led them to view religious liberty as one of humankind's natural rights—a right as natural and as significant as those of thought and expression. Each individual freedom was an essential part of the whole; none could be—none should be—isolated or targeted or curbed.

PATRICK HENRY'S CRUSADE

The road to religious freedom was not easy. In 1777, after a meeting at the Rising Sun Tavern in Fredericksburg, Virginia,

Jefferson wrote a statute for religious freedom within the state. He drafted a bill, but it took almost a decade to become law. Opinion on both sides of the establishment question was strong—many believers saw no compelling reason to give up the flow of tax dollars—but the tide favored the more liberally minded.

The events leading to the passage of the Virginia statute came to a head in 1784, when John Blair Smith, a Presbyterian clergyman and president of the private Hampden-Sydney College in Prince Edward County, petitioned the state legislature for public dollars on behalf of the Hanover Presbytery. Madison and Jefferson joined forces. "The legitimate powers of government extend to such acts only as are injurious to others," Jefferson, who was in Paris, once said. "But it does me no injury for my neighbor to say there are twenty gods, or no God. It neither picks my pocket nor breaks my leg." Madison, on the scene in Virginia, noted, "Whilst we assert for ourselves a freedom to embrace, to profess and to observe the religion which we believe to be of divine origin, we cannot deny an equal freedom to those whose minds have not yet yielded to the evidence which has convinced us."

Patrick Henry, then a lawmaker, disagreed. (By this time Jefferson and Madison had fallen out with Henry and opposed him on other issues. "What we have to do I think is devoutly to pray for his death," Jefferson wrote Madison of Henry at one point.) Henry's current proposal was to pay for "teachers of the Christian religion" with public money; Henry was the bill's chief sponsor, but he was elected governor in November 1784, a move that took him out of the legislature. With this opening, Madison struck in 1785, writing a "Memorial and Remonstrance" on the subject of state support for churches. When religious and civil power were intertwined, Madison said, "What have been its fruits? More or less in all places, pride and indolence in the clergy, ignorance and servility in the laity; in both, superstition, bigotry and persecution."

At one point the pro-Christian forces in Virginia tried to put Jesus in the middle of Jefferson's bill by including the phrase "Jesus Christ, the holy author of our religion," but the sectarians were beaten back, Jefferson said, "by a great majority," and his bill became law in January 1786.

BEN FRANKLIN'S PLEA

The next year, 1787, brought the Constitutional Convention, a reaction to the failure of the government established by the post-Revolution Articles of Confederation. "Our affairs seem to lead to some crisis, something that I cannot foresee or conjecture," John Jay wrote George Washington. "I am uneasy and apprehensive, more so than during the war."

Physically unassuming, habitually dressed in black, James Madison was, the historian Charles Mee wrote, "a small man, no bigger, it was said, than half a piece of soap—frail, fearful to travel for what it might do to his health. Shy, pale, reticent, a bookish man, with a small high-pitched voice, awkward in debate, he always depended . . . on thorough preparation, and his baggage was stuffed with books and notes." There was much to carry about, for there was much to decide. The crush of business was heavy, and the question of religion—perhaps mercifully—was apparently discussed only briefly at the Convention. The reason was largely political: the document had to get through the stateratifying conventions before it could become what William Gladstone admiringly called "the most wonderful work ever struck off at a given time by the brain and purpose of man." And so the drafters at Philadelphia made their bets. "The framers believed that any constitutional provisions that might be interpreted by the states as a usurpation of the states' long-held jurisdiction over religion would spell certain defeat of the Constitution in the ratification process," wrote the historian Derek H. Davis. As it turned out, religion would still find its way into the thick of the ratification debate, partly because some Americans objected to the godlessness of what the scholars Isaac Kramnick and R. Laurence Moore call "the godless Constitution."

Despite the debates then and since, history has proven Madison and his colleagues largely right: in hindsight, a secular successor document to the Delcaration of Independence made a great deal of sense, and there is no arguing with the Constitution's durability. In a way, the making of the Constitution and the subtle political and personal forces at work on Madison and the others foreshadowed how statesmen would have to balance God and government for years to come. Given the choice to tack toward the secular or the sectarian, they chose to practice what they had been preaching about severing church from state while creating a culture in which religion would rise or fall on its own merits.

And yet even the most single-minded advocates of religious freedom were personally motivated and inspired by religious convictions. One man said this of the creation of the Constitution: "It is impossible for the man of pious reflection not to perceive in it a finger of that Almighty hand which has been so frequently and signally extended to our relief in the critical stages of the revolution." The author of these words? Not a clergyman nor an avowed churchman, but James Madison, in Federalist No. 37.

The elusive, shape-shifting Franklin was even more sentimental than Madison about God's hand in the framing of the new government. He did not mean to imply, he said, that "our General Convention was divinely inspired when it formed the new federal Constitution. . . . [Y]et I must own that I have so much faith in the general government of the world by Providence, that I can hardly conceive a transaction of such momentous importance to the welfare of millions now existing, and to exist in the posterity of a great nation, should be suffered to pass without being in some degree influenced, guided, and governed by that omnipotent, omnipresent, and beneficent Ruler, in whom all inferior Spirits live, and move, and have their Being." (Franklin borrowed the last phrase from Saint Paul.)

At a particularly fierce period of debate in late June 1787, when agreement seemed distant, Benjamin Franklin spoke up. In a passionate, intelligent, and measured tone, Franklin reminded the Convention of what God had done for America thus far—and, as the biographer Walter Isaacson noted, simultaneously reminded his divided colleagues that it was time to rise above politics and make a new country. "We indeed seem to feel our own want of political wisdom, since we have been running all about in search of it," Franklin said, adding:

In this situation of this assembly, groping, as it were, in the dark, to find political truth, and scarce able to distinguish it when presented to us, how has it happened, sir, that we have not hitherto once thought of humbly applying to the father of lights to illuminate our understandings? In the beginning of the contest with Britain, when we were sensible of danger, we had daily prayers in this room for the divine protection! Our prayers, sir, were heard; and they were graciously answered. All of us who were engaged in the struggle must have observed frequent instances of a superintending providence in our favor.

Drawing again on his life and long years of service, his knowledge of scripture and of history, Franklin went on:

I have lived, sir, a long time; and the longer I live, the more convincing proofs I see of this truth, *that God governs in the affairs of men!* And if a sparrow cannot fall to the ground without his notice, is it probable that an empire can rise without his aid? We have been assured, sir, in the sacred writings, that except the lord build the house, they labor in vain that build it. I firmly believe this; and I also believe that without his concurring aid, we shall succeed in this political building no better than the builders of Babel: we shall be divided by our little partial local interests, our projects will be confounded and we ourselves shall become a reproach and a byword down to future ages. And what is worse, mankind may hereafter, from this unfortunate instance, despair of establishing government by human wisdom, and leave it to chance, war and conquest.

His argument done, his case made, Franklin asked that a prayer be said each succeeding day. The delegates, however, were curiously unmoved. *"The Convention except three or four persons thought prayers* unnecessary!!" Franklin noted gloomily.

Power, not God, was at the center of the constitutional struggle—power between large and small states, between branches of government, between different visions of the rights of man. Jonas Phillips, a Jew, wrote the only petition the Constitutional Convention received on religious freedom, saying that "the Israelites will think themselves happy to live under a government where all religious societies are on an equal footing." In the end, unlike the Declaration, the Constitution failed to mention God, nor did it invoke any synonym for a divine power or author.

In two substantive ways, however, religion and religious freedom were protected and advanced in these summer weeks. First, the government issued the Northwest Ordinance of Friday, July 13, 1787, to set policy for the expanding country. "No person demeaning himself in a peaceable and orderly manner shall ever be molested on account of his mode of worship or religious sentiments in the said territory," the ordinance read, and, in a subsequent article, it said flatly: "Religion, morality, and knowledge being necessary to good government and the happiness of mankind, schools and the means of education shall forever be encouraged."

Meanwhile, the Constitution prohibited any religious requirement for federal officeholders, which meant the government could not force public officials to be believers of any sort or condition—an enormous stride in the cause of religious freedom, given the context of the times. The lieutenant governor of Connecticut, Oliver Wolcott, reflected: "Knowledge and liberty are so prevalent in this country that I do not believe that the United States would ever be disposed to establish one religious sect and lay all others under legal disabilities. But as we know not what may take place hereafter, and any such test would be exceedingly injurious to the rights of free citizens, I cannot think it altogether superfluous to add a clause which secures us from the possibility of such oppression."

In a speech after the Convention, Benjamin Rush reverted to the imagery of public religion. Rush said he believed that "the hand of God was employed in this work, as that God had divided the Red Sea to give a passage to the children of Israel" or had delivered "the ten commandments on Mount Sinai!" (Some, presumably from the camp that failed to rally to Franklin, thought Rush had gone too far and criticized him for the remarks, but Rush was working within what was now a well-established tradition.)

DIVIDE AND CONQUER

The Constitution went to a diverse nation for approval. "They are a mixture of English, Scotch, Irish, French, Dutch, Germans, and Swedes," wrote J. Hector St. John de Crèvecoeur. "From this promiscuous breed, that race now called Americans has arisen." In describing American religious habits, de Crèvecoeur observed in practice what Madison was writing about in theory. Catholics, Lutherans, Deists, Calvinists, and Quakers were all living together. "Thus all sects are mixed, as well as all nations; thus religious indifference is imperceptibly disseminated from one end of the continent to the other, which is at present one of the strongest characteristics of the Americans," de Crèvecoeur wrote.

What he called indifference, however, could also be seen as

mutual forbearance and respect among the panoply of peoples consumed with the task of settling a continent. "Persecution, religious pride, the love of contradiction, are the food of what the world commonly calls religion," de Crèvecoeur wrote. "These motives have ceased here; zeal in Europe is confined; here it evaporates in the great distance it has to travel; there it is a grain of powder inclosed; here it burns away in the open air and consumes without effect."

James Madison was counting on just that. In Federalist No. 10, published on Thursday, November 22, 1787, he made the critical distinction between a democracy and a republic—a distinction that would protect the rights and freedoms Americans think of as hallmarks of American democracy. In a republic, the business of government is delegated to a few representatives of a people spread out over a large space. These two characteristics—delegated power and geographic scope—stood the best chance, Madison wrote, of curbing the excesses of momentary passions and checking the interests of motivated factions. In Madison's view, the American Constitution offered a "republican remedy" for most of the problems likely to afflict a growing national enterprise like the United States. The Senate would balance the House; the presidency the Congress; the judiciary the legislative and executive branches; the states the federal establishment.

In making his case for curbing the power of a handful to impose its will on the rest of the nation, Madison turned first to something he knew was close to the hearts of his readers: religion. "A religious sect may degenerate into a political faction in a part of the confederacy," Madison wrote, "but the variety of sects dispersed over the entire face of it must secure the national councils against any danger from that source." The diversity of interests, and of checks and balances, Madison was saying, would keep a particular extreme cause from overwhelming the general good. Such was the genius of the Republic. As much noise as a given faction or party (or church) might make over an issue, that faction or party (or church) was constrained by the Constitution from carrying the day unless it could convince enormous numbers of people in different states and at different levels of government of the wisdom of its cause. To use Madison's imagery, a brush fire in one part of the Union had little chance of burning out of control nationally without widespread support—which would mean the brush fire was not a brush fire but the will of a great number of people.

Madison opened his argument with religion, but moved quickly to other issues as well. "A rage for paper money, for an abolition of debts, for an equal division of property, or for any other improper or wicked project will be less apt to pervade the whole body of the union than a particular member of it; in the same proportion as such a malady is more likely to taint a particular county or district, than an entire state." A shrewd insight into human nature, and into politics. Religion remained an abiding concern of Madison's, though, and in an October 1787 letter to Jefferson Madison wrote: "When indeed religion is kindled into enthusiasm, its force, like that of other passions, is increased by the sympathy of the multitude. But enthusiasm is only a temporary state of religion, and whilst it lasts will hardly be seen with pleasure at the helm." In a way, Madison, and America, needed de Crèvecoeur to be right: the more churches there were, the less chance there was of any one faith coming to play too large a role in politics. "*Divide et impera* [divide and conquer], the reprobated axiom of tyranny," Madison wrote Jefferson, "is, under certain qualifications, the only policy by which a republic can be administered on just principles." Like any other interest, the religious interest was part of the whole, a whole that respected it but did not favor it. "If men were angels, no government would be necessary," Madison wrote in Federalist No. 51 on Wednesday, February 6, 1788. "If angels were to govern men, neither external nor internal controls on government would be necessary." As things are, neither men nor government are intrinsically angelic, and thus a republic is necessary to give us at least a chance of working our way through the shadows and ambitions of the world toward the right. "Justice is the end of government," Madison said. "It is the end of civil society."

The climate around ratification was one of high drama and deep seriousness. The men who were to decide whether to accept the work of Philadelphia were thoughtful and thorough. There were, of course, partisan fights and newspaper skirmishes—*The Federalist Papers* are a collection of journalistic columns written in defense of the Constitution—but on the whole, the debates were conducted with a sense of grace and a spirit of generosity. "The constitution proposed to your acceptance is designed not for yourselves alone, but for generations yet unborn," Thomas Greenleaf, writing as "Brutus," said in the *New York Journal* on Thursday, November 1, 1787. On Wednesday, January 9, 1788, the *Massachusetts Sentinel* greeted an expected vote by its convention with a plea at once religious and patriotic: "May the GREAT IDEA fill the mind of every member of this honourable body that Heaven on this auspicious occasion favours America. . . ."

Even skeptics leavened their doubts with hope and pragmatism. "Whether this is the best possible system of government, I will not pretend to say," Francis Hopkinson wrote Jefferson in July 1788. "Time must determine; but I am well persuaded that without an efficient federal government, the states must in a very short time sink into contempt & the most dangerous confusion." Benjamin Gale, an anti-Federalist, said the Constitution was "an artful, dark, mysterious, complex, expensive form of government." He thought it would be ratified, though, and controlling the president would require the "shedding of *Blood.*" Still, most believed the Constitution worth the gamble. "While some have boasted it as a work from Heaven, others have given it a less righteous origin and charged it to the great old devil," Gouverneur Morris wrote a friend in February 1788. ". . . I have many reasons to believe that it was the work of plain honest men and such I think it will appear. Faulty it must be, for what is perfect?"

A WAR ON CHRISTIAN OATHS

Not everyone was so sanguine. There were religious fears that the document was too secular. In Connecticut, the statesman William Williams thought the preamble should be rewritten to acknowledge the nation's dependence on the Almighty, and proposed this language:

> *We the people of the United States, in a firm belief of the being and perfections of the one living and true God, the creator and supreme Governor of the World, in His universal providence and the authority of His laws: that He*

will require of all moral agents an account of their con-
duct, that all rightful powers among men are ordained of,
and mediately derived from God, therefore in a depen-
dence on His blessing and acknowledgement of His effi-
cient protection in establishing our Independence, whereby
it is become necessary to agree upon and settle a Constitu-
tion of federal government for ourselves, and in order to
form a more perfect union, etc., as it is expressed in the
present introduction, do ordain, etc.

Officeholders, Williams believed, should be compelled to
ascribe to those words, thus creating a religious test. Williams's
position drew fire from Oliver Ellsworth, who styled himself
"Landholder" in the *Connecticut Courant* on Monday, December 17, 1787. To force a civil or military officer to make his communion or go to church is to abridge his rights, he argued. "A
test in favor of any one denomination of Christians would be to
the last degree absurd in the United States," Ellsworth wrote.
"If it were in favor of either Congregationalists, Presbyterians,
Episcopalians, Baptists, or Quakers, it would incapacitate more
than three-fourths of the American citizens for any public office. . . ."

William Williams thought "the Federal Constitution has had
so calm, dispassionate, and rational a discussion, and so happy
an issue" that he claimed to be surprised when he read
Ellsworth's criticism. Writing in the *American Mercury* on
Monday, February 11, 1788, Williams defended himself by recounting what had happened in the state convention. If a man
could not swear allegiance to Christianity, Williams said, then
he should not be in government. Even more important to him,

he claimed, was that the new preamble "be the voice of the great body of the people and an acknowledgement proper and highly becoming them to express on this great and only occasion, and, according to the course of Providence, one means of obtaining blessings from the Most High." It had been a lonely stand in the state convention. Seeing that it was "so difficult and dubious to get it inserted," Williams said, he had dropped his objection. "I thought it was my duty to make the observations in this behalf, which I did, and to bear my testimony for God," he wrote, arguing the question of a Christian oath for federal officials was a legitimate thing to raise in debate over ratification. In closing, Williams said he would no longer reply to missives signed by pseudonyms like "Landholder."

Williams's foes, though, were having too much fun at this point to let the matter die. They were almost gleeful in their attacks. Writing as "Elihu" a week later, a correspondent seized on Williams's thought that God required "an acknowledgement proper" in the Constitution. "A low mind may imagine that God, like a foolish old man, will think himself slighted and dishonored if he is not complimented with a seat or a prologue of recognition in the Constitution, but those great philosophers who formed the Constitution had a higher idea of the perfection of that INFINITE MIND which governs all worlds than to suppose they could add to his honor or glory, or that He would be pleased with such low familiarity or vulgar flattery."

Elihu made an effective countercase. "The most shining part, the most brilliant circumstance in honor of the framers of the Constitution, is their avoiding all appearance of craft, declining to dazzle even the superstitious by a hint about grace ghostly knowledge," he said. "They come to us in the plain la

guage of common sense and propose to our understanding a system of government as the invention of mere human wisdom; no deity comes down to dictate it, not even a God appears in a dream to propose any part of it." According to the Declaration of Independence, the rights being protected by the creation of the constitutional system came from God. In a way, the entire exercise was an act of faith.

Religious freedom was also said to be good for both democracy and business. Writing to reassure people in the western counties of Pennsylvania, Tench Coxe argued that both the churchly and the political realms would flourish in the fresh air of liberty—and freedom, he argued, would lead to economic progress. "The liberality and virtue of America in establishing perfect equality and freedom among all religious denominations and societies, will no doubt produce to us a great reward, for when news of it shall reach the oppressed dissenters from the establishment churches of Britain, Ireland, Holland, Germany, France, Spain, and Italy, and they shall find it encourages both protestants and catholics, they will at once cry out, America is the '*land of promise.*'"

"WE HAVE BECOME A NATION"

Friday, July 4, 1788, was a beautiful day in Philadelphia. Benjamin Rush appreciatively noted the "pleasant and cooling breeze," and the clear sky full of stars after darkness fell. The festivities to celebrate the Constitution's ratification were cheerful and thronged, and Rush was ecstatic about the symbolism of a new day in religious affairs. "The Clergy formed a very agreeable part of the Procession—They manifested, by their attendance, their sense of the connection between religion and good

government," Rush said. There were seventeen in all, and they marched in sets, arm in arm. "Pains were taken to connect ministers of the most dissimilar religious principles together, thereby to show the influence of a free government in promoting Christian charity," Rush said. "The Rabbi of the Jews [Jacob Raphael Cohen of Mikve Israel], locked in the arms of two ministers of the gospel, was a most delightful sight. There could not have been a more happy emblem contrived of that section of the new constitution which opens all its power and offices alike not only to every sect of Christians, but to worthy men of every religion."

Rush heard many remark: "Heaven was on the federal side of the question." He added his own musings: "I do not believe that the Constitution was the offspring of inspiration, but I am as perfectly satisfied that the union of the states, in its form and adoption, is as much the work of divine providence as any of the miracles recorded in the old and new testament were the effects of a divine power. 'Tis done! We have become a nation."

Rush was not the only one to read such significance into the day. "Scarcely any who composed a part of the procession made a more conspicuous figure than the clergy, who displayed a complete triumph over religious prejudices," another observer said. "The Jew joined the Christian; the Episcopalian the Presbyterian . . . all walked arm in arm, exhibiting a proof of worldly affection, and testifying to their approbation of the new constitution."

THE BILL OF RIGHTS

Many saw the hand of God in the Constitution's construction and adoption. ". . . I am convinced this is the Lord's doing, and it is marvelous in our eyes," said "a Connecticut farmer" in the *Connecticut Courant* on Monday, January 28, 1788. Perhaps, but "Z," in the *Independent Chronicle* in Massachusetts, fretted about the lack of specified liberties. "If the rights of conscience, for instance, are not sacredly reserved to the people, what security will there be, in case the government should have in their heads a predilection for any one sect in religion? What will hinder the civil power from erecting a national system of religion, and committing the law to a set of lordly priests . . . ?"

The Bill of Rights was the answer to such concerns. After the ratification of the Constitution in 1789, the framers returned to work to formulate a list of more specific rights. The final Senate version of the religion clause of the First Amendment read: "Congress shall make no law establishing articles of faith or a mode of worship, or prohibiting the free exercise of religion." In a conference between the Senate and the House, lawmakers agreed to a broader clause, which is the one that ultimately passed: "Congress shall make no law respecting an establishment of religion, nor prohibiting the free exercise thereof." The difference is important: the Senate version may have left the door open to the government's playing a larger role in religious affairs so long as it could successfully argue it was not meddling specifically with "articles of faith" or "modes of worship."

The time was approaching when Washington would have to decide whether to accept the presidency. Writing him in 1788, John Armstrong, Sr., an elderly correspondent, advised Washington to think of the people's voice as the Lord's. Of the rightness of the choice, Armstrong said, "there need be little hesitation amongst the citizens, but not so with you; persuaded as I am, it will cost you much anxious thought—nevertheless if the call of God is manifested to you in a plenary or unanimous call of the people, I hope that will obviate every objection. . . ." It did. Washington left Mount Vernon on Thursday, April 16, 1789, and made his way to New York, the new capital.

The Founders were aware that they were designing a government for a pluralistic nation—a country in which people of different faiths had to live together. When Washington was inaugurated in New York on Thursday, April 30, 1789, Gershom Seixas, of Shearith Israel, was listed among the city's clergy (there were fourteen ministers in New York at the time)—a sign of respect. In an earlier message to Governor George Clinton, the synagogue had subtly reminded the new country's leadership that "though the Society we belong to is but small, when compared with other religious societies, yet, we flatter ourselves that none has manifested a more zealous attachment . . . in the late war with Great Britain . . . and we now look forward with pleasure to the happy days we expect to enjoy under a Constitution wisely framed to preserve the inestimable blessings of civil and religious liberty." The next year, Washington wrote his landmark letter to the Hebrew Congregation of Newport, Rhode Island. "May the children of the stock of Abraham, who dwell in this land continue to merit and enjoy the good will of the other inhabitants;—while every one shall sit in safety under his own vine and fig tree and there shall be none to make him afraid."

The allusion to the vine and fig tree comes from the fourth chapter of the Book of Micah, in a prophetic vision of order and mercy and justice. A remarkable document—gracious, ecumenical, democratic. To read the entire biblical passage Washington had in mind suggests the scope of the Founders' commitment to religious liberty:

But in the last days it shall come to pass, that the mountain of the house of the Lord shall be established in the top of the mountains, and it shall be exalted above the hills; and people shall flow unto it.

And many nations shall come, and say, Come, and let us go up to the mountain of the Lord, and to the house of the God of Jacob; and he will teach us of his ways, and we will walk in his paths: for the law shall go forth of Zion, and the word of the Lord from Jerusalem.

And he shall judge among many people, and rebuke strong nations afar off; and they shall beat their swords into plowshares, and their spears into pruning hooks: nation shall not lift up a sword against nation, neither shall they learn war any more.

But they shall sit every man under his vine and under his fig tree; and none shall make them afraid: for the mouth of the Lord of hosts hath spoken it.

For all people will walk every one in the name of his god, and we will walk in the name of the Lord our God for ever and ever.

The image of every man being free from fear, comforted by the shade of his own conscience, is vivid and enduring, and places the ideal and the reality of liberty and mutual understanding at the heart of the American tradition from the first year of the first presidency.

The times in which Washington governed the young nation were intellectually rich and even thrilling; Wordsworth's lines commemorating the French Revolution—"Bliss was it in that dawn to be alive,/But to be young was very heaven!"—resonate more than two centuries later because they strike us as both romantic and true. The old ways of life were giving way, and the people, not princes or prelates, were taking control of the destinies of nations. "We have it in our power to begin the world over again," Thomas Paine wrote in *Common Sense*. "A situation similar to the present has not happened since the days of Noah until now."

A TREATY WITH ISLAM

The nation's religious identity—or codified lack thereof—played a role in foreign policy. In the waters off Tripoli, pirates were making sport of American shipping near the Barbary Coast in the 1790s. Toward the end of his second term, Washington sent Joel Barlow, the diplomat-poet, to Tripoli to settle matters, and the resulting treaty, finished after Washington left office, bought a few years of peace. An interesting element of this long-ago document lies in Article 11, which reads: "As the government of the United States of America is not in any sense founded on the Christian Religion;—as it has in itself no character of enmity against the laws, religion or tranquility of Musselmen,—and as the said States never have entered into any war or act of hostility against any Mehomitan nation, it is declared by the parties that no pretext arising from religious opinions shall ever produce an interruption of harmony existing between the two countries."

The Senate ratified the treaty at the recommendation of President John Adams. There is no record of any debate about Article 11, one that defines the federal government as secular, not religious, and which most likely has roots in the American awareness of the Crusades and the ever-present threat that religious fervor in foreign lands could fuel attacks on America. By declaring the United States a secular nation, the president, the secretary of state, and the Senate—through two administrations, for negotiations had only begun under Washington—were doing what the Founders had thus far done best in the construction of the Constitution and the Bill of Rights: they were seeking to learn from, and thus avoid, the mistakes of the past. Violence between Christian monarchs and Islamic powers in the Holy Land had been a recurring feature of life for five hundred years, and the rise of seafaring technology meant that Americans, Europeans, and Islamic peoples would be increasingly encountering one another as different regions of the world were linked by a growing network of global commerce—hence the problem of Muslim piracy against American shipping far from American shores.

Using religion for partisan political ends—to divide voters by painting the opposing candidate as immoral or unfaithful—became part of American political life even before the nineteenth century was a year old. In the election of 1800, when Jefferson challenged Adams, Jefferson's foes, mostly New England Federalists, used his unorthodox religious views against him: "GOD—AND A RELIGIOUS PRESIDENT or . . . JEFFERSON—AND NO GOD," one newspaper said. Yet Jefferson managed to defeat Adams.

On the first day of 1802, Jefferson answered a letter from the Danbury Baptist Association in Connecticut with an eye toward reassuring believers that he was no enemy of God or God's people. "Believing with you that religion is a matter which lies solely between Man & his God . . . ," Jefferson said,

"I contemplate with sovereign reverence that act of the whole American people which declared that *their* legislature should make no law respecting an establishment of religion, or prohibiting the free exercise thereof, thus building a wall of separation between Church & State."

The metaphor of the wall between church and state would not take a central place in the American political or legal culture for another century and a half. Jefferson unabashedly called on God for guidance and blessing in difficult times. In his second inaugural address, he charted the relationship between God and America in some detail, and asked God to begin a new chapter in that story: "I shall need, too, the favor of that Being in whose hands we are, who led our forefathers, as Israel of old, from their native land, and planted them in a country flowing with all the necessaries and comforts of life. . . ."

INTUITIVE ETHICS

The American mind was not so enlightened that it was able to rise above perpetuating and protecting the evil of slavery, the chief moral compromise of the Founding era—a compromise that would lead to civil war in less than a century. Whatever his faults—slaveholding among them—Patrick Henry saw the paradox. "It is not a little surprising that Christianity, whose chief excellence consists in softening the human heart, in cherishing & improving its finer feelings, should encourage a practice so totally repugnant to the first impression of right & wrong," he said.

Henry was talking about intuitive ethics—that men have the innate capacity to assess the justice of something whether they act in accordance with that assessment or not. Some things simply strike us as right, and some as wrong. Many of the Founding Fathers chose to understand the moral sense as divinely inspired and implanted; others, such as Voltaire or the Paine of *The Age of Reason,* argued that civility and generosity flourished in spite of religious institutions or instruction. Neither argument is ironclad. The Founders could not prove that God endowed us with a sense of right and wrong in the way they might be able to prove, for instance, that fire is hot. Coming to the debate so long after the sundry religions of the world had dominated human affairs, Voltaire and Paine had no convincing way to make the case that religion had not contributed to the development of ethics. Do men act kindly toward one another because of beliefs in the gods, or God; or do they do so naturally, aware only of other men and the immediate sensory universe? It is an unanswerable question; religion has been with us so long that it is an element in the air we breathe.

How, then, could so many avowedly religious people choose to live in a country that allowed slavery? Why did the still, small voice of conscience fail to speak to more Americans sooner? One test for rendering moral judgment on the past with the hindsight afforded by history (as Arthur Schlesinger, Jr., has said, "Righteousness is easy, also cheap, in retrospect") is whether contemporary voices were making the case for doing the right thing. In the case of slavery, they were indeed. "Shall we hold the sword in one hand to defend our just rights as men; and grasp chains with the other to enslave the inhabitants of Africa?" asked Reverend Samuel Stillman in 1779. "Forbid it heaven!—Forbid it all the freeborn sons of this western world!" The Quakers were early abolitionists; in 1807 the British banned the transatlantic slave trade, and in 1833 abolished slavery in Britain and all her colonies. In America, however, the voices were not convincing enough—not yet.

THE QUEST FOR EQUALITY

At the Shearith Israel synagogue, Gershom Seixas was apparently less than enthusiastic about the War of 1812. But in remarks to his congregation when asked to raise money to help the conflict's American victims, he spoke of the duties of democracy in the language of covenant: duly elected leaders who make decisions through the mechanics of government, with its checks and balances, deserve public support despite the reservations of the religious. No one is above the law, even those who may invoke the name of God in disagreeing with a public action. "To the citizens at large it is sufficient for us to know that our rulers are chosen to be the judges on all affairs concerning the welfare of their constituents," Seixas said. "They, the ruling powers, have declared war, and it is our bounden duty to act as true and faithful citizens, to support and preserve the honor, dignity, and the independence of the United States of America, that they may bear equal rank among the nations of the earth." In other words, even if one's faith led to the level of a conscientious objection—in which case American tradition finds ways in times of war for the objectors to serve in nonviolent spheres of the national effort—the state gives the opinion of the religious no special standing. The importance of such a custom lies in the freedom it gives officials of the government to conduct the affairs of the nation without having to seek the sanction of any church. Religious values may influence the conduct of the government, just as other values may, and leaders frequently seek support or informal blessing from religious figures before or after embarking on a possibly controversial course. But in the end, the decision is the government's to make—which is precisely what the Founders wanted.

Seixas's rise in the clerical and academic circles of New York in the first decade and a half of the nineteenth century—he became a trustee of Columbia, which struck a medal in his honor at his death—was a sign that there was a good chance the tolerant rhetoric of the Revolutionary era would become reality, at least for the handful of Jews in the country. Still, obstacles remained. Though the Constitution specifically banned religious tests in the federal sphere, Christian oaths were in effect in some state constitutions, oaths that any officeholder had to take in order to serve.

North Carolina was an early field of battle for the clash between revolutionary rhetoric and political and cultural reality. Jacob Henry, a Jew, was elected to the state house in 1808 but he was blocked the following year because the law required him to be a Protestant and to accept the divine authority of the Old and New Testaments. A standoff ensued, with Christian lawmakers refusing to seat him. "Governments only concern the actions and conduct of man, and not his speculative notions," Henry told the legislature. "Who among us feels himself so exalted above his fellows as to have a right to dictate to them any mode of belief? Will you bind the conscience in chains, and fasten conviction upon the mind in spite of the conclusions of reason and of those ties and habitudes which are blended with every pulsation of the heart?"

It was an appeal to common sense, for many feel just that exalted, and always have. His next point was stronger and could resonate with even the most convinced believer: "Will you drive from your shores and from the shelter of your constitution all who do not lay their oblations on the same altar, observe the same ritual, and subscribe to the same dogmas? If so, which among the various sects into which we are divided shall be the favored one?" In closing, Henry reached into Christian tradition to make the case for equal rights for Jewish Americans, saying that no one could "subscribe more sincerely than myself to the maxim, 'whatever ye would that men should do unto you do ye so even unto them, for such is the law and the prophets.' " The words were Jesus', from Matthew.

Such fights worked around the country. Jonathan Sarna noted that by 1840, twenty-one of the nation's twenty-six states accorded Jews "formal political equality," and the others were not far behind.

POLITICS AND PLAGUES

The age of Andrew Jackson—he served as president from 1829 to 1837—was a time of religious revival and growing nationalism. On July 4, 1827—a midsummer Wednesday—one of the leading Protestant clergymen of the day, Ezra Stiles Ely, preached a controversial sermon in Philadelphia, one which was soon published and spread around the country. Its title could not have been clearer: "The Duty of Christian Freemen to Elect Christian Rulers." Arguing for the formation of a "Christian party in politics," Ely, who was supporting Jackson in the 1828 presidential election, said, "Every ruler should be an avowed and sincere friend of Christianity. He should know and believe the doctrines of our holy religion, and act in conformity to its precepts. . . ." Reading the sermon, Jackson sensed danger in Ely's extreme words. There was a time for the state and a time for the church—but both at once meant trouble. In a deft reply, Jackson wrote: "All true Christians love each other, and while here below ought to harmonize; for all must unite in the realms above." Having given faith its due, he acknowledged the centrality of individual freedom in religious matters. "Amongst the greatest blessings secured to us under our Constitution," Jackson told Ely, "is the liberty of worshipping God as our conscience dictates."

When Jackson was asked to officially join the Presbyterian Church in his years in public life, he declined; he did not want his opponents to be able to say he was using religion to get ahead in politics. Such a stance feels quaint now, but he was being guided by the Founders' example. Though Jackson himself was careful to keep faith and government in separate spheres, it was not easy. (This was also the era in which Joseph Smith founded the Church of Jesus Christ of Latter-day Saints, the Mormon faith.)

God became an issue of contention during the 1832 congressional session as Jackson and Henry Clay, who was challenging the president for reelection in November, squared off over church and state amid a deadly plague. The trouble had begun in Quebec, when a ship arrived from Europe in June 1832. Forty-two of the passengers were dead or dying from cholera, a communicable illness caused by the bacterium *Vibrio cholerae*, which strikes the intestines, leading to diarrhea, vomiting, and, in the worst cases, death through dehydration. Spread through food and water, cholera hit New York with such ferocity that the mayor canceled the Fourth of July parade; 2,565 people in the city soon died. In June, Clay proposed that the president declare a day of prayer and fasting to seek divine relief from the outbreak.

The resolution was good politics—people in the afflicted states might be grateful, and religious believers who were undecided in the presidential race could see Clay's initiative as evidence of a good soul who shared the essence of their faith. A woman styling herself as "a Daughter of Massachusetts" wrote Clay "to offer you my sincere acknowledgement for your recent noble and spirited avowal of your belief of the Christian religion, and your reverence for its precepts; and I can assure you, Sir, that a large majority of the daughters of the descendants of the Pilgrims unite with me in the same sentiment."

As he had done when Ely made the case for the election of "Christian Rulers," though, Jackson was reluctant to mix God and government so overtly. Reading the establishment clause of the First Amendment in its strictest sense, Jackson said he too believed in "the efficacy of prayer," but felt that the president of the United States should "decline the appointment of any period or mode" of religious activity. (So had Jefferson.) "I could not do otherwise without transcending those limits which are prescribed by the Constitution for the President," Jackson had said earlier in June, "and without feeling that I might in some degree disturb the security which religion now enjoys in this country in its complete separation from the political concerns of the General Government."

Let the people, or even the states, tend to matters of faith. "It is the province of the pulpits and the state governments to recommend the mode by which the people may best attest their reliance on the protecting arm of the almighty in times of great public distress," Jackson said. "Whether the apprehension that cholera will visit our land furnishes a proper occasion for their solemn notice, I must therefore leave to their own consideration." Jackson's reluctance to carry the presidency into the religious realm reflected the view that the church risked corruption by contact with the government—that believers should avoid the entanglements of a sinful world. Other evangelical believers, of course, saw the work of the faithful differently, holding that it was the duty of the Christian to put the Gospel into action. Jackson was more broad-minded, and ecumenical, in his vision of God and man. "I am no sectarian, though a lover of the Christian religion," he said while in the White House. "I do not believe that any who shall be so fortunate as to be received to heaven through the atonement of our blessed Savior will be asked whether they belonged to the Presbyterian, the Methodist, the Episcopalian, the Baptist, or the Roman Catholic [faiths]. All Christians are brethren, and all true Christians know they are such *because they love one another.* A true Christian *loves all,* immaterial to what sect or church he may belong." Jackson meant what he said, and he was prepared to veto Clay's day-of-prayer-and-fasting bill if it reached the White House. Before that could happen, the resolution was tabled in the House.

What could not be tabled was the growing storm over slavery. When Jackson put down a potential rebellion by South Carolina over tariffs—the tax issue was really a stand-in for slavery, for the agrarian South was worried that rising federal power would one day give the abolitionists their way—he saw what was coming. The South Carolinians, led by John C. Calhoun, had tried to press the doctrine of nullification, arguing that a state had a right to suspend the enforcement of a federal law within its borders if it believed the law unconstitutional. Jackson saw the campaign as the beginning of disunion and fought it, but he knew he had won only a battle, not the war. "The nullifiers in the South intend to blow up a storm on the subject of the slave question," Jackson wrote a friend. "This ought to be met, for be assured these men would do any act to destroy the union and form a southern confederacy bounded, north, by the Potomac river." The letter was dated Tuesday, April 9, 1833. Twenty-eight Aprils later, troops loyal to the newly formed Confederate States of America fired on Fort Sumter in Charleston Harbor.

III. LET US DIE TO MAKE MEN FREE

THE CIVIL WAR, LINCOLN, AND DARWIN

*I now leave, not knowing when, or whether ever, I may
return, with a task before me greater than that which
rested upon Washington. Without the assistance of that
Divine Being who ever attended him, I cannot succeed.
With that assistance I cannot fail.*

—ABRAHAM LINCOLN, FAREWELL ADDRESS AT
SPRINGFIELD, ILLINOIS, FEBRUARY 11, 1861

*There is a serene Providence which rules the fate of
nations. . . . It makes its own instruments, creates the
man for the time, trains him in poverty, inspires his
genius, and arms him for his task.*

—RALPH WALDO EMERSON,
"ORATION ON THE DEATH OF LINCOLN," APRIL 19, 1865

*A*braham Lincoln had been president for little more than a
month when the Civil War broke out. In a February 1861 stop at
Independence Hall in Philadelphia en route to Washington to
take office, he had linked the present crisis to the deliberations
over Jefferson's handiwork in that long-ago summer of 1776. "I
have never had a feeling politically that did not spring from the

sentiments embodied in the Declaration of Independence," he said to a cheering crowd. "I have often inquired of myself, what great principle or idea it was that kept this Confederacy so long together. It was not the mere matter of the separation of the colonies from the mother land; but something in that Declaration giving liberty, not alone to the people of this country, but hope to the world for all future time." Soaking up the applause— Lincoln had polled less than 50 percent of the vote and there seemed little hope of averting war—he ruminated on the rights "Nature's God" had given a country now facing its greatest test. The Declaration's significance, he said, lay in the "promise that in due time the weights should be lifted from the shoulders of all men, and that *all* should have an equal chance." Though he had been making similar remarks at several stops on his journey, he used a familiar orator's device and claimed to have been unprepared to speak—a ploy that made one seem all the more spontaneously eloquent—and concluded, "but I have said nothing but what I am willing to live by, and, in the pleasure of Almighty God, die by." Two weeks later, in his inaugural address of March 4, 1861, Lincoln begged the nation for forbearance, asking for "intelligence, patriotism, Christianity, and a firm reliance on Him, who has never yet forsaken this favored land."

In another inaugural address, this one delivered in Montgomery, Alabama, in February, Confederate President Jefferson Davis had called on the same Lord for different purposes. "Reverently let us invoke the God of our Fathers to guide and protect us in our efforts," Davis said, beseeching the Almighty for aid in tearing apart what Lincoln had called "this favored land." And so both sides marched forth, each convinced God was on its side. But He could not be—could He?

It was a question that haunted Lincoln throughout the war. "The will of God prevails," he wrote in a note to himself during the conflict, adding a dirgelike succession of sentences: "In great contests each party claims to act in accordance with the will of God. Both <u>may</u> be, and one <u>must</u> be wrong. God can not be <u>for</u>, and <u>against</u> the same thing at the same time. . . . By his mere quiet power on the minds of the now contestants, He could have either <u>saved</u> or <u>destroyed</u> the Union without a human contest. Yet the contest began. And having begun He could give the final victory to either side any day. Yet the contest proceeds."

The God Lincoln wrote of was the God of the Founders, a God engaged in the fits and starts of American history. He was no amorphous source of intelligence, no Platonic form, but an active, involved, and consummately mysterious Lord whose will was at work in the world. The fate of man, Lincoln mused, was to be at God's mercy, and to hope to live in such a way that would find favor with the Almighty.

A PROMISE KEPT

On Monday, September 22, 1862, in a meeting of his Cabinet on the second floor of the White House, Lincoln seemed a bit embarrassed. He was trying to explain the timing of the Emancipation Proclamation, but was not sure anyone else would understand. It had been a vicious and frightening military season; the previous Wednesday, at Antietam, in Maryland, would go down in history as the bloodiest day of the war. But the Union had won the battle, stopping the Confederate advance. Now, facing his Cabinet, Lincoln told them what he was going to do—and why. According to Treasury Secretary Salmon P. Chase's diary, Lincoln said: "When the Rebel Army was at Frederick, I determined, as soon as it should be driven out of Maryland, to issue a Proclamation of Emancipation. . . . I said nothing to anyone, but I made a promise to myself, and (hesitating a little) to my Maker."

He had given his word to God, Lincoln said, and that was that. "The Rebel Army is now driven out, and I am going to fulfill that promise." Chase's account is supported by others: President Lincoln chose to emancipate the slaves at that particular moment because, he said, he had made a deal with the Almighty.

Secretary of the Navy Gideon Welles recalled the meeting the same way Chase did. Lincoln called them together and said the slaves were to be freed. "He had, he said, made a vow, a covenant, that if God gave us the victory in the approaching battle (which had just been fought) he would consider it his duty to move forward in the cause of emancipation." Lincoln knew his listeners might be skeptical or puzzled, but there it was. "We might think it strange, he said, but there were times when he felt uncertain how to act; that he had in this way submitted the disposal of matters when the way was not clear to his mind what he should do. God had decided this question in favor of the slave. He was satisfied he was right—was confirmed and strengthened by the vow and its results; his mind was fixed, his decision made."

Thirty years before, in the Age of Jackson, Tocqueville heard an American clergyman utter these words at a public gathering: "O Lord! Never turn thy face away from us; permit us always to be the most religious people as well as the most free." In Lincoln's understanding, God required, first, a guile-lessness and purity of purpose, and in exchange would relieve the country of fear and sustain her through the fires of war, and the penance he was exacting. Then, and only then, might light come from darkness.

PRAYING TO THE SAME GOD

On Saturday, March 4, 1865, standing at the East Front of the Capitol, Lincoln took the presidential oath for the second time and delivered a brief but epochal address. America was finishing its fourth year of civil war. What Lincoln knew, though, and what informed the words he had written out to read to the nation, was that the roots of the war could be traced back much farther than the showdown at Sumter.

Reflecting on his first inaugural in 1861, Lincoln said, "One eighth of the whole population were colored slaves, not distributed generally over the Union, but localized in the Southern part of it. These slaves constituted a peculiar and powerful interest. All knew that this interest was, somehow, the cause of the war." North and South, Lincoln said, "both read the same Bible, and pray to the same God; and each invokes His aid against the other. It may seem strange that any men should dare to ask a just God's assistance in wringing their bread from the sweat of other men's faces; but let us judge not that we be not judged. The prayers of both could not be answered; that of neither has been answered fully. The Almighty has His own purposes."

Lincoln's words were an honest, even brutal acknowledgment that man is not always able to arrange the world as he

would like. The religious see this plight as the inevitable consequence of the Fall and, as Lincoln noted, as the workings of the
mysterious mind of God; the secular as the vagaries of fate or
chance. Whether viewed through the lens of faith or the prism
of secularism, the point is the same: we are subject to forces beyond our control.

For Lincoln, such a vision did not absolve us of moral responsibility. "Let us have faith that right makes might, and in
that faith, let us, to the end, dare to do our duty as we understand it," he said at New York's Cooper Union on Monday,
February 27, 1860. And Lincoln's second inaugural makes the
case that Americans cannot expect the blessings and protec-

During the Civil War, President Lincoln agonized over how both North and South
could think God was on each one's side. In the Emancipation Proclamation, which
Lincoln is here pictured reading before the Cabinet, Lincoln begged for "the
gracious favor of Almighty God" as he at last freed the slaves. *(Bettmann/Corbis)*

tion of God without also answering for their transgressions against him.

A melancholy man who never joined a church, Lincoln intuitively understood the drama of sin and redemption better than most traditional believers. Lincoln's God is neither benign nor sunny but a Lord calling his people to account. "If we shall suppose that American slavery is one of those offences which, in the providence of God, must needs come," Lincoln said, "but which, having continued through His appointed time, He now wills to remove, and that He gives to both North and South, this terrible war, as the woe due to those by whom the offence came, shall we discern therein any departure from those divine attributes which the believers in a Living God always ascribe to Him?"

Americans, Lincoln was saying, must take God altogether. The nation's public religion, based as it was on a God who is attentive to history and has it in his power to affect our course, cannot only be a source of sunshine and comfort; it is also hard and demanding, for it requires us to do unto others as we would have them do unto us.

The Living God who delivered Israel from Egypt or who raised Jesus from the dead was also the Living God who mocked Job in his suffering and inexplicably withdrew his favor from Saul in order to make David king. Visiting war on America in the middle of the nineteenth century, then, did not mark, in Lincoln's view, "any departure from those divine attributes which the believers in a Living God always ascribe to Him," for those attributes included both reward and punishment. "Fondly do we hope—fervently do we pray—that this mighty scourge of war may speedily pass away," Lincoln said. "Yet, if God wills that it continue, until all the wealth piled by the bond-man's two hundred and fifty years of unrequited toil shall be sunk, and until every drop of blood drawn with the lash, shall be paid by another drawn with the sword, as was said three thousand years ago, so still it must be said: 'the judgments of the Lord, are true and righteous altogether.' "

The eloquence of Lincoln's address can conceal the starkness of his message. Read carefully, the speech is startling in its religiosity and its insistence that the events of this world are linked to the will and mind of a God who presides outside time and space. Here is a president of the United States, waging a civil war in which his countrymen are the only casualties, quoting the Nineteenth Psalm—"the judgments of the Lord are true and righteous altogether"—to say that an indefinite struggle would be not only divinely ordained but just, for America was being summoned to account for its sins against the human beings it had long enslaved. Eleven days later, answering a congratulatory message about the speech, Lincoln said he understood that the address was not going to be "immediately popular," but he was confident he had done right. "Men are not flattered by being shown that there has been a difference of purpose between the Almighty and them," Lincoln wrote. "To deny it, however, in this case, is to deny that there is a God governing the world. It is a truth which I thought needed to be told. . . ."

Lincoln believed he was acting in the humane religious tradition of the Declaration. "This was their majestic interpretation of the economy of the Universe," he said of the Founders' view of what Hamilton had called mankind's "sacred rights." "This was their lofty, and wise, and noble understanding of the justice of the Creator to His creatures," Lincoln said. "Yes, gentlemen, to *all* His creatures, to the whole great family of man. In their enlightened belief, nothing stamped with the Divine image and likeness was sent into the world to be trodden on, and degraded, and imbruted by its fellows. They grasped not only the whole race of man then living, but they reached forward and seized upon the farthest posterity." Lincoln always kept a sense of perspective about himself and about man's place in the larger order of things. When a "somewhat pompous and cocksure clergyman," the historian William J. Wolf wrote, called at the White House, Lincoln remarked, "Well, gentlemen, it is not often one is favored with a delegation *direct* from the Almighty."

In a crushing personal loss, Willie, the Lincolns' son, died in 1862. On being told of the nation's prayers, the grieving president was gracious. "I am glad to hear that," he said. "I want them to pray for me. I need their prayers. I will try to go to God with my sorrows. . . ." Grief became all too familiar as the war continued. Writing to a mother who lost two sons fighting for the Union, Lincoln offered the only reassurance he could: that her children had given their lives for the good of others, the noblest sacrifice a man could make. "I feel how weak and fruitless must be any words of mine which should attempt to beguile you with the grief of a loss so overwhelming," Lincoln said. "But I cannot refrain from tendering to you the consolation that may be found in the thanks of the Republic they died to save. I pray that our Heavenly Father may assuage the anguish of your bereavement, and leave you only the cherished memory of the loved and lost, and the solemn pride that must be yours, to have laid so costly a sacrifice upon the altar of Freedom."

Religion was a weapon used by both North and South to

justify their very different causes, a tragic reality Lincoln saw clearly. The usual story of abolition runs something like this: The religious fervor of the Second Great Awakening spread out from the churches of the North to the pages of William Lloyd Garrison's *Liberator,* slowly awakening the nation's conscience and bracing the North for the coming struggle. The religious nature of the Union cause was captured in this verse of Julia Ward Howe's 1861 "Battle Hymn of the Republic":

> *In the beauty of the lilies Christ was born across the sea,*
> *With a glory in His bosom that transfigures you and me:*
> *As He died to make men holy, let us die to make men free;*
> *While God is marching on.*
> *Glory! Glory! Hallelujah! Glory! Glory! Hallelujah!*
> *Glory! Glory! Hallelujah! While God is marching on.*

It takes nothing away from the power of Ward's hymn to note that the real story of abolition was more than a clash between faithful Northerners and godless Southerners. The slaveholders were far from godless—which offers a cautionary tale about the uses of religion in public life.

SCRIPTURE AND SLAVERY

"If slavery is not wrong," Lincoln once said, "then nothing is wrong." In coming to this conclusion, he used not only scripture but reason, history, and experience—in short, he was deploying his natural gifts to their fullest as he struggled to see the right, as he put it in the second inaugural, "as God gives us to see the right." The Bible is rarely a safe sole source on specific political matters, for, as Shakespeare wrote, "The devil can cite Scripture for his purpose." Abolitionists cited Exodus and Deuteronomy to help make the case against slavery. ("Whoever steals a man, whether he sells him or is found in possession of him, shall be put to death," reads Exodus 21:16.)

Pro-slavery advocates had their own biblical ammunition. The central text was Genesis 9:25–27, a bizarre episode involving a drunken Noah and his grandson. Noah had three sons: Shem, Ham, and Japheth. After the Flood, Noah planted a vineyard, then drank too deeply of its fruits (perhaps understandably, given what he had just been through). According to the account in Genesis, the old man passed out in his tent, naked, only to be discovered by Ham, who told his brothers of it. The brothers, Shem and Japheth, went to their father, and carefully covered him while keeping their eyes averted from him. Once he awoke, Noah was furious to learn Ham had seen him, and cried, "Cursed be Canaan [a son of Ham's]; a slave of slaves shall he be to his brothers." A tradition developed that the "sons of Ham" were dark-skinned, and thus was born one of the roots of the biblical defense of slavery. In the New Testament, Saint Paul's admonitions for slaves to obey their masters were singled out as somehow having more force than the whole weight of the Gospels and the rest of the canon, which was that "ye are all one in Christ Jesus." Reverend Devereux Jarratt, an Anglican priest, represented a widespread view that slaves (or "servants," in the euphemistic culture of the South) were born to a certain station and role in life by God's design. "Upon the whole, God hath set the members in the body, every one as it hath pleased him, and in such order and subserviency one to another, that the *eye cannot say unto the hand, I have no need of thee, nor the head to the feet, I have no need of you.*"

Frederick Douglass experienced the bitter mix of slavery and faith firsthand. During the summer of 1832, in Talbot County, Maryland, Douglass's master went to a Methodist revival meeting and, Douglass recalled, "there experienced religion." On hearing the news, Douglass said that he hoped that the conversion might lead to emancipation or, failing that, at least to a gentler life for the slaves on the place. "I was disappointed in both these respects," Douglass wrote. Christianity "neither made him to be humane to his slaves, nor to emancipate them. If it had any effect on his character, it made him more cruel and hateful in all his ways; for I believe him to have been a much worse man after his conversion than before."

Why? How could the Gospel have had such a perverse effect? "Prior to his conversion," Douglass said, "he relied upon his own depravity to shield and sustain him in his savage barbarity; but after his conversion, he found religious sanction and support for his slaveholding cruelty." The master became a model of public piety, hosting traveling ministers and conspicuously holding household prayers, especially when there were guests.

A young slave woman who had been severely burned as a child—Douglass calls her "Henny"—paid the heaviest price for the master's newfound religious zeal. After tying her up, the master would whip her with "a heavy cowskin upon her naked shoulders, causing the warm red blood to drip; and, in justification of the bloody deed, he would quote this passage of Scripture—'He that knoweth his master's will, and doeth it not, shall be beaten with many stripes.' " The verse is found in the Gospel of Luke.

Religion is more than a familiarity with and purported application of scripture: it is also an attitude of belief formed by tradition, reason, and experience. While Douglass's master could pick up one brand of Christianity and use it to fuel his own cruelty, a more thoughtful Christian like John Quincy Adams, the former president who was elected to the House of Representatives from Massachusetts in his post–White House years, could choose precisely the opposite course on the slavery question and believe that he was fighting under "the standard of Almighty God." As Adams decided to take on the Supreme Court appeal of slaves who mutinied aboard the *Amistad* in 1841, he confided his fears and his faith to his diary: "I find impulses of duty upon my own conscience, which I cannot resist, while on the other hand, the magnitude, the danger, the insurmountable burden of labour to be encountered in the undertaking to touch upon the slave-trade. No one else will undertake it. . . . The world, the flesh, and all the devils in hell are arrayed against any man, who now, in this North-American Union, shall dare to join the standard of Almighty God, to put down the African slave-trade, and what can I, upon the verge of my seventy-fourth birthday, with a shaking hand, a darkening eye, a drowsy brain, and with all my faculties dropping from me, one by one, as the teeth are dropping from my head, what can I do for the cause of God and man? for the progress of human emancipation? for the suppression of the African slave-trade? Yet my conscience presses me on—let me but die upon the breach."

Adams was taking his stand not on some narrow biblical ground, nor had he tried to use religion to defend what so many believed to be morally indefensible. As he said in his diary, he believed the "African slave-trade" wrong—contrary to the "cause of God and man." It was a view taken after a lifetime of service to the nation and contemplation of philosophy, poetry, theology, and politics—the view of a man who, as the shadows lengthened, not only felt but thought that the right thing to do, however unpopular, would win him treasure in heaven if not on earth. Adams represented a particular breed of believer, one who takes solace in scripture but does not necessarily think the Bible is the only field of battle in life's wars.

BIBLICAL BATTLES

If anything, competing scriptural citations stand a good chance of exacerbating tensions and fueling unhealthy, possibly destructive passions, for if both sides fight with what each considers the inerrant word of God, it is difficult to see how such battles can be reasonably settled. What is essential—and what has long been part of religious intellectual traditions—is to draw not only on scripture but on reason and on experience when contemplating the nature and problems of the world.

In the seventeenth-century battle between the Catholic hierarchy and Galileo over whether the earth revolved around the sun or vice versa, it was Galileo—a Christian—who understood better than his persecutors how to reconcile apparent contradictions between faith and science. "If Scripture cannot err," he said, "certain of its interpreters and commentators can and do so in many ways." In other words, if reason leads humankind to discover a truth that seems to be incompatible with the Bible, then the interpretation of scripture should give way to the rational conclusion. In this Galileo was echoing Augustine, who wrote, "If it happens that the authority of Sacred Scripture is set in opposition to clear and certain reasoning, this must mean that the person who [interprets scripture] does not understand

it correctly." Such is the intellectual footwork of a believer unprepared to allow the possibility that the Bible might be fallible,
but Augustine's work enables thinking Christians to take advantage of scientific and social advances without surrendering
the authority of revelation. Guided by these lights, believers
have (however slowly) removed the biblical support for the
ideas that the earth, not the sun, is the physical center of the universe, that women are property—and that slavery is divinely
sanctioned.

The lesson is that purely religious arguments may not be
sufficient to get us to the right result. The faithful should see
that God meant for them to use reason as well as revelation as
they make their way through the world. The secular need to
note the moral component of any cause and should not dismiss
it even if the religious and the moral course happen to be the
same. Lincoln recognized that the battle between good and evil,
light and dark, is never ending, and that we will not always be
able to tell where the combatants' loyalties truly lie by the words
they speak. "The struggle of today is not altogether for today—
it is for a vast future also," Lincoln said in late 1861.

Postwar events proved him a prophet. After Appomattox,
one would have thought that our public religion would have
been like this: grounded on the principle that all men are created equal, in the image of God, and are by right worthy to be
treated fairly and equitably, loving and being loved in the spirit
of the second great commandment. Like a drinker who cannot
resist just one more bender, though, the South could not help itself once federal troops left the region after Reconstruction.
Segregation became the order of the day, and racism once more
overrode whatever gentler impulses a chastened Southern reli-

gious sensibility might have had. Deliverance would require decades in the wilderness of discrimination and hate, the blood of prophets and martyrs, and finally progress toward a Promised Land—a century after the Civil War.

THE CHRISTIAN AMENDMENT

Lincoln's use of religion to discuss the war, explain its causes, and point the way ahead raises a key question: What if a president were not as brilliant or as judicious as he was in framing the affairs of the nation in theological language and imagery? We have seen how slaveholders could cloak injustice in godly garb. Once the cause of the Union was depicted in holy terms—that, in Julia Ward Howe's words, soldiers should die to make men free in a Christ-like sacrifice—was America at risk of seeing a president's theological vision take a theocratic turn? Of course it was. The line between theology and theocracy, between public religion and consuming religious fervor that could distort the delicate American balance between religious and civic life, is a very thin one. Yet history shows that leaders in even the most difficult of crises have managed to practice public religion and preserve freedom of religion at the same time. Such may not be the case forever, but it has been thus far, and Lincoln's experience is telling, for he had the opportunity to go much farther than he did, and he resisted it.

The opening to steer the country in a more explicitly Christian direction came to him in the work of an organization of Christians who believed that many problems could be solved if the Constitution were changed to acknowledge the nation's dependence on God—not on providence, or even just the God of

Abraham, but God the Father of the Holy Trinity. In Xenia, Ohio, and Sparta, Illinois, in 1863, ministers gathered to debate the measure, and on Wednesday, February 10, 1864, they came together to ask President Lincoln and the Congress to support the passage of the following amended Preamble:

> We, the people of the United States, humbly acknowledging Almighty God as the source of all authority and power in civil government, the Lord Jesus Christ, as the Ruler among the nations, and His revealed will as of supreme authority, in order to constitute a Christian government, and in order to form a more perfect union. . . .

As the historian Morton Borden told it, Lincoln met the delegation politely. "Gentlemen," he replied after hearing the group's resolution read out, "the general aspect of your movement I cordially approve. In regard to particulars I must ask time to deliberate, as the work of amending the Constitution should not be done hastily. I will carefully examine your paper in order more fully to comprehend its contents than is possible from merely hearing it read, and will take such action upon it as my responsibility to my Maker and our country demands." Warm words, but nothing was behind them. On Capitol Hill, the chairman of the House Judiciary Committee said the amendment was "unnecessary and injudicious, at this time, at any rate," and took no further action. *Unnecessary and injudicious:* good words, and a good test for such things.

Lincoln brought a generosity of spirit to his dealings with Jewish concerns as well. First, in 1862, he agreed to open military chaplaincies to Jews after an energetic effort by the Board of

Delegates of American Israelites. That was July; in December, General U. S. Grant, then headquartered in Mississippi, issued General Order 11, which expelled Jews from the states under his control. It had been decided that "Jews, as a class" were responsible for smuggling. Lincoln had the order revoked, later telling Jewish leaders that "to condemn a class is, to say the least, to wrong the good with the bad. I do not like to hear a class or nationality condemned on account of a few sinners." A battle won, the war went on. In 1866, the Reconstruction loyalty oath for Southerners was to be sworn on the "Holy Evangelists," meaning the Gospels, another sectarian move Jewish leaders had to beat back.

A DEATH ON GOOD FRIDAY

Friday, April 14, 1865, Walt Whitman recalled years later, "seems to have been a pleasant one throughout the whole land—the moral atmosphere pleasant too—the long storm, so dark, so fratricidal, full of blood and doubt and gloom, over and ended at last by the sun-rise of such an absolute National victory, and utter break-down of Secessionism—we almost doubted our own senses!" Lee had surrendered; the rebellion was over. Then, after nightfall, Lincoln was murdered at Ford's Theater.

That the assassination took place on Good Friday, at the time of Passover, in the closing weeks of a war of liberation from the sins of the past was lost on no one. In Hartford, Connecticut, the Baptist minister C. B. Crane said the murder was "the aftertype of the tragedy which was accomplished on the first Good Friday, more than eighteen centuries ago, upon the eminence of Calvary in Judea." At Shearith Israel, Jacques Judah

Lyons, the rabbi, prayed, "We bewail the sudden removal from our midst of the good, the honest Abraham Lincoln. . . ." A casualty of war as much as any soldier who fell in combat, in his anguish and his struggle, Lincoln, like Jefferson, was a kind of mirror for many of his followers. Lincoln once wrote that "probably it is to be my lot to go on in a twilight, feeling and reasoning my way through life, as questioning, doubting Thomas did." It is intriguing that Lincoln chose the apostle Thomas as an example, because for all his initial uncertainty and skepticism, when Thomas beholds the risen Jesus, he exclaims, "My Lord and my God!" A small sign, perhaps, that somewhere in his soul Lincoln held out a hope that at the end of the feeling, the reasoning, the questioning, and the doubting, he, too, would emerge from the twilight, sure and certain of a divine order. One thing is sure and certain: because of Lincoln's intellectual and emotional engagement with the idea of God, America emerged from the gloom of war not only intact, but stronger and freer.

CHAMPIONS OF THE CENTER

Predictably, Americans used that strength and freedom to keep on arguing with one another. The push for the Christian amendment gave Robert Ingersoll, the agnostic lawyer, lecturer, and leader of the "free thought" movement, occasion to make the case against not only public religion but religion in general. Though he went farther than most Americans did then or do now, Ingersoll brought passion and clarity to the ongoing defense of liberty of conscience. If Americans amended the Constitution to "acknowledge the existence and supremacy of God," he wondered, then would the government enforce the new law? "Will it be a crime to deny the existence of this constitutional God?" Ingersoll asked. "Can the offender be proceeded against in the criminal courts? Can his lips be closed by the power of the state? Would not this be the inauguration of religious persecution?" As it turned out, Ingersoll's darkest fears never came to pass.

That is because the republican system worked. If more Americans had truly wanted such an amendment, they could have brought more pressure to bear on Congress and the president. Those uncomfortable with allusions to the Almighty in public life may find reassurance in this story, for it illustrates the value of liberty for every side. The faithful were free to petition. The president and the Senate declined to be lobbied into something they found "unnecessary and injudicious." Thus the moderate nature of the country's public religion was protected. And it did not take a Lincoln to resist the Christian amendment. Despite attempts to press the amendment in the second half of the nineteenth century, no president thought it a reasonable thing to do. The center held.

That center has always had its quiet champions. As presidents go, John Tyler is rarely spoken of—he was no Jefferson, no Lincoln—but he was a significant bridge figure between those two great men on the question of public religion. An Episcopalian from Virginia who succeeded William Henry Harrison in the White House, Tyler served from 1841 until 1845. Like Jefferson, he was a kind of Deist who believed that reason offered rewards; like Lincoln, he was somewhat stoic. "The person who is a stranger to sickness is equally a stranger to the highest enjoyments of health," Tyler once wrote his daughter.

"So . . . I have brought myself to believe that the variableness in the things of the world [is] designed by the Creator for the happiness of His creatures." His tendency to the philosophical—he said that "the person who justly contemplates the wise order of Providence can alone possess a just idea of the Deity"—led him to a spirit of religious tolerance, perhaps on the grounds that man can only contemplate the ways of God, not fully grasp them.

When Harrison died in 1841, Tyler spoke of "Christian people" as he asked for a national day of prayer. A Jewish American, Jacob Ezekiel of Richmond, asked Tyler for an "explanation . . . as may meet the views of those who do not profess Christianity though believers in the Supreme Being of the world." In reply, Tyler was gracious. He apparently realized his mistake and was honest about it. He had not intended, he told Ezekiel, "to exclude any portion of my fellow citizens from a cordial union in the solemnities of that occasion. . . . For the people of whom you are one, I can feel none other than profound respect. The wisdom which flowed from the lips of your prophets has in time past, and will continue for all time to come, to be a refreshing fountain of moral instruction to mankind— while holy records bear witness of Divine favors and protection of the God of Abraham and of Isaac and of Jacob, God of the Christian and Israelite, to his chosen people—may I then hope, sir, that this explanation will remove all difficulties, and that your voice and the voices of all your brethren will ascend to our Common Father in supplication and prayer on the day I have suggested."

Later in his term, in July 1843, Tyler offered his thoughts on religion and freedom: "The United States have adventured upon a great and noble experiment, which is believed to have been hazarded in the absence of all previous precedent—that of total separation of church and state. No religious establishment *by law* exists among us. The conscience is left free from all restraint and each is permitted to worship his Maker after his own judgment. . . . The Mohammedan, if he were to come among us, would have the privilege guaranteed to him by the constitution to worship according to the Koran; and the East Indian might erect a shrine to Brahma if it so pleased him. Such is the spirit of toleration inculcated by our political institutions." Tyler added: "The Hebrew persecuted and down trodden in other regions takes up his abode among us with none to make him afraid." As the United States grew ever more diverse, visions like Tyler's became ever more relevant.

THE KNOW-NOTHINGS

The story of America understandably tends to be told through the narratives of shooting wars—the Revolution, the War of 1812, the Civil War, World War I, World War II, the Cold War, Korea, Vietnam, and, of late, the war against the Taliban and against Saddam Hussein's Iraq. But wars of culture—sometimes loud, sometimes quiet—are often as important in the hearts and minds of the people caught up in such conflicts.

One battle that began in the nineteenth century and lasted well into the twentieth was over the place of Catholicism in American life—a long-running struggle that further underscores how the country has faced the issue of pluralism throughout its history, not just recently. From the 1830s to the 1850s, Catholic immigration was enormous, and nativist Protestants reacted badly, consumed by ancient prejudices against "popery" and worried about the effects of the influx of immigrants into the country. This was the age of the anti-Catholic, anti-immigrant Know-Nothing party, so called because members were to be known to one another only in secret (denying the existence of the movement—to say you knew nothing about it—was a hallmark). In his brilliant and provocative 2002 book, *Separation of Church and State,* University of Chicago law professor Philip Hamburger places the origins of the popular American understanding of separation of church and state squarely in the middle of the Protestant backlash against Catholics. As parochial schools sought public funding (partly on the ground that the "common schools," as they were known, were essentially Protestant, with Bible readings and prayers), Protestants suddenly became enamored of separation of church and state. Hamburger quotes one contemporary anti-Catholic cry:

> *And shall our Common Schools, the republic's strongest hope*
> *Be wielded by deceitful Priests, a Bishop or the Pope?*

JESUS AND DARWIN

For the Victorians on both sides of the Atlantic, the age was one of great faith and great doubt. In England, the poet Matthew Arnold, son of Reverend Thomas Arnold of Rugby School and godson of Reverend John Keble, a key figure in the Oxford Movement, lost his religion and, in the poem "Dover Beach," captured some of the feelings of the growing ranks of the agnostic. In Arnold's verses, written in 1867, the narrator says:

The Sea of Faith
Was once, too, at the full, and round earth's
    shore
Lay like the folds of a bright girdle furled.
But now I only hear
Its melancholy, long, withdrawing roar,
Retreating, to the breath
Of the night-wind, down the vast edges drear
And naked shingles of the world.

Ah, love let us be true
To one another! For the world, which seems
To lie before us like a land of dreams,
So various, so beautiful, so new,
Hath really neither joy, nor love, nor light,
Nor certitude, nor peace, nor help for pain;
And we are here as on a darkling plain
Swept with confused alarms of struggle and
    flight,
Where ignorant armies clash by night.

"Dover Beach" is a hardy perennial—the nineteenth century's version of Yeats's "Second Coming," often quoted to evoke the bloodshed and chaos of the twentieth—but Arnold is a fitting voice to hear because two of the most important forces which created waves that came to crash on the shores of American thought and life originated in the Old World. First, from Germany and France, there was the rise of scholarly interest in the historical nature of the Bible and of the life of Jesus and, second, from England, the 1859 publication of Charles Darwin's *The Origin of Species.*

Albert Schweitzer's influential *Quest of the Historical Jesus,* published in 1906, was arguably the first broadly popular summary of about two centuries of work by scholars to separate the Jesus of history (the figure who was born and lived in first-century Judea) from the Christ of faith (the "anointed one" of God, which is the translation of the Greek CHRISTOS). The search, and its implications for calling into question the literal, factual accuracy of the Gospels, was in fact even older than Schweitzer's book led many to believe. As Charlotte Allen wrote in *The Human Christ: The Search for the Historical Jesus,* modern biblical criticism had really begun around 1678, with the French Catholic Richard Simon, who analyzed the scriptures with an eye toward what the Vatican would later call "literary forms." Once the Bible was seen as the product of human hands and hearts, not directly of God, a reader was then free to, and was right to, understand its content using critical methods. The story of the Creation in six "days," for instance, could be looked at anew as a possible metaphor or analogy, or one could try to trace the derivation and meaning of "day" in different texts. A Protestant, Johann Albrecht Bengel, was also essential in this Enlightenment period of learning to bringing the faculty of reason and intellect to the business of scriptural interpretation. Such religious founders of the critical movement were soon eclipsed by more glamorous Deists such as Voltaire and Thomas Chubb, who found the "quest" a useful weapon in their war against what they saw as the inventions of the institutional church. (The debates, as we have seen, influenced Jefferson and Franklin.)

George Eliot's English translation of the German David Friedrich Strauss's *Life of Jesus Critically Examined* was published in 1846, a work calling the most essential tenets of biblical believers into serious question. As the Bible was under what the most conservative Christians thought was assault from European intellectuals, Darwin published *The Origin of Species* in 1859. America was otherwise engaged with the Civil War in those years, but Darwinian thought, easily caricatured by critics as irreligious and blasphemous, also roiled the American faithful.

Many religious believers, while challenged by Darwin's findings, managed to reconcile their faith with the idea of evolution by acknowledging the mysterious ways of God and holding that at some unknown juncture in the making of the species, God invested his creatures with a soul. Experience shows that there need be no stalemate between religion and science; the faithful have met and risen to intellectual difficulties from age to age. In his Gifford Lectures in 1973–74—the same forum at Edinburgh University in which William James delivered *The Varieties of Religious Experience* in 1901 and 1902—the historian Owen Chadwick plumbed what he called "The Secularization of the European Mind in the Nineteenth Century." At least one of his observations on the effect of the rise of Darwinism on religion also applied to the American mind. "Let us suppose ourselves back, to have been born about 1840, of a church-going family but not especially pious, an educated family but not especially scientific," Chadwick said. "We learn at mother's knee that the seven days of Genesis Chapter I are not to be taken literally, and Noah's flood too for it would not have covered the whole earth. . . . We should probably have thought Adam and Eve to be as historical as Caesar and Calpurnia. We should feel no tug between school-learning and religious practice." Chadwick was articulating an intellectually sophisticated—widespread, but still sophisticated—point of view.

There was a tug-of-war between "school-learning and religious practice," though, and in America it led to the Scopes Trial in Dayton, Tennessee, in 1925. The struggle continues to occupy many cultural warriors who choose not to take Augustine's counsel to heart: if the mind discerns new truths incompatible with standing scriptural interpretations, then it is the interpretation that is wrong, not the truth.

"A CHRISTIAN NATION"

The politics of religion can be irresistible to public figures, including clergy. The role of ministers in politics was always complicated. Even before the Revolution, colonists were anxious about the possibility of Anglican bishops' coming to settle in America; in the seventeenth century, "bishops, wielded enormous political as well as spiritual power," wrote the historian Edwin S. Gaustad. "Bishops were officers of the state, members of the powerful House of Lords, agents of persecution and oppression"—and even in the eighteenth century, "the very thought of religious officials wielding similar powers in America inflamed the colonists' passions to great heights and contributed to their readiness to sever their ties with England."

In the nineteenth century, one of the most important revivalists in American history, Charles Finney, was a fascinating, tireless figure. In 1821, he was studying law in Adams, New York, when, he recalled, the "Holy Spirit descended upon me in a manner that seemed to go through me, body and soul. I could feel the impression, like a wave of electricity, going through and through me. Indeed it seemed to come in waves and waves of liquid love. . . . It seemed like the very breath of God." An architect of what we think of as the Christian revival meeting, Finney, the historian Mark A. Noll wrote, "succeeded in joining evangelical religion to social reform," from abolition to temperance to coeducation at Oberlin College. Finney said that "the great business of the church is to reform the world—to put away every kind of sin," and he believed the faithful were "bound to exert their influence to secure a legislation that is in accordance with the law of God."

Finney put the cause of the church before anything else, including his own comfort. When he moved from New York to teach theology at Oberlin, he was, Noll wrote, "so pressed for funds that he was forced to sell 'my traveling trunk, which I had used in my evangelistic labors.' " So be it, Finney said: "if help did not come," he noted, "I should assume that it was best that it should not."

But not every prominent evangelist was a Charles Finney. In the twentieth century, there was Billy Sunday, a hugely popular revival preacher who, in the words of the scholar William Martin, "thought the Christian life required little more than adhering to dominant political and economic orthodoxies and upholding the moral standards of the Anglo-Saxon Protestant middle class." Sunday supported Prohibition, called on presidents, sold war bonds to back the American effort in World War I, and attacked progressive reform movements as "godless social service nonsense." His foreign-policy views were equally unsubtle. "I tell you it is Bill against Woodrow, Germany against America, Hell against Heaven," he said of Kaiser Wilhelm II and World War I—a war, Sunday said, to defeat a "bunch of pretzel-chewing sauerkraut spawn of blood-thirsty Huns." Father Charles Coughlin, a Catholic priest, built a vast national following through regular radio broadcasts. (He was, *Fortune* said in 1934, "just about the biggest thing that ever happened to radio.") Coughlin started the 1930s supporting Franklin Roosevelt; before the decade was out, Coughlin had turned virulently anti-Semitic, which finally ruined his media career. The fundamentalist Gerald B. Winrod followed a similar arc into the abyss, shifting from the fight against the teaching of evolution to attacking Jews in his publication *Defender*.

Dark odysseys like Coughlin's and Winrod's make the old Baptist tradition of securing the spiritual from the temporal by encouraging distance between religion and politics seem all the more appealing. The movement was born, it is true, partly out of self-interest: the Baptists were a persecuted minority, and if they could convince the Anglican and Congregationalist majorities in the Revolutionary era to leave them alone, then the persecution would stop. John Leland was an eloquent advocate of the Madison-Jefferson view, as was Isaac Backus, a Baptist who wrote in 1779: "Nothing can be true religion but voluntary obedience unto his revealed will, of which each rational soul has an equal right to judge for itself. . . ."

Religious issues in the public sphere are perennial. Sensing an opportunity in the anti-Catholic sentiment of the day, President Grant went to Des Moines in the autumn of 1875 and called for new constitutional action to prevent aid to parochial schools. "If we are to have another contest in the near future of our national existence, I predict that the dividing line will not be Mason and Dixon's, but it will be between patriotism and intelligence on one side, and superstition, ambition and ignorance on the other," Grant said. "Encourage free schools, and resolve that not one dollar appropriated to them shall be applied to the support of any sectarian school. . . . Leave the matter of religion to the family altar, the church, and the private school, supported entirely by private contribution. Keep the Church and State forever separate."

Unless, of course, one was talking about the Protestant church, which was, in this view, rightfully intertwined with the public schools. James G. Blaine of Maine, a Republican congressman soon to become a senator and with hopes of becoming president, took specific legislative action, proposing a revision of the religion clause of the First Amendment: "No state shall make any law respecting an establishment of religion or prohibiting the free exercise thereof; and no money raised by taxation in any State for the support of public schools, or derived from any public fund therefore, nor any public lands devoted thereto, shall ever be under the control of any religious sect, nor shall any money so raised or lands so devoted be divided between religious sects or denominations." Neither Grant nor Blaine succeeded—another example, as in the age of Lincoln, of the broad middle realizing that the republican mechanisms of government were sufficient to the task of governing.

Enough Americans had detected what was really going on. The separation argument was largely a cover for politicians to play to the Protestant majority, but the Protestant majority did not seem willing to undo the work of the Founders. Still, for those on the conservative side, immigration, biblical scholarship, and evolution were factors in late-nineteenth- and early-twentieth-century efforts by Christians to turn the American republic into their port in the storm of modernity. Jonathan Sarna quotes a late-nineteenth-century assertion by the Presbyterian minister Isaac A. Cornelison, who said America was "a state without a church but not without a religion." So far, so good, but then Cornelison outran the Founders and their moderate heirs: "Christianity in a proper sense is the established religion of this nation; established, not by statute law, it is true, but by a law equally valid, the law in the nature of things, the law of necessity, which law will remain in force so long as the great mass of the people are Christian." In 1892, a unanimous Supreme Court said, "[W]e find everywhere a clear recognition of the same truth: . . . this is a Christian nation."

COLONEL ROOSEVELT'S CREED

Yet America was not a "Christian nation" except in the sense that it was a nation populated by people who identified themselves as Christians. Words have consequences, and there is a distinction—an essential one—between being a "Christian nation" and being one whose public religion allows religious values, Christian or otherwise, to shape its manners and morals.

Properly understood and applied, public religion can be a force for good, and was as the twentieth century began. The country was in the midst of the reforming Progressive Era. From temperance to Sunday closing laws, many of the movements of the age were helped along by reformers who saw good works as a critical element of Christianity. The faith of one of progressivism's champions, Theodore Roosevelt, was of a piece with the more orthodox of the Founders: he believed works were as important, if not more important, than words—

men, he thought, echoing a biblical text, "shall be judged by their fruits."

On an early autumn day in 1907, Roosevelt, known as the "Colonel" from his Rough Rider days, showed up early for the laying of the cornerstone of the Cathedral of Saints Peter and Paul, the grand Gothic church on Wisconsin Avenue in Washington that was to become known as the National Cathedral. The bishop of London was also there, *The New York Times* reported, and used the trowel that had laid the cornerstone of the Capitol. In a speech, Roosevelt addressed himself largely to Christians, challenging them to put the Gospel into action, saying that "the real field for rivalry among and between the creeds comes in the rivalry of the endeavor to see which can render best service to mankind. . . ." A lover of books—he read constantly and wrote dozens of them—Roosevelt would, a friend recalled, carry the Bible along on camping trips while at Harvard. "Some folks read the Bible to find an easier way into Heaven," the friend, Bill Sewall, said. But "Theodore reads it to find the right way and how to pursue it."

As president he relished his claim on the attention of his vast flock. "I am charged with being a preacher," Roosevelt once said. "Well, I suppose I am. I have such a bully pulpit." One of his causes was to undo the Civil War–era insertion of the phrase "In God We Trust" on the country's currency. Roosevelt's motives were religious, not secular: he believed the practice came "dangerously close to sacrilege." The phrase had begun to appear on American money during Salmon Chase's tenure as Treasury secretary, but Roosevelt thought the custom was, he said, "from every standpoint profoundly to be regretted." To invoke God as a defender of liberty and of America was a good thing, Roosevelt believed, but to him the motto on the money seemed mindless, even, in the words of one of his biographers, blasphemous. "It is a motto which it is indeed well to have inscribed on our great national monuments, in our temples of justice, in our legislative halls, and in buildings such as those at West Point and Annapolis—in short, wherever it will tend to arouse and inspire a lofty emotion in those who look thereon," Roosevelt wrote a New York minister who was lobbying for retaining the phrase on the currency. "But it seems to me eminently unwise to cheapen such a motto by use on coins, just as it would be to cheapen it by use on postage stamps, or in advertisements." A noble argument—which Roosevelt lost.

At heart, though, TR was more about deeds than words. "I know not how philosophers may ultimately define religion," he once said, "but from Micah to James it has been defined as service to one's fellowmen rendered by following the great rule of justice and mercy, of wisdom and righteousness." He had the Epistle of Saint James in mind: "but be ye doers of the word, and not hearers only. . . . Ye see then how that by works a man is justified, and not by faith only." Franklin, Jefferson, and Adams believed the same. Such are the kinds of views that wear well and tend to have the best influence in American politics, for they appeal to godliness without requiring a confession of faith in a particular vision of God.

A BULLY DEFENSE OF LIBERTY

Partisanship, however, poses a constant threat to civility, particularly on religious questions. In 1908, when William Howard Taft was running to succeed Roosevelt, who had chosen not to seek another term (a decision he would come to regret), Roosevelt found himelf devising replies to religiously motivated attacks on Taft, a Unitarian. "There is considerable opposition to him . . . on account of his religious views," noted Taft's opponent, William Jennings Bryan. "Think of the United States with a President who does not believe that Jesus Christ was the Son of God, but looks upon our immaculate Savior as a . . . low, cunning imposter!" the *Penecostal Herald* said in July 1908.

Reaching back into history, Roosevelt sought to reassure "Will," as he called Taft in an August 1908 letter written from Oyster Bay. "I would simply say that you decline to permit any such gross violation of the first principles of our government as an effort to make you subscribe to any given principles of dogmatic theology before counting you as eligible to receive votes," TR wrote Taft. He should say, too, Roosevelt went on, "that the same attack was made upon Lincoln as being a nonorthodox Christian as upon you, and far severer attacks upon Jefferson."

Roosevelt grew more furious as Election Day approached. In an October letter to a correspondent who had asked him to advise Taft to speak out on the religious question, Roosevelt pounded his beloved bully pulpit. "If there is one thing for which we stand in this country, it is for complete religious freedom and for the right of every man to worship his Creator as his conscience dictates," Roosevelt said. "It is an emphatic negation of this right to cross-examine a man on his religious views before being willing to support him for office. Is he a good man, and is he fit for the office? These are the only questions which there is a right to ask, and to both of these in Mr. Taft's case, the answer must be in the affirmative." Roosevelt then spoke of his experience with such questions in the White House. "In my own Cabinet there are at present Catholic, Protestant and Jew—the Protestants being of various denominations," he said. "I am incapable of discriminating between them, or of judging any one of them save as to the way in which he performs his public duty."

Finally, after the campaign, in yet another letter on the subject, Roosevelt sounded ever more Madisonian. "Discrimination against the holder of one faith means retaliatory discrimination against men of other faiths," he said. "The inevitable result of entering upon such a practice would be an abandonment of our real freedom of conscience and a reversion to the dreadful conditions of religious dissension which in so many lands have proved fatal to true liberty, to true religion, and to all advance in civilization." In his penultimate paragraph, Roosevelt offered both prediction and benediction:

> I believe that this Republic will endure for many centuries. If so there will doubtless be among its Presidents Protestants and Catholics, and, very probably at some time, Jews. I have consistently tried while President to act in relation to my fellow Americans of Catholic faith as I hope that any future President who happens to be a Catholic will act towards his fellow Americans of Protestant faith. Had I followed any other course I should have felt that I was unfit to represent the American people.

In the end Bryan lost—which meant, if one takes the *Pentecostal Herald*'s argument at face value, that Americans were more comfortable with a president who did not believe in the divinity of Jesus than with one who took the Bible literally, and who would die shortly after defending that Bible in a hot Tennessee courtroom in 1925.

THE PIOUS WILSON

A new test of church and state came from the middle of the country in 1913. The city of Gary, Indiana, devised a plan under which children in public schools could be "released" from classes to take religious instruction off school property. Opinion was divided within American Judaism, but in a personal letter, Samuel Schulman, a leading New York rabbi, wrote movingly of the dilemma facing religious minorities. "In America, we have a unique and, therefore very delicate problem," he said.

> We, of course, want to keep religion, Bible reading, hymn singing out of the public schools. At the same time we know that there is not enough efficient moral and religious education in the country. . . . Jews make a mistake in thinking only of themselves and assuming always a negative and critical attitude. They must supplement that negative attitude with a constructive policy. Otherwise, they will soon be classed in the minds of the Christian men and women in this country with the free-thinkers and with those who have no interest in the religious education of the youth. That, of course, is undesirable both because it is contrary to our genius as Jews and also contrary to the real spirit of Americanism, which while not ecclesiastical, and separates Church from State, has always been religious.

The man who became president the year the Gary plan was proposed, Woodrow Wilson, would have agreed with much of Schulman's letter, for Wilson believed in the exercise of justice and the rights of the small against the large, the weak against the strong. The son of a Presbyterian clergyman, Wilson sounded like a professor with a preacherly streak, or, perhaps, a preacher with a professorial streak. Neither was especially good for a politician, but Wilson helped bring a missionary—his critics would say messianic—dimension to American life and policy. "Here is the nation God has builded by our hands," Wilson said on the fiftieth anniversary of Lincoln's Gettysburg Address. "What shall we do with it?"

Slow to engage in World War I, Wilson ultimately saw much for America to do abroad. William McKinley and TR were, of course, no retiring isolationists. What Wilson brought to the imperial impulses already in evidence in Washington in 1913 was an overtly moral tone and ministerial zeal at a time of global conflict. The American instinct to project power, both hard and soft, in faraway places is based on many factors, but one is what is rather awkwardly known as Wilsonianism, which is itself linked to public religion. "It is a fearful thing to lead this great peaceful people into war, into the most terrible and disastrous of all wars, civilization itself seeming to be in the balance," Wilson told Congress in April 1917. "But the right is more precious than peace, and we shall fight for the things which we have always carried nearest our hearts . . . the day has come when America is privileged to spend her blood and her might for the principles that gave her birth and happiness and the peace which she has treasured. God helping her, she can do no other."

It was not a far leap for Wilson from the personal to the public. "My life would not be worth living if it were not for the driving power of religion, for faith, pure and simple. . . . [N]ever for a moment have I had one doubt about my religious beliefs.

There are people who believe only so far as they understand—that seems to me presumptuous and sets their understanding as the standard of the universe."

In his Fourteen Points Address to Congress on Tuesday, January 8, 1918, ten months and three days before the Armistice, Wilson articulated a moral vision of foreign policy, one whose tone was in the tradition of public religion. The unifying theme of American policy, he said in conclusion, "is the principle of justice to all peoples and nationalities, and their right to live on equal terms of liberty and safety with one another, whether they be strong or weak." For Wilson there was something apocalyptic about the struggle: "The moral climax of this the culminating and final war for human liberty has come, and they are ready to put their own strength, their own highest purpose, their own integrity and devotion to the test." As we know all too well, this was not the culminating and final war for human liberty. Wilson's assumption that he was leading the climactic battle to, as he put it elsewhere, make the world safe for democracy, shows the dangers of investing the crises of one's present time with grandiosity, which can understandably happen to a president or a people who are engaged heart and soul in a struggle for the survival of cherished ideals.

Toward the end of his life, Wilson faced foes who thought little of him. William Howard Taft called him "a ruthless hypocrite." Afflicted by a stroke, crushed in his hopes for an effective League of Nations, Wilson took a view of politics and fate different from Lincoln's. For the martyr of the Civil War, the ways of God were mysterious, the destiny of men and their designs vulnerable. On Armistice Day 1923, with only a few months to live, Wilson said he was confident about the future.

"I am not one of those that have the least anxiety about the triumph of the principles I have stood for," he said. "I have seen fools resist Providence before, and I have seen their destruction. . . . That we shall prevail is as sure as that God reigns."

Lincoln thought differently; in his eyes, it was the will of God that prevailed, not the will of God's creatures. Nevertheless, Wilson's high-mindedness, global engagement, fierce political drive, and religious rhetoric shaped American politics for a decade—and beyond, for his young assistant secretary of the navy, Franklin D. Roosevelt, had watched the president closely, and learned from him. Ten years later, Franklin Roosevelt would bring his cousin Theodore's energy and Wilson's idealism to the White House at an hour when God seemed very far away.

IV. IMPERFECT THOUGH WE ARE

WARS AGAINST THE GREAT DEPRESSION, TOTALITARIANISM, AND JIM CROW

People are going to die here. I'm going to die here.

—JOHN LEWIS, THE EDMUND PETTUS BRIDGE, SELMA, ALABAMA, MARCH 7, 1965

Believing the Bible as I do, I would find it impossible to stop preaching the pure saving gospel of Jesus Christ and begin doing anything else—including the fighting of communism, or participating in civil rights reforms. . . . Preachers are not called to be politicians but to be soul winners.

—REVEREND JERRY FALWELL, THOMAS ROAD BAPTIST CHURCH, LYNCHBURG, VIRGINIA, MARCH 21, 1965

*W*herever he was, Franklin Roosevelt liked to be in charge—even in church. He was a "frustrated clergyman at heart," one of his sons once remarked. Like Washington and Jefferson, Roosevelt was vestryman of his parish, St. James in Hyde Park, New York. The joke in town, wrote the foreign correspondent John Gunther, was "This is Roosevelt's church, once God's."

For a man who was curious about so many things, Roosevelt was not theologically deep. When Eleanor asked him whether he believed the tenets of the Episcopal faith in which he had been raised, he said, "I really never thought about it. I think it is just as well not to think about things like that too much." He loved the Twenty-third Psalm, the Sermon on the Mount, and the thirteenth chapter of Corinthians I; he liked the rhythms and comfort of ritual, inviting his old headmaster Reverend Endicott Peabody, the Rector of Groton, to officiate at his wedding and to lead services in Washington. Asked once about his creed, Roosevelt replied, "I am a Christian and a Democrat—that's all." (John Gunther reports that Roosevelt was careful not to take the Lord's name in vain. On Election Day 1944, in Hyde Park, Roosevelt got stuck in his voting booth and he called out, "The damn thing won't work"—not, he claimed, "the god-damned thing," which some people thought he had said.) To him the problems of the here and now were sufficient trouble for the day. "He never talked about his religion or his beliefs and never seemed to have any intellectual difficulties about what he believed," Eleanor Roosevelt recalled.

After Roosevelt became president, on Saturday, March 4, 1933, he turned to scripture again and again—subtly but surely—as he spoke to a nation hobbled by the Great Depression. His inaugural address is justly remembered for its ringing assertion that "the only thing we have to fear is fear itself," but the speech is also notable for its dependence on the Bible and biblical precepts. Speaking of "our common difficulties," he was grateful, he said, that "[t]hey concern, thank God, only material things." The American spirit would carry them through this "dark hour," Roosevelt said, then drew on the Books of Exodus and of Joshua: "We are stricken by no plague of locusts," he said. "Compared with the perils which our forefathers conquered because they believed and were not afraid, we have still much to be thankful for." Attacking big businessmen in stark terms, Roosevelt referred to them as "money changers," and alluded to Proverbs as he reassured the country that the time had come to look ahead, not back. Mere profit seekers, he said, "have no vision, and when there is no vision the people perish." He then argued for a renewed sense of the moral life: "Happiness lies not in the mere possession of money; it lies in the joy of achievement, in the thrill of creative effort. The joy and moral stimulation of work no longer must be forgotten in the mad chase of evanescent profits." Overly idealistic, perhaps, but Roosevelt then returned to Jesus' second great commandment, recasting it for a people bereft of confidence. "These dark days will be worth all they cost us," he said, "if they teach us that our true destiny is not to be ministered unto but to minister to ourselves and to our fellow men." He was speaking the language of public religion: Americans were on a pilgrimmage and would face snare after snare in the wilderness, but there was the promise of deliverance.

The hope that mercy and charity could truly make a difference was a real one. "We face the arduous days that lie before us in the warm courage of the national unity; with the clear consciousness of seeking old and precious moral values; with the clean satisfaction that comes from the stern performance of duty by old and young alike." Those old and precious values were not necessarily religious ones, but they were religious in the eyes and, Roosevelt hoped, in the hearts of the faithful.

Charles Peters grew up in Charleston, West Virginia, during the New Deal and turned thirteen as World War II was beginning at the end of the decade. Writing about his own experience in his book about Roosevelt and Wendell Willkie's 1940 campaign, *Five Days in Philadelphia,* Peters, the founding editor of

The Washington Monthly, saw Roosevelt's religion as essential to his presidency. He had beaten polio, which gave him confidence, but something else was at work, too. "Another source of Roosevelt's faith in the future—and of his ability to communicate with his fellow citizens—was the Christianity he shared with a great majority of them," Peters wrote.

Peters understood what Eleanor Roosevelt had meant when she said FDR had no intellectual qualms about his beliefs. "This was certainly true of the Peters family and of most of the Christians we knew," he wrote. "We did not dwell on doubts that may have fleetingly passed through our minds as we considered Noah and the Ark, Jonah and the whale, and Moses at the Red Sea. We believed in the Ten Commandments and most of all in the Golden Rule. Roosevelt saw the New Deal as applied Christianity."

Something else helped in the 1930s, too: the experiment with Prohibition ended the year FDR moved into the White House. To Peters, whose father spent two Sunday mornings a month driving into the hills to see his bootlegger, the experience of God-fearing believers acting illegally actually had a beneficial effect. "Tens of millions of Christians were violating not only man's law, but what a great many of their preachers had told them was God's law," Peters wrote. "Memory of the experience seemed to breed—for a while at least—humility, tolerance, and a merciful attitude towards other sinners."

GATHERING STORM

As the decade wore on, the rise of Nazi Germany became a consuming concern—but for many Americans, it was not consuming enough. Adolf Hitler had taken over Germany in January 1933 and soon began persecutions of Jews and other minorities, persecutions that were only prologue to the Holocaust of World War II. Some in America were part of the problem: Father Charles Coughlin, for example, attacked what he called Roosevelt's "Jew Deal." As late as 1941, Charles Lindbergh blamed the Jews and the British for pulling America toward war. And as the historian Michael Beschloss wrote in his book *The Conquerors,* even Roosevelt, as noble and fair-minded as he was, could think and speak in racial and ethnic terms. "You know this is a Protestant country, and the Catholics and Jews are here under sufferance," an indignant Secretary of the Treasury Henry Morgenthau recorded Roosevelt saying to him and to Leo Crowley, an official who was Catholic, in the aftermath of Pearl Harbor. (Roosevelt could also seem the most tolerant and forbearing of men. To a correspondent inquiring whether FDR had Jewish ancestors, Roosevelt replied: "In the dim past they may have been Jews or Catholics or Protestants. What I am more interested in is whether they were good citizens and believers in God. I hope they were both.")

If our public religion holds that we have special responsibilities because of the gifts we have received from God, how can we explain the nation's long period of isolation at the outset of World War II, at a time when the moral stakes were utterly clear—or were at least utterly clear to people like Winston Churchill? Did Americans have a duty to protect the divinely ordained values of innocent people who were being crushed by the Nazis? Yes, they—we—did, and we fell short. Our failing, as in other instances, was miserable. But we will always be vulnerable to national sin in the way individuals are vulnerable to personal sin. The point of America as constructed by the Founders was, as Jefferson put it, to fix essential rights in the eternal because history has taught us that the spirit of the times is changeable, and can shift from good to evil with little or no warning. In securing freedom of religion—which is really freedom of thought—and freedom of speech, the Founding Fathers created a national milieu in which those who saw the right when others did not had the liberty to bear witness to the truth as they understood it, in the hope that the rest of us might come to glimpse it, too.

On the eve of America's much belated entry into World War II, Reinhold Niebuhr, a Protestant clergyman and professor at Union Theological Seminary in New York, wrote a piece called "The Christian Faith and the World Crisis," which he published on February 10, 1941. In it he talked about why isolationism was so strong, and what Christianity could do to move the nation in the proper direction—to throw its force behind the British and the defeated peoples of the conquered nations in Europe. Too many American Christians, Niebuhr argued, were suffering from utopianism, an idea that "war could be eliminated if only Christians and other men of good will refused resolutely enough to have anything to do with conflict." Speaking for like-minded believers, Niebuhr wrote, "In our opinion this utopianism [has] contributed to the tardiness of the democracies in defending themselves against the perils of a new barbarism, and (in America at least) it is easily compounded with an irresponsible and selfish nationalism."

His words illuminate the religious grounds for defending freedom, even if that defense meant, as it did, killing other creatures of God. "Love must be regarded as the final flower and fruit of justice," he said; "however, when it is substituted for justice it degenerates into sentimentality and may become the accomplice of tyranny." Niebuhr continued:

... We are well aware of the sins of all the nations, including our own, which have contributed to the chaos of our era. We know to what degree totalitarianism represents false answers to our own unsolved problems—political, economic, spiritual.

Yet we believe the task of defending the rich inheritance of our civilization to be an imperative one, however much we might desire that our social system were more worthy of defense. We believe that the possibility of correcting its faults and extending its gains may be annulled for centuries if this external peril is not resolutely faced. We do not find it particularly impressive to celebrate one's sensitive conscience by enlarging upon all the well-known evils of our western world and equating them with the evils of the totalitarian systems. . . . We think it dangerous to allow religious sensitivity to obscure the fact that Nazi tyranny intends to annihilate the Jewish race, to subject the nations of Europe to the dominion of a "master" race, to extirpate the Christian religion, to annul the liberties and legal standards that are the priceless heritage of ages of Christian and humanistic culture, to make truth the prostitute of political power, to seek world dominion through its satraps and allies, and generally to destroy the very fabric of our western civilization.

A STERN SERMON

In August 1941, six months after Niebuhr's plea, Roosevelt secretly met with Churchill on warships at Placentia Bay, off Newfoundland. The president and the prime minister believed in personal diplomacy, and both were anxious to size up the other; for a few days they smoked and chatted and thrashed out issues such as American supplies for Britain. History remembers the rendezvous for two things that were not high on the lists of the military officers and diplomats there to do business: the Atlantic Charter and a Sunday morning service aboard HMS *Prince of Wales*.

The Atlantic Charter was a public declaration of the common aims of the two democracies—chiefly, as the document said, that "all the men in all the lands may live out their lives in freedom from fear and want." Britain and America were not opposing the Axis powers, the charter said, for "aggrandizement, territorial or other" but because "they respect the right of all peoples to choose the form of government under which they will live; and they wish to see sovereign rights and self government restored to those who have been forcibly deprived of them."

The pageantry of the Sunday service gave ceremonial shape to those noble principles. The lesson was from Joshua: "Be strong and of a good courage; be not afraid . . . for the Lord thy God is with thee whithersoever thou goest." Churchill wept as the company—a mixture of British and American sailors—prayed and sang. "Every word seemed to stir the heart," Churchill recalled. There were three hymns: "Onward, Christian Soldiers," "Eternal Father, Strong to Save," and the opening one, a paraphrase of Psalm 90 by Isaac Watts, which expressed dependence on providence:

> *O God, our help in ages past,*
> *Our hope for years to come,*
> *Be Thou our guide while troubles last,*
> *And our eternal home.*

Roosevelt was roused by the service. "If nothing else had happened while we were here," he said to his son Elliott afterward, "that would have cemented us. 'Onward, Christian Soldiers.' We *are* Christian soldiers, and we *will* go on, with God's help."

When news and pictures of the morning were released to the wider world, even those who would ordinarily have been alienated by the heavily Anglican imagery were moved. "Even if it was the Protestant Church militant, not ecumenical, the service was emblematic of the gathering of the forces of the English-speaking peoples," said Joseph P. Lash, a close friend of Eleanor Roosevelt who became a significant Roosevelt biographer. Lash's accommodation with the *Prince of Wales* scene mirrors the way many Americans react to sectarian services held in times of national crisis or celebration: uneasy unless there is a spirit of ecumenism (ministers of non-Christian faiths, for example) but essentially comfortable with ceremonies intended to underscore values of liberty, justice, and democracy.

"And so, all that is implied in the fact that you and Churchill met, in the circumstances under which, and the aims for which you met, that is the vital achievement from which all else will flow," Supreme Court Justice Felix Frankfurter wrote Roosevelt. " 'We will live by symbols,' as we cannot too often recall.

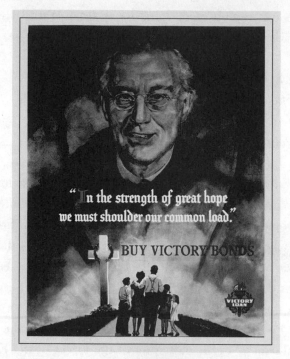

"In the strength of great hope we must shoulder our common load."

BUY VICTORY BONDS

VICTORY LOAN

Franklin Roosevelt loved playing the role of national pastor. On D-Day, June 6, 1944, he led the nation in reading a prayer of his own composition as America sought divine blessing on the vast amphibious operation against Nazi-occupied Europe. (© *Snark/Art Resource, N.Y.*)

And you two in that ocean . . . in the setting of that Sunday service, give meaning to the conflict between civilization and arrogant brute challenge, and give promise, more powerful and binding than any formal treaty could, that civilization has claims and resources that tyranny will not be able to overcome, because it will find that force and will and the free spirit of man are more powerful than force and will alone." The cause of freedom was unfolding to the music of faith.

Ultimately, though, events—not a collective act of American conscience—pressed the country into war against Nazism and

Japanese militarism. Four months later, after Pearl Harbor and Hitler's subsequent declaration of war on the United States, Churchill was at the White House, planning strategy with Roosevelt for a two-front global war.

On New Year's Day 1942, the two traveled by car to Christ Church in Alexandria, Virginia, where the rector, Reverend Edward Randolph Welles, took the pulpit amid a service of Morning Prayer.

In cassock and surplice, the priest looked benign enough, but as he began to preach his words rang out across the old nave with strength. Saying America's "greatest sin" was its "international irresponsibility," Welles spoke sternly of his own people—and his own president. "Nationally we have been like the priest and the Levite in the story of the Good Samaritan—we have passed by on the other side when we have seen other nations in need or peril, or we have given them aid at the end of a 3,000-mile pole, fearful of involving ourselves in danger or drastic sacrifice. We have wanted other nations to pay the supreme price for human liberty while we gave them dollar credits!"

He was only getting started. "That is not the way of Jesus Christ. He endured His cross and we nationally must accept our cross, too." In plain language, in the tradition of Lincoln's calling America to account, Welles told Roosevelt and Churchill:

I believe that this present world struggle is at its core a spiritual struggle, and that much of the evil is on our side. We Americans need to be purged and cleansed individually and nationally before we are worthy to survive. But imperfect though we are (and we must repent and turn to God if we are to be saved) it is important that we discern the vast difference between our aims and those of the

Nazis. . . . The Nazi regime scorns freedom and honesty and purity and love of one's neighbor. . . . Let us pray: for pardon for past shortcomings; for power for the present task of achieving victory; and, finally, for peace. I am convinced that we and our Allies shall win the war; let us pray, and not today only, but every day from now on, that God will help us win a new era of peace, a peace built upon the only basis which can produce enduring justice and truth: the Fatherhood of God and the brotherhood of all mankind.

Welles's words are striking for their lack of sentimentality. Here is no mindless patriot, no reflexive Christian soldier. At the outset of America's full engagement in the deadliest war in history—one that would end only with the use of atomic weapons on large civilian populations in Japan, weapons constructed on the authority of the two leaders sitting in the pews of Christ Church on this Sunday morning—a man of God was arguing that victory required something in addition to arms and strategy and battlefield bravery. He was saying that humility and virtue were preconditions for believers to reasonably ask God for what Roosevelt had called "absolute victory" on the day after Pearl Harbor. We were not going to win because it was our destiny, Welles implied, but only if we acknowledged our own sins and, in theological terms, made ourselves worthy of the responsibilities of triumph.

COMMUNISM, KIERKEGAARD, AND FDR

Later that day FDR and Churchill were to join the other Allies against Hitler in signing a "Declaration by the United Nations,"

which laid out the general principles of the war effort. One was religious freedom, but the negotiations over the cause had been anything but simple. Roosevelt had had a long-running debate with Moscow about the issue, beginning with the 1933 talks over America's recognition of the Soviet Union. According to Labor Secretary Frances Perkins, Roosevelt was talking with the Soviet official Maxim Litvinov about the fate of religion under Communist rule. As Perkins recalled, Roosevelt said:

> Well now, Max, you know what I mean by religion. You know what religion gives a man. You know the difference between the religious and the irreligious person. Why, you must know, Max. You were brought up by pious parents. Look here, some time you are going to die, and when you come to die, Max, you are going to remember your old father and mother—good, pious Jewish people who believed in God and taught you to pray to God. You had a religious bringing up, and when you come to die, Max, that's what is going to come before you, that is what you are going to think about, that's what you are going to grasp for. You know it's important.

The conversation was still going on now, nearly a decade later. Over the 1941–1942 holidays, Roosevelt and Churchill were trying to make the cause of religious freedom explicit in the New Year's Day declaration. Litvinov had been resisting the insertion of the religion clause; he wanted "freedom of conscience." Roosevelt fought back, the speechwriter Robert Sherwood recalled, saying, "[T]he traditional Jeffersonian principle of religious freedom was so broadly democratic that it included the right to have no religion at all—it gave to the individual the right to worship any God he chose or no god." FDR carried the day, and the final document said the Allies were at war because they were "convinced that complete victory over their enemies is essential to defend life, liberty, independence, and religious freedom." Churchill was impressed by Roosevelt's theological victory over Litvinov and jokingly offered to make Roosevelt the archbishop of Canterbury if Roosevelt lost his next race. "I did not however make any official recommendation to the Cabinet or the Crown upon this point," Churchill said, "and as he won the election in 1944 it did not arise."

Banter aside, religion and religious liberty were important to Roosevelt and helped shape his abiding conviction in the idea and the reality of human progress. The ease with which he appealed to religion, Frances Perkins said, "explains many of the attitudes Roosevelt took and much of his faith in the possibilities of man, whom he never thought of as divorced from God in his struggle to improve life upon this planet. He saw the betterment of life and people as part of God's work, and he felt that man's devotion to God expressed itself by serving his fellow men."

In his first State of the Union address after America joined the war, Roosevelt turned a favorite phrase of Hitler's against the Führer. The Germans, Hitler had long argued, were seeking greater *Lebensraum,* or "living room"—hence their aggression in Europe. Speaking before Congress on Tuesday, January 6, 1942, Roosevelt taunted Hitler from afar. The world, Roosevelt said, was "too small to provide adequate 'living room' for both Hitler and God." America fought, he said, for what Americans had always fought: in defense of the founding ideal that "God created man in his own image."

Roosevelt savored history—especially American history, a story in which his own family had played such a large part. In moments of difficulty, his mind tended to dart back into the past in search of examples to help him exhort a people weary from the Depression and frightened by the war. In the bleak winter months after Pearl Harbor, when nothing was going right for the Allies, he summoned the spirit of the patriots of Valley Forge, reminding a Washington's Birthday audience that, as Thomas Paine had written in 1776, " 'Tyranny, like hell, is not easily conquered.' "

As the war went on and he became older and ever frailer, Roosevelt seemed to become more reflective than usual. In early 1944, dining in the White House with Reverend Howard Johnson, a curate from St. John's, the beautiful Episcopal parish on Lafayette Square, Roosevelt found himself enjoying a wide-ranging literary and theological conversation. As Frances Perkins recalled it, Roosevelt and Johnson spoke of Dorothy Sayers, the British author who wrote books about religion as well as her Lord Peter Wimsey series of mysteries (FDR knew the latter, but had not heard of the former). Talk turned to Søren Kierkegaard, whom Johnson had studied, and Roosevelt listened with interest, taking time in the midst of war to muse about theology and philosophy.

Every year Roosevelt attended a special service at St. John's to commemorate his first inauguration, and Johnson was to plan the 1944 liturgy. The priest decided to include a controversial prayer, one entitled "Prayer for Our Enemies." The other clergy at St. John's, Perkins recalled, scoffed at their junior colleague. "The White House would never authorize it in wartime," Perkins wrote. "[I]t would be misunderstood throughout the country; the publicity would be terrible, since the Christian injunction to pray for our enemies was scarcely understood, even by Christians in this country." When Roosevelt read over the proposed service, however, he scribbled a note next to the prayer: "Very good—I like it." FDR recognized that humility, not hubris, was the proper posture for a nation whose sons were under fire.

Gathering in the church at 10:30 on the morning of Saturday, March 4, 1944, the president of the United States, his Cabinet, and the senior officials of a nation at war bowed their heads as these words were said:

Most loving Father, who by thy Son Jesus Christ hast taught us to love our enemies and to pray for them, we beseech thee, give to those who are now our enemies the light of thy Holy Spirit. Grant that they and we, being enlightened in conscience and cleansed from every sin, may know and do thy will, and so be changed from foes to friends united in thy service; through Jesus Christ our Lord. Amen.

THE D-DAY PRAYER

The drinks were strong, the company congenial, the evenings lovely and moonlit. On the first weekend of June 1944, Roosevelt slipped away from Washington to spend a few days at Kenwood, the estate of his aide General Edwin "Pa" Watson in the rolling hills outside Charlottesville, Virginia. It was a favorite spot of Roosevelt's, so much so that Watson built a simple but comfortable guest house for the president. Accompanied by his cousin Margaret "Daisy" Suckley, his daughter Anna, and her husband, John Boettiger, Roosevelt had important business to take care of as he tried to relax for a few days: across the Atlantic, in southern England, Allied forces were preparing to launch Overlord, the cross-channel operation that Churchill called "the most complicated and difficult that has ever taken place." The reckoning was at hand; D-day, what the Allies hoped to be the beginning of the end of Hitler's Fortress Europe, was scheduled for Monday, June 5. Twenty thousand men might die in the first waves to strike the beaches of Normandy; failure would be catastrophic, perhaps bringing down Churchill's government in London, costing Roosevelt the presidential election in November, and giving the Nazis world enough and time to finish the work they had begun in the death camps of Eastern Europe and possibly complete an atomic bomb of their own. If there were ever a moment for prayer, no matter what one's conviction or creed, Roosevelt thought, this was it.

Feeling at home among family and friends, Roosevelt began composing a prayer to read to the nation on the day of the invasion. The result, delivered by the president over the radio on the evening of Tuesday, June 6, 1944—the attack had been delayed for a day because of the weather—was an eloquent, six-minute-long appeal to a superintending providence.

> Almighty God: Our sons, pride of our nation, this day have set upon a mighty endeavor, a struggle to preserve our Republic, our religion and our civilization, and to set free a suffering humanity.

Lead them straight and true; give strength to their arms, stoutness to their hearts, steadfastness in their faith.

They will need Thy blessings. Their road will be long and hard. For the enemy is strong. He may hurl back our forces. Success may not come with rushing speed, but we shall return again and again; and we know that by Thy grace, and by the righteousness of our cause, our sons will triumph.

They will be sore tried, by night and by day, without rest—until the victory is won. The darkness will be rent by noise and flame. Men's souls will be shaken with the violences of war.

For these men are lately drawn from the ways of peace. They fight not for the lust of conquest. They fight to end conquest. They fight to liberate. They fight to let justice arise, and tolerance and good-will among all Thy people. They yearn but for the end of battle, for their return to the haven of home.

Some will never return. Embrace these, Father, and receive them, Thy heroic servants, into Thy kingdom. . . .

With Thy blessing, we shall prevail over the unholy forces of our enemy. Help us to conquer the apostles of greed and racial arrogances. Lead us to the saving of our country, and with our sister nations into a world unity that will spell a sure peace—a peace invulnerable to the schemings of unworthy men. And a peace that will let all men live in freedom, reaping the just rewards of their honest toil.

Thy will be done, Almighty God.

Amen.

The White House released the text to the afternoon newspapers with the request that the audience—estimated at one hundred million Americans—read it along with the president. If that estimate is right, then on that Tuesday in June, Franklin Roosevelt led what was, at the time, one of the largest single mass prayers in human history.

The moment invested the sacrifice of so many young lives with the peculiarly religious combination of hope and humility. Their mission could not have been nobler—before the year was out, the same men liberated Nazi death camps—and Roosevelt, confronted with the nearly unthinkable responsibility of sending so many lives into harm's way, chose not to take the occasion to justify the war or to offer the troops platitudinous praise. Like Lincoln before him in the fading weeks of the Civil War, Roosevelt thought it wise to draw on the language and ritual of public religion to do the best one could at an hour when events were beyond the control of any president: help Americans see the crisis in the largest possible context, reminding them that nothing would be easy but that the cause was worth the sacrifice.

Roosevelt knew his audience. "With uncanny oneness of gesture," *Newsweek* said, "America turned to prayer." From dawn forward, correspondents wired word of spontaneous religious devotion back to the magazine's headquarters in New York. Churches and synagogues were full. A girl knelt in prayer at an intersection in Detroit. In Covington, Kentucky, women said the rosary. A family in Coffeyville, Kansas, fell to their knees on their front porch. In Corpus Christi, Texas, the parents of fifty soldiers crawled two blocks on their hands and knees in an act of penance. *Time* magazine agreed. "Across the land, generally, the mood was solemn," it said. "There was no sudden fear, as on that September morning in 1939 when the Germans marched into Poland; no sudden hate, as on Pearl Harbor day. This time, moved by a common impulse, the casual churchgoers as well as the devout went to pray."

The Allies were fighting for many things in World War II, among them the cause of spreading the rights and insights of our own Founding to other parts of the world. As Roosevelt was preparing his 1941 State of the Union speech, he was at work with his aides Samuel Rosenman, Robert Sherwood, and Harry Hopkins. As Rosenman recalled it, the president said to his secretary, "Dorothy, take a law," and began: "We must look forward to a world based on four essential freedoms. The first is freedom of speech and expression—everywhere in the world. The second is freedom of every person to worship God in his own way—everywhere in the world. The third is freedom from want. . . . The fourth is freedom from fear. . . ."

The section complete, Hopkins objected to the phrase "everywhere in the world."

"That covers an awful lot of territory, Mr. President," Rosenman recalled Hopkins saying. "I don't know how interested Americans are going to be in the people of Java."

Roosevelt came right back at Hopkins: "I'm afraid they'll have to be some day, Harry. The world is getting so small that even the people in Java are getting to be our neighbors now."

POSTWAR PIETY

On the day Roosevelt died, Thursday, April 12, 1945, Vice President Harry Truman had been on the job eight days shy of three months. The world was still at war. Hitler would not commit suicide until eighteen days later, and progress on the atomic bomb—about which Truman knew little when he was summoned to the White House from Sam Rayburn's hideaway office on Capitol Hill—was uncertain. "There have been few men in all history the equal of the man into whose shoes I am stepping," Truman told an Associated Press reporter the next morning. "I pray God I can measure up to the task." Later that day, after a lunch on Capitol Hill, Truman paused with reporters on his way back to the White House. "Boys, if you ever pray, pray for me now," he said. "I don't know whether you fellows ever had a load of hay fall on you, but when they told me yesterday what had happened, I felt like the moon, the stars, and all the planets had fallen on me."

On the Monday after Roosevelt's death—the thirty-second president had been buried between the hedges of his mother's rose garden by the rector of St. James the day before—Truman gave his first address to Congress. His peroration was in the spirit of Washington, Adams, Jefferson, and Roosevelt, and it shared, too, the humility of Lincoln's rhetoric. "At this moment I have in my heart a prayer," Truman said. "As I have assumed my duties, I humbly pray Almighty God, in the words of King Solomon: 'Give therefore Thy servant an understanding heart to judge Thy people, that I may discern between good and bad: for who is able to judge this Thy so great a people?' I ask only to be a good and faithful servant of my Lord and my people."

There it was again, at the midpoint of what Henry Luce called the American Century, as Nazi death camps were being liberated and, in the desert of New Mexico, the Atomic Age was about to begin: an American president invoking the story of Israel. It is doubtful that Truman thought about the implication of his choice of scripture: Solomon was the son of God's beloved David, and many Americans felt as many Israelites may have when the great king died—uncertain, worried, and somewhat skeptical of the man who had assumed the throne. Yet what had begun with Reverend Duché and Psalm Thirty-five on that frightening day in Philadelphia in 1774 unfolded yet again— words of supplication and reverence offered to the Almighty, in the hope and with the prayer that he might protect us.

Within two years, however, an intriguing and enduring pattern emerged. As the nation grew more broadly religious, fueled in part by the Cold War against "godless Communism," the Supreme Court, led by Justice Hugo Black, the former Klansman from Alabama, excavated Jefferson's letter to the Danbury Baptists and with it his wall between church and state—or at least what the court thought his wall was. In 1947, in a decision that actually upheld some aid to parochial schools, Black wrote a crucial paragraph in his majority opinion in the case of *Everson v. Board of Education of the Township of Ewing (New Jersey) et al.*

The "establishment of religion" clause of the First Amendment means at least this: Neither a state nor the Federal Government can set up a church. Neither can pass laws which aid one religion, aid all religions, or prefer one religion over another. Neither can force nor influence a person [to] go to or remain away from church against his will or force him to profess a belief or disbelief in any religion. No person can be punished for entertaining or professing religious beliefs or disbeliefs, for church attendance or non-attendance. . . . In the words of Jefferson, the clause against establishment of religion by law was intended to erect "a wall of separation between Church and State."

Black concluded: "The First Amendment has erected a wall between church and state. That wall must be kept high and impregnable. We could not approve the slightest breach."

In *McCollum v. Board of Education,* an Illinois atheist argued that allowing religious teachers to come into public schools to offer religious instruction breached just that wall. The court agreed, thus building on the principles outlined in Black's *Everson* opinion, and an apparent judicial trend toward separation was by now well under way. Against this tide, the National Association of Evangelicals, understandably but hopelessly proposed adding Jesus to the Constitution: "This nation divinely recognizes the authority and law of Jesus Christ, Savior and Ruler of Nations, through whom are bestowed the blessings of Almighty God." The amendment was offered in 1947 and again in 1954, to no avail.

The late 1940s and '50s were also the years in which Billy Graham was filling stadiums and making his first visits to the White House, when President Eisenhower opened Cabinet meetings with prayer (on one occasion, however, deep into a session, he said, "Jesus Christ! We forgot the prayer!"), when Congress voted to make "In God We Trust" the national motto, and the phrase "under God" was added to the Pledge of Allegiance—all signs of a vital public religion.

The Supreme Court's move toward putting more distance between private religion and the public sphere on specific questions of law and the rise of what was called "Piety Along the Potomac" were simultaneous. As the postwar world took shape at home and abroad, with the court's growing interest in separation, the stirrings of civil rights, the rise of a more geographically mobile culture, and the pervasive fear of nuclear attack, Americans found comfort in the rituals of public religion as an antidote to the changes around them.

"INTERFAITH IN ACTION"

Eisenhower was an easy target for scholars who tend to look down on the public religion of a generic God. Writing in 1955, the sociologist Will Herberg noted Americans' *"faith in faith"*—the italics were his—and defined "the American Way of Life" as a collection of beliefs, rituals, and symbols that "commends itself to the American as the right, the good, and the true in actual life. It embraces such seemingly incongruous elements as sanitary plumbing and freedom of opportunity, Coca-Cola and an intense faith in education—all felt as moral questions relating to the proper way of life." To some, Eisenhower seemed unsophisticated—bland, platitudinous, unaware of complexity. Faith produced important values, Eisenhower once said: "Honesty, decency, fairness, service—all that sort of thing." It was the kind of answer that made the intelligentsia chuckle ruefully.

As usual, though, reading Eisenhower in context reveals that the Supreme Commander of the liberation of Europe, like other great presidents, was often underestimated. At the Waldorf-Astoria on Park Avenue in New York on Monday, December 22, 1952, president-elect Eisenhower—he had just defeated Adlai Stevenson in November—was discussing the Cold War in remarks before a meeting of the directors of the Freedoms Foundation. Contrasting the United States with the Soviet Union, Eisenhower recalled thinking how "hopeless" it had been to talk to a Red Army officer he knew about the differences between American democracy and Soviet Communism. There was no point in trying to explain the United States, Eisenhower said, to a man who had no sense of faith, for "our form of government is founded on religion." The premise of the nation was spiritual, not secular. "Our ancestors who formed this government said, . . . 'We hold that all men are endowed by their Creator. . . .' Not by the accident of birth, not by the color of their skins or by anything else, but 'all men are endowed by their Creator,' " Eisenhower stated. "In other words, our form of government has no sense unless it is founded in a deeply felt religious faith, and I don't care what it is. With us of course it is the Jud[e]o-Christian concept but it must be a religion that [believes] all men are created equal. . . . Even those among us who are, in my opinion, so silly as to doubt the existence of an Almighty, are still members of a religious civilization, because the Founding Fathers said it was a religious concept that they were trying to translate into the political world." Eisenhower understood something many Americans do not quite grasp even now: that "Nature's God" resides at the center of the Founding.

He also used a term—"Judeo-Christian"—that was growing in popularity in mid-twentieth-century America but actually dated back to the last year of the nineteenth. As the scholar Mark Silk noted, the phrase first appeared in the *Literary Guide* in 1899 to connote Christianity's debt to Judaism in the first century. George Orwell used the term in 1939; by 1941, in response to rising anti-Semitism in America, moderate and liberal Christians adopted "Judeo-Christian" to encapsulate the two traditions' shared values of individual worth, rule of law, and common decency. While some Jews worried the phrase threatened to subsume Judaism, other Jewish leaders and liberal Protestants such as Reinhold Niebuhr were undertaking theological work to chart the common ground between the two faiths. (As Islam grew in the United States, the search for such ground would widen to include Muslims.) John Adams had anticipated some of this. "It has pleased the Providence of the first Cause, the Universal Cause, that Abraham should give religion not only to Hebrews but to Christians and Mahomitans, the greatest part of the modern civilized world," he wrote in 1818.

In 1948, the government offered its sanction to the Judeo-Christian idea, issuing a postage stamp to commemorate the Protestant, Catholic, and Jewish chaplains of the USS *Dorchester,* an American troop ship sunk in 1943. The ship's four chaplains surrendered their own life jackets to save others and went down with the ship—"arm and arm in prayer," survivors recalled. The stamp read: "Interfaith in action."

There were worse things to sanction and celebrate; still, many devout believers made something of an industry of diminishing the manifestations of public faith, arguing that bland religion was no religion at all. "Remember the float representing religion in President Eisenhower's inaugural parade?" the *Episcopal Church News* wrote. "Standing for all religions, it had the symbols of none, and it looked like nothing whatsoever in Heaven above, or in the earth beneath, except possibly an oversized model of a deformed molar left over from some dental exhibit." Quoting these words in a 1954 piece in *The Reporter* magazine, William Lee Miller said that "the content of official religion is bound to be thin; the commitment to it is also apt, now and then, to be hollow. Where everybody professionally believes something, then for some the belief may be a bit more professional than real."

That is certainly so, but it is a price the country was willing to pay in order to enjoy the benefits of public religion in the Tocqueville tradition rather than go down the darker path of Puritan excesses of the seventeenth century in New England, which may be more orthodox but which belongs in the private, not the public, sphere. Serious believers will always find public religion wanting—lighter on substance, perhaps, than they would like, or vague to the point of meaninglessness. But part of the American gospel is that such lamentations should take place in churches or homes, not in the public arena. "This is the first principle of democracy: that the essential things in men are the things they hold in common, not the things they hold separately," G. K. Chesterton once remarked, and the defense of democracy, including its allowance for differences and divergent opinions, is bound to the defense of faith, for freedom is like oxygen to religion. Without liberty for all, some one sect or creed might crush all the others, and history tells us that no earthly victory is ever final—so he who crushes may one day be crushed. Religious liberty frees a society from the threat of such strife.

ISLAM IN WASHINGTON

The Eisenhowers were quick to take off their shoes. In late June 1957, the president and his wife, Mamie, were driven from the White House to the opening of the new Islamic Center on Massachusetts Avenue in Washington. Ambassadors from the Arab League had told Eisenhower's staff that the president and

In 1957, President and Mrs. Eisenhower doffed their shoes as a sign of respect as they toured the new Islamic Center in Washington, D.C. "And I should like to assure you, my Islamic friends, that under the American Constitution, under American tradition, and in American hearts, this center, this place of worship, is just as welcome as could be a similar edifice of any other religion," Eisenhower said. *(AP Images)*

the first lady needed only to slip cloth coverings over their shoes as they toured the prayer room (which faces Mecca), but the Eisenhowers cheerfully skipped the intermediate course, with Eisenhower covering his socks and Mamie padding around wearing her nylons.

The symbolism of the shoes was matched by some extemporaneous remarks of the president's. Listening were the representatives of Saudi Arabia, Afghanistan, Egypt, Indonesia, Iran, Iraq, Jordan, Libya, Morocco, Pakistan, Sudan, Syria, Tunisia, Turkey, and Yemen. Departing from his prepared text, Eisenhower said, "And I should like to assure you, my Islamic friends, that under the American Constitution, under American tradition, and in American hearts, this center, this place of worship, is just as welcome as could be a similar edifice of any other religion. Indeed, America would fight with her whole strength for your right to have here your own church and worship according to your own conscience. This concept is indeed part of America, and without that concept we would be something else than what we are." Soothing words and good intentions, but there was a small yet telling moment that showed cross-cultural understanding would require careful attention to detail: the American dignitaries' shoes—those of congressmen, senators, Supreme Court justices, and diplomats—were, *The Washington Post* reported, hopelessly mixed together, leaving men like the eighty-nine-year-old senator from Rhode Island, Theodore Green, struggling to find his wingtips.

THE KENNEDY MOMENT

Nearly half a century on, Ted Sorensen could still remember the letters: a flood of them, from all over, attacking John Kennedy's Catholicism in the 1960 presidential campaign. "The single biggest obstacle to his election was his religion," said Sorensen, Kennedy's speechwriter and special counsel. "You should have seen the hate mail that came in, both from rednecks and from liberal intellectuals who should have known better." At a distance it is striking to read Kennedy's speeches and remarks: far from dodging religious subjects or muting his mentions of God, Kennedy frequently alluded to the Almighty, cited scripture, and carried on the tradition of framing America as a nation charged not only with protecting its own liberties but, in Kennedy's phrase, with projecting them in order to "truly light the world."

There was some irony in John Kennedy's finding himself in the role of a pioneering Catholic. In a conversation with one of JFK's sisters, Frank Pakenham, a writer and politician who was the seventh Earl of Longford, once mentioned he might write a book about President Kennedy's personal religion. As Arthur Schlesinger, Jr., recalled, the sister's reply was terse: "That will be a very short book." When I asked Ted Sorensen what he thought Kennedy meant when he spoke of God, the response was also quick. "The honest answer is I don't know," Sorensen said. "He was intent on not wearing his religion on his sleeve."

In the arena, where he could not help but address the question of his Catholicism, Kennedy faced what was called "the religious issue" with grit, grace, and wit. At a meeting of the American Society of Newspaper Editors in Washington on Thursday, April 21, 1960, he said he did not want to be the first Catholic president—he wanted to be president, and he happened to have been born a Catholic. "I have made it clear that I strongly support—out of conviction as well as constitutional obligation—the guarantees of religious equality provided by the First Amendment; and I ask only that these same guarantees be extended to me," he told the editors. He challenged them to avoid reflexive labels. "Can we justify analyzing voters as well as candidates strictly in terms of their religion?" Referring to the Wisconsin primary, Kennedy chided journalists for their obsession with faith. "I think the voters of Wisconsin objected to being categorized simply as either Catholics or Protestants. . . . I think they objected to being accosted by reporters outside of political meetings and asked one question only—their religion—not their occupation or education or philosophy or income, only their religion." A student of history and a lover of politics, Kennedy was astute about the electorate. "For voters are more than Catholics, Protestants, or Jews," he said. "They make up their minds for many diverse reasons, good and bad. To submit the candidates to a religious test is unfair enough—to apply it to the voters themselves is divisive, degrading, and wholly unwarranted." Tough, smart words, putting the press on notice while his campaign—like all campaigns—strategized and maneuvered, thinking of blocs of voters.

He could also be extremely funny about his religion, using humor to smooth the edges of the wedge. (He had done the same with the subject of his family's wealth, joking that his father, Joseph P. Kennedy, had told him not to buy a single vote more than was necessary because "I'll be damned if I'll pay for a landslide.") At a Democratic event in the Bronx the same month he addressed the editors in Washington, Kennedy claimed to have spoken recently with Francis Cardinal Spellman, the powerful archbishop of New York. "I sat next to Cardinal Spellman at dinner the other evening, and asked him what I should say when voters question me about the doctrine of the pope's infallibility. 'I don't know, Senator,' the Cardinal told me. 'All I know is he keeps calling me Spillman.' "

Finally, on Monday, September 12, 1960, before the Greater Houston Ministerial Association, Kennedy made his most profound remarks on the subject—remarks with roots in the battle Madison had fought against Patrick Henry in Virginia nearly two centuries before.

> I believe in an America that is officially neither Catholic, Protestant, nor Jewish—where no public official either requests or accepts instructions on public policy from the pope, the National Council of Churches, or any other ecclesiastical source—where no religious body seeks to impose its will directly or indirectly upon the general populace or the public acts of its officials—and where religious liberty is so indivisible that an act against one church is treated as an act against all.
>
> For while this year it may be a Catholic against whom the finger of suspicion is pointed, in other years it has been, and may someday be again, a Jew—or a Quaker— or a Unitarian—or a Baptist. It was Virginia's harassment of Baptist preachers, for example, that helped lead to Jefferson's Statute of Religious Freedom. Today I may be the victim—but tomorrow it may be you—until the whole fabric of our harmonious society is ripped at a time of great national peril.
>
> Finally, I believe in an America where religious intolerance will someday end—where all men and all churches are treated as equal—where every man has the same right to attend or not attend the church of his choice—where

John Kennedy, shown here leaving St. John's Church with Reverend John C. Harper and Right Reverend William F. Creighton in 1963, was comfortable speaking of public life in religious terms. His inaugural address quoted Isaiah and Paul, and concluded that "on earth, God's work must truly be our own." *(AP Images)*

there is no Catholic vote, no anti-Catholic vote, no bloc voting of any kind—and where Catholics, Protestants, and Jews, at both the lay and pastoral level, will refrain from those attitudes of disdain and division which have so often marred their works in the past, and promote instead the American ideal of brotherhood.

In his inaugural, drawing on Jefferson, Kennedy used public religion to distinguish between America and the Soviet Union, saying that God, not man, was the author of freedom. "When he spoke of human rights coming 'from the hand of God,' he was illustrating a big difference between us and the totalitarian system we were then opposing, which believed that the rights were granted by the state," said Sorensen. With hope triumphing over experience in the service of rhetoric, Kennedy called on the Communist world to act charitably in its sphere as the Free World would in its. "Let both sides unite to heed in all corners of the earth the command of Isaiah—to 'undo the heavy burdens [and] let the oppressed go free.' " He did not see statecraft as magical or easy; life, as Augustine had said long before, was a pilgrimage, and the work of the world was never fully done. Kennedy knew that and, with admirable political candor, said so. "All this will not be finished in the first one hundred days. Nor will it be finished in the first one thousand days, nor in the life of this administration, nor even perhaps in our lifetime on this planet. But let us begin." What gave life meaning, what imbued politics with honor and drama was the notion that, in the work of hands and hearts, Americans might make their own lives and those of others gentler and freer.

Now the trumpet summons us again—not as a call to bear arms, though arms we need—not as a call to battle, though embattled we are—but as a call to bear the burden of a long twilight struggle, year in and year out, "rejoicing in hope, patient in tribulation"—a struggle against the common enemies of man: tyranny, poverty, disease, and war itself. . . . With a good conscience our only sure reward, with history the final judge of our deeds, let us go forth to lead the land we love, asking His blessing and His help, but knowing that here on earth God's work must truly be our own.

The quotation calling for good cheer among a people enveloped by a cold war—"rejoicing in hope, patient in tribulation"—is from the powerful twelfth chapter of Saint Paul's Epistle to the Romans, a chapter that closes with these words: "Be not overcome of evil, but overcome evil with good."

There was, naturally, a political and cultural calculus to Kennedy's rhetoric. "The allusions to God in his speeches were a deliberate attempt to make himself sound like any other Christian American," said Sorensen. There was something else at work, too. Kennedy loved the drama of history; like Churchill, to whom he granted an honorary American citizenship in 1963, he envisioned himself as a great actor in the pageant of time. It was partly because of his abiding historical imagination that Kennedy's rhetoric drew so heavily on public religion, for God was a character in the national story, as was Kennedy, and to play scenes with him invested the moment with the highest conceivable stakes.

As the president drew on theocentric imagery, the Supreme Court was about to set many religious conservatives off once again. On Monday, June 25, 1962, Justice Hugo Black leaned forward in his seat on the bench and read the majority opinion ruling that the State of New York could not have an official prayer read in public school classrooms. Written by the New York Board of Regents, the prayer was brief and nondenominational, assuming only the existence of a deity: "Almighty God, we acknowledge our dependence upon Thee, and we beg Thy blessing upon us, our parents, our teachers and our country." The objecting parents believed the prayer, one "composed by government officials as part of a governmental program to further religious beliefs," was unconstitutional, and once the court agreed, many Christian critics immediately said un-Christian things. "They put the Negroes in the schools and now they've driven God out," Congressman George Andrews of Alabama told *The New York Times*. A Republican representative from New York, Frank J. Becker, called it "the most tragic decision in the history of the United States," apparently judging *Dred Scott* not quite as bad. In a statement, former president Herbert Hoover—at the venerable age of eighty-eight—declared the ruling a "disintegration of one of the most sacred of American heritages" and called for "an amendment to the Constitution which establishes the right to religious devotion in all governmental agencies—national, state or local."

In a press conference, Kennedy was cool and judicious. "The Supreme Court has made its judgment, and a good many people obviously will disagree with it. . . . But I think it is important, if we are going to maintain our constitutional principle, [to] support the Supreme Court decisions even when we may not agree with them," he said. Then, sensibly, he went on: "In addition, we have in this case a very easy remedy and that is to pray ourselves. I would think that it would be a welcome reminder to every American family that we can pray a good deal more at home, we can attend our churches with a good deal more fidelity, and we can make the true meaning of prayer much more important in the lives of all of our children." There were scattered voices of support for this middle course, the one marked out by the Founders. "It is wrong for the churches to expect the government to implement their teachings," Reverend William B. Sperry of Detroit's Christ Episcopal Church said in *Time*—words that would have pleased Roger Williams. In Schenectady, New York, the magazine reported, the Methodist Church put up a sign saying that the "place for specific teaching and formal practice of religion is in the home and in the church."

The court was not yet done. In an eight-to-one decision in June 1963, the justices ruled—not surprisingly, given the trend since *Everson* in 1947—that reciting the Lord's Prayer and reading the Bible in public schools was unconstitutional. In a United Press International bulletin from Stuttgart, Germany, where he was leading crusades, Billy Graham passionately protested the ruling. "I am shocked at the Supreme Court's decision," he said. "Prayers and Bible reading have been a part of American public school life since the Pilgrims landed at Plymouth Rock." Leaving aside whether public school devotionals as understood in 1963 were part of the life of Plymouth Plantation during the hard years, Graham was voicing the feelings of millions. "At a time when moral decadence is evident on every hand, when race tension is mounting, when the threat of Communism is growing, when terrifying new weapons of destruction are being created, we need more religion, not less." Graham's closing point: "Eighty percent of the American people want Bible reading and prayer in the schools. Why should the majority be so severely penalized by the protests of a handful?"

Because that is what America does: within reason, it is dedicated to the religious idea that we are all created equal and are entitled, by the laws of God, not just of men, to protection from the pressures of the majority. An Indiana Republican congress-man, Richard L. Roudebush, followed Herbert Hoover's lead from the year before and said he would propose an amendment to overturn the court's decision. "Congress must act if our Christian heritage is to be preserved for future generations," he said. And Strom Thurmond of South Carolina predictably chalked the ruling up as "another major triumph for the forces of secularism and atheism."

The extremes, while colorful and quotable, were just that: the extremes. The line most people seem to draw is one of grace and civility. No one should be forced, as a matter of routine, to participate in (or even have to choose not to participate in, by leaving a classroom) a religious exercise that makes him uncomfortable. Are legislators made uneasy by prayers at the opening of a session? They are grown-ups and can decide whether to leave or stay or pay attention or read the paper. Should presidents and other public officials refrain from allusions to God in the context of public religion because some people in their audience, either at hand or beyond, are atheists or secularists? One could make arguments either way, but the cultural reality—one with strong historical foundations from the Founding—is that such allusions are important to enough Americans, and particularly to those making the allusions, that evocations of God are as much a part of the American tradition as is liberty from coercion.

Public religion was at the center of the remarks President Kennedy was on his way to deliver to a luncheon at the Dallas Trade Mart on Friday, November 22, 1963. Had he lived to speak them, they would have been in keeping with his, and the country's, long and eloquent record of religious evocations.

"We in this country, in this generation, are—by destiny rather than choice—the watchmen on the walls of world freedom. We ask, therefore, that we may be worthy of our power and responsibility, that we may exercise our strength with wisdom and restraint, and that we may achieve in our time and for all time the ancient vision of 'peace on earth, goodwill toward men,' " Kennedy's text read. "That must always be our goal, and the righteousness of our cause must always underlie our strength"—a point Lincoln would have recognized and agreed with. "For as was written long ago," Kennedy was to conclude, " 'except the Lord keep the city, the watchman waketh but in vain.' "

The source of Kennedy's climactic quotation was the King James Version of the 127th Psalm.

RECKONING AT SELMA

With the president who was to have given that speech dead, his successor, Lyndon B. Johnson, stepped off *Air Force One* to address the nation in the November night. "I ask for your help—and God's," he said on the tarmac, his breath misty in the autumn cold.

Johnson liked things *big*—big cars, big dreams, big ideas. America as nothing less than the New Israel was just right for him—his only regret, perhaps, was that God had used Moses, not him, as his interlocutory. Writing his essay on civil religion for the Winter 1967 issue of *Daedalus,* Robert Bellah quoted Johnson's 1965 inaugural to illustrate the theme of America as a Promised Land that would illumine the world. "They came here—the exile and the stranger, brave but frightened—to find a place where a man could be his own man," Johnson said. "They made a covenant with this land. Conceived in justice, written in liberty, bound in union, it was meant one day to inspire the hopes of all mankind; and it binds us still. If we keep its terms, we shall flourish."

A test of those terms soon arrived. On Sunday, March 7, 1965, in Alabama, John Lewis and Hosea Williams, two of Martin Luther King, Jr.'s lieutenants in the war against Jim Crow, were leading a march from Selma to Montgomery. Lewis, just 25 years old—a native of tiny Troy, Alabama, who had been ordained a Baptist minister at age 18—was wearing a light raincoat. He was there because of God: he had joined the movement out of religious conviction, and it was faith that kept him going, through all the taunts and all the threats. "Without religion—without the example of Christ, who sacrificed for others—as the foundation of the movement, it would have been impossible for us to endure the setbacks, and to hope, and to go on," Lewis recalled. "It was religion that got us on the buses for the Freedom Rides; we were in Selma that day because of our faith."

As they set out through town, he was struck by the unusual atmospherics. "It was somber and subdued," Lewis wrote in his memoir, *Walking with the Wind,* "almost like a funeral procession." They went down Water Street and made their way to the base of the Edmund Pettus Bridge. It is still there, with its steel canopy and steep rise. At the top of the bridge, Lewis stopped. "There, facing us at the bottom of the other side, stood a sea of blue-helmeted, blue-uniformed Alabama state troopers, line after line of them, dozens of battle-ready lawmen stretched from one side of U.S. Highway 80 to the other." The marchers would not turn around. Peaceably, unarmed, committed to nonviolence, Lewis and Williams led the way to the bottom of the bridge. "We were prepared to die," Lewis told me four decades later. "Dr. King had taught us to use the teachings of Jesus and the techniques of Gandhi, and we knew the price we might have to pay in blood." With a bullhorn, Major John Cloud said: "You have two minutes to turn around and go back to your church." Years later, after the beatings and the pain, Lewis recalled every detail of what ensued: "We couldn't go forward. We couldn't go back. There was only one option left that I could see."

"We should kneel and pray," Lewis said to Williams.

But the lawmen had already made up their minds. Cloud or-

On Sunday, March 7, 1965, John Lewis and Hosea Williams led a peaceful march across the Edmund Pettus Bridge in Selma, Alabama; confronted by white Alabama lawmen, they knelt to pray as the authorities fired tear gas and began to beat the innocent. It became known as "Bloody Sunday"—but led to the Voting Rights Act later that year. (© 1965 *Spider Martin/The Spider Martin Civil Rights Collection. All rights reserved. Used with permission.*)

dered his men forward. It was, Lewis said, "like a human wave, a blur of blue shirts and billy clubs and bullwhips." He heard a woman scream: "Get 'em! *Get* the niggers!" A trooper struck Lewis on the left side of the head, and he fell to the asphalt; soon he was inhaling tear gas, C-4. "I began choking, coughing," Lewis wrote. "I couldn't get air into my lungs. I felt as if I was taking my last breath."

As television cameras rolled and still cameras clicked, Lewis, lying on the ground, fighting for oxygen, believed the end had come. "This is it," he remembered thinking. "People are going to die here. *I'm* going to die here."

Lewis felt a kind of calm; he recalled worrying about the others—about Hosea, and his comrades stretching back toward the bridge—but an odd sense of tranquility was coming over him. "I was ready to die," he told me. "I really thought I saw death when I was lying on that pavement. I really did. It was peaceful, somehow." Mercifully, he survived, and by ten that night, Lewis, his wound treated at Good Samaritan Hospital, was sedated and slipped off to sleep. He only heard later about what happened that evening. ABC's Frank Reynolds interrupted the film *Judgment at Nuremberg* to show the assault on Lewis and his fellow marchers. "The images were stunning—scene after scene of policemen on foot and on horseback beating defenseless American citizens," Lewis wrote. "Many viewers thought this was somehow part of the movie. It seemed too strange, too ugly to be real. It *couldn't* be real."

The day became known as Bloody Sunday. The movement organized in the black churches of the South, led by ministers of God such as Lewis, King, and Ralph Abernathy, was a moral struggle and a religious one, informed and shaped by biblical thought and language. Eight days later President Johnson went to Congress to propose a voting rights act.

The president's speech that night, one which has since entered the American canon, nearly did not happen. After a long liquid dinner party at the house of Arthur Schlesinger, Jr., in Washington, Richard Goodwin went home to bed on the evening of Sunday, March 14, 1965. A speechwriter and advisor to President Johnson, Goodwin thought he had little to do; the major piece of business in the White House, the drafting of Johnson's address to Congress in the wake of Bloody Sunday, had been assigned to another speechwriter. When Johnson woke up in the White House that Monday morning, he asked Jack Valenti: "How's Dick coming with the speech?"

"He's not doing it," Valenti replied. "I assigned it to Horace Busby."

As Goodwin recalled the story, "Johnson sat upright, his voice raised in sudden anger: 'The hell you did. Don't you know a liberal Jew has his hand on the pulse of America? And you assign the most important speech of my life to a Texas public relations man? Get Dick to do it. And now!' "

Goodwin arrived at the White House about 9:30 a.m., and suddenly found himself staring at his typewriter. "It just came," he recalled—cadences from scripture, echoes of Lincoln, the language of the marchers in the streets. Johnson was reading the speech page by page as they came out of the typewriter. "The biblical imagery is part of the American tradition, no matter what your personal beliefs are," Goodwin told me forty years later. "The Old Testament, the New Testament, it is all woven into who we are, Christian, Jew, or whatever. Religious metaphors and religious language form a kind of common bond in America—you can think of it either in literal or literary terms. Even if you are basically secular, the ideals and principles that come out of religion are essentially what we all should share: what is the right thing to do, what is just, what is fair. Most Americans believe there is a higher power at work, whether they call it God or not, and I was trying to frame the civil rights question in terms of what was right, what was just, what was fair—and that was, to me at least, and certainly to Johnson, partly religious."

"At times history and fate meet at a single time in a single place to shape a turning point in man's unending search for freedom," Johnson said that evening. "So it was at Lexington and Concord. So it was a century ago at Appomattox. So it was last week in Selma, Alabama." Later Johnson intoned the first three words of the great spiritual: "We *shall* overcome."

The opening sentences of the address, lines in which Johnson explained his mission in simple, powerful, declarative terms, are much less well known. "I speak tonight for the dignity of man and the destiny of democracy," he said. "I urge every member of both parties, Americans of all religions and of all colors, from every section of this country, to join me in that cause." As he defended dignity and democracy, he needed to summon Americans of all religions, for many white Christians remained morally blind to racism, often defending it, as had their forebears, on biblical grounds. Johnson, in his thick Texas voice, was having none of it:

Rarely are we met with a challenge, not to our growth
or abundance, or our welfare or our security, but rather
to the values and the purposes and the meaning of our

beloved nation. The issue of equal rights for American Negroes is such an issue. And should we defeat every enemy, and should we double our wealth and conquer the stars, and still be unequal to this issue, then we will have failed as a people and as a nation. For, with a country as with a person, "what is a man profited if he shall gain the whole world, and lose his own soul?" . . .

Above the pyramid on the great seal of the United States it says in Latin, "God has favored our undertaking." God will not favor everything that we do. It is rather our duty to divine His will. But I cannot help believing that He truly understands and that He really favors the undertaking that we begin here tonight.

In the house of a Selma dentist, a recuperating John Lewis watched the address with King. Always self-effacing, Lewis credited King with preparing the way for the message Johnson was to deliver. "Dr. King had transformed the streets of Selma, of Montgomery, of Birmingham, and the steps of the Lincoln Memorial into one huge pulpit," Lewis recalled, and the nation was about to hear from a president who had absorbed King's gospel of equality before the law.

"I was deeply moved," Lewis wrote. "Lyndon Johnson was no politician that night. He was a man who spoke from his heart. His were the words of a statesman and more; they were the words of a poet." If he were a poet, he was one with a theological streak, for the idea that God "truly understands and . . . really favors the undertaking that we begin here tonight" suggests that we live in a world governed by an attentive God who

198 | JON MEACHAM

has given us free will but also the instinct to try to, as Johnson phrased it, "divine His will."

Johnson's quotation from Jesus—"what is a man profited if he shall gain the whole world, and lose his own soul?"—comes from a critical chapter of the Gospel of Matthew. Like Bloody Sunday—a day of sin that led to at least a partial national redemption—the passage from Matthew is about both hope and hardship. In it Jesus makes an ultimate promise. "Thou art Peter," he says to the man hitherto known as Simon Barjona, "and upon this rock I will build my church; and the gates of hell shall not prevail against it." Then, only a few verses later, Jesus is clear that nothing will be easy for those who choose, as he has and as John Lewis did, to reverse the usual human order of things and find strength in weakness, or win victory without violence. "If any man will come after me," Jesus says, "let him deny himself, and take up his cross, and follow me. For whosoever will save his life shall lose it: and whosoever will lose his life for my sake shall find it." The very next verse is the one Johnson quoted. He understood the centrality of paradox, that, as in his hero Franklin Roosevelt's cherished Beatitudes, the first shall be last and the last first. "We will guard against violence," Johnson said that night, "knowing it strikes from our hands the very weapons which we seek—progress, obedience to law, and belief in American values." Values that, in Johnson's mind and in that of his country's, were religious.

Two weeks after Bloody Sunday, on March 21, 1965, at Thomas Road Baptist Church in Lynchburg, Virginia, the congregation's thirty-one-year-old pastor, Reverend Jerry Falwell, preached a sermon he would come to regret. "Believing the

Bible as I do, I would find it impossible to stop preaching the pure saving gospel of Jesus Christ, and begin doing anything else—including the fighting of communism, or participating in civil rights reforms," Falwell said. "As a God-called preacher, I find that there is no time left after I give the proper time and attention to winning people to Christ. Preachers are not called to be politicians but to be soul winners." That was Falwell's view when ministers were marching for equality for black people. In little more than a decade, however, Falwell would change his mind about preachers and politics.

V. THE FIGHT WAS ON!

THE MARTYRDOM OF DR. KING, THE RISE OF A NEW RIGHT, AND REAGAN'S DELICATE BALANCE

*We shall overcome because the arc of a moral universe
is long, but it bends toward justice.*

—REVEREND MARTIN LUTHER KING, JR., SUNDAY,
MARCH 31, 1968, WASHINGTON NATIONAL CATHEDRAL

*Yes, let us pray for the salvation of all of those who live in
that totalitarian darkness—pray they will discover the
joy of knowing God. But until they do, let us be aware
that while they preach the supremacy of the state, declare
its omnipotence over individual man, and predict its
eventual domination of all peoples on the earth, they are
the focus of evil in the modern world.*

—RONALD REAGAN, REMARKS ON THE SOVIET UNION
TO THE NATIONAL ASSOCIATION OF EVANGELICALS,
MARCH 8, 1983

*D*epressed and somewhat adrift, Martin Luther King, Jr., was
having a hard time sleeping as the winter of 1968 came to an
end. In Washington, his plans for a massive Poor People's Campaign to call for economic justice were in disarray. In Memphis,

his first march with striking sanitation workers had degenerated into a riot when young black radicals—not, as in the old days, white state troopers—broke his nonviolent ranks. The WHITES ONLY signs had been taken down and, following the civil- and voting-rights triumphs of 1964 and 1965, King felt lost. "Dr. King kept saying, 'Where do we go? How do we get there?' " John Lewis recalls.

In 1968 King was trying to build an interracial coalition to end the war in Vietnam and force major economic reforms. He understood that the clarity of the conflicts of Birmingham and Selma was gone and sensed the tricky racial and political terrain ahead. At the March on Washington in August 1963, King had spoken of the Founding in moving and metaphorical terms. "When the architects of our republic wrote the magnificent words of the Constitution and the Declaration of Independence, they were signing a promissory note to which every American was to fall heir," King had said. But America, King said, had "given the Negro people a bad check, a check which has come back marked 'insufficient funds.' " He knew the country was now embarking on a long twilight struggle against poverty and violence—necessarily more diffuse, and more arduous, than the fight against Jim Crow. He realized that jealousies among reformers, always high, would grow even worse; once the target shifted to poverty, it would be difficult to replicate the drama that had led to the landmark legislation of the middle of the decade. On the streets, the Black Power movement thought King's philosophy of nonviolence was out of date. Within the system King fared little better. "The years before '68 were a time when people in Detroit would call us to march for civil rights—come to Chicago, come to L.A.," Jesse

202 | JON MEACHAM

Jackson said. "But by the '70s, you had mayors who were doing the work every day."

King took the change in climate hard. On the last weekend of March 1968, he was back in Atlanta from Memphis after the sanitation riot. Sitting in his study at Ebenezer Baptist Church, King fretted and contemplated a fast—a genuine sacrifice for a man who joked about how his collars were growing tighter. King mused about getting out of the full-time movement, maybe becoming president of Morehouse College. Then his spirits started to rise. "He preached himself out of the gloom," said Jackson. "We must turn a minus into a plus," King said, "a stumbling block into a steppingstone—we must go on anyhow." Early the next morning he left for Washington, where he was to preach at the National Cathedral.

"THE SONS OF GOD WILL SHOUT FOR JOY"

Sunday, March 31, 1968, was cloudy with a threat of rain in the capital. King climbed the thirteen steps into the cathedral's ten-foot-high pulpit, one carved from stone that had come from Canterbury Cathedral. Its panels depict scenes from the story of the English Bible, and includes an image of the barons and King John with Magna Carta, the great Western document that began shifting power from the rulers to the ruled. Lifting his eyes, King would have seen the vast stained-glass Rose Window on the west wall and the flags of the fifty states of the Union hanging in parallel rows high atop the great nave. He was pleased to note, too, that the church was crowded: like politicians and actors, preachers love a full house.

He made the most of the moment. Like John Winthrop,

King spoke of Americans as inexorably linked one to another. "We are tied together in the single garment of destiny, caught in an inescapable network of mutuality," King said. "And whatever affects one directly affects all indirectly. For some strange reason, I can never be what I ought to be until you are what you ought to be. And you can never be what you ought to be until I am what I ought to be. This is the way God's universe is made; this is the way it is structured."

We are, King said, called to do right, to seek justice, to alleviate poverty. "Ultimately a great nation is a compassionate nation," he said. "America has not met its obligations and its responsibilities to the poor." At the heart of his sermon was the religious idea of ultimate judgment—that we are not only moral agents on earth who should be kind and generous for the sake of being kind and generous but that if we are not, we will face a reckoning beyond time. A secular speaker can urge an audience toward benevolence on humane or rational grounds. A preacher has something more: the promise (or threat) of future reward or punishment. "One day we will have to stand before the God of history, and we will talk in terms of things we've done," King said. "Yes, we will be able to say we built gargantuan bridges to span the seas. We built gigantic buildings to kiss the skies. Yes, we made our submarines to penetrate oceanic depths. We brought into being many other things with our scientific and technological power." His voice echoing across the Gothic church, he went on, evoking the teachings of Jesus: "It seems that I can hear the God of history saying, 'That was not enough! But I was hungry, and ye fed me not. I was naked, and ye clothed me not. I was devoid of a decent sanitary house to live in, and ye provided no shelter for me. And consequently, you cannot enter the kingdom of greatness. If ye do it unto the least of these, my brethren, ye do it unto me.' That's the question facing America today."

So many questions: questions of race and poverty, war and peace. They were, King said, problems of the spirit, and any answer, according to King, would be found in the central American force: liberty. To him there was no distinction between the promises of the Declaration of Independence and the laws of the Lord. "We're going to win our freedom because both the sacred heritage of our nation and the eternal will of the Almighty God are embodied in our echoing demands," he said. "And so, however dark it is, however deep the angry feelings are, and however violent the explosions are, I can still sing 'We Shall Overcome.' We shall overcome because the arc of a moral universe is long, but it bends toward justice." Finally, citing the Revelation of Saint John the Divine, King evoked "a new Jerusalem . . . a new day of justice and brotherhood and peace. And that day the morning stars will sing together, and the sons of God will shout for joy. God bless you." With those words he turned and stepped back down to the floor of the nave. He had four days to live.

He was a prophet and a martyr, crying for justice so that the world might become more like what many people believed God wanted it to be. He was a minister of the Gospel; others who suffered and died to deliver America from its sins of slavery or bigotry or segregation were the children of Israel; others who put on the uniform of America to deliver the world from the evils of totalitarianism or injustice were asked to fight the good fight not because of their faith but because of the nation's faith in liberty and in human rights.

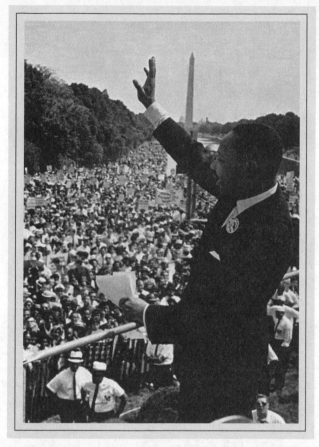

In his sermon at the Lincoln Memorial during the March on Washington, Martin Luther King, Jr., called America to live up to the promise at the heart of the Declaration of Independence—that God had created all men equal. *(AP Images)*

King's call had always been for a fulfillment of the Founders' will—to make good on the "promissory note" he had spoken of at the Lincoln Memorial—and no more. In the jammed cathedral (those who could not fit inside listened to the service over loudspeakers outside or in St. Alban's parish down the hill), the organ swelled, and the congregation sang:

Once to every man and nation,
    comes the moment to decide,
In the strife of truth with falsehood,
    for the good or evil side;
Some great cause, some great decision,
    offering each the bloom or blight,
And the choice goes by forever,
    'twixt that darkness and that light. . . .

By the light of burning martyrs,
    Christ, Thy bleeding feet we track,
Toiling up new Calvaries ever
    with the cross that turns not back;
New occasions teach new duties,
    ancient values test our youth;
They must upward still and onward,
    who would keep abreast of truth. . . .

Upward still and onward went King, back to Memphis, where, at dusk on the following Thursday, April 4, he was shot down as he stepped from Room 306 of the Lorraine Motel, falling backward on the balcony. The Passion of Martin Luther King, Jr., was complete, and the promise of the Founding closer to fulfillment.

In his eulogy for King at Atlanta's Ebenezer Baptist Church on April 9, Benjamin Mays, the retired president of Morehouse, linked King with figures who did what God intended for them to do, whatever the price, whatever the hardship: Jesus, Saint Paul, the founders of ancient Israel: "Moses leading a rebellious people to the Promised Land; Jesus dying on a cross; Galileo on his knees recanting at seventy; Lincoln dying of an assassin's bullet; Woodrow Wilson crusading for a League of Nations; Martin

Luther King, Jr., fighting for justice for garbage collectors—none of these men were ahead of their time," said Mays. "With them the time is always ripe to do that which is right and that which needs to be done."

Like the Founders, King had confronted a world he found wanting, and he changed it. Like them, he did not perfect it; no one could, or can. And like them, he drew on the City of God in order to transform the City of Man—not to create a theocracy or to force beliefs on others, but to make a claim on the moral sense of the nation, a sense shaped by, but not limited to, familiar faiths. The men of the American Revolution had done this in making the case for independence and for the God-given natural rights of man; so had Lincoln, as he fought to save the Union and to extend the recognition of those rights to the slaves whom the Founders had left in chains; so had Franklin Roosevelt, in marshaling the forces of government to help the downtrodden at home and to defeat tyranny and totalitarianism abroad. Now, burying King, Mays rightly ranked the thirty-nine-year-old Baptist preacher with the great deliverers of history. "He belonged to the world and to mankind," Mays said of King. "Now, he belongs to posterity."

One hundred and three Aprils before, Secretary of War Edwin Stanton had said much the same of the murdered Lincoln: "Now he belongs to the ages." Mays had a more recently martyred president on his mind, though. "I close by saying to you what Martin Luther King, Jr., believed: 'If physical death was the price he had to pay to rid America of prejudice and injustice, nothing could be more redemptive.' And to paraphrase the words of the immortal John Fitzgerald Kennedy, permit me to say that Martin Luther King, Jr.'s unfinished work on earth must truly be our own."

THE AGE OF ROE

As the war in Vietnam wore on, President Lyndon B. Johnson decided enough was enough. On the evening of King's morning sermon at the National Cathedral, Johnson announced that he would not seek reelection. Richard Nixon won the presidential race that November, and while most Americans remember Nixon for Watergate (or, if they are feeling charitable, for the opening to China), for an important slice of the country the most memorable day of Nixon's presidency was not June 17, 1972 (the break-in) or August 9, 1974 (his resignation and South Lawn farewell), but Tuesday, January 23, 1973: the day newspapers carried word of the Supreme Court's decision in *Roe v. Wade*.

In many papers the story was not the lead; former President Johnson had died on January 22, and his obituaries filled the papers. Reading the *Lynchburg News* on that winter morning in Virginia, though, Jerry Falwell had no trouble deciding which story was more important. As he recalled it, he "read and reread" the story of the *Roe* opinion, the decision opening the way to legal abortions in the first trimester of pregnancy. Mesmerized by the court's ruling, Falwell said he was consumed with "growing horror and disbelief," and could not bring himself to go in to breakfast. As his coffee cooled, he recalled, "I sat there staring at the *Roe v. Wade* story, growing more and more fearful of the consequences of the Supreme Court's act and wondering why so few voices had been raised against it." There were some exceptions: "Already, leaders of the Catholic Church had spoken courageously in opposition to the Court's decision; but the voices of my Protestant Christian brothers and sisters,

Billy Graham and Vice President Richard Nixon lunch in Washington in March 1960. The evangelist would come to regret his proximity to Nixon during Watergate; the scandal—and Graham's realization that Nixon was not the man he thought he was—would lead Graham to later take more care around politicians. *(AP Images)*

especially the voices of evangelical and fundamentalist leaders, remained silent." That would soon change—radically.

As he weighed plunging into politics to fight abortion and, later, a host of other things, Falwell knew he had a consistency issue. When the questions had been civil rights, back in the mid-1960s, he had preached against ministers' entering the fray, saying "government could be trusted to correct its own ills." In a memoir, Falwell quoted himself telling a national clergy convention that "Our role as pastors and Christian leaders is to attend to the spiritual needs of our people." Following in the Leland-Backus tradition, Falwell was a Baptist separationist. "Serving the church and letting government take care of itself had been my lifelong policy and the policy of my Christian friends and family," Falwell said, looking back. If the memoir is to be believed, Falwell genuinely debated, however briefly, the issues relevant to a preacher's partisan engagement. There was much to learn about the game, he knew, and he "became concerned that taking a political stand, even on my own time, might divide our growing congregation. I pastored a pluralistic church where people could hold various political views and still be one in Christ. Already the nation was being terribly divided over the issue of abortion. Would that also happen to my congregation?"

Ultimately, of course, Falwell overcame his initial doubts and emerged as a central figure in the latest manifestation of an overtly religious political movement. Abandoning Leland and Backus, Falwell and Reverend Pat Robertson (who ran for president in 1988) became heirs of Ezra Stiles Ely, Billy Sunday, Charles Coughlin, and Gerald Winrod, emerging as leaders of well-organized, largely media-savvy campaigns to, in their view, take America back from liberals, secularists, gays, judges, or whoever struck them as undesirable at any given moment.

BILLY GRAHAM'S DILEMMA

One evangelist who had deep reservations about the kind of political action Falwell was contemplating was the world's most prominent Protestant preacher: Billy Graham. An intriguing figure in the story of postwar American public religion, Graham was seemingly ubiquitous, befriending presidents of both parties and spending so much time in the White House family quarters that the first President George Bush once asked him to give some visiting lawmakers a guided tour.

Never particularly strident or fundamentalist—as a college student Graham dropped out of Bob Jones College, forerunner of South Carolina's hard-line Bob Jones University—Graham nevertheless spoke out on political and cultural issues for a long time, and his association with presidents had worldly implications. From Eisenhower on, politicians who were seen with Graham were invested with a kind of religious aura, and Graham apparently never met a famous person he did not like. It is easy—too easy—to be cynical about Graham, to consign him to the role of pastor to the powerful. His decades of ministry, however, show him to have been at once a maker and a mirror of the nation's public religion, from Cold War millennialism to the suburban sunniness of the conservative counterculture in the sixties and seventies.

Eloquent and driven, tireless and able to bring calm to the most turbulent of personal moments—a hallmark of a great pastor—Graham spent decades preaching the Gospel message around the world. He has spent as many decades at the highest levels, forging friendships with politicians and businessmen—friendships that often seem to have revolved around golf and prayer.

For many years Graham tried to have things both ways, dabbling in direct political involvement while feeling he should remain above the partisan fray. Early on, when Eisenhower was considering running for president, Graham visited him on trips to France and to Colorado to urge him to join the race. From Denver's Brown Palace Hotel in the summer of 1952, Eisenhower wrote a letter about Graham. "Billy Graham came to see me here on Friday the 1st, and earlier in Paris," Eisenhower told Governor Arthur B. Langlie of Washington on August 11, 1952. "I quite agree with you regarding his remarkable ability to reach millions of our people with a spiritual message. . . . Since all pastors must necessarily take a nonpartisan approach, it would be difficult to form any formal organization of religious leaders to work on our behalf." But the old general had a tactical thought about that. "However, this might be done in an informal way."

The next year, Graham sent President Eisenhower reports of a hugely successful crusade in Dallas. "Enclosed are newspaper clips of the great service last evening when 75,000 people were in attendance," Graham wrote. "This was the largest evangelistic meeting in the history of the Christian church." He was not boasting, Graham said, but wanted the president to understand the feelings in the country. "I am only informing you of these things to indicate the great spiritual hunger there is in America," he wrote Eisenhower. "People are hungry for God."

In 1960, he drafted a piece for *Life* magazine about "Nixon as a man" to run late in Nixon's race against Kennedy—a piece that would probably be read as an endorsement—and immediately regretted sending the article to New York. Then, miraculously, Henry Luce, the publisher, killed it to protect Graham from appearing too partisan. ("God had intervened!" Graham recalled, a comparison Luce would have liked.) Instead Graham wrote on why Christians should be sure to vote. Evoking the Cold War, Graham said: "Even now we are wrestling with the forces of anti-Christ on a worldwide scale. . . . We Americans need to decide this election, as it were, on our knees." When Kennedy won, Graham forged a relationship with him, and when Johnson became president, Graham spent a great deal of time around LBJ. "Preacher, pray for me," Johnson would say to Graham, and then the president would fall to his knees.

Graham's connection with Nixon marked a turning point for the evangelist, moving him further from the temporal realm and back toward the spiritual. He and Nixon were, Graham thought, good friends, but as Watergate broke and the White House tapes—which, among many other things, recorded Nixon's propensity for profanity—emerged, Graham was confused and hurt. "Looking back these forty-five years later, considering all that has intervened, I wonder whether I might have exaggerated his spirituality in my own mind," Graham wrote of Nixon in 1997. "But then, in my presence, he always made ready references to his mother's faith and the Bible that she loved so much." It is not particularly surprising Nixon would speak in such terms and of such things to Graham, and even at the time, at some level, Graham sensed something was astray. "Where religion was concerned with him," Graham wrote of Nixon, "it was not always easy to tell the difference between the spiritual and the sentimental. In retrospect, whenever he spoke about the Lord, it was in pretty general terms."

In one 1972 conversation captured by the White House taping system, Graham found himself agreeing with an anti-Semitic Nixon about alleged Jewish control of the media. "A lot of the Jews are great friends of mine," Graham said. "They swarm around me and are friendly to me because they know that I'm friendly with Israel. But they don't know how I really feel about what they are doing to this country."

When the conversations were released in 2002, Graham said he could not recall the episode and sought forgiveness and reconciliation: "Racial prejudice, anti-Semitism, or hatred of anyone with different beliefs has no place in the human mind or heart." Jewish leaders, many of whom appreciated his support of Israel and his refusal to join other evangelicals in calling for the conversion of the Jews, accepted his apology. "Much of my life has been a pilgrimage—constantly learning, changing, growing and maturing," Graham said. "I have come to see in deeper ways some of the implications of my faith and message, not the least of which is in the area of human rights and racial and ethnic understanding."

The significance of Graham's journey from flirting with partisanship to a more pastoral role is that the more distance he put between himself and the strife of the political arena, the more able he became to serve as a unifying figure within public religion. "It is true that we are a pluralistic nation," Graham said during a 1985 sermon at Washington National Cathedral. "We have a Constitution which guarantees to all of us human freedoms, of which religious freedom is foremost. In America any and all religions have the right to exist and to propagate what they stand for. We enjoy the separation of church and state, and no sectarian religion has ever been—and we pray God, ever will be—imposed upon us." He shared the Founders' vision that religion and morality were connected, continuing:

> It is most often in religion that the world finds its value systems and its moral guidance. In the past few years I've

been many places where the masses of people were looking wistfully for Moses (the Ten Commandments) and
Christ to show them the way. Only the living God can fill
the moral vacuum that exists in our world.

In our pluralistic state we have learned to live with
each other and to respect each other's religious and political convictions. But at the same time, whatever our religious convictions may be, we're all aware that we're
dependent on a power higher than our own. . . .

There's a truth reiterated throughout the teachings of
the various religions, but especially in the Bible, that no
man rules except by the will of God. There's a mandate
that is higher than the ballot box, and it comes from God.
We have a responsibility not only to all the people of
America and to the people of the world, but also we have
a great responsibility to the God of our fathers. And
someday, as we stand before Him, we will have to give an
account.

For Graham, then, politics became "hot-button issues" to be
avoided. "At my age," he said when he was eighty-seven, "I have
one message": the Gospel.

"AMERICA BACK TO GOD"

In the years Graham was moving away from the arena, Falwell
and others were charging into it. Religion—public and private—
was unavoidable in the bicentennial year of 1976. In the presidential campaign, Jimmy Carter, a Southern Baptist from Plains,
Georgia, won the Democratic nomination, and suddenly the

216 | JON MEACHAM

term "born-again Christian" was in currency. Like Woodrow Wilson, Carter could be austere and inflexible; a politician who knew Carter for a long time once said Carter was "as stubborn as a South Georgia turtle." Faith was a critical part of Carter's life, but he belonged to the long tradition of Baptist separationists and understood the subtleties of American public religion.

In the days before he took office, Carter was having what he called "second thoughts." As president-elect, he had been pondering which Bible verse to cite in his 1977 inaugural and was leaning toward II Chronicles 7:14: "If my people, which are called by my name, shall humble themselves, and pray, and seek my face, and turn from their wicked ways; then will I hear them from heaven, and will forgive their sin, and will heal their land." Carter worried, however, about "how those who did not share my beliefs might misunderstand and react to the words 'wicked' and 'sin.'" Instead he chose Micah 6:8: "He hath showed thee, O man, what is good; and what doth the Lord require of thee, but to do justly, and to love mercy, and to walk humbly with thy God." Reflecting on the inaugural address in his memoirs, Carter thought Micah "held the reminder of the need to seek God's help and guidance as we sought to improve our commitment to justice and mercy. After Watergate, we would need a sense of remembered history, deriving our strength from our nation's diversity, its resilience, and its moral values."

Sensitivity to how all Americans, not only those of a particular tradition, may react to religious language is essential. In the White House, Carter drew on Jefferson and Roger Williams to explain the distinctions a religious officeholder had to make in order to be true to the spirit of the Founding. "Separation is specified in the law, but for a religious person . . . you can't divorce religious beliefs from public service. At the same time, of course, in public office you cannot impose your own religious beliefs on others."

Given the large-scale failures of his administration and the crisis of confidence they produced, Carter's handling of public religion at the highest levels may be one of his most useful legacies. In his long post-presidency, Carter recalled being asked "whether my Christian beliefs ever conflicted with my secular duties as president." His reply: "There were a few inconsistencies, but I always honored my oath to 'preserve, protect, and defend the Constitution of the United States.' For instance, I have never believed that Jesus Christ would approve either abortions or the death penalty, but I obeyed such Supreme Court decisions to the best of my ability, at the same time attempting to minimize what I considered to be their adverse impact." In his 1976 campaign book, *Why Not the Best?,* Carter quoted Reinhold Niebuhr: "The sad duty of politics is to establish justice in a sinful world."

The sinfulness of the world was much on the minds of Jerry Falwell and other evangelicals during the Bicentennial. "I got me a Bible in one hand and *Old Glory* in the other and went up and down the streets and across the coliseums in this country," he told his congregation later. "I said, 'I've been quiet as long as I'm going to be quiet!' "

Capitalizing on the patriotic sentiment of the Bicentennial, Falwell seized the moment to portray America as wholly Christian. Traveling the nation with seventy performers from his Liberty Baptist College (later Liberty University), Falwell went to 141 cities to put on a musical called *I Love America;* he would preach, too, "calling America back to God," he recalled. "We reminded the tens of thousands who watched our program that we were living in a nation threatened by godlessness. We warned them that our leaders were making decisions that could destroy the moral foundations upon which the country was built." Then Falwell added: "About that time, a Gallup poll discovered that 34 percent of the American public professed to be born-again Christians. We were mobilizing a potential army numbering in the tens of millions. The fight was on!"

An important front in that fight was the full-immersion retrospective baptism of the Founders. "Somehow I thought the separation doctrine existed to keep the church out of politics," Falwell wrote. "I was wrong. In fact, to our nation's forefathers, especially Thomas Jefferson and his colleagues from our state of Virginia, the separation of church and state had been designed to keep the government from interfering with the church. Never during the founding years of this great democracy had our forefathers meant to distance the government from the truths of the Christian faith or to prohibit Christians from applying Biblical principles in their influence on the state." Those Virginian authors of the Statute of Virginia of Religious Freedom and of the Memorial and Remonstrance Against Religious Assessments, not to mention the first president of the United States, would be surprised indeed to find that their intention had been to keep the workings of government close to "the truths of the Christian faith."

One of the key differences between Martin Luther King, Jr.'s use of black churches in the 1950s and 1960s and the campaigns launched from white evangelical pulpits in the 1970s can be seen in King's and Falwell's contrasting readings of history. King called on the nation to keep the promise it made in the

Declaration of Independence—to treat *all* men equally. Falwell, on the other hand, said he was trying to guide the nation back to a path from which it had allegedly strayed—a case predicated on the notion, contradicted by history, that the United States was created in a sectarian spirit. "Any diligent student of American history finds that our great nation was founded by godly men upon godly principles to be a Christian nation," Falwell wrote in a 1980 manifesto titled *Listen, America!* In a Moral Majority report a few years later, Falwell's organization called for "an old-fashioned, God-honoring, *Christ-exalting* revival to turn America back to God."

Such talk is precisely what the Founders, who took care to root the country's rights in the gifts of "Nature's God," hoped to avoid. But the legend Falwell was helping to create endures. Tim LaHaye, the coauthor of the hugely popular bestselling *Left Behind* novels, wrote a book making the same case called *Faith of Our Founding Fathers,* and evangelical organizations produce books, videos, DVDs, and websites devoted to the theme of "America's Godly Heritage." From the mid-1970s forward, the pervasiveness of what is commonly called the religious right led many Americans to think armies of evangelical Christians were a new factor in political life. That they were not does not mean the center should take them any less seriously.

REAGAN'S MISSION

One man who knew exactly how seriously to take evangelicals— at first to their pleasure, later to their chagrin—was Ronald Reagan, a man of serious but eclectic religious beliefs whose wife, Nancy, found comfort in astrology. The opening pages of Bob

A man comfortable with the language of good and evil, Ronald Reagan was a favorite of evangelical voters. While governor of California, he posed with wife, Nancy, and children, Patti and Ron, for their annual family Christmas photo, just several months after a house guest prophesized that Reagan would one day become president. *(© Bettmann/Corbis)*

Slosser's 1984 book about Reagan, *Reagan Inside Out,* are among the most peculiar in the annals of presidential biography. A journalist who became a vice president of Pat Robertson's Christian Broadcasting Network (and coauthored a book with

Robertson), Slosser recounted a Sunday afternoon in Sacramento in October 1970. Reagan was midway through his eight years as governor of California, and Pat Boone, the entertainer, had brought a few prominent evangelicals to meet the Reagans. At one point someone suggested a prayer, and the Reagans and their five guests formed a circle and held hands. George Otis, a Christian businessman, was on Reagan's left and began to speak.

"The Holy Spirit came upon me and I knew it," Otis recalled. "In fact, I was embarrassed. There was this pulsing in my arm. And my hand—the one holding Governor Reagan's hand—was shaking. I didn't know what to do."

Then, Slosser reported, Otis's voice "spoke specifically to Ronald Reagan and referred to him as 'My son.' . . . His 'labor' was described as 'pleasing.' . . . The foyer was absolutely still and silent. The only sound was George's voice. Everyone's eyes were closed. 'If you walk uprightly before Me, you will reside at 1600 Pennsylvania Avenue.' The words ended. The silence held for three or four seconds. Eyes began to open and the seven rather sheepishly let go of hands. Reagan took a deep breath and turned and looked into Otis's face. All he said was a very audible 'Well!' "

Ten years later, shortly after Reagan defeated Carter, Boone called Reagan and asked if the president-elect recalled "the time we joined hands and prayed, and we had a sense you were being called to something higher." Reagan, Slosser reports, answered immediately, "Of course I do."

Reagan was a man of many parts. With vision and determination, he made himself into the greatest of politicians and the deftest of statesmen, a president who bent the nation, and the world, to his will. His religious faith was certainly a factor in his rise to power—and in his resilience after being shot in his seventieth year. He soldiered on, never giving in, believing he had been spared for a purpose.

Like his hero Franklin Roosevelt, Reagan loved playing pastor in America's public religion. Commemorating the Allied victory at Normandy for which FDR had prayed so fervently forty years before, Reagan stood on the French coast in 1984. "These are the boys of Pointe du Hoc," he said, hailing the Rangers who helped spearhead the liberation. "These are the men who took the cliffs." His voice catching with emotion, Reagan said, "The men of Normandy had faith that what they were doing was right, faith that they fought for all humanity, faith that a just God would grant them mercy on this beachhead—or on the next."

He spoke with such grace, such conviction, and such power that only the most cynical observers recalled that Reagan himself had spent World War II in Hollywood, making training films. That day at Normandy—and all the other days of his remarkable public life—Reagan was doing what he did best: making Americans believe in a vision of the nation as a beacon of light in a world of darkness, as the home of an essentially brave and good people. He loved citing Winthrop's image of America as a "city upon a hill," adding a Reaganesque visual element to the phrase: in Reagan's formulation, America became "a shining city on a hill."

The real Reagan was a romantic at heart. He saw the world as a cosmic struggle between good and evil, but he did not think it would all end in doom and destruction. The boy who had been a lifeguard in the 1920s became the man who believed he would save the planet from both totalitarianism and nuclear war. He thought he could, by personal persuasion, convince Moscow that it was on the wrong side of history, and help Americans believe in themselves and in their special role in the life of the world.

With his sense of destiny also came a fascination with the theology of the End Times, an interesting quirk, to say the least, for a president of the United States in the Nuclear Age. (There are three times as many references to Armageddon in the index of Lou Cannon's landmark biography *President Reagan: The Role of a Lifetime* as there are to affirmative action—six to two.) The year after his visit from Boone and Otis, Reagan, according to Cannon, told the president pro tem of the California senate that "for the first time ever, everything is in place for the battle of Armageddon and the second coming of Christ." It was to be a recurring theme. "We may be the generation that sees Armageddon," Reagan said on Jim and Tammy Faye Bakker's PTL network in 1980. After leaving office, Reagan told Cannon that "strange weather things" could signal the last days.

In the hillside Reagan library in Simi Valley, California, there are six folders whose three-hundred-odd pages shed light on the mind of the man so often and so wrongly caricatured as an unserious movie star turned politician. The aging pages are the sundry drafts and memoranda related to a speech Reagan delivered nearly a quarter century ago to the annual convention of the National Association of Evangelicals meeting in Orlando, Florida. The address, given at three o'clock in the afternoon on Tuesday, March 8, 1983, is remembered, if at all, for Reagan's repetition of the phrase "evil empire" to describe the Soviet Union, a term he had used the year before in remarks to the House of Commons in London.

But the draft of the Orlando talk, which Reagan edited in his own hand the weekend before—a seventeen-page, typed, double-spaced draft on file in the library—reveals Reagan as much more than simply a cold warrior. Assiduously going through the speech word by word with a pen, he was thinking widely, historically, and theologically. Well versed in public religion, he quoted William Penn, Jefferson, Washington, and Tocqueville (whom he edited rather harshly, changing some words to make them sound better). Reagan argued that "the great triumph of our Founding Fathers" was that, as Penn said, "men who will not be ruled by God will be ruled by tyrants." He had instant recall of telling anecdotes about prayer and presidents, and he is clearly striving to soften the harsher sections of the speech. From memory, he inserts an old story about Lincoln: "I feel as Abe Lincoln felt when he said, 'I have been driven many times to my knees by the overwhelming conviction that I had nowhere else to go.' "

The draft, by speechwriter Tony Dolan, originally included this line: "Those of us in the political world need to be reminded that our fast-paced existence can sometimes be an obstacle to quiet reflection and deep commitment, that we can easily forget the ideas and principles that brought us into the public arena in the first place."

Scratching through those words, Reagan made the point more sunnily: "I tell you truly there are a great many God fearing, dedicated, noble men & women in public life. Yes, we need your help to keep us ever mindful of the ideas and principles that brought us into the public arena in the first place." It was a masterful stroke, at once saluting those in politics and investing the audience with a crucial role. Rather than put down those in politics in order to score points with those in the pulpits, Reagan lifted everyone, kicking aside the speechwriter's "obstacle."

Reagan dealt with abortion, school prayer, and other issues important to the evangelical audience, and he was clearly thinking of the virtues of life and of the difficulties of how to live as he moved through the text, tinkering along the way. "There is sin and evil in the world," the draft said, "and we are enjoined by scripture and the Lord Jesus to oppose it with all our might." In an elegant section, the speech acknowledged the nation's own moral accountability for discrimination. "We must never go back," Reagan said. "There is no room for racism, anti-semitism or other forms of ethnic and racial hatred in this country."

Those words were the speechwriter's, but the grace note was Reagan's: "The commandment given us is clear & simple—'Thou shalt love thy neighbor as thyself,' " the president added in his small, neat handwriting.

Turning abroad, the draft took a hard but humane line with the Soviets. Denouncing them for a remark of Lenin's that, as Reagan rendered it, "morality is entirely subordinate to the interests of class war," he still held out hope for redemption. "This does not mean we should isolate ourselves and refuse to seek an understanding with them," Reagan scribbled on the page. "I intend to do everything I can to persuade them of our peaceful intent. . . . At the same time, however, they must be made to understand we will never compromise our principles & standards. We will never give away our freedom. We will never abandon our belief in God."

The Reagan who emerges from this document was a tolerant, principled leader, speaking declaratively and honestly about broad American convictions. He thought that America's love of liberty and reverence for the Almighty would always carry the day, and he was unembarrassed to say so. "I believe this because the source of our strength in the quest for human freedom is not material but spiritual, and, because it knows no limitation, it must terrify and ultimately triumph over those who would en-slave their fellow man." Just over six years later the Berlin Wall would come down; two years after that the Soviet Union ceased to exist. There were many reasons for these grand historical shifts, but one was that people who were enslaved longed for the kind of freedom America has nurtured—a kind of freedom Ronald Reagan intuitively understood. In his closing words to the evangelicals in the Citrus Crown Ballroom of the Sheraton Twin Towers Hotel in Orlando in 1983, he used an old favorite: "One of our Founding Fathers, Thomas Paine, said, 'We have it within our power to begin the world over again.' We can do it, doing together what no one church could do by itself."

When Reagan died after a long, noble battle with Alzheimer's disease, he was brought to Washington for a state funeral. At the National Cathedral, not far from where Martin Luther King, Jr., preached his last Sunday sermon, Supreme Court Justice San-dra Day O'Connor was asked to read an ancient text that had meant the world to Reagan. It was not from the Bible. It was John Winthrop's "Model of Christian Charity"—American scripture that, like the nation's public life, is sacred in its way.

VI. OUR HOPE FOR YEARS TO COME

HISTORY, RELIGION, AND COMMON SENSE

*I have but one lamp by which my feet are guided; and
that is the lamp of experience. I know of no way judging
the future but by the past.*

—PATRICK HENRY

*Our particular principles of religion are a subject of
accountability to our God alone. I inquire after no
man's, and trouble none with mine; nor is it given to us
in this life to know whether yours or mine, our friend's
or our foe's, are exactly the right.*

—THOMAS JEFFERSON

James Madison, always sickly, survived them all. He lived to
bury Franklin, Washington, Jefferson, and Adams. In his great
old age at Montpelier, his house not far from Jefferson's Monticello, Madison wore a cap and gloves with his dressing gowns to
keep himself warm. His beloved wife, Dolley, said, "my days are
devoted to nursing and comforting my sick patient." But his
mind was sharp through the long twilight. In private notes he
kept in his retirement, he mused about the complexities of life in
a republic full of religious people.

"The Constitution of the U.S. forbids everything like an establishment of a national religion," Madison wrote; he was debating whether the appointment of congressional chaplains was compatible with the First Amendment and with the ideal of religious liberty. "In strictness the answer on both points must be in the negative," Madison acknowledged.

Both pragmatic and wise, though, Madison concluded that "as the precedent is not likely to be rescinded, the best that can now be done may be to apply to the Constitution the maxim of the law, de minimis non curat"—Latin for "the law does not concern itself with trifles." It was not a fight worth fighting; it was a case, in other words, where the wall of separation was very low to the ground indeed.

In his final days in May and June of 1836, his biographer Ralph Ketcham recounted, Madison sipped sherry with his doctor, dictated letters (his hands were crippled by rheumatism), and read over the pages of a forthcoming biography of Thomas Jefferson. Like Jefferson, his friend of a half century, Madison was a man of complicated religious views; intensely private about his theology, he did say that he had long held that "belief in a God All Powerful wise and good is so essential to the moral order of the world and to the happiness of man that arguments which enforce it cannot be drawn from too many sources."

His own sources were eclectic. In a document composed for publication after his death called "Advice to My Country," Madison wrote: "The advice nearest to my heart and deepest in my conviction is that the Union of the States be cherished and perpetuated." He had given much of his life to the creation and preservation of the Union; as president he and his wife had

For half a century, fellow Virginians Thomas Jefferson and James Madison worked together to create the new nation and to secure the rights of religious freedom. *(© Bettmann/Corbis)*

faced death when the British invaded Washington and took the White House in the War of 1812. Madison loved the Union, he loved liberty, and he loved the Constitution, and he believed—even perhaps prayed—that the Constitution would preserve both Union and liberty. "Let the open enemy to [the Union] be regarded as a Pandora with her box opened," Madison wrote in his farewell "Advice," "and the disguised one, as the Serpent creeping with his deadly wiles into Paradise." The images that most readily came to him when he contemplated his life's work, then, were both classical and biblical—one myth from the Greeks, the other from the Garden.

After Madison died, on Tuesday, June 28, 1836, he was, like Jefferson, buried in an Episcopal service. His slaves, it was reported, cried out in grief when the priest commended the body to the ground with the words, "earth to earth, ashes to ashes, dust to dust. . . ."

Greek, Jewish, Christian—Madison was fascinated by religion, because he was fascinated by humanity. "There appears to be in the nature of man," he once said, something that "ensures his belief in an invisible cause of his present existence, & an anticipation of his future existence." The Union he loved could not be preserved without vigilance. Freedom was hard won but easily lost, particularly when, Madison said, humankind had so many "propensities & susceptibilities in the case of religion," always a potential source of tyranny and discord.

Madison knew that Americans down the ages would confront what he called "the danger of a direct mixture of religion & civil government." The Founders deployed reason and history to defeat the danger by creating a nation in which both religion and politics could play their proper roles in the larger American experiment.

Yet the work of America is never done. "We shall leave the world with many consolations," wrote Madison's fellow Founder John Adams. "It is better than we found it." Adams was right, but he also knew, as Machiavelli wrote in his *History of Florence,* that "in human affairs nothing should be perpetual or quiet." So it is with America, for each generation faces the danger of extremism that Madison spoke of—and each generation must defeat it anew.

TRANSCENDING TRAGEDY

In the last book of Homer's *Iliad*, after years of interminable war, Priam, King of Troy, and Achilles, the mightiest of the Greeks, meet in the night, two foes finding communion in their grief. In darkness they weep together for all that they have lost, for the beloved kith and kin who have fallen in the ceaseless battle. Priam was in the Greek camp on bleak business: to ask for the mutilated corpse of his son. With respect, Achilles tells Priam, "The heart in you is iron," and asks the old man to sit with him for a while. The awful truth, Achilles mused, was that "There is not any advantage to be won from grim lamentation," for in the world they knew there was nothing but tragedy: pain and death are the inescapable lot of man. "Such is the way the gods spun life for unfortunate mortals," Achilles says, "that we live in unhappiness, but the gods themselves have no sorrows."

Writing to Adams about grief in the summer of 1816, Jefferson said, "I see that, with the other evils of life, it is destined to temper the cup we are to drink." Then Jefferson quoted Achilles' words from the rendezvous with Priam:

Two urns by Jove's high throne have ever stood,
The source of evil one, one of good;
From thence the cup of mortal man he fills,
Blessings to these, to those distributes ills;
To most he mingles both.

Yet both Jefferson and Adams held out hope that they, too, might one day live as Achilles' gods, as immortals with "no sorrows." They relished the idea that they, with Madison, Washington, Franklin, and all their old comrades-in-arms, would be together beyond the grave, watching how history dealt with the work of their years. "We shall only be lookers-on, from the clouds above, as we . . . look down on the labors, the hurry, the bustle of the ants and bees," Jefferson once wrote Adams. It was with "more readiness than reluctance," Jefferson said, that he anticipated such a reunion in the afterlife. "May we meet there again, in Congress, with our ancient colleagues," he wrote Adams, "and receive with them the seal of approbation, 'Well done, good and faithful servants' "—words Jesus used in a parable in the Gospel of Matthew which promised the reward of "the joy of thy lord."

THE TYRANNY OF THE PRESENT

A grasp of history is essential for Americans of the center who struggle to decide how much weight to assign a religious consideration in a public matter. To fail to consult the past consigns us to what might be called the tyranny of the present—the mistaken idea that the crises of our own time are unprecedented and that we have to solve them without experience to guide us. Subject to such a tyranny, we are more likely to take a narrow or simplistic view, or to let our passions get the better of our reason. If we know, however, how those who came before us found the ways and means to surmount the difficulties of their age, we stand a far better chance of acting in the moment with perspective and measured judgment. Light can neither enter into nor emanate from a closed mind.

The intensity with which the religious right attempts to conscript the Founders into their cause indicates the importance the movement ascribes to historical benediction by association with the origins of the Republic. If Falwell and his seventy performers, or Tim LaHaye in his *Faith of Our Founding Fathers,* can convince enough people that America was a Christian nation that has lost its way, the more legitimate their efforts in the political arena seem.

The problem with their reading of history is that it is wrong. There is no doubt, as we have seen, that the Founders lived in and consciously bequeathed a culture shaped and sustained by public religion, one that was not Christian or Jewish or Muslim or Buddhist but was simply transcendent, with reverence for the "Creator" and for "Nature's God."

To hope, as some secularists do, that faith will one day withdraw from the public sphere, if only this presidential candidate or that Supreme Court nominee comes to power, is futile. Humankind could not leave off being religious even if it tried. The impulse is intrinsic. "We and God have business with each other; and in opening ourselves to his influence our deepest destiny is fulfilled," William James told his scholarly audience in Edinburgh. "The universe . . . takes a turn genuinely for the worse or for the better in proportion as each one of us fulfills or evades God's demands." To James, "the instinctive belief of mankind" is that "God is real since he produces real effects."

James quoted Professor James H. Leuba of Bryn Mawr College: "The truth of the matter can be put in this way: *God is not known, he is not understood; he is used*—sometimes as a meat-purveyor, sometimes as moral support, sometimes as friend, sometimes as an object of love. If he proves himself useful, the religious consciousness asks for no more than that. Does God really exist? How does he exist? What is he? are so many irrelevant questions." Such a verdict, James pointed out, offered religion vindication, for it showed that religion "must exert a permanent function, whether . . . it be true or false." The task of a republic like ours is to draw the best we can out of faith's "permanent function" while avoiding the worst.

The worst was on vivid display two days after the terrorist attacks of September 11, 2001. As rescue workers were still struggling through tons of rubble trying to account for the innocents who lost their lives on that brilliant blue Tuesday in New York, Washington, and in the skies over Pennsylvania, Pat Robertson invited Jerry Falwell to appear with him on Robertson's *700 Club* television broadcast. The resulting conversation was the grimmest imaginable.

> FALWELL: . . . [T]he Lord has protected us so wonderfully these 225 years. And since 1812, this is the first time that we've been attacked on our soil, and by far the worst results. And I fear, as Donald Rumsfeld, the Secretary of Defense, said yesterday, that this is only the beginning. And with biological warfare available to these monsters— the Husseins, the Bin Ladens, the Arafats—what we saw on Tuesday, as terrible as it is, could be miniscule [*sic*] if, in fact, God continues to lift the curtain and allow the enemies of America to give us probably what we deserve.
>
> ROBERTSON: Jerry, that's my feeling. I think we've just seen the antechamber to terror. We haven't even begun to see what they can do to the major population.
>
> FALWELL: The ACLU's got to take a lot of blame for this.
>
> ROBERTSON: Well, yes.
>
> FALWELL: And, I know that I'll hear from them for this. But, throwing God out successfully with the help of the

federal court system, throwing God out of the public square, out of the schools. The abortionists have got to bear some burden for this because God will not be mocked. And when we destroy 40 million little innocent babies, we make God mad. I really believe that the pagans, and the abortionists, and the feminists, and the gays and the lesbians who are actively trying to make that an alternative lifestyle, the ACLU, People For the American Way—all of them who have tried to secularize America— I point the finger in their face and say "you helped this happen."

ROBERTSON: Well, I totally concur, and the problem is we have adopted that agenda at the highest levels of our government. And so we're responsible as a free society for what the top people do. And the top people, of course, is the court system.

FALWELL: Pat, did you notice yesterday the ACLU, and all the Christ-haters, the People For the American Way, NOW, etc. were totally disregarded by the Democrats and the Republicans in both houses of Congress as they went out on the steps and called out to God in prayer and sang "God Bless America" and said "let the ACLU be hanged"? In other words, when the nation is on its knees, the only normal and natural and spiritual thing to do is what we ought to be doing all the time—calling upon God.

ROBERTSON: Amen. . . .

Falwell and Robertson do not, of course, represent all of evangelical Christianity. Extreme secularists have not helped matters either, with harsh words designed to wound and deride religious believers. For much of the sixties and seventies, Madalyn Murray O'Hair, one of the plaintiffs in the 1963 Supreme Court case that ruled mandatory classroom prayer and Bible reading unconstitutional, was a prominent cultural figure. Founder of a group called American Atheists, she became, *Life* magazine said in 1964, "the most hated woman in America" for her bitter attacks on religion. When one of her sons converted to Christianity and turned on his mother, O'Hair disowned him. In a speech laced with profanity at Memphis State University in Tennessee in 1986, O'Hair taunted believers. "Judeo-Christianity is basically a philosophy of life which espouses tenets that are anti-education, anti-science, anti-peace, anti-woman, anti-human sexuality, and anti-life," she said, adding: "Religion—all religions—create a world of make-believe. . . . No god ever gave any man anything, nor answered any prayer, nor ever will."

O'Hair and two of her relatives disappeared in 1995; they were killed, dismembered, and secretly buried on a Texas ranch as a result of an extortion-kidnapping scheme. It took nearly six years for authorities to locate the family's remains. When O'Hair's minister son learned that the bodies had been found, he said: "She was an evil person who led many to hell. That is hard for me to say about my own mother but it is true." Her contempt for believers lives on in Internet postings. "God was sitting on his ass in Nowhere," she said of the story of Creation in her Memphis State address, "since at that time there wasn't even a universe, for hundreds of millions of years without an idea in his head, picking his nose and farting, when suddenly he became bored one moment in particular and said, in clear Hebrew, 'From nothing I will create something,' and he created the entire universe (whatever that may be) for the express purpose of creating you in his own image, complete down to the belly button." These were, she said, "foolish" ideas. Voices like Robertson's, Falwell's, and O'Hair's come from the farthest fringes, but they reach many ears.

HUMILITY AND HISTORY

Can religion be a force for unity, not division, in the nation and in the world? The Founders thought so, and so must we. As a force in the affairs of nations it must be managed and marshaled for good, for faith will be with us, as the scriptures say, to the end of the age. For many, reverence for one's own tradition is not incompatible with respect for the traditions of others. Elizabeth I is said to have remarked that she did not wish to make windows into men's souls—sound counsel for any era. We should be careful not to turn into people like the minister in the New England story told by the Columbia University scholar Jacques Barzun. Two Protestants from different denominations, one a minister, the other a layman, met and discussed the differences between their faiths. The two talked amicably, and as they parted, the minister said, "Yes, we both worship the same God, you in your way and I in His."

Humility and a sense of history are our best hopes of avoiding the self-satisfaction of that (probably) apocryphal minister. It is easier to speak of such things in the abstract than it is to apply them in particular. Interpreting and ruling on the establishment and free-exercise clauses of the First Amendment will never be simple; there is no convenient three-point plan to offer as a way forward. Instead faith and politics and religion and public life will present each generation with dilemmas that are, in Augustine's phrase, so old and so new.

There is nearly universal agreement on this point from

thoughtful observers. Here are three examples—one from a scholar of Judaism, another from two scholars of secularism, and yet another from three scholars of Christianity. "In their dreams, most Jews long for an America where they and their neighbors can live as equals, safe from the fire and brimstone of the Christian state and the desolate barrenness of the secular one. How best to achieve such a society, however, remains an unsolved riddle," wrote Jonathan Sarna. "Our argument . . . is that the Constitution created a secular state. It is a precious but confused legacy, one that Americans have fought over since the beginning of the Republic," said Kramnick and Moore in *The Godless Constitution.* "No easy solutions from the past are going to resolve the profound questions which surround us—of life and death, truth and morality, peace and justice," wrote Mark Noll, Nathan Hatch, and George Marsden in *The Search for Christian America.*

Cases about religious holiday displays and prayers in public places as well as issues such as abortion about which so many have deeply held religious beliefs will always play a part in campaigns and in the courts. The Founders knew this, which is why their system of checks and balances remains so essential, for it creates a world in which it is likely that the center, not the extremes, will hold sway. "Reasonable minds can disagree about how to apply the Religion Clauses in a given case," wrote Justice Sandra Day O'Connor. "But the goal of the Clauses is clear: to carry out the Founders' plan of preserving religious liberty to the fullest extent possible in a pluralistic society. By enforcing the Clauses, we have kept religion a matter for the individual conscience, not for the prosecutor or the bureaucrat. At a time when we see around the world the violent consequences of the assumption of religious authority by government, Americans may count themselves fortunate: Our regard for constitutional boundaries has protected us from similar travails, while allowing private religious exercise to flourish."

In her sensible words, O'Connor was working within an old tradition. In 1952, Justice William O. Douglas wrote an opinion in which he used perhaps the most important phrase to bear in mind amid what George Eliot called the "dim lights and tangled circumstance" of the world: "common sense."

"There cannot be the slightest doubt that the First Amendment reflects the philosophy that Church and State should be separated. . . ." Douglas wrote, adding:

> The First Amendment, however, does not say that, in every and all respects there shall be a separation of Church and State. Rather, it studiously defines the manner, the specific ways, in which there shall be no concert or union or dependency one on the other. That is the common sense of the matter. Otherwise the state and religion would be aliens to each other—hostile, suspicious, and even unfriendly. Churches could not be required to pay even property taxes. Municipalities would not be permitted to render police or fire protection to religious groups. Policemen who helped parishioners into their places of worship would violate the Constitution. Prayers in our legislative halls; the appeals to the Almighty in the messages of the Chief Executive; the proclamations making Thanksgiving Day a holiday; "so help me God" in our courtroom oaths—these and all other references to the Almighty that run through our laws, our public ritu-

als, our ceremonies would be flouting the First Amendment. A fastidious atheist or agnostic could even object to the supplication with which the Court opens each session: "God save the United States and this Honorable Court."

Yes, a fastidious atheist or agnostic could indeed do that, and would probably be right in the strictest sense of the First Amendment, for if one is going to be logically precise about it, then being compelled to hear mentions of or see images of God or even being exposed to the most general religious belief in civic forums or rituals is a form of religious coercion. Douglas's point is one in defense of public religion—that there is a collective cultural consensus, grounded in "common sense," allowing for the kinds of broad religious expression one hears in presidential and public rhetoric.

For all the talk about the separation of church and state and the power of precedent, the right decision in a case involving religion and the Constitution is a little like the late justice Potter Stewart's description of hard-core pornography: we cannot say precisely what it is, but we know it when we see it. In 1971, about a quarter century after the Supreme Court evoked the wall metaphor, Chief Justice Warren E. Burger—a Nixon appointee— honestly acknowledged the eternal truth at the heart of the constitutional battles over politics and religion: "the line of separation, far from being a 'wall,' is a blurred, indistinct, and variable barrier depending on all the circumstances of a particular relationship." A piece of advice Jefferson gave his nephew in 1787 applies to us all: "Fix reason firmly in her seat, and call to her tribunal every fact, every opinion. . . . Your own reason is the only oracle given you by heaven, and you are answerable not for the rightness but uprightness of the decision." May that heavenly gift bring clarity to earthly riddles.

Madison saw all this coming. "I must admit . . . ," he wrote, "that it may not be easy in every possible case to trace the line of separation between the rights of religion and the Civil authority with such distinctness as to avoid collisions & doubts on unessential points." And so the experiment goes on.

PERMIT THE TWILIGHT

G. K. Chesterton once said America seemed to think of herself as "a nation with the soul of a church," which, if the soul of a church is a source of grace, civility, and charity, is not necessarily a bad thing. Chesterton's views on private religion also shed light on public religion. For him, personal belief was rooted in both mind and heart. "Reason is itself a matter of faith," he wrote in his 1908 book *Orthodoxy*. "It is an act of faith to assert that our thoughts have any relation to reality at all." Chesterton described himself as an "ordinary" man when it came to religion, and in his early-twentieth-century words he echoed the sentiments of the eighteenth-century Founding Fathers. "I am ordinary in the correct sense of the term, which means the acceptance of an order; a Creator and the Creation, the common sense of gratitude for Creation, life and love as gifts permanently good, marriage and chivalry as laws rightly controlling them. . . ." Elsewhere, he added, "The ordinary man has always been sane because the ordinary man has always been a mystic. He has permitted the twilight. He has always had one foot in earth and the other in fairyland. He has always left himself free to doubt his gods; but (unlike the agnostic of to-day) free also to believe in them. He has always cared more for truth than for consistency. If he saw two truths that seemed to contradict each other, he would take the two truths and the contradiction along with them. His spiritual sight is stereoscopic, like his physical sight: he sees two different pictures at once and yet sees all the better for that." In America, public religion requires a similar habit of mind: we must permit the twilight.

Many committed secularists in our own age have largely made their peace with public religion. "Those of us who are Jeffersonian separatists live more or less easily with the accumulated chinks in the wall of separation like prayer at the beginning of legislative or judicial sessions, 'In God We Trust' on our money and as our nation's motto," wrote Kramnick and Moore in *The Godless Constitution*. "In remembering that Jefferson did in fact found human rights on a Creator's intentions, we should pick fights carefully and not ever imagine that references to God will or should disappear from public rhetoric."

The religious, meanwhile, must always ask themselves whether their political undertakings honor what the twentieth-century theologian Paul Tillich called their "ultimate concern." Putting faith into action can be a good thing so long as the true end of belief is not compromised or corrupted in the fire of battle. The antiabortion protester who assassinates a physician is a powerful if extreme example of someone so consumed by fanaticism, not faith, that he loses his way with unspeakably tragic results. Such extremists are not Christians but pagans worshipping the gods of self-righteousness and violence rather than the Lord of history and love. "Idolatry is the elevation of a preliminary concern to ultimacy," Tillich wrote in words that should serve as a wise warning to all those tempted to put the issues of the moment above charity and humility.

The temptation to do so is great, and sometimes understandable. A Christian who opposes abortion or the death penalty sees any kind of accommodation as nothing less than a capitulation to the forces of death. A secularist who fears that believers blinded by faith will impose their values on the rest of the country thinks the religious rituals in public life may be the thin edge of the wedge.

Why, some Christians ask, must the majority be silenced or made to feel as though their beliefs and customs are to go unremarked or uncelebrated simply because a minority—and probably a tiny minority at that—believe something different? One religious reply is that a true Christian ought to be more interested in making the life of the world gentle for others than he should be in asserting the dominance of his own faith. The power of the story of Jesus' Passion lies in its paradoxes: he confounded the world, and the world's expectations, by bringing light from darkness, strength from weakness, and life from death. The Sermon on the Mount is about reversing the understood order of things. If the first shall be last and the last first, then who are Christians to exert power over others by the sword or the purse or the polling place?

Pope John Paul II struck the perfect tone about religion and politics in his first encyclical, *Redemptor Hominis*. "The Church . . . has no weapons at her disposal apart from those of the spirit, of the word and of love. . . . For this reason she does not cease to implore . . . everybody in the name of God and in the name of man: Do not kill! Do not prepare destruction and extermination for each other! Think of your brothers and sisters who are suffering hunger and misery! Respect each other's dignity and freedom!"

When he was governor of New York—the office once held by both Theodore and Franklin Roosevelt—Mario Cuomo, a Democrat and a Catholic, spoke at Notre Dame on the dilemma facing a faithful politician torn between the teachings of his church and what he believed to be best for civil society. Quoting John Paul's *Redemptor Hominis,* Cuomo said, "The weapons of the word and of love are already available to us; we need no statute to provide them." He also cited a letter of the American bishops that explored the distinction between a church's engaging in the world on behalf of broad moral ends and entangling itself in specific policies or the politics of a particular moment. "We recognize that the Church's teaching authority does not carry the same force when it deals with technical solutions involving particular means as it does when it speaks of principles or ends," the bishops wrote. "People may agree in abhorring an injustice, for instance, yet sincerely disagree as to what practical approach will achieve justice. Religious groups are as entitled as others to their opinion in such cases, but they should not claim that their opinions are the only ones that people of good will may hold."

The Republic is not a church, but it is a Republic filled with churches. Let the religious speak but encourage them not to shout; let them argue, but encourage them not to brawl. The system the Founders built allows for religious considerations to play a role in politics in the same measure—no greater, no smaller—as any other consideration, whether geographical, economic, or cultural. Washington, Jefferson, Madison, Adams, Franklin, Jay, and their comrades could have chosen to draw on the examples of Jamestown, Plymouth, or Massachusetts Bay, but they did not. Virginia's early "Laws Divine, Moral and Martial" tried to regulate not only the business of civil society but of men's minds and souls—and history had taught the revolutionary generation that the former was difficult enough without quixotically attempting the latter.

Americans of the new millennium may find the notion that they should profitably follow the lead of a gaggle of dead white men from the eighteenth century quaint or unconvincing, but it is neither. The Founders got some things wrong, particularly slavery, but they were on the mark about much, including religion and politics. The sound and fury of our own time could be calmed by grasping what they had to say about the role of faith in the nation. Respect religion, hear it out, learn from it, then let the work of the country unfold as the parties to the republican contract—the Constitution—will have it. In a letter to Abigail with advice for his sons, John Adams wrote, "Let them revere nothing but Religion, Morality, and Liberty"—a useful exhortation for the nation, too.

Two objections are often raised when discussing applying the wisdom of the Founders. One is that they were creating a government for a nation that was almost entirely Protestant; the men of Philadelphia or Mount Vernon or Monticello or Montpelier, this argument runs, could not have anticipated the pluralism of twenty-first-century America. Yet for their time and place, the diversity of sects, though mostly Christian, amounted to a more diverse country than we tend to think. "The bosom of America," Washington said, was to be "open to receive . . . the oppressed and persecuted of all nations and religions; whom we shall welcome to a participation of all our rights and privileges. . . . They may be Mohometans, Jews or Christians of any sect, or they may be atheists." Jefferson saw diversity as a national virtue, not a vice. "Our country has been the first to prove to the world two truths the most salutary to human society," Jefferson said: "that man can govern himself, and that religious freedom is the most effective anodyne against religious dissension: the maxims of civil government being reversed in that of religion, where its true form is 'divided we stand, united we fall.' " They expected their system to be tested by people of many different creeds—and they expected America to pass, which it has.

America has grown more powerful as we have expanded our definition of the mainstream, going from strength to strength as freedom has spread to blacks, to women, to immigrants, and to any who felt excluded from the vital center of American democracy. In the first years of the twenty-first century we are the strongest nation in human history—and the most religiously, ethnically, and racially diverse. And so the Founders were, as usual, right when they chose the nation's first motto in the summer of 1776: *E Pluribus Unum*—"out of many, one."

The second argument against looking back in order to move ahead is that the issues we now confront were unimaginable to the men who made America. Abortion, bioethics, stem-cell research, euthanasia, the rights of homosexuals, the teaching of the theory of evolution versus creationism or intelligent design—these were not part of the world of the Founders. What light, some say, could the eighteenth century possibly shed on such questions well over two hundred years later? Yet the Founders hoped they were constructing a republic that would withstand the vicissitudes of time and chance and would, with amendment, endure. Why else work so hard, think so deeply, argue so closely, and design so carefully a government that would check passions, thus raising the odds that it would serve Americans from age to age?

The Founders were also men of enormous sophistication and accomplishment, and they knew how rapidly the world could change, for theirs had been a convulsive age of revolution in science, in philosophy, in political thinking, and in economics. This is not to say that John Adams had an opinion about reproductive rights, or that a judge can decide a bioethical case by consulting James Madison's views on twenty-first-century technology. It is to say, however, that the Founders' decision to nurture a public piety and treat faith as one force among many to be honored but heeded only in the measure sensible citizens of the day chose to assign it stands as an epochal accomplishment according to the standards by which we judge such things.

Democracy is easy; republicanism is hard. Democracy is fueled by passion; republicanism is founded on moderation. Democracy is loud, raucous, disorderly; republicanism is quiet, cool, judicious—and that we still live in its light is the Founders' most wondrous deed.

THE GOOD FIGHT

Shortly before noon on a cool spring day in April 1943, Franklin Roosevelt left the White House with his wife, Eleanor, and Mrs. Edith Wilson for the brief journey to dedicate the newly constructed Jefferson Memorial. A reporter for *The Washington Post* noticed that the early Japanese cherry blossoms were already fading as Roosevelt doffed his dark cape and rose to face the monument. Five thousand people were on hand. Right Reverend Henry St. George Tucker, the presiding bishop of the Episcopal Church in America, stepped to the microphones for a moment of prayer. As the people in the crowd bowed their heads and listened to the bishop's words, guards wearing the costumes of Continental Army soldiers stood at attention before the memorial's Ionic columns. How like Jefferson to be fixed forever in a classical temple, modeled after the Pantheon of Rome, dedicated by a man of Christ in the capital of a nation fighting a global war to protect our own liberty and to project the rights of "Nature's God" to all the world. Asking the audience to join him, Bishop Tucker thanked God for "raising up thy servant, Thomas Jefferson, to be a leader in the cause of freedom to which the Nation was dedicated at its birth."

It was the president's turn. His braces locked in place, his big hands holding the rostrum, Roosevelt gazed up at the great statue of Jefferson. Sculpted from plaster—the bronze would have to wait until after the war—the nineteen-foot-tall Jefferson looked rather defiant, his feet set as if ready to stride forward at any moment, his strong, stern face staring out toward the White House. Jefferson, Roosevelt told the crowd, was an "apostle of freedom" who saw that "men who will not fight for liberty can lose it. We, too, have faced that fact."

Americans would not shrink from wars against tyranny and terror. Jefferson, Roosevelt said, "lived in a world in which freedom of conscience and freedom of mind were battles still to be fought through—not principles already accepted of all men." Roosevelt paused. "We, too, have lived in such a world."

A cold wind blew off the Potomac, but Roosevelt, in his gray suit coat, did not seem to notice. He had a sermon to preach.

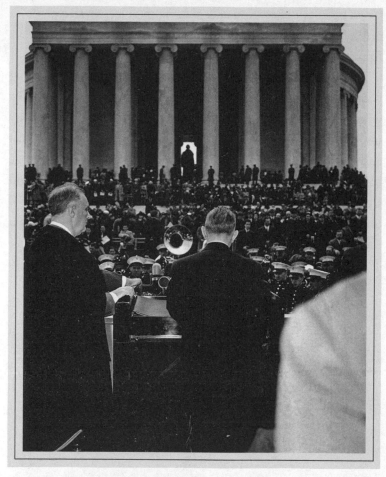

On April 13, 1943, a cool springtime Tuesday in the midst of World War II, President Roosevelt and two bishops dedicated the Jefferson Memorial. Jefferson knew, FDR said, that "men who will not fight for liberty can lose it." *(AP Images)*

"Thomas Jefferson believed, as we believe, in man. He believed, as we believe, that men are capable of their own government and that no king, no tyrant, no dictator can govern for them as wisely as they can govern for themselves," said Roosevelt. "He believed, as we believe, in certain inalienable rights. He, as we, saw those principles and freedoms challenged. He fought for them, as we fight for them."

The preservation of American liberty is the most demanding of tasks, requiring unrelenting work and a resilient spirit, but to whom much is given, much is expected. Roosevelt closed by quoting words expressing what he called Jefferson's "noblest and most urgent meaning," the sentence carved inside the frieze of the marble monument: "I have sworn upon the altar of God eternal hostility against every form of tyranny over the mind of man." In a voice from the past, a vow worth keeping in our own time, and for all times.

APPENDIX A

IN THEIR OWN WORDS:
SELECTED DOCUMENTS ON RELIGION IN AMERICA

ENGLISH TRANSLATION OF PRAYER FOR PEACE OF CONGREGATION
SHEARITH ISRAEL DURING THE REVOLUTION, NEW YORK CITY

Congregation Shearith Israel, the first Jewish congregation in New York, was led by Reverend Gershom Seixas, who carried the community's Torah scrolls out of the city when the British were advancing during the war. The following is an excerpt from a prayer the congregation used during America's fight for independence. The "president" referred to in the text is the presiding officer of the Continental Congress.

O Great, tremendous, mighty, high, & Exalted King of Israel, Lord of Hosts. . . . He that is near to all those that call upon him, He that answereth those that fear him, when called on in time of their distress: May he bless, guard, preserve, assist, shield, save, supremely exalt and aggrandize to a high degree His Excellency the President, & the Honorable Delegates of the United States of America, in Congress Assembled; His Excellency George Washington, Captain, General, & Commander in Chief of the Federal Army of these States. . . . [A]nd all Kings & Potentates in alliance with North America.

May the Supreme King of Kings, through his infinite mercies, preserve & grant them Life and deliver them from all manner of trouble & injury, fixing and establishing them in their several departments in peace and tranquility.

May the Supreme King of Kings, through his infinite mercies, save and prosper the men of these United States, who are gone forth to War; the Lord of Hosts be the shield of those who are armed for war by land, and for those who are gone in ships to war on the seas. May the Lord fight for them; May they, their rulers, their leaders, and all their allies joining them in battle, equally experience thy

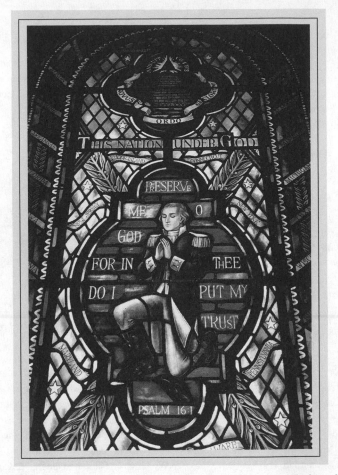

THIS NATION UNDER GOD

PRESERVE

ME   O

GOD

FOR IN   THEE

DO I   PUT MY

TRUST

PSALM 16:1

Washington was apparently not a conventionally believing Christian. The legends of his piety are most likely just that—legends—but he frequently spoke of providence and believed in the value of religion as a force for moral conduct. *(Meditation Chapel, U.S. Capitol Building, © Carrie Devorah, God in the Temples of Government)*

goodness, and may thy angels have in charge and save them from death and all manner of distress.

May the Supreme King of Kings implant among them amity, brotherly love, peace and sociableness. Let not their lips speak evil, nor their tongues utter deceit. May their troops go forth without duplicity when they have taken counsel together to war against those that seek their injury. May the supreme King of Kings through his infinite mercies impart his divine wisdom to the rulers of these United States, and grant them a spirit of just council and true valor, so that they may [be] enabled to support their determinations with wisdom and judgment. . . .

We beseech thee, O most gracious and merciful King, to whom peace pertaineth, that thou wilt cause us to enjoy a firm peace and tranquility, & spread over us the tabernacle of peace everlastingly, & speedily permit that among us may be heard the voice of Him who bringeth glad tidings, announcing that "The Redeemer Cometh to Zion." Amen. So may it be.

JEFFERSON'S VIRGINIA STATUTE FOR RELIGIOUS FREEDOM

First drafted after a meeting at the Rising Sun Tavern in Fredericksburg, Virginia, in 1777, Thomas Jefferson's statute underwent some editing through the years—first introduced to the General Assembly during Jefferson's governorship in 1779, it did not pass until January 16, 1786, in the form below.

I. **WHEREAS** Almighty God hath created the mind free; that all attempts to influence it by temporal punishments or burthens, or by civil incapacitations, tend only to beget habits of hypocrisy and meanness, and are a departure from the plan of the Holy author of our religion, who being Lord both of body and mind, yet chose not to propagate it by coercions on either, as it was in his Almighty power to do; that the impious presumption of legislators and rulers, civil as well as ecclesiastical, who being themselves but fallible and uninspired men, have assumed dominion over the faith of others, setting up their own opinions and modes of thinking as the only true and infallible, and as such endeavouring to impose them on others, hath established and maintained false religions over the greatest part of the world, and through all time; that to compel a man to furnish contributions of money for the propagation of opinions which he disbelieves, is sinful and tyrannical; that even the forcing him to support this or that teacher of his own religious persuasion, is depriving him of the comfortable liberty of giving his contributions to the particular pastor, whose morals he would make his pattern, and whose powers he feels most persuasive to righteousness, and is withdrawing from the ministry those temporary rewards, which proceeding from an approbation of their personal conduct, are an additional incitement to earnest and unremitting labours for the instruction of mankind; that our civil rights have no dependence on our religious opinions, any more than our opinions in physics or geometry; that therefore the proscribing any citizen as unworthy of the public confidence by laying upon him an incapacity of being called to offices of trust and emolument, unless he profess or renounce this or that religious opinion, is depriving him injuriously of those privileges and advantages to which in common with his fellow-citizens he has a natural right; that it tends only to corrupt the principles of that religion it is meant to encourage, by bribing with a monopoly of worldly honours and emoluments, those who will externally profess and conform to it; that though indeed these are criminal who do not withstand such temptation, yet neither are those innocent who lay the bait in their way; that to suffer the civil magistrate to intrude his powers into the field of opinion, and to restrain the profession or propagation of principles on supposition of their ill tendency, is a dangerous fallacy, which at once destroys all religious liberty, because he being of course judge of that tendency will make his opinions the rule of judgment, and approve or condemn the sentiments of others only as they shall square with or differ from his own; that it is time enough for the rightful purposes of civil government, for its officers to interfere when Principles break out into overt acts against peace and good order; and finally, that truth is great and will prevail if left to herself, that she is the proper and sufficient antagonist to error, and has nothing to fear from the conflict, unless by human interposition disarmed of her natural weapons, free argument and debate, errors ceasing to be dangerous when it is permitted freely to contradict them:

II. Be it enacted by the General Assembly, that no man shall be compelled to frequent or support any religious worship, place or ministry whatsoever, nor shall be enforced, restrained, molested, or burthened in his body or goods, nor shall otherwise suffer on account of his religious opinions or belief; but that all men shall be free to profess, and by argument to maintain, their opinion in matters of religion, and that the same shall in no wise diminish, enlarge or affect their civil capacities.

III. And though we well know that this assembly, elected by the people for the ordinary purposes of legislation only, have no power to restrain the acts of succeeding assemblies, constituted with powers equal to our own, and that therefore to declare this act to be irrevocable would be of no effect in law; yet we are free to declare, and do declare, that the rights hereby asserted are of the natural rights of mankind, and that if any act shall hereafter be passed to repeal the present, or to narrow its operation, such act will be an infringement of natural right.

MADISON'S MEMORIAL AND REMONSTRANCE AGAINST RELIGIOUS ASSESSMENTS

In 1785, James Madison wrote the following "Memorial and Remonstrance" in opposition to Patrick Henry's proposed law to use state funds in Virginia to pay

"Teachers of the Christian Religion." Madison thought such a bill "a dangerous abuse of power."

MEMORIAL AND REMONSTRANCE AGAINST RELIGIOUS ASSESSMENTS

To the Honorable the General Assembly
Of the Commonwealth of Virginia
A Memorial and Remonstrance

We the subscribers, citizens of the said Commonwealth, having taken into serious consideration, a Bill printed by order of the last Session of General Assembly, entitled "A Bill establishing a provision for Teachers of the Christian Religion," and conceiving that the same if finally armed with the sanctions of a law, will be a dangerous abuse of power, are bound as faithful members of a free State to remonstrate against it, and to declare the reasons by which we are determined. We remonstrate against the said Bill,

1. Because we hold it for a fundamental and undeniable truth, "that Religion or the duty which we owe to our Creator and the manner of discharging it, can be directed only by reason and conviction, not by force or violence." The Religion then of every man must be left to the conviction and conscience of every man; and it is the right of every man to exercise it as these may dictate. This right is in its nature an unalienable right. It is unalienable, because the opinions of men, depending only on the evidence contemplated by their own minds, cannot follow the dictates of other men: It is unalienable also, because what is here a right towards men, is a duty towards the Creator. It is the duty of every man to render to the Creator such homage and such only as he believes to be acceptable to him. This duty is precedent, both in order of time and degree of obligation, to the claims of Civil Society. Before any man can be considered as a member of Civil Society, he must be considered as a subject of the Governor of the Universe: And if a member of Civil Society, who enters into any subordinate Association, must always do it with a reservation of his duty to the general authority; much more must every man who becomes a member of any particular Civil Society, do it with a saving of his allegiance to the Universal Sovereign. We maintain therefore that in matters of Religion, no man's right is abridged by the institution of Civil Society, and that Religion is wholly exempt from its cognizance. True it is, that no other rule exists, by which any question which may divide a Society, can be ultimately determined,

but the will of the majority; but it is also true that the majority may trespass on the rights of the minority.

2. Because if religion be exempt from the authority of the Society at large, still less can it be subject to that of the Legislative Body. The latter are but the creatures and viceregents of the former. Their jurisdiction is both derivative and limited: it is limited with regard to the co-ordinate departments, more necessarily is it limited with regard to the constituents. The preservation of a free government requires not merely, that the metes and bounds which separate each department of power be invariably maintained; but more especially, that neither of them be suffered to overleap the great Barrier which defends the rights of the people. The Rulers who are guilty of such an encroachment, exceed the commission from which they derive their authority, and are Tyrants. The People who submit to it are governed by laws made neither by themselves, nor by an authority derived from them, and are slaves.

3. Because it is proper to take alarm at the first experiment on our liberties. We hold this prudent jealousy to be the first duty of citizens, and one of the noblest characteristics of the late Revolution. The freemen of America did not wait till usurped power had strengthened itself by exercise, and entangled the question in precedents. They saw all the consequences in the principle, and they avoided the consequences by denying the principle. We revere this lesson too much soon to forget it. Who does not see that the same authority which can establish Christianity, in exclusion of all other Religions, may establish with the same ease any particular sect of Christians, in exclusion of all other Sects? That the same authority which can force a citizen to contribute three pence only of his property for the support of any one establishment, may force him to conform to any other establishment in all cases whatsoever?

4. Because the bill violates that equality which ought to be the basis of every law, and which is more indispensable, in proportion as the validity or expediency of any law is more liable to be impeached. If "all men are by nature equally free and independent," all men are to be considered as entering into Society on equal conditions; as relinquishing no more, and therefore retaining no less, one than another, of their natural rights. Above all are they to be considered as retaining an "*equal* title to the free exercise of Religion according to the dictates of conscience." Whilst we assert for ourselves a freedom to embrace, to profess and to observe the Religion which we believe to be of divine origin, we cannot deny an equal freedom to those whose minds have not yet yielded to the evidence which has convinced us. If this freedom be abused, it is an offense against God, not against man: To God, therefore, not to man, must an account of it be rendered. As the Bill violates equality by subjecting some to peculiar burdens, so it violates the same principle, by granting to others pecu-

liar exemptions. Are the Quakers and Menonists the only sects who think a compulsive support of their religions unnecessary and unwarrantable? Can their piety alone be intrusted with the care of public worship? Ought their Religions to be endowed above all others, with extraordinary privileges by which proselytes may be enticed from all others? We think too favorably of the justice and good sense of these denominations to believe that they either covet pre-eminences over their fellow citizens, or that they will be seduced by them from the common opposition to the measure.

5. Because the bill implies either that the Civil Magistrate is a competent Judge of Religious truth; or that he may employ Religion as an engine of Civil policy. The first is an arrogant pretension falsified by the contradictory opinions of Rulers in all ages, and throughout the world: the second an unhallowed perversion of the means of salvation.

6. Because the establishment proposed by the Bill is not requisite for the support of the Christian Religion. To say that it is, is a contradiction to the Christian Religion itself, for every page of it disavows a dependence on the powers of this world: it is a contradiction to fact; for it is known that this Religion both existed and flourished, not only without the support of human laws, but in spite of every opposition from them; and not only during the period of miraculous aid, but long after it had been left to its own evidence, and the ordinary care of Providence: Nay, it is a contradiction in terms; for a Religion not invented by human policy, must have pre-existed and been supported, before it was established by human policy. It is moreover to weaken in those who profess this Religion a pious confidence in its innate excellence and the patronage of its Author; and to foster in those who still reject it, a suspicion that its friends are too conscious of its fallacies, to trust it to its own merits.

7. Because experience witnesseth that ecclesiastical establishments, instead of maintaining the purity and efficacy of Religion, have had a contrary operation. During almost fifteen centuries has the legal establishment of Christianity been on trial. What have been its fruits? More or less in all places, pride and indolence in the Clergy; ignorance and servility in the laity; in both, superstition, bigotry and persecution. Enquire of the Teachers of Christianity for the ages in which it appeared in its greatest lustre; those of every sect, point to the ages prior to its incorporation with Civil policy. Propose a restoration of this primitive state in which its Teachers depended on the voluntary rewards of their flocks, many of them predict its downfall. On which side ought their testimony to have greatest weight, when for or when against their interest?

8. Because the establishment in question is not necessary for the support of Civil Government. If it be urged as necessary for the support of Civil Government only as it is a means of supporting Religion, and it be not necessary for the lat-

ter purpose, it cannot be necessary for the former. If Religion be not within the cognizance of Civil Government, how can its legal establishment be said to be necessary to civil Government? What influence in fact have ecclesiastical establishments had on Civil Society? In some instances they have been seen to erect a spiritual tyranny on the ruins of Civil authority; in many instances they have been seen upholding the thrones of political tyranny; in no instance have they been seen the guardians of the liberties of the people. Rulers who wished to subvert the public liberty, may have found an established clergy convenient auxiliaries. A just government instituted to secure & perpetuate it needs them not. Such a government will be best supported by protecting every citizen in the enjoyment of his Religion with the same equal hand which protects his person and his property; by neither invading the equal rights of any Sect, nor suffering any Sect to invade those of another.

9. Because the proposed establishment is a departure from that generous policy, which, offering an asylum to the persecuted and oppressed of every Nation and Religion, promised a lustre to our country, and an accession to the number of its citizens. What a melancholy mark is the Bill of sudden degeneracy? Instead of holding forth an asylum to the persecuted, it is itself a signal of persecution. It degrades from the equal rank of Citizens all those whose opinions in Religion do not bend to those of the Legislative authority. Distant as it may be in its present form from the Inquisition, it differs from it only in degree. The one is the first step, the other the last in the career of intolerance. The magnanimous sufferer under this cruel scourge in foreign Regions, must view the Bill as a Beacon on our Coast, warning him to seek some other haven, where liberty and philanthropy in their due extent, may offer a more certain repose from his troubles.

10. Because it will have a like tendency to banish our Citizens. The allurements presented by other situations are every day thinning their number. To superadd a fresh motive to emigration, by revoking the liberty which they now enjoy, would be the same species of folly which has dishonoured and depopulated flourishing kingdoms.

11. Because it will destroy that moderation and harmony which the forbearance of our laws to intermeddle with Religion has produced amongst its several sects. Torrents of blood have been spilt in the old world, by vain attempts of the secular arm, to extinguish Religious discord, by proscribing all difference in Religious opinions. Time has at length revealed the true remedy. Every relaxation of narrow and rigorous policy, wherever it has been tried, has been found to assuage the disease. The American Theatre has exhibited proofs that equal and compleat liberty, if it does not wholly eradicate it, sufficiently destroys its malignant influence on the health and prosperity of the State. If with

the salutary effects of this system under our own eyes, we begin to contract the bounds of Religious freedom, we know no name that will too severely reproach our folly. At least let warning be taken at the first fruits of the threatened innovation. The very appearance of the Bill has transformed that "Christian forbearance, love and charity," which of late mutually prevailed, into animosities and jealousies, which may not soon be appeased. What mischiefs may not be dreaded, should this enemy to the public quiet be armed with the force of a law?

12. Because the policy of the bill is adverse to the diffusion of the light of Christianity. The first wish of those who enjoy this precious gift ought to be that it may be imparted to the whole race of mankind. Compare the number of those who have as yet received it with the number still remaining under the dominion of false Religions; and how small is the former! Does the policy of the Bill tend to lessen the disproportion? No; it at once discourages those who are strangers to the light of revelation from coming into the Region of it; and countenances by example the nations who continue in darkness, in shutting out those who might convey it to them. Instead of levelling as far as possible, every obstacle to the victorious progress of truth, the Bill with an ignoble and unchristian timidity would circumscribe it with a wall of defence against the encroachments of error.

13. Because attempts to enforce by legal sanctions, acts obnoxious to so great a proportion of Citizens, tend to enervate the laws in general, and to slacken the bands of Society. If it be difficult to execute any law which is not generally deemed necessary or salutary, what must be the case, where it is deemed invalid and dangerous? and what may be the effect of so striking an example of impotency in the Government, on its general authority?

14. Because a measure of such singular magnitude and delicacy ought not to be imposed, without the clearest evidence that it is called for by a majority of citizens, and no satisfactory method is yet proposed by which the voice of the majority in this case may be determined, or its influence secured. "The people of the respective counties are indeed requested to signify their opinion respecting the adoption of the Bill to the next Session of Assembly." But the representation must be made equal, before the voice either of the Representatives or of the Counties will be that of the people. Our hope is that neither of the former will, after due consideration, espouse the dangerous principle of the Bill. Should the event disappoint us, it will still leave us in full confidence, that a fair appeal to the latter will reverse the sentence against our liberties.

15. Because, finally, "the equal right of every citizen to the free exercise of his Religion according to the dictates of conscience" is held by the same tenure with all our other rights. If we recur to its origin, it is equally the gift of nature; if we

weigh its importance, it cannot be less dear to us; if we consult the "Declaration of those rights which pertain to the good people of Virginia, as the basis and foundation of Government," it is enumerated with equal solemnity, or rather studied emphasis. Either then, we must say, that the will of the Legislature is the only measure of their authority; and that in the plenitude of this authority, they may sweep away all our fundamental rights; or, that they are bound to leave this particular right untouched and sacred: Either we must say, that they may controul the freedom of the press, may abolish the trial by jury, may swallow up the Executive and Judiciary Powers of the State; nay that they may despoil us of our very right of suffrage, and erect themselves into an independent and hereditary assembly: or, we must say, that they have no authority to enact into law the Bill under consideration. We the subscribers say, that the General Assembly of this Commonwealth have no such authority: And that no effort may be omitted on our part against so dangerous an usurpation, we oppose to it, this remonstrance; earnestly praying, as we are in duty bound, that the Supreme Lawgiver of the Universe, by illuminating those to whom it is addressed, may on the one hand, turn their councils from every act which would affront his holy prerogative, or violate the trust committed to them: and on the other, guide them into every measure which may be worthy of his [blessing, may re]dound to their own praise, and may establish more firmly the liberties, the prosperity, and the Happiness of the Commonwealth.

WASHINGTON'S LETTER TO THE HEBREW CONGREGATION AT NEWPORT

In August 1790, about eighteen months into his presidency, George Washington wrote the following to the Hebrew Congregation at Newport, Rhode Island, succinctly articulating his vision of religious liberty in the new nation.

18 August, 1790
Gentlemen:

While I received with much satisfaction, your address replete with expressions of esteem, I rejoice in the opportunity of assuring you, that I shall always retain grateful remembrance of the cordial welcome I experienced on my visit to Newport, from all classes of citizens.

The reflection on the days of difficulty and danger which are past is rendered the more sweet, from a consciousness that they are succeeded by days of uncommon prosperity and security.

If we have wisdom to make the best use of the advantages with which we are now favored, we cannot fail, under the just administration of a good government, to become a great and happy people.

The citizens of the United States of America have a right to applaud themselves for having given to mankind examples of an enlarged and liberal policy: a policy worthy of imitation. All possess alike liberty of conscience and immunities of citizenship.

It is now no more that toleration is spoken of, as if it were by the indulgence of one class of people, that another enjoyed the exercise of their inherent natural rights. For, happily, the Government of the United States, which gives to bigotry no sanction, to persecution no assistance, requires only that they who live under its protection should demean themselves as good citizens, in giving it on all occasions their effectual support.

It would be inconsistent with the frankness of my character not to avow that I am pleased with your favorable opinion of my administration and fervent wishes for my felicity.

May the children of the stock of Abraham who dwell in this land continue to merit and enjoy the good will of the other inhabitants;—while every one shall sit in safety under his own vine and fig tree and there shall be none to make him afraid.

May the father of all mercies scatter light and not darkness upon our paths, and make us all in our several vocations useful here, and in His own due time and way everlastingly happy.

WASHINGTON'S FAREWELL ADDRESS

In 1796, as he retired from two terms as president, Washington issued a farewell address warning Americans against the "baneful effects of the spirit of party," by which he meant the prospect of excessively partisan or narrow interests coming to play too large a role in the Republic. In a brief but interesting discussion of religion and morality, excerpted below, Washington linked religion to morality and virtue, and in turn linked the cultivation of virtue to education.

Of all the dispositions and habits which lead to political prosperity, religion and morality are indispensable supports. In vain would that man claim the tribute of patriotism, who should labor to subvert these great pillars of human happiness, these firmest props of the duties of men and citizens. The mere politician, equally with the pious man ought to respect and to cherish them. A volume could not trace all their connections with private and public felicity. Let it simply be asked: Where is the security for property, for reputation, for life, if the sense of religious obligation desert the oaths, which are the instruments of investigation in courts of justice? And let us with caution indulge the supposition, that morality can be maintained without religion. Whatever may be conceded to the influence of refined education on minds of peculiar structure, reason and experience both forbid us to expect that national morality can prevail in exclusion of religious principle.

It is substantially true that virtue or morality is a necessary spring of popular government. The rule indeed extends with more or less force to every species of free government. Who that is a sincere friend to it can look with indifference upon attempts to shake the foundation of the fabric?

Promote then as an object of primary importance, institutions for the general diffusion of knowledge. In proportion as the structure of a government gives force to public opinion, it is essential that public opinion should be enlightened.

TREATY OF PEACE AND FRIENDSHIP BETWEEN THE UNITED STATES
AND THE BEY AND SUBJECTS OF TRIPOLI OF BARBARY

In 1796, the American diplomat Joel Barlow negotiated a treaty between the United States and the Islamic nation of Tripoli of Barbary. The negotiations began under George Washington and the treaty went to the Senate in the first months of John Adams's administration. It passed unanimously on June 7, 1797, after being read aloud. The treaty, including Article 11, was widely discussed and published.

Article 11. As the government of the United States of America is not in any sense founded on the Christian Religion,—as it has in itself no character of enmity against the laws, religion or tranquility of Musselmen [Muslims],—and as the said States never have entered into any war or act of hostility against any Mehomitan [Muslim] nation, it is declared by the parties that no pretext arising from religious opinions shall ever produce an interruption of the harmony existing between the two countries.

CORRESPONDENCE BETWEEN THE DANBURY BAPTIST ASSOCIATION OF
CONNECTICUT AND PRESIDENT THOMAS JEFFERSON,
OCTOBER 1801–JANUARY 1802

After the ferociously divisive presidential election of 1800—one in which issues of culture and religion played leading parts—the Baptists of Danbury, Connecticut, wrote President Jefferson a letter expressing their thanks for his steadfast defense of religious liberty even in the face of political pressure to grant religion and religious organizations a larger sphere of influence in public life. Jefferson's reply includes the phrase "wall of separation," wording that echoed the Anglican divine Richard Hooker, Roger Williams, and the British thinker James Burgh, and which was popularized in the twentieth century when Justice Hugo Black quoted Jefferson in a 1947 case before the United States Supreme Court.

LETTER OF THE DANBURY BAPTIST ASSOCIATION OF CONNECTICUT TO PRESIDENT JEFFERSON, OCTOBER 7, 1801

Sir,

Among the many million in America and Europe who rejoice in your election to office, we embrace the first opportunity which we have enjoyed in our collective capacity since your inauguration, to express our great satisfaction, in your appointment to the chief magistracy in the United States: And though our mode of expression may be less courtly and pompous than what many others clothe their addresses with, we beg you, sir, to believe, that none are more sincere.

Our sentiments are uniformly on the side of religious liberty—that religion is at all times and places a matter between God and individuals—that no man ought to suffer in name, person, or effects on account of his religious opinions—that the legitimate power of civil government extends no further than to punish the man who works ill to his neighbor. But, sir, our constitution of government is not specific. Our ancient charter, together with the laws made coincident therewith, were adopted as the basis of our government at the time of our revolution; and such had been our laws and usages, and such still are; that religion is considered as the first object of legislation; and therefore what religious privileges we enjoy (as a minor part of the state) we enjoy as favors granted, and not as inalienable rights; and these favors we receive at the expense of such degrading acknowledgements, as are inconsistent with the rights of freemen. It is not to be wondered at therefore, if those, who seek after power and gain under the pretense of government and religion should reproach their fellow man—should reproach their Chief magistrate, as an enemy of religion, law and good order because he will not, dare not assume the prerogative of Jehovah and make laws to govern the kingdom of Christ.

Sir, we are sensible that the president of the United States, is not the national legislator, and also sensible that the national government cannot destroy the laws of each state; but our hopes are strong that the sentiments of our beloved president, which have had such genial effect already, like the radiant beams of the sun, will shine and prevail through all these states and all the world till hierarchy and tyranny be destroyed from the earth. Sir, when we reflect on your past services, and see a glow of philanthropy and good will shining forth in a course of more than thirty years we have reason to believe that America's God has raised you up to fill the chair of state out of that goodwill which he bears to the millions which you preside over. May God strengthen you for the arduous task which providence and the voice of the people have called you to sustain and support you and your administration against all the predetermined opposition of those who wish to rise to wealth and importance on the poverty and subjection of the people.

And may the Lord preserve you safe from every evil and bring you at last to his heavenly kingdom through Jesus Christ our Glorious Mediator.

JEFFERSON'S REPLY, JANUARY 1, 1802

Gentlemen:

The affectionate sentiments of esteem and approbation which you are so good as to express towards me on behalf of the Danbury Baptist association, give me the highest satisfaction. My duties dictate a faithful and zealous pursuit of the interests of my constituents, & in proportion as they are persuaded of my fidelity to those duties, the discharge of them becomes more and more pleasing.

Believing with you that religion is a matter which lies solely between Man & his God, that he owes account to none other for his faith or his worship, that the legitimate powers of government reach actions only, & not opinions, I contemplate with sovereign reverence that act of the whole American people which declared that their legislature should "make no law respecting an establishment of religion, or prohibiting the free exercise thereof," thus building a wall of separation between Church & State. Adhering to this expression of the supreme will of the nation in behalf of the rights of conscience, I shall see with sincere satisfaction the progress of those sentiments which tend to restore to man all his natural rights, convinced he has no natural right in opposition to his social duties.

I reciprocate your kind prayers for the protection & blessing of the common father and creator of man, and tender you for yourselves & your religious association, assurances of my high respect & esteem.

RABBI MAX LILIENTHAL ON "GOD, RELIGION, AND OUR AMERICAN CONSTITUTION," DECEMBER 1870

This sermon is a powerful response to the mid-to-late-nineteenth-century movement to add a "Christian Amendment" to the Constitution—a campaign led by an evangelical Christian organization called the National Reform Association. A Reform rabbi in Cincinnati, Lilienthal was an eloquent voice in the cause of preserving the Founding Fathers' intentions about church and state.

What do the reverend gentlemen mean and intend by inserting the name of God into our constitution? Was the Almighty Ruler of All Nations less God and Father because His holy name was not mentioned in that holy instrument? Was he less worshipped, less revered and adored by the American people, because the fathers of 1776 wisely refrained from meddling with religious matters?

Yes, what do they mean and intend by trying to declare by a new amendment to the constitution this nation to be a Christian nation? . . .

What kind of a Christian nation shall this people be, according to the desire of these reverend gentlemen, a Catholic or a Protestant one? Which one? These gentlemen do not come out in their true colors; they of course mean a Protestant Christian nation. They have as yet too much genuine regard for the American spirit of religious liberty that they shall come forward and declare, we mean a Protestant Christian nation. But do they not by this assertion throw down the gauntlet to the Catholic Church, which ever increases in power, and challenge her to a deadly combat? Or do they presume to avert by such a declaration the dangers they fear from the ever-increasing influence of the Catholic clergy? Do they pretend to put a check on the formidable growth of the Church by adding such an amendment to the constitution?

They will accomplish thereby neither the one nor the other. They will only add fuel to the threatening fire and put the denominational antagonists into a well-defined array; they will thereby only drill and prepare them for a contest which by such agitations will rather be accelerated than avoided.

No, my friends, an old, true adage says: "Let well enough alone." Our country is in no need of a better name than free America, and our people of no better name than that of an American nation. There is glory enough in the name "I am an American." There is security enough against all threatening dangers in our constitution. It will protect and shield us against all temporal or spiritual intrigues and machinations. Let us not willfully jeopardize its might and power, its wise and well-meant guarantees; let us cling to it at any price as it reads and stands; let us hold firmly to the entire separation of church and state and our beloved country will not only prosper and succeed as heretofore, but will always lead the van of human liberty and civilization. . . .

ROBERT INGERSOLL'S DEFINITION OF SECULARISM

The great voice of nineteenth-century free thought, Ingersoll was a prolific writer and orator. In the following 1887 essay for The Independent Pulpit *of Waco, Texas, he eloquently relates his understanding of the secular creed.*

Secularism is the religion of humanity; it embraces the affairs of this world; it is interested in everything that touches the welfare of a sentient being; it advocates attention to the particular planet in which we happen to live; it means that each individual counts for something; it is a declaration of intellectual independence; it means that the pew is superior to the pulpit, that those who bear the burdens shall have the profits and that they who fill the purse shall hold the strings. It is a protest against theological oppression, against ecclesiastical tyranny, against being the serf, subject or slave of any phantom, or of the priest of any phantom. It is a protest against wasting this life for the sake of one that we know not of. It proposes to let the gods take care of themselves. It is another name for common sense; that is to say, the adaptation of means to such ends as are desired and understood.

Secularism believes in building a home here, in this world. It trusts to individual effort, to energy, to intelligence, to observation and experience rather than to the unknown and the supernatural. It desires to be happy on this side of the grave.

Secularism means food and fireside, roof and raiment, reasonable work and reasonable leisure, the cultivation of the tastes, the acquisition of knowledge, the enjoyment of the arts, and it promises for the human race comfort, independence, intelligence, and above all liberty. It means the abolition of sectarian feuds, of theological hatreds. It means the cultivation of friendship and intellectual hospitality. It means the living for ourselves and each other; for the present instead of the past, for this world rather than for another. It means the right to express your thought in spite of popes, priests, and gods. It means that impudent idleness shall no longer live upon the labor of honest men. It means the destruction of the business of those who trade in fear. It proposes to give serenity and content to the human soul. It will put out the fires of eternal pain. It is striving to do away with violence and vice, with ignorance, poverty and disease. It lives for the ever present today, and the ever coming tomorrow. It does not believe in praying and receiving, but in earning and deserving. It regards work as worship, labor as prayer, and wisdom as the savior of mankind. It says to every human being, Take care of yourself so that you may be able to help others; adorn your life with the gems called good deeds; illumine your path with the sunlight called friendship and love.

Secularism is a religion, a religion that is understood. It has no mysteries, no mumblings, no priests, no ceremonies, no falsehoods, no miracles, and no persecutions. It considers the lilies of the field, and takes thought for the morrow. It says to the whole world, Work that you may eat, drink, and be clothed; work that you may enjoy; work that you may not want; work that you may give and never need.

APPENDIX B

SCRIPTURE AND STATE:
THE PRESIDENTS' CHOICE OF INAUGURAL BIBLE VERSES

According to the Architect of the Capitol, there are records of a president having the Bible on which he was sworn into office opened to a specific passage for thirty-four of the inaugurations in American history. (For presidents not listed below, the information is either unknown or the Bible was opened, the Architect's office reports, at random.) I have chosen to use the King James Version of the Holy Bible's translation in each case. If the passage was an entire chapter of a book, I have transcribed the first verse and an additional one to give a sense of the whole.

Martin Van Buren, 1837
PROVERBS 3:17: "Her ways are ways of pleasantness, and all her paths are peace."

Andrew Johnson, 1865
PROVERBS 21: "The king's heart is in the hand of the Lord, as the rivers of water: he turneth it whithersoever he will. . . . He that followeth after righteousness and mercy findeth life, righteousness, and honour."

Ulysses S. Grant, 1873
ISAIAH 11:1–3: "And there shall come forth a rod out of the stem of Jesse, and a Branch shall grow out of his roots: And the spirit of the Lord shall rest upon him, the spirit of wisdom and understanding, the spirit of counsel and might, the spirit of knowledge and of the fear of the Lord; And shall make him of quick understanding in the fear of the Lord: and he shall not judge after the sight of his eyes, neither reprove after the hearing of his ears. . . ."

Rutherford B. Hayes, 1877

PSALM 118:11–13: "They compassed me about; yea, they compassed me about: but in the name of the Lord I will destroy them. They compassed me about like bees; they are quenched as the fire of thorns: for in the name of the Lord I will destroy them. Thou hast thrust sore at me that I might fall: but the Lord helped me."

James A. Garfield, 1881

PROVERBS 21:1: "The king's heart is in the hand of the Lord, as the rivers of water: he turneth it whithersoever he will."

Chester A. Arthur, 1881

PSALM 31:1–3: "In thee, O Lord, do I put my trust; let me never be ashamed: deliver me in thy righteousness. Bow down thine ear to me; deliver me speedily: be thou my strong rock, for an house of defence to save me. For thou art my rock and my fortress; therefore for thy name's sake lead me, and guide me."

Benjamin Harrison, 1889

PSALM 121:1–6: "I will lift up mine eyes unto the hills, from whence cometh my help. My help cometh from the Lord, which made heaven and earth. He will not suffer thy foot to be moved: he that keepeth thee will not slumber. Behold, he that keepeth Israel shall neither slumber nor sleep. The Lord is thy keeper: the Lord is thy shade upon thy right hand. The sun shall not smite thee by day, nor the moon by night."

Grover Cleveland, 1893

PSALM 91:12–16: "They shall bear thee up in their hands, lest thou dash thy foot against a stone. Thou shalt tread upon the lion and adder: the young lion and the dragon shalt thou trample under feet. Because he hath set his love upon me, therefore will I deliver him: I will set him on high, because he hath known my name. He shall call upon me, and I will answer him: I will be with him in trouble; I will deliver him, and honour him. With long life will I satisfy him, and show him my salvation."

William McKinley, 1897

CHRONICLES II 1:10: "Give me now wisdom and knowledge, that I may go out and come in before this people: for who can judge this thy people, that is so great?"

William McKinley, 1901

PROVERBS 16: "The preparations of the heart in man, and the answer of the tongue, is from the Lord. . . . A man's heart deviseth his way: but the Lord directeth his steps."

Theodore Roosevelt, 1905
JAMES 1:22–23: "But be ye doers of the word, and not hearers only, deceiving your own selves."

William Howard Taft, 1909
KINGS I 3:9–11: "Give therefore thy servant an understanding heart to judge thy people, that I may discern between good and bad: for who is able to judge this thy so great a people? And the speech pleased the Lord, that Solomon asked this thing. And God said unto him, Because thou hast asked this thing, and hast not asked for thyself long life; neither hast asked riches for thyself, nor hast asked the life of thine enemies; but hast asked for thyself understanding to discern judgment; Behold, I have done according to thy words: lo, I have given thee a wise and an understanding heart; so that there was none like thee before thee, neither after thee shall any arise like unto thee."

Woodrow Wilson, 1913
PSALM 119: "Blessed are the undefiled in the way, who walk in the law of the Lord. Blessed are they that keep his testimonies, and that seek him with the whole heart."

Woodrow Wilson, 1917
PSALM 46: "God is our refuge and strength, a very present help in trouble. Therefore will not we fear, though the earth be removed, and though the mountains be carried into the midst of the sea. . . . The Lord of hosts is with us; the God of Jacob is our refuge. Selah. Come, behold the works of the Lord, what desolations he hath made in the earth. He maketh wars to cease unto the end of the earth; he breaketh the bow, and cutteth the spear in sunder; he burneth the chariot in the fire. Be still, and know that I am God: I will be exalted among the heathen, I will be exalted in the earth."

Warren G. Harding, 1921
MICAH 6:8: "He hath showed thee, O man, what is good; and what doth the Lord require of thee, but to do justly, and to love mercy, and to walk humbly with thy God?"

Calvin Coolidge, 1925
JOHN 1: "In the beginning was the Word, and the Word was with God, and the Word was God. . . . And the Word was made flesh, and dwelt among us, (and we beheld his glory, the glory as of the only begotten of the Father,) full of grace and truth."

Herbert Hoover, 1929
PROVERBS 29:18: "Where there is no vision, the people perish: but he that keepeth the law, happy is he."

Franklin D. Roosevelt, 1933, 1937, 1941, 1945
CORINTHIANS I:13: "Though I speak with the tongues of men and of angels, and have not charity, I am become as sounding brass, or a tinkling cymbal. . . . And now abideth faith, hope, charity, these three; but the greatest of these is charity."

Harry S. Truman, 1949 (Truman used two Bibles)
MATTHEW 5:3–11: "Blessed are the poor in spirit: for theirs is the kingdom of heaven. Blessed are they that mourn: for they shall be comforted. Blessed are the

At his 1949 inauguration, Harry Truman was sworn in on two Bibles—one opened to the Beatitudes, the other to the Ten Commandments. *(© Bettmann/Corbis)*

meek: for they shall inherit the earth. Blessed are they which do hunger and thirst after righteousness: for they shall be filled. Blessed are the merciful: for they shall obtain mercy. Blessed are the pure in heart: for they shall see God. Blessed are the peacemakers: for they shall be called the children of God. Blessed are they which are persecuted for righteousness' sake: for their's is the kingdom of heaven. Blessed are ye, when men shall revile you, and persecute you, and shall say all manner of evil against you falsely, for my sake."

EXODUS 20:3–17: "Thou shalt have no other gods before me. Thou shalt not make unto thee any graven image, or any likeness of any thing that is in heaven above, or that is in the earth beneath, or that is in the water under the earth: Thou shalt not bow down thyself to them, nor serve them: for I the LORD thy God am a jealous God, visiting the iniquity of the fathers upon the children unto the third and fourth generation of them that hate me; And shewing mercy unto thousands of them that love me, and keep my commandments. Thou shalt not take the name of the LORD thy God in vain; for the LORD will not hold him guiltless that taketh his name in vain. Remember the sabbath day, to keep it holy. Six days shalt thou labour, and do all thy work: But the seventh day is the sabbath of the LORD thy God: in it thou shalt not do any work, thou, nor thy son, nor thy daughter, thy manservant, nor thy maidservant, nor thy cattle, nor thy stranger that is within thy gates: For in six days the LORD made heaven and earth, the sea, and all that in them is, and rested the seventh day: wherefore the LORD blessed the sabbath day, and hallowed it. Honour thy father and thy mother: that thy days may be long upon the land which the LORD thy God giveth thee. Thou shalt not kill. Thou shalt not commit adultery. Thou shalt not steal. Thou shalt not bear false witness against thy neighbour. Thou shalt not covet thy neighbour's house, thou shalt not covet thy neighbour's wife, nor his manservant, nor his maidservant, nor his ox, nor his ass, nor any thing that is thy neighbour's."

Dwight D. Eisenhower, 1953 (Eisenhower used two Bibles)
PSALM 127:1: "Except the Lord build the house, they labour in vain that build it: except the Lord keep the city, the watch waketh but in vain."
CHRONICLES II 7:14: "If my people, which are called by my name, shall humble themselves, and pray, and seek my face, and turn from their wicked ways; then will I hear from heaven, and will forgive their sin, and will heal their land."

Dwight D. Eisenhower, 1957
PSALM 33:12: "Blessed is the nation whose God is the Lord; and the people he hath chosen for his own inheritance."

Richard Nixon, 1969 and 1973
ISAIAH 2:4: "And he shall judge among the nations, and shall rebuke many people: and they shall beat their swords into plowshares, and their spears into pruning-hooks: nation shall not lift up sword against nation, neither shall they learn war any more."

Gerald R. Ford, 1974
PROVERBS 3:5–6: "Trust in the Lord with all thine heart; and lean not unto thine own understanding. In all thy ways acknowledge him, and he shall direct thy paths."

Jimmy Carter, 1977
MICAH 6:8: "He hath showed thee, O man, what is good; and what doth the Lord require of thee, but to do justly, and to love mercy, and to walk humbly with thy God?"

Ronald Reagan, 1981 and 1985
CHRONICLES II 7:14: "If my people, which are called by my name, shall humble themselves, and pray, and seek my face, and turn from their wicked ways; then will I hear from heaven, and will forgive their sin, and will heal their land."

George H.W. Bush, 1989
MATTHEW 5: "And seeing the multitudes, he went up into a mountain: and when he was set, his disciples came unto him: And he opened his mouth, and taught them, saying: Blessed are the poor in spirit: for theirs is the kingdom of heaven. . . . Be ye therefore perfect, even as your Father which is in heaven is perfect."

Bill Clinton, 1993
GALATIANS 6:8: "For he that soweth to his flesh shall reap corruption; but he that soweth to the Spirit shall of the Spirit reap life everlasting."

Bill Clinton, 1997
ISAIAH 58:12: "And they that shall be of thee shall build the old waste places: thou shalt raise up the foundations of many generations; and thou shalt be called, The repairer of the breach, The restorer of paths to dwell in."

George W. Bush, 2005
ISAIAH 40:31: "But they that wait upon the Lord shall renew their strength; they shall mount up with wings as eagles; they shall run, and not be weary; and they shall walk, and not faint."

SOURCES: Jacques Judah Lyons Collection, American Jewish Historical Society, New York and Newton Centre, Massachusetts; Henning, W. W., ed. *Statutes At Large of Virginia.* Vol. 12 (1823), 84–86; Rutland, Robert A., ed. *The Papers of James Madison.* Vol. 8. (Chicago, 1973), 298–304; Twohig, Dorothy, ed. *The Papers of George Washington: Presidential Series.* Vol. 6. (Charlottesville, 1996), 284–85; Fitzpatrick, John C., ed. *The Writings of George Washington.* Vol. 35. (Washington, D.C., 1940), 229; The Avalon Project. Yale Law School: The Barbary Treaties, 1796–1816. "Treaty of Peace and Friendship, Signed at Tripoli, Nov. 4, 1796"; Library of Congress; Sarna, Jonathan D. and David G. Dalin, eds. *Religion and State in the American Jewish Experience* (Notre Dame, 1997), 169–170; http://www.infidels.org /library/historical/robert_ingersoll/; http://memory.loc.gov/ammem/pihtml/pibible .html

SOURCE NOTES

INTRODUCTION: AMERICAN GOSPEL

3   "The God who gave"   Thomas Jefferson, *Writings* (New York, 1984), 122. Readers should note that, for the sake of clarity, I have frequently modernized the spelling and punctuation of quotations from earlier centuries. I have occasionally retained the original when it seemed important to convey the speaker or writer's meaning.

3   "Religion and liberty must flourish or fall"   Frank Moore, ed. *The Patriot Preachers of the American Revolution. With Biographical Sketches.* (New York, 1862), 105. Smith, an Episcopal priest who was also a professor and provost of the College of Philadelphia, entitled his work "The Crisis of American Affairs." (Ibid., 92.) At the time of this sermon, delivered on June 23, 1775, at Christ Church in Philadelphia, Smith saw the Revolutionary struggle in biblical terms: "As clay in the potter's hands, so are the nations in the hands of him, the everlasting Jehovah! He lifteth up, and he casteth down—he resisteth the proud, and giveth grace to the humble—he will keep the feet of his saints—the wicked shall be silent in darkness, and by strength shall no man prevail. . . . For my part, I have long been possessed with a strong and even enthusiastic persuasion, that Heaven has great and gracious purposes toward this continent, which no human power or human device shall be able finally to frustrate. Illiberal or mistaken plans of policy may distress us for a while, and perhaps sorely check our growth; but if we maintain our own virtue; if we cultivate the spirit of liberty among our children; if we guard against the snares of luxury, venality and corruption, the genius of America will still rise triumphant, and that with a power at last too mighty

for opposition. This country will be free—nay, for ages to come a chosen seat of freedom, arts, and heavenly knowledge, which are now either drooping or dead in most countries of the old world." (Ibid., 107–110.) Smith, however, "could never warm to the cause of independence," wrote Ellis Sandoz, "and was driven out of Pennsylvania in 1779" before returning at the end of his life. (Ellis Sandoz, ed. *Political Sermons of the American Founding Era, 1730–1805,* I [Indianapolis, 1998], 816.) By 1784, however, Smith was striking the same notes he had struck in 1775. In "A Sermon Preached Before a Convention of the Episcopal Church" in Maryland on June 22, 1784, Smith said, "Thus, with the truth in our heads and love in our hearts; with zeal and public spirit; with a concern for liberty, civil and religious; with industry and economy; with a strict care for the education of youth and their nurture and admonition in the fear of the Lord; this American land shall become a great and glorious empire! Transported at the thought, I am born into future days! I see this new world rising in her glory, and behold period still brightening upon period. Where depths of gloomy wilderness now extend and shut out even beams of day, I behold polished villas and religious domes spreading around." (Ibid., 833.)

3   the courthouse bell in Charlottesville tolled   Recollections of Andrew K. Smith, of the General Land Office, Charlottesville *Weekly Chronicle,* Friday, October 15, 1875, Jefferson Papers Project, Retirement Series, Monticello. According to James A. Bear, Jr., Smith's account in the *Weekly Chronicle* is "the only written source telling of T. J.'s funeral." (James A. Bear, Jr., "The Last Few Days in the Life of Thomas Jefferson," *The Magazine of Albemarle County History,* Vol. 32, 1974, 77.) The national reaction was moving. In Washington, a newspaper wrote, "Thomas Jefferson is no more! . . . His history may be read in a nation's eyes—his eulogy beams on the surface of everything that is admirable and peculiar in the principles of our governments." (*Daily National Inquirer,* Friday, July 7, 1826.)

3   Thomas Jefferson was dead   Dr. Robley Dunglison's "Ana," College of Physicians of Philadelphia, Robley Dunglison Papers, are the handwritten recollections of Jefferson's doctor about Jefferson's last days. Thomas Jefferson Randolph's "Account of TJ's Last Illness and Death," July 4, 1826, University of Virginia, Edgehill-Randolph Papers, is Jefferson's grandson's version of events. Nicolas P. Trist to Joseph Coolidge, "His bed side, July 4th, 1826," University of Virginia, Correspondence of Ellen Wayles Randolph Coolidge, is a letter written several hours before the end. See also Henry S. Randall, *The Life of Thomas Jefferson,* III (New York, 1858), 542–552; Dumas Malone, *Jefferson and His Time: The Sage of Monticello* (New York, 1981), 479–499; Bear, "The Last Few Days in the Life of

Thomas Jefferson," *The Magazine of Albemarle County History,* Vol. 32, 63–79; *Daily National Inquirer,* Friday, July 7, 1826; and *Richmond Enquirer* of Friday, July 7, 1826; Friday, July 14, 1826; and Friday, October 27, 1826.

3   at ten minutes to one   Thomas Jefferson Randolph's "Account," July 4, 1826. Dunglison reports the death occurred "about one o'clock."

4   "I am of a sect by myself"   Albert Ellery Bergh, ed. *The Writings of Thomas Jefferson,* XV (Washington, D.C., 1904), 203. The context is a letter from Jefferson to Ezra Stiles dated June 25, 1819.

4   he once spent a few evenings in the White House   Dickinson W. Adams and others, eds. *Jefferson's Extracts from the Gospels: "The Philosophy of Jesus" and "The Life and Morals of Jesus,"* Papers of Thomas Jefferson, Second Series (Princeton, NJ, 1983). The introduction to this volume is indispensable for those trying to make sense of Jefferson's religious views, and I am grateful to Jefferson Looney of the Jefferson Papers Project, Retirement Series, for his guidance on this point. Eugene R. Sheridan, *Jefferson and Religion* (Charlottesville, VA, 1998), is also essential reading as is Paul K. Conkin, "The Religious Pilgrimage of Thomas Jefferson," in Peter Onuf, ed. *Jeffersonian Legacies* (Charlottesville, VA, 1993), 19–49. Randall, *The Life of Thomas Jefferson,* III, 451–452. See also Jefferson, *Writings,* 1300–1304, 1372–1373; Edwin S. Gaustad, *Sworn on the Altar of God: A Religious Biography of Thomas Jefferson* (Grand Rapids, MI, 1996), 123–131; Charles B. Sanford, *The Religious Life of Thomas Jefferson* (Charlottesville, VA, 1984), 102–104.

4   through the Gospels   Thomas Jefferson, *The Jefferson Bible: The Life and Morals of Jesus of Nazareth* (Boston, 1989), 18.

4   with a razor   Ibid., 149.

4   waved away talk of the Holy Trinity   Gaustad, *Sworn on the Altar of God,* 139.

4   "Ideas must be distinct"   Ibid.

4   Neither conventionally devout nor wholly unbelieving   It would be a mistake to try to portray Jefferson as anything approaching an orthodox Christian. In his essay in *Jeffersonian Legacies,* Conkin wrote this of the Semitic monotheistic tradition: "A masculine god created the world and all that inhabit it, and such a god also controlled or planned the history of his creation. Jefferson never doubted such a creative and providential god, even when he tried without success to understand the views of authentic atheists. This cosmology remained the foundation of his private religious beliefs and a support both for objective knowledge and moral confidence." Jefferson, however, rejected the divinity of Jesus, though he did believe in an afterlife.

He was also, Conkin wrote, a great reader of Stoic and Epicurean philosophy. (Conkin, "The Religious Pilgrimage of Thomas Jefferson," in Onuf, ed. *Jeffersonian Legacies*, 20–21.) "Jefferson's religious beliefs never cohered," Conkin wrote (Ibid., 45), and "One has to note that, in the most strict sense of the label, Jefferson was never a Christian, for he never believed that Jesus was the promised Messiah, the Christ, although at times he turned the word Christ (a status term) into a proper name. He never bestowed any special authority upon Jesus beyond the power of his message." (Ibid., 46.) I think Conkin is clearly right, but it is interesting to read Randall, in the middle of the nineteenth century, offering this view: "Mr. Jefferson was a public professor of his belief in the Christian religion. In all his most important early state papers, such as his Summary View of the Rights of British America, his portion of the Declaration made by Congress on the causes of taking up arms, the Declaration of Independence, the draft of a Constitution for Virginia, etc., there are more or less pointed recognitions of God and Providence. In his two Inaugural Addresses as President of the United States, and in many of his annual messages he makes the same recognitions—clothes them on several occasions in the most explicit language—substantially avows the God of his faith to be the God of revelation—declares his belief in the efficacy of prayer, and the duty of ascriptions of praise to the Author of all mercies—and speaks of the Christian religion as professed in his country as a benign religion, evincing the favor of Heaven." (Randall, *The Life of Thomas Jefferson*, III, 553–554.)

It's true that Jefferson was not quite as unconventional as perhaps even he liked to think. Despite charges from his partisan opponents that he was an "atheist" and "a French infidel" (on the eve of the 1800 presidential election, a New York clergyman decried Jefferson in a pamphlet called "The Voice of Warning to Christians On the Ensuing Election"), Jefferson openly professed belief. Raised in the Anglican world of colonial Virginia, he was baptized and married in his parish, graduated from the church's College of William and Mary, served as a vestryman, owned and traveled with a well-worn Book of Common Prayer, contributed to different churches, and designed a new one for the nearby parish. He invoked God in his inaugural addresses and as president attended Sunday services in the chamber of the House of Representatives, lending the prestige of his office to religious gatherings. (See Randall, *The Life of Thomas Jefferson, II*, and *The Life of Thomas Jefferson, III*; Gaustad, *Sworn on the Altar of God;* Sanford, *The Religious Life of Thomas Jefferson;* and James H. Hutson, *The Founders on Religion: A Book of Quotations* (Princeton, NJ, 2005).

Randall, in *The Life of Thomas Jefferson*, III, 555, reported: "He at-

tended church with as much regularity as most of the members of the congregation—sometimes going alone on horseback, when his family remained
at home. He generally attended the Episcopal Church, and when he did so,
always carried his prayer-book, and joined in the responses and prayers of
the congregation. He was baptized into the Episcopal Church in his infancy;
he was married by one of its clergymen; his wife lived and died a member of
it; his children were baptized into it, and when married were married according to its rites; its burial services were read over those of them who pre-
ceded him to the grave, over his wife, and finally over himself." (Ibid., 555.)

5   the legacy of the Founding   I am indebted to many authors who have
done excellent work on faith, the Founding, and the presidency, and my
book draws on, among others: Alfred Owen Aldridge, *Benjamin Franklin
and Nature's God* (Durham, NC, 1967); Robert N. Bellah, *Beyond Belief: Essays on Religion in a Post-Traditionalist World* (Berkeley, CA, 1991); Robert
N. Bellah and Phillip E. Hammond, *Varieties of Civil Religion* (San Francisco, 1980); Paul F. Boller, Jr., *George Washington and Religion* (Dallas,
1963); Morton Borden, *Jews, Turks, and Infidels* (Chapel Hill, NC, 1984);
Jon Butler, *Awash in a Sea of Faith: Christianizing the American People*
(Cambridge, MA, 1990); Norman Cousins, *"In God We Trust": The Reli-
gious Beliefs and Ideas of the American Founding Fathers* (New York, 1958);
Derek H. Davis, *Religion and the Continental Congress, 1774–1789: Contri-
butions to Original Intent* (New York, 2000); Edwin S. Gaustad, *Faith of the
Founders: Religion and the New Nation, 1776–1826* (Waco, TX, 2004);
Gaustad, *Sworn on the Altar of God: A Religious Biography of Thomas Jef-
ferson,* Edwin S. Gaustad and Leigh Schmidt, *The Religious History of
America: The Heart of the American Story from Colonial Times to Today,* re-
vised ed. (San Francisco, 2002); Edwin S. Gaustad, and with revisions by
Mark A. Noll, eds. *A Documentary History of Religion in America,* 3rd ed., 2
vols. (Grand Rapids, MI, 2003); Ronald Hoffman and Peter J. Albert, eds.,
Religion in a Revolutionary Age (Charlottesville, VA, 1994); Robert H. Hor-
witz, ed. *The Moral Foundations of the American Republic* (Charlottesville,
VA, 1986); James H. Hutson, *Religion and the Founding of the American Re-
public* (Washington, D.C.; 1998); James H. Hutson, ed., *The Founders on
Religion* (Princeton, NJ, 2005); James H. Hutson, ed. *Religion and the New
Republic: Faith in the Founding of America* (Lanham, MD, 2000); Susan Ja-
coby, *Freethinkers: A History of American Secularism* (New York, 2004);
Isaac Kramnick and R. Laurence Moore, *The Godless Constitution: A Moral
Defense of the Secular State* (New York, 2005); Frank Lambert, *The Found-
ing Fathers and the Place of Religion in America* (Princeton, NJ, 2003);
William Lee Miller, *The First Liberty: America's Foundation in Religious*

Freedom (Washington, D.C., 2003); Alan Mittleman, Robert Licht, and Jonathan D. Sarna, eds. *Jews and the American Public Square: Debating Religion and Republic* (Lanham, MD, 2002); Mark A. Noll, Nathan O. Hatch, and George M. Marsden, *The Search for Christian America* (Colorado Springs, CO, 1989); John T. Noonan, Jr., *The Lustre of Our Country: The American Experience of Religious Freedom* (Berkeley, CA, 1998); Russell E. Richey and Donald G. Jones, eds. *American Civil Religion* (New York, 1974); Richard V. Pierard and Robert D. Linder, *Civil Religion & the Presidency* (Grand Rapids, MI, 1989); Sanford, *The Religious Life of Thomas Jefferson;* Jonathan D. Sarna, *American Judaism: A History* (New Haven, CT, 2004); Jonathan D. Sarna and David G. Dalin, eds. *Religion and State in the American Jewish Experience* (Notre Dame, IN, 1997); William J. Wolf, *The Almost Chosen People: A Study of the Religion of Abraham Lincoln* (Garden City, NY, 1959).

5   the problem of church and state   I particularly drew on, among others: Thomas J. Curry, *The First Freedoms: Church and State in America to the Passage of the First Amendment* (New York, 1986); Terry Eastland, ed. *Religious Liberty in the Supreme Court: The Cases That Define the Debate over Church and State* (Grand Rapids, MI, 1993); Bette Novit Evans, *Interpreting the Free Exercise of Religion: The Constitution and American Pluralism* (Chapel Hill, NC, 1997); Philip Hamburger, *Separation of Church and State* (Cambridge, MA, 2002); Leonard W. Levy, *The Establishment Clause: Religion and the First Amendment* (Chapel Hill, NC, 1994).

6   the Jeffersonian "wall of separation between church and state"   The finest, most thorough assessment of the origins and uses of the wall metaphor is Daniel L. Dreisbach, *Thomas Jefferson and the Wall of Separation Between Church and State* (New York, 2002).

6   as though Washington, Adams, Jefferson, and Franklin were cheerful Christian soldiers   For a penetrating scholarly discussion of this issue, see Noll, Hatch, and Marsden, *The Search for Christian America;* for examples, see, for instance, Tim LaHaye, *Faith of Our Founding Fathers: A Comprehensive Study of America's Christian Foundations* (Green Forest, AR, 1994). LaHaye's argument: "If we sit back and let the secularizers continue to dominate the government, the courts, the media, and education, those guarantees will be lost. Fortunately, a groundswell of concerned citizens is getting involved. They are becoming so informed that they will wrest control of this nation from the hands of the secularizers and place it back into the hands of those who founded this nation, citizens who had a personal and abiding faith in the God of the Bible." (Ibid., 15.)

6   "the better angels of our nature"   Abraham Lincoln, *Abraham Lincoln:*

Speeches and Writings, 1859–1865 (New York, 1989), 224. The quotation is from the first inaugural's beautiful closing paragraph: "I am loth to close. We are not enemies, but friends. We must not be enemies. Though passion may have strained, it must not break our bonds affection. The mystic chords of memory, stretching from every battlefield, and patriot grave, to every living heart and hearthstone, all over this broad land, will yet swell the chorus of the Union, when again touched, as surely they will be, by the better angels of our nature." (Ibid.)

7   his doctor said, with "all the striking characteristics"   Dr. Robley Dunglison's "Ana," College of Physicians of Philadelphia, Robley Dunglison Papers.

7   "All eyes are opened"   Jefferson, *Writings,* 1517. This moving letter of June 24, 1826, written to Roger C. Weightman, the mayor of Washington, D.C., has long been cited as the final letter of Jefferson's life—hailed, in the words of Jefferson Looney, editor and project director of the Papers of Thomas Jefferson, Retirement Series, as "a masterly ending to the approximately 18,000 letters penned by the third president." But as Looney reported in the *Virginia Magazine of History and Biography* in 2004, Jefferson wrote at least two other letters after his epistle to Weightman—and one that has recently come to light concerns the importation of wine. As Looney wrote: "Where the Weightman letter attests to the continuing faith of the public Jefferson in the enduring value of the American experiment with democracy, the [letter about the wine] speaks to the private Jefferson who to the last could not deny himself imported luxury goods. . . ." (J. Jefferson Looney, "Thomas Jefferson's Last Letter," *Virginia Magazine of History and Biography* 112, no. 2 [2004], 178–184.)

7   first draft of the Declaration of Independence   Jefferson, *Writings,* 19–24. I also learned much about the Declaration from the following books: Allen Jayne, *Jefferson's Declaration of Independence: Origins, Philosophy, and Theology* (Lexington, KY, 1998); Pauline Maier, *American Scripture: Making the Declaration of Independence* (New York, 1997); Carl L. Becker, *The Declaration of Independence: A Study in the History of Political Ideas* (New York, 1942); and Garry Wills, *Inventing America: Jefferson's Declaration of Independence* (Garden City, NY, 1978).

7   Aristotle and Cicero   Jefferson, *Writings,* 1501.

7   John Locke   Ibid.

7   Algernon Sidney   Ibid.

7   Joseph Priestley, and Lord Bolingbroke   Jayne, *Jefferson's Declaration of Independence,* 86, 165. See also Joseph Priestley, *Essay of the First Principles of Government and on the Nature of Political, Civil and Religious Liberty* (Whitefish, MT, 2003).

8   Franklin rephrased and rearranged   Aldridge, *Benjamin Franklin and Nature's God,* 7. See also Cousins, *"In God We Trust,"* 21.

8   recalled falling sound asleep   Ibid., 16.

8   influenced by Deism   Henry F. May, *The Enlightenment in America* (New York, 1976), 116–132. The following were, in May's formulation, "conventional deistic affirmations: belief in a supreme being, rewards and punishment, and a future state." (Ibid., 128.) See also Peter Gay, ed. *Deism: An Anthology* (Princeton, NJ, 1968).

8   *The Age of Revelation*   Elias Boudinot, *The Age of Revelation* (Philadelphia, 1801).

8   John Adams considered the ministry   Cousins, *"In God We Trust,"* 76.

8   a Unitarian   Ibid., 75.

8   confessed a weakness   Hutson, ed. *The Founders on Religion,* 96.

9   Franklin helped advance the career of John Carroll   Scott McDermott, *Charles Carroll of Carrollton: Faithful Revolutionary* (New York, 2002), 206.

9   Jefferson read Aeschylus, Sophocles, Euripides, and the Bible   Randall, *The Life of Thomas Jefferson,* III, 539.

9   "A few hours more, Doctor"   Ibid., 543.

9   Jefferson took his medicine for the last time   Nicholas P. Trist to Joseph Coolidge, "His bed side, July 4th, 1826," University of Virginia, Correspondence of Ellen Wayles Randolph Coolidge. The medicine was laudanum, which, Thomas Jefferson Randolph reported, "caused his slumbers to be disturbed and dreamy." (Randall, *The Life of Thomas Jefferson,* III, 544.)

9   "Oh God!"   Nicholas P. Trist to Joseph Coolidge, "His bed side, July 4th, 1826," University of Virginia, Correspondence of Ellen Wayles Randolph Coolidge.

9   "a tone of impatience"   Ibid.

9   Jefferson declined: "No! nothing more"   Ibid.

9   he gestured as though he were once again writing   Randall, *The Life of Thomas Jefferson,* III, 544.

9   he gave his grandson instructions   Thomas Jefferson Randolph's "Account of TJ's Last Illness and Death," July 4, 1826, University of Virginia, Edgehill-Randolph Papers. The *Richmond Enquirer* of July 7, 1826, also reported: "It is said that in the course of last week he calmly gave directions about his coffin & internment." In Jefferson's last days, he once woke with something of a start, thinking he had heard the name of the Reverend Frederick Hatch, the local Episcopal priest. Told no, Mr. Hatch was not there, Jefferson settled back down for another nap, saying, "I have no objection to see him, as a kind and good neighbor." (Randall, *The Life of Thomas Jeffer-*

son III, 543.) Randall's source, Thomas Jefferson Randolph, added: "The impression made upon my mind at the moment was, that his religious opinions having been formed upon mature study and reflection, he had no doubts upon his mind, and therefore did not desire the attendance of a clergyman; I have never since doubted the correctness of the impression then taken." (Ibid.) In his piece in *The Magazine of Albemarle County History*, James Bear writes that Jefferson said he did not want to see Hatch "as a man of the cloth," citing George Tucker as the source. (Bear, "The Last Days in the Life of Thomas Jefferson," *The Magazine of Albemarle County History*, Vol. 32, 71.) The relevant pages of Tucker's book, however, do not have the quotation Bear claimed it did. (See George Tucker, *The Life of Thomas Jefferson*, II [Philadelphia, 1837], 495.) Tucker's account tracks with Randall's: "The impression upon the by-standers was that he did not wish to avail himself of Mr. Hatch's clerical functions." (Ibid.) Yet his connection to and affection for Reverend Hatch is also documented in Randall, *The Life of Thomas Jefferson*, III, 545, where Randall referred to Hatch as Jefferson's "friend." Jefferson was also a contributor to Hatch and the parish.

9   said that everyone hoped   Ibid.

9   With a smile, Jefferson replied, "Do you imagine"   Ibid.

9   Once we left "our sorrows and suffering bodies"   Hutson, ed. *The Founders on Religion*, 10.

9   "ascend in essence"   Ibid.

9   He was thinking of his beloved wife   Randall, *The Life of Thomas Jefferson*, III, 545.

9   as he went "to his fathers"   A facsimile of the whole poem was published in *The New York Times* on July 4, 1954, on the occasion of its sale at auction. Entitled "A death-bed adieu," Jefferson wrote: "Life's visions are vanished, it's [sic] dreams are no more. / Dear friends of my bosom, why bathed in tears? / I go to my fathers; I welcome the shore, / which crowns all my hopes, on which buries my cares, / Then farewell my dear, my lov'd daughter, Adieu! / The last pang of life is in parting from you! / Two Seraphs await me, long shrouded in death; / I will bear them your love on my last parting breath." (*The New York Times*, July 4, 1954, from the "Death" file of the Jefferson Library, Monticello.)

10   hearing him repeat the song of Simeon   Randall, *The Life of Thomas Jefferson*, III, 547. Dr. Dunglison says he never heard Jefferson use the phrase "Nunc dimittis," the Latin for "Lord, now lettest thou . . ." (Dr. Robley Dunglison's "Ana," College of Physicians of Philadelphia, Robley Dunglison Papers.) Despite his feeling to the contrary, however, the doctor could not have heard everything in those last weeks and days, and Randall had a

family report. Moreover, Jefferson's apparent fondness for the passage was well known enough that it was mentioned as his "favorite quotation" in the *Richmond Enquirer* of July 7, 1826. The confusion may have come from a report that Jefferson had spoken the Latin phrase, when Randall is clear that the family told him Jefferson spoke the words in English.

10   is told he will not die until he sees Christ   Luke 2:25–35, King James Version.

10   low stone wall   Bear, "The Last Few Days of the Life of Thomas Jefferson," 77.

10   wooden coffin   Ibid.

10   Reverend Frederick Hatch   Randall, *The Life of Thomas Jefferson*, III, 545.

10   The day was wet   Ibid.

10   planks were placed over the grave   Bear, "The Last Few Days of the Life of Thomas Jefferson," 77.

10   " ' "I am the resurrection" ' "   Ibid., 78. At a memorial service in Richmond, the Right Reverend Richard Channing Moore, the Episcopal Bishop of Virginia, offered a prayer in keeping with Anglican tradition: "We thank thee, heavenly father, for the civil and religious blessings with which as a nation thou hast favored us—for that form of government which secures to us liberty . . . and protects us in the enjoyment of the sacred rights of conscience." Alluding to the death of John Adams, which occurred on the same day as Jefferson's, Bishop Moore closed: "Place beneath them the everlasting arms of thy love—may they find a shelter in every American heart; never leave them nor forsake them for a moment; and at last, Oh take them, blessed Jesus, to a better world. We ask these blessings, thou God of love, for Jesus Christ sake.—*Amen.*" (*Richmond Enquirer,* Friday, July 14, 1826.)

10   for which "I wish most to be remembered"   Thomas Jefferson, "Design for Tombstone and Inscription," Thomas Jefferson Papers, Library of Congress.

11   for which he had lived   Ibid.

11   *"Whereas Almighty God hath created the mind free"*   usinfo.state.gov/usa/infousa/facts/democrac/42.htm. Jefferson's first draft opened this way: "Well aware that the opinions and belief of men depend not on their own will, but follow involuntarily the evidence proposed to their minds; that Almighty God hath created the mind free, and manifested his supreme will that free it shall remain by making it altogether insusceptible of restraint; that all attempts to influence it by temporal punishments, or burdens, or by civil incapacitations, tend only to beget habits of hypocrisy and meanness, and are a departure from the plan of the holy author of our religion, who being lord both of body and mind, yet chose not to propagate it by coercions on ei-

ther, as was in his Almighty power to do, but to extend it by its influence on reason alone." By the time it passed, the "Almighty God hath created" line provided the first words of the bill. (Jefferson, *Writings*, 346.)

11   it fell to his neighbor James Madison to carry it through   Miller, *The First Liberty*, 66–125, is a full and interesting account.

11   "Whilst we assert for ourselves"   James Madison, *Writings* (New York, 1999), 31.

11   was "meant to comprehend, within the mantle of its protection"   Jefferson, *Writings*, 40.

11   George Washington would not kneel to pray   Boller, *George Washington and Religion*, 32–33.

11   not known to take communion   Ibid., 33.

11   "the hand of Providence"   Cousins, *"In God We Trust,"* 54.

11   "time enough"   Ibid.

12   he fathered at least one child with a woman he owned and controlled   Jan Ellen Lewis and Peter S. Onuf, eds. *Sally Hemings and Thomas Jefferson: History, Memory, and Civil Culture* (Charlottesville, VA, 1999), and Annette Gordon-Reed, *Thomas Jefferson and Sally Hemings: An American Controversy* (Charlottesville, VA, 1997).

12   hated Catholicism   Walter Stahr, *John Jay: Founding Father* (New York, 2005), 41–42; 78–79. At the Constitutional Convention, Jay tried, Stahr writes, "to deprive Catholics of the right to own land or participate in government, unless they swore that 'no pope, priest, or foreign authority on earth' could 'absolve the subjects of this state from the allegiance to the same.' " (Ibid., 78.)

12   At a crowded party in France   Cousins, *"In God We Trust,"* 364.

12   one of the more orthodox   Ibid., 360.

12   speaking "freely and contemptuously"   Ibid., 364.

12   serious, sometimes overly grave   Stahr, *John Jay: Founding Father,* 367. Stahr wrote that Jay was "serious, sober, even severe." (Ibid.) Norman Cousins wrote: "It is said that the British had been confidentially advised that John Jay could 'bear any opposition to what he advances, provided that regard is shown his abilities,' and that 'John Jay's weak side is Mr. Jay.' " (Cousins, *"In God We Trust,"* 359.)

12   "In the course of it"   Cousins, *"In God We Trust,"* 364.

12   a Puritan who looked askance at other faiths   Ibid., 345. "These Quakers are in general a sly artful people," Adams once wrote, "not altogether destitute, as I conceive, of worldly views in their religious professions." (Ibid.)

12   "Neither religion nor liberty"   John K. Alexander, *Samuel Adams: America's Revolutionary Politician* (Lanham, MD, 2002), 221.

12   "The Catholics thought him almost a Catholic"   Aldridge, *Benjamin Franklin and Nature's God,* 8.

12   "He that spits against the wind"   Albert Henry Smyth, ed. *The Writings of Benjamin Franklin,* IX (New York, 1907), 521. There is debate over whether this letter was to Thomas Paine or to someone else. For an excellent summary of the controversy—and a strong case that Paine was the correspondent—see Walter Isaacson, *Benjamin Franklin: An American Life* (New York, 2003), 562–563.

12   a Harvard-educated clergyman   David McCullough, *John Adams* (New York, 2001), 56.

12   her mother had not thought much   Ibid. McCullough wrote: "According to traditional family accounts, the match was strongly opposed by Abigail's mother. She was a Quincy, the daughter of old John Quincy, whose big hilltop homestead, known as Mount Wollaston, was a Braintree landmark. Abigail, it was thought, would be marrying beneath her." (Ibid.)

12   a dysentery epidemic   Ibid., 26.

12   divine retribution for slavery   Ibid.

13   set aside an hour   Patricia Brady, *Martha Washington* (New York, 2005), 188–189.

13   "praying and reading"   Ibid.

13   popular works by Anglican divines   Ibid., 201–202.

13   the *Works of Josephus*   Ibid.

13   Franklin's parents and siblings   Walter Isaacson, ed. *A Benjamin Franklin Reader* (New York, 2003), 119–122.

13   "uneasiness"   Ibid., 120.

13   his eclectic theology   Ibid., 119. Isaacson wrote: "Franklin's freethinking and unorthodox religious views, especially his belief that salvation was more likely to come by doing good works than merely through God's grace alone, unnerved his family." (Ibid.)

13   like to read the Bible   Bliss Isely, *The Presidents: Men of Faith* (New York, 1953), 44 45.

13   would plunge naked   Jack Shepherd, *The Adams Chronicles: Four Generations of Greatness* (Boston, 1975), 302.

13   before attending his weekly Sunday church service   John Quincy Adams diary, 29 April 1827, Adams Family Papers, Massachusetts Historical Society, Boston.

13   Andrew Jackson summoned   John F. Marszalek, *The Petticoat Affair: Manners, Mutiny, and Sex in Andrew Jackson's White House* (New York, 1997), 101–102.

13   an alleged extramarital pregnancy   Ibid., 93–94.

13 charged with being "a scoffer at religion" Wolf, *The Almost Chosen People*, 69.

13 delivered by his opponent in the race, Reverend Peter Cartwright Ibid., 70.

13 "All who do not wish" Ibid., 71.

13 Only Lincoln kept his seat Ibid.

13 "May I inquire of you" Ibid.

13 "I am going to Congress" Ibid.

13 a purported exchange Ibid., 140.

14 "that Almighty Being who rules over the universe" George Washington, *Writings* (New York, 1997), 731. The quotation is from Washington's first inaugural.

14 *homo religiosus* Mircea Eliade, *The Sacred and the Profane: The Nature of Religion* (New York, 1959) is a landmark study of the human instinct for the religious.

14 "All men," said Homer, "need the gods" Homer, *The Odyssey*, trans. Robert Fagles (New York, 1996), 109.

14 Washington improvised "so help me, God" Douglas Southall Freeman, *George Washington: A Biography*, vol. 6 (New York, 1954), 192.

14 one of God's impenetrable mysteries Lincoln, *Speeches and Writings, 1859–1865*, 359; 686–687. See also Wolf, *The Almost Chosen People*, 143–159.

14 a prayer he had written *The New York Times*, June 7, 1944.

14 opened Cabinet meetings with prayers Pierard and Linder, *Civil Religion & the Presidency*, 201.

14 "the focus of evil in the modern world" Remarks of the president to the 41st Annual Convention of the National Association of Evangelicals, Orlando, Florida, March 8, 1983. White House Office of Speech Writing: Speech drafts, National Assoc. of Evangelicals (Orlando) (Dolan) March 8, 1983, folders 1–6, Ronald Reagan Presidential Library.

15 "We have done what we had to do" Richard Reeves, *President Reagan: The Triumph of Imagination* (New York, 2005,) 320.

16 there is no thing new The Book of Ecclesiastes, 1:9.

16 In 1822, Jefferson worried aloud Gaustad, *Sworn on the Altar of God*, 168.

16 charity toward all About 80 percent of Americans say they are some kind of Christian. (The Gallup Poll, May 2–5, 2005.) When asked "what, if any, is your religious preference—are you Protestant, Roman Catholic, Jewish, Mormon, Muslim, or an Orthodox religion such as the Greek or Russian Orthodox Church?," 48 percent identified themselves as Protestant, 7 percent as nonspecific Christian, and 25 percent as Catholic. Two percent iden-

tified themselves as Jewish, 1 percent as Orthodox, 2 percent as Mormon, 8 percent as none, and less than 1 percent as Muslim/Islam. Other figures of interest: fifty-eight percent believe "religion can answer all or most of today's problems"; only 23 percent think such a notion "largely out-fashioned and out of date." (The Gallup Poll, April 18–21, 2005.) Forty-eight percent have had a "born again" Christian experience, and 52 percent have tried to encourage others to believe in Jesus Christ. (The Gallup Poll, May 2–5, 2005.) A few other figures of interest: Eighty-two percent of Americans say Jesus was God or the Son of God, not another religious leader like Mohammed or Buddha. Seventy-nine percent believe in the Virgin Birth. Fifty-five percent say every word of the Bible is literally true, that the events it describes actually happened. (The Newsweek Poll, December 2–3, 2004.) Seventy-eight percent say Jesus physically rose from the dead; 75 percent say that he was sent to Earth to absolve mankind of its sins. (The Newsweek Poll, March 17–18, 2005.)

16   For the left   Secularists feel surrounded and are lashing out in ways that are far from charitable or respectful of the benignly held beliefs of a vast swath of the country. In her *Freethinkers: A History of American Secularism,* for example, Susan Jacoby wrote of her unease with President George W. Bush's remarks to the nation from the Washington National Cathedral on September 14, 2001, three days after the terrorist attacks of September 11. "Delivering an address indistinguishable from a sermon, replacing the language of civic virtue with the language of faith, the nation's chief executive might as well have been the Reverend Bush. . . . [He] felt perfectly free to ignore Americans who adhere to no religious faith, whose outlook is predominately secular, and who interpret history and tragedy as the work of man rather than God. There was no speaker who represented my views. . . . It is one of the great unresolved paradoxes of American history that religion has come to occupy such an important place in the communal psyche and public life of a nation founded on the separation of church and state." (Ibid, 2–4.) Bush was commemorating the dead in a customary way in a customary place—a cathedral that Theodore Roosevelt helped begin and in which Woodrow Wilson is buried. Yet secularists are clearly exercised. One piece of statistical evidence tends to support Jacoby's view: Gallup figures show a rising unease with the tide of belief in America. Thirty-three percent—a third of the nation—would like to see organized religion have less influence in the country (the highest figure since pollsters began asking the question in 2001), and a quarter (25 percent) are dissatisfied with religion's role and would like to see less. (The Gallup Poll, January 3–5, 2005.)

17   For the right   Many conservative Christians are being no more rational or moderate about the debate over religion's role in public life than many secularists are. A few examples: during a court case over whether public school stu-

dents in Dover, Pennsylvania, should be told of the "intelligent design" alternative to Darwin's theory of evolution, Richard Thompson, president and chief counsel of the Thomas More Law Center, said: "America's culture has been influenced by Christianity from the very beginning, but there is an attempt to slowly remove every symbol of Christianity and religious faith in our country. This is a very dangerous movement because what will ultimately happen is, out of sight, out of mind." (*The New York Times,* November 4, 2005.) When the United States Supreme Court ruled that some government displays of the Ten Commandments on public property were unconstitutional, former Alabama chief justice Roy Moore said, "When you deny God, as this Court is doing, you slowly lose your rights to life, liberty, and property." (*The Birmingham News,* June 28, 2005.) "The long war on Christianity in America continues today on the floor of the House of Representatives," Republican congressman John N. Hostettler of Indiana said during a June 20, 2005, debate on an amendment asking the Air Force Academy to come up with a plan to limit "coercive and abusive" proselytizing. He said the war "continues unabated with aid and comfort to those who would eradicate any vestige of our Christian heritage being supplied by the usual suspects, the Democrats." (*The Washington Post,* July 3, 2005.) One hopes the country might heed these words of Richard John Neuhaus, the distinguished Catholic priest and editor-in-chief of the journal *First Things:* "There is a very big difference between tolerating others because nobody has the truth and being convinced of the truth that we are to love those with whom we disagree about the truth." (*First Things,* November 2005, 62.) Well put—and these words apply to anyone for whom the radical course of unconditional, forgiving love lies at the center of faith or, in the absence of faith, at the center of life.

17 "O the depth of the riches"   Romans 11: 33–34 (RSV).

17 alluded to   Isaiah 40: 13–14 (RSV).

17 "There are more things"   William Shakespeare, *Hamlet,* Act I, scene V.

17 "I hate polemical"   Cousins, *"In God We Trust,"* 104.

19 "gives . . . bigotry no sanction"   Washington, *Writings,* 767.

19 a treaty with the Muslim nation of Tripoli   Borden, *Jews, Turks, and Infidels,* 76–79.

19 "the equal rights of citizenship"   McDermott, *Charles Carroll of Carrollton,* 206.

19 "As mankind becomes more liberal"   Ibid., 206–207. See also Boller, *George Washington and Religion,* 183–184.

19 The wall metaphor   Dreisbach, *Thomas Jefferson and the Wall of Separation Between Church and State,* 71–82, is a terrific history of the term.

20 what Benjamin Franklin called "public religion"   Isaacson, ed. *A Benjamin Franklin Reader,* 144.

20   In 1749, laying out his thoughts on the proper education of the young
     Ibid., 139–146.
21   "Morality, by descanting"   Ibid., 143.
21   "*History* will also afford"   Ibid., 144.
21   "I believe in one God"   Ibid., 376–378.
22   holds that there is a God   To talk about "public religion" in the way I am
     defining it inevitably draws on Robert N. Bellah's essay "Civil Religion in
     America" and the four decades of scholarship that piece spawned. Bellah
     quoted President John F. Kennedy's heavily theological inaugural address to
     buttress his points: "With a good conscience our only sure reward, with his-
     tory the final judge of our deeds," Kennedy said, "let us go forth to lead the
     land that we love, asking His blessing and His help, but knowing that here
     on earth God's work must truly be our own." Such allusions to the Almighty,
     Bellah wrote, could be seen as "a sentimental nod that serves largely to pla-
     cate the more unenlightened members of the community before a discussion
     of the really serious business with which religion has nothing whatever to
     do." The problem with a dismissive interpretation of words and ideas like
     Kennedy's is that it fails to take account of the true nature of ritual in human
     affairs. It is dangerous, Bellah reminds us, to wave something away as " 'only
     a ritual.' What people say on solemn occasions need not be taken at face
     value, but it is often indicative of deep-seated values and commitments that
     are not made explicit in the course of everyday life."
22   "as Israel of old"   Jefferson, *Writings,* 523.
23   how to conduct themselves   There can be tension between religious lib-
     erty and the imperative some Christians feel to evangelize. First, a word of
     definition. "In a generic sense," the scholar Randall Balmer wrote in his in-
     dispensable *Encyclopedia of Evangelism* (Waco, TX, 2004), "an evangelical
     is someone who believes, first, in the centrality of the conversion or 'Born
     Again' experience as the criterion for entering the kingdom of heaven. Sec-
     ond, an evangelical is someone who takes the Bible seriously as God's reve-
     lation to humanity; an evangelical is inclined, more often than not, to
     interpret the Bible literally. Defined in this broad fashion, *evangelical* refers
     to a vast number of people; recent estimates put that number as high as 40 to
     46 percent of the population in the United States, for example. Within that
     broader definition, however, are various permutations of evangelicals: fun-
     damentalists, pentecostals, charismatics, and those in the holiness tradi-
     tion." (Ibid., 236.)
         As the Inquisition, pogroms, crusades, and centuries of sins and short-
     comings show, there is much for Christians to regret about the evil done in
     the name of the church. But there is also a Christian tradition of forebear-
     ance and tolerance. "Go ye therefore, and teach all nations, baptizing them

in the name of the Father, and of the Son, and of the Holy Ghost," the risen Jesus tells his disciples in Matthew, "teaching them to observe all things whatsoever I have commanded you." (Matthew 28:19–20 [KJV].) They were sent forth, note, to *teach,* not to conquer, and the Jesus of the gospels res- olutely refuses to resort to the means of this world—either the clash of arms or the passions of politics—to further his ends. After the miracle of the loaves and fishes, the dazzled throng thought they had found their earthly messiah. "When Jesus therefore perceived that they would come and take him by force, to make him a king, he departed again into a mountain himself alone," according to the Gospel of John. (John 6:15 [KJV].) In Gethsemane, Matthew writes, one of Jesus' followers draws a sword and slices off the ear of one of the arresting party, but Jesus says, "Put up thy sword." (Matthew 26:51–52 [RSV].) Later, before Pilate, he says: "My kingdom is not of this world: if my kingdom were of this world, then would my servants fight." (John 18:36 [KJV].)

In two important documents, *Dignitatis Humanae* and *Nostra Aetate* (both available on the Vatican website), the Catholic Church lays out a firm and compelling vision of both the significance of religious freedom and of generous relations between the church and non-Christian religions. In *Dig- nitatis Humanae,* promulgated by Pope Paul VI on December 7, 1965, the Second Vatican Council wrote: "The disciple is bound by a grave obligation toward Christ, his Master, ever more fully to understand the truth received from Him, faithfully to proclaim it, and vigorously to defend it, never—be it understood—having recourse to means that are incompatible with the spirit of the Gospel."

The council also said: "The religious acts whereby men, in private and in public and out of a sense of personal conviction, direct their lives to God transcend by their very nature the order of terrestrial and temporal affairs. Government therefore ought indeed to take account of the religious life of the citizenry and show it favor, since the function of government is to make provision for the common welfare. However, it would clearly transgress the limits set to its power, were it to presume to command or inhibit acts that are religious."

In the *Nostra Aetate,* promulgated on October 28, 1965, the council wrote: "The Church reproves, as foreign to the mind of Christ, any discrim- ination against men or harassment of them because of their race, color, con- dition of life, or religion. . . . [T]his sacred synod ardently implores the Christian faithful to 'maintain good fellowship among the nations' (I Peter 2:12), and, if possible, to live for their part in peace with all men [14], so that they may truly be sons of the Father who is in heaven [15]."

There have been objections by serious believers' objection to public invocations of a generic God. The sociologist Will Herberg laid out this critique of a public or civil religion that revolves around what Jefferson called "Nature's God" and what most of the rest of us have spent almost two and a half centuries after the Declaration simply calling "God": "To see America's civil religion as somehow standing above or beyond the biblical religions of Judaism and Christianity, and Islam too, and somehow including them and finding a place in [civil religion's] overarching unity," he said, "is idolatry, however innocently held and whatever may be the subjective intentions of the believers." (Richey and Jones, eds. *American Civil Religion*, 87.) To my mind, the proposition articulated by Herberg can be true only if one takes the strictest conceivable view of the claims of one's own private religious faith. I think many people, even those of deep private faith within a particular tradition, are prepared to accept that there is much mystery about the will and purposes of God, that there are things which pass all human understanding, and that religious liberty in the public sphere is a public good. No one, Jefferson once said, should "be uneasy . . . about the different roads we may pursue . . . to that our last abode." (Gaustad, *Sworn on the Altar of God*, 201.)

23   rooted in Leviticus   Leviticus 19:18 (KJV).
23   "I exhort, therefore"   I Timothy 2:1 (KJV).
23   "Beloved, let us love"   I John 4:7–8 (KJV).
24   the Almighty shall "swallow up"   Isaiah 25:8 (RSV).
24   "see through a glass, darkly"   I Corinthians 13:12 (KJV).
24   "nations do not worship"   Noonan, *The Lustre of Our Country*, 246.
24   once told some visiting ministers   Wolf, *The Almost Chosen People*, 128.
24   As King George III's British troops moved toward New York City   Sarna, *American Judaism*, 33.
25   what they called their "exile"   Ibid., 36.
25   Armed with the Torah scrolls   Ibid., 33.
25   "the sacred cause of America"   Ibid., 36.
25   "We cried unto the Lord"   Prayer in Hebrew, *Publications of the American Jewish Historical Society*, vol. 27, American Jewish Historical Society.
25   Robert N. Bellah published a landmark essay   Bellah, *Beyond Belief: Essays on Religion in a Post-Traditionalist World*, 168–189. See also C. H. Barfoot and G. T. Sheppard, "Prophetic vs. Priestly Religion," *Review of Religious Research* 22 (1980): 2–17; Martin E. Marty, "Two Kinds of Two Kinds of Civil Religion" in Richey and Jones, eds. *American Civil Religion*, 139–160; and Marty, *The Public Church: Mainline-Evangelical-Catholic* (New York, 1981).

There is much scholarship on civil religion and its subsets. A very good summary of the scholarly discussion and controversies is in Martin E. Marty, *A Nation of Behavers* (Chicago, 1976), 180–203. Marty wittily wrote: "The term 'Civil Religion' appears only in books, articles, or reports of theologians, sociologists, and social critics. Once or twice politicians have used it in the public sector, where it has not yet grasped the imagination. The term would inspire only bemusement and puzzlement in the neighborhood tavern, St. Boniface Parish, or a meeting of the American Legion." (Ibid., 182.) That may be so even now, thirty years later, but the academic work on the subject is fascinating. In their *Civil Religion & the Presidency,* Pierard and Linder trace the history of the idea from antiquity forward with grace and skill, making the distinction between "prophetic" and "priestly" civil religion. "In a functional sense," they wrote, "the prophet stands before the people and speaks to them the necessary (and sometimes unpleasant) words from God, but the priest stands before God and speaks on behalf of the people. The prophet focuses on judgment and repentance while the priest pronounces words of comfort, praise, and celebration. . . . Whatever its emphasis, prophetic or priestly, American civil religion represents an alliance between politics and religion at the national level, resting on a politicized ideological base: (1) there is a God; (2) his will can be known and fulfilled through democratic procedures; (3) America has been God's primary agent in modern history; and (4) the nation is the chief source of identity for Americans in both a political and religious sense." (Ibid., 24–25.) See also Marty, "Two Kinds of Two Kinds of Civil Religion" in Richey and Jones, eds., *American Civil Religion.* Marty's "two kinds of two kinds" are the following: the first kind is transcendent, in which, Marty wrote, "a transcendent deity is seen as the pusher or puller of the social process." The second kind is "national self-transcendence," in which, Marty wrote, the conversation moves from a transcendent deity's "promise *to* America" to "the promise *of* America." Both "kinds" have "priestly" and "prophetic" styles. (Ibid., 144–156.) Bellah himself addressed the issue of civil religion again in, among other works, Robert N. Bellah, *The Broken Covenant: American Civil Religion in Time of Trial* (Chicago, 1992).

Another important work in this area is John T. Noonan, Jr.'s *The Lustre of Our Country: The American Experience of Religious Freedom.* His discussion of Bellah and of Emile Durkheim is brilliant, and, as noted above, he made the following essential point: "Civil religion is a construct, a synthesis that plausibly explains some American practices but obscures the place of persons in creating the practices. Nations do not worship, persons do. . . . Attention needs to be focused on the intentions of those fulfilling the roles assigned to them in what is described as civil religion." (Ibid., 246.) For the full range of scholarly debate on civil religion, see also Richey and Jones, eds. *American Civil Religion.*

25   "a set of beliefs"   Ibid., 171.

25   "Europe is Egypt"   Ibid., 175.

25   not, he said, "in any specific sense"   Ibid.

25   has deep roots   Pierard and Linder, *Civil Religion & the Presidency,* 30–64, is an excellent discussion.

25   In antiquity Plato   Ibid., 36.

25   in *The Discourses*   Niccolò Machiavelli, *The Discourses,* ed. Bernard Crick (New York, 2003), 9–10. Machiavelli, whose book was a commentary on Livy's history of republican Rome, apparently began his *Discourses* in 1515; they were unpublished until roughly four years after his death on June 21, 1527, appearing in print in 1531–1532. (Ibid.)

25   the Romans "turned to"   Ibid., 139. Machiavelli went on to write: "It was religion that facilitated whatever enterprise the senate and the great men of Rome designed to undertake. Whoever runs through the vast number of exploits performed by the people of Rome as a whole, or by many of the Romans individually, will see that its citizens were more afraid of breaking an oath than of breaking the law, since they held in higher esteem the power of God than the power of man." (Ibid.)

25   Rousseau coined the term   Bellah, *Beyond Belief,* 172. See also Victor Gourevitch, ed. *Rousseau: The Social Contract* and other later political writings (Cambridge, 1997), 150–151. Rousseau saw civil religion in purely utilitarian terms, thinking such a religion would support the sovereign of a given state. "There is therefore a purely civil profession of faith the articles of which it is up to the Sovereign to fix, not precisely as dogmas of Religion but as sentiments of sociability, without which it is impossible to be either a good citizen or a loyal subject. . . . The dogmas of the civil Religion ought to be simple, few in number, stated with precision, without explanations or commentary. The existence of the powerful, intelligent, beneficent, prescient, and provident Divinity, the life to come, the happiness of the just, the punishment of the wicked, the sanctity of the social Contract and the Laws; these are the positive dogmas." Rousseau made an interesting case for tolerance as well: "Wherever theological intolerance is allowed, it is impossible for it not to have some civil effect; and as soon as it does, the Sovereign is no longer Sovereign, even in the temporal sphere: from then on Priests are the true masters; Kings are but their officers." (Ibid.)

25   Washington, who envisioned a republic   Hutson, ed. *The Founders on Religion,* 193.

25   in which "religion and morality"   Washington, *Writings,* 971.

25   "A volume could not trace"   Ibid.

27   America's "great struggle"   Lincoln, *Speeches and Writings, 1859–1865,*
      209.

27   God's "almost chosen people"   Ibid. The occasion was an address to the
      New Jersey Senate in Trenton on February 21, 1861.

27   "And let us with caution"   Washington, *Writings,* 971.

28   any number of secular sources   See, for instance: Simon Blackburn,
      Ethics: A Very Short Introduction (New York, 2003); Peter Singer, ed., *A
      Companion to Ethics* (Oxford, 1991); Lewis Vaughn and Austin Dacey, *The
      Case for Humanism* (Lanham, MD, 2003); Erik J. Weilenberg, *Value and
      Virtue in a Godless Universe* (Cambridge, 2005). Even some theories pred-
      icated on the existence of God separate morality from a belief in Him. In his
      The Elements of Moral Philosophy (New York, 2003), James Rachels has a
      strong chapter entitled "Does Morality Depend on Religion?" in which he
      describes natural-law thinking, a tradition that runs from antiquity to St.
      Thomas Aquinas, "the world is a rational order with values and purposes
      built into its very nature," Rachels wrote. (Ibid., 53.) A case in point: "Con-
      sider, for example, the duty of beneficence," Rachels wrote. "We are
      morally required to be concerned for our neighbor's welfare as well as for
      our own. Why? According to the Theory of Natural Law, beneficence is
      natural for us, considering the kind of creatures we are. We are by our na-
      ture social creatures who want and need the company of other people. It is
      also part of our natural makeup that we care about others. Someone who
      does not care at all for others—who really does not care, through and
      through—is seen as deranged, in the terms of modern psychology, as a so-
      ciopath. A malicious personality is defective, just as eyes are defective if
      they cannot see. And, it may be added, this is true because we were created
      by God, with a specific 'human' nature, as part of his overall plan for the
      world." (Ibid., 55.) We discern what is natural—and thus what is right—
      through reason, which is a divine gift to all human beings, regardless of
      whether they choose to believe in God or not. This leads to the following
      conclusion: "The religious believer has no special access to moral truth.
      The believer and the nonbeliever are in the same position. God has given
      both the same powers of reasoning; and so believer and nonbeliever alike
      may listen to reason and follow its directives. . . . In an important sense,
      this leaves morality independent of religion." (Ibid., 57.)
          Most systems of secular ethics end up in the same place as most religious
      teachings: do not lie, cheat, steal, or otherwise do harm. The difference is that
      such laws are not understood as God-given. Much of modern ethics grapples
      with the problem of how to act in the absence of a divinely sanctioned code of

conduct. (Singer, ed., *A Companion to Ethics,* 147.) Many philosophers, perhaps most significantly Immanuel Kant, located morality wholly within human reason and free will—which, he held, exist independently of any outside authority such as God. The foundation of Kant's philosophy is "the categorical imperative," which says, "act only on the maxim through which you can at the same time will that it be a universal law." (Ibid., 177.) In the nineteenth century, John Stuart Mill and advocates of utilitarianism—which holds that conduct is moral when it maximizes happiness for the greatest number—also believed that morality is rationally, not divinely, determined. (Ibid., 152.) More recent ethics tend to focus less on individual reason as the source of morality and more on the cooperation between people. Such "social contract theories" try to reconcile free will and the importance of a just society. (Ibid., 156.) John Rawls, for example, bases his theory of justice on the question of how people would structure society if they knew nothing about their station in life. Behind the "veil of ignorance," he wrote, reasonable people would conclude that the best society is one predicated on human rights. (Ibid., 265.) Peter Singer's *A Companion to Ethics* provides an excellent overview of major ethical systems, and I am grateful to Austin Dacey for his guidance on these points.

28   "Without religion"   Hutson, ed. *The Founders on Religion,* 115.

28   "Religion I hold"   Ibid., 147. On the whole, Adams' view of Christianity was more positive than that of Jefferson, Franklin, and Washington. In his diary on August 14, 1796, Adams wrote: "One great advantage of the Christian religion is that it brings the great principle of the law of nature and nations—Love your neighbor as yourself, and do to others as you would that others should do to you—to the knowledge, belief, and veneration of the whole people. Children, servants, women, and men are all professors in the science of public and private morality. No other institution for education, no kind of political discipline, could diffuse this kind of necessary information so universally among all ranks and descriptions of citizens." (Cousins, *"In God We Trust,"* 99–100.)

28   drafting a plan for educating   Hutson, ed. *The Founders on Religion,* 120.

28   In a draft of Washington's   Ibid., 147. Hamilton's faith is a subject of much interesting biography. In his book *Alexander Hamilton* (New York, 2004), Ron Chernow is particularly good on the subject, especially in depicting Hamilton's last hours. Wounded and dying, Hamilton told his wife: *"Remember, my Eliza, you are a Christian."* He also asked the Episcopal bishop of New York, Benjamin Moore, to give him holy communion. The bishop hesitated but finally did so; afterward, Chernow wrote, Hamilton "lay back serenely and declared that he was happy." (Ibid., 706–708.)

28   "A virtuous heretic"   Hutson, ed. *The Founders on Religion*, 147.

29   "On the dogmas of religion"   Thomas Jefferson to Matthew Carey, November 11, 1816. The Library of Congress American Memory project, http://memory.loc.gov/cgi-bin/query/P?mtj:20:./temp/~ammem_8TBq:: The Thomas Jefferson Papers Series 1, General Correspondence, 1651–1827.

29   "If we did a good act"   Hutson, ed. *The Founders on Religion*, 22.

29   "The Creator would, indeed"   Thomas Jefferson to Thomas Law, June 13, 1814, Thomas Jefferson Papers, Library of Congress.

29   "the moral sense is"   Thomas Jefferson to John Adams, October 14, 1816. Lester J. Cappon, ed. *The Adams-Jefferson Letters*, vol. 2 (Chapel Hill, N.C., 1959), 492.

30   "morality *must* fall"   Hutson, ed. *The Founders on Religion*, 192.

30   Adams believed that "every man"   Cousins, *"In God We Trust,"* 105.

30   "For, I am certain"   Ibid.

30   "a lustre to our country"   Madison, *Writings*, 33.

30   *"Real* Christians"   Hutson, ed. *The Founders on Religion*, 197.

30   the colony had a bell made   Edwin S. Gaustad, *Proclaim Liberty Throughout All The Land: A History of Church and State in America* (New York, 2003), ix.

30   "Proclaim liberty"   Leviticus 25:10 (KJV). The verse: "And ye shall hallow the fiftieth year, and proclaim liberty throughout all the land unto all the inhabitants thereof: it shall be a jubilee unto you."

31   "The God who gave us life"   Jefferson, *Writings*, 122.

31   "The sacred rights of mankind"   Cousins, *"In God We Trust,"* 326.

32   "Let every man speak freely without fear"   Barbara A. McGraw and Jo Renee Formicola, eds. *Taking Religious Pluralism Seriously: Spiritual Politics on America's Sacred Ground* (Waco, TX, 2005), 199.

33   "Our fathers founded"   Tim Page, ed. *What's God Got to Do with It?: Robert Ingersoll on Free Thought, Honest Talk, and the Separation of Church and State* (Hanover, NH, 2005), 22.

33   attended Fourth of July ceremonies at the Capitol   Allan Nevins, ed. *The Diary of John Quincy Adams, 1794–1845: American Diplomacy, and Political, Social, and Intellectual Life, from Washington to Polk* (New York, 1969), 357.

33   slipping off to work   Ibid., 358.

33   "a strange and very striking coincidence"   Ibid.

33   came a letter   Ibid. His sister-in-law wrote him that "my father's end was approaching," John Quincy Adams noted. (Ibid.)

33   terrible midsummer heat   Ibid., 359. The president was agitated; the

news of his father's decline had hit him hard. The night before he left Washington was long and miserable. "I was up, in anxiety and apprehension, till near midnight," he said. "The suddenness of the notice of my father's danger was quite unexpected. Some weeks since, my brother had written to me that he was declining, though not so as to occasion immediate alarm; and my intention had been to visit him about the beginning of the next month. I had flattered myself that he would survive this summer, and even other years." (Ibid.)

34   Stopping for breakfast at Waterloo   Ibid. Afterward, Adams told his diary: "My father had nearly closed the ninety-first year of his life—a life illustrious in the annals of his country and of the world. He had served to great and useful purpose his nation, his age, and his God. He is gone, and may the blessing of Almighty God have attended him to his account!" (Ibid.)

34   "The time, the manner, the coincidence"   Ibid., 360.

34   "grateful and silent adoration"   Ibid.

34   Adams hoped that one day   Ibid.

34   "I must ever believe"   Bergh, ed. *The Writings of Thomas Jefferson*, XIV (Washington, D.C., 1904), 197–198. The remark came in a letter from Jefferson to Miles King, September 26, 1814.

34   On a summer day in 1816 at Monticello   Gaillard Hunt, ed. *The First Forty Years of Washington Society* (New York, 1965), 126–128.

34   Margaret Bayard Smith   Ibid., v–ix.

34   it might be "the last time"   Ibid., 79.

34   she now wrote Jefferson   Ibid., 126.

35   "I never told my religion"   Ibid., 127.

35   "For it is in our lives"   Ibid.

CHAPTER ONE: GOD AND MAMMON

37   "For we must consider"   Richard S. Dunn and Laetitia Yeandle, eds. *The Journal of John Winthrop, 1630–1649*, abridged edition (Cambridge, MA, 1996), 10. This quotation from Winthrop's lay sermon is drawn from Dunn and Yeandle's abridged edition of Winthrop's journal, an edition in which they modernized his spelling, punctuation, and capitalization. Dunn and Yeandle are also the editors, with James Savage, of what they call a "full-scale, unabridged, old-spelling edition." (See Dunn, Savage, and Yeandle, eds. *The Journal of John Winthrop, 1630–1649*, unabridged edition [Cambridge, MA, 1996]). There is some scholarly question about when Winthrop wrote the sermon (and presumably delivered it). One school of thought holds that

Winthrop delivered it at sea, as a cover note in another person's hand found with the sermon says: "On Boarde the Arrabella, On the Attlantick Ocean. By the Honorable John Winthrop, Esquire. In His passage, (with the great Company of Religious People, of which Christian Tribes he was the Brave Leader and famous Governor;) from the Island of Great Brittaine, to New-England in North America. Anno 1630." (Dunn and Yeandle, eds. *The Journal of John Winthrop,* abridged edition, 1.) Dunn and Yeandle also cite Hugh J. Dawson's argument that, as they write, "JW actually wrote and delivered this discourse before embarking for America, and that his friends circulated the piece in manuscript in England after he left." For this case, see Hugh J. Dawson, "John Winthrop's Rite of Passage: The Origins of the 'Christian Charitie' Discourse," *Early American Literature* 26 (1991), 219–231. I am indebted to Dunn and Yeandle for this account of the controversy.

37   "No man . . . can be so stupid"   John Milton, *Complete Poems and Major Prose,* ed. Merritt Y. Hughes (New York, 1957), 754.

37   In the North Atlantic   William Bradford, *Of Plymouth Plantation, 1620–1647* (New York, 1981), 66–71. I am indebted to Nathaniel Philbrick for his generous guidance on questions related to the *Mayflower.*

37   a storm at sea   Ibid., 66–71.

37   going to die   Ibid., 67.

38   came within sight of Cape Cod   Ibid., 68.

38   "they were not a little joyful"   Ibid.

38   "they fell upon their knees"   Ibid., 69.

38   suggested his own generation's epitaph   Ibid., 71.

38   one of the hired sailors—a "proud"   Ibid., 66.

38   Bradford was not unhappy   Ibid.

38   "But it pleased God"   Ibid.

38   "a special work"   Ibid.

38   "a city upon a hill"   Francis J. Bremer, *John Winthrop: America's Forgotten Founding Father* (New York, 2003), 180.

39   "they committed themselves to the will of God"   Bradford, *Of Plymouth Plantation,* 67.

39   "The civilization of New England"   Tocqueville, *Democracy in America,* 32.

40   "Soon after the Reformation"   Cousins, *"In God We Trust,"* 90. The remark came in a letter to Nathan Webb, October 12, 1755.

41   the First Charter of Virginia   Charles W. Eliot, ed. *Harvard Classics: American Historical Documents* (New York, 1910), 43: 51–61.

41   "so noble a work"   Ibid., 52.

41   would carry the "Christian religion"   Ibid.

41   take possession of "all the Lands"   Ibid.

41   "dig, mine, and search"   Ibid., 56.

41   "Robbery or Spoil"   Ibid., 59.

41   "pursue"   Ibid., 60.

42   was "their color, when all their aim was"   John Smith, *Captain John Smith: A Select Edition of His Writings*, ed. Karen Ordahl Kupperman (Chapel Hill, NC, 1988), 281.

42   three ships—the *Discovery*, the *Godspeed*   James Horn, *A Land As God Made It: Jamestown and the Birth of America* (New York, 2005), 39–54. See also Ed Southern, ed. *The Jamestown Adventure: Accounts of the Virginia Colony, 1605–1614* (Winston-Salem, NC, 2004), ix–x.

42   built a makeshift chapel   Kupperman, ed. *Captain John Smith*, 81. Smith wrote: "When I first went to Virginia, I well remember we did hang an awning (which is an old sail) to three or four trees to shadow us from the sun. Our walls were rails of wood, our seats unhewed trees, till we cut planks, our pulpit a bar of wood nailed to two neighboring trees. In foul weather we shifted into an old rotten tent, for we had few better . . . this was our church, till we built a homely thing like a barn, set upon cratchets, covered with rafts, sedge, and earth, so was also the walls . . . we had daily Common Prayer morning and evening, every Sunday two sermons, and every three months the holy Communion, till our minister died." (Ibid.)

42   two or three years before "more preachers came"   Ibid.

42   Within weeks of the Jamestown landing   Horn, *A Land As God Made It*, 52. The assaulting force, Horn wrote, "was an alliance of five tribes—Quiyoughcohannocks, Weyanocks, Appomattocs, Paspaheghs, and Kiskiacks, about two hundred warriors in all. . . . The Indians came right up to the camp and shot their arrows through the tents, wounding twelve of the English, two of whom later died." (Ibid.)

42   Smith went on an expedition   Ibid., 60–71, is a thorough and entertaining account of Smith's experience.

42   and saved from execution   Ibid., 68–69, is a convincing dissection of the Pocahontas-Smith mythology.

42   he found only a third of the original company   Ibid., 75.

42   In June 1609, Sir Thomas Gates was sent   Ibid., 157.

42   "Laws Divine, Moral and Martial"   Ibid., 181.

43   On Monday, July 24, 1609, a hurricane struck   Ibid., 158.

43   The *Sea Venture* fought the storm   Ibid., 159.

43   "Prayers might well be"   Louis B. Wright, ed. *A Voyage to Virginia in 1609: Two Narratives, Strachey's 'True Reportory' and Jourdain's Discovery of the Bermudas,* (Charlottesville, VA, 1964), 6.

43   the ship came upon a reef   Ibid., 15.

43   150 or so survivors   Ibid., 16.

43   built two boats out of the wreckage   Ibid., 57–58.

43   *Deliverance* and *Patience*   Ibid.

43   on Monday, May 23, 1610   Ibid., 63.

43   Shakespeare is said to have drawn on it   Ibid., ix.

43   imposed martial law   Ibid., 181.

43   "Laws Divine, Moral and Martial"   Southern, ed. *The Jamestown Adventure,* 178–194.

43   "upon pain of death"   Ibid., 181.

43   Those who failed to come to services   Ibid., 181–182.

43   Sodomy, incest, rape, and adultery   Ibid., 183.

43   fornication led only   Ibid.

43   To disobey the governor   Ibid., 184.

44   "a new birth of freedom"   Lincoln, *Speeches and Writings, 1859–1865,* 536. The quotation is from the Gettysburg Address, delivered on November 19, 1863. The full sentence: "It is rather for us to be here dedicated to the great task remaining before us—that from these honored dead we take increased devotion to that cause for which they gave the last full measure of devotion—that we here highly resolve that these dead shall not have died in vain—that this nation, under God, shall have a new birth of freedom—and that government of the people, by the people, and for the people, shall not perish from the earth." (Ibid.)

44   took delivery of black slaves   Kenneth M. Stampp, *The Peculiar Institution: Slavery in the Ante-Bellum South* (New York, 1956), 17–18. Stampp wrote: "When a 'Dutch man of warre' brought the first cargo of twenty 'negars' to Virginia in 1619, John Rolfe and his neighbors sanctioned a trade and tapped a source of labor that had been familiar to some Europeans for nearly two centuries." (Ibid., 18.)

44   "African diaspora"   Albert J. Raboteau, *Slave Religion: The "Invisible Institution" in the Antebellum South* (New York, 1978), is a superb account. See also Milton S. Sernett, ed. *African American Religious History: A Documentary Witness* (Durham, NC, 1999), for a collection of firsthand narratives.

44   Some slaves were Muslims   Raboteau, *Slave Religion,* 46–47.

44   practiced native African religions   This is Raboteau's essential argument in *Slave Religion*. He wrote: "In the New World slave control was based on the eradication of all forms of African culture because of their power to unify the slaves and thus enable them to resist or rebel. Nevertheless, African beliefs and customs persisted and were transmitted by slaves to their descendants. Shaped and modified by a new environment, elements of African

folklore, music, language, and religion were transplanted in the New World by the African diaspora. Influenced by colonial European and indigenous native American cultures, aspects of the African heritage have contributed, in greater or lesser degree, to the formation of various Afro-American cultures in the New World. One of the most durable and adaptable constituents of the slave's culture, linking African past with American present, was his religion. It is important to realize, however, that in the Americas the religions of Africa have not been merely preserved as static 'Africanisms' or as archaic 'retentions.' The fact is that they have continued to develop as living traditions putting down new roots in new soil, bearing new fruit as unique hybrids of American origin. African styles of worship, forms of ritual, systems of belief, and fundamental perspectives have remained vital on this side of the Atlantic, not because they were preserved in a 'pure' orthodoxy but because they were transformed. Adaptability, based upon respect for spiritual power wherever it originated, accounted for the openness of African religions to syncretism with other religious traditions and for the continuity of a distinctively African religious consciousness. At least in some areas of the Americas, the gods of Africa continued to live—in exile." (Ibid., 4–5.)

44   another scholar, Jon Butler   Butler, *Awash in a Sea of Faith,* 129–163, is an excellent discussion of these issues, as is Butler's essay in Hoffman and Albert, eds. *Religion in a Revolutionary Age,* 1–30.

45   "reason, justice & humanity"   Hutson, ed. *The Founders on Religion,* 206.

45   to consider the Christianization of   Francis Paul Prucha, *The Great Father: The United States Government and the American Indians* (Lincoln, NE, 1984), 10. Prucha's book is a landmark account of this long and painful history.

45   Massachusetts looked to "win"   Ibid.

46   "The great distinguishing feature"   Ibid., 11.

46   1622 in Virginia and by 1637 in New England   Ibid., 13. In Virginia, Prucha writes, "the Indians under Opechancanough rose up against the white settlers who had invaded their lands and quickly killed a quarter to one-third of the population. English reaction was immediate and vengeful." Then, "soon after, in New England, the Pequot War of 1637 began formal conflicts between the Indians and the English." (Ibid.)

46   voyage of the *Arbella*   Bremer, *John Winthrop,* 188–191.

46   "Now the only way"   Dunn and Yeandle, eds. *The Journal of John Winthrop,* abridged edition, 9–10.

48   "There are two rules"   Ibid., 2.

48   "Every party"   Lambert, *The Founding Fathers and the Place of Religion in America,* 76.

48   "shall have free liberty to keep away"   Edwin S. Gaustad, *Liberty of Conscience: Roger Williams in America* (Valley Forge, PA, 1999), 43.

48   In 1630 . . . the colony provided for   Edmund S. Morgan, *Roger Williams: The Church and the State* (New York, 1967), 75.

48   In 1631, it limited the suffrage   Ibid., 76.

49   In 1635 came an order   Ibid., 75.

49   nonmembers should . . . "help pay"   Ibid.

49   "The ministers have great power"   Ibid., 78. "Before Roger Williams founded Rhode Island," Morgan writes, "there was probably no place in the western world where clergymen were as carefully cut off from political power as in Massachusetts Bay." (Ibid., 79.) "The colony was not a theocracy in the usual sense of a rule by priests. But in the sense of a rule by God, through agents who steadily searched His Word and sought to apply it to every situation, Massachusetts aspired to be a theocracy." (Ibid., 84.)

49   came to the colony in 1634   Dunn and Yeandle, eds. *The Journal of John Winthrop,* abridged edition, 105. See also Eve LaPlante, *American Jezebel: The Uncommon Life of Anne Hutchinson, the Woman Who Defied the Puritans* (San Francisco, 2004).

49   Conversant with the Bible   LaPlante, *American Jezebel,* 41–44.

49   became a popular religious figure   Ibid., 47–49.

49   arguing in favor of the doctrine   Ibid., 50–55.

49   an "Antinomian"   Dunn and Yeandle, eds. *The Journal of John Winthrop,* abridged edition, 106–107.

49   on trial for heresy   La Plante, *American Jezebel,* 272.

49   informed the court that God   Dunn and Yeandle, eds., *The Journal of John Winthrop,* abridged edition, 133.

49   "ruin us and our posterity"   Ibid.

49   "I desire to know"   Ibid.

50   suffered a terrible miscarriage   Ibid., 146.

50   Winthrop wrote to Dr. John Clarke   Ibid., 146–147.

51   Mrs. Hutchinson moved from Rhode Island   Ibid., 239.

51   "These people had cast off"   Ibid.

51   In the last journal entry of the man's life   Ibid., 344–345.

52   Maryland, founded by a powerful Catholic family   J. Moss Ives, *The Ark and the Dove: The Beginnings of Civil and Religious Liberties in America* (New York, 1936), tells this story well. See also Ronald Hoffman, *Princes of Ireland, Planters of Maryland: A Carroll Saga, 1500–1782* (Chapel Hill, NC, 253), and McDermott, *Charles Carroll of Carrollton,* 19–22.

52   Religious Toleration Act in 1649   McDermott, *Charles Carroll of Carrollton,* 20.

52   the term "Quaker" was coined in England   Margery Post Abbott, *Historical Dictionary of the Friends (Quakers)* (Lanham, MD, 2003), 233.

52   George Fox, one of the founders   Ibid., 105–107.

52   tended "to tremble at the word of God"   Ibid., 233.

52   "Inner Light" . . . and experience God directly   Noll, *America's God*, 28–29; Mark A. Noll, *A History of Christianity in the United States and Canada* (Grand Rapids, MI, 1992), 67–68.

52   a welcome champion in William Penn   Noll, *A History of Christianity in the United States and Canada*, 66–68. See also Martin E. Marty, *Pilgrims in Their Own Land: The 500 Years of Religion in America* (Boston, 1984), 86–89.

52   the eloquent 1670 "The Great Case"   Gaustad and Schmidt, *The Religious History of America*, 85.

52   was to be a "holy experiment"   Noll, *A History of Christianity in the United States and Canada*, 67.

53   Connecticut's Code of 1650   Tocqueville, *Democracy in America*, 38–39.

53   "If any man"   Ibid., 38.

53   "the legislator, forgetting completely"   Ibid., 39.

53   Cotton Mather, a minister at Boston's   Noll, *America's God*, 21–22; Lambert, *The Founding Fathers and the Place of Religion in America*, 73–74.

53   Mather believed America was in   Michael Warner, comp. *American Sermons: The Pilgrims to Martin Luther King Jr.* (New York, 1999), 195–214. In this sermon, Mather said: "Let us now make a good and a right use, of the prodigious *descent*, which the *Devil*, in *Great Wrath*, is at this day making upon our Land." (Ibid., 195.)

53   Jonathan Edwards's "Sinners in the Hands"   Ibid., 347–364. For discussion of Edwards and his significance, see also: Richard L. Bushman, ed. *The Great Awakening: Documents on the Revival of Religion, 1740–1745* (Chapel Hill, NC, 1970), 121–127, 153–157; Hoffman and Albert, eds. *Religion in a Revolutionary Age*, 6–8; Marty, *Pilgrims in Their Own Land*, 112–117; Noll, *America's God;* Noll, *The Rise of Evangelicalism*. Wilson H. Kimnach, Kenneth P. Minkema, and Douglas A. Sweeney, eds. *The Sermons of Jonathan Edwards: A Reader* (New Haven, CT, 1999), is also illuminating.

53   "The Wonders of the Invisible World"   Warner, comp. *American Sermons*, 195.

53   "If you do not by a speedy"   Ibid., 214.

54   Roger Williams, a minister who   Gaustad, *Liberty of Conscience*, 20–23.

54   mostly interested in saving the church   Morgan, *Roger Williams*, 86–114, is a thorough discussion.

54   "Render to Caesar"   Mark 12:17 (KJV).

54   "hedge or wall of separation"   Gaustad, *Liberty of Conscience*, 207; Hamburger, *Separation of Church and State*, 38–45. Hamburger quoted a partic-

ularly interesting line of Williams's: "And hence it is true, that a *Christian Captaine, Christian, Merchant, Physitian, Lawyer, Pilot, Father, Master,* and (so consequently) *Magistrate,* &c. is no more a *Captaine, Merchant, Physitian, Lawyer, Pilot, Father, Master, Magistrate,* &c. then a *Captaine, Marchant,* &c. of any other Conscience or Religion," and "A *Pagan* or *Antichristian Pilot* may be as skillful to carry the Ship to its desired Port, as any *Christian Mariner* or *Pilot.*" (Ibid., 42.)

54   Constantine's conversion early in the fourth century   Morgan, *Roger Williams,* 96–97.

54   Williams's goal "was not freedom of thought"   Ibid., 141.

54   "the gardens of Christ's churches turned"   Ibid., 96.

54   the year Henry VIII broke with Rome   Diarmaid MacCulloch, *The Reformation: A History* (New York, 2003), 193–98. MacCulloch's book is excellent, far-reaching, and deep. Madeleine Gray, *The Protestant Reformation: Belief, Practice and Tradition* (Portland, OR, 2003), offers an accessible overview.

55   Henry's daughter Mary, a Catholic   MacCulloch, *The Reformation* 272–283.

55   sister and successor, Elizabeth   Ibid., 277–283.

55   a century of civil strife   Ibid., 503–515.

55   "I commend that man"   Morgan, *Roger Williams,* 128.

55   Williams was exiled   Dunn and Yeandle, eds. *The Journal of John Winthrop,* abridged edition, 76–79, 85; Gaustad, *Liberty of Conscience,* 44–46.

55   his embattled life   Irwin H. Polishook, ed. *Roger Williams, John Cotton and Religious Freedom: A Controversy in New and Old England* (Englewood Cliffs, NJ, 1967) chronicles an important element of that life.

55   "At Providence also the devil"   Dunn and Yeandle, eds. *The Journal of John Winthrop,* abridged edition, 150.

55   a wife-beating husband's anger at Williams   Ibid., 150–151.

55   What changed?   Hoffman and Albert, eds. *Religion in a Revolutionary Age,* 1–30, is particularly strong on this subject. The essay "Coercion, Miracle, Reason: Rethinking the American Religious Experience in the Revolutionary Age" by Jon Butler includes this wonderful paragraph discussing religion in America after 1720: "Denominational deviations further tangled the American spiritual thicket. The doctrinal variety that simultaneously energized and plagued seventeenth-century Puritanism found heightened expression in the eighteenth century. Arianism (denial that Christ was consubstantial with God), Arminianism (denial of the Calvinist doctrine of predestination), Behmenism (attachment to the doctrines of the German

mystical Pietist Jacob Boehme), Chiliasm (attachment to the importance of the thousand-year reign of Christ), Origenism (belief in universal salvation), Pelagianism (denial of the doctrine of original sin), Socinianism (denial of Christ's divinity), as well as diverse views on the resurrection of the body, hell, eternal punishment, and the validity of particular rituals all took root in eighteenth-century America." (Ibid., 13–14.)

56 John Toland's *Christianity Not Mysterious*   Philip McGuinness, Alan Harrison, and Richard Kearney, eds. *John Toland's Christianity Not Mysterious: Text, Associated Works and Critical Essays* (Dublin, 1997), is an excellent source for Toland's thought and its place in intellectual history.

56 America was becoming religiously diverse   Ibid. For interesting accounts of the pre-Revolutionary and Revolutionary eras, see also Roger Finke and Rodney Stark, *The Churching of America, 1776–1990: Winners and Losers in Our Religious Economy* (New Brunswick, NJ, 1992), 22–53; Gaustad and Schmidt, *The Religious History of America*, 3–138; Noll, *A History of Christianity in the United States and Canada*, 7–141. Another fine book in this area is Alan Taylor, *American Colonies* (New York, 2001).

56 Studying the stories   See, for instance, Jefferson, *Writings*, 123–327; Ralph Ketcham, *James Madison: A Biography* (Charlottesville, VA, 1990), 58.

57 "You are happy"   Madison, *Writings*, 9.

57 "They cast their eyes on these new countries"   Jefferson, *Writings*, 283.

57 He knew of New England's history   Ibid.

57 persecution of   Ibid.

57 need "for the recovery and establishment"   *Journal of the Continental Congress, 1774–1789, Saturday, June 17, 1774*. See original document at *American Memory* on the Library of Congress website, www.loc.gov.

57 writing his *Notes*   Jefferson, *Writings*, 124.

57 Query XVII   Jefferson, *Writings*, 283–287.

57 "The first settlers"   Ibid., 283.

58 the Quakers were a particular target   Ibid.

58 the human costs of a 1705 act   Ibid., 284–285.

58 "religious slavery"   Ibid., 285.

58 "two-thirds of the people"   Ibid., 283.

58 In 1654, the French ship *Ste. Catherine*   Sarna, *American Judaism*, 1–2. See also Jonathan D. Sarna, ed. *The American Jewish Experience* (New York, 1986), 5–17, and William Pencak, *Jews & Gentiles in Early America, 1654–1800* (Ann Arbor, MI, 2005).

59 enormous courage and resilience   Sarna, *American Judaism*, 1–8.

59 "The Jews . . . would nearly all"   Fritz Hirschfeld, *George Washington and the Jews* (Newark, NJ, 2005), 13.

59   "the deceitful race"   Ibid.

59   directing him to allow settlers   Sarna, *American Judaism,* 2.

59   Shearith Israel   Ibid., 12–20.

59   "Whereas in so many other diaspora"   Ibid., 28.

59   began referring to their flocks   Ibid., 29.

60   "O Lord: the God of our Fathers"   Jacques Judah Lyons Collection, Box 1, American Jewish Historical Society.

60   "It is error alone"   Jefferson, *Writings,* 286.

60   "When a religion is good"   Aldridge, *Benjamin Franklin and Nature's God,* 192

60   some private *Notes on Religion* jotted down in 1776   Julian P. Boyd, ed. *The Papers of Thomas Jefferson,* I (Princeton, NJ, 1950), 546.

61   "that faculty whereby man"   John Locke, *An Essay Concerning Human Understanding,* ed. Peter H. Nidditch (Oxford, 1975), 668.

61   "Nothing that is contrary to"   Ibid., 696.

62   religious liberty "the chief characteristic mark of the true Church"   John Locke, *The Selected Political Writings of John Locke,* ed. Paul E. Sigmund (New York, 2005), 126.

62   "men's striving for power and empire"   Ibid.

62   "I esteem it above all things"   Ibid., 129.

62   Musing amid the Revolution   Jefferson, *Writings,* 283–287; the passage is from his *Notes on the State of Virginia,* composed in 1781 and 1782.

62   "I doubt whether the people of this country"   Ibid., 287.

63   "It can never be too often repeated"   Ibid.

CHAPTER TWO: AND NONE SHALL BE AFRAID

64   "The cause in which America is now in arms"   Sandoz, ed. *Political Sermons of the American Founding Era, 1730–1805,* I, 549. The full quotation from the sermon is: "If your cause is just—you may look with confidence to the Lord and entreat him to plead it as his own. You are all my witnesses, that this is the first time of my introducing any political subject into the pulpit. At this season however, it is not only lawful but necessary, and I willingly embrace the opportunity of declaring my opinion without any hesitation, that the cause in which America is now in arms is the cause of justice, of liberty, and of human nature." (Ibid.) As we will see in the discussion of his role in Madison's life, Witherspoon is a critical figure in early American history. Derek Davis wrote: "Witherspoon's influence was enormous. The only clergyman to sign the Declaration, Witherspoon counted among his pupils one

future president (Madison), one vice president, twenty-one senators, twenty-nine representatives, and thirty-three judges. Nine of the fifty-five delegates to the 1787 Constitutional Convention had been his pupils." (Davis, *Religion and the Continental Congress*, 275.)

64   "Ye Sovereigns of the European world"   Tench Coxe, "A Friend of Society and Liberty: Pennsylvania Gazette, 23 July," in Merrill Jensen, ed., *The Documentary History of the Ratification of the Constitution*, vol. 18, *Commentaries on the Constitution, Public and Private: 10 May to 13 September 1788*, ed. John P. Kaminski and Gaspare J. Saladino (Madison, WI, 1995), 282.

64   the inaugural session of the Continental Congress   Davis, *Religion and the Continental Congress*, 73–76, tells the story of the Congress's first days.

64   Carpenters' Hall in Philadelphia, an elegant Georgian brick building   John L. Cotter, *The Buried Past: An Archaeological History of Philadelphia* (Philadelphia, 1993), 97.

64   Thomas Cushing, a lawyer from Boston   Davis, *Religion and the Continental Congress*, 73; see also Letter from John Adams to Abigail Adams, 16 September 1774 [electronic edition]. *Adams Family Papers: An Electronic Archive*. Massachusetts Historical Society. http://www.masshist.org/ digitaladams/, and Alexander, *Samuel Adams*, 139–140.

65   that "because we were so divided in religious sentiments"   Letter from John Adams to Abigail Adams, 16 September 1774 [electronic edition]. *Adams Family Papers: An Electronic Archive*.

65   Jay, a future warden of Trinity Church on Wall Street   Stahr, *John Jay: Founding Father*, 233.

65   leader in Christ Church Parish in Charleston   John A. Garraty and Marc C. Carnes, eds. *American National Biography* (New York, 1991), 19: 131–133.

65   "Mr. S. Adams arose"   Letter from John Adams to Abigail Adams, 16 September 1774 [electronic edition]. *Adams Family Papers: An Electronic Archive*. See also Alexander, *Samuel Adams*, 139.

66   a onetime tax collector   Alexander, *Samuel Adams*, 9.

66   "As neither reason requires"   William V. Wells, *Life and Public Services of Samuel Adams* (Boston, 1865), 1: 502.

66   "the horrible rumor of the cannonade of Boston"   Letter from John Adams to Abigail Adams, 16 September 1774 [electronic edition]. *Adams Family Papers: An Electronic Archive*.

66   rumors would prove   Alexander, *Samuel Adams*, 139.

66   dressed in clerical garb   Letter from John Adams to Abigail Adams, 16 September 1774 [electronic edition]. *Adams Family Papers: An Electronic Archive*.

66   at once stunned and moved   Ibid.

66   "I never saw a greater effect"   Ibid.

67   "It has had an excellent effect"   Ibid.

67   young man in Orange County   Ketcham, *James Madison,* 61. See also Garry Wills, *James Madison* (New York, 2002), 14–17.

67   devoured a friend's letters   Ketcham, *James Madison,* 61–62.

67   notable for its "glowing patriots"   Ibid., 61.

67   to "illuminate the minds"   Ibid.

67   Madison had been a sickly child   Ibid., 51–52. See also Wills, *James Madison,* 14–15.

67   "a constitutional liability"   Ketcham, *James Madison,* 51.

67   his affliction changed the course of his life   Wills, *James Madison,* 15–16.

67   Born to Virginia gentry   Ketcham, *James Madison,* 1–5.

67   was held back a year   Wills, *James Madison,* 15.

67   with a tutor who was an alumnus   Ibid., 15–16.

67   under John Witherspoon, a Presbyterian clergyman   Ibid., 15–17. See also Ketcham, *James Madison,* 25–50, and Noll, *America's God,* 124–130, for additional discussions of Witherspoon and his place in American religious and political history.

67   Scottish Enlightenment   Wills, *Inventing America: Jefferson's Declaration of Independence,* discusses the influence of the Scottish Enlightenment on Jefferson. See also Noll, *America's God,* 93–103.

68   offered "free and equal liberty"   Ketcham, *James Madison,* 30.

68   the Anglican establishment imprisoned dissenting preachers   Ibid., 57–58.

68   argued against the oppression   Ibid.

68   reports a legend that "young Madison"   Miller, *The First Liberty,* 6.

68   "that diabolical Hell conceived principle"   Ketcham, *James Madison,* 57.

68   "So I leave you"   Ibid.

68   Madison read George Mason's version   Miller, *The First Liberty,* 6.

68   "That as religion, or the duty which we owe"   Gaustad, *Faith of the Founders,* 174. For a discussion of Article XVI, see also Miller, *The First Liberty,* 4–8; Robert A. Rutland, *George Mason: Reluctant Statesman* (Baton Rouge, LA, 1980), 60; Ketcham, *James Madison,* 71–73.

69   "toleration" bothered Madison   Miller, *The First Liberty,* 6.

69   He seems to have asked Patrick Henry   Ketcham, *James Madison,* 72.

69   legislative to-ing and fro-ing   Miller, *The First Liberty,* 6–7.

69   "That religion"   Helen Hill, *George Mason: Constitutionalist* (Cambridge, MA, 1938), 138.

69   The vote on Virginia's declaration   Philip B. Kurland and Ralph Lerner, eds. *The Founders' Constitution* (Chicago, 1987), 1: 6–7.

69   "Although it is not clear"   Miller, *The First Liberty*, 7.

70   He and his wife, Martha, lost a year-and-a-half-old daughter   Dumas Malone, *Jefferson and His Time*, vol. 1, *Jefferson the Virginian* (Boston, 1948), 210. The little girl's name was Jane Randolph Jefferson.

70   away for several months on political business   Ibid., 211–212.

70   he became agitated   Ibid., 213.

70   "The suspense under which I am"   Ibid.

70   They were fine   Ibid., 214. Malone wrote: "They were in the best of hands; but his fears about his wife's health had started." (Ibid.)

70   biographers speculate that there was a miscarriage   Ibid., 216. According to Malone, a friend urged Jefferson to bring Martha to Philadelphia for the next session of Congress, but, Malone wrote, "she was in no condition to go. It would have been unlike [Jefferson] to give any further explanation, but the chances are that she carried other children than those who finally appeared upon the record and that there were mishaps which went unmentioned." (Ibid.)

70   tried to comfort himself with details of life at Monticello   Ibid., 215.

70   stocking deer   Ibid.

70   drinking good Madeira   Ibid.

70   tending to his stables   Ibid.

70   on Sunday, March 31, 1776, Jefferson's mother died   Ibid., 216.

70   her collapse from a stroke   Ibid.

70   quickly followed by his own   Ibid. Malone wrote: "This [March 31] was just about the date that he had expected to return to Congress, but in the meantime he himself fell ill and was incapacitated for some five weeks longer. The report got around that he was suffering from an inveterate headache which had a hard name; probably it was what we now call migraine." (Ibid.)

70   "the greatest question . . . "   John Adams, *The Political Writings of John Adams*, ed. George W. Carey (Washington, D.C., 2000), 651. The remark comes from a July 3, 1776, letter to Abigail Adams. Another, cleaner version of this quotation can be found in Irving, *George Washington*, 245.

71   he arrived, Adams recalled, with   Randall, *The Life of Thomas Jefferson*, I, 144.

71   intensely curious about what was happening in Williamsburg   Malone, *Jefferson the Virginian*, 218.

72   debating Virginia's Declaration of Rights   Curry, *The First Freedoms*, 135; Miller, *The First Liberty*, 4–17; Rutland, *George Mason*, 43–67; See also Jefferson, *Writings*, 34–35, for Jefferson's observations on the fury of the ongoing debates over religious freedom in Virginia.

72   sent down his own draft   Malone, *Jefferson the Virginian*, 236.

72   "All persons shall have full and free"   Jefferson, *Writings*, 344.

72   rented rooms   Malone, *Jefferson the Virginian*, 216.

72   a bedroom where he slept   Ibid.

72   a small portable writing desk   Ibid.

72   On Friday, June 7, 1776, Richard Henry Lee of Virginia moved for a declaration   Davis, *Religion and the Continental Congress*, 95.

72   A committee of five was appointed   Jefferson, *Writings*, 17.

72   Jefferson was asked to put pen to paper   Malone, *Jefferson the Virginian*, 220. Many years later Adams and Jefferson had differing memories about exactly how it came to pass that Jefferson wrote the document. John H. Hazelton, *The Declaration of Independence: Its History* (New York, 1970), 141–146.

72   adjourned to his quarters at Seventh   Malone, *Jefferson the Virginian*, 220–221. Malone noted that there were seventeen days between the appointment of the committee on June 11 and the presentation of the draft declaration to Congress on June 28. (Ibid., 220.)

72   The document, he said, was "intended"   Jefferson, *Writings*, 1501. He made this remark in a letter to Henry Lee on May 8, 1825.

72   synthesis of the "sentiments of the day"   Ibid.

73   "When in the course of human events"   For the final Declaration, see www.archives.gov/national-archives-experience/charters/declaration-transcript.html. See also Maier, *American Scripture*, for an excellent account of the Declaration.

73   two more allusions to the Almighty   Jefferson, *Writings*, 23–24.

73   Jefferson's draft   The Declaration's significance is a subject of scholarly debate, with some arguing that the Constitution and the Bill of Rights are more important. But I would argue that the Declaration should have pride of place, given that its composition, passage, and signing marked the irrevocable step toward a new nation. (Why the joking about hanging otherwise? [see page 76]). Of the Declaration John Adams wrote Abigail: "You will see in a few days a Declaration setting forth the causes which have impelled us to this mighty revolution, and the reasons which will justify it in the sight of God and man. . . . You will think me transported with enthusiasm, but I am not. I am well aware of the toil, and blood, and treasure, that it will cost us to maintain this declaration, and support and defend these states. Yet, through all the gloom, I can see the rays of ravishing light and glory. I can see that the end is more than worth all the means, and that posterity will triumph in that day's transaction, even although we should rue it, which I trust in God we shall not." (Carey, ed. *The Political Writings of John Adams*, 651–654.)

73   went to the Congress on Friday, June 28   Malone, *Jefferson the Virginian*, 220.

73   believe that it was sacred scripture   Randall, *The Life of Thomas Jefferson*, I, 177–178.

74   Franklin—another writer—detected the truth   Ibid., 178.

74   to "assume among"   Jefferson, *Writings*, 19.

74   based more on a religion of reason   Jayne, *Jefferson's Declaration of Independence*, 9–61, is particularly illuminating on the Declaration's religious nature.

74   "The Liberty of a People is the gift of God and Nature"   Algernon Sidney, *Discourses Concerning Government*, ed. Thomas G. West (Indianapolis, 1996), 510.

74   a reply to a treatise   Ibid., xvi.

75   Jefferson's God   Sanford, *The Religious Life of Thomas Jefferson*, 93.

75   "watches over our country's freedom"   Ibid.

75   "We are not a world ungoverned"   Ibid.

75   "I write with freedom"   Ibid., 90.

75   met again to discuss a seal   Davis, *Religion and the Continental Congress*, 137–140. See also Malone, *Jefferson the Virginian*, 242–243.

76   John Hancock of Massachusetts   Harlow Giles Unger, *John Hancock: Merchant King and American Patriot* (New York, 2000), 240–241.

76   bedeviled by horseflies   James Parton, *Life of Thomas Jefferson* (New York, 1971), 191.

76   "swarms of flies"   Ibid.

76   "the silk-stockinged legs"   Ibid.

76   Jefferson loved the story   Randall, *The Life of Thomas Jefferson*, I, 153.

76   the delegates immediately voted to suppress the standard Anglican prayer   Ketcham, *James Madison*, 70.

76   directing congregations to ask God   Ibid.

77   "The bells rung all day"   Unger, *John Hancock*, 242.

77   took part in a kind of riot   Irving, *George Washington*, 246–247.

77   full of religious people   Mark A. Noll charted the "confluence" of several different intellectual, political, and theological forces in the Founding era. "By the late eighteenth century most Americans . . . shared both a mistrust of intellectual authorities inherited from previous generations and a belief that true knowledge arose from the use of one's own senses—whether the external senses for information about nature and society or the moral sense for ethical and aesthetic judgments," Noll wrote. "Most Americans were thus united in the conviction that people had to think for themselves in order to know science, morality, economics, politics, and especially theology." According to Noll, the American synthesis was unique and powerful: "To sum up a situation that many historians now

take for granted: after the 1780s, republicanism (wherever found along a continuum from classical to liberal) had come to prevail in America; very soon thereafter, commonsense principles (whether defined in elite or populist terms) were almost as widely spread; and in the same post-Revolutionary period, Protestant evangelicalism (however divided into contending sects) became the dominant American religion." (Noll, *America's God,* 12–13.)

77   Washington laced his military orders   Cousins, *"In God We Trust,"* 50–52, is illustrative.

77   "Let every face brighten"   Boller, *George Washington and Religion,* 54.

77   every man was "accountable to God alone"   Ibid., 170.

77   "ought to be protected"   Ibid.

78   William White, who knew Washington   Ibid., 32–33.

78   "I do not believe that"   Ibid., 89.

78   Washington attended services at St. Paul's   Irving, *George Washington,* 652.

79   "From the beginning, politics and religion"   Tocqueville, *Democracy in America,* 275.

79   "The magistrate is to govern the *state*"   Moore, ed. *The Patriot Preachers of the American Revolution,* 284.

79   "I do not know if all Americans have faith in their religion"   Tocqueville, *Democracy in America,* 280.

79   Interviewing clergyman after clergyman   Ibid., 283.

80   "[In] allying itself"   Ibid., 284.

80   "If the Americans, who change their head of state"   Ibid., 285.

80   "In Europe, Christianity has permitted itself"   Ibid., 288.

80   Franklin and Jefferson played with the idea of America as a New Israel   Davis, *Religion and the Continental Congress,* 138.

80   "hardened, sullen tempered Pharoah of England"   Thomas Paine, *Collected Writings* (New York, 1995), 29.

80   Reverend George Duffield spoke of the "American Zion"   Moore, ed. *The Patriot Preachers of the American Revolution,* 349.

81   Washington was Joshua   Ibid., 361–362.

81   the king of France, Cyrus   Ibid., 365.

81   When on the afternoon of July 4   Ibid.

81   "Moses standing on the shore"   Ibid., 138. Davis's discussion of the committee's work—Jefferson proposed a combined Israel/Anglo-Saxon theme, Adams "The Judgment of Hercules"—is interesting and well told. (Ibid., 137–144).

81   a depiction of "the Children"   Ibid.

81   The final seal   Ibid., 143–144. See also "The Great Seal of the United

States," United States Department of State, Bureau of Public Affairs, September 1996.

81   The *Annuit Coeptis* phrase comes from Virgil   The website www.Great Seal.com, authored by John D. MacArthur, offers a thorough and interesting telling of the history of the seal.

82   A classicist, Thomson   Ibid. Both "The Great Seal of the United States" publication and www.GreatSeal.com report Thomson's classical background.

82   the Founders honored "the many signal"   Ibid.

82   appointing chaplains, opening legislative sessions   Davis, *Religion and the Continental Congress,* 73–93, offers a thorough discussion of these issues and their significance.

82   the last state (Massachusetts) disestablished   John D. Cushing, "Notes on Disestablishment in Massachusetts, 1780–1833," *William and Mary Quarterly,* 3rd ser., 26 (April 1969), 169–90.

83   He and Adams once clashed on the floor   McCullough, *John Adams,* 113–114.

83   Benjamin Rush recalled   Ibid.

84   after a meeting at the Rising Sun Tavern   John T. Goolrick, *Old Homes and History Around Fredericksburg* (Richmond, VA, 1929), 28. George Washington and John Paul Jones were also regulars. Washington once told his diary: "Evening at the Rising Sun. Lost money as usual. The boys at Fredericksburg are too smart for me." (Ibid., 27–28.)

85   events leading to the passage   Curry, *The First Freedoms,* 136–148. See also Ketcham, *James Madison,* 162–168; Lambert, *The Founding Fathers,* 209–210; Henry Mayer, *A Son of Thunder: Patrick Henry and the American Republic,* (New York, 1986), 359–364; and Miller, *The First Liberty,* 24–67, for accounts of the history of Virginia's Statute for Religious Freedom.

85   John Blair Smith   Mayer, *A Son of Thunder,* 360. See also Herbert Clarence Bradshaw, *History of Hampden-Sydney College; From the Beginnings to the Year 1856* (Durham, NC 1976), 78–87.

85   "The legitimate powers of government"   Jefferson, *Writings,* 285.

85   "Whilst we assert for ourselves"   Madison, *Writings,* 31.

85   "What we have to do I think"   Mayer, *A Son of Thunder,* 359.

85   Henry's current proposal was   Ketcham, *James Madison,* 162. See also Madison, *Writings,* 760–761, for his recollections of Henry's maneuverings.

85   elected governor in November 1784   Mayer, *A Son of Thunder,* 362. See also Ketcham, *James Madison,* 163, for Madison's undisguised pleasure, in Ketcham's words, that "the orator's departure from the Assembly would be 'a circumstance very inauspicious to his offspring,' Madison reported to James Monroe." (Ibid.)

85   writing a "Memorial and Remonstrance"   Madison, *Writings,* 29–36.

86   "What have been its fruits?"   Ibid., 32.

86   the pro-Christian forces . . . "of our religion"   Jefferson, *Writings,* 40.

86   by including the phrase "Jesus Christ, the holy author of our religion"
      Ibid.

86   "by a great majority"   Ibid.

86   became law in January 1786   Davis, *Religion and the Continental Congress,* 35.

86   "Our affairs seem to lead"   Irving, *George Washington,* 639.

86   "a small man"   Charles Mee, *Genius of the People* (New York, 1987), 7.

86   The reason was largely political   Davis, *Religion and the Continental Congress,* 203.

87   "the most wonderful work"   Ibid., 3–4.

87   "The framers believed"   Ibid., 203–204.

87   religion would still find its way   Ibid., 204.

87   "the godless Constitution" Kramnick and Moore, *The Godless Constitution,* 24.

87   "It is impossible"   Hutson, ed. *The Founders on Religion,* 77.

88   "our General Convention"   Ibid., 76–77.

88   At a particularly fierce period of debate   Isaacson, ed. *A Benjamin Franklin Reader,* 362.

88   Walter Isaacson noted   Isaacson, *Benjamin Franklin: An American Life,* 451–452.

88   "We indeed seem to feel our own want"   Isaacson, ed. *A Benjamin Franklin Reader,* 362.

89   "I have lived, sir, a long time"   Ibid., 362–363.

89   asked that a prayer be said   Ibid., 363.

90   *"The Convention except three or four"*   Ibid.

90   Jonas Phillips, a Jew, wrote the only petition   Mittleman, Sarna, and Licht, eds. *Jews and the American Public Square,* 51.

90   the Constitution failed to mention God   Lambert, *The Founding Fathers and the Place of Religion in America,* 246–251.

90   issued the Northwest Ordinance   Gaustad, *Faith of the Founders: Religion and the New Nation,* 116–117; for the key elements of the ordinance's text, see ibid., 155–156.

90   prohibited any religious requirement for federal officeholders   Davis, *Religion and the Continental Congress,* 35–37.

90   The lieutenant governor of Connecticut, Oliver Wolcott, reflected   Jensen, *The Documentary History of the Ratification of the Constitution,* vol. 3, 557–558.

90   "Knowledge and liberty"   Ibid., 558.

91   he believed that "the hand of God"   Jensen, *The Documentary History of the Ratification of the Constitution*, vol. 18, 269.

91   "They are a mixture"   J. Hector St. John de Crèvecoeur, *Letters from an American Farmer and Sketches of Eighteenth-Century America* (New York, 1981), 68.

91   Catholics, Lutherans, Deists   Ibid., 73–76.

91   "Thus all sects are mixed"   Ibid., 76.

92   "Persecution, religious pride"   Ibid.

92   published on Thursday, November 22, 1787   Madison, *Writings,* 167.

92   critical distinction between   Ibid., 164–167.

92   a "republican remedy"   Ibid., 298.

92   "A religious sect"   Ibid., 297.

93   "A rage for paper money"   Ibid.

93   "When indeed religion is kindled"   Ibid., 151.

93   *"Divide et impera"*   Ibid.

94   "If men were angels"   Ibid., 295.

94   "Justice is the end of government"   Ibid., 298.

94   "The constitution proposed to your acceptance"   Jensen, *The Documentary History of the Ratification of the Constitution*, vol. 13, *Commentaries on the Constitution, Public and Private: 21 February to 7 November 1787,* ed. John P. Kaminski and Gaspare J. Saladino (Madison, WI, 1981), 524–525.

94   "May the GREAT IDEA"   Jensen, *The Documentary History of the Ratification of the Constitution*, vol. 15, *Commentaries on the Constitution, Public and Private: 18 December 1787 to 31 January 1788,* ed. John P. Kaminski and Gaspare J. Saladino (Madison, WI, 1984), 565.

95   "Whether this is the best possible system"   Jensen, *The Documentary History of the Ratification of the Constitution*, vol. 18, 270–271.

95   the Constitution was "an artful, dark, mysterious"   Jensen, *The Documentary History of the Ratification of the Constitution*, vol. 3, *Delaware, New Jersey, Georgia, Connecticut* (Madison, WI, 1978), 459.

95   controlling the president would require the "shedding of *Blood*"   Ibid.

95   "While some have boasted it"   Jensen, *The Documentary History of the Ratification of the Constitution*, vol. 16, 171.

95   William Williams thought the Preamble   Jensen, *The Documentary History of the Ratification of the Constitution*, vol. 3, 589. See also Lambert, *The Founding Fathers and the Place of Religion in America,* 3–4.

95   "We the people of the United States"   Jensen, *The Documentary History of the Ratification of the Constitution*, vol. 3, 589.

96   Oliver Ellsworth, who styled himself "Landholder"   Ibid., 329.

96   "A test in favor"   Ibid., 499.

96 Williams thought "the Federal Constitution"   Ibid., 588–590.

97 Writing as "Elihu" a week later   Ibid., 591–592.

98 Tench Coxe argued that both   Jensen, *The Documentary History of the Ratification of the Constitution*, vol. 18, 278–285.

98 the "pleasant and cooling breeze," and the clear sky full of stars   Ibid., 266. See pages 261–269 for the complete letter.

98 "The Clergy formed a very agreeable part"   Ibid., 265.

99 There were seventeen in all   Ibid.

99 "Pains were taken"   Ibid.

99 "Heaven was on the federal side of the question"   Ibid., 266.

99 "Scarcely any who composed a part of the procession"   Ibid., 269.

99 "I am convinced this is the Lord's doing"   Jensen, *The Documentary History of the Ratification of the Constitution*, vol. 3, 586.

100 fretted about the lack of specified liberties   Jensen, *The Documentary History of the Ratification of the Constitution*, vol. 4, *Massachusetts*, ed. John P. Kaminski and Gaspare J. Saladino (Madison, WI, 1997), 374.

100 "If the rights of conscience"   Ibid.

100 The final Senate version   Davis, *Religion and the Continental Congress*, 20. As Davis and other scholars have pointed out, however, this language, in Davis's words, had "the unmistakable meaning of prohibiting acts that prefer one church or sect over other—clearly a narrow intent."

100 In a conference between   Ibid., 20–21.

100 The difference is important   It is also the subject of endless debate. The "broad" interpretation is also, Davis wrote, occasionally known as the "separationist" interpretation. It was this view that Justice Black endorsed in the Everson case (in 1947). See Davis, *Religion and the Continental Congress*, 9–24, for a summary of the scholarly debate on the question.

100 think of the people's voice as the Lord's   Jensen, *The Documentary History of the Ratification of the Constitution*, vol. 16, *Commentaries on the Constitution, Public and Private: 1 February to 31 March 1788*, ed. John P. Kaminski and Gaspare J. Saladino (Madison, WI, 1986), 149.

101 Washington left Mount Vernon on   George Washington, *The Diaries of George Washington*, ed. Donald Jackson and Dorothy Twohig, vol. 5, *July 1786–December 1789* (Charlottesville, VA, 1979), 445.

101 Gershom Seixas, of Shearith Israel   Sarna, *American Judaism*, 40–41. Sarna wrote: "When press accounts, in 1789, listed [Seixas] as one of just fourteen ministers serving the city upon the inauguration of George Washington, he knew he had succeeded [in his bid for recognition for the synagogue]. Though ranked at the very bottom of that list, below the Baptist minister, the fact that a 'Jewish minister' was mentioned at all indicates a

heightened degree of acceptance. That same year, when Shearith Israel's cemetery experienced dangerous cave-ins, 'Gentile and Jew vied with one another to save the burial ground from disaster,' according to the cemetery's historian. . . . All of this goes to show that the world of American religion, opened up with the leveling of restrictive colonial laws and monopolistic church establishments, extended the boundaries of legitimate faiths to embrace Jews in new ways. Neither prejudice nor legal restrictions completely disappeared, of course. Even supporters of Jewish rights, like Thomas Jefferson, poured scorn on what he believed Jews stood for—their theology, morality, and doctrine. Outside of the few cities where Jews and Christians dwelt side by side, most people had no direct knowledge of Jews at all. Still, even where Jews had not yet settled, the principles underlying the Constitution inevitably affected their position. Privileges once accorded only to favored denominations of Protestants now applied far more broadly." (Ibid., 41.)

101   that "though the Society we belong"   Ibid.

101   "May the children of the stock of Abraham"   Washington, *Writings,* 767.

102   "But in the last days"   Micah 4:1–5 (KJV).

102   "Bliss was it in that dawn"   John Morley, ed. *The Complete Poetical Works of William Wordsworth* (New York, 1888), 267. The poem goes on to speak of the stage on which men found themselves able to live out their lives: "the very world, which is the world / Of all of us,—the place where in the end / We find our happiness, or not at all!" (Ibid.) Most of the Founders would not have fully agreed with Wordsworth on this point, for a central tenet of America's public religion was that there was some greater glory beyond time, toward which all men were moving.

103   "We have it in our power"   Paine, *Collected Writings,* 52.

103   pirates were making sport   James Woodress, *A Yankee's Odyssey: The Life of Joel Barlow* (Philadelphia, 1958), 153–186.

103   Washington sent Joel Barlow   Ibid., 154. Washington's verdict on Barlow: "It has ever been my opinion from the little I have seen and from what I have heard of Mr. Barlow that his abilities are adequate to any employment; & . . . there can be little doubt of his fitness as a negotiator." (Ibid.) Hamburger, *Separation of Church and State,* 134–135, notes Barlow was also a friend of Jefferson's and quotes some lines of Barlow's poetry. Borden, *Jews, Turks, and Infidels,* 76–79, adds interesting detail to the episode.

103   "As the government of the United States"   Boller, *George Washington and Religion,* 87–88. See also Lambert, *The Founding Fathers and the Place of Religion in America,* 238–241, and Paul A. Rahe, *Republics Ancient and Modern: Classical Republicanism and the American Revolution* (Chapel Hill, NC, 1992), 753.

103   The Senate ratified the treaty   Noll, *America's God,* 498. Noll wrote: "In 1796 Joel Barlow, a radical deist and friend of Tom Paine, negotiated a treaty with Tripoli in which he inserted an article in the English (but not the Arabic) text asserting that 'the government of the United States of America is not in any sense founded on the Christian religion.' Mild protests were heard, but not in the United States Senate, which approved the treaty without a dissenting vote." (Ibid.)

104   the election of 1800   John Ferling, *Adams vs. Jefferson: The Tumultuous Election of 1800* (New York, 2004), is a vivid account. See also Bernard A. Weisberger, *America Afire: Jefferson, Adams, and the Revolutionary Election of 1800* (New York, 2000).

104   "GOD—AND A RELIGIOUS PRESIDENT"   Ferling, *Adams vs. Jefferson,* 154.

104   On the first day of 1802, Jefferson answered a letter   Dreisbach, *Thomas Jefferson and the Wall of Separation Between Church and State,* 1–8, introduces his excellent book on Jefferson's metaphor.

104   with an eye toward reassuring believers   Ibid., 25–26.

104   "Believing with you that religion"   Ibid., 1–2. See also Jefferson, *Writings,* 510.

105   charted the relationship between God and America   Jefferson, *Writings,* 523. His concluding paragraph is striking for its humility and its admission that much lies beyond not only Jefferson's power but his understanding as well: "I shall now enter on the duties to which my fellow citizens have again called me, and shall proceed in the spirit of those principles which they have approved. I fear not that any motives of interest may lead me astray; I am sensible of no passion which could seduce me knowingly from the path of justice; but the weakness of human nature, and the limits of my own understanding, will produce errors of judgment sometimes injurious to your interests. I shall need, therefore, all the indulgence I have heretofore experienced—the want of it will certainly not lessen with increasing years. I shall need, too, the favor of that Being in whose hands we are, who led our forefathers, as Israel of old, from their native land, and planted them in a country flowing with all the necessaries and comforts of life; who has covered our infancy with his providence, and our riper years with his wisdom and power; and to whose goodness I ask you to join with me in supplications, that he will so enlighten the minds of your servants, guide their councils, and prosper their measures, that whatsoever they do, shall result in your good, and shall secure to you the peace, friendship, and approbation of all nations." (Ibid.)

105   "I shall need, too"   Ibid.

105 "It is not a little surprising"   Mayer, *A Son of Thunder,* 166–170. Mayer wrote: "Patrick Henry bought and sold his share of slaves, and fears of slave uprisings filled his neighborhood as they did any other. . . . He was a man skilled at political gesture, brave in defiance of convention, but on the question of slavery he would follow the common path of least resistance and, like his contemporaries, only squirm in private agony about what he knew to be a public wrong." (Ibid.)

106 "Righteousness is easy"   Arthur M. Schlesinger, Jr. *A Life in the Twentieth Century: Innocent Beginnings, 1917–1950* (Boston, 2000), 311.

106 "Shall we hold the sword"   Moore, ed. *The Patriot Preachers of the American Revolution,* 285–286.

106 in 1807 the British banned   James Trager, *People's Chronology* (New York, 1992), 366.

107 in 1833 abolished slavery   Ibid., 412.

107 apparently less than enthusiastic   Jacob Rader Marcus, *The Handsome Young Priest in the Black Gown: The Personal World of Gershom Seixas* (Cincinnati, 1970), 13.

107 "To the citizens at large"   Ibid.

108 Seixas's rise in the clerical and   Ibid., 22–24. See also Sarna, *American Judaism,* 40.

108 struck a medal in his honor   Marcus, *The Handsome Young Priest,* 26.

108 Christian oaths were still in effect   Borden, *Jews, Turks, and Infidels,* 23–52.

108 North Carolina was an early field   Sarna and Dalin, eds. *Religion and State in the American Jewish Experience,* 82–85. See also Joseph L. Blau and Salo W. Baron, eds. *The Jews of the United States, 1790–1840: A Documentary History,* I (New York, 1963), 28–32.

108 "Governments only concern"   Sarna and Dalin, eds. *Religion and State in the American Jewish Experience,* 84.

108 "Will you drive from your shores"   Ibid.

109 no one could "subscribe more sincerely"   Ibid., 85

109 by 1840, twenty-one of the nation's   Sarna and Dalin, eds. *Religion and State in the American Jewish Experience,* 4.

109 a time of religious revival   Daniel Feller, *The Jacksonian Promise: America, 1815–1840* (Baltimore, 1995), 1–32, describes the nationalist sentiment of the age; Feller's account of religion, 95–117, is also illuminating. See also Butler, *Awash in a Sea of Faith,* 225–256, a fascinating overview of America's religious experience from the post-Revolutionary period to the years before the Civil War, and Arthur M. Schlesinger, Jr., *The Age of Jackson* (Boston, 1950).

109 Ezra Stiles Ely, preached a controversial   Joseph L. Blau, " 'The Chris-

tian Party in Politics,' " *The Review of Religion,* XI (November, 1946), 18–36. See also Bertram Wyatt-Brown, "Prelude to Abolitionism: Sabbatarian Politics and the Rise of the Second Party System," *The Journal of American History,* LVIII (June, 1971), 323–326. John F. Marszalek, *The Petticoat Affair,* is also interesting on Ely and his (largely unsuccessful) maneuverings in Andrew Jackson's Washington.

109   "Every ruler should be an avowed"   Ezra Stiles Ely, *The Duty of Christian Freemen to Elect Christian Rulers: A Discourse* (Philadelphia, 1828). As Joseph Blau noted, Ely anticipated objections to his case. "It deprives no man of his right for me to prefer a Christian to an Infidel," Ely said. "If Infidels were the most numerous electors, they would doubtless elect men of their own sentiments; and unhappily such men not infrequently get into power in this country, in which ninety-nine hundredths of the people are believers in the divine origin and authority of the Christian religion. . . . Have we not as much liberty to be supporters of the Christian cause by our votes, as others have to support anti-Christian men and measures?" (Blau, " 'The Christian Party in Politics,' " 24.)

The Ely "Christian rulers" episode came at a time when Christians in America were seeing more and more connections between religion and politics. (See Charles I. Foster, *An Errand of Mercy: The Evangelical United Front, 1790–1837* [Chapel Hill, NC, 1960.]) Foster wrote: "As the 1840s approached, the idea of God's government, under which American liberty prospered, fused naturally with the more nationalistic notion of manifest destiny. God's government served best as a vague, general assumption because of its conflict with the secularism of the founding fathers and its threat to freedom. Whenever it found explicit expression and application it caused trouble." (Ibid., 56.) The missionary work of the American Bible Society, the American Sunday-School Union, and later campaigns for Sunday laws and to suspend Sunday mails (in deference to the Christian Sabbath) were all factors in American life from roughly the Age of Jackson through Prohibition.

For strong treatments of these subjects, see, for instance: Foster, *An Errand of Mercy*; Gaines M. Foster, *Moral Reconstruction: Christian Lobbyists and the Federal Legislation of Morality, 1865–1920* (Chapel Hill, NC, 2002); Jacoby, *Freethinkers,* 78–81; and Schlesinger, *The Age of Jackson,* 137–140. Schlesinger is particularly good on the fight over the Sunday mails, in which Kentucky senator Richard M. Johnson wrote what Schlesinger called "a resounding statement of religious liberty." In arguing against the notion that the government should, in effect, sanctify the Christian Sabbath by the legislative act of suspending a government service on that day, Johnson wrote:

"It is not the legitimate province of the legislature to determine what religion is true, or what false. Our government is a civil, and not a religious institution." (Ibid., 139.) Sarna and Dalin, eds. *Religion and State in the American Jewish Experience,* 139–165, is also illuminating. As Jacoby pointed out in *Freethinkers,* a reduction in Sunday mail delivery ultimately came "for nonreligious reasons, after the 1844 invention of the telegraph provided a more efficient form of business communication." (Ibid., 80.)

110   "All true Christians love each other"   Andrew Jackson, *The Papers of Andrew Jackson,* ed. Sam B. Smith and Harriet Chappell Owsley, vol. 6, ed. Harold D. Moser and J. Clint Clifft (Knoxville, TN, 2002), 358–359.

110   "Amongst the greatest blessings"   Ibid., 358.

110   to be able to say he   James Parton, *The Life of Andrew Jackson,* III (Boston, 1866), 101. Parton reported the following scene between Andrew and Rachel Jackson: "One Sunday morning, a communion Sunday, in 1826 or 1827, as they were walking toward the little Hermitage church, she besought him to dally no longer with his sense of duty, but, then and there, that very hour, in their own little church, to renounce the world and all its pomps and vanities, and partake of the communion with her. He answered, 'My dear, if I were to do that now, it would be said, all over the country, that I had done it for the sake of political effect. My enemies would all say so. I can not do it *now,* but I promise you that when once more I am clear of politics I will join the church.' " (Ibid.) Which he did: see Ibid., 647–648.

110   Joseph Smith founded the Church of   Richard Lyman Bushman, *Joseph Smith: Rough Stone Rolling* (New York, 2005). See also R. Laurence Moore, *Religious Outsiders and the Making of Americans* (New York, 1986), 25–47.

110   The trouble had begun in Quebec   Parton, *Life of Andrew Jackson,* vol. 3, 418–420.

110   Forty-two of the passengers   Ibid., 419.

110   the bacterium *Vibrio cholerae,* which strikes   *Shorter Oxford English Dictionary on Historical Principles,* vol. 1 (New York, 2002), 400.

110   hit New York with such ferocity   Parton, *Life of Andrew Jackson,* vol. 3, 419.

110   In June, Clay proposed   Robert V. Remini, *Henry Clay: Statesman for the Union* (New York, 1991), 396–397.

111   was good politics   Remini, *Henry Clay: Statesman for the Union,* 397.

111   A woman styling herself   Henry Clay, *The Papers of Henry Clay,* ed. James F. Hopkins and Mary W. M. Hargreaves, vol. 8, *Candidate, Compromiser, Whig: March 5, 1829–December 31, 1836,* ed. Robert Seager II and Melba Porter Hay (Lexington, KY 1984), 549.

111   he too believed in "the efficacy of prayer"   Andrew Jackson, *Correspondence of Andrew Jackson,* ed. John Spencer Bassett (Washington, D.C., 1929), 4: 447.

111   "I could not do otherwise"   Ibid.

111   "It is the province"   Ibid.

112   "I am no sectarian"   Ibid., 256.

112   was prepared to veto Clay's   Robert V. Remini, *Andrew Jackson and the Course of American Freedom, 1822–1832* (New York, 1981), 361.

112   the resolution was tabled in the House   Remini, *Henry Clay: Statesman for the Union,* 397. John Quincy Adams moved that the bill be tabled. (Ibid.)

112   Jackson put down a potential rebellion   William W. Freehling, *Prelude to Civil War: The Nullification Controversy in South Carolina, 1816–1836* (New York, 1965) is an excellent account.

112   the tax issue was really a stand-in   Ibid.

113   "The nullifiers in the South"   Jackson, *Correspondence of Andrew Jackson,* 5: 56. The letter was to Jackson's Tennessee friend and confidant John Coffee.

CHAPTER THREE: LET US DIE TO MAKE MEN FREE

114   "I now leave"   Lincoln, *Speeches and Writings,* 199.

114   "There is a serene Providence"   Ralph Waldo Emerson, *The Essential Writings of Ralph Waldo Emerson,* ed. Brooks Atkinson (New York, 2000), 833.

114   In a February 1861 stop   Lincoln, *Speeches and Writings,* 213–214.

115   Two weeks later   Ibid., 223.

115   President Jefferson Davis had called   Shelby Foote, *The Civil War: A Narrative, Fort Sumter to Perryville* (New York, 1958), 40–41.

115   "Reverently let us"   Ibid.

116   "The will of God prevails"   Lincoln, *Speeches and Writings,* 359. Lincoln secretary John Hay found the document among Lincoln's papers after the president's death and dated it around September 1862. (Ronald C. White, Jr., *Lincoln's Greatest Speech: The Second Inaugural* [New York, 2002], 209.) For discussions of Lincoln's faith and theological views, see, for instance, Allen C. Guelzo, *Abraham Lincoln: Redeemer President* (Grand Rapids, MI, 1999), a fascinating account; David Herbert Donald, *Lincoln* (New York, 1995), 15, 33, 48–49, 74–75, 114, 337, 514–515, 566–568; White, *Lincoln's Greatest Speech,* 96–97, 98, 121, 122–128, 144–149, 163, 167–168, 172–173, 179, 193, 194, 201, 202–203, 210.

116   in a meeting of his Cabinet   Wolf, *The Almost Chosen People,* 17–20. See also Foote, *The Civil War: A Narrative, Fort Sumter to Perryville,* 704–710.

116   a vicious and frightening   Foote, *The Civil War: A Narrative, Fort Sumter to Perryville,* 685–700.

117   According to Treasury Secretary   Wolf, *The Almost Chosen People,* 18–19.

117   "The Rebel Army is now"   Ibid., 19.

117   Chase's account is supported   Ibid., 17–20.

117   Secretary of the Navy   Ibid., 19.

117   "He had, he said"   Ibid.

117   "We might think"   Ibid.

117   Tocqueville heard an American clergyman   Tocqueville, *Democracy in America,* 277. Also fascinating is Butler, *Awash in a Sea of Faith,* 293–295.

118   On Saturday, March 4, 1865, standing at the East Front   Donald, *Lincoln,* 565–568. For close analysis of the second inaugural, there is the excellent book by Ronald White, cited above. For an insightful discussion of the role religion played in the ranks on both the Union and Confederate sides, see James M. McPherson, *For Cause & Comrades: Why Men Fought in the Civil War* (New York, 1997), particularly 62–76.

118   "One eighth of the whole population"   Lincoln, *Speeches and Writings,* 686–687.

119   "Let us have faith that right makes might"   Ibid., 130.

120   "If we shall suppose that American slavery"   Ibid., 687.

120   "any departure from those divine attributes"   Ibid.

120   "Fondly do we hope"   Ibid.

121   the Nineteenth Psalm   Psalm 19:9 (KJV).

121   Eleven days later, answering a congratulatory message   Ibid., 689.

121   "This was their majestic interpretation"   Wolf, *The Almost Chosen People,* 96–97.

122   "somewhat pompous and cocksure"   Ibid., 128–129.

122   being told of the nation's prayers   Ibid., 122.

122   "I feel how weak"   Ibid., 123–124.

123   "If slavery is not wrong"   Lincoln, *Speeches and Writings, 1859–1865,* 585.

123   "as God gives us to see the right"   Ibid., 687.

124   "The devil"   William Shakespeare, *The Merchant of Venice,* Act I, Scene iii.

124   Abolitionists cited Exodus and Deuteronomy   John R. McKivigan and Mitchell Snay, eds. *Religion and the Antebellum Debate over Slavery* (Athens, GA, 1998), 8. See also ibid., 70–71, and James Oakes, *The Ruling Race: A History of American Slaveholders* (New York, 1982), 96–122. In *Religion and the Antebellum Debate over Slavery,* Robert P. Forbes sums up the

biblical debate about slavery well: "To the contemporary reader, the Bible's position on slavery is ambiguous and contradictory. On the one hand, a host of passages paint the institution in a negative light and impose stiff sanctions on certain practices related to it. Most notably on the antislavery side of the ledger, the book of Exodus provides a classic paradigm of the passage from slavery to freedom. Deuteronomy 24:7 condemns 'man-stealing' as a capital offense, and another passage forbids the Israelites to return an escaped slave to his master (23:15–16). On the proslavery side, however, both the Hebrew Scriptures and the New Testament portray societies not only tolerant of, but economically dependent upon slave labor; the institution is never condemned outright, even by Jesus, while Saint Paul explicitly enjoins slaves' obedience. In a pitched battle of exegesis, as generations of controversy would prove, pro- and antislavery controversialists could generally match each other verse for verse and interpretation for interpretation." (McKivigan and Snay, eds. *Religion and the Antebellum Debate over Slavery*, 71.)

124   Pro-slavery advocates had their own biblical ammunition   McKivigan and Snay, eds. *Religion and the Antebellum Debate over Slavery*, 15–16. See also ibid., 42–44. For an excellent discussion of the religious defense of slavery, see also Mitchell Snay, *Gospel of Disunion: Religion and Separatism in the Antebellum South* (Chapel Hill, NC, 1997), 53–109.

124   Saint Paul's admonitions for slaves to obey their masters   McKivigan and Snay, eds. *Religion and the Antebellum Debate over Slavery*, 71, 113; and 145–149.

124   "ye are all one in Christ Jesus"   Galatians 3:28 (KJV). The full verse reads: "There is neither Jew nor Greek, there is neither bond nor free, there is neither male nor female: for ye are all one in Christ Jesus."

124   Devereux Jarratt, an Anglican priest, represented   McKivigan and Snay, eds. *Religion and the Antebellum Debate over Slavery*, 41.

124   "Upon the whole"   Ibid.

125   During the summer of 1832   John W. Blassingame, John R. McKivigan, and Peter P. Hinks, eds. *Narrative of the Life of Frederick Douglass, An American Slave Written by Himself* (New Haven, CT, 2001), 43.

125   "I was disappointed"   Ibid.

125   "Prior to his conversion"   Ibid.

125   a model of public piety   Ibid., 44.

125   woman who had been   Ibid., 44–45.

125   "Henny"   Ibid., 44.

125   After tying her up   Ibid.

125   " 'He that knoweth his master's will' "   Ibid., 44. Douglass's quotation is a slight paraphrase of Luke 12:47 (KJV): "And that servant, which knew his

lord's will, and prepared not *himself*, neither did according to his will, shall be beaten with many *stripes*."

126   the Supreme Court appeal of slaves   Leonard L. Richards, *The Life and Times of Congressman John Quincy Adams* (New York, 1986), 135–139.

126   "I find impulses"   John Quincy Adams Diary, March 29, 1841, Adams Family Papers, Massachusetts Historical Society, Boston.

127   the seventeenth-century battle between the Catholic hierarchy and Galileo George Weigel, *Witness to Hope: The Biography of John Paul II* (New York, 1999), 629–631, is a wise and judicious telling of the Galileo episode. On October 31, 1992, John Paul II received the report of a papal commission on the Galileo case, saying that the church had made an "objective error" by refusing to allow Galileo's work to be taught. Weigel wrote: "What had been learned from this experience? It could not be blithely assumed, the Pope said, that something like this would never happen again. The Church was not going away, and neither was science. . . . History, literary studies, biblical interpretation, philosophy, and theology had all had to reexamine their procedures and their age-old assumptions because of the scientific method. . . . In confronting scientific advances, theologians and pastors 'ought to show a genuine boldness, avoiding the double trap of a hesitant attitude and of hasty judgment' about new scientific discoveries. It was essential for theologians 'to keep themselves informed of scientific advances in order to examine . . . whether or not there are reasons for taking them into account in their reflection or for introducing changes in their teaching.' At the same time, the Pope proposed, everyone should recognize that the Galileo affair had become a 'sort of myth' which had helped to 'anchor a number of scientists of good faith in the idea that there was an incompatibility between the spirit of science and its rules of research . . . and the Christian faith.' That, in turn, had led to 'a tragic mutual incomprehension,' based on the notion of 'a fundamental opposition between science and faith.' That could not be true, for as Pope Leo XIII had written, 'Truth cannot contradict truth.' If that seemed to be happening, a mistake had been made somewhere. There were different ways of knowing the truth about the human person and the human place in the cosmos. A genuine humanism respected that diversity, and celebrated the plurality of intellectual methods necessary to probe the human condition in its marvelous complexity. Science and theology were 'two realms of knowledge' that should not regard themselves as locked inexorably in opposition." (Ibid., 630–631.)

127   "If Scripture cannot err"   John Paul II, "Lessons of the Galileo Case," *Origins* 22:22 (November 12, 1992), 372.

127 "If it happens that the authority of Sacred Scripture"   Ibid., 369–373; the quotation from Augustine is found on 372.

128 "The struggle of today"   Lincoln, *Speeches and Writings*, 297.

129 an organization of Christians   Foster, *Moral Reconstruction*, 2. The organization went by different names through the years. According to Foster, it began life as the National Association for the Amendment of the Constitution and ultimately became the National Reform Association. (Ibid.)

130 In Xenia, Ohio, and Sparta, Illinois   Ibid., 22.

130 on Wednesday, February 10, 1864   Ibid.

130 "We, the people of the United States"   Ibid. For discussions of the Christian Amendment, see also Borden, *Jews, Turks, and Infidels*, 66–74; Mittleman, Sarna, and Licht, eds. *Jews and the American Public Square*, 53–54; Sarna and Dalin, eds. *Religion and State*, 134–136, 167–174.

130 Lincoln met   Borden, *Jews, Turks, and Infidels*, 69.

130 "Gentlemen"   Ibid.

130 chairman of the House Judiciary Committee   Foster, *Moral Reconstruction*, 22–23.

130 "unnecessary and injudicious"   Ibid., 22.

130 in 1862, he agreed to open military chaplaincies   Sarna and Dalin, eds. *Religion and State in the American Jewish Experience*, 129–131.

131 Grant, then headquartered in Mississippi   Sarna, *American Judaism*, 120.

131 General Order 11, which expelled Jews   Ibid.

131 "Jews, as a class" were responsible   Ibid., 120–121.

131 Lincoln had the order revoked   Ibid., 121. Sarna reported a "revealing but unverifiable later tradition" in which one of the expelled Jews, Cesar Kaskel of Paducah, Kentucky, had the following exchange with Lincoln: "And so the children of Israel were driven from the happy land of Canaan?" Lincoln said. "Yes, and that is why we have come unto Father Abraham's bosom, asking protection," Kaskel said. "And this protection they shall have at once," Lincoln replied. It is doubtful such a conversation took place, but the fact that the tradition took shape and endured suggests how highly many American Jews regarded Lincoln. (Ibid.)

131 "to condemn a class is"   Ibid.

131 the Reconstruction loyalty oath   Sarna and Dalin, eds. *Religion and State in the American Jewish Experience*, 8.

131 Walt Whitman recalled years later   Walt Whitman, *Complete Poetry and Collected Prose* (New York, 1982), 1041.

131 took place on Good Friday   Thomas Reed Turner, *Beware the People Weeping: Public Opinion and the Assassination of Abraham Lincoln* (Baton

Rouge, LA, 1982), 77–89. Turner wrote: "Because Lincoln was assassinated on Good Friday, many religious parallels were drawn. Several ministers [said] . . . the assassination was the blackest crime, save one, that had ever been committed in the world. The exception was the Crucifixion upon Calvary." (Ibid., 82–83.)

131 In Hartford, Connecticut, the Baptist minister C. B. Crane said   Guelzo, *Abraham Lincoln*, 440. For reaction to the assassination, see also Carolyn L. Harrell, *When the Bells Tolled for Lincoln: Southern Reaction to the Assassination* (Macon, GA, 1997).

132 "We bewail the sudden removal from our midst"   Prayers on the death of Abraham Lincoln, Jacques Judah Lyons Collection, Box 6, American Jewish Historical Society.

132 "probably it is to be my lot"   Guelzo, *Abraham Lincoln*, 155–156.

132 "My Lord and my God!"   John 20:28 (KJV).

132 to "acknowledge the existence and supremacy of God"   Tim Page, ed. *What's God Got to Do with It?* 30.

133 Like Jefferson, he was a kind of Deist   Robert Seager II, *And Tyler Too: A Biography of John & Julia Gardiner Tyler* (New York, 1963), 109.

133 "The person who is a stranger to sickness"   Oliver Perry Chitwood, *John Tyler: Champion of the Old South* (New York, 1939), 434–435.

134 "the person who justly contemplates"   Seager, *And Tyler Too,* 109.

134 a spirit of religious tolerance   Ibid., 108–109.

134 spoke of "Christian people"   Sarna and Dalin, eds. *Religion and State in the American Jewish Experience,* 121.

134 A Jewish American, Jacob Ezekiel   Ibid.

134 "to exclude"   Ibid., 122.

134 "The United States have adventured"   Ibid., 123.

135 the place of Catholicism in American life   Hamburger, *Separation of Church and State,* 191–251.

136 the anti-Catholic, anti-immigrant Know-Nothing party   Ibid., 218–219.

136 *And shall our Common Schools*   Ibid., 224.

136 the poet Matthew Arnold   Lionel Trilling, *Matthew Arnold* (New York, 1982), 36.

137 *The Sea of Faith*   Jerome Hamilton Buckley and George Benjamin Woods, eds. *Poetry of the Victorian Period* (Chicago, IL, 1965), 499.

138 had really begun around 1678   Charlotte Allen, *The Human Christ: The Search for the Historical Jesus* (New York, 1998), 74–75. I have drawn on Allen's excellent book for my discussion of the role biblical criticism played in American faith.

138 the Vatican would later call   *Dei Verbum,* available on the Vatican website,

is the church's "Dogmatic Constitution on Divine Revelation." Promulgated by Pope Paul VI on November 18, 1965, *Dei Verbum* is, in the words of the Second Vatican Council, the Catholic Church's "authentic doctrine on divine revelation and how it is handed on, so that by hearing the message of salvation the whole world may believe, by believing it may hope, and by hoping it may love." The document says that "everything asserted by the inspired authors or sacred writers must be held to be asserted by the Holy Spirit" and scripture therefore "must be acknowledged as teaching solidly, faithfully and without error that truth which God wanted put into sacred writings for the sake of salvation." It goes on to make this point: "However, since God speaks in Sacred Scripture through men in human fashion, the interpreter of Sacred Scripture, in order to see clearly what God wanted to communicate to us, should carefully investigate what meaning the sacred writers really intended, and what God wanted to manifest by means of their words. To search out the intention of the sacred writers, attention should be given, among other things, to 'literary forms.' For truth is set forth and expressed differently in texts which are variously historical, prophetic, poetic, or of other forms of discourse. The interpreter must investigate what meaning the sacred writer intended to express and actually expressed in particular circumstances by using contemporary literary forms in accordance with the situation of his own time and culture. For the correct understanding of what the sacred author wanted to assert, due attention must be paid to the customary and characteristic styles of feeling, speaking and narrating which prevailed at the time of the sacred writer, and to the patterns men normally employed at that period in their everyday dealings with one another."

138   Johann Albrecht Bengel   Allen, *The Human Christ,* 75.

138   Deists such as Voltaire   Ibid., 75–77.

138   George Eliot's English translation   Ibid., 160–164.

139   Owen Chadwick plumbed   Owen Chadwick, *The Secularization of the European Mind in the Nineteenth Century* (New York, 1975).

139   "Let us suppose ourselves back"   Ibid., 182.

140   the Scopes Trial in Dayton   Edward J. Larson, *Summer for the Gods: The Scopes Trial and America's Continuing Debate over Science and Religion* (Cambridge, MA, 1997), is a particularly strong book on the subject.

140   the possibility of Anglican bishops' coming   Gaustad, *Proclaim Liberty Throughout All the Land,* 16–20.

140   "bishops wielded"   Ibid., 17.

140   "the very thought"   Ibid.

140   one of the most important revivalists   Nathan O. Hatch, *The Democratization of American Christianity* (New Haven, CT, 1989), 196–201, captures

Finney's religious importance well. Three other books on Finney are of particular note: Charles E. Hambrick-Stowe, *Charles G. Finney and the Spirit of American Evangelicalism* (Grand Rapids, MI, 1996); Charles Finney, *Experiencing the Presence of God* (New Kensington, PA, 2000); and Helen Wessel, ed. *The Autobiography of Charles Finney* (Minneapolis, 1977).

140 a fascinating, tireless figure   Noll, *A History of Christianity in the United States and Canada,* 174–178.

140 In 1821, he was studying law   Ibid., 175.

140 the "Holy Spirit descended"   Jon Butler, Grant Wacker, and Randall Balmer, *Religion in American Life: A Short History* (New York, 2003), 196.

141 An architect of what we think of   Noll, *A History of Christianity in the United States and Canada,* 174–176.

141 "succeeded in joining"   Ibid., 174. He also, Noll wrote, "formalized ties between conservative theology and industrial wealth that still characterize evangelical culture." (Ibid., 174–175.)

141 abolition to temperance to coeducation   Ibid., 174.

141 "the great business"   William Martin, *With God on Our Side: The Rise of the Religious Right in America* (New York, 1996), 5.

141 moved from New York   Noll, *A History of Christianity in the United States and Canada,* 178.

141 "so pressed for funds"   Ibid.

141 "if help did not come"   Ibid.

141 "thought the Christian life"   Ibid., 9. See also Marty, *Pilgrims in Their Own Land,* 352–353.

141 supported Prohibition, called on presidents   Ibid., 9–10.

141 attacked progressive reform   Marty, *Pilgrims in Their Own Land,* 352.

141 "I tell you"   Ibid., 370.

141 a "bunch of pretzel-chewing"   Ibid.

142 Father Charles Coughlin   Marty, *Pilgrims in Their Own Land,* 396–400, offers a fine description of Coughlin's rise and fall.

142 *Fortune* said in 1934   Ibid., 396.

142 supporting Franklin Roosevelt   Martin, *With God on Our Side,* 19.

142 turned virulently anti-Semitic   Ibid.

142 Gerald B. Winrod followed a similar arc   Ibid., 19–20.

142 shifting from the fight   Marty, *Pilgrims in Their Own Land,* 396.

142 his publication *Defender*   Martin, *With God on Our Side,* 19–20.

142 The movement was born   McGraw and Formicola, eds. *Taking Religious Pluralism Seriously: Spiritual Politics on America's Sacred Ground,* 196–198.

142 advocate of the Madison-Jefferson view   Ibid., 199.

142   a Baptist who wrote in 1779   Ibid., 197.
142   "Nothing can be true religion"   Ibid., 198.
142   Grant went to Des Moines   Hamburger, *Separation of Church and State*, 322.
142   "If we are to have another contest"   Ibid.
143   James G. Blaine . . . took specific legislative action   Ibid., 297–98.
143   The separation argument   As noted above, I am indebted to Hamburger's *Separation of Church and State* for this line of thinking.
144   America was "a state without a church"   Mittleman, Licht, and Sarna, eds. *Jews and the American Public Square*, 50.
145   "shall be judged"   *The New York Times*, July 3, 1907.
145   showed up early   *The New York Times*, September 30, 1907.
145   carry the Bible along on camping trips while at Harvard   William Henry Harbaugh, *Power and Responsibility: The Life and Times of Theodore Roosevelt* (New York, 1961), 214.
145   "Some folks"   Ibid.
145   "I am charged with being a preacher"   Pierard and Linder, *Civil Religion & the Presidency*, 305.
145   motives were religious, not secular   Elting E. Morison, ed. *The Letters of Theodore Roosevelt*, vol. 5 (Cambridge, Mass., 1952), 842.
145   "dangerously close to sacrilege"   Ibid.
145   had begun to appear on American money   Jacoby, *Freethinkers*, 106–108.
145   "from every standpoint"   Morison, ed. *The Letters of Theodore Roosevelt*, vol. 5, 842.
146   in the words of one of his biographers   Nathan Miller, *Theodore Roosevelt: A Life* (New York, 1992), 427.
146   "It is a motto"   Morrison, ed. *The Letters of Theodore Roosevelt*, vol. 5, 842.
146   a New York minister   Ibid.
146   "But it seems to me"   Ibid. An important part of this issue for Roosevelt was the "spirit of levity" with wich the motto was often treated in political battles over money. "Everyone must remember the innumerable cartoons and articles based on phrases like 'In God we trust for the other eight cents'; 'In God we trust for the short weight'; . . . and so forth and so forth. Surely I am well within bounds when I say that a use of the phrase which invites constant levity of this type is most undesirable." (Ibid., 842–843.)
146   "I know not how philosophers"   Harbaugh, *Power and Responsibility*, 215.
146   "but be ye doers of the word"   James 1:22 (KJV).
146   a decision he would come to regret   Patricia O'Toole, *When Trumpets*

Call: Theodore Roosevelt After the White House (New York, 2005), is an excellent study of TR's restless, and largely unhappy, post-presidency.

147 "There is considerable" Louis W. Koenig, *Bryan: A Political Biography of William Jennings Bryan* (New York, 1971), 448. Koenig wrote: "Many a cleric criticized Taft for being not a Christian but a Unitarian. Indignantly they stressed that no man who denied the divinity of Christ was fit to be President of the United States." (Ibid.)

147 "Think of the United States" Paul W. Glad, *The Trumpet Soundeth: William Jennings Bryan and His Democracy* (Lincoln, NE, 1960), 117.

147 sought to reassure "Will" Elting E. Morison, ed. *The Letters of Theodore Roosevelt,* vol. 6 (Cambridge, MA, 1952), 1200. Another line of assault on Taft turned on his alleged pro-Catholic bias, an impression produced, Roosevelt believed, by the fact that Taft "acted fairly toward the Catholic Church in Philippine matters [as governor-general]." (Ibid., 1285.)

147 "I would simply say" Ibid, 1200.

147 "that the same attack" Ibid.

147 "If there is one thing" Morison, ed. *The Letters of Theodore Roosevelt,* 1290. The letter, dated October 16, 1908, was to Starr H. Beatty. TR's first draft of this letter, which is published in Ibid., 1289–1290, is even more colorful.

147 "In my own Cabinet" Ibid., 1290.

148 "Discrimination against the holder" Ibid., 1334. The letter, dated November 6, 1908, was to J. C. Martin, whom the editors of the TR correspondence identified as "a piano dealer of Dayton, Ohio."

148 "I believe that this Republic" Ibid., 1335.

149 The city of Gary, Indiana, devised Sarna and Dalin, eds. *Religion and State in the American Jewish Experience,* 19–20.

149 Samuel Schulman, a leading New York Ibid., 20.

150 "Here is the nation" Woodrow Wilson, *The Papers of Woodrow Wilson,* ed. Arthur S. Link (Princeton, NJ, 1978), 28: 25.

150 "It is a fearful thing" Wilson, *The Papers of Woodrow Wilson* (Princeton, NJ, 1983), 41: 526.

150 "My life would not be worth living" "Diary of Nancy Saunders Toy" in Wilson, *The Papers of Woodrow Wilson* (Princeton, NJ, 1980), 32: 8.

151 a moral vision of foreign policy Wilson, *The Papers of Woodrow Wilson* (Princeton, NJ, 1984), 45: 534–539.

151 "The moral climax" Ibid., 539.

151 make the world safe for democracy Wilson, *The Papers of Woodrow Wilson,* 41: 525.

151 William Howard Taft called him Dalin and Kolatch, *The Presidents of the United States and the Jews,* 143.

152 "I am not one of those that have the least anxiety"   Wilson, *The Papers of Woodrow Wilson* (Princeton, NJ, 1993), 68: 469.

CHAPTER FOUR: IMPERFECT THOUGH WE ARE

153 "People are going to die here"   John Lewis with Michael D'Orso, *Walking with the Wind: A Memoir of the Movement* (New York, 1998), 328.

153 "Believing the Bible as I do"   Jerry Falwell, *Strength for the Journey: An Autobiography* (New York, 1987), 290.

153 was a "frustrated clergyman at heart"   James Roosevelt and Sidney Shalett, *Affectionately, F.D.R.: A Son's Story of a Lonely Man* (New York, 1959), 99–101. I have drawn on my *Franklin and Winston: An Intimate Portrait of an Epic Friendship* (New York, 2003), 27–28, for these points about Roosevelt and his ecclesiastical sensibility.

153 The joke in town   John Gunther, *Roosevelt in Retrospect: A Profile in History* (New York, 1950), 79.

154 When Eleanor asked him whether he believed   Gunther, *Roosevelt in Retrospect,* 79. "He was not, as we know, at all introspective, and problems of dogma were miles outside his province; he never explored the why of things, even the giant why of belief itself," wrote Gunther. "He disliked the institutional side of religion; his basic approach was ethical." (Ibid., 78.)

154 He loved the Twenty-third Psalm   Eleanor Roosevelt, *This I Remember* (New York, 1949), 346. "Franklin always felt that a president should consider himself an instrument chosen by the people to do their bidding, but that he should also consider that as president he had an obligation to enlighten and lead the people," Eleanor Roosevelt recalled. (Ibid., 67.) She also said: "I always felt that my husband's religion had something to do with his confidence in himself. As I have said, it was a very simple religion. He believed in God and in his guidance. He felt that human beings were given tasks to perform and with those tasks the ability and strength to put them through. He could pray for help and guidance and have faith in his own judgment as a result. The church services that he always insisted on holding on Inauguration Day, anniversaries and whenever a great crisis impended were the expression of his religious faith. I think this must not be lost sight of in judging his acceptance of responsibility and his belief in his ability to meet whatever crisis had to be met." (Ibid., 69–70.)

154 "I am a Christian"   Frances Perkins, *The Roosevelt I Knew* (New York, 1946), 330.

154 got stuck in his voting booth   Gunther, *Roosevelt in Retrospect,* 80.

154 not, he claimed, "the goddamned thing"   Ibid.

154   "He never talked about"   Eleanor Roosevelt, *This I Remember*, 346–347.

154   His inaugural address   Franklin D. Roosevelt, *The Public Papers and Addresses of Franklin D. Roosevelt*, vol. 2, *The Year of Crisis, 1933* (New York, 1938), 11–16.

155   Charles Peters grew up in Charleston   Charles Peters, *Five Days in Philadelphia* (New York, 2005), 5.

156   "Another source of Roosevelt's faith"   Ibid., 13.

156   "This was certainly true"   Ibid., 13–14.

156   To Peters, whose father spent   Ibid., 14.

156   "Tens of millions of Christians"   Ibid., 14–15.

157   what he called Roosevelt's "Jew Deal"   Michael Beschloss, *The Conquerors: Roosevelt, Truman and the Destruction of Hitler's Germany, 1941–1945* (New York, 2002), 41.

157   Charles Lindbergh blamed the Jews   Meacham, *Franklin and Winston*, 127. The occasion was a speech in Des Moines, Iowa, in September 1941 in which Lindbergh said that "the three most important groups which have been pressing this country toward war are the British, the Jewish and the Roosevelt Administration." See also *The New York Times*, September 12, 1941.

157   "You know this is a Protestant country"   Beschloss, *The Conquerors*, 51.

157   "In the dim past"   Pierard and Linder, *Civil Religion & the Presidency*, 173.

158   "The Christian Faith and the World Crisis"   Reinhold Niebuhr, *Christianity and Crisis: A Bi-Weekly Journal of Christian Opinion*, February 10, 1941.

158   were suffering from utopianism   Ibid.

158   "In our opinion"   Ibid.

159   "Love must be regarded"   Ibid.

160   Roosevelt secretly met with Churchill   There are many accounts of the meeting. I drew on the research I did for my *Franklin and Winston*, which included the original "Order of Service, August 10th, 1941," President's Official File 200-1-R: Trips of the President: Cruise on the USS AUGUSTA, Aug. 1941, Franklin D. Roosevelt Presidential Library and Museum, Hyde Park, New York. See also H. V. Morton, *Atlantic Meeting: An Account of Mr. Churchill's Voyage in H.M.S. Prince of Wales, in August, 1941, and the Conference with President Roosevelt Which Resulted in the Atlantic Charter* (New York, 1943), and Theodore A. Wilson, *The First Summit: Roosevelt & Churchill at Placentia Bay, 1941* (Lawrence, KS, 1991).

160   The Atlantic Charter was   Frank Freidel, *Franklin D. Roosevelt: A Rendezvous with Destiny* (Boston, 1990).

160   "all the men in all the lands"   Ibid., 388.

160 for "aggrandizement, territorial or other"   Ibid., 387.

160 "they respect the right of all"   Ibid.

160 The lesson was from Joshua   "Order of Service, August 10th, 1941," President's Official File 200-1-R: Trips of the President: Cruise on the USS AUGUSTA, Aug. 1941, FDRL. The verse quoted is Joshua 1:9 (KJV).

160 Churchill wept   Morton, *Atlantic Meeting*, 114.

160 "Every word seemed to stir the heart"   Winston S. Churchill, *The Second World War: The Grand Alliance* (Boston, 1950), 432.

160 three hymns   "Order of Service, August 10th, 1941," President's Official File 200-1-R: Trips of the President: Cruise on the USS AUGUSTA, Aug. 1941, FDRL.

161 *O God, our help*   *The English Hymnal*, 450.

161 "If nothing else had happened"   Meacham, *Franklin and Winston*, 116.

161 "Even if it was the Protestant Church militant"   Joseph P. Lash, *Roosevelt and Churchill, 1939–1941: The Partnership That Saved the West* (New York, 1976), 396.

161 "And so, all that is implied"   Max Freedman, ed. *Roosevelt & Frankfurter: Their Correspondence, 1928–1945* (Boston, 1967), 612–613. The letter is dated August 18, 1941; Roosevelt cited it in a press conference when he returned from the meeting.

163 New Year's Day 1942   Edward Randolph Welles, *Pardon, Power, Peace: A Sermon Preached . . . On the Occasion of the National Day of Prayer, January 1st, 1942* (Baltimore, 1942).

163 in cassock and surplice   Details drawn from news photographs of Roosevelt and Churchill at Christ Church, Alexandria, January 1, 1942.

163 "greatest sin"   Welles, *Pardon, Power, Peace*, 6.

163 "Nationally we"   Ibid.

163 "That is not the way"   Ibid., 7.

163 "I believe that this present world struggle"   Ibid., 8–9.

164 "absolute victory"   *The New York Times*, December 9, 1941.

165 "Well now, Max"   Perkins, *The Roosevelt I Knew*, 143.

165 Over the 1941–1942 holidays   The story of the "Declaration by the United Nations" is well told in many places. I drew on Robert E. Sherwood, *Roosevelt and Hopkins: An Intimate History* (New York, 1948), 447–453; Lash, *Roosevelt and Churchill*, 16–20; and my own work in Meacham, *Franklin and Winston*, 156–158, which included an interview with the late Trude Lash, Joseph Lash's widow, who was in the White House at the time of these events.

165 Litvinov had been resisting   Sherwood, *Roosevelt and Hopkins*, 448–449.

165 he wanted "freedom of conscience"   Ibid., 449.

165 Robert Sherwood recalled, saying "[T]he"   Ibid.

166   they were "convinced that"   *The New York Times,* January 3, 1942.

166   Churchill was impressed   Meacham, *Franklin and Winston,* 156–157.
       Churchill's memories of the episode are in his *The Grand Alliance,* 683.

166   The ease with which   Perkins, *The Roosevelt I Knew,* 143.

166   "explains many of the attitudes"   Ibid., 143–144.

166   was "too small"   Pierard and Linder, *Civil Religion & the Presidency,* 181.

166   that "God created man"   Ibid.

167   reminding a Washington's Birthday audience   Sherwood, *Roosevelt and
       Hopkins: An Intimate History,* 503–504. Roosevelt said: "For eight years
       General Washington and his Continental Army were faced continually with
       formidable odds and recurring defeats. Supplies and equipment were lack-
       ing. In a sense, every winter was a Valley Forge. Throughout the Thirteen
       States there existed Fifth Columnists—selfish men, jealous men, fearful
       men, who proclaimed that Washington's cause was hopeless, that he should
       ask for a negotiated peace." (Ibid., 504.)

167   "Tyranny, like hell"   Ibid., 504.

167   dining in the White House   Perkins, *The Roosevelt I Knew,* 146–147.

167   spoke of Dorothy Sayers   Ibid., 147.

167   Talk turned to Søren Kierkegaard   Ibid.

167   Johnson was to plan the 1944 liturgy   Ibid., 148.

167   "Prayer for Our Enemies"   "The Order of the Service for Saturday,
       March 4, 1944, on the Eleventh Anniversary of the Inauguration of Franklin
       D. Roosevelt as President of the United States," Files of St. John's Episcopal
       Church, Lafayette Square, Washington, D.C.

167   The other clergy   Perkins, *The Roosevelt I Knew,* 148.

167   "The White House would never"   Ibid., 148–149.

168   scribbled a note   Ibid., 149.

168   "Very good—I like it"   Ibid.

168   Gathering in the church at 10:30 on the morning   "The Order of the Ser-
       vice for Saturday, March 4, 1944, on the Eleventh Anniversary of the Inau-
       guration of Franklin D. Roosevelt as President of the United States," Files of
       St. John's Episcopal Church, Lafayette Square, Washington, D.C.

168   "Most loving Father"   Ibid.

168   the evenings lovely and moonlit   Geoffrey C. Ward, ed. *Closest Compan-
       ion: The Unknown Story of the Intimate Friendship Between Franklin Roo-
       sevelt and Margaret Suckley* (Boston, 1995), 307–308.

169   that Churchill called "the most complicated"   Martin Gilbert, *Churchill:
       A Life* (New York, 1991), 777.

169   Twenty thousand men might die   Mary Soames, *Clementine Churchill:
       The Biography of a Marriage* (Boston, 1979), 468.

169   six-minute-long appeal   This was the amount of time it took Roosevelt to

read the prayer on D-day; the audio is available at the Franklin D. Roosevelt Presidential Library website at www.fdrlibrary.marist.edu.

169   "Almighty God"   *The New York Times,* June 7, 1944.

171   The White House released the text   Ibid.

171   one hundred million   *Newsweek,* June 19, 1944. See also Stephen E. Ambrose, *D-Day: June 6, 1944: The Climactic Battle of World War II* (New York, 1994), 491.

171   "With uncanny oneness"   *Newsweek,* June 19, 1944, 36.

171   Churches and synagogues   Ibid.

171   A girl knelt in prayer   Ibid.

171   In Covington, Kentucky, women said the rosary   Ibid.

171   A family in Coffeyville, Kansas, fell   Ibid.

171   In Corpus Christi, Texas, the parents   Ibid.

171   "Across the land, generally"   *Time,* June 12, 1944, 21.

172   Roosevelt was preparing his 1941 State of the Union   Samuel I. Rosenman, *Working With Roosevelt* (New York, 1952), 262–265.

172   "Dorothy, take a law"   Ibid., 263.

172   "We must look forward"   Ibid.

172   The section complete, Hopkins objected   Ibid.

172   "That covers"   Ibid.

172   "I'm afraid they'll have to be"   Ibid., 264. Hopkins got the message, and he understood Roosevelt in ways few others did. "You and I are for Roosevelt because he's a great spiritual figure, because he's an idealist, like Wilson, and he's got the guts to drive through against any opposition to those ideals," Hopkins once told Robert Sherwood. "Oh—he sometimes tries to appear tough and cynical and flippant, but that's an act he likes to put on, especially at press conferences. He wants to make the boys think he's hardboiled. Maybe he fools some of them, now and then—but don't ever let him fool you, or you won't be any use to him. You can see the real Roosevelt when he comes out with something like the Four Freedoms. And don't get the idea that those are any catch phrases. *He believes them!* He believes they can be practically attained. That's what you and I have got to remember in everything we may be able to do for him." (Sherwood, *Roosevelt and Hopkins: An Intimate History,* 266.)

172   the day Roosevelt died   There are many fascinating accounts of Roosevelt's last hours and of the world's reaction to his death. See, for instance, Ward, ed. *Closest Companion*; Bernard Asbell, *When F.D.R. Died* (New York, 1961); and James MacGregor Burns, *Roosevelt: The Soldier of Freedom* (New York, 1970).

172   Vice President Harry Truman had been on the job   David McCullough, *Truman* (New York, 1992), 333–340, covers Truman's brief vice presidency.

172   Hitler would not commit suicide until eighteen days later   Martin Gilbert, *The Second World War: A Complete History* (New York, 1989), 680–681.

173   progress on the atomic bomb   McCullough, *Truman,* 289–291, makes the case that Truman understood the broad outlines of the Manhattan Project, quoting both a conversation Truman had with Secretary of War Henry Stimson and a 1943 letter Truman wrote describing "a secret weapon that will be a wonder." (Ibid., 289–290.)

173   "There have been few men"   Ibid., 352.

173   after a lunch on Capitol Hill   Ibid., 353.

173   "Boys, if you ever pray"   Ibid.

173   hedges of his mother's rose garden   Burns, *Roosevelt: The Soldier of Freedom,* 612.

173   "At this moment I have"   McCullough, *Truman,* 360.

173   what Henry Luce called   W. A. Swanberg, *Luce and His Empire* (New York, 1972), 180.

174   Solomon was the son   The story of Saul, David, and Solomon is the central drama of I Samuel, II Samuel, and I Kings 1-11; Solomon dies at the conclusion of I Kings 11.

174   the nation grew more broadly religious   Noll, *A History of Christianity in the United States and Canada,* 438–444; Marty, *Pilgrims in Their Own Land,* 403–405.

174   Justice Hugo Black, the former Klansman   Robert S. Alley, ed. *The Supreme Court on Church and State* (New York, 1988), 37–71, prints the opinions of the justices in *Everson v. Board of Education, 330,* U.S. 1 (1947). For various views on the case, the reemergence of the wall metaphor, and applications of the Establishment Clause, see, for instance: Hamburger, *Separation of Church and State,* 454–478, and Leonard W. Levy, *The Establishment Clause: Religion and the First Amendment* (Chapel Hill, NC, 1994), 149–154.

174   The "establishment of religion" clause of the First Amendment   Alley, ed. *The Supreme Court on Church and State,* 11–15

175   "The First Amendment has erected a wall"   Ibid., 46.

175   In *McCollum v. Board of Education,* an Illinois atheist   Alley, ed. *The Supreme Court on Church and State,* 173–183, prints the McCollum opinions. For a full account and analysis of the case, see also Hamburger, *Separation of Church and State,* 472–478. Philip Hamburger noted the ironies of the decision. "Whereas in Everson Protestants had sought to prevent children in Catholic schools from receiving state aid for busing, in McCollum an atheist aimed to prevent mostly Protestant children from receiving time-released religious instruction in public schools," he wrote. "It was a pattern

already evident in the nineteenth century, when Protestants initially popularized separation, and then anti-Christian secularists and other theological liberals insisted upon their expanded understanding of it. This time, however, because of greater popular support and because of the substitution of the judicial for the amendment process, a relatively secular version prevailed." (Ibid.)

175   proposed adding Jesus to the Constitution   Kramnick and Moore, *The Godless Constitution,* 148.

175   offered in 1947 and again in 1954   Ibid.

175   Billy Graham was filling stadiums   William Martin, *A Prophet With Honor: The Billy Graham Story* (New York, 1991), 89–120, describes the beginnings of Graham's popular ministry.

175   making his first visits   Billy Graham, *Just As I Am: The Autobiography of Billy Graham* (San Francisco, 1997), xvii–xxiii, is Graham's self-deprecating account of his appointment with President Truman.

175   "Jesus Christ! We forgot the prayer!"   William Bragg Ewald, Jr., *Eisenhower the President: Crucial Days, 1951–1960* (Englewood Cliffs, NJ, 1981), 13.

175   Congress voted to make "In God"   Richard H. Jones, " 'In God We Trust' and the Establishment Clause," 31 *Journal of Church and State* (Autumn 1989): 381.

175   "under God" was added to the Pledge   Derek H. Davis, "The Pledge of Allegiance and American Values," 45 *Journal of Church and State* (Autumn 2003): 657. See also Lee Canipe, "Under God and Anti Communist: How the Pledge of Allegiance Got Religion in Cold War America," 45 *Journal of Church and State* (Spring 2003): 305.

175   what was called "Piety Along the Potomac"   Will Herberg, *Protestant-Catholic-Jew: An Essay in American Religious Sociology* (Garden City, NY, 1955), 93. The phrase is William Lee Miller's in "Piety Along the Potomac," *The Reporter,* August 17, 1954.

176   *"faith in faith"*   Herberg, *Protestant-Catholic-Jew,* 89.

176   "the American Way of Life"   Ibid., 74–75.

176   "commends itself"   Ibid., 75.

176   "Honesty, decency, fairness"   Pierard and Linder, *Civil Religion & the Presidency,* 200.

176   At the Waldorf-Astoria   *The New York Times,* December 23, 1952. I am also indebted to a witty and illuminating piece on the strange history of the Eisenhower quotation by the scholar Patrick Henry. See Patrick Henry, " 'And I Don't Care What It Is': The Tradition-History of a Civil Religion Proof-Text," *The Journal of the American Academy of Religion,* 1981 XLIX: 35–49.

176   thinking how "hopeless"   Ibid.

177   "our form of government"   Ibid.

177   "Our ancestors who"   Ibid.

177   growing in popularity   Mark Silk, "Notes on the Judeo-Christian Tradition in America," *American Quarterly* 36 (Spring 1984), 65. See also Herberg, *Protestant-Catholic-Jew,* 82–98. (Herberg's footnotes are a great joy); Herberg, "Judaism and Christianity: Their Unity and Difference," *The Journal of Bible and Religion* 21 (April, 1953), 67–79; and Paul Tillich, "Is There a Judeo-Christian Tradition?" *Judaism: A Quarterly Journal of Jewish Life and Thought* 1 (April 1952), 106–109. In crisp and clear prose, Tillich answers the question he posed in the affirmative while also noting the fundamental differences between the two. Jews and Christians share a belief in one God, a God who is righteous and just, and history is the story of the journey toward God: "God is manifest through the historical event. In the history of mankind, He [God] fights and conquers the anti-divine forces. History has an end in the double sense of goal and finish. In a unique, irreversible process, history drives towards this end, which combines ultimate judgment and ultimate fulfillment, the two great themes of Jewish-Christian eschatology. Nobody, I think, can doubt the justification of the hypen [between "Judeo" and "Christian"] at this point." (Ibid., 108.) On the other hand, Tillich noted, Christians believe the kingdom of God has arrived "though visible only for the Spiritual eye"; in Judaism, Tillich wrote, "*expectation* is the basic attitude. . . . Those differences cannot be denied and must not be underestimated." (Ibid., 109.)

177   dated back to the last year   Silk, "Notes on the Judeo-Christian Tradition in America." *American Quarterly* 36 (Spring 1984), 65.

177   first appeared in the *Literary Guide*   Ibid.

177   George Orwell used the term   Ibid., 66.

177   by 1941, in response to rising anti-Semitism   Ibid.

177   some Jews worried the phrase   Ibid., 68–69. Silk characterized Trude Weiss-Rosmarin's argument in her 1943 book *Judaism and Christianity: The Differences* this way: "Making Jewish-Christian amity depend on a shared religious identity was 'a totalitarian aberration' fundamentally at odds with the pluralistic principles of democracy. Judaism and Christianity were *not* basically one: her book sought to spell out the profound differences between them. She was not the last Jewish writer to perceive in 'Judeo-Christian' a syncretizing threat to the survival of Judaism." (Ibid.)

178   other Jewish leaders   Ibid., 68–71. To make the point about shared values, Silk quoted Julian Morgenstern, president of Reform Judaism's Hebrew Union College, who made the following remarks in 1942: "Today we

realize, as never since Christianity's birth, how intimate are the relations of the two religions, so intimate and insoluble that they are truly, basically one, that they have a common descent, a common vision, hope, mission, face a common foe and a common fate, must achieve a common victory or share a common death." (Ibid., 68.)

178   theological work to chart   In Niebuhr's 1955 *The Self and the Dramas of History*—which Silk described as "his last major theological work"— Niebuhr wrote: "The essence of the Christian faith is drawn from the Hebraic, particularly the prophetic, interpretation of life and history. . . ." (Ibid., 71.) As a historical matter, Jonathan Sarna wrote, the "Judeo-Christian" formulation "entered the lexicon as the standard liberal term for the idea that Western values rest on a religious consensus. In the face of worldwide antisemitic efforts to stigmatize and destroy Judaism, influential Christians and Jews in America labored to uphold it, pushing Judaism from the margins of American religious life toward its very center." (Sarna, *American Judaism*, 267.)

178   "It has pleased the Providence"   Hutson, ed. *The Founders on Religion*, 127.

178   In 1948, the government offered   Sarna, *American Judaism*, 267. I am indebted to Sarna's recounting of the *Dorchester* story, which he called "oft-repeated and somewhat romanticized," but the larger meaning is clear: in the aftermath of the war and the Holocaust, many Americans were looking for ways to dramatize what they held in common, not what separated them. Again, Tillich, writing in 1952, is interesting in this context. Even allowing for the important differences between Jews and Christians, Tillich said, "If some one shaped and nourished by the Hindu or the Buddhist or the Confucian or the Greek tradition were to hear what I have said, would he not be astonished at the identity of structure at all points, and at the identity of content in most? Would he not, if he compared all this with his own tradition, answer the question: Is there a Jewish-Christian tradition?, with an unhesitating and unambiguous, Yes? I think he would!" (Tillich, "Is There a Judeo-Christian Tradition?" *Judaism: A Quarterly Journal of Jewish Life and Thought* 1 [April 1952].)

178   "arm and arm in prayer"   Ibid.

178   "Remember the float"   Miller, "Piety Along the Potomac," *The Reporter*, August 17, 1954, 27.

178   "the content of official religion is bound to be thin"   Ibid.

179   "This is the first principle of democracy"   G. K. Chesterton, *Orthodoxy* (New York, 2001), 43.

179   were quick to take off   *The New York Times*, June 29, 1957.

342 | SOURCE NOTES

180   the Eisenhowers cheerfully skipped   Ibid.

181   the representatives of Saudi Arabia, Afghanistan   Ibid.

181   Departing from his prepared text   Ibid.

181   the American dignitaries' shoes   *The Washington Post,* June 29, 1957.

181   Ted Sorensen could still remember   Author interview with Theodore C.
Sorensen.

181   "The single biggest obstacle"   Ibid.

182   "truly light the world"   John F. Kennedy, *"Let the Word Go Forth": The
Speeches, Statements, and Writings of John F. Kennedy, 1947 to 1963,* comp.
Theodore C. Sorensen (New York, 1988), 14.

182   In a conversation with one of JFK's sisters   Author interview with Arthur
Schlesinger, Jr.

182   "That will be a very short book"   Ibid.

182   "The honest answer is I don't know"   Author interview with Theodore
C. Sorensen.

182   what was called "the religious issue"   Kennedy, *"Let the Word Go Forth,"*
124.

182   a meeting of the American Society   Ibid., 125–130.

182   he said he did not want   Ibid., 125.

182   "I have made it clear"   Ibid., 127.

183   "Can we justify"   Ibid.

183   "I think the voters of Wisconsin"   Ibid.

183   "For voters are more than"   Ibid., 127–128.

183   "I'll be damned"   Robert Dallek, *An Unfinished Life: John F. Kennedy,
1917–1963* (Boston, 2003), 231.

183   a Democratic event in the Bronx   Kennedy, *"Let the Word Go Forth,"* 130.

184   before the Greater Houston Ministerial Association   Ibid., 130–136.

184   "I believe in an America"   Ibid., 131.

186   "When he spoke of human rights"   Author interview with Theodore C.
Sorensen.

186   "Let both sides unite"   Kennedy, *"Let the Word Go Forth,"* 14.

186   "All this will not be finished"   Ibid., 14–15.

186   "Now the trumpet summons us again"   Ibid., 14–15.

187   "rejoicing in hope, patient in tribulation"   The Epistle of Paul to the Romans, 12:12 (KJV).

187   "Be not overcome of evil"   Ibid., 12:21 (KJV).

187   "The allusions to God in his speeches"   Author interview with Theodore
C. Sorensen.

187   Justice Hugo Black leaned forward   *Newsweek,* July 9, 1962.

187   Written by the New York Board   *The New York Times,* June 26, 1962.

187 "Almighty God, we acknowledge"   Ibid.

188 one "composed by government officials"   Ibid.

188 "They put the Negroes in the schools"   Ibid.

188 "the most tragic decision"   *Newsweek*, July 9, 1962.

188 declared the ruling a "disintegration"   Ibid.

188 called for "an amendment to the Constitution"   *The New York Times*, June 27, 1962.

188 "The Supreme Court has made its judgment"   Kennedy, *"Let the Word Go Forth,"* 140.

189 "It is wrong for the churches"   *Time*, July 6, 1962.

189 In Schenectady, New York   Ibid.

189 In an eight-to-one decision   Alley, ed. *The Supreme Court on Church and State*, 204–224.

189 from Stuttgart, Germany, where he was   *The New York Times*, June 18, 1963.

190 "Congress must act"   Ibid.

191 "We in this country, in this generation"   Kennedy, *"Let the Word Go Forth,"* 404–405.

191 "I ask for your help—and God's"   Lyndon B. Johnson, *Public Papers of the Presidents of the United States: Lyndon B. Johnson; Containing the Public Messages, Speeches, and Statements of the President, 1963–1964* (Washington, D.C., 1965) 1: 1.

191 his essay on civil religion   Bellah, *Beyond Belief*, 175.

192 Sunday, March 7, 1965   Lewis with D'Orso, *Walking with the Wind*, 335–362. My account of that day and its ramifications is drawn from Congressman Lewis's wonderful memoir and is informed by several conversations I have been privileged to have with him about Selma and President Johnson over the years.

192 ordained a Baptist minister   Author interview with John Lewis.

192 was wearing a light raincoat   Lewis with D'Orso, *Walking with the Wind*, 325.

192 He was there because of God   Author interview with John Lewis.

192 "Without religion—without the example of Christ"   Ibid.

192 "It was somber and subdued"   Lewis with D'Orso, *Walking with the Wind*, 338.

192 went down Water Street   Ibid.

192 "There, facing us"   Ibid., 326.

193 "We were prepared to die"   Author interview with John Lewis.

193 With a bullhorn, Major John Cloud   Lewis with D'Orso, *Walking with the Wind*, 339.

193 "We couldn't go forward"   Ibid., 327.

193 Cloud ordered his men forward   Ibid.

194 "like a human wave"   Ibid.

194 "Get 'em!"   Ibid.

194 A trooper struck Lewis   Ibid.

194 inhaling tear gas, C-4   Ibid.

194 As television cameras rolled   Ibid., 329.

194 "This is it"   Ibid., 328.

194 "People are going to die here"   Ibid.

194 Lewis felt a kind of calm   Author interview with John Lewis.

194 worrying about the others—about Hosea   Ibid.

194 "I was ready to die"   Ibid.

194 "I really thought I saw death"   Ibid.

194 treated at Good Samaritan Hospital   Lewis with D'Orso, *Walking with the Wind*, 330.

194 ABC's Frank Reynolds interrupted the film   Ibid., 331.

194 "The images were stunning"   Ibid.

195 Eight days later President Johnson   Lyndon B. Johnson, *Public Papers of the Presidents of the United States: Lyndon B. Johnson; Containing the Public Messages, Speeches, and Statements of the President, 1965* (Washington, D.C., 1966) 1: 281–287.

195 The president's speech that night   Richard N. Goodwin, *Remembering America: A Voice from the Sixties* (New York, 1988), 324–339, tells the story of the speech in vivid and compelling terms.

195 a long liquid dinner party   Author interview with Richard Goodwin.

195 thought he had little to do   Ibid.

195 When Johnson woke up   Goodwin, *Remembering America*, 326–327.

195 "How's Dick coming"   Ibid., 326.

195 "He's not doing it"   Ibid.

195 "Johnson sat upright"   Ibid., 326–327.

195 arrived at the White House about 9:30   Author interview with Richard Goodwin.

195 "It just came"   Ibid.

195 reading the speech page by page   Ibid.

195 "The biblical imagery"   Ibid.

195 "The Old Testament"   Ibid.

196 "At times history and fate"   Johnson, *Public Papers of the Presidents of the United States, 1965,* vol. 1, 281.

196 "We *shall* overcome"   Ibid., 284.

196 "I speak tonight for the dignity of man"   Ibid., 281.

196 "Rarely are we met"   Ibid., 281–282.

197 "Above the pyramid"   Ibid., 287.

197 In the house of a Selma dentist   Lewis with D'Orso, *Walking with the Wind*, 354.

197 "Dr. King had transformed"   Author interview with John Lewis.

198 a critical chapter of the Gospel   Matthew 16 (KJV).

198 "Thou art Peter"   Matthew 16:18 (KJV).

198 "If any man will come after me"   Matthew 16:24 (KJV).

198 "We will guard against violence"   Johnson, *Public Papers of the Presidents of the United States, 1965*, vol. 1, 285.

198 Jerry Falwell, preached a sermon   Falwell, *Strength for the Journey*, 289–291. The sermon, which Falwell calls "Ministers and Marches," is sometimes referred to as "Ministers and Marchers." For other discussions of the sermon, see Susan Friend Harding, *The Book of Jerry Falwell: Fundamentalist Language and Politics* (Princeton, NJ, 2000), 21–23, and Cal Thomas and Ed Dobson, *Blinded by Might: Why the Religious Right Can't Save America* (Grand Rapids, MI, 1999), 69. The Thomas-Dobson book is particularly good, and I am grateful to Cal Thomas for talking these issues over with me.

198 "Believing the Bible as I do"   Falwell, *Strength for the Journey*, 290.

CHAPTER FIVE: THE FIGHT WAS ON!

200 "We shall overcome because the arc"   "Remaining Awake Through a Great Revolution," Sermon Delivered by the Reverend Martin Luther King, Jr., Sunday, March 31, 1968, Cathedral Archives of Washington National Cathedral. Here and below, I am quoting from a transcript by Margaret Shannon, Cathedral Choral Society Program Annotator, in March 1998 using the audiotape recording made by the sound engineer of Washington National Cathedral on Sunday, March 31, 1968. Many published versions of the sermon have King saying, "the arc of the moral universe is long," but I have relied on the cathedral's transcription of the actual sermon.

200 "Yes, let us pray for the salvation"   White House Office of Speech Writing: Speech drafts, National Assoc. of Evangelicals (Orlando) (Dolan) March 8, 1983, folders 1–6, Ronald Reagan Library.

200 Depressed and somewhat adrift   Coretta Scott King, *My Life with Martin Luther King, Jr.* (New York, 1969), 309. For this section, I have drawn on reporting and writing I did for a *Newsweek* piece commemorating the 30th anniversary of King's assassination. (*Newsweek,* April 6, 1998, 43–47.) For moving accounts of King's last years, see also Taylor Branch, *At Canaan's Edge: America in the King Years, 1965–1968* (New York, 2006), and David J.

Garrow, *Bearing the Cross: Martin Luther King, Jr., and the Southern Leadership Conference* (New York, 1986).

200 having a hard time sleeping *Newsweek,* April 6, 1998, 43.

200 were in disarray Ibid.

201 degenerated into a riot Coretta Scott King, *My Life with Martin Luther King, Jr., 308–311.*

201 "Dr. King kept saying" Author interview with John Lewis.

201 "When the architects" Josh Gottheimer, ed. *Ripples of Hope: Great American Civil Rights Speeches* (New York, 2003), 230.

201 "The years before '68" Author interview with Jesse Jackson.

202 in his study at Ebenezer Baptist Church Ibid.

202 who joked about how his collars Jim Bishop, *The Days of Martin Luther King, Jr.* (New York, 1971), 56.

202 King mused about Author interview with Jesse Jackson.

202 "He preached himself out of the gloom" Ibid.

202 Early the next morning Garrow, *Bearing the Cross,* 618.

202 Sunday, March 31, 1968, was *The Washington Post,* March 31, 1968.

202 the thirteen steps Detail courtesy of Elizabeth Mullen, Washington National Cathedral.

202 ten-foot-high pulpit Ibid.

202 scenes from the story of Ibid.

202 the church was crowded "Martin Luther King, Jr., and Washington Cathedral," *The Cathedral Age,* Summer 1968, Washington National Cathedral Archives. It was, *The Cathedral Age* said, "the largest group of people the cathedral has ever held." (Ibid.)

203 "We are tied together" "Remaining Awake Through a Great Revolution," Martin Luther King, Jr., Washington National Cathedral Archives.

203 "Ultimately a great nation" Ibid.

203 "One day we will have to stand" Ibid.

204 "We're going to win our freedom" Ibid.

204 "a new Jerusalem" Ibid.

204 He had four days to live When the dean of the National Cathedral, Francis Sayre, got word of King's assassination in Memphis on the following Thursday, April 4, he consulted with the Bishop of Washington and, at 10:45 on Saturday morning, telegraphed Coretta Scott King, offering to bury her husband in a sepulcher in the cathedral. "The family considered the matter carefully and appreciatively, but finally sent me word that the elder Dr. Martin Luther King wished his son's remains to be buried in southern soil," Sayre recalled. "They, thus, gracefully declined. That was the day before the service in Atlanta. . . . How right it would have been

had the decision been otherwise, for King had outgrown his southern soil and become one of the great Americans who should be buried in a place where all could honor his memory." (Washington National Cathedral Archives.)

205　those who could not fit inside　"Martin Luther King, Jr., and Washington Cathedral," *The Cathedral Age,* Summer 1968.

205　St. Alban's parish　Ibid.

206　*Once to every man and nation*　Notes on the Cathedral Service on Sunday, March 31, 1968, Washington National Cathedral Archives.

206　shot down as he stepped　Garrow, *Bearing the Cross,* 623–624.

206　"Moses leading a rebellious people"　*The New York Times,* April 10, 1968.

207　"He belonged to the world"　Ibid.

207　"Now he belongs to the ages"　Carl Sandburg, *Abraham Lincoln: The War Years* (New York, 1939), 4: 297.

207　"I close by saying to you"　*The New York Times,* April 10, 1968.

208　Reading the *Lynchburg News*　Falwell, *Strength for the Journey,* 334–335.

210　"government could be trusted"　Ibid., 337.

210　telling a national clergy convention　Ibid., 338.

210　"Serving the church"　Ibid.

210　much to learn about the game　Ibid., 339.

211　George Bush once asked him　Billy Graham, *Just As I Am,* 592.

211　Graham dropped out of Bob Jones College　William Martin, *A Prophet with Honor: The Billy Graham Story* (New York, 1991), 66–70.

212　Graham visited him on trips to France　Graham, *Just As I Am,* 188–190.

212　"Billy Graham came to see me"　Dwight D. Eisenhower to Honorable Arthur B. Langlie, August 11, 1952, PPF 1052, Graham, Billy; Box 966, White House Central Files-President's Personal File, Dwight D. Eisenhower Presidential Library, Abilene, Kansas.

212　"Enclosed are newspaper clips"　Billy Graham to Dwight D. Eisenhower, June 29, 1953, PPF 1052, Graham, Billy; Box 966, White House Central Files-President's Personal File, Dwight D. Eisenhower Presidential Library, Abilene, Kansas.

212　"I am only informing you"　Ibid.

212　drafted a piece for *Life*　Graham, *Just As I Am,* 392.

212　immediately regretted sending　Ibid., 392–393.

212　killed it to protect Graham　Ibid., 393.

212　"God had intervened!"　Ibid.

212　why Christians should be sure to vote　Ibid.

213　"Even now we are wrestling"　Billy Graham, " 'We Are Electing a President of the World,' " *Life,* November 7, 1960.

213 "Preacher, pray for me"   Graham, *Just As I Am,* 412.

213 would fall to his knees   Ibid.

213 "Looking back"   Ibid., 442.

213 one 1972 conversation captured by the White House   *The New York Times,* March 17, 2002.

213 "A lot of the Jews"   Ibid.

214 Graham said he could not recall   Ibid.

214 "Racial prejudice, anti-Semitism, or hatred"   Ibid.

214 Jewish leaders, many of whom appreciated   *Newsweek,* July 4, 2005.

214 "Much of my life"   *The New York Times,* March 17, 2002.

214 "It is true that we are a pluralistic nation"   "A Nation Under God," address given by Billy Graham, Presidential Prayer Service, January 20, 1985, Washington National Cathedral, Files of the Billy Graham Evangelistic Association. Responding to a question from me about what God Graham prays to when Graham is praying in the public square of American life, Graham's spokesman, A. Larry Ross, replied: "While in the public square, Mr. Graham is praying to the One who is God over all creation and the Lord of all nations and peoples—whether or not they recognize Him as such. Though Mr. Graham is always mindful of individuals from other faiths attending or in the media audience, he always offers those prayers as a follower of Jesus, whom he acknowledges as Mighty God and Prince of Peace." (Letter of A. Larry Ross to author, November 18, 2005.) Mr. Ross wrote: "Several days ago I had a meeting with Mr. Graham, during which . . . I was able to pose to him your question relating to which God he is addressing when he prays publicly. My response, on his behalf, is as follows. . . ." (Ibid.) I also put the question to the Reverend Rick Warren, pastor of Saddleback Church in Lake Forest, California. "I have to be the pastor of everybody—not a politician," Warren said. "I don't mind people violently disagreeing with me as long as they are civil about it. The problem of late has been that both extremes have been uncivil, and that's not good for anybody. I think any Muslim, any Hindu, any Jew has every right to try to convince me they're right." On public prayer in civic settings, Warren said: "Does anybody really think anybody has ever converted because of 'under God' in the Pledge or because of 'In God We Trust' on the currency? No, of course not. But there is a civil religion in this country. When I pray in certain settings, like a legislative session, I, as a Protestant, will pray in Jesus' name, recognizing that we are a nation of many faiths. But I have to pray in the name of my savior, though I am certainly not saying everybody has to agree with me and have the same savior." (Author interview.)

215 "At my age"   *Newsweek,* July 4, 2005.

216 "as stubborn as a South Georgia turtle"   Jimmy Carter, *Why Not the Best?* (Nashville, TN, 1975), 161.

216 what he called "second thoughts"   Jimmy Carter, *Keeping Faith: Memoirs of a President* (New York, 1982), 19.

216 leaning toward II Chronicles 7:14   Ibid.

216 Carter worried, however, about "how those"   Ibid.

216 Micah "held the reminder of the need"   Ibid., 20.

216 "Separation is specified in the law"   Jimmy Carter, *Our Endangered Values: America's Moral Crisis* (New York, 2005), 58–59. The remarks are from a 1978 speech.

217 recalled being asked "whether my Christian beliefs"   Ibid., 57.

217 "The sad duty of politics"   Carter, *Why Not the Best?* Epigraph

217 "I got me a Bible"   *The Washington Post,* September 27, 1984.

217 Capitalizing on the patriotic sentiment   Noll, Hatch, and Marsden, *The Search for Christian America,* has a thorough and incisive account of the Christian conservatives' use of the 1976 milestone.

217 Traveling the nation with seventy performers   Falwell, *Strength for the Journey,* 345–347.

217 "calling America back"   Ibid., 345–346.

218 "The fight was on!"   Ibid., 347.

218 "Somehow I thought"   Ibid., 337.

219 "Any diligent student of American history"   Jerry Falwell, *Listen, America!* (New York, 1980), 25.

219 In a Moral Majority report   *The Washington Post,* September 27, 1984.

219 a book making the same case   LaHaye, *Faith of Our Founding Fathers.*

219 books, videos, DVDs, and websites devoted   Wallbuilders.com, under the direction of David Barton, is perhaps the most notable of these.

219 Bob Slosser's 1984 book about Reagan   Bob Slosser, *Reagan Inside Out* (Waco, TX, 1984).

221 a Sunday afternoon in Sacramento   Ibid., 13–15.

221 Ten years later   Ibid., 20.

222 "These are the boys of Pointe"   Ronald Reagan, *Public Papers of the Presidents of the United States: Ronald Reagan; Containing the Public Messages, Speeches, and Statements of the President, 1984* (Washington, D.C., 1986), 1: 817–819.

222 The real Reagan was a romantic   For this section I have drawn on my reporting and writing for my obituary of President Reagan, "American Dreamer," *Newsweek,* June 14, 2005.

223 three times as many references   Lou Cannon, *President Reagan: The Role of a Lifetime* (New York, 1991), 843–844.

223 told the president pro tem   Ibid., 248.

223 "We may be the generation"   Ibid.

223 "strange weather things"   Ibid.

223   six folders   White House Office of Speech Writing: Speech drafts, "National Assoc. of Evangelicals (Orlando) (Dolan) March 8, 1983, folders 1–6, Ronald Reagan Library.

223   given at three o'clock   Ibid.

223   a term he had used   "Address to Members of the British Parliament, June 8, 1982." The Public Papers of President Ronald W. Reagan. Ronald Reagan Presidential Library. http://www.reagan.utexas.edu/archives/speeches/1982/60882a.htm.

224   Reagan edited in his own hand   The document I am describing is dated "March 5, 1983, Noon," and is clearly a draft Reagan worked on. I am grateful to Richard Darman for his guidance and counsel. (White House Office of Speech Writing: Speech drafts, "National Assoc. of Evangelicals [Orlando] [Dolan] March 8, 1983, folders 1–6, Ronald Reagan Library.)

224   quoted William Penn   Ibid., 2–3.

224   edited rather harshly   Ibid.

224   "the great triumph"   Ibid., 2.

224   "I feel as Abe Lincoln felt"   Ibid., 1.

224   "Those of us"   Ibid., 2.

224   "I tell you truly"   Ibid.

225   "There is sin"   Ibid., 11.

225   "We must never"   Ibid., 12.

225   "The commandment given"   Ibid.

225   as Reagan rendered it, "morality is"   Ibid., 14.

225   "This does not mean"   Ibid.

225   "I intend to do everything"   Ibid.

226   "I believe this because"   Ibid., 17.

226   Citrus Crown Ballroom   The remarks released by the Office of the Press Secretary on March 8, 1983, include the details of the venue.

226   "One of our Founding Fathers"   "Remarks at the Annual Convention of the National Association of Evangelicals in Orlando, Florida, March 8, 1983." The Public Papers of President Ronald W. Reagan. Ronald Reagan Presidential Library. http://www.reagan.utexas.edu/archives/speeches/1983/30883b.htm.

226   Supreme Court Justice Sandra Day O'Connor   The Washington Post, June 12, 2004. Former President George H. W. Bush also spoke movingly at the Reagan funeral. In the course of researching this book, I talked with the senior President Bush about faith and politics, and asked him why he had chosen to open his 1989 inaugural address with a prayer. "I wanted to have the tone that we are one nation, under God, and that prayer is good," Bush told me. "It put a good emphasis on what was in my heart." Beyond the ceremonial, I asked, under what circumstances was prayer a genuine part of life in the White

House? "Prayer was important, especially when you are sending people into battle; presidents have the ultimate responsibility of risking the lives of other people's sons and daughters. It troubled me, and we prayed about it—prayed with Billy Graham about it." Asked whether religion was much on his mind in his four years in office, Bush said: "I felt lifted by faith. I don't know how you could cope in the presidency without a sense of a larger power, of a larger destiny, of something bigger than your own ambitions, your own passions, your own plans, your own problems. Belief in God, for me at least, gave me hope, and kept me going. I didn't show it very much—don't like to talk about it—and maybe I should have been a little more open, a little clearer about my heartbeat. But I felt it—felt it very, very strongly." And, finally, a thought in the Jefferson-Adams tradition of pondering the afterlife: "As you get to be an older guy," Bush said, "you think about what lies over the horizon. It's just natural—you think about what Heaven's like, and hope like hell that you get there." (Author interview with George H. W. Bush, November 5, 2005.)

CHAPTER SIX: OUR HOPE FOR YEARS TO COME

227 "I have but one lamp"   Alex Barnett, ed. *Words That Changed America* (Guilford, CT, 2003), 5–8.

227 "Our particular principles of religion"   Randall, *The Life of Thomas Jefferson*, III, 405.

227 survived them all   Franklin died in 1790, Washington in 1799, and Jefferson and Adams in 1826.

227 Madison wore a cap and gloves   Ketcham, *James Madison*, 659–660.

227 Dolley, said "my days are devoted"   Ibid., 668.

227 private notes he kept   Madison, *Writings*, 745–770. These are known as Madison's Detached Memoranda.

228 "The Constitution of the U.S."   Ibid., 762.

228 "In strictness"   Ibid.

228 concluded that "as the precedent"   Ibid., 788. The letter, dated July 10, 1822, was to Edward Livingston.

228 sipped sherry   Ketcham, *James Madison*, 669.

228 dictated letters (his hands were crippled)   Ibid., 659.

228 read over the pages   Ibid., 669. The biography, by George Tucker, was of particular interest to Madison. Two days after Jefferson's death, on July 6, 1826, Madison had written Nicholas P. Trist: "We are more than consoled for the loss, by the gain to him; and by the assurance that he lives and will live in the memory and gratitude of the wise & good, as a luminary of Science, as a

votary of liberty, as a model of patriotism, and as a benefactor of human kind. In these characters, I have known him, and not less in the virtues & charms of social life, for a period of fifty years, during which there has not been an interruption or diminution of mutual confidence and cordial friendship, for a single moment in a single instance." (Madison, *Writings,* 811–812.)

228 intensely private about his theology   Ketcham, *James Madison,* 667.

228 long held that "belief in a God"   Ibid.

228 a document composed for publication   Madison, *Writings,* 866.

228 he and his wife had faced death   Ketcham, *James Madison,* 575–581, describes the British burning of Washington.

229 "Let the open enemy"   Madison, *Writings,* 866.

230 buried in an Episcopal service   Ketcham, *James Madison,* 670.

230 His slaves, it was reported   Ibid. Ketcham cites James Barbour as the source of the detail.

230 "There appears to be in the nature of man"   Hutson, ed. *The Founders on Religion,* 189–190.

230 had so many "propensities & susceptibilities"   Ibid., 190.

230 "the danger of a direct mixture"   Madison, *Writings,* 761. The line is found in his Detached Memoranda.

230 "We shall leave the world"   Cousins, *"In God We Trust,"* 113.

230 Machiavelli wrote in his *History of Florence*   Ibid., 97.

231 In the last book of Homer's *Iliad*   *The Iliad of Homer,* trans. Richmond Lattimore (Chicago, 1951), 475–496.

231 "The heart in you is iron"   Ibid., 489.

231 "There is not"   Ibid.

231 "Such is the way"   Ibid.

231 Writing to Adams about grief   Braden, ed. *"Ye Will Say I Am No Christian": The Thomas Jefferson/John Adams Correspondence on Religion, Morals, and Values* (Amherst, New York, 2006), 174. The letter was dated August 1, 1816, from Monticello.

231 "I see that"   Ibid.

231 *Two urns by Jove's high throne*   Ibid.

232 "We shall only"   Hutson, ed. *The Founders on Religion,* 10.

232 "May we meet there again"   Braden, ed. *"Ye Will Say I Am No Christian,"* 224.

232 reward of "the joy"   Matthew 25:21 (KJV).

232 Falwell and his seventy performers   Falwell, *Strength for the Journey,* 345.

233 Tim LaHaye in his *Faith*   LaHaye, *Faith of Our Founding Fathers.*

233 "We and God have business"   William James, *The Varieties of Religious Experience: A Study in Human Nature* (New York, 1994), 561.

233 "the instinctive belief of mankind"   Ibid.

233   "God is real since he produces"   Ibid.

233   James quoted Professor James H. Leuba   Ibid., 550–551.

233   "must exert a permanent"   Ibid., 551.

234   "[T]he Lord has protected us so wonderfully"   Partial Transcript of Comments from the Thursday, September 13, 2001, edition of the "700 Club," U.S. Newswire, Inc., September 13, 2001.

236   *Life* magazine said in 1964   *Life,* June 19, 1964. "The Most Hated Woman in America" was the headline of the *Life* piece. (Ibid.)

236   a speech laced with profanity   The address, entitled "Fundamentalism," is available online at http://www.infidels.org/library/modern/madalyn_ohair/fundie.html. The American Atheists Inc. website also has information on O'Hair.

236   disappeared in 1995   The Associated Press, December 8, 1999.

236   killed, dismembered, and secretly buried   Cox News Service, January 28, 2001. See also *The Washington Post,* July 29, 2001, for a piece on O'Hair by Stephen Bates.

236   "She was an evil person"   *The Washington Post,* July 29, 2001.

236   "God was sitting on his ass"   http://www.infidels.org/library/modern/madalyn_ohair/fundie.html

237   "foolish" ideas   Ibid.

237   Elizabeth I is said to have remarked   Full quotation can be found at the Royal Family's website at www.Royal.gov.uk.

237   the minister in the New England story   Jacques Barzun, *From Dawn to Decadence: 500 Years of Western Cultural Life* (New York, 2000), 31.

237   so old and so new   Augustine, *Confessions,* 10:27:38.

238   "In their dreams"   Mittleman, Licht, and Sarna, eds. *Jews and the American Public Square,* 64.

238   "Our argument . . . is that"   Kramnick and Moore, *The Godless Constitution,* 200.

238   "No easy solutions from the past"   Noll, Hatch, and Marsden, *The Search for Christian America,* 154–155. They add: "At the same time, we may not hide behind the complexities, ambiguities, and uncertainties of history as an excuse for inaction." (Ibid., 155.)

238   "Reasonable minds can disagree"   *McCreary County, Kentucky et al Petitioners v. American Civil Liberties Union of Kentucky et al* 545 U.S. (2005). Case decided June 27, 2005.

239   In 1952, Justice William O. Douglas   Alley, ed. *The Supreme Court on Church and State,* 185–186. The case was *Zorach v. Clauson.*

239   "dim lights"   George Eliot, *Middlemarch* (London, 1872), 1.

239   "There cannot be the slightest doubt"   Alley, ed. *The Supreme Court on Church and State,* 185–186. The ruling allowed students to be excused from

public school property to attend voluntary religious instruction elsewhere. Douglas also wrote in the opinion: "We are a religious people whose institutions presuppose a Supreme Being. We guarantee the freedom to worship as one chooses. We make room for as wide a variety of beliefs and creeds as the spiritual needs of man deem necessary. We sponsor an attitude on the part of government that shows no partiality to any one group and that lets each flourish according to the zeal of its adherents and the appeal of its dogma. When the state encourages religious instruction or cooperates with religious authorities by adjusting the schedule of public events to sectarian needs, it follows the best of our traditions. For it then respects the religious nature of our people and accommodates the public service to their spiritual needs. To hold that it may not would be to find in the Constitution a requirement that the government show a callous indifference to religious groups. That would be preferring those who believe in no religion over those who do believe. Government may not finance religious groups nor undertake religious instruction nor blend secular and sectarian education nor use secular institutions to force one or some religion on any person. But we find no constitutional requirement which makes it necessary for government to be hostile to religion and to throw its weight against efforts to widen the effective scope of religious influence. The government must be neutral when it comes to competition between sects. It may not thrust any sect on any person. It may not make a religious observance compulsory. It may not coerce anyone to attend church, to observe a religious holiday, or to take religious instruction. But it can close its doors or suspend its operations as to those who want to repair to their religious sanctuary for worship or instruction. No more than that is undertaken here." (Ibid., 186–187.)

240   For all the talk   John T. Noonan, Jr.'s work is essential and enlightening on the questions of religion and the Constitution. He wrote: "The problem is, Can you have a nation without a national religion? Rhetoric says, Of course. Realities are different—observe the employment of prayer and the celebration of religious holidays by all three branches [of government]; the tax exemption of religious bodies and the draft exemption of the clergy and certain conscientious objectors; the integration of religion into the armed services, whose chapels and chaplains, bibles and torahs and sacramental stock are provided at governmental expense according to congressional appropriation and appropriate service regulation. And when the nation actually goes to war, its leaders call on God to grant it victory. . . . Religion is entangled with government." (Noonan, *The Lustre of Our Country*, 7.) In this lovely, learned book, Noonan—scholar and judge—also wrote that "the experiment [in religious freedom, particularly free-exercise] goes on. Final answers are premature." (Ibid.)

240 "the line of separation"   John T. Noonan, Jr., and Edward McGlynn Gaffney, Jr. *Religious Freedom: History, Cases, and Other Materials on the Interaction of Religion and Government* (New York, 2001), 693. Burger was writing for the court in the case that produced the much-debated "Lemon Test" for religion cases involving the Establishment Clause. Burger suggested this standard: "First, the statute must have a secular legislative purpose; second, its principal or primary effect must be one that neither advances nor inhibits religion; finally, the statute must not foster 'an excessive government entanglement with religion.' " (Ibid.)

240 "Fix reason"   Hutson, ed. *The Founders on Religion*, 187. The full quotation includes this line: "Question with boldness even the existence of a god because, if there be one, he must more approve the homage of reason than that of blindfolded fear." (Ibid.)

241 "I must admit"   Hutson, ed. *The Founders on Religion*, 64. In his fascinating book *Divided By God: America's Church-State Problem—And What We Should Do About It* (New York, 2005), Noah Feldman recounts the history of church-state tensions with grace and insight. In the search for answers, Feldman concluded: "They have it much easier in France, for example, where . . . constitutionalized strong secularism . . . simply rejects the notion that religion is an inherently meaningful source of values, and so can easily conclude that religion can be excluded from the public sphere altogether. It is also simpler in many Muslim countries where constitutions declare Islam to be a principal source of legislation and, correspondingly, do not institutionally separate religion from government. Our experiment will have to avoid both extremes. We want to acknowledge the centrality of religion to many citizens' values while keeping religion and government in some important sense distinct.

"Despite the gravity of the problem, I believe that the history of church and state in America . . . does point toward an answer. Put simply, it is this: offer greater latitude for public religious discourse and religious symbolism, and at the same time insist on a stricter ban on state funding of religious institutions and activities. Such a solution would both recognize religious values *and* respect the institutional separation of religion and government as an American value in its own right." (Ibid., 236–237.) While I continue to believe more in the Potter Stewart test, I thing Professor Feldman is to be commended for trying to impose some order on the chaos of religion and government, and I am grateful to him for discussing these issues with me.

241 "a nation with the soul of a church"   G. K. Chesterton, *The Collected Works of G. K. Chesterton*, ed. George J. Marlin and others, vol. 21, *What I Saw in America, The Resurrection of Rome, Sidelights* (San Francisco, 1990), 45.

241 "Reason is itself"   Chesterton, *Orthodoxy*, 29.

241 "I am ordinary"   Ibid., xvii.

241 "The ordinary man has always been sane"   Ibid., 23.

242 "Those of us who are Jeffersonian separatists"   Kramnick and Moore, *The Godless Constitution*, 197.

242 their "ultimate concern"   Paul Tillich, *Systematic Theology*, I (Chicago, 1951), 11–12. Tillich wrote: "Ultimate concern is the abstract translation of the great commandment: 'The Lord, our God, the Lord is one; and you shall love the Lord your God with all your heart, and with all your soul and with all your mind, and with all your strength.' The religious concern is ultimate; it excludes all other concerns from ultimate significance; it makes them preliminary. The ultimate concern is unconditional, independent of any conditions of character, desire, or circumstance. The unconditional concern is total: no part of ourselves or of our world is excluded from it; there is no 'place' to flee from it. The total concern is infinite: no moment of relaxation or rest is possible in the face of a religious concern which is ultimate, unconditional, total, and infinite." (Ibid.)

242 "Idolatry is the elevation"   Ibid., 13.

243 "The Church . . . has no weapons"   Mario Cuomo, *More Than Words: The Speeches of Mario Cuomo* (New York, 1993), 47–48.

244 "The weapons of the word"   Ibid., 48.

244 "We recognize that"   Ibid., 44.

245 a letter to Abigail with advice   Hutson, ed. *The Founders on Religion*, 48. Of his sons John and Charles, Adams also wrote in this April 15, 1776, letter: "Take care that they don't go astray. Cultivate their minds, inspire their little hearts, raise their wishes. Fix their attention upon great and glorious objects, root out every little thing, weed out every meanness, make them great and manly. Teach them to scorn injustice, ingratitude, cowardice, and falsehood." (Ibid.)

245 "The bosom of America"   Ibid., 120–121.

246 "Our country has been"   Ibid., 136–137.

247 Shortly before noon   *The Washington Post*, April 14, 1943.

247 left the White House   Ibid.

247 the early Japanese cherry blossoms   Ibid.

247 Five thousand people   *The New York Times*, April 14, 1943.

248 Henry St. George Tucker . . . stepped   *The Washington Post*, April 14, 1943.

248 guards wearing the costumes of Continental   *The New York Times*, April 14, 1943.

248 modeled after the Pantheon of Rome   Merrill D. Peterson, *Jefferson Memorial: An Essay* (Washington, D.C., 1998), 11.

248 Tucker thanked God for "raising up" *The Washington Post,* April 14, 1943.

248 His braces locked in place Ibid.; details drawn from the *Post*'s Harris and Ewing photograph. Because of his infantile paralysis, Roosevelt had to use steel braces which locked at the knee in order to walk with a cane in one hand and assisted by an aide or son on the other side. (Freidel, *Franklin D. Roosevelt: A Rendezvous with Destiny,* 47.) When putting his braces in place or getting in or out of a wheelchair, he would admonish photographers: "No movies of me getting out the machine, boys"—and they respected his wishes. (Ibid.) For a brilliant account of Roosevelt's struggle with polio and its psychological effects, see Geoffrey C. Ward, *A First-Class Temperament: The Emergence of Franklin Roosevelt* (New York, 1989).

248 Roosevelt gazed up *The Washington Post,* April 14, 1943.

248 Sculpted from plaster *Time,* April 12, 1943.

248 the bronze would have to wait Ibid.

248 nineteen-foot-tall Ibid.

248 looked rather defiant, his feet set Author observation.

248 an "apostle of freedom" *The New York Times,* April 14, 1943.

248 "lived in a world" Ibid.

248 cold wind blew off the Potomac *The Washington Post,* April 14, 1943.

248 in his gray suit coat Ibid.

249 "Thomas Jefferson believed" *The New York Times,* April 14, 1943.

250 Jefferson's "noblest and most urgent meaning" Ibid.

250 "I have sworn upon the altar" Jefferson, *Writings,* 1082. The quotation comes from a September 23, 1800, letter to Benjamin Rush written from Monticello. Jefferson, who was then challenging President Adams's reelection, was under attack by his Federalist foes for being irreligious. The political climate was particularly charged in the wake of the XYZ Affair, a diplomatic skirmish with France that led to a chaotic period in the United States in which patriotic feeling ran high, prompting the passage of the Alien and Sedition Acts. In such a nativist, anti-French atmosphere, Jefferson seems to have believed that some denominations harbored ambitions to advance their interests and take on a more public role, including receiving government sanction as the favored faith. Some clergy, Jefferson told Rush, had "a very favorite hope of obtaining an establishment of a particular form of Christianity thro' the U.S.; and as every sect believes its own form the true one, every one perhaps hoped for his own, but especially the Episcopalians & Congregationalists. The returning good sense of our country threatens . . . their hopes, & they believe that any portion of power confided to me, will be exerted in opposition to their schemes. And they believe rightly." (Ibid., 1081–1082).

BIBLIOGRAPHY

MANUSCRIPT COLLECTIONS

- Adams Family Papers, Massachusetts Historical Society, Boston, Massachusetts
- Correspondence of Ellen Wayles Randolph Coolidge, University of Virginia, Charlottesville, Virginia
- Robley Dunglison Papers, College of Physicians of Philadelphia, Philadelphia, Pennsylvania
- Edgehill-Randolph Papers, University of Virginia, Charlottesville, Virginia
- The Dwight D. Eisenhower Presidential Library, Abilene, Kansas
- The Billy Graham Evangelistic Association, Charlotte, North Carolina
- Andrew Jackson Papers, Library of Congress, Washington, D.C.
- Thomas Jefferson Papers, Library of Congress, Washington, D.C.
- Collections of the Lyndon B. Johnson Presidential Library, Austin, Texas
- Presidential Correspondence Files, John F. Kennedy Library, Boston, Massachusetts
- Jacques Judah Lyons Collection, American Jewish Historical Society, New York and Newton Centre, Massachusetts
- Files of St. John's Episcopal Church, Lafayette Square, Washington, D.C.
- The Ronald Reagan Presidential Library, Simi Valley, California
- Franklin D. Roosevelt Papers, Franklin D. Roosevelt Presidential Library and Museum, Hyde Park, New York
- Margaret Suckley Papers, Wilderstein Collection, Rhinebeck, New York
- Washington National Cathedral Archives, Washington National Cathedral, Washington, D.C.

BOOKS AND ARTICLES CONSULTED

Adams, John. *Papers of John Adams.* Edited by Robert J. Taylor, Mary-Jo Kline, and Gregg L. Lint. The Adams Papers: Series III, General Correspondence and Other Papers of the Adams Statesmen. Vol. 1, *September 1755–October 1773.* Cambridge: Belknap Press of Harvard University Press, 1977.

———. *The Political Writings of John Adams.* Edited by George W. Carey. Conservative Leadership Series. Washington, D.C.: Regnery Publishing, 2000.

Adams, John Quincy. *The Diary of John Quincy Adams, 1794–1845: American Political, Social and Intellectual Life from Washington to Polk.* Edited by Allan Nevins. New York: Longmans, Green, 1928.

———. *Memoirs of John Quincy Adams, Comprising Portions of His Diary from 1795 to 1848.* Edited by Charles Francis Adams. 12 vols. Philadelphia: J. B. Lippincott & Co., 1874–1877.

Albanese, Catherine L. *Sons of the Fathers: The Civil Religion of the American Revolution.* Philadelphia: Temple University Press, 1976.

Aldridge, Alfred Owen. *Benjamin Franklin and Nature's God.* Durham, NC: Duke University Press, 1967.

Alexander, John K. *Samuel Adams: America's Revolutionary Politician.* American Profiles. Lanham, MD: Rowman & Littlefield Publishers, 2002.

Allen, Charlotte. *The Human Christ: The Search for the Historical Jesus.* New York: Free Press, 1998.

Alley, Robert S., ed. *The Supreme Court on Church and State.* New York: Oxford University Press, 1988.

Amar, Akhil Reed. *America's Constitution: A Biography.* New York: Random House, 2005.

———. *The Bill of Rights: Creation and Reconstruction.* New Haven: Yale University Press, 1998.

Ambrose, Stephen E. *D-Day, June 6, 1944: The Climactic Battle of World War II.* New York: Simon & Schuster, 1994.

Appleby, Joyce. *Inheriting the Revolution: The First Generation of Americans.* Cambridge: Belknap Press of Harvard University Press, 2000.

Aquinas, Saint Thomas. *On Faith and Reason.* Edited by Stephen F. Brown. Indianapolis: Hackett Publishing Co., 1999.

Asbell, Bernard. *When F.D.R. Died.* New York: Holt, Rinehart and Winston, 1961.

Augustine, Saint. *The City of God.* Translated by Marcus Dods. New York: Modern Library, 1993.

———. *Confessions.* Translated by Henry Chadwick. Oxford World's Classics. New York: Oxford University Press, 1998.

Bailyn, Bernard. *The Ideological Origins of the American Revolution.* Cambridge: Belknap Press of Harvard University Press, 1967.

————. *To Begin the World Anew: The Genius and Ambiguities of the American Founders.* New York: Alfred A. Knopf, 2003.

————, comp. *The Debate on the Constitution: Federalist and Antifederalist Speeches, Articles, and Letters During the Struggle Over Ratification.* 2 vols. The Library of America. New York: Library of America, 1993.

Balmer, Randall. *Encyclopedia of Evangelicalism.* Waco, TX: Baylor University Press, 2004.

Barnes, Jonathan, ed. *The Cambridge Companion to Aristotle.* New York: Cambridge University Press, 1995.

Barzun, Jacques. *From Dawn to Decadence: 500 Years of Western Cultural Life, 1500 to the Present.* New York: HarperCollins Publishers, 2000.

Becker, Carl. *The Declaration of Independence: A Study in the History of Political Ideas.* New York: Alfred A. Knopf, 1942.

Beecher, Lyman. *Autobiography.* Edited by Barbara M. Cross. The John Harvard Library. 2 vols. Cambridge: Belknap Press of Harvard University Press, 1961.

Bellah, Robert N. *Beyond Belief: Essays on Religion in a Post-Traditional World.* New York: Harper & Row, 1970.

————. *The Broken Covenant: American Civil Religion in Time of Trial.* 2nd ed. Chicago: University of Chicago Press, 1992.

Bellah, Robert N. and Phillip E. Hammond. *Varieties of Civil Religion.* San Francisco: Harper & Row, 1980.

Berger, Peter L., ed. *The Desecularization of the World: Resurgent Religion and World Politics.* Washington, D.C.: The Ethics and Public Policy Center, 1999.

Berlin, Ira. *Many Thousands Gone: The First Two Centuries of Slavery in North America.* Cambridge: Belknap Press of Harvard University Press, 1998.

Beschloss, Michael. *The Conquerors: Roosevelt, Truman and the Destruction of Hitler's Germany, 1941–1945.* New York: Simon & Schuster, 2002.

Bishop, Jim. *The Days of Martin Luther King, Jr.* New York: G. P. Putnam's Sons, 1971.

Blackburn, Simon, ed. *Ethics: A Very Short Introduction.* New York: Oxford University Press, 2003.

Blau, Joseph L., and Salo W. Baron, eds. *The Jews of the United States, 1790–1840: A Documentary History.* 3 vols. New York: Columbia University Press, 1963.

Bobrick, Benson. *Angel in the Whirlwind: The Triumph of the American Revolution.* New York: Simon & Schuster, 1997.

Bolingbroke, Henry St. John, Viscount. *The Works of Lord Bolingbroke.* Reprints of Economic Classics. 4 vols. New York: A. M. Kelley, 1967.

Boller, Paul F. *George Washington and Religion.* Dallas: Southern Methodist University Press, 1963.

Bonomi, Patricia U. *Under the Cope of Heaven: Religion, Society, and Politics in Colonial America.* New York: Oxford University Press, 1986.

Boorstin, Daniel J. *The Americans: The National Experience.* New York: Random House, 1965.

Borden, Morton. *Jews, Turks, and Infidels.* Chapel Hill: University of North Carolina Press, 1984.

Bradford, William. *Of Plymouth Plantation, 1620–1647.* Modern Library College Editions. Introduction by Francis Murphy. New York: Modern Library, 1981.

Bradshaw, Herbert Clarence. *History of Hampden-Sydney College.* Vol. 1, *From the Beginnings to the Year 1856.* Durham, NC: Fisher-Harrison Corp., Seeman Printery Division, 1976.

Branch, Taylor. *At Canaan's Edge: America in the King Years, 1965–68.* New York: Simon & Schuster, 2006.

———. *Parting the Waters: America in the King Years, 1954–63.* New York: Simon & Schuster, 1988.

———. *Pillar of Fire: America in the King Years, 1963–65.* New York: Simon & Schuster, 1998.

Brant, Irving. "Madison and the Prayer Case." *New Republic* 147 (July 30, 1962): 18–20.

Breitman, Richard. *Official Secrets: What the Nazis Planned, What the British and Americans Knew.* New York: Hill and Wang, 1998.

Bremer, Francis J. *John Winthrop: America's Forgotten Founding Father.* New York: Oxford University Press, 2003.

Brodsky, Alyn. *Benjamin Rush: Patriot and Physician.* New York: Truman Talley Books, 2004.

Buckley, Jerome Hamilton, and George Benjamin Woods, eds. *Poetry of the Victorian Period.* 3rd ed. Chicago: Scott, Foresman and Co., 1965.

Buckley, Thomas E. "After Disestablishment: Thomas Jefferson's Wall of Separation in Antebellum Virginia." *Journal of Southern History* 61 (August 1995): 445–80.

———. "Evangelicals Triumphant: The Baptists' Assault on the Virginia Glebes, 1786–1801." *William and Mary Quarterly,* 3rd ser., 45 (January 1988): 33–69.

Bulliet, Richard W. *The Case for Islamo-Christian Civilization.* New York: Columbia University Press, 2004.

Bullock, Steven C. *Revolutionary Brotherhood: Freemasonry and the Transformation of the American Social Order, 1730–1840.* Chapel Hill: Published for the Institute for Early American History and Culture, Williamsburg, Virginia, by the University of North Carolina Press, 1996.

Burns, James MacGregor. *Roosevelt: The Lion and the Fox.* New York: Harcourt, Brace and Co., 1956.

———. *Roosevelt: The Soldier of Freedom.* New York: Harcourt Brace Jovanovich, 1970.

———. *The Vineyard of Liberty: The American Experiment.* New York: Alfred A. Knopf, 1982.

Bushman, Richard L. *From Puritan to Yankee: Character and the Social Order in Connecticut, 1690–1765.* Cambridge: Harvard University Press, 1967.

———. *Joseph Smith: Rough Stone Rolling.* New York: Alfred A. Knopf, 2005.

Butler, Jon. *Awash in a Sea of Faith: Christianizing the American People.* Studies in Cultural History. Cambridge: Harvard University Press, 1990.

———. *Becoming America: The Revolution Before 1776.* Cambridge: Harvard University Press, 2000.

Butler, Jon, Grant Wacker, and Randall Balmer. *Religion in American Life: A Short History.* New York: Oxford University Press, 2003.

Bynum, William B. " 'The Genuine Presbyterian Whine': Presbyterian Worship in the Eighteenth Century." *American Presbyterians* 74 (Fall 1996): 157–70.

Cannon, Lou. *President Reagan: The Role of a Lifetime.* New York: Simon & Schuster, 1991.

Carnes, Jim. *Us and Them: A History of Intolerance in America.* New York: Oxford University Press, 1996.

Carter, Jimmy. *Keeping Faith: Memoirs of a President.* New York: Bantam Books, 1982.

———. *Our Endangered Values: America's Moral Crisis.* New York: Simon & Schuster, 2005.

———. *Why Not the Best?* Nashville: Broadman Press, 1975.

Carter, Stephen L. *The Culture of Disbelief: How American Law and Politics Trivialize Religious Devotion.* New York: Basic Books, 1993.

———. *The Dissent of the Governed: A Mediation on Law, Religion, and Loyalty.* The William E. Massey, Sr., Lectures in the History of American Civilization. Cambridge: Harvard University Press, 1998.

———. *God's Name in Vain: The Wrongs and Rights of Religion in Politics.* New York: Basic Books, 2000.

Cayton, Mary Kupiec. "Who Were the Evangelicals?: Conservative and Liberal Identity in the Unitarian Controversy in Boston, 1804–1833." *Journal of Social History* 31 (Fall 1997): 85–107.

Chadwick, Henry. *The Church in Ancient Society: From Galilee to Gregory the Great.* Oxford History of the Christian Church. New York: Oxford University Press, 2001.

———. *The Early Church.* Revised ed. Penguin History of the Church. New York: Penguin Books, 1993.

Chadwick, Owen. *The Secularization of the European Mind in the Nineteenth Century: The Gifford Lectures in the University of Edinburgh for 1973–4.* New York: Cambridge University Press, 1975.

Chernow, Ron. *Alexander Hamilton.* New York: Penguin Press, 2004.

Cherry, Conrad, ed. *God's New Israel: Religious Interpretations of American Destiny.* Rev. ed. Chapel Hill: University of North Carolina Press, 1998.

Chesterton, G. K. *The Collected Works of G. K. Chesterton.* Edited by George J. Marlin and others. Vol. 21, *What I Saw in America. The Resurrection of Rome. Sidelights.* San Francisco: Ignatius Press, 1990.

———. *Orthodoxy.* Image Books ed. New York: Doubleday, 2001.

Church, Forrest, ed. *The Separation of Church and State: Writings on a Fundamental Freedom by America's Founders.* Boston: Beacon Press, 2004.

Churchill, Winston S. *The Second World War.* 6 vols. Boston: Houghton Mifflin, 1948–1953. Vol. 1, *The Gathering Storm,* 1948. Vol. 2, *Their Finest Hour,* 1949. Vol. 3, *The Grand Alliance,* 1950. Vol. 4, *The Hinge of Fate,* 1950. Vol. 5, *Closing the Ring,* 1951. Vol. 6, *Triumph and Tragedy,* 1953.

Clay, Henry. *The Papers of Henry Clay.* Edited by James F. Hopkins and Mary W. M. Hargreaves. Vol. 8, *Candidate, Compromiser, Whig: March 5, 1829–December 31, 1836.* Edited by Robert Seager II and Melba Porter Hay. Lexington: University Press of Kentucky, 1984.

Clinton, Bill. *My Life.* New York: Alfred A. Knopf, 2004.

Colish, Marcia L. *Medieval Foundations of the Western Intellectual Tradition, 400–1400.* Yale Intellectual History of the West. New Haven: Yale University Press, 1997.

Commager, Henry Steele. *The Empire of Reason: How Europe Imagined and America Realized the Enlightenment.* Garden City, NY: Anchor Press/Doubleday, 1977.

Conkin, Paul K. "The Religious Pilgrimage of Thomas Jefferson." In *Jeffersonian Legacies,* edited by Peter S. Onuf, 19–49. Charlottesville: University Press of Virginia, 1993.

Cousins, Norman, ed. *In God We Trust: The Religious Beliefs and Ideas of the American Founding Fathers.* New York: Harper & Brothers, 1958.

Cuomo, Mario. *More Than Words: The Speeches of Mario Cuomo.* New York: St. Martin's Press, 1993.

Curry, Thomas J. *Farewell to Christendom: The Future of Church and State in America.* New York: Oxford University Press, 2001.

———. *The First Freedoms: Church and State in America to the Passage of the First Amendment.* New York: Oxford University Press, 1986.

Cushing, John D. "Notes on Disestablishment in Massachusetts, 1780–1833." *William and Mary Quarterly,* 3rd ser., 26 (April 1969): 169–90.

Dahl, Curtis. "The Clergyman, the Hussy, and Old Hickory: Ezra Stiles Ely and the Peggy Eaton Affair." *Journal of Presbyterian History* 52 (Summer 1974): 137–55.

Dalin, David G., and Alfred J. Kolatch. *The Presidents of the United States and the Jews.* Middle Village, NY: Jonathan David Publishers, 2000.

Dallek, Robert. *An Unfinished Life: John F. Kennedy, 1917–1963*. Boston: Little, Brown and Co., 2003.

Dallimore, Arnold A. *George Whitefield: God's Anointed Servant in the Great Revival of the Eighteenth Century*. Westchester, IL: Crossway Books, 1990.

Davies, Samuel. *Sermons*. Edited by Thomas Gibbons. Vol. 2. Pittsburgh: Soli Deo Gloria Publications, 1995.

Davis, Derek H. *Religion and the Continental Congress, 1774–1789: Contributions to Original Intent*. Religion in America Series. New York: Oxford University Press, 2000.

Dewey, John. *A Common Faith*. New Haven: Yale University Press, 1934.

Dionne, E. J., Jr., Jean Bethke Elshtain, and Kayla M. Drogosz, eds. *One Electorate Under God?: A Dialogue on Religion and American Politics*. Washington: D.C.: Brookings Institution Press, 2004.

Donald, David Herbert. *Lincoln*. New York: Simon & Schuster, 1995.

Douglass, Frederick. *Narrative of the Life of Frederick Douglass, an American Slave*. Edited by John W. Blassinghame, John R. McKivigan, and Peter P. Hinks. New Haven: Yale University Press, 2001.

Dreisbach, Daniel L. *Thomas Jefferson and the Wall of Separation Between Church and State*. Critical America. New York: New York University Press, 2002.

Eastland, Terry, ed. *Religious Liberty in the Supreme Court: The Cases That Define the Debate Over Church and State*. Washington, D.C.: Ethics and Public Policy Center, 1993.

Eck, Diana L. *A New Religious America: How a "Christian Country" Has Now Become the World's Most Religiously Diverse Nation*. San Francisco: HarperSan Francisco, 2001.

Edwards, Jonathan. *The Sermons of Jonathan Edwards: A Reader*. Edited by Wilson H. Kimnach, Kenneth P. Minkema, and Douglas A. Sweeney. New Haven: Yale University Press, 1999.

Eisenhower, Dwight D. *At Ease: Stories I Tell to Friends*. Garden City, NY: Doubleday & Co., 1967.

———. *The White House Years*. 2 vols. Garden City, NY: Doubleday & Co., 1963–1965. Vol. 1, *Mandate for Change, 1953–1956*, 1963. Vol. 2, *Waging Peace, 1956–1961*, 1965.

Eliade, Mircea. *The Sacred and the Profane: The Nature of Religion*. Translated from the French by Willard R. Trask. New York: Harcourt, Brace and Co., 1959.

Ellis, Joseph J. *American Sphinx: The Character of Thomas Jefferson*. New York: Alfred A. Knopf, 1997.

———. *Founding Brothers: The Revolutionary Generation*. New York: Alfred A. Knopf, 2000.

———. *His Excellency: George Washington*. New York: Alfred A. Knopf, 2004.

Emerson, Ralph Waldo. *The Essential Writings of Ralph Waldo Emerson.* Edited by Brooks Atkinson. New York: Modern Library, 2000.

Ewald, William Bragg, Jr. *Eisenhower the President: Crucial Days, 1951–1960.* Englewood Cliffs, NJ: Prentice-Hall, 1981.

Falwell, Jerry. *America Can Be Saved!: (Jerry Falwell Preaches on Revival).* Murfreesboro, TN: Sword of the Lord Publishers, 1979.

———. *Listen, America!* Garden City, NY: Doubleday & Co., 1980.

———. *Strength for the Journey: An Autobiography.* New York: Simon & Schuster, 1987.

Federer, William J. *America's God and Country: Encyclopedia of Quotations.* Coppell, TX: Fame Publishing, 1994.

———. *The Ten Commandments and Their Influence on American Law: A Study in History.* St. Louis: Amerisearch, 2003.

Feldman, Noah. *Divided By God: America's Church-State Problem—And What We Should Do About It.* New York: Farrar, Straus and Giroux, 2005.

Feller, Daniel. *The Jacksonian Promise: America, 1815–1840.* The American Moment. Baltimore: Johns Hopkins University Press, 1995.

Ferling, John. *Adams vs. Jefferson: The Tumultuous Election of 1800.* Pivotal Moments in American History. New York: Oxford University Press, 2004.

Finke, Roger, and Rodney Stark. *The Churching of America, 1776–1990: Winners and Losers in Our Religious Economy.* New Brunswick, NJ: Rutgers University Press, 1992.

Finney, Charles G. *The Autobiography of Charles G. Finney.* Condensed and edited by Helen Wessel. Minneapolis: Bethany House Publishers, 1977.

———. *Experiencing the Presence of God.* New Kensington, PA: Whitaker House, 2000.

Fischer, David Hackett. *Liberty and Freedom.* America: A Cultural History. New York: Oxford University Press, 2005.

Fleming, Thomas J. *One Small Candle: The Pilgrims' First Year in America.* New York: W. W. Norton & Co., 1964.

Foner, Eric, ed. *The New American History.* Revised and expanded ed. Critical Perspectives on the Past. Philadelphia: Temple University Press, 1997.

Foote, Shelby. *The Civil War: A Narrative.* 3 vols. New York: Random House, 1958–1974. Vol. 1, *Fort Sumter to Perryville,* 1958. Vol. 2, *Fredericksburg to Meridian,* 1963. Vol. 3, *Red River to Appomattox,* 1974.

Ford, Gerald R. *A Time to Heal: The Autobiography of Gerald R. Ford.* New York: Harper & Row, 1979.

"Forum." *William and Mary Quarterly,* 3rd ser., 56 (October 1999): 775–824. Includes: Hutson, James H. "Thomas Jefferson's Letter to the Danbury Baptists: A Controversy Rejoined," pp. 775–90; O'Neil, Robert M. "The 'Wall of Separation' and Thomas Jefferson's Views on Religious Liberty," pp. 791–94;

Buckley, Thomas E. "Reflections on a Wall," pp. 795–800; Gaustad, Edwin S. "Thomas Jefferson, Danbury Baptists, and 'Eternal Hostility,' " pp. 801–4; Dreisbach, Daniel L. "Thomas Jefferson and the Danbury Baptists Revisited," pp. 805–16; Kramnick, Isaac, and R. Laurence Moore, "The Baptists, the Bureau, and the Case of the Missing Lines," pp. 817–22; Hutson, James H. "James H. Hutson Responds," pp. 823–24.

Foster, Charles I. *An Errand of Mercy: The Evangelical United Front, 1790–1837.* Chapel Hill: University of North Carolina Press, 1960.

Foster, Gaines M. *Moral Reconstruction: Christian Lobbyists and the Federal Legislation of Morality, 1865–1920.* Chapel Hill: University of North Carolina Press, 2002.

Franklin, Benjamin. *A Benjamin Franklin Reader.* Edited by Walter Isaacson. New York: Simon & Schuster, 2003.

Freehling, William W. *Prelude to Civil War: The Nullification Controversy in South Carolina, 1816–1836.* New York: Harper & Row, 1966.

Freidel, Frank. *Franklin D. Roosevelt.* 4 vols. Boston: Little, Brown and Co., 1952–1973. Vol. 1, *The Apprenticeship,* 1952. Vol. 2, *The Ordeal,* 1954. Vol. 3, *The Triumph,* 1956. Vol. 4, *Launching the New Deal,* 1973.

———. *Franklin D. Roosevelt: A Rendezvous with Destiny.* Boston: Little, Brown and Co., 1990.

Fuller, Robert C. *Religious Revolutionaries: The Rebels Who Reshaped American Religion.* New York: Palgrave/Macmillan, 2004.

Garrow, David J. *Bearing the Cross: Martin Luther King, Jr., and the Southern Christian Leadership Conference.* New York: William Morrow and Co., 1986.

Gaustad, Edwin S. *Faith of the Founders: Religion and the New Nation, 1776–1826.* Waco, TX: Baylor University Press, 2004.

———. *Proclaim Liberty Throughout All the Land: A History of Church and State in America.* New York: Oxford University Press, 2003.

———. *Sworn on the Altar of God: A Religious Biography of Thomas Jefferson.* Library of Religious Biography. Grand Rapids, MI: William B. Eerdmans Publishing Co., 1996.

Gaustad, Edwin S., and Philip L. Barlow. *New Historical Atlas of Religion in America.* New York: Oxford University Press, 2001.

Gaustad, Edwin S., and Leigh Schmidt. *The Religious History of America: The Heart of the American Story from Colonial Times to Today.* Revised ed. San Francisco: HarperSanFrancisco, 2002.

Gaustad, Edwin S., ed., with revisions by Mark A. Noll. *A Documentary History of Religion in America.* 3rd ed. 2 vols. Grand Rapids, MI: William B. Eerdmans Publishing Co., 2003. Vol. 1, *To 1877.* Vol. 2, *Since 1877.*

Gay, Peter. *The Enlightenment: An Interpretation.* 2 vols. New York: Alfred A.

Knopf, 1966–1969. Vol. 1, *The Rise of Modern Paganism*, 1966. Vol. 2, *The Science of Freedom*, 1969.

Genovese, Michael A. *The Power of the American Presidency, 1789–2000*. New York: Oxford University Press, 2001.

Gilbert, Martin. *Churchill: A Life*. New York: Henry Holt and Co., 1991.

———. *The Second World War: A Complete History*. New York: Henry Holt and Co., 1989.

Glad, Paul W. *The Trumpet Soundeth: William Jennings Bryan and His Democracy*. Lincoln, Nebraska: University of Nebraska Press, 1960.

Gomez, Michael A. *Black Crescent: The Experience and Legacy of African Muslims in the Americas*. New York: Cambridge University Press, 2005.

Goodwin, Richard N. *Remembering America: A Voice from the Sixties*. Boston: Little, Brown and Co., 1988.

Goolrick, John T. *Old Homes and History Around Fredericksburg: The Northern Neck and the Southside, Stafford and Spotsylvania Counties and Battle Sketches*. Richmond, VA: Garrett & Massie, 1929.

Gottheimer, Josh, ed. *Ripples of Hope: Great American Civil Rights Speeches*. New York: Basic Civitas Books, 2003.

Graham, Billy. *Just As I Am: The Autobiography of Billy Graham*. San Francisco: HarperSanFrancisco, 1997.

———. "We Are Electing a President of the World." *Life* 49 (November 7, 1960): 109–10.

Grant, James. *John Adams: Party of One*. New York: Farrar, Straus and Giroux, 2005.

Grant, Ulysses S. *Personal Memoirs of U. S. Grant*. Edited by E. B. Long. 2nd Da Capo Press ed. New York: Da Capo Press, 2001.

Gray, Madeleine. *The Protestant Reformation: Belief, Practice, and Tradition*. Portland, OR: Sussex Academic Press, 2003.

Green, John C., Mark J. Rozell, and Clyde Wilcox, eds. *The Christian Right in American Politics: Marching to the Millennium*. Religion and Politics Series. Washington, D.C.: Georgetown University Press, 2003.

Grenz, Stanley. *Isaac Backus—Puritan and Baptist: His Place in History, His Thought, and Their Implications for Modern Baptist Theology*. NABPR Dissertation Series. Macon, GA: Mercer University Press, 1983.

Grizzard, Frank E., Jr. *The Ways of Providence: Religion and George Washington*. Buena Vista, VA: Mariner Publishing, 2005.

Guelzo, Allen C. *Abraham Lincoln: Redeemer President*. Grand Rapids, MI: William B. Eerdmans Publishing Co., 1999.

Gunther, John. *Roosevelt in Retrospect: A Profile in History*. New York: Harper & Brothers, 1950.

Gurn, Joseph. *Charles Carroll of Carrollton, 1737–1832*. New York: P. J. Kennedy & Sons, 1932.

Gushee, David P. *The Righteous Gentiles of the Holocaust: A Christian Interpretation.* Minneapolis: Fortress Press, 1994.

Hall, Kermit L., ed. *The Oxford Guide to United States Supreme Court Decisions.* New York: Oxford University Press, 1999.

Hambrick-Stowe, Charles E. *Charles G. Finney and the Spirit of American Evangelicalism.* Library of Religious Biography. Grand Rapids, MI: William B. Eerdmans Publishing Co., 1996.

Hamburger, Philip. *Separation of Church and State.* Cambridge: Harvard University Press, 2002.

Hamilton, Alexander. *Writings.* The Library of America. New York: Library of America, 2001.

Hamilton, James E. "John Witherspoon: Foundations for a Threatened Tradition." *Christianity Today* 21 (November 5, 1976): 12–15.

Hampton, Vernon B. *Religious Background of the White House.* Boston: The Christopher Publishing House, 1932.

Harbaugh, William Henry. *Power and Responsibility: The Life and Times of Theodore Roosevelt.* New York: Farrar, Straus and Cudahy, 1961.

Harding, Susan Friend. *The Book of Jerry Falwell: Fundamentalist Language and Politics.* Princeton: Princeton University Press, 2000.

Harrell, Carolyn L. *When the Bells Tolled for Lincoln: Southern Reaction to the Assassination.* Macon, GA: Mercer University Press, 1997.

Harris, Sam. *The End of Faith: Religion, Terror, and the Future of Reason.* New York: W. W. Norton & Co., 2004.

Haskins, James. *The Life and Death of Martin Luther King, Jr.* New York: Lothrop, Lee & Shepard, 1977.

Hatch, Nathan O. *The Democratization of American Christianity.* New Haven: Yale University Press, 1989.

———. *The Sacred Cause of Liberty: Republican Thought and the Millennium in Revolutionary New England.* New Haven: Yale University Press, 1977.

Hazelton, John H. *The Declaration of Independence: Its History.* Da Capo Press Reprints in American Constitutional and Legal History. New York: Da Capo Press, 1970.

Henry, Carl F. H. "Of Bicentennial Concerns and Patriotic Symbols." *Christianity Today* 20 (July 2, 1976): 14–19.

Henry, Patrick. " 'And I Don't Care What It Is': The Tradition-History of a Civil Religion Proof-Text," *Journal of the American Academy of Religion* 49 (March 1981): 35–49.

Herberg, Will. *Protestant-Catholic-Jew: An Essay in American Religious Sociology.* Garden City, NY: Doubleday & Co., 1955.

Herndon, William H., and Jesse W. Weik. *Abraham Lincoln: The True Story of a Great Life.* 2 vols. New York: D. Appleton & Co., 1917.

Heschel, Abraham Joshua. *Moral Grandeur and Spiritual Audacity: Essays.* Edited by Susannah Heschel. New York: Farrar, Straus and Giroux, 1996.

Hirschfeld, Fritz. *George Washington and the Jews.* Newark: University of Delaware Press, 2005.

Hodgson, Marshall G. S. *Rethinking World History: Essays on Europe, Islam, and World History.* Edited by Edmund Burke III. Studies in Comparative World History. New York: Cambridge University Press, 1993.

Hoffman, Ronald, in collaboration with Sally D. Mason. *Princes of Ireland, Planters of Maryland: A Carroll Saga, 1500–1782.* Chapel Hill: Published for the Omohundro Institute of Early American History and Culture, Williamsburg, Virginia, by the University of North Carolina Press, 2000.

Hoffman, Ronald, and Peter J. Albert, eds. *Religion in a Revolutionary Age.* Perspectives on the American Revolution. Charlottesville: Published for the United States Capitol Historical Society by the University Press of Virginia, 1994.

Hofstadter, Richard. *The American Political Tradition and the Men Who Made It.* New York: Alfred A. Knopf, 1948.

Holifield, E. Brooks. *Theology in America: Christian Thought from the Age of the Puritans to the Civil War.* New Haven: Yale University Press, 2003.

Homer. *The Iliad.* Translated by Richmond Lattimore. Chicago: University of Chicago Press, 1951.

———. *The Odyssey.* Translated by Robert Fagles. New York: Viking, 1996.

Hoobler, Dorothy, and Thomas Hoobler. *Captain John Smith: Jamestown and the Birth of the American Dream.* Hoboken, NJ: John Wiley & Sons, 2005.

Horn, James. *A Land As God Made It: Jamestown and the Birth of America.* New York: Basic Books, 2005.

Horwitz, Robert H., ed. *The Moral Foundations of the American Republic.* 3d ed. Charlottesville: University Press of Virginia, 1986.

Huntington, Samuel P. *The Clash of Civilizations and the Remaking of World Order.* New York: Simon & Schuster, 1996.

———. *Who Are We?: The Challenges to America's National Identity.* New York: Simon & Schuster, 2004.

Hutchinson, Paul. "The President's Religious Faith." *Christian Century* 71 (March 24, 1954): 362–69.

Hutson, James H. *Religion and the Founding of the American Republic.* Washington, D.C.: Library of Congress; Hanover, NH: University Press of New England, 1998.

———, ed. *The Founders on Religion: A Book of Quotations.* Princeton: Princeton University Press, 2005.

———, ed. *Religion and the New Republic: Faith in the Founding of America.* Lanham, MD: Rowman & Littlefield Publishers, 2000.

Irving, Washington. *George Washington: A Biography.* Abridged and edited by Charles Neider. Garden City, NY: Doubleday & Co., 1976.

Isaac, Rhys. *The Transformation of Virginia, 1740–1790.* Chapel Hill: Published for the Institute of Early American History and Culture, Williamsburg, Virginia, by the University of North Carolina Press, 1982.

Israel, Jonathan I. *Radical Enlightenment: Philosophy and the Making of Modernity, 1650–1750.* New York: Oxford University Press, 2001.

Jackson, Andrew. *Correspondence of Andrew Jackson.* Edited by John Spencer Bassett. Vols. 4 and 5. Washington, D.C.: Carnegie Institution of Washington, 1929, 1931.

———. *The Papers of Andrew Jackson.* Edited by Sam B. Smith and Harriet Chappell Owsley. Vol. 6. Edited by Harold D. Moser and J. Clint Clifft. Knoxville: University of Tennessee Press, 2002.

Jacoby, Susan. *Freethinkers: A History of American Secularism.* New York: Metropolitan Books, 2004.

Jaffa, Harry V., with Bruce Ledewitz, Robert L. Stone, and George Anastaplo. *Original Intent and the Framers of the Constitution: A Disputed Question.* Washington, D.C.: Regnery Gateway, 1993.

James, William. *The Varieties of Religious Experience: A Study in Human Nature.* New York: Modern Library, 1994.

———. *The Will to Believe and Other Essays in Popular Philosophy, and Human Immortality.* New York: Dover Publications, 1956.

Jayne, Allen. *Jefferson's Declaration of Independence: Origins, Philosophy, and Theology.* Lexington: University Press of Kentucky, 1998.

Jefferson, Thomas. *Jefferson's Extracts from the Gospels: "The Philosophy of Jesus" and "The Life and Morals of Jesus."* Edited by Dickinson W. Adams and others. The Papers of Thomas Jefferson. Second Series. Princeton: Princeton University Press, 1983.

———. *Writings.* The Library of America. New York: Literary Classics of the United States, 1984.

———. *The Writings of Thomas Jefferson.* Edited by Andrew A. Lipscomb and Albert Ellery Bergh. Vol. 15. Washington, D.C.: Thomas Jefferson Memorial Association of the United States, 1904.

Jefferson, Thomas, and John Adams. *"Ye Will Say I Am No Christian": The Thomas Jefferson/John Adams Correspondence on Religion, Morals, and Values.* Edited by Bruce Braden. Amherst, NY: Prometheus Books, 2005.

Jefferson, Thomas, and James Madison. *Jefferson and Madison on the Separation of Church and State: Writings on Religion and Secularism.* Edited by Lenni Brenner. Fort Lee, NJ: Barricade Books, 2004.

Jensen, Merrill, ed. *The Documentary History of the Ratification of the Constitu-*

tion. Vol. 2, *Pennsylvania.* Vol. 3, *Delaware, New Jersey, Georgia, Connecticut.* The following volumes are edited by John P. Kaminski and Gaspare J. Saladino: Vol. 4, *Massachusetts.* Vol. 10, *Virginia.* Vol. 13, *Commentaries on the Constitution, Public and Private: 21 February to 7 November 1787.* Vol. 15, *Commentaries on the Constitution, Public and Private: 18 December 1787 to 31 January 1788.* Vol. 16, *Commentaries on the Constitution, Public and Private: 1 February to 31 March 1788.* Vol. 18, *Commentaries on the Constitution, Public and Private: 10 May to 13 September 1788.* Madison: State Historical Society of Wisconsin, 1976, 1978, 1981, 1984, 1986, 1993, 1995, 1997.

Johnson, Lyndon B. *Public Papers of the Presidents of the United States: Lyndon B. Johnson; Containing the Public Messages, Speeches, and Statements of the President; 1963–64 and 1965.* Washington, D.C.: U.S. Government Printing Office, 1965–1966.

———. *The Vantage Point: Perspectives of the Presidency, 1963–1969.* New York: Holt, Rinehart and Winston, 1971.

Johnson, Paul. *A History of Christianity.* Touchstone ed. New York: Simon & Schuster, 1995.

———. *A History of the Jews.* New York: Perennial Library, 1988.

———. *Modern Times: The World from the Twenties to the Nineties.* New York: Perennial Classics, 2001.

Johnson, Thomas H. *The Oxford Companion to American History.* New York: Oxford University Press, 1966.

Kammen, Michael, ed. *The Origins of the American Constitution: A Documentary History.* New York: Penguin Books, 1986.

Kauffman, Michael W. *American Brutus: John Wilkes Booth and the Lincoln Conspiracies.* New York: Random House, 2004.

Kelly, J.N.D. *Early Christian Doctrines.* San Francisco: Harper & Row, 1978.

Kennedy, John F. *"Let the Word Go Forth": The Speeches, Statements, and Writings of John F. Kennedy, 1947 to 1963.* Selected by Theodore C. Sorensen. New York: Delacorte Press, 1988.

———. *Public Papers of the Presidents of the United States: John F. Kennedy; Containing the Public Messages, Speeches, and Statements of the President, 1961–1963.* 3 vols. Washington, D.C.: U.S. Government Printing Office, 1962–1964.

Ketcham, Ralph. *James Madison: A Biography.* Charlottesville: University Press of Virginia, 1990.

———, ed. *The Anti-Federalist Papers and the Constitutional Convention Debates.* New York: New American Library, 1986.

King, Coretta Scott. *My Life with Martin Luther King, Jr.* New York: Holt, Rinehart and Winston, 1969.

Koenig, Louis W. *Bryan: A Political Biography of William Jennings Bryan.* New York: G. P. Putnam's, 1971.

Kohut, Andrew, and others. *The Diminishing Divide: Religion's Changing Role in American Politics.* Washington, D.C.: Brookings Institution Press, 2000.

Kramnick, Isaac, and R. Laurence Moore. *The Godless Constitution: A Moral Defense of the Secular State.* New York: W. W. Norton & Co., 2005.

Kunhardt, Dorothy Meserve, and Philip B. Kunhardt, Jr. *Twenty Days: A Narrative in Text and Pictures of the Assassination of Abraham Lincoln and the Twenty Days and Nights That Followed—the Nation in Mourning, the Long Trip Home to Springfield.* New York: Harper & Row, 1965.

Kunhardt, Philip B., Jr., Philip B. Kunhardt III, and Peter W. Kunhardt. *Lincoln: An Illustrated Biography.* New York: Alfred A. Knopf, 1992.

Kutler, Stanley I., ed. *Abuse of Power: The New Nixon Tapes.* New York: Free Press, 1997.

Lacey, Michael J., ed. *Religion and Twentieth-Century American Intellectual Life.* Woodrow Wilson Center Series. Washington, D.C.: Woodrow Wilson International Center for Scholars; New York: Cambridge University Press, 1989.

LaHaye, Tim. *Faith of Our Founding Fathers: A Comprehensive Study of America's Christian Foundations.* Green Forest, AR: Master Books, 1994.

Lambert, Frank. *The Founding Fathers and the Place of Religion in America.* Princeton: Princeton University Press, 2003.

LaPlante, Eve. *American Jezebel: The Uncommon Life of Anne Hutchinson, the Woman Who Defied the Puritans.* San Francisco: HarperSanFrancisco, 2004.

Larson, Edward J. *Summer for the Gods: The Scopes Trial and America's Continuing Debate over Science and Religion.* Cambridge: Harvard University Press, 1997.

Lash, Joseph P. *Roosevelt and Churchill, 1939–1941: The Partnership That Saved the West.* New York: W. W. Norton & Co., 1976.

Latourette, Kenneth Scott. *Christianity in a Revolutionary Age: A History of Christianity in the Nineteenth and Twentieth Centuries.* Vol. 4, *The Twentieth Century in Europe: The Roman Catholic, Protestant, and Eastern Churches.* New York: Harper & Brothers, 1961.

Layman, Geoffrey. *The Great Divide: Religious and Cultural Conflict in American Party Politics.* Power, Conflict, and Democracy. New York: Columbia University Press, 2001.

Leepson, Marc. *Saving Monticello: The Levy Family's Epic Quest to Rescue the House That Jefferson Built.* New York: Free Press, 2001.

Levy, Leonard W. *The Establishment Clause: Religion and the First Amendment.* 2nd ed., revised. Chapel Hill: University of North Carolina Press, 1994.

———. *Origins of the Bill of Rights.* Contemporary Law Series. New Haven: Yale University Press, 1999.

Lewis, Bernard. *The Muslim Discovery of Europe.* New York: W. W. Norton & Co., 2001.

————. *What Went Wrong?: Western Impact and Middle Eastern Response*. New York: Oxford University Press, 2002.

Lewis, John, with Michael D'Orso. *Walking with the Wind: A Memoir of the Movement*. New York: Simon & Schuster, 1998.

Lincoln, Abraham. *Abraham Lincoln: Speeches and Writings*. Vol. 2, *1859–1865*. The Library of America. New York: Library of America, 1989.

Locke, John. *An Essay Concerning Human Understanding*. Edited by Peter H. Nidditch. The Clarendon Edition of the Works of John Locke. Oxford: Clarendon Press, 1975.

————. *The Selected Political Writings of John Locke*. Edited by Paul E. Sigmund. A Norton Critical Edition. New York: W. W. Norton & Co., 2005.

Looney, J. Jefferson. "Thomas Jefferson's Last Letter." *Virginia Magazine of History and Biography* 112 (Spring 2004): 178–84.

Madison, James. *Writings*. The Library of America. New York: Library of America, 1999.

Maier, Pauline. *American Scripture: Making the Declaration of Independence*. New York: Alfred A. Knopf, 1997.

Malone, Dumas. *Jefferson and His Time*. 6 vols. Boston: Little, Brown and Co., 1948–1981. Vol. 1, *Jefferson the Virginian*, 1948. Vol. 2, *Jefferson and the Rights of Man*, 1951. Vol. 3, *Jefferson and the Ordeal of Liberty*, 1962. Vol. 4, *Jefferson the President: First Term, 1801–1805*, 1970. Vol. 5, *Jefferson the President: Second Term, 1805–1809*, 1974. Vol. 6, *The Sage of Monticello*, 1981.

Mancall, Peter C., ed. *Envisioning America: English Plans for the Colonization of North America, 1580–1640*. The Bedford Series in History and Culture. Boston: Bedford Books of St. Martin's Press, 1995.

Marcus, Jacob Rader. *The Handsome Young Priest in the Black Gown: The Personal World of Gershom Seixas*. Cincinnati: American Jewish Archives, 1970.

Marsden, George M. *Fundamentalism and American Culture: The Shaping of Twentieth Century Evangelicalism, 1870–1925*. New York: Oxford University Press, 1980.

Marshall, Paul Victor. *One, Catholic, and Apostolic: Samuel Seabury and the Early Episcopal Church*. New York: Church Publishing, 2004.

Marszalek, John F. *The Petticoat Affair: Manners, Mutiny, and Sex in Andrew Jackson's White House*. New York: Free Press, 1997.

Martin, William. *A Prophet with Honor: The Billy Graham Story*. New York: William Morrow and Co., 1991.

————. *With God on Our Side: The Rise of the Religious Right in America*. New York: Broadway Books, 1996.

Marty, Martin E. *Modern American Religion*. 3 vols. Chicago: University of

Chicago Press, 1986–1996. Vol. 1, *The Irony of It All, 1893–1919*, 1986. Vol. 2, *The Noise of Conflict, 1919–1941*, 1991. Vol. 3, *Under God, Indivisible, 1941–1960*, 1996.

———. *A Nation of Behavers.* Chicago: University of Chicago Press, 1976.

———. *The One and the Many: America's Struggle for the Common Good.* The Joanna Jackson Goldman Memorial Lecture on American Civilization and Government. Cambridge: Harvard University Press, 1997.

———. *Pilgrims in Their Own Land: 500 Years of Religion in America.* Boston: Little, Brown and Co., 1984.

———. *The Public Church: Mainline, Evangelical, Catholic.* New York: Crossroad Publishing Co., 1981.

———. *Religion, Awakening and Revolution.* Faith of Our Fathers. Wilmington, NC: Consortium Books, 1977.

———. *When Faiths Collide.* Blackwell Manifestos. Malden, MA: Blackwell Publishers, 2005.

Marty, Martin E., and R. Scott Appleby, eds. *Fundamentalisms Observed.* The Fundamentalism Project. Chicago: University of Chicago Press, 1991.

Mathews, Donald G. *Religion in the Old South.* Chicago History of American Religion. Chicago: University of Chicago Press, 1977.

May, Henry F. *The Enlightenment in America.* New York: Oxford University Press, 1976.

Mayer, Henry. *A Son of Thunder: Patrick Henry and the American Republic.* New York: Franklin Watts, 1986.

Mays, Benjamin E. *Born to Rebel: An Autobiography.* New York: Charles Scribner's Sons, 1971.

McCoy, Drew R. *The Last of the Fathers: James Madison and the Republican Legacy.* New York: Cambridge University Press, 1989.

McCullough, David. *John Adams.* New York: Simon & Schuster, 2001.

———. *1776.* New York: Simon & Schuster, 2005.

———. *Truman.* New York: Simon & Schuster, 1992.

McDermott, Scott. *Charles Carroll of Carrollton: Faithful Revolutionary.* New York: Scepter Publishers, 2002.

McDonald, Forrest. *Novus Ordo Seclorum: The Intellectual Origins of the Constitution.* Lawrence: University Press of Kansas, 1985.

McGraw, Barbara A., and Jo Renee Formicola, eds. *Taking Religious Pluralism Seriously: Spiritual Politics on America's Sacred Ground.* Waco, TX: Baylor University Press, 2005.

McGreevy, John T. *Catholicism and American Freedom: A History.* New York: W. W. Norton & Co., 2003.

McKenzie, Steven L. *How to Read the Bible: History, Prophecy, Literature—Why*

Modern Readers Need to Know the Difference, and What It Means for Faith Today. New York: Oxford University Press, 2005.

McKivigan, John R., and Mitchell Snay, eds. *Religion and the Antebellum Debate over Slavery*. Athens: University of Georgia Press, 1998.

McPherson, James M. *Battle Cry of Freedom: The Civil War Era*. The Oxford History of the United States. New York: Oxford University Press, 1988.

———. *For Cause and Comrades: Why Men Fought in the Civil War*. New York: Oxford University Press, 1997.

Meacham, Jon. *Franklin and Winston: An Intimate Portrait of an Epic Friendship*. New York: Random House, 2003.

Miller, Perry. *Errand into the Wilderness*. Cambridge: Belknap Press of Harvard University Press, 1984.

———. *The Life of the Mind in America: From the Revolution to the Civil War*. New York: Harcourt, Brace & World, 1965.

———. *The New England Mind: From Colony to Province*. Cambridge: Belknap Press of Harvard University Press, 1983.

———. *The New England Mind: The Seventeenth Century*. Cambridge: Harvard University Press, 1983.

Miller, Perry, and Thomas H. Johnson, eds. *The Puritans*. Rev. ed. Harper Torchbooks. The Academy Library. 2 vols. New York: Harper & Row, 1963.

Miller, Robert T., and Ronald B. Flowers. *Toward Benevolent Neutrality: Church, State, and the Supreme Court*. 5th ed. 2 vols. Waco, TX: Markham Press Fund of Baylor University Press, 1996.

Miller, William Lee. *The First Liberty: America's Foundation in Religious Freedom*. Expanded and updated. Washington, D.C.: Georgetown University Press, 2003.

———. "Piety Along the Potomac." *Reporter* 11 (August 17, 1954): 25–28.

Milton, John. *Complete Poems and Major Prose*. Edited by Merritt Y. Hughes. New York: Macmillan Publishing Company, 1957.

Mittleman, Alan, Robert Licht, and Jonathan D. Sarna, eds. *Jewish Polity and American Civil Society: Communal Agencies and Religious Movements in the American Public Sphere*. Lanham, MD: Rowman & Littlefield Publishers, 2002.

———, eds. *Jews and the American Public Square: Debating Religion and Republic*. Lanham, MD: Rowman & Littlefield Publishers, 2002.

Moore, Frank, ed. *The Patriot Preachers of the American Revolution. With Biographical Sketches. 1766–1783*. New York: Charles T. Evans, 1862.

Moore, R. Laurence. *Religious Outsiders and the Making of Americans*. New York: Oxford University Press, 1986.

Morgan, Edmund S. *American Slavery, American Freedom: The Ordeal of Colonial Virginia*. New York: W. W. Norton & Co., 1975.

———. *The Gentle Puritan: A Life of Ezra Stiles, 1727–1795.* New Haven: Published for the Institute of Early American History and Culture, Williamsburg, Virginia, by Yale University Press, 1962.

———. *The Puritan Dilemma: The Story of John Winthrop.* Edited by Oscar Handlin. The Library of American Biography. Boston: Little, Brown and Co., 1958.

———. *Roger Williams: The Church and the State.* New York: Harcourt, Brace & World, 1967.

Morone, James A. *Hellfire Nation: The Politics of Sin in American History.* New Haven: Yale University Press, 2003.

Morris, Edmund. *The Rise of Theodore Roosevelt.* New York: Coward, McCann & Geoghegan, 1979.

———. *Theodore Rex.* New York: Random House, 2001.

Moynahan, Brian. *The Faith: A History of Christianity.* New York: Doubleday, 2002.

Murray, John Courtney. *We Hold These Truths: Catholic Reflections on the American Proposition.* New York: Sheed and Ward, 1960.

Murrow, Edward R., comp. *This I Believe: The Living Philosophies of One Hundred Thoughtful Men and Women in All Walks of Life.* Edited by Edward P. Morgan. New York: Simon & Schuster, 1952.

Neuhaus, Richard John. *Christian Faith and Public Policy: Thinking and Acting in the Courage of Uncertainty.* Minneapolis: Augsburg Publishing House, 1977.

———. *The Naked Public Square: Religion and Democracy in America.* Grand Rapids, MI: William B. Eerdmans Publishing Co., 1986.

Neusner, Jacob, ed. *God's Rule: The Politics of World Religions.* Washington, D.C.: Georgetown University Press, 2003.

Neusner, Jacob, Bruce Chilton, and William Graham. *Three Faiths, One God: The Formative Faith and Practice of Judaism, Christianity, and Islam.* Boston: Brill Academic Publishers, 2002.

Niebuhr, Reinhold. *The Essential Reinhold Niebuhr: Selected Essays and Addresses.* Edited by Robert McAfee Brown. New Haven: Yale University Press, 1986.

———. *Faith and History: A Comparison of Christian and Modern Views of History.* New York: Charles Scribner's Sons, 1949.

Niven, John. *Salmon P. Chase: A Biography.* New York: Oxford University Press, 1995.

Nixon, Richard M. *RN: The Memoirs of Richard Nixon.* New York: Grosset & Dunlap, 1978.

Nöel Hume, Ivor. *The Virginia Adventure: Roanoke to James Towne: An Archaeological and Historical Odyssey.* The Virginia Bookshelf. Charlottesville: University Press of Virginia, 1997.

Noll, Mark A. *America's God: From Jonathan Edwards to Abraham Lincoln.* New York: Oxford University Press, 2002.

———. *A History of Christianity in the United States and Canada.* Grand Rapids, MI: William B. Eerdmans Publishing Co., 1992.

———. *Religion and American Politics: From the Colonial Period to the 1980s.* New York: Oxford University Press, 1990.

———. *The Rise of Evangelicalism: The Age of Edwards, Whitefield and the Wesleys.* A History of Evangelicalism. Downers Grove, IL: InterVarsity Press, 2003.

———. *The Scandal of the Evangelical Mind.* Grand Rapids, MI: William B. Eerdmans Publishing Co., 1994.

———. *Turning Points: Decisive Moments in the History of Christianity.* Grand Rapids, MI: Baker Books, 1997.

Noll, Mark A., Nathan O. Hatch, and George M. Marsden. *The Search for Christian America.* Westchester, IL: Crossway Books, 1983.

Noonan, John T., Jr. *The Lustre of Our Country: The American Experience of Religious Freedom.* Berkeley: University of California Press, 1998.

Noonan, John T., Jr., and Edward McGlynn Gaffney, Jr. *Religious Freedom: History, Cases, and Other Materials on the Interaction of Religion and Government.* New York: Foundation Press, 2001.

Norris, Pippa, and Ronald Inglehart. *Sacred and Secular: Religion and Politics Worldwide.* Cambridge Studies in Social Theory, Religion, and Politics. New York: Cambridge University Press, 2004.

Novick, Peter. *The Holocaust in American Life.* Boston: Houghton Mifflin, 1999.

Oakes, James. *The Ruling Race: A History of American Slaveholders.* New York: Alfred A. Knopf, 1982.

O'Connor, Flannery. *The Habit of Being: Letters.* Edited by Sally Fitzgerald. New York: Farrar, Straus and Giroux, 1979.

O'Toole, Patricia. *When Trumpets Call: Theodore Roosevelt After the White House.* New York: Simon & Schuster, 2005.

Paine, Thomas. *Collected Writings.* The Library of America. New York: Library of America, 1995.

Parton, James. *Life of Andrew Jackson.* Vol. 3. Boston: Ticknor and Fields, 1866.

———. *Life of Thomas Jefferson.* The American Scene: Comments and Commentators. New York: Da Capo Press, 1971.

Pearson, Roger. *Voltaire Almighty: A Life in Pursuit of Freedom.* New York: Bloomsbury Publishing, 2005.

Pelikan, Jaroslav. *The Christian Tradition: A History of the Development of Doctrine.* Vol. 1, *The Emergence of the Catholic Tradition (100–600).* Chicago: University of Chicago Press, 1971.

——. *Credo: Historical and Theological Guide to Creeds and Confessions of Faith in the Christian Tradition.* New Haven: Yale University Press, 2003.

——. *Jesus Through the Centuries: His Place in the History of Culture.* New Haven: Yale University Press, 1985.

Pencak, William. *Jews and Gentiles in Early America, 1654–1800.* Ann Arbor: University of Michigan Press, 2005.

Perkins, Frances. *The Roosevelt I Knew.* New York: Viking Press, 1946.

Perry, Ralph Barton. *Characteristically American: Five Lectures Delivered on the William W. Cook Foundation at the University of Michigan, November–December 1948.* William W. Cook Foundation Lectures. New York. Alfred A. Knopf, 1949.

Peters, Charles. *Five Days in Philadelphia: The Amazing "We Want Wilkie!" Convention of 1940 and How It Freed FDR to Save the Western World.* New York: PublicAffairs, 2005.

Peters, F. E. *The Monotheists: Jews, Christians, and Muslims in Conflict and Competition.* 2 vols. Princeton: Princeton University Press, 2003. Vol. 1, *The Peoples of God.* Vol. 2, *The Words and Will of God.*

Peterson, Merrill D. *The Great Triumvirate: Webster, Clay, and Calhoun.* New York: Oxford University Press, 1987.

——. *The Jefferson Image in the American Mind.* New York: Oxford University Press, 1960.

——. *Jefferson Memorial: An Essay.* National Park Handbooks. Washington, D.C.: U.S. Department of the Interior, 1998.

——. *Thomas Jefferson and the New Nation: A Biography.* New York: Oxford University Press, 1970.

Pfeffer, Leo. *Church, State, and Freedom.* Revised ed. Boston: Beacon Press, 1967.

Polishook, Irwin H. *Roger Williams, John Cotton, and Religious Freedom: A Controversy in New and Old England.* American Historical Sources Series: Research and Interpretation. Englewood Cliffs, NJ: Prentice-Hall, 1967.

Polkinghorne, John. *The Faith of a Physicist: Reflections of a Bottom-Up Thinker; The Gifford Lectures for 1993–4.* Minneapolis: Fortress Press, 1996.

——. *Faith, Science and Understanding.* New Haven: Yale University Press, 2000.

Porter, Roy. *Flesh in the Age of Reason.* New York: W. W. Norton & Co., 2004.

Price, David. *Love and Hate in Jamestown: John Smith, Pocahontas, and the Heart of a New Nation.* New York: Alfred A. Knopf, 2003.

Priestley, Joseph. *Essay of the First Principles of Government and on the Nature of Political, Civil and Religious Liberty.* Whitefish, MT: Kessinger Publishing, 2003.

Prucha, Francis Paul. *The Great Father: The United States Government and the American Indians.* 2 vols. Lincoln: University of Nebraska Press, 1984.

Raboteau, Albert J. *Canaan Land: A Religious History of African Americans*. New York: Oxford University Press, 2001.

Rachels, James. *The Elements of Moral Philosophy*. 4th ed. New York: McGraw-Hill Higher Education, 2003.

Rakove, Jack N. *Original Meanings: Politics and Ideas in the Making of the Constitution*. New York: Alfred A. Knopf, 1996.

Randall, Henry Stephens. *The Life of Thomas Jefferson*. The American Scene. 3 vols. New York: Da Capo Press, 1972.

Ratzinger, Joseph Cardinal [Pope Benedict XVI]. *Introduction to Christianity*. Translated by J. R. Foster. San Francisco: Ignatius Press, 1990.

———. *Many Religions—One Covenant: Israel, the Church and the World*. Translated by Graham Harrison. San Francisco: Ignatius Press, 1999.

———. *Truth and Tolerance: Christian Belief and World Religions*. Translated by Henry Taylor. San Francisco: Ignatius Press, 2004.

Reagan, Ronald. *An American Life*. New York: Simon and Schuster, 1990.

———. *Public Papers of the Presidents of the United States: Ronald Reagan; Containing the Public Messages, Speeches, and Statements of the President, 1984*. Vol. 1. Washington, D.C.: U. S. Government Printing Office, 1986.

Reagan, Ronald, with Richard G. Hubler. *Where's the Rest of Me?* New York: Duell, Sloan and Pearce, 1965.

Reeves, Richard. *President Reagan: The Triumph of Imagination*. New York: Simon & Schuster, 2005.

Remini, Robert V. *Andrew Jackson and the Course of American Freedom, 1822–1832*. New York: Harper & Row, 1981.

———. *Henry Clay: Statesman for the Union*. New York: W. W. Norton & Co., 1991.

Richey, Russell E. and Donald G. Jones, eds. *American Civil Religion*. New York: Harper & Row, 1974.

Rittner, Carol, Stephen D. Smith, and Irena Steinfeldt, eds. *The Holocaust and the Christian World: Reflections on the Past, Challenges for the Future*. New York: Continuum, 2000.

Roosevelt, Eleanor. *This I Remember*. New York: Harper & Brothers, 1949.

Roosevelt, Franklin D. *The Public Papers and Addresses of Franklin D. Roosevelt*. Compiled by Samuel I. Rosenman. Vol. 2, *The Year of Crisis, 1933*. New York: Random House, 1938.

Roosevelt, James, and Sidney Shalett. *Affectionately, F.D.R.: A Son's Story of a Lonely Man*. New York: Harcourt, Brace and Co., 1959.

Rosenman, Samuel I. *Working with Roosevelt*. New York: Harper & Brothers, 1952.

Rountree, Helen C. *Pocahontas, Powhatan, Opechancanough: Three Indian Lives Changed by Jamestown*. Charlottesville: University of Virginia Press, 2005.

Rousseau, Jean-Jacques. *The Social Contract and Other Later Political Writings.* Edited and translated by Victor Gourevitch. New York: Cambridge University Press, 1997.

Russett, Cynthia Eagle. *Darwin in America: The Intellectual Response, 1865–1912.* San Francisco: W. H. Freeman, 1976.

Rutland, Robert A. *George Mason: Reluctant Statesman.* Williamsburg in America Series. Baton Rouge: Louisiana State University Press, 1980.

Sanford, Charles B. *The Religious Life of Thomas Jefferson.* Charlottesville: University Press of Virginia, 1984.

Sarna, Jonathan D. *American Jews and Church-State Relations: The Search for "Equal Footing."* New York: American Jewish Committee, Institute of Human Relations, 1989.

———. *American Judaism: A History.* New Haven: Yale University Press, 2004.

———. *Jacksonian Jew: The Two Worlds of Mordecai Noah.* New York: Holmes & Meier Publishers, 1981.

———. ed. *Minority Faiths and the American Protestant Mainstream.* Urbana: University of Illinois Press, 1998.

Sarna, Jonathan D., and David G. Dalin. *Religion and State in the American Jewish Experience.* Nortre Dame, IN: University of Notre Dame Press, 1997.

Sarna, Jonathan D., Benny Kraut, and Samuel K. Joseph, eds. *Jews and the Founding of the Republic.* New York: Markus Wiener Publishers, 1985.

Sarna, Jonathan D., and Ellen Smith, eds. *The Jews of Boston: Essays on the Occasion of the Centenary (1895–1995) of the Combined Jewish Philanthropies of Greater Boston.* Boston: The Philanthropies, 1995.

Satz, Ronald N. *American Indian Policy in the Jacksonian Era.* Lincoln: University of Nebraska Press, 1974.

Scaer, David P. "The Civil War of 1776." *Christianity Today* 20 (July 2, 1976): 12–14.

Schaaf, Gregory. *Franklin, Jefferson, and Madison: On Religion and the State.* U.S. Constitution and Bill of Rights Series. Santa Fe: CIAC Press, 2004.

Schlesinger, Arthur M., Jr. *The Age of Jackson.* Boston: Little, Brown and Co., 1950.

———. *A Thousand Days: John F. Kennedy in the White House.* Boston: Houghton Mifflin, 1965.

Sernett, Milton C., ed. *African American Religious History: A Documentary Witness.* 2nd ed. The C. Eric Lincoln Series on the Black Experience. Durham, NC: Duke University Press, 1999.

Sharansky, Natan, with Ron Dermer. *The Case for Democracy: The Power of Freedom to Overcome Tyranny and Terror.* New York: PublicAffairs, 2004.

Shaw, Mark R. "The Spirit of 1740." *Christianity Today* 20 (January 2, 1976): 7–8.

Shepherd, Jack. *The Adams Chronicles: Four Generations of Greatness*. Boston: Little, Brown and Company, 1975.

Sheridan, Eugene R. *Jefferson and Religion*. Monticello Monograph Series. Charlottesville, VA: Thomas Jefferson Memorial Foundation, 1998.

Sherrill, Rowland A., ed. *Religion and the Life of the Nation: American Recoveries*. Urbana: University of Illinois Press, 1990.

Sherwood, Robert E. *Roosevelt and Hopkins: An Intimate History*. New York: Harper & Brothers, 1948.

Sidney, Algernon. *Discourses Concerning Government*. Revised ed. Edited by Thomas G. West. Indianapolis: Liberty Fund, 1996.

Silk, Mark. "Notes on the Judeo-Christian Tradition in America." *American Quarterly* 36 (Spring 1984): 65–85.

Singer, Peter, ed. *A Companion to Ethics*. Oxford: Blackwell Publishers, 1991.

Slosser, Bob. *Reagan Inside Out*. Waco, TX: Word Books, 1984.

Smith, Adam. *Wealth of Nations*. Edited by Edwin Cannan. The Modern Library of the World's Best Books. New York: Modern Library, 1937.

Smith, Gary Scott, ed. *God and Politics: Four Views on the Reformation of Civil Government: Theonomy, Principled Pluralism, Christian America, National Confessionalism*. Phillipsburg, NJ: Presbyterian and Reformed Publishing Co., 1989.

Smith, Jean Edward. *John Marshall: Definer of a Nation*. New York: Henry Holt and Co., 1996.

Smith, John. *Captain John Smith: A Select Edition of His Writings*. Edited by Karen Ordahl Kupperman. Chapel Hill: Published for the Institute of Early American History and Culture by the University of North Carolina Press, 1988.

Smith, Margaret Bayard. *The First Forty Years of Washington Society in the Family Letters of Margaret Bayard Smith*. Edited by Gaillard Hunt. American Classics. New York: Frederick Ungar Publishing Co., 1965.

Smith, Richard Norton. *Patriarch: George Washington and the New American Nation*. Boston: Houghton Mifflin, 1993.

Smith, Steven D. *Foreordained Failure: The Quest for a Constitutional Principle of Religious Freedom*. New York: Oxford University Press, 1995.

Snay, Mitchell. *Gospel of Disunion: Religion and Separatism in the Antebellum South*. New York: Cambridge University Press, 1993; Chapel Hill: University of North Carolina Press, 1997.

Soames, Mary. *Clementine Churchill: The Biography of a Marriage*. Boston: Houghton Mifflin, 1979.

Sorensen, Theodore C. *Kennedy*. New York: Harper & Row, 1965.

Southern, Ed, ed. *The Jamestown Adventure: Accounts of the Virginia Colony,*

1605–1614. Real Voices, Real History Series. Winston-Salem, NC: John F. Blair, Publisher, 2004.

St. John de Crèvecoeur, J. Hector. *Letters from an American Farmer and Sketches of Eighteenth-Century America*. Edited by Albert E. Stone. New York: Penguin Books, 1981.

Stahr, Walter. *John Jay: Founding Father*. New York: Hambledon and London, 2005.

Stampp, Kenneth M. *The Peculiar Institution: Slavery in the Ante-Bellum South*. New York: Vintage Books, 1989.

Stark, Rodney. *For the Glory of God: How Monotheism Led to Reformations, Science, Witch-Hunts, and the End of Slavery*. Princeton: Princeton University Press, 2003.

———. *One True God: Historical Consequences of Monotheism*. Princeton: Princeton University Press, 2001.

———. *The Rise of Christianity: How the Obscure, Marginal Jesus Movement Became the Dominant Religious Force in the Western World in a Few Centuries*. San Francisco: HarperSanFrancisco, 1997.

Stokes, Anson Phelps. *Church and State in the United States*. 3 vols. New York: Harper & Brothers, 1950.

Storing, Herbert J., with the editorial assistance of Murray Dry. *What the Anti-Federalists Were For*. Chicago: University of Chicago Press, 1981.

Stump, Eleonore, and Norman Kretzmann, eds. *The Cambridge Companion to Augustine*. New York: Cambridge University Press, 2001.

Swanberg, W. A. *Luce and His Empire*. New York: Charles Scribner's Sons, 1972.

Sweet, William Warren. *Religion in the Development of American Culture, 1765–1840*. New York: Charles Scribner's Sons, 1952.

Taylor, Alan. *American Colonies*. The Penguin History of the United States. New York: Viking, 2001.

Thomas, Cal, and Ed Dobson. *Blinded by Might: Can the Religious Right Save America?* Grand Rapids, MI: Zondervan Publishing House, 1999.

Tillich, Paul. *Systematic Theology*. Vol. 1, *Reason and Revelation. Being and God*. Chicago: University of Chicago Press, 1951.

Tocqueville, Alexis de. *Democracy in America*. Translated and edited by Harvey C. Mansfield and Delba Winthrop. Chicago: University of Chicago Press, 2000.

Todd, Charles Burr. *Life and Letters of Joel Barlow, LL.D., Poet, Statesman, Philosopher, with Extracts from His Works and Hitherto Unpublished Poems*. New York: G. P. Putnam's Sons, 1886.

Trilling, Lionel. *Matthew Arnold*. The Works of Lionel Trilling. New York: Oxford University Press, 1982.

Truman, Harry S. *Memoirs.* 2 vols. Garden City, NY: Doubleday & Co., 1955–56. Vol. 1, *Year of Decisions,* 1955. Vol. 2, *Years of Trial and Hope,* 1956.

Tulis, Jeffrey K. *The Rhetorical Presidency.* Princeton: Princeton University Press, 1987.

Tully, Grace G. *F.D.R., My Boss.* New York: Charles Scribner's Sons, 1949.

Turner, Thomas Reed. *Beware the People Weeping: Public Opinion and the Assassination of Abraham Lincoln.* Baton Rouge: Louisiana State University Press, 1982.

Unger, Harlow Giles. *John Hancock: Merchant King and American Patriot.* New York: John Wiley & Sons, 2000.

Urofsky, Melvin I. *The Levy Family and Monticello, 1834–1923: Saving Thomas Jefferson's House.* Monticello Monograph Series. Charlottesville, VA: Thomas Jefferson Foundation, 2001.

Van Doren, Carl. *Benjamin Franklin.* New York: Viking Press, 1938.

Vaughn, Lewis and Austin Dacey. *The Case for Humanism.* Lanham, MD: Rowman & Littlefield, 2003.

Wallace, Anthony F. C. *The Long, Bitter Trail: Andrew Jackson and the Indians.* A Critical Issue. New York: Hill and Wang, 1993.

Ward, Geoffrey C., ed. *Closest Companion: The Unknown Story of the Intimate Friendship Between Franklin Roosevelt and Margaret Suckley.* Boston: Houghton Mifflin, 1995.

———. *A First-Class Temperament: The Emergence of Franklin Roosevelt.* New York: Harper & Row, 1989.

Warner, Michael, comp. *American Sermons: The Pilgrims to Martin Luther King Jr.* The Library of America. New York: Library of America, 1999.

Washington, George. *The Diaries of George Washington.* Edited by Donald Jackson and Dorothy Twohig. Vol. 5, *July 1786–December 1789.* Charlottesville: University Press of Virginia, 1979.

———. *Writings.* Selected by John H. Rhodehamel. The Library of America. New York: Library of America, 1997.

Watson, Harry L. *Liberty and Power: The Politics of Jacksonian America.* New York: Hill and Wang, 1990.

Weigel, George. *The Cube and the Cathedral: Europe, America, and Politics Without God.* New York: Basic Books, 2005.

———. *The Truth of Catholicism: Ten Controversies Explored.* New York: Cliff Street Books, 2001.

———. *Witness to Hope: The Biography of Pope John Paul II.* New York: Cliff Street Books, 1999.

Weisberger, Bernard A. *America Afire: Jefferson, Adams, and the Revolutionary Election of 1800.* New York: HarperCollins Publishers, 2000.

———. *They Gathered at the River: The Story of the Great Revivalists and Their Impact upon Religion in America*. Boston: Little, Brown and Co., 1958.

Welles, Edward Randolph. *Pardon, Power, Peace: A Sermon Preached . . . On the Occasion of the National Day of Prayer, January 1st, 1942*. Baltimore, 1942.

White, Ronald C., Jr. *Lincoln's Greatest Speech: The Second Inaugural*. New York: Simon & Schuster, 2002.

Whitefield, George. *Select Sermons of George Whitefield*. With an account of his life by J. C. Ryle. London: Banner of Truth Trust, 1958.

Whitman, Walt. *Complete Poetry and Collected Prose*. The Library of America. New York: Literary Classics of the United States, 1982.

Wielenberg, Erik J. *Value and Virtue in a Godless Universe*. New York: Cambridge University Press, 2005.

Wilcox, Clyde. *Onward Christian Soldiers?: The Religious Right in American Politics*. 2nd ed. Dilemmas in American Politics. Boulder, CO: Westview Press, 2000.

Wilentz, Sean. *The Rise of American Democracy: Jefferson to Lincoln*. New York: W. W. Norton & Co., 2005.

Wilken, Robert L. *The Christians As the Romans Saw Them*. New Haven: Yale University Press, 1984.

Wills, Garry. *Inventing America: Jefferson's Declaration of Independence*. Garden City, NY: Doubleday & Co., 1978.

———. *James Madison*. The American Presidents Series. New York: Times Books, 2002.

———. *Lincoln at Gettysburg: The Words That Remade America*. New York: Simon & Schuster, 1992.

———. *Under God: Religion and American Politics*. New York: Simon & Schuster, 1990.

Wilson, A. N. *God's Funeral: A Biography of Faith and Doubt in Western Civilization*. New York: Ballantine Books, 2000.

Wilson, John F. *Public Religion in American Culture*. Philadelphia: Temple University Press, 1979.

Wilson, Woodrow. *The Papers of Woodrow Wilson*. Edited by Arthur S. Link. Vols. 28, 41, 45, and 68. Princeton: Princeton University Press, 1978, 1983, 1984, 1993.

Winthrop, John. *The Journal of John Winthrop, 1630–1649*. Edited by Richard S. Dunn and Laetitia Yeandle. Abridged ed. The John Harvard Library. Cambridge: Belknap Press of Harvard University Press, 1996.

Wofford, Harris. *Of Kennedys and Kings: Making Sense of the Sixties*. New York: Farrar, Straus and Giroux, 1980.

Wood, Gordon S. *The Creation of the American Republic, 1776–1787*. Chapel Hill: Published for the Institute of Early American History and Culture at Williamsburg, Virginia, by the University of North Carolina Press, 1969.

Wood, James E., Jr., ed. *The First Freedom: Religion and the Bill of Rights*. Waco, TX: J. M. Dawson Institute of Church-State Studies, Baylor University, 1990.

Woodress, James. *A Yankee's Odyssey: The Life of Joel Barlow*. Philadelphia: J. B. Lippincott Co., 1958.

Wright, Louis B., ed. *A Voyage to Virginia in 1609; Two Narratives: Strachey's "True Repertory" and Jourdain's Discovery of the Bermudas*. Jamestown Documents. Charlottesville, VA: Published for the Association for the Preservation of Virginia Antiquities by the University Press of Virginia, 1964.

Wuthnow, Robert. *The Struggle for America's Soul: Evangelicals, Liberals, and Secularism*. Grand Rapids, MI: William B. Eerdmans Publishing Co., 1989.

Wyman, David S. *The Abandonment of the Jews: America and the Holocaust, 1941–1945*. New York: Pantheon Books, 1984.

Zagorin, Perez. *How the Idea of Religious Toleration Came to the West*. Princeton: Princeton University Press, 2003.

MAGAZINES, JOURNALS, AND NEWSPAPERS

American Academy of Religion
American Quarterly
The Birmingham (AL) *News*
The Cathedral Age
Charlottesville (VA) *Weekly Chronicle*
Christianity Today
The Christian Century
Christianity and Crisis: A Bi-Weekly Journal of Christian Opinion
First Things
The Journal of Bible and Religion
Journal of Church and State
Journal of Presbyterian History
Journal of Social History
Judaism: A Quarterly Journal of Jewish Life and Thought
The Magazine of Albemarle County History
The New Republic
The New York Times
Newsweek
The Reporter

The Review of Religion
Review of Religious Research
Richmond (VA) *Enquirer*
Time
(Washington, D.C.) *National Intelligencer*
The Washington Post
The William and Mary Quarterly

AUTHOR'S NOTE

AND ACKNOWLEDGMENTS

In choosing to explore the connections between religion and public life, I have failed to follow the example of Thomas Jefferson, who, when asked to publish something on the subject in 1815, replied: "I not only write nothing on religion, but rarely permit myself to speak on it, and never but in a reasonable society." He was not, of course, being wholly serious. Few men in our history have been as thoughtful about faith as Jefferson, and his surviving writings on the topic, from letters to legislation to his versions of the Gospels, are compelling. Yet there was, and is, something to his reluctance to engage the issues too publicly, for little is more emotional and vexing than how much religious expression in a democracy is appropriate and how much is too much. My hope in writing this book was to try to make some contribution toward swelling the ranks of those in what Jefferson called "reasonable society"—readers willing to approach these questions with a historical sensibility, an analytical mind, and, at the risk of sentimentality, an open heart.

This book is not a work of historical or theological scholarship, though it draws on both traditions. As I write in the Introduction, it is an essay that covers a great deal of territory quickly and briefly. I recognize the perils of this approach: some will wonder why complex issues are treated simply, or not addressed at all. My aim, however, was not to be comprehensive but to give readers a sense of the scope and nature of a debate that is even older than the Republic. I hope that those who are interested or intrigued will look to the books listed in the Source Notes and the Bibliography for more detailed discussions and fuller arguments. Readers should also know that in the text, for the sake of clarity, I generally modernized the spelling and have punctuation of quotations from past centuries.

The choice to conclude the narrative with Ronald Reagan was a careful one. I generally hold to what I call the Beschloss Rule, my name for the distinguished historian Michael Beschloss's opinion that only after twenty or thirty years does one begin to have enough information to evaluate a president. That kind of interval also allows the passions of the day to cool, events to take their course, and thus enables historians to render judgments in greater tranquility and, hopefully, with greater perspective and understanding. I think, however, that readers will have little trouble applying the conclusions I draw from history to their own interpretations of the presidencies of Bill Clinton and George W. Bush. (I did make one exception to the Beschloss Rule, quoting from an interview I did for this book with the senior President Bush in the Source Notes.)

There is a large, interesting, and vibrant world of scholarship on religion and public life in America. Martin E. Marty, the Fairfax M. Cone Distinguished Service Professor Emeritus at the University of Chicago, graciously read and commented on my manuscript, offering warm support and wise counsel. Edwin S. Gaustad, professor emeritus of history and religious studies at the University of California Riverside, was equally kind and helpful. Both men are magisterial figures, authors of many canonical works on the history of religion in America and how faith has shaped the nation's politics and culture. I am honored and humbled that they so generously read my pages. I am also indebted to Jon Butler, dean of the Graduate School of Arts and Sciences at Yale University, not only for his wonderful books but for taking time to advise me on several crucial points.

James H. Hutson, chief of the Manuscript Division at the Library of Congress and the author of several indispensable books about faith and the Founding, read and commented on my manuscript; I am grateful for his time, insights, and thoughtfulness. Derek H. Davis, director of the J. M. Dawson Center of Church-State Relations at Baylor University and editor of the *Journal of Church and State,* also read a draft and offered many useful suggestions. Professor Davis's *Religion and the Continental Congress* is essential reading. The scarily prolific and wise Mark A. Noll, the Carolyn and Fred McManis Professor of Christian Thought at Wheaton College, is the author of numerous invaluable works, and he generously talked with me about many of the issues discussed in this book. Philip Hamburger, the John P. Wilson Professor of Law at the University of Chicago and author of the landmark *Separation of Church and State,* was kind and helpful. Albert J. Raboteau, the Henry W. Putnam Professor of Religion at Princeton University, generously discussed the history of the African American experience with me. Jonathan D. Sarna is a historian of enormous depth and range; his work on Judaism in America from it beginnings to the present day is rich, compelling, thorough, and essential. He is the Joseph H. and Belle R. Braun Professor of American Jewish History at Brandeis University and chairs the Academic Board of the Jacob Rader Marcus Center of the American Jewish Archives. Professor Sarna was welcoming and generous to me, and I am grateful to him. My friend George Weigel, the papal biographer and Catholic theologian, is a kind and keenly intelligent source of wisdom. I am also grateful to the distinguished writer and historian Karen Armstrong; to Alan Brinkley, historian, friend, and provost of Columbia University; to Noah Feldman, professor of law at New York University School of Law and author of the fascinating book *Divided by God: America's Church-State Problem—And What We Should Do About It;* to the writer Susan Jacoby, author of the provocative *Freethinkers: A History of American Secularism;* to the philosopher Austin Dacey of the Center for Inquiry's New York City office; to the Pulitzer Prize–winning Martin Luther King, Jr., biographer David J. Garrow; to Dean William A. Graham of the Harvard Divinity School; to Paula Fredriksen, the Aurelio Professor of the Appreciation of Scripture at Boston University; to Reverend Barry W. Lynn of Americans United for Separation of Church and State; and to Dr. R. Albert Mohler, Jr., president of the Southern Baptist Theological Seminary in Louisville, Kentucky. All of them have been helpful to me in thinking through the issues touched on in these pages.

I am fortunate in my friends, and I owe them debts I cannot repay. They selflessly made time in their very full lives to read this book with care. Michael Beschloss was, as always, a steady counselor, reassuring confidant, and trusted reader. He is the best of friends and the most generous of colleagues. David

McCullough graciously agreed to read the entire manuscript, giving me wise counsel on several points. I am grateful to him, to his wife, Rosalee, and to their daughter, Dorie Lawson, for their generosity. The gifted Nathaniel Philbrick generously advised me on *Mayflower*-related issues. Tom Brokaw, Walter Isaacson, Elaine Pagels, Charles Peters, and Arthur Schlesinger, Jr., were magnificent as ever.

Many people at libraries and archives were helpful in unearthing material about different aspects of religion and politics. One of the great joys of this kind of work is the hunt for what Randolph Churchill, the prime minister's son and his first official biographer, called "lovely grub"—fresh historical documents and nuggets. At Monticello, I am grateful to Jefferson Looney and Lisa Francavilla at the Jefferson Papers Project, Retirement Series, for mining their archives for details about Jefferson's last days and his funeral. At the Library and Archives of the American Jewish Historical Society, Lyn Slome, the director, was welcoming and generous. At Washington National Cathedral, Margaret Shannon, Beth Mullen, and Miriam Zanders were gracious and helpful in finding the archival material I needed to reconstruct Martin Luther King, Jr.'s last Sunday sermon; many thanks to them, and to the cathedral's dean, the Very Reverend Samuel T. Lloyd III. I am also grateful to Robert Clark of the Franklin D. Roosevelt Library and Museum, Hyde Park, New York (Bob thought he was done with me, only to have me appear on his doorstep once again); to Valoise Armstrong of the Dwight D. Eisenhower Presidential Library, Abilene, Kansas; to Stephen Plotkin of the John F. Kennedy Presidential Library in Boston, Massachusetts; to the staffs of the Lyndon B. Johnson Presidential Library in Austin, Texas, and the Ronald Reagan Presidential Library in Simi Valley, California; and to Linda and Duane Watson of the Margaret Suckley Papers, Wilderstein Collection, Rhinebeck, New York. A. Larry Ross kindly posed some questions to Reverend Billy Graham on my behalf and provided me information from the Graham files; Larry is unfailingly helpful, and I am indebted to him. R. Malcolm-Woods took the trouble to provide me with a copy of the sermon her stepfather, Reverend Edward Randolph Welles, delivered at Christ Church, Alexandria, on New Year's Day 1942, to a congregation that included Franklin Roosevelt and Winston Churchill. Hayden G. Bryan, executive director for operations at St. John's Church, LaFayette Square, kindly helped me with documents relating to President Roosevelt's inaugural anniversary service of March 4, 1944. Thanks as well to Tom Flynn, the director of the Robert Green Ingersoll Birthplace Museum in Dresden, New York. Celeste Walker was greatly helpful with the Adams Family Papers at the Massachusetts Historical Society.

In the end, of course, any mistakes are my own, and the lovely people who have helped me bear no responsibility for anything I may have gotten wrong or for points with which they disagree.

I am blessed—and I am not using that word loosely—in my friendship with John Lewis, the congressman from Georgia whose personal courage and steadfast faith changed the nation forever. He faced death in order to set a people free and has led an exemplary life of service to America and to Americans of all races and creeds. As always, I am indebted to him for talking with me about the role of religion in the civil-rights movement and for recounting the events of Bloody Sunday, one of the great turning points of the twentieth century.

I am grateful to former president George H. W. Bush for sharing his thoughts with me about faith and the presidency. A man of grace and dignity, President Bush has served the nation from his earliest years, in combat and at the highest levels, and I appreciate his warmth and his generosity. Jean Becker, his able and tireless chief of staff, is a good friend. Theodore C. Sorensen, President Kennedy's former special counsel, kindly discussed the late president's rhetoric with me. Richard N. Goodwin generously spoke with me about the making of President Johnson's "We Shall Overcome" address to Congress. Richard Darman helped me understand President Reagan's working style as I analyzed Reagan's personal edits of a draft of his March 1983 speech to the National Association of Evangelicals. Reverend Billy Graham generously replied to questions, and it was a pleasure to meet with him during his New York crusade in the summer of 2005. Reverend Rick Warren took time to speak with me at length about the challenges of being a Christian pastor in a nation with an ecumenical public religion. The commentator Cal Thomas, coauthor of the important book *Blinded by Might: Can the Religious Right Save America?*, discussed the question of politics and religion with me. William E. Brock III, the former Tennessee senator, Republican National Committee chairman, and Cabinet officer, shared memories of conversations between the Republican Party and Evangelical Christians, as did Roger Semerad, a former White House aide who worked with Brock at the RNC in the late 1970s. I drew on a decade of work for *Newsweek* in the course of the book, particularly research and reporting that I undertook for our obituary of Ronald Reagan and for a project I did with my colleague and friend Vern E. Smith, the magazine's longtime Atlanta bureau chief, to commemorate the thirtieth anniversary of Martin Luther King, Jr.'s assassination.

At *Newsweek,* my colleagues Jonathan Alter, Deidre Depke, Kathy Deveny, Howard Fineman, Daniel Klaidman, Marcus Mabry, Lisa Miller, Tom Watson, Kenneth L. Woodward, and Fareed Zakaria were generous in listening to my musings and helping in other ways. I am lucky to be able to work with them and with everyone else at the magazine every day. The indomitable Lally Weymouth is a wonderful friend and journalistic force. I am also grateful to Steve Luxenberg and Steve Mufson of *The Washington Post* for giving me the chance to write about some of these subjects in their pages. And Maria Campbell's kind invitation to deliver the Bowen Lectures in North Carolina was a spur in thinking through the argument of the book. Bernard McGuirk and Brian Williams generously endured my early chatterings on the topic, and Chris Matthews has taught me much about politics, both in his books and in his commentaries on the Washington scene. For their kindness, I am also grateful to Shaima Ally, Reverend Maryetta Anschutz, Julia Baird, Simon Barnett, David Bradley, Reverend Chloe Breyer, Tina Brown, Damien Donck, Barbara Epstein, Betsy Fischer, Doris Kearns Goodwin, Kelli Grant, Tammy Haddad, Hope Hartman, Brenda Jones, Eric Katzman, Raina Kelley, Alice Mayhew, Deborah Millan, Andrea Mitchell, Michelle Molloy, Laurie Morris, Carey Newman, David Olivenbaum, Anna Quindlen, Sally Quinn, Julia Reed, Dale Richardson, Douglas Robbe, William Safire, Barry Shrage, Evelyn Small, Reverend Robert Stafford, Lynn Staley, Steve Walkowiak, Professor the Reverend Canon J. Robert Wright, and Iva Zoric. The staff of the *Newsweek* Research Center is unfailingly kind and guides me and my colleagues through the denser forests of the news and of history; many thanks to Lisa Bergstraum, Judy Ganeles, Rena Kirsch, Tony Skaggs, Susan Szeliga, Ruth Tenenbaum, and Sam Register. With unfailing good cheer, Becca Pratt again rescued me from sundry technological disasters and, with the ever-generous Ignacio Kleva, took time on a winter's afternoon to pull me somewhere within hailing distance of twenty-first-century computing. And Barbara DiVittorio generously takes care of a great deal of my life with enormous skill and seemingly endless patience, for which I thank her.

For permission to quote from documents, speeches, sermons, and prayers, I am grateful to the American Jewish Historical Society, New York and Newton Centre, Massachusetts, and to the Estate of Martin Luther King, Jr.

With her preternaturally impressive editorial eye and good judgment, Louisa Thomas did wonderful work searching archives, checking my facts, and reading the manuscript with care; when she argued with me, I listened—and always learned something. Jack Bales again proved himself a master of bibliographical detail, taking time from his own projects to help me. I am thankful for his thoroughness and enthusiasm.

Mike Hill was indispensable: a tireless, cheerful, and wise researcher and, most important, a friend. A man of grace and insight, Mike is not only an astute navigator of archival collections and libraries but is himself turning into a walking library, fluid and knowledgeable about the nooks and crannies of American history. He is the best.

In a way, the genesis of this book can be traced back nearly twenty years, when Herbert Wentz introduced me to Robert

Bellah's idea of civil religion, an idea that brought together two subjects of enduring fascination: God and politics. Since then, Herbert has been the most constant and forbearing of teachers and friends, always willing, as he puts it, to "come out and play" by debating different propositions and sharpening my thinking.

At Random House, my editor, the marvelous Kate Medina, was brilliant, reassuring, and fun. She focused the project when it most needed it, and edited with grace and skill. I am fortunate to have pitched up on her shores, and for that, and for so much else, I owe the formidable Amanda Urban, who was, as ever, wonderful, wise, and funny—and one can ask for nothing more than that. Kate Medina's team of Robin Rolewicz and Abby Plesser is a force to be reckoned with. Both were terrific—intelligent, gracious, and able. Sally Marvin and Dennis Ambrose have generously endured two books with me; they are the best. At Random House I am also indebted to Karen Richardson and Deborah Posner for their copyediting; to Carol Poticny for her photo research; and to Pei Koay for book design. Jonathan Karp brought me to Random House, and I value his friendship and his keen mind. And I am grateful to Gina Centrello for her enduring interest, confidence, and support.

To work for Donald Graham, Rick Smith, and Mark Whitaker is a great blessing. *Newsweek* plays an essential role in the life of the nation, and I am fortunate to be a part of the company and the magazine they have created and nurtured. Ann McDaniel and Evan Thomas remain the most steadfast of friends and editors, and I treasure their affection and generosity of spirit.

To Keith, as always, I owe the most. Fortunately, her patience seems to know no limits, which is a good thing for me. This

AUTHOR'S NOTE AND ACKNOWLEDGMENTS | 399

book is dedicated to our children, Mary and Sam; may they come of age in a world both secure and serene. Near the end of his life, Jefferson wrote a letter of advice to a young namesake: "Adore God. . . . Love your neighbor as yourself; and your country more than life. Be just. Be true. Murmur not at the ways of providence and the life into which you have entered will be a passage to one of eternal and ineffable bliss." Such is our hope for our children, too: that they will love their country and their God, do good, and always make their way through the darkness to find what John Henry Newman called "a safe lodging, and a holy rest, and peace at the last."

AFTERWORD

"For now we see through a glass, darkly; but then face to face . . ."
—1 CORINTHIANS 13:12

When I was working on *American Gospel,* I called the forty-first president of the United States, George H. W. Bush—an Episcopalian, and far more reticent about matters of theology than his son—to ask him whether religion had been much on his mind in his four years in the White House. "I felt lifted by faith," the former president told me. "I don't know how you could cope in the presidency without a sense of a larger power, of a larger destiny, of something bigger than your own ambitions, your own passions, your own plans, your own problems. Belief in God, for me at least, gave me hope and kept me going. I didn't show it very much—don't like to talk about it—and maybe I should have been a little more open, a little clearer about my heartbeat. But I felt it—felt it very, very strongly." To feel strongly yet to act humbly—how very admirable, and how very American.

I wrote the book you are holding in the hope that a recovery of the past might enable us to put the storms of the present in perspective—that we, in our time, could draw lessons from recalling how the Founding Fathers and more than two centuries of

American presidents understood the delicate, sometimes corrosive, sometimes corrective connection between faith and politics. (The scriptural justifications for slavery are an example of the corrosive; the use of moral arguments drawn from the Bible and from the American canon to combat Jim Crow is an instance of the corrective.)

The reaction to the hardcover edition was not quite what I expected. I was prepared for the extremes—the ferociously secular and the ferociously evangelical—to strike from both sides, with the more liberal readers saying I was, as the psychologists might say, enabling the religious, and the more conservative arguing that I was really in sympathy with the left because I may appear soft on the fundamentals of faith. I do not believe either point to be the case, but that is what I thought I would hear.

Instead, hearteningly, most people who took the time to write—and I am grateful to them all—seemed to appreciate my attempt to steer a middle course. Yes, I got a few e-mails suggesting that I was really in the evangelicals' pocket, and a few others regretting that I did not seem to have accepted Jesus as my personal savior (if I had, these critics said, I could not possibly argue that America was not a "Christian nation"). On the whole, though, the responses I received reflected a hunger for a more moderate conversation about religion and public life. *American Gospel* was respectfully received by the Anti-Defamation League and by Focus on the Family, by National Public Radio and by Fox News Channel, by Al Franken and by Billy Graham. The center, it seems, can hold—or at least it stands a decent chance of holding amid the political and cultural winds of the moment.

As a Southerner, I stand with Faulkner: "The past is never dead," he wrote in *Requiem for a Nun*. "It's not even past." Historical circumstances may change, but human nature is constant. John Adams's vanity is recognizable to us; so is George Washington's insecurity, and Thomas Jefferson's curiosity, and Benjamin Franklin's need for personal reinvention. Ecclesiastes tells us that there is no thing new under the sun—a case of biblical overstatement, perhaps, but a point one should not entirely dismiss. The utility of the past, I believe, lies in how it speaks to us as we struggle to play our parts in the long story of the world.

The chapter in which we are living is one marked by extremism in the name of God. In talking to audiences about *American Gospel,* I was frequently asked what relevance the American experience has for the Islamic world, where theocracy is prevalent. There is nothing simple about projecting any of our values around the globe. To do so is the work of many years, and it begins, I think, as so many things do, with a story—in this case, our story: the story of how a young nation overcame its worst instincts and saw the historical and theological truth that freedom is the greatest of virtues, and it is from freedom that all else flows, from justice to faith to prosperity.

In the bloody twentieth century, the poet Robert Penn Warren wrote:

Tell me a story.
In this century, and moment, of mania,
Tell me a story.
Make it a story of great distances, and starlight. . . .
Tell me a story of deep delight.

America has a story to tell about religious freedom. Our tale is far from perfect, and it is not always delightful, for our history is stained with evil and bloodshed and discrimination, from slavery to Jim Crow to our perennial failure to lift up the poorest among us. But it is still, even so, a good story, for we have survived the storms of six centuries—from the founding of Virginia in the sixteenth to the first years of the twenty-first—and remain, for all our faults, what John Winthrop called a "city upon a hill."

In that city, we must vigilantly guard against religiously tinged strife. Christians who think that the more secular, or even just the more liberal, are godless, are as wrong as secularists who believe the more religious, or even just the more conservative, are superstitious zealots.

I have a particular view of what the public conversation about faith and culture should be like, as *American Gospel* shows. The religious must be humble, for faith is a matter of accepting mystery, of acknowledging, with Saint Paul, that "for now we see through a glass, darkly; but then face to face . . ." Not *now*, but *then*, beyond time. And the secular must respect others as others should respect the secular—fully and unreservedly. If the conversation begins with either side antagonizing the other, then there is no way forward; civility is a precious virtue, and one we must preserve and practice.

That, in a way, was my aim in writing this book: to encourage those of us who are still in the arena of history to treat one another with respect, to defend liberty, and to nurture a culture of generosity. Sentimental? Yes, I suppose it is, but such was the work undertaken by the Founding Fathers and carried on by Americans of goodwill, and I would prefer to be called an idealist rather than a cynic any day.

Six days after the attacks of September 11, 2001, the senior President Bush was in his small office on Walker's Point, the family's compound in Kennebunkport, Maine, answering his mail. I had sent word to the former president asking for a *Newsweek* interview in the aftermath of the slaughter; as a wartime leader himself, he would have, I thought, much to say about the forces bearing down on his son, the incumbent. Gentlemanly as always, however, Bush declined, saying he did not want to talk about things that might complicate life for the White House. His reply was not unexpected, but the last line of his dignified note struck me as particularly poignant in those days of anxiety: "Please say a prayer for our beloved son, The President."

Our beloved son, The President: It was a revealing formulation, one that mixed the personal and the political. For the former president, as for the nation, the shock of the violence underscored the centrality of the ties of affection while simultaneously turning our attention abroad, to the wider world in which the caves of Afghanistan are linked to the canyons of Manhattan. History had come calling out of a brilliant blue sky, and, for a moment at least, the nation stood united. The ensuing years have brought discord, division, and a charged debate over the means and ends of both the power of the nation and of the presidency—and of the making of such arguments there shall be no end. It would be wonderfully American to struggle to conduct these arguments in a spirit of grace—and equally American to try to agree that saying a prayer for our president, whoever he (or, to be sure, she) may be, can do no harm, and might, just might, do some good.

—SEPTEMBER 11, 2006
NEW YORK CITY

INDEX

Page numbers in *italics* refer to illustrations.

JON MEACHAM is the editor of *Newsweek*. A graduate of The University of the South in Sewanee, Tennessee, he is the author of the *New York Times* bestseller *Franklin and Winston: An Intimate Portrait of an Epic Friendship*. Meacham lives in New York City with his wife and two children.

ABOUT THE TYPE

This book was set in Bulmer, a typeface designed in the late eighteenth century by the London type cutter William Martin. The typeface was created especially for the Shakespeare Press, directed by William Bulmer; hence the font's name. Bulmer is considered to be a transitional typeface, containing characteristics of old-style and modern designs. It is recognized for its elegantly proportioned letters, with their long ascenders and descenders.